D0722276

Yi Kwang-su and Modern Korean Literature: *Mujŏng*

"Hongji-dong Sanjang Hwa," ink and watercolor on paper, 1971, by Wŏlchŏn Chang U-sŏng. The painting depicts the house where Yi Kwang-su lived from 1934-39, and was published in volume four of the *Yi Kwang-su Chŏnjip* (1971).

Yi Kwang-su and Modern Korean Literature
Mujŏng

Ann Sung-Hi Lee

East Asia Program
Cornell University
Ithaca, New York 14853

The Cornell East Asia Series is published by the Cornell University East Asia Program (distinct from Cornell University Press). We publish affordably priced books on a variety of scholarly topics relating to East Asia as a service to the academic community and the general public. Standing orders, which provide for automatic notification and invoicing of each title in the series upon publication, are accepted.

If after review by internal and external readers a manuscript is accepted for publication, it is published on the basis of camera-ready copy provided by the volume author. Each author is thus responsible for any necessary copyediting and for manuscript formatting. Address submission inquiries to CEAS Editorial Board, East Asia Program, Cornell University, Ithaca, New York 14853-7601.

The translation and publication of this book was supported by a grant from the Korea Literature Translation Institute. The publication was also supported by the Sunshik Min Endowment for the Advancement of Korean Literature, Korea Institute, Harvard University. The cover design was made possible by a donation from Mr. and Mrs. I.H. Cho.

Number 127 in the Cornell East Asia Series
Copyright © 2005 by Ann Sung-hi Lee. All rights reserved
ISSN 1050-2955
ISBN-13: 978-1-885445-37-7 hc / ISBN-10: 1-885445-37-7 hc
ISBN-13: 978-1-885445-27-8 pb / ISBN-10: 1-885445-27-X pb
Library of Congress Control Number: 2005922988

23 22 21 20 19 18 17 16 15 14 13 12 11 10 09 08 05   9 8 7 6 5 4 3 2 1

Cover characters from original newspaper printing of Yi Kwang-su, *Mujŏng. Maeil Sinbo*, 1 January 1917. Facsimile reprint. Seoul: Kyŏngin Munhwasa, 1984. Cover painting: "Hongji-dong Sanjang Hwa," by Wŏlchŏn Chang U-sŏng, 1971. Cover design by Sumi Shin.

The paper in this book meets the requirements for permanence of ISO 9706:1994.

Contents

Acknowledgments

I thank Gari Ledyard for having been my graduate school advisor and mentor at Columbia University. The late Edward Wagner and the late Marshall Pihl advised my undergraduate research at Harvard University, where I wrote my undergraduate thesis about *Mujŏng*. I did some of the research for this book with the help of a Fulbright-Hays dissertation grant, and a grant from the Joint Committee of the Social Science Research Council and the American Council of Learned Societies. I would like to thank the University of Washington for providing me with a Royalty Research Fund grant and a junior faculty development quarter. A summer fellowship from the Academy of Korean Studies in 1996 gave me the opportunity to pursue further research. I have benefited from talking with Mike Shin, Jina Kim, Mee-hwa Lee, Hye-jin Juhn Sidney, Jemma Song and Yoko Uchida about literary theory and Korean literature. Clark Sorensen encouraged me to continue the process of revising my manuscript for publication. Jim Palais read the manuscript and offered many helpful suggestions. Lee Ki-moon allowed me to audit his classes at Seoul National University and use the SNU library, introduced me to Korean scholars, and gave me many helpful research materials. Kim Yun-sik and Ku In-hwan too were kind enough to let me to audit their classes at SNU. Edward Seidensticker and Bob Hymes helped me to continue my research over the years. Jeff Riegel gave me funds to go to New York City for my dissertation defense. Roh Yang-hwan shared with me textual materials that he collected while compiling and editing my grandfather's collected works. Yoon-whan Choe advised me about library materials at the University of Washington, and helped me with my research questions. I thank the libraries at Yonsei University and Korea University for giving me access to materials there. I thank Mr. Kim Yeong-weon of Yonsei University Library for helping me obtain a copy of the facsimile reprint of the 1918 Sinmungwan edition of *Mujŏng*. I would also like to thank Cappy Hurst, Chang Yun-sik, Hong Il-sik, Kim Kichung, Kim Ho-sun, Kim Nam-gil, Kim Sŏng-gon, Young-key Kim Renaud, Ross King, David

Knechtges, Paik Nak-chung, Peter Nosco, Joy Kim, Bob and Younghi Ramsey, Michael Robinson, Suh Dae-sook, John Treat, Sohn Ho-min, and Kenneth Wells for their scholarly advice, support and encouragement.

I thank the scholars without whose work I could not have written this book, though I am responsible for any mistakes.

Introduction

In this introduction, I discuss how early modern Korean writer Yi Kwang-su (1892–1950) wrote about literature, and depicted gendered subjectivity. Yi wrote twenty-seven novels, numerous short stories, poetry, articles, essays, plays and translations. His writings shared with *sinsosŏl* or early modern "new fiction" the enlightenment ideology of social, economic, political and cultural reform for Korean self-strengthening and independence. Yi participated in the March First Independence Movement (1919), writing the February 8th Declaration of Independence that was read at a Korean student demonstration in Tokyo. He then went to Shanghai and wrote press releases that were sent to Chinese and English language newspapers, in order to publicize the March First Independence Movement. After the March First movement, Yi worked as a reporter for the *Tongnip Sinmun* (the Independent), the official newspaper for the Shanghai Provisional Government (SPG), which overseas Korean nationalists organized in Shanghai. Yi also participated in an SPG committee to compile materials about the history of the Korean independence movement. Tosan An Ch'ang-ho[1] introduced Yi, moreover, to the Hŭngsadan (Corps for the Advancement of Scholars).[2]

After participating in the Korean overseas independence movement in Shanghai, Yi left Shanghai in early spring, 1921, to return to Korea. Though arrested in Sŏnch'ŏn on his way into Korea, he was released. This made Koreans think that he had renounced the independence movement. Yi began to write collaborationist texts under the Minami regime (1936–1942). However, Yi continued to write literature in vernacular Korean.

---

1. Koreans could have a polite name (*cha*), and a literary name or pen name (*ho*), in addition to their surname and given name. Tosan was An Ch'ang-ho's literary name.
2. See Michael Edson Robinson, *Cultural Nationalism in Colonial Korea, 1920–1925* (Seattle: University of Washington Press, 1988), 66. The Hŭngsadan sought to nurture competencies in the individual, and organize individuals into collective strength.

1

Ideologies of enlightenment can become hegemonic.[3] Yi Kwang-su has at times been considered a canonical writer, and often has been identified with Japanese imperialism itself. Indeed, one could try to identify Yi with Japanese imperialism. However, trying not to essentialize what it is to be Korean, I have tried to focus on a Korean writer's subjectivity, with emphasis on literary texts.[4] I discuss Yi's literary thought, and his views of literature as a means of enlightenment. Yi thought of Korean literature as being part of an ideology of nationalist reform. Cultural nationalists such as Yi sought to achieve Korean national independence by means of gradual social and cultural reform.[5] Although enlightenment ideology had been used by Japan to justify Japanese imperialism, reiteration of such enlightenment discourse by Korean colonial subalterns created a different understanding of that discourse.[6] I consider these new understandings, and the context of Yi's writings. I discuss Yi's life from 1892 to 1917;[7] his thought on language and literature; his early writings from 1909 to 1917; early modern Korean

3. Brian O'Connor, ed., *The Adorno Reader* (Oxford, UK: Blackwell Publishers, 2000), 155. I would like to thank Jina Kim for discussing Adorno's theory of the dialectics of enlightenment, in my Korean 532 class at the University of Washington, Winter quarter 2002. Henry Em has observed that certain Korean nationalist views of history and nation have suppressed nondominant perspectives. Henry H. Em, "Minjok as a construct," in ed. Gi-wook Shin and Michael Robinson, *Colonial Modernity in Korea* (Cambridge: Harvard University Asia Center, 1999), 337.
4. Lydia Liu discusses the role of non-European subjectivity in translingual practice. Language acquires new meanings and uses when translated into other languages; recognizing the significance of non-Western subjectivities in translation helps overcome the positivist dualism of "oppressor" and "victim." Lydia Liu, *Translingual Practice: Literature, National Culture, and Translated Modernity—China, 1900–1937* (Stanford: Stanford University Press, 1995).
5. For a discussion of Korean cultural nationalism, cf. Michael Robinson, *Cultural Nationalism in Colonial Korea, 1920–1925* (Seattle: University of Washington Press, 1988).
6. Homi Bhabha, *The Location of Culture* (London and New York: Routledge, 1994), 86. I would like to thank Ann Choi for bringing to my attention the importance of the trope of the "double" in postcolonial studies. I have also learned much from Henry Em's discussions of Homi Bhabha at the Southern California Korean Studies Colloquium, organized by Eun Mee Kim in 1992.
7. Yi died during the Korean War. The North Korean People's Army took Yi from his home in Seoul on July 12, 1950. Chung Wha Lee, *Kŭriun Abŏnim Ch'unwŏn* (Seoul: Usinsa, 1993), 130. According to former North Korean official Chŏng Sang-jin, who lived in Alma Ata, Kazakhstan when he was interviewed in 1991, the North Korean army took Yi from Seoul to P'yŏngyang, and when the North Koreans retreated from United Nations forces in mid-October 1950, the North Koreans took Yi and other prisoners on foot towards what is now Chagang Province. Yi wrote to North Korean official Hong Myŏng-hŭi, who was in Kanggye. Hong had Yi brought to his lodgings, but Yi died after several days. Former North Korean official, Pak Kil-lyong, residing in Kazakhstan when interviewed in 1991, has said that when Yi's condition grew worse, Hong had him moved to a hospital in Manp'o, about fifteen km from Kanggye, and Yi died in early December 1950, of frostbite and tuberculosis. Kim Kuk-hu, "Ch'unwŏn Yi Kwang-su Osimnyŏnmal Manp'o Pyŏngwŏn sŏ Pyŏngsa," *Chungang Ilbo* July 26, 1991: 1. According to Professor Suh Dae-sook of the University of Hawaii, a former North Korean official named Valentin Pak has said that Yi Kwang-su wrote to then Minister of Education Paek Nam-un while Yi was being taken north, but died before help reached him. Personal interview, University of Hawaii, May 1988.

literature; language and Korean literature; and Yi's first novel *Mujŏng* (The Heartless). The book includes a complete translation of *The Heartless*. There are various theories as to when modernity began in Korean literature. Some literary historians have believed that modern Korean literature began around the time of the Kabo reforms in 1894. The Kabo reforms were social reforms imposed with Japanese force. In *Chosŏn Munhaksa* (A History of Korean Literature, 1922), An Cha-san wrote that "contemporary" Korean literature had begun after the Kabo reforms of 1894;[8] the Kabo reforms had started a new culture, and a new literature had emerged from this new culture. An emphasized the publication of Yu Kil-chun's *Sŏyu Kyŏnmun* (Things Seen and Heard While Traveling in the West, 1895) for its use of a *kukhanmun* or mixed Korean and Sino-Korean style, and its introduction of Western civilization (*sŏyang munmyŏng*). An referred to fiction before the Kabo reforms as "traditional fiction" (*ku sosŏl*), and later fiction as the "new fiction" (*sinsosŏl*). An thought that the "new fiction" differed from traditional Chosŏn dynasty fiction in that it did not consider literature as a means of idle amusement, but was concerned with genuine life issues.[9]

Im Hwa used Marxist theory to discuss Korean literature. Im emphasized Marxist concepts such as "base" and "superstructure," and thought there could be no discussion of a superstructure such as literature without examining its base.[10] Im called the literature of the period between the Kabo reforms and the literature of Ch'oe Nam-sŏn and Yi Kwang-su a "transitional period," and characterized this literature as enlightenment literature.[11] In *Chosŏn Sinmunhaksaron Sasŏl* (A Preface to a History of the New Korean Literature, 1935), Im discussed Korean literature from the literature of Yi In-jik and Yi Hae-jo, to early proletariat literature. Im used the Marxist concept of dialectics, moreover, to describe how the literature of Yi In-jik and Yi Hae-jo "developed" into the literature of Yi Kwang-su, and how Yi's literature led to the Naturalist literature of Kim Tong-in, Yŏm Sang-sŏp and Hyŏn Chin-gŏn.[12] Im thought that Korea during the late nineteenth to early twentieth centuries had not developed material conditions adequate for achieving an autonomous modernization process, and therefore ended up modernizing through the introduction of foreign culture. Im

8. Kim Yŏng-min, "Han'guk Munhaksa ŭi Kŭndae wa Kŭndaesŏng: Kŭndae Ch'ogi Sŏsa Munhak Yangsik ŭi Kŭndaesŏng ŭl Chungsim ŭro," in *20 Segi Han'guk Munhak ŭi Pansŏng kwa Chaengjŏm*, ed. Munhak kwa Sasang Yŏn'guhoe (Seoul: Somyŏng Ch'ulp'an, 1999), 13.
9. The writer wrote about reality (*hyŏnsil*), and not a world of fantasy (*kongsanggye*), and subjectively expressed his or her beliefs. The writer thereby became the "center" of the "people's thought" (*kungmin sasang*). Ibid.
10. Yang Mun-gyu, "Han'guk Kŭndae Munhaksaron ŭi Insik kwa Chaengjŏm," in *20 Segi Han'guk Munhak ŭi Pansŏng kwa Chaengjŏm*, 36.
11. Kim Yŏng-min, "Han'guk Munhaksa," 16.
12. Yang Mun-gyu, "Han'guk Kŭndae Munhaksaron," 37.

discussed the underdeveloped nature of the material base of feudal Korea. From Im's perspective, the process of enlightenment that took place after the Kabo reforms had not taken place on a foundation of the reform of traditional culture or a thorough rethinking of the legacies of traditional culture, but amounted only to the unilateral "transplantation" (isik) and "imitation" (mobang) of European civilization.[13] This was nevertheless the means through which a "new Korean culture" (Chosŏn sinmunhwa) was formed, Im argued. Im used the term "new literature" (sinmunhak) to refer to the literature of Ch'oe Nam-sŏn and Yi Kwang-su, and added that he used the term "new literature" to problematize the foreign nature of this literature.

In Chosŏn Sosŏlsa (A History of Korean Fiction, 1933), Kim T'ae-jun used the term early modern fiction (kŭndae sosŏl) to refer to fiction written during the reigns of Yŏngjo (1724–1776) and Chŏngjo (1776–1800) and afterwards.[14] In discussing early modern fiction, Kim emphasized the fiction of the Sirhak or "Practical Learning" school of thought, particularly the fiction of Yŏnam Pak Chi-wŏn.[15] Kim included, moreover, fiction in classical Chinese such as Changhwa Hongnyŏn Chŏn (The Story of Chang-hwa and Hong-nyŏn),[16] and the work Ch'unhyang Chŏn (The Story of Ch'unhyang), a work of vernacular sung and spoken narrative (p'ansori). Critics who agree with Kim T'ae-jun perceive a social consciousness in these works that they consider modern.[17] Literary historian Chŏn Kwang-yong has recognized aspects of modernity in Sirhak thought, but adds that Sirhak writers were scholars of the ruling class, and that Sirhak thought did not become popularized. In contrast, Chŏn says, modernization during the late nineteenth century and afterwards obtained popular participation, and continued to take place.[18]

Ch'oe Wŏn-sik has criticized efforts to find modernity in eighteenth-century Korean literature, and has argued that modern Korean literature began in the period 1905 to 1910, which Ch'oe refers to as the nationalist enlightenment period (aeguk kyemonggi).[19] Ch'oe does not think that any

13. Kim Yŏng-min, "Han'guk Munhaksa," 15.
14. Ibid., 17–19.
15. Sirhak thought advocated improving the livelihood of the people through reform of government institutions; agriculture; and promotion of commerce and industry. Cf. James Palais, Confucian Statecraft and Korean Institutions: Yu Hyŏng-wŏn and the Late Chosŏn Dynasty (Seattle: University of Washington, 1996).
16. Changhwa Hongnyŏn Chŏn (The Story of Chang-hwa and Hong-nyŏn) was a suspense novel (kongan) set in P'yŏngan Province during the reign of Hyojong (1649–1659), about two sisters. Kim Tong-ni et al., ed., Han'guk Munhak Taesajŏn (Seoul: Munwŏn'gak, 1973), 891.
17. Writing in the 1950s, Paek Ch'ŏl too saw modernity in eighteenth-century Korean literature. Paek argued that Koreans had used Euro-centric criteria of modernity, and had not considered modern aspects of Korean culture. Kim Yŏng-min, "Han'guk Munhaksa," 20–22.
18. Chŏn Kwang-yong, "Han'guk Kŭndae Sosŏl ŭi Yŏksajŏk Chŏn'gae," in Chŏn Kwang-yong, ed., Han'guk Hyŏndae Sosŏlsa Yŏn'gu (Seoul: Minŭmsa, 1984), 11.
19. Kim Yŏng-min, "Han'guk Munhaksa," 33–4.

significant modern Korean literature can be found in the period between the Kabo reforms and 1905. Literary critics such as Cho Yŏn-hyŏn think that Korean literature of the 1910s was early modern because it was apolitical and only literary. Cho was influenced by the New Criticism, which focused on structural aspects of literature and the verbal object as an entity unto itself.[20] Cho thus defined modern Korean literature as that which was "pure literature" (*sunsu munhak*).[21] Cho Dong-il, however, has defined modern Korean literature as that written in the vernacular, in the genres of lyric poetry, fiction and drama; that which takes as its subject the actual lives of the people; and literature that circulates as a printed product. Such literature, Cho says, began after the March First Independence Movement (1919).[22]

It is evident that Korean literary historians have set forth competing narratives of modern Korean literary history. In this book, I will focus my research Korean literature from the late nineteenth century to 1917, and the writings of Yi Kwang-su in particular. This is not to privilege theories that modern Korean literature began during this period. I will not discuss issues of modernity in eighteenth and early- to mid-nineteenth-century Korean literature simply because I thought it more feasible to focus my research on the late nineteenth century to 1917. I will discuss selected literary narratives of this period.

A BIOGRAPHY OF YI KWANG-SU: THE EARLY YEARS (1892–1917)

Yi Kwang-su was born on the first day of the second month, 1892,[23] in the village of Iksŏng, in the town of Kalsan, Chŏngju County, North P'yŏngan Province, to Yi Chong-wŏn (b. 1850)[24] and his third wife, a woman with the surname Kim (b. 1870).[25]

20. Stanley E. Fish, "Literature in the Reader: Affective Stylistics," *Reader-Response Criticism*, in ed. Jane P. Tompkins (Baltimore: Johns Hopkins University Press, 1980), 75.
21. Yang Mun-gyu, "Han'guk Kŭndae Munhaksaron," 45.
22. Ibid., 53.
23. The family register (*hojŏk*) gives the birth date as the first day of the second month, 1892, *sŏgi* (Western calendar). The clan genealogy gives the birth date as the first day of the second month, the year *imjin* [1892], but does not specify whether the day and month are given by the lunar or Western calendar. *Sŏwŏn Anwŏn Taegunp'a Chŏnju Yi Ssi Sebo* (Seoul: P'yŏngan Pukto Chŏngjugun Yiŏn Silli Chokpo P'yŏnch'anhoe, 1976), 155. In 1979, Edward Wagner of Harvard University helped me to trace Yi's lineage in the genealogy.
24. *Sŏwŏn Anwŏn Taegunp'a Chŏnju Yi Ssi Sebo*, 155.
25. Yi Kwang-su does not mention her name, and in the genealogy she is identified only by her father's name, Kim Wŏn-sŏp; her clan seat, Ch'ungju; and the year she was born. She was Yi Chong-wŏn's third wife. There are discrepancies, however, between Yi's memoirs and the genealogy. Only two wives of Yi Chong-wŏn are mentioned in the genealogy, i.e. a woman surnamed Hong (b. 1850; died the tenth day of the third month, 1882), and a woman surnamed Kim. According to Yi Kwang-su, Yi Chong-wŏn's second wife gave birth to a daughter, then died. Yi Chong-wŏn married his first wife when he was fourteen (Western age); she died three years later. His second wife gave birth to a daughter; then she too died. Yi Kwang-su, *Na:*

The family traced its lineage to a branch of the Chŏnju Yi clan. Members of the Chŏnju Yi in the north had distinguished themselves as a whole in terms of performance in the civil service examination,[26] but it is unlikely that any attained high office.[27] The genealogy of Yi's clan branch attributes official titles to several members, but these may have been purchased, honorary titles, conferred posthumously.[28] At any rate, neither Yi's father nor his grandfather passed the civil service examination, and the family lived in poverty.

The head of our household was my grandfather. He had never tried to take the civil service examination, and since his youth had always delighted in poetry, calligraphy and wine. In his middle age, he took a *kisaeng*[29] concubine, no longer wore a cap over his topknot, and started a wine house. He was known even in the neighboring county for his impressive physique and strength, and as a man who appreciated the finer arts of living—he was a painter, and a man who could hold his own in drinking. His father was a scholarly gentleman in whose name a memorial gate honoring his filial piety had been built. My grandfather's paternal uncle passed the civil service examination and held the title of

Sonyŏn P'yŏn, Seoul: Saenghwalsa, 1947; reprint, *Yi Kwang-su Chŏnjip*, ed. Noh Yang-hwan, vol. 6 (Samjungdang, 1971), 439. Cited in Kim Yun-sik, *Yi Kwang-su wa Kŭ ŭi Sidae*, vol. 1 (Seoul: Han'gilsa, 1976), 20. Yi Chong-wŏn was thirty-four (Western age) when he married his third wife, who was fourteen (Western age). Yi Kwang-su, "Uri Ŏmŏni nŭn Namukkun lŏssŏ," *Sin Yŏsŏng* (December 1933); reprint, *Munhak Sasang* (December 1978), 309. Cited in Kim Yun-sik, 20.

26. A study of the Chŏnju Yi clan by Edward Wagner indicated that members of the Chŏnju Yi residing in the northern provinces accounted for 12% of all passers nationwide for the Chŏnju Yi in the period 1776–1875. Chŏnju Yi members in P'yŏngan Province in particular accounted for 76% of all north Korean passers in the clan for the period 1776–1875, and 9% of all passers nationwide. Edward Wagner, "The Civil Service Examination Process as Social Leaven: the Case of the Northern Provinces in the Yi Dynasty," paper presented at the International Symposium Commemorating the 30th Anniversary of Korean Liberation, Seoul, Korea, August 11–20, 1975.

27. There was regional discrimination against northerners. Kyung Moon Hwang studies regionalism as a factor of discrimination in Chosŏn dynasty Korea. Kyung Moon Hwang, "Bureaucracy in the Transition to Modern Democracy: Secondary Status Groups and the Transformation of Government and Society, 1880–1930," (Ph.D. diss., Harvard University, 1997).

28. The particular sub-lineage (within the Chŏnju Yi clan) to which Yi Kwang-su belonged included only a few examination passers. Among the twenty generations of descendants in the direct line of descent from Tongnam kun (the first member of the Anwŏn branch to move to Chŏngju) to Yi Kwang-su, there were only two passers of the *chinsakwa*, or Literary Licentiate examination (an intermediate level of the civil service examination), one passer of the *munkwa* (the highest level of the civil service examination), and two *mukwa* (military examination) passers.

29. *Kisaeng* were female entertainers. Cf. Kathleen Louise McCarthy, "*Kisaeng* in the Koryŏ Period," (Ph.D. diss., Harvard University, 1991). Kathleen McCarthy, "*Kisaeng* in the Koryŏ Period," *Korean Culture* 15, no. 2 (Summer 1994), 4–13.

sagan or censor; one of my great-grandfather's cousins passed the civil service exam and held the title of *sŭngji*; my great-great-grandfather passed the civil service examination and held the title of *changnyŏng*.[30]

Others referred to his family as "*changnyŏng* Yi's family" because Yi's great-great grandfather had held the title of *changnyŏng*. Yi's family was also known as the "Seoul house" because his ancestors had spent the most time in the capital. Some also called his family the "house with the front gate" because his great-grandfather and one of his ancestors eight generations[31] earlier had been honored for their filial piety; their front gate had been painted red, and a sign was posted at the front gate with the honoree's name and the words "a filial son."[32] As the family grew poorer, however, Yi's father sold the house with the front gate. The family moved to a thatched hut, and the sign that had hung over the outer gate of the old house was wrapped in paper and put aside. Yi himself realized that the nicknames that others had used to refer to his family "may have been appropriate until my grandfather's generation, but more recently it was only used by elderly people, or when people deliberately wanted to express respect for our family."

The poorer his family became, the more conscious Yi seems to have become of their poverty and of the economic disparity between his family and their relatives. He likened his family's declining fortunes to the decline of Korea, and felt himself the descendant of an enervated family and nation, "born at a time when the Korean nation was in a state of decline, and my family fortunes too were at a low ebb." After selling the big house, the family moved several times, "from a big house to a smaller one, and from there to an even smaller house, and again several times afterwards, moving five times within a period of fourteen to fifteen years." As Yi noted, "the sixth time, my father moved from this world to the next."

Yi's father Chong-wŏn drank heavily, and was regarded by his son as "somewhat incompetent and stupid." He took the *ch'osi* or preliminary exam for the civil service examination, but flunked subsequent examinations, and "took up drinking as his occupation."[33] Eventually shunned by relatives, and sought out only by debt collectors, Yi's father seemed to have become "a

---

30. Yi Kwang-su, "Kŭ ŭi Chasŏjŏn," *Chosŏn Ilbo* 22 December 1936–1 May 1937; reprint, *Yi Kwang-su Chŏnjip*, vol. 6 (1971), 299.
31. Yi's ancestor eight generations removed was Inch'an (1689–1737), who passed the Literary Licentiate examination, and was honored with a commemorative "Gate of Filial Piety" (*hyohaeng chongnyŏ*). Inch'an held the perhaps posthumous title of *sungnyŏng ch'ambong*, a junior fifth rank office in the Royal House Administration. *Kyŏngguk Taejŏn*, kwŏn 1.
32. Yi Kwang-su, *Na: Sonyŏn P'yŏn* (Seoul: Saenghwal sa, 1947); reprint, *Yi Kwang-su Chŏnjip*, vol. 6 (1971), 438.
33. Yi Kwang-su, "Kŭ ŭi Chasŏjŏn," 299.

man of no use to the world."[34] Yi began to regard his father with pity rather than respect. Chong-wŏn was devoted to his only son, and patiently took care of him through his son's frequent illnesses. As Yi would remember, "my father was a man of little greed aside from drink; I was the one thing which he was greatly attached to and treasured."[35] When Yi was sick, his father "would not leave the house, but slept by my side, not even going out to his study. He would light a sesame seed oil lamp and lie down beside me, without undoing the ties on his trouser legs, and would sleep with his head on a round wooden pillow. The sesame seed oil lamp was a sign of his solicitude, and the wooden pillow was meant to keep him from sleeping too soundly." Chong-wŏn even looked the other way when the boy's maternal grandmother would come to their home and hold shamanistic healing ceremonies, although Chong-wŏn disapproved of shamanism. Yi's father also began to visit a Buddhist temple to make offerings to the Buddha, and took his son along. Chong-wŏn had his son get vaccinations. "Nowadays everyone gets vaccinations, but it was not that way fifty years ago," Yi wrote. Chong-wŏn had a geomancer look at the family's ancestral burial sites, too; according to geomancy, the location of ancestral burial sites could affect a family's fortunes. When Yi once caught dysentery, his father kept constant vigil by the sick boy's side, heating warm stones to place on his stomach, changing the diapers that the boy had to wear because of the disease, and administering medicine. As Yi recovered, Chong-wŏn played chess and dominoes with him and tutored him in Confucian ritual. "He showed me books like the *Sarye P'yŏllam, Sangnye*,[36] *and Ch'ŏn'gi Taeyo*.[37] It was during this time that I learned about the capping ceremony, marriage ritual, funerary ritual and rituals for ancestral worship, and memorized the ritual readings made at ceremonies for the ancestors."[38]

Yi's mother was fourteen when she married Chong-wŏn.[39] As the wife of the eldest male descendant of the lineage, she was responsible for the duty of preparing food for Neo-Confucian rituals. This was a burdensome duty,

34. Yi Kwang-su, *Na: Sonyŏn P'yŏn*, 478.
35. Ibid., 440.
36. *Sarye P'yŏllam* (Convenient Overview of the Four Rites) was a book about rituals for capping ceremonies, marriage and funerals. The book was edited by Yi Chae during the reign of Sukchong in the Chosŏn dynasty, and published in 1844 (the tenth year of Hŏnjong). A revised edition was published in 1900 (Kwangmu 4). *Sangnye*: This may refer to the *Sangnye Piyo* (Comprehensive Summary of Funerary Ritual). This was originally published in 1621 (the thirteenth year of Kwanghaegun), and was a compilation by Sin Ŭi-gyŏng, adding various commentaries to the text of Zhu Xi's *Jia I* (Family Ritual).
37. The title *Ch'ŏn'gi Taeyo* means "Outline of the Workings of Heaven that Govern the Universe."
38. Yi Kwang-su, *Na: Sonyŏn P'yŏn*, 480.
39. Fourteen, Western age. Yi Kwang-su, "Uri ŏmŏni nŭn namukkun iŏssŏ, *Sin yŏsŏng* (December 1933); reprint, *Munhak Sasang* (December 1978), 309. Cited in Kim Yun-sik, 20.

since the household observed ceremonies honoring up to four generations of ancestors, as often as fifteen times a year.[40]

On the day we observed the ceremony for my four great-great grandparents, my distant uncles and cousins would gather at our house and help prepare the food for the ceremonies. Nevertheless, my mother was, after all, the wife of the principal heir of the lineage and thus responsible for the preparations. The more helpless my mother realized herself to be because of her youth, the more anxious her young heart must have been. The families of two of my distant uncles would come to our house for my three great-grandparents' ceremonies, and my paternal uncle and his wife would come for my late grandmother's services, but there were still two ceremonies which my poor, young mother had to prepare all by herself, and those were for my father's two former, deceased wives.[41]

My father first married when he was fifteen, but became a widower three years later. His second wife died after giving birth to a daughter. My own mother was his third wife. Father never took part himself in the commemorative services for his two former wives, but I remember that mother bathed and changed her clothes for those services just as she would for any of the other ancestral services.[42]

Yi's family eventually became too poor to perform the rituals, however, and began selling off family heirlooms, including the family ritual utensils.

gThe women of the family nurtured Yi Kwang-su's love for literature during his childhood. Folk songs his cousins sang left a vivid impression, as did the vernacular stories his grandmother and cousins read. His grandmother had poor eyesight and often asked her five-year-old grandson to read traditional vernacular storybooks (*iyagi ch'aek*) to her, for which she rewarded him with food and lavish praise. "Perhaps it was her habit that stimulated my own interest in literature," he wrote later. "Grandmother's praise fed my vanity, and I kept reading."[43] After his grandmother died, one

---

40. "We held ancestral ceremonies ten times a year, sometimes as often as two times in a single month. If one included the ancestral observations held on the four or five other holidays (e.g. the days of the vernal and autumnal equinox, Hansik day, etc.) we held ceremonies some fifteen times a year." Yi Kwang-su, *Na: Sonyŏn P'yŏn*, 439.

41. According to Yi Kwang-su's memoir, his father Chong-wŏn married three times. Only two of his wives, however, are mentioned in the clan genealogy, i.e. Hong (1850–1882), and Yi's mother, Kim (b. 1870). Although no date is given in the genealogy for Kim's death, Yi wrote in his memoirs that his mother and father both died of cholera when he was eleven years old by Korean count; that would be the year 1902.

42. Yi Kwang-su, *Na: Sonyŏn P'yŏn*, 439.

43. Yi Kwang-su, "Tananhan Pansaeng ŭi Tojŏng," *Chogwang* April–June 1937; reprint, *Yi Kwang-su Chŏnjip*, vol. 8 (1971), 445.

of his older cousins, his *samjong nunim* (a female cousin descended from a common great-great grandfather), became his tutor in literature. She read aloud to him from vernacular texts of *Wŏlbonggi* (The Story of Moon Mountain), *Ch'angsŏn Kamŭirok* (A Story to Illuminate Virtue and Move Through Righteousness) and *Sa Ssi Namjŏng Ki* (The Record of Madame Sa's Righteous Journey to the South). Yi wrote a story when he was nine or ten, and showed it to his other cousins. He also read some Chinese literature. "The only literary works among the works I read in classical Chinese," he wrote, "were untitled Chinese *shi* poems, *Ma Shang Xiao Shi,*[44] and *Guwen Zhenbao.*[45] I read the *Shi Zhuan*[46] when I was eleven or twelve."

The women in his family introduced him to shamanism, an influence from which he would later rebel. His maternal grandmother held shamanistic rituals whenever she went to Yi's home, though she took care to avoid her son-in-law on those visits, since he disapproved of her beliefs. According to his grandmother, "there were many spirits to placate, since our house was an old one."[47] When the family's fortunes deteriorated, someone told them that it was because no one in their family observed shamanistic or Buddhist rituals any more after Yi's maternal grandmother died.

Yi's father died of cholera in 1902, when Yi was ten years old.[48] Yi's mother died of cholera soon afterwards.[49] Yi's one-year-old sister, Ŏnnyŏn, was given away by relatives as a *minmyŏnŭri*, or a girl who is taken into a family and raised as a future daughter-in-law; she died of dysentery about one year later, at the age of two.[50] Yi's other sister went to stay with their grandfather, Yi Kŏn-gyu.

Yi found compassion and respect among members of the Tonghak or "Eastern learning" religion (renamed Ch'ŏndogyo, or "the Heavenly Way" in 1905). A Tonghak leader named Sŭng I-dal took pity on Yi and introduced him to Pak Ch'an-myŏng, another Tonghak leader.[51] Yi worked as a

44. This could refer to a book of poems by Song Zhi-wen of the early Tang dynasty. One of the poems in the book begins with a phrase that includes the words "on horseback" (*ma shang*); Koreans therefore referred to the book as *Masang Tang Ŭm* (The "On Horseback" Tang Poems).
45. An anthology of poetry from the Former Han dynasty to the Song dynasty. 20 *juan*.
46. This could be Commentaries on the "Classic of Poetry" (*Shi Jing*), or could refer to the "Classic of Poetry" itself.
47. Yi Kwang-su, *Na*, 440.
48. Yi was eleven years old in the Korean way of counting age. Koreans followed the Chinese practice of adding a year to one's age on New Year's day, as well as on one's birthday. Yi Kwang-su, "Kŭŭi Chasŏjŏn," 321.
49. Yi wrote in *Na* that his mother became sick with cholera the day after Yi's father died, and passed away one week later. Cf. *Na*, p. 483. In another work he wrote that she died ten days after his father. "Son'garak," *Yŏngdae* no. 2 (September 1924); reprint, *Yi Kwang-su Chŏnjip*, vol. 8 (1971), 236.
50. She was three years old in the Korean way of counting age, but actually two years old. Yi Kwang-su, "Ŏrin Yŏnghon," *Yŏngdae* no. 3 (October 1924); reprint, *Yi Kwang-su Chŏnjip*, vol. 8 (1971), 241. Yi had another younger sister.
51. Yi Kwang-su, *Na ŭi Kobaek* (Seoul: Ch'unch'usa, 1948); reprint, *Yi Kwang-su Chŏnjip*, vol.

secretary to Pak Ch'an-myŏng. He copied letters from Seoul and Tokyo, for distribution among Tonghak members. Yi observed among Tonghak members an ethos of serving others.[52] Yi attributed to Tonghak members a spirit of humility and kindness, nationalism, and belief in equality and nonviolence. Koreans seemed to consider arrogance and affectation signs of elite social status. Tonghak leaders, in contrast, did not disdain humility and kindness.

Yi also identified Tonghak as influential in his personal development as a nationalist. Tonghak thought was not nationalist per se, Yi wrote, but it was nationalist in that it sought to first realize within the Korean nation and among the Korean people the world to which it aspired. Tonghak resisted the "invasionism" that seemed to follow Catholicism.[53] The world of Tonghak would be achieved not through violent revolution, but through *ch'angdo*, or spreading the way of Tonghak, peacefully and spiritually. According to Yi, the nonviolent March First Independence Movement was based on Tonghak principles. Yi's Tonghak background provided a foundation for his later interest in Tolstoy and Gandhi's beliefs in nonviolent resistance.[54]

In 1905, Yi went to Seoul and, though just a youth of thirteen years, became an instructor in a school in Sogong-dong that was run by Pak Ch'an-myŏng. At the time there was no completed railroad between Seoul and Sinŭiju, so Yi walked from Chŏngju to Chinnamp'o, then took a steamboat to Inch'ŏn, then a train from Inch'ŏn to Namdaemun in Seoul.[55] In Seoul, Yi cut his hair short and wore Western clothes. The school was in a large, traditional-style Korean house. Yi taught Japanese, though his only qualification was that he had memorized a book called *Irŏ Tokhak* (Self-taught Japanese). The students studied Japanese and math. Their objective was to go to Japan to learn about "railroads and steamboats." This was due to the influence of Son Pyŏng-hŭi.

In Seoul, Yi and the students were devoted readers of newspapers, through which "we were able to satisfy our thirst for information about the fate of our nation, the situation in the Russo-Japanese war, and overall circumstances throughout the world. We read editorials by Yu Kŭn, Chang Chi-yŏn and Pak Ŭn-sik as though they were the Bible. Sin Ch'ae-ho would set forth his incisive arguments in the *Taehan Maeil Sinbo* (The Korea Daily News) two or three years later. An Ch'ang-ho founded the *Taehan Maeil Sinbo* as the official newspaper of the Sinminhoe (New People's Association), which he organized after he returned from the United States."

7 (1971), 224.
52. Ibid.
53. Yi Kwang-su, *Na ŭi Kobaek*, 226.
54. Michael Robinson discusses Korean readings and misreadings of Gandhi. Michael Robinson, *Cultural Nationalism in Colonial Korea*, 74, 76, 79, 95, 96–97, 101.
55. Yi Kwang-su, *Na ŭi Kobaek*, 221.

Newspapers were delivered in the morning by dignified-looking men in traditional horsehair hats and *turumagi*.[56] Yi said that sometimes he would go directly to the newspaper company and buy a paper, instead of waiting for delivery.

The students at the school where Yi taught were the sons of members of the Chinbohoe *(*Progressive Society),[57] and were from P'yŏngan, Hwanghae, Hamgyŏng and Kyŏnggi Provinces. The Chinbohoe had been organized by Yi Yong-gu and other Tonghak followers, upon instructions from Tonghak founder Son Pyŏng-hŭi in September 1904.[58] When the Korean government tried to suppress the Chinbohoe because of its Tonghak origins, the Chinbohoe joined forces with the Ilchinhoe (Unity and Progress Society) in December 1904. Yi Kwang-su was one of several students selected by Son Pyŏng-hŭi to go to Tokyo on a fellowship from the Ilchinhoe in August 1905; this was after Son Pyŏng-hŭi and the Chinbohoe had joined forces with the Ilchinhoe, and three months before the Protectorate Treaty of 1905, in which Korea lost diplomatic sovereignty to Japan. Son and his followers left the Ilchinhoe after Yi Yong-gu and the organization openly supported the Protectorate Treaty, which was concluded in November 1905.[59]

Yi attended Tokai gijuku in 1905, and Taisei chūgakkō in 1906[60] while preparing to take entrance examinations for Meiji Gakuin, a Presbyterian school in Tokyo. In 1906, he also joined the T'aegŭk Hakhoe (T'aegŭk Academic Association), a nationalist organization of overseas Korean students in Japan, and heard nationalist activist An Ch'ang-ho speak to a gathering of students in Tokyo.[61] Yi's examination preparations were interrupted in 1906 when the Ilchinhoe ended its scholarship program. Yi returned to Korea.

While in Korea, Yi met his first love, a girl named Siltan. He had gone to the home of maternal relatives in his hometown, Chŏngju, in the middle of the first lunar month, 1907. His grandmother and his maternal uncles had all died; only his cousin's wife was left. His cousin's wife had three daughters. On the thirteenth or fourteenth day of the month, a group of girls came over

---

56. A *turumagi* is a Korean coat worn by men over their clothes. Cf. Koryŏ Taehakkyo Minjok Munhwa Yŏn'guso, *Han'guk Minsok Taegwan*, vol. 2 (Seoul: Kodae Minjok Munhwa Yŏn'guso, 1982), 218.
57. The Chinbohoe was organized in August 1904 by Yi Yong-gu. For a discussion of Tonghak and political participation, cf. Jim Palais, "Political participation in Korea." *Journal of Korean Studies* 1:106–107.
58. Jim Palais, "Political Participation in Korea," 108.
59. Ibid.
60. Yi Kwang-su, "Na ŭi Sasip Pansaenggi," *Sinin Munhak* August 1935: 18, cited in Kim Yun-sik, *Yi Kwang-su wa Kŭ ŭi Sidae*, vol. 1 (Seoul: Han'gilsa, 1986), 140.
61. Kim Yŏng-dŏk, "Ch'unwŏn ŭi Kidokkyo Immun kwa kŭ Sasang kwa ŭi Kwan'gye Yŏn'gu, in *Yi Kwang-su Yŏn'gu*, vol. 1, ed. Tongguk Taehakkyo Pusŏl Han'guk Munhwa Yŏn'guso (Seoul: T'aehaksa, 1984), 169. First published in *Han'guk Munhwa Yŏn'gu Nonch'ong* vol. 5, no. 1 (Seoul: Ewha University, 1965).

to play. They played a Korean game of hide-and-seek called *sullae chapki*, in which someone is designated the robber and someone the blindfolded person who has to catch the robber; everyone else stands in a circle and joins hands, and lifts their joined hands by turn to form an open gate for the robber to run through. Yi felt attracted to one of the girls who was visiting. Her name was Siltan, and she was fifteen years old (fourteen years old, Western age). She was the daughter of Yi's father's second wife's cousin's daughter.[62]

Her face was dark, as though tanned by the sun, but her body, and the contours of her face made her dark skin look beautiful. Her face was round, and her nose, mouth and eyes were all lovely in form and proportion. Her black hair, plaited in one long braid, reached almost to her heels, and when she ran, her braid, tied at the end with a silk ribbon that was imprinted with a pattern of silver chrysanthemums and ornamented with an ochre-colored hair pin, swung to and fro with a clicking noise.[63]

Although Siltan seemed "completely indifferent to the fact that I was a male," Yi felt that he had experienced love for the first time. "The love that I felt for Siltan that night was a love I had never imagined before, and it was the first time I had ever experienced such a love."[64] Yi walked her home, and they embraced on the way, frightened by a sound in the woods.

Yi went back to Japan in 1907, when the Korean government assumed responsibility for supporting former Ilchinhoe scholarship students in Tokyo.[65] He studied at Shirayama Gakusha, in order to continue preparing for the entrance examination to Meiji Gakuin. He was admitted to Meiji Gakuin in the fall of 1907, and attended the school until his graduation in 1910.

Yi began to write for the student journal *Sonyŏn* (Boys), published and edited by Yuktang Ch'oe Nam-sŏn.[66] Yi had met Ch'oe in Tokyo, through Hong Myŏng-hŭi. The journal *Sonyŏn* used a mixed script of the Korean alphabet and Sino-Korean characters, and published poetry, fiction, and articles on various subjects such as art, politics, history and economics. Ch'oe was also a member of the Ch'ŏngnyŏn haguhoe (Youth Student Association), an organization inspired by An Ch'ang-ho.[67] According to Yi's memoirs, seven or eight youths had gathered to form a group called the

62. Yi Kwang-su, *Na: Sonyŏn p'yŏn* (Seoul: Saenghwalsa, 1947); reprint, *Yi Kwang-su Chŏnjip*, vol. 6 (1971), 465. Cited in Kim Yun-sik, *Yi Kwang-su wa kŭ ŭi sidae*, 88.
63. Yi Kwang-su, *Na: Sonyŏn p'yŏn*, 458–9.
64. Ibid., 465.
65. Kim Yun-sik, *Yi Kwang-su wa Kŭ ŭi Sidae*, 141–143.
66. For a study of Ch'oe Nam-sŏn, cf. Chizuko Takeuchi, "Ch'oe Nam-sŏn: History and Nationalism in Modern Korea," (Ph.D. diss., University of Hawaii at Manoa, 1988).
67. Kenneth Wells, *New God, New Nation: Protestants and Self-Reconstruction Nationalism in Korea 1896–1937* (Honolulu: University of Hawaii Press, 1990), 66–67.

Sonyŏnhoe (Boys' Association). The group grew to about twenty members who were all seventeen or eighteen years old. *Sonyŏn* was published from November 1908 to May 1911, when it was banned after publishing an article that opposed the Japanese annexation of Korea. [68] According to Yi's memoirs, the third or fourth issue came to the attention of the Japanese police, and he and the others (not specified) were summoned to the Police Station. They had to listen to some kind of broadcast warning, and then were released, but they were under police surveillance from then on. "We realized clearly that our magazine would be subject to surveillance by Japanese police, but we were also able to regard ourselves with a kind of pride." [69]

From 1909 to 1917, Yi wrote several short stories in various journals, in which he experimented with literary styles, eventually developing a modern vernacular style. Yi's first work of fiction, "Ai ka" (Is This Love?) was published in the Meiji Gakuin newsletter, the *Shiragane Gakuhō*. [70] "Ŏrin Hŭisaeng" (The Young Sacrifice), an adaptation of a Russian work, was published in the February and May issues of *Sonyŏn* in 1910, the short story "Mujŏng" (The Heartless) in March and April 1910 in the *Taehan Hŭnghakpo* (Journal of the Society to Encourage Learning), [71] and "Hŏnsinja" (A Person of Dedication) in the August 1910 issue of *Sonyŏn*. [72]

Marriage

Yi graduated from Meiji Gakuin in March 1910, [73] and passed the entrance examination for Daiichi High School but interrupted his studies to return to Korea to visit his ailing grandfather. While in Korea, he married his first wife Paek Hye-sun in a traditional arranged marriage.

I was returning home from my uncle's house . . . when I met a man named Sŏngjae, who was from the same clan as I, and of my grandfather's generation, hobbling towards my uncle's house looking for me. He was an old man over sixty years old, and walked with a long walking staff. I knew he was a poor scholar of Chinese who had been on good terms with my late father.

He had traveled dozens of miles on his aged limbs to see me about none other than the question of my marriage. He told me that an old man named S, who had been a drinking companion of my father's, was on his

68. Kim Tong-ni et al., *Han'guk Munhak Taesajŏn* (Seoul: Munwŏn'gak, 1973), 339.
69. Yi Kwang-su, *Na ŭi Kobaek*, 229.
70. "Ai ka" in Kurokawa Sō, ed., *Chōsen*, vol. 3 of *'Gaichi' no Nihongo Bungaku sen* (Tokyo: Shinjuku Shobō, 1996), 21–26.
71. *Taehan Hŭnghakpo* nos. 11–12; reprint, *Yi Kwang-su Chŏnjip*, vol. 1 (1978), 556–561.
72. *Sonyŏn* vol. 3, no. 8; reprint, *Yi Kwang-su Chŏnjip*, vol. 1 (1978), 565–568.
73. Yi Kwang-su, "Tananhan Pansaeng ŭi Tojŏng," *Chogwang* (April–June 1937); reprint, *Yi Kwang-su Chŏnjip*, vol. 8 (1978), 448. Yi said he graduated from Meiji Gakuin when he was nineteen years old, in the "third month of the year kyŏngsul (1910)."

deathbed and was saying that he would not close his eyes in peace until he had gotten me as his son-in-law and entrusted his young daughter to me.

I followed Sŏngjae along the dark streets—it was the end of the seventh lunar month—and across icy paths through the fields, to S's house. S grabbed my hand and said in a barely audible voice, "I am a friend of your father's. I trust only you. My daughter is not much out of the ordinary, but I believe in you and no one else. I will close these eyes trusting only in you." His tongue had already grown numb, and his speech was slurred. I found myself answering, "Yes." Perhaps it was because I am easily moved. I did not have the courage to refuse this dying man's request. I would not have had the courage to refuse anything he asked of me.

Then one day, in the eighth lunar month, I put on indigo trousers, a jade green jacket, and a ceremonial cap, and was carried in a palanquin to the bride's house, where the rites were performed.[74]

Yi was unhappy in the marriage, though, and left for Tokyo again. Once in Tokyo, he felt conscience-stricken, and returned to Chŏngju, only to leave within days after his arrival. Paek Hye-sun gave birth to a son Chin-gŭn.[75] Yi and Paek were eventually divorced, though, and Yi married a woman named Hŏ Yŏng-suk in 1921.[76]

Osan

After graduating from middle school, Yi gave up the idea of continuing his education, and decided to return to Korea to teach. He and his friends "had no heart for studying. Our minds were troubled by the urgent awareness that the future of our country hung in the balance."[77] Yi felt somewhat disappointed when Ch'oe Nam-sŏn and Hong Myŏng-hŭi seemed unimpressed by his decision to be a teacher. He thought they did not appreciate the importance of education. He himself had doubts about whether or not he was making a good decision. He thought he might be stuck in the countryside forever.

---

74. Yi Kwang-su, "Kŭ ŭi Chasŏjŏn," 338.
75. Chin-gŭn's date of birth on the *hojŏk* (family register) in the Seoul District Public Procurator's Office is August 4, 1915. He married Cho Tŏk-sun April 9, 1938. According to the *chokpo* (family genealogy), Chin-gŭn lived from 1913 to 1950.
76. Hŏ Yŏng-suk gave birth to two sons and two daughters: Pong-gŭn (May 30, 1927–February 22, 1934), Yŏng-gŭn (spelled Yung-keun, b. September 26, 1929); Chŏng-nan (spelled Chung-nan, b. September 24, 1933); and Chŏng-hwa (spelled Chung Wha, b. December 31, 1934). These are the official family register dates, except for Chung Wha's birthday, which my father says was incorrectly reported by my grandfather on the register as January 31, 1935.
77. Yi Kwang-su, *Na ŭi Kobaek*, 229.

He returned to Korea to accept a teaching offer at Osan Hakkyo, a school founded by Namgang Yi Sŭng-hun (1864–1930),[78] in Chŏngju County, North P'yŏngan Province. While traveling to Chŏngju, he witnessed the segregation of Korean and Japanese passengers in separate train cars. This made him indignant, and he strengthened his resolve to be a teacher and educate Koreans to better their lives.[79] The incident further motivated Yi to help Koreans improve their lives and situation.

Osan was one of five schools in P'yŏngan Province. The others were Sungsil Chung Hakkyo in P'yŏngyang; Taesŏng Hakkyo, founded by Tosan An Ch'ang-ho, in P'yŏngyang; Yangsil Hagwŏn in Ŭiju; and Sinsŏng Chung Hakkyo in Sŏnch'ŏn.[80] Sungsil and Sinsŏng were run by Western missionaries. Yangsil existed in name only, and had no substantial operations. Taesŏng and Osan were the only schools run by Koreans. All of the schools, however, sought to provide nationalist education. According to Yi's memoirs, the Western missionaries at Sungsil and Sinsŏng Middle Schools gave Korean instructors the freedom to teach what they wanted to teach. Osan specifically sought to nurture nationalist leaders.

Namgang Yi Sŭng-hun founded Osan in 1907. Originally a merchant in Chŏngju, he had decided to dedicate himself to the education of the Korean people as a way of strengthening the Korean nation. He had funded the Kangmyŏng Ŭisuk,[81] an elementary school, and had begun working to establish a modern middle school too. When Confucian scholars at the Confucian academy (*hyanggyo*) in Chŏngju refused to help Namgang start Osan, the governor (*kwanch'alsa*) of North P'yŏngan Province, Pak Sung-bong, sympathized with Namgang, and intervened, persuading the scholars who ran the Confucian academy to donate land to help fund the new school. The school opened on December 24, 1907.[82]

Soon after the annexation of Korea to Japan in 1910, Yi Sŭng-hun was arrested in connection with the Sinminhoe (New People's Association) incident.[83] The Sinminhoe incident was called by the Japanese the

78. Namgang was Yi Sŭng-hun's pen name, Sŭng-hun was his polite name, and his given name was In-hwan.

79. Yi Kwang-su, *Na ŭi Kobaek*, 230.

80. Ibid., 231.

81. Kim To-t'ae, *Namgang Yi Sŭng-hun Chŏn* (Seoul: Mungyosa, 1950), 201.

82. When Governor Pak left for another post, local Confucian scholars ousted Namgang and tried to run the school themselves. The Confucians wanted to close Osan Middle School, and just run an elementary school. Namgang decided to sell all of his property, and donate the money to Osan Hakkyo. He returned lands donated by the local Confucian academy. The Confucians then agreed to leave the school.

83. The Sinminhoe was a secret society formed with the purpose of attaining Korean independence. It sought to carry out educational, industrial and youth activities, within the bounds of law. The Sinminhoe published the *Taehan Maeil Sinbo* under the name of Ernest Bethell, an Englishman. Cf. Chŏng Chin-sŏk, *Taehan Maeil Sinbo wa Paesŏl: Han'guk Munje e Taehan Yŏngil Oegye* (Seoul: Nanam, 1987). An Ch'ang-ho published the newspaper after he

"conspiracy to assassinate governor general Terauchi." As many as seven hundred people were arrested, and one hundred and five were prosecuted; it thus is also referred to as the "Incident of the 105." Most of the people involved were in education or the church. Schoolmaster Yi Sŭng-hun, moreover, was an important official in the New People's Association, responsible for North P'yŏngan Province.[84] The colonial government used the charges of a conspiracy to assassinate governor general Terauchi, as a pretext to arrest Korean nationalists and suppress their activities.

Yi became responsible for administering Osan Hakkyo. He taught the local evening school, moreover, in addition to teaching forty-two hours a week during the day, in math, language and other subjects. Several hundred people had been arrested in connection with the Sinminhoe incident, so there were few people to serve as teachers. Yi earned ten wŏn per month and once received a *turumagi*, or Korean-style, long, outer coat made of ramie. The teachers lived on rice and bean paste. Yi also managed the neighborhood association (*tonghoe*) that Yi Sŭng-hun had organized in Yŏng-dong. Men and women had equal rights in the neighborhood association. They could vote, and participate in discussion. Under Yi Sŭng-hun's influence, there were many Christian converts in the neighborhood, and they agreed to take Sundays off for rest and spiritual cultivation. In evening school, Yi taught people in the neighborhood how to read the newspaper and the Bible. He taught women in particular; they all gained enough literacy to read the Bible in Korean.

In 1913, when Yi returned from teaching summer school in Ungch'on, Kyŏngsang Province, he learned that some people were trying to have him removed from Osan Hakkyo for having taught about Tolstoy. Yi's critics considered Tolstoy's views of Christianity heretical. Yi was accused of having corrupted students' faith in Christianity. On his way back from Ungch'ŏn, Yi had visited Yi Sŭng-hun in jail, and reported about the school. Namgang advised him to stay on at the school until he was out of prison. Yi could not stay at the school due to his critics, though, and left. He had thought of leaving the school, but could not because of his sense of obligation to Namgang; now, however, he felt that the movement to oust him freed him to leave the school.

returned to Korea from the United States. He published the newspaper with Yi Kap, Yi Tong-nyŏng, Chŏn Tŏk-ki and Yang Ki-t'ak. Yu Tong-yŏl and Kim Hong-nyang sought to establish a military academy in Manchuria in 1908 or 1909, as a project of the Sinminhoe. Other Sinminhoe projects included the Taesŏng School in P'yŏngyang, the T'aegŭk sŏgwan—a publishing company, and the Masandong Chagi Hoesa (Masandong Porcelain Company). Yi Kwang-su, *Na ŭi Kobaek*, 229.
84. Yi Kwang-su, *Na ŭi Kobaek*, 235.

Yi decided to travel. He thought of the fact that many Koreans had gone into exile outside of Korea because of the Japanese occupation. Yi also felt compelled to leave by the increasingly pervasive presence of Japanese hegemony in Korea. Yi left Chŏngju in November 1913, with hopes of traveling through China and then visiting colonized nations such as Vietnam, India, Persia and Egypt, to see the situations there and how the peoples there were seeking national independence.[85] Yi's travel was motivated by the desire to overcome colonialism; this contrasts with Orientalist travel, which seeks to conquer and colonize. Yi traveled in order to learn about ways in which other colonized peoples were trying to regain national sovereignty.

At first, Yi planned on going to Mukden by train. He took a train from Chŏnju to Andong in Manchuria. He spent one night there, and the next day happened to meet Chŏng In-bo, who was on his way from Shanghai to Seoul to seek funds. Chŏng gave Yi thirty *yuan* of Chinese money and told him that Hong Myŏng-hŭi and several others were in Shanghai, and that he himself would be returning to Shanghai. Chŏng said that the north was cold just then, and advised Yi to go to Shanghai first. Yi used most of the money to buy a ticket for a boat to Shanghai, and an outfit of Chinese clothing, made of blue cotton.

He took an English boat, which later became a secret meeting place for Koreans from the Shanghai Provisional Government, and from Korea. "Now I was outside the jurisdiction of the Japanese police," he wrote in his memoirs. The room that he stayed in on the boat was freezing cold. He met several Koreans all of whom were going to Shanghai. The boat was supposed to go through Chefoo and Qingdao, then on to Shanghai, but for some reason, they had to disembark at Yinkow, and wait a week for a boat called the Wenzhou. Yi had no money, so a Korean named Ch'a Kwan-ho paid for his food. At Pudong, they disembarked and boarded a small boat, crossed the Huangpu River, and got off at Huangpu tan.

In his narratives about China, Yi wrote about the Korean overseas nationalist community in Shanghai. Yi went to the home of Wi Hye-rim, and received directions to where Hong Myŏng-hŭi was staying on Baierbulu. Hong Myŏng-hŭi was living in a two-story house. Hoam Mun Il-p'yŏng[86] lived on the first floor. Hong Myŏng-hŭi, Cho Yong-ŭn and two other people lived on the second floor.

In January 1914, Yegwan Sin Sŏng advised Yi that the overseas Korean newspaper in San Francisco, the *Sin Han Minbo* (New Korean People's Newspaper) was looking for a writer. The newspaper was published by the nationalist organization, the Kungminhoe (The Korean National Asso-

---

85. Yi Kwang-su, *Na ŭi Kobaek*, 238.
86. Hoam was Mun Il-p'yŏng's literary name.

ciation).[87] Sin gave him five hundred wŏn, and told him to go to the United States. Yi thus gave up his plans of traveling through Asia, and decided to try to go to the United States through Europe. Sin wrote letters of introduction to Wŏlsong Yi Chong-ho in Vladivostok, and to Ch'ujŏng Yi Kap in Muling, Jilin Province.[88] Yi left Shanghai in January 1914, after having stayed in Shanghai for a little over a month.

He took a Russian boat to Vladivostok,[89] then traveled by train to Heilongjiang Province, where he stayed with Yi Kap for a month.[90] Continuing west, he then took the trans-Siberian railway to Chita. The vast expanses of Siberia would later appear in Yi's novel *Yujŏng* (Emotion, 1933). Yi stayed in Chita for a year, waiting to receive funds from the Kungminhoe to fund the rest of his trip to the United States. Yi postponed his plans to go the United States after receiving a letter about a factional dispute in the United States among overseas Koreans. An organization called the Kungmin yŏnmaeng (Citizens' Alliance) had claimed Yi as a member, prompting the rival Kungminhoe to demand a public statement from Yi disavowing any connection with the Kungmin yŏnmaeng. Yi refused, however, since the Kungmin yŏnmaeng had been organized by a former middle school classmate of his. Yi stayed on in Chita until August 1914, when World War I began and Yi was forced to cancel his plans to travel to the United States through Europe. He returned instead to Korea.

Vladivostok

In *Na ŭi Kobaek* (My Confessions, 1948), Yi wrote about Korean nationalists he met in Vladivostok who were trying to organize nationalist movements outside of Korea to recover Korean national independence. When he reached Vladivostok, he went first to Sin Han Ch'on (New Korea Village).[91] There, he was questioned suspiciously, and his belongings

87. Yi Kwang-su, "Tananhan Pansaeng ŭi Tojŏng," *Chogwang* April–June 1936; reprint, *Yi Kwang-su Chŏnjip*, ed. Noh Yang-hwan, vol. 8 (Seoul: Usinsa, 1978), 449. The overseas independence organizations the Hanin Hapsŏng Hyŏphoe (United Korean Society) and Kongnip Hyŏphoe (Mutual Assistance Association) had merged to form the Kungminhoe (Korean Community Association) on February 1, 1909 in San Francisco. The Kungminhoe was renamed the Taehan Kungminhoe (Korean National Association) in 1912, and chapters organized in Hawaii, the United States, Mexico, Siberia and Manchuria. John K. Hyun, *A Condensed History of the Kungminhoe: the Korean National Association (1903–1945)* (Seoul: Koryŏ Taehakkyo Minjok Munhwa Yŏn'guso, 1986), 4. I have used Hyun's translations of organization names.
88. Yi Kwang-su, *Na ŭi Kobaek* (Seoul: Ch'unch'usa, 1948); reprint, *Yi Kwang-su Chŏnjip*, ed. Noh Yang-hwan, vol. 7 (Seoul: Samjungdang, 1971), 242.
89. Yi Kwang-su, "Haesamwi rosŏ," *Ch'ŏngch'un* no. 6 (1 March 1915), 79–83; reprint, *Yi Kwang-su Chŏnjip*, vol. 9 (1978), 137–139. "Tananhan Pansaeng ŭi Tojŏng," *Chogwang* April–June 1936; reprint, *Yi Kwang-su Chŏnjip*, vol. 8 (Seoul: Usinsa, 1978), 449.
90. Yi Kwang-su, "Tananhan Pansaeng ŭi Tojŏng," *Chogwang* April–June 1936, 449.
91. For a study of Sinhanch'on, cf. Yun Pyŏng-sŏk, "Yŏnhaeju esŏ ŭi Minjok Undong kwa Sinhanch'on," *Han'guk Minjok Undongsa Yŏn'gu* 3 (1989), cited in Pak Hwan, *Rŏsia Hanin*

searched, until three people who recognized him appeared. Kim Ip, Yun Hae and Kim Ha-gu[92] had read his work in the Korean student journals *Sonyŏn* (Boys), *Ch'ŏngch'un* (Youth) and *T'aegŭk Hakpo* (The Scholarly Journal of the T'aegŭk Society).[93] Yi met with Yi Chong-ho, with Kim Ha-gu's help.

According to Yi's memoirs, Yi Chong-ho had been a founding member of the Sinminhoe (New People's Association) in 1908, with Tosan An Ch'ang-ho, Yi Kap, Yi Tong-nyŏng and Yi Tong-hwi. The Sinminhoe sought to promote Korean industry and education, and nurture Korean nationalist leaders.[94] While in Russia Yi Kwang-su wrote articles for the *Kwŏnŏp Sinmun*, which was published in Vladivostok, and the *Taehanin Chyŏnggyobo*, which was published in Chita.

Returning to Korea in 1914

When World War I began, Yi could not continue with his plans to reach the United States through Europe. In August 1914, Yi returned to Korea.

Yi taught again at Osan Hakkyo, and wrote for *Saepyŏl* (New Star) and *Ch'ŏngch'un* (Youth) magazines, published and edited by Yuktang Ch'oe Nam-sŏn. Yi's writings included a short story entitled "Kim Kyŏng" in *Ch'ŏngch'un* no. 6 (1 March 1915); an article about Yi's travels in Shanghai in 1913, published in *Ch'ŏngch'un* nos. 3–4; an account of a visit to Posŏng Middle School (*Ch'ŏngch'un* no. 3); an essay about ethics and philosophy, entitled "Tongjŏng" (Compassion) (*Ch'ŏngch'un* no. 3); and the lyrics that he wrote for the Osan school song, entitled "Sae Ai" (New Child) (*Ch'ŏngch'un* no. 3). An interviewer later asked Yi whether or not *Ch'ŏngch'un* paid for his manuscripts; Yi replied, "How could a magazine that only printed two to three thousand copies afford to pay manuscript fees?"[95]

Minjok Undongsa (Seoul: T'amgudang, 1995), 12.

92. Kim Ha-gu was from the county of Myŏnch'ŏn, in North Hamgyŏng Province. He worked as a reporter for the *Haejo Sinmun*, which was the first Korean newspaper in Russia and was published February 26, 1908 to May 26, 1908. Pak Hwan, *Rŏsia Hanin Minjok Undongsa*, 19. Kim Ha-gu studied at Waseda University, in the department of political science and economics, with financial help from Yi Chong-ho. Pak Hwan, p. 32. After attending Waseda, Kim Ha-gu worked as an instructor at Kitokkyo Pot'ong Hakkyo (Christian Elementary School). He went into exile in Vladivostok in July 1912. Pak Hwan, 152.

93. The *t'aegŭk* image used in the name of this organization referred to the Taoist image of *yin* and *yang* on the Korean flag, and was a nationalist symbol. Cf. Chapter 2, n. 139.

94. Arthur Gardner, "The Korean Nationalist Movement and An Ch'ang-ho, Advocate of Gradualism," (Ph.D. diss., University of Hawaii, 1979), 41–58. Cited in Michael Robinson, *Cultural Nationalism in Colonial Korea, 1920–1925* (Seattle: University of Washington Press, 1988), 41. It was Yi Chong-ho who obtained a secret letter from the Kwangmu emperor to give to Yi Chun to present at the Hague. Yi Kwang-su, *Na ŭi Kobaek*, 243.

95. Yi Kwang-su, "*Mujŏng* tŭng Chakp'um ŭl Ŏ Hada," *Samch'ŏlli* January 1937; reprint, *Yi Kwang-su Chŏnjip*, vol. 10 (Seoul: Samjungdang, 1971), 521.

Yi went to Japan in 1915, and began studying in the liberal arts division of Waseda University in September 1915. He received financial support, either from Chungang High School, where An Chae-hong was dean, or from educator and entrepreneur Kim Sŏng-su (1891–1955); Yi mentioned both in a 1936 interview.[96] After completing the freshman preparatory program at Waseda, Yi entered the philosophy department. He published poetry and essays in January, 1916, in a book edited by Ch'oe Nam-sŏn entitled *Simun Tokpon* (A Reader of Modern Writing), and began publishing articles in the *Maeil Sinbo* (Daily News); these included travelogues, and essays about literature, education, agriculture, and social reform.

Yi began writing his first novel *Mujŏng* (The Heartless)[97] during his second year at Waseda University. He received five wŏn per installment from the *Maeil Sinbo*. The novel was published in the newspaper from January 1 to June 14, 1917. Nakamura Kentarō was editor-in-chief, and Sŏnu Il and Yi Sang-hyŏp were also working there.[98]

KOREAN LITERATURE FROM THE LATE NINETEENTH TO EARLY TWENTIETH CENTURIES

The sinsosŏl

The *sinsosŏl* or "new fiction" genre of early modern Korean literature dated from 1906 to the 1930s.[99] Yi Chae-sŏn has identified the work "Illyŏmhong," by Irhak Sanin, as the first *sinsosŏl*; this work was published in the *Taehan Ilbo* (Korea Daily News), from January 23 to February 18, 1906.[100]

---

96. Ibid.
97. Please see Chapter 4 for an explanation of the meaning of the word *mujŏng*. Peter H. Lee translated the title as "The Heartless," in *Korean Literature: Topics and Themes* (Tucson: University of Arizona Press, 1965), 112; and in Peter H. Lee, comp. and ed., *Modern Korean Literature: An Anthology* (Honolulu: University of Hawaii Press, 1990), xvi. Kim Kichung translated the title as "The Heartless," when translating an excerpt from the novel. Cf. Yi Kwang-su, "The Heartless," trans. Kim Kichung, in *Modern Korean Literature: An Anthology*, comp. and ed. Peter H. Lee (Honolulu: University of Hawaii Press, 1990), 2–15. Chung Chong-wha translated the title as "Indifference," in *Modern Korean Literature: An Anthology, 1908–1965*, ed. Chung Chong-wha (New York: Columbia University Press, 1995), xv.
98. Yi Kwang-su, "Tananhan Pansaeng ŭi Tojŏng," 445–457.
99. Yi Chae-su includes certain works published in the 1920s and 1930s in the genre of *sinsosŏl*. Cf. Yi Chae-su, *Han'guk Sosŏl Yŏn'gu* (1969). Cited in Hwang Chŏng-hyŏn, *Sinsosŏl Yŏn'gu*, 17. Jina Kim discusses *sinsosŏl* as part of commodity culture, and, moreover, presents research about the word *sin* (new) and *modŏn* (modern). Jina Kim, "Language, Commodity and the City: The Production of Urban Literature in Colonial Korea," *Seoul Journal of Korean Studies* 16 (December 2003): 39–74.
100. Yi Chae-sŏn, "Kaehwagi ŭi Uguk Sosŏl," in Min Pyŏng-su, Cho Tong-il, Yi Chae-sŏn, *Kaehwagi ŭi Uguk Munhak* (Seoul: Sin'gu Munhwasa, 1974), 134. *Illyŏmhong* may have been an adaptation of a Chinese work, which itself was an adaptation or translation of a Western work; Yi Chae-sŏn found a work with the same title listed as a translation, or adaptation, in a history

Chŏng Hyŏn-jŏn speculates that the term *sinsosŏl* may have been used in Korean to make a distinction between modern and premodern literature.[101] Chŏn Kwang-yong shares this hypothesis when interpreting the Chinese character *sin* (new) in *sinsosŏl* as expressing the innovativeness of foreign culture, rejection of premodern culture, and interest in the new.[102] As Yi Chae-sŏn has observed, though, how different were the *sinsosŏl* from Chosŏn dynasty fiction? Yi suggests that the term *sinsosŏl* may have been used to refer to foreign elements in the *sinsosŏl*, but not necessarily the complete departure from traditional literature. There were many continuities between the *sinsosŏl* and premodern Korean fiction. The plot was often contrived. There was not much character development.[103] The traditional theme of lovers who are separated and then reunited appeared often in *sinsosŏl*. There were continuities between the *sinsosŏl* and the novel of the "aristocratic hero" (*kwijokjŏk yŏngung sosŏl*) in the story of the main character who passes through ordeals in order to attain success.[104] Yi Chae-sŏn concurs with Chŏn Kwang-yong on the "novelty" of the *sinsosŏl*. *Sinsosŏl* such as *Tears of Blood* satisfied consumers' fascination with the "new."[105] Newspapers published fiction in order to sell more papers.[106] This profit motive created a publishing environment favorable for *sinsosŏl*. Many *sinsosŏl* were published in newspapers. An article in the *Hwangsŏng Sinmun* on January 12, 1901 reported that there were five newspaper companies in Korea at the time, and estimated the number of newspaper readers at no more than three thousand, but added that readership would increase with time and the growing sophistication of the reading public.

Sinsosŏl were written by professional writers and journalists. Pak Yŏng-un, who wrote the novel *Ongnyŏndang* (Jade Lotus Pavilion), referred to himself as a *kija*, or journalist, in an advertisement for his novel *Kŭmsanwŏl* (Gold Mountain Moon).[107] *Sinsosŏl* writers were enlightenment advocates who sought to promote popular enlightenment and national

of Qing fiction, *Wan Qing Xiaoshuo Shi*, by He Ying.
101. Hwang Chŏng-hyŏn, *Sinsosŏl Yŏn'gu*, 16. See also Yi Chae-sŏn, *Han'guk Kaehwagi Sosŏl Yŏn'gu*, 11.
102. Chŏn Kwang-yong, "Han'guk Kŭndae Sosŏl ŭi Yŏksajŏk Chŏn'gae," in *Han'guk Hyŏndae Sosŏlsa Yŏn'gu*, ed. Chŏn Kwang-yong (Seoul: Minŭmsa, 1984), 12.
103. Hwang Chŏng-hyŏn, *Sinsosŏl Yŏn'gu*, 78.
104. Cho Dong-il, *Sinsosŏl ŭi Munhaksajŏk Sŏnggyŏk* (1973), cited in Hwang Chŏng-hyŏn, *Sinsosŏl Yŏn'gu*, 18.
105. Yi Chae-sŏn, *Han'guk Kaehwagi Sosŏl Yŏn'gu*, 9.
106. Ibid., 21.
107. *Kyŏngnam Ilbo* 22 November 1912. Cited in Yi Chae-sŏn, *Han'guk Kaehwagi Sosŏl Yŏn'gu*, 44. For a discussion of *sinsosŏl* writers as journalists, see Cho Yŏn-hyŏn, *Han'guk Hyŏndae Munhaksa* (1964); *Han'guk Sin Munhak Ko* (1966). Cited in Hwang Chŏng-hyŏn, *Sinsosŏl Yŏn'gu*, 16.

self-strengthening through their writings in newspapers, journals and books.[108]

The main characters of *sinsosŏl* were often poor students, and commoners or citizens of low social status. The novel *Hyŏngwŏl* (Firefly Moon) depicts a peasant youth named Kang P'ir-yŏng, who is from an impoverished family of tenant farmers. Kang decides that he does not want to farm, and wants an education.[109] In most *sinsosŏl*, the student is easily admitted to a school, and graduates first in the class. The character Kim Kwan-il in *Tears of Blood* just sets off to study in the United States, leaving the reader "bewildered," as literary critic Hwang Chŏng-yŏn has said. Where does he get the money to go there? How does he get into school? These questions are never answered in *Tears of Blood*. *Hyŏngwŏl* is more realistic; Kang P'ir-yŏng struggles to get into school, and supports himself through school working as a laborer. During class, he is so exhausted from work that he has difficulty staying awake. Kang P'ir-yŏng has no benefactor, moreover, who puts him through school; he has to work to put himself through school.

The novel of domestic intrigue was a kind of *sinsosŏl* that resembled traditional domestic comedy, while offering modern social criticism. It was similar to traditional novels in the themes of rivalry between wife and concubine, and the persecution of virtuous characters by scheming enemies. It was like traditional court case literature, in the depiction of crime and punishment. The novel of domestic intrigue, however, advocated education for women, reform of traditional marriage customs, abolition of concubinage, and free love.

T'oronch'e sosŏl[110] or "debate-style fiction" was a genre of sinsosŏl that was written in the form of dialogue. Characters were described in the beginning of the work, and thereafter identified in parentheses or not at all. This genre used dialogue more as a forum for ideological and political discussion, than for character development or narrative purposes.[111]

---

108. Yu Yang-sŏn, "Kuhanmal Sahoe Sasang ŭi Sosŏrhwa Yangsang," *Chindan Hakpo* no. 59 (1985): 122.
109. Hwang Chŏng-hyŏn, *Sinsosŏl Yŏn'gu*, 124.
110. For studies of the *t'oronch'e sosŏl*, see Kim Chung-ha, "Kaehwagi sosŏl 'Kŏbu Ohae' Sogo," *Suryŏn Ŏmun Nonjip* 5 December 1975. Kim Chung-ha, "Kaehwagi T'oronch'e Sosŏl Yŏn'gu," *Kwanak Ŏmun Yŏn'gu* 3 (1978). Cited in Hwang Chŏng-hyŏn, *Sinsosŏl Yŏn'gu*, 19.
111. Yi Ho-suk has observed the use of dialogue as a means of editorializing, in the writings of early modern Korean woman writer Na Hye-sŏk. Na wrote a story entitled "Pubu kan ŭi Mundap" (Questions and Answers Between a Husband and Wife). See Yi Ho-suk, "Wiakchŏk Chagi Pangŏ Kije rosŏ ŭi Erot'ijŭm: Na Hye-sŏk Non," in *P'eminijŭm kwa Sosŏl Pip'yŏng*, ed. Han'guk Yŏsŏng Sosŏl Yŏn'guhoe (Seoul: Han'gilsa, 1995), 90–91.

Historical fiction

Early modern Korean historical fiction eulogized nationalists, used historical allegory to comment on the present, and offered instruction for the purpose of national self-strengthening. Korean historical fiction was often based on works that were written in Chinese. These Chinese works, moreover, were sometimes influenced by Japanese translations of western modernity. The Korean work *Raran puin chŏn* about Madame Roland[112] was a Korean translation of Liang Qichao's *Jinshi Dii Nujie, Lolan Furen Zhuan* (A Biography of the First Heroine of Modern Times, Madame Roland).[113] Pak Ŭn-sik, Sin Ch'ae-ho and Chang Chi-yŏn, moreover, who wrote Korean historical fiction, were educated in classical Chinese and sought access to modernity through the Chinese language.[114] Books written in Chinese, or written by foreign missionaries in China writing in Chinese, had been the most influential foreign books in Korea from 1870 to 1880; this influence continued in 1890 to 1900, though Japanese influence steadily increased.[115] As Kang Yŏng-ju has noted, though, there was a difference between Korean historical fiction that glorified imperialists such as Bismarck, Napoleon and Peter the Great, and historical fiction about nationalists such as Joan of Arc, William Tell, and Mazzini.[116] Sin Ch'ae-ho wrote about Korean historical figures who had fought foreign invasion. Sin wrote *Ŭlchi Mundŏk* (1908), which was about the Koguryŏ general who defeated the Sui invasion of Koguryŏ in 612, and *Yi Sun-sin Chŏn* (The Life of Yi Sun-sin, 1908), which depicted the Chosŏn dynasty admiral who fought the Japanese invasion of Korea in 1592–1597.[117]

Fiction about righteous armies

The short story "So Kŭmgang" (Little Kŭmgang Mountain, 1910), by an author who wrote under the pseudonym of Pinghŏ cha, depicts an *ŭibyŏng* or

112. Theresa Hyun, *Writing Women in Korea* (Honolulu: University of Hawaii Press, 2004), 36. Hyun discusses legends about the lives of European heroines translated into Korean at the beginning of the twentieth century.
113. Yi Chae-sŏn, *Han'guk Kaehwagi Sosŏl Yŏn'gu* (Seoul: Ilchogak, 1972), 148–149. Liang's translation was based on an 1886 Japanese translation. Kim Pyŏng-ch'ŏl, *Han'guk Kŭndae Pŏnyŏk Munhaksa Yŏn'gu* (Seoul: Ŭryu Munhwasa, 1975 and 1988), 231–234. Cited in Theresa Hyun, *Writing Women in Korea*, 36.
114. Yi Sŏn-yŏng, *Yŏksa Chŏn'gi Sosŏl* (Seoul: Asea Munhwasa, 1979) 7. Cited in Hwang Chŏng-hyŏn, *Sinsosŏl Yŏn'gu* (Seoul: Chimmundang, 1997), 222–223.
115. Yi Kwang-nin, *Han'guk Kaehwasa Yŏn'gu* (Seoul: Ilchogak, 1969) 28–34, cited in Yi Chae-sŏn, *Han'guk Kaehwagi Sosŏl Yŏn'gu*, 30.
116. Kang Yŏng-ju, *Han'guk Yŏksa Sosŏl ŭi Chae Insik* (Seoul: Ch'angjak kwa Pip'yŏngsa, 1991), 24.
117. Cf. Michael Robinson, "National Identity and the Thought of Sin Ch'ae-ho: *Sadaejuŭi* and *Chuch'e* in History and Politics," *Journal of Korean Studies* 5 (1984): 121–42. I attended a talk given by Henry Em in 1994 about Sin Ch'ae-ho, at the Southern California Korean Studies Colloquium.

"righteous army" that fought against Japanese colonialism. Published in the *Taehan Minbo* (Korean People's Newspaper) from January 14 to March 6, 1910, the story portrays rebellion in Kangwŏn Province. The story depicts a fictional group of vigilantes based in a cave on Pogae Mountain in Kangwŏn Province.[118] The group emigrates to western Jian dao in order to start an overseas independence movement.

LANGUAGE AND KOREAN LITERATURE

The project of constructing a history of language and literature is a tautological one, in that the ideological constructs of history, language and literature that are used to form the project determine the results. A book about modern literary history privileges the notions of subjectivity, and writing as equivalent to speech.[119] I will discuss here Korean language and literature from the late nineteenth to the early twentieth centuries, but acknowledge the ideological nature of such a narrative.

Early modern Korean literature emerged from traditions of literature written in Chinese characters, the Korean alphabet, and mixed styles using both Chinese characters and the Korean alphabet. Classical Chinese was used as the principal literary medium in Korea until as recently as the early twentieth century. Koreans essentially wrote in a foreign language different from their own; the Korean language is not related to the Sino-Tibetan family of languages, and the agglutinative nature of the language differs

118. The Sogŭmgang group draws its leadership from military men and progressives. The tale of the Kangwŏn Province rebels seems to have been based on actual popular uprisings of "righteous armies" in the late nineteenth to early twentieth centuries in Kangwŏn Province. Rebellion broke out nationwide in January, 1896 in reaction to the Japanese imposed ordinance of November 15, 1895 requiring Koreans to cut off their topknots; the ordinance was a Westernizing measure that outraged Confucians who viewed the body as a sacred legacy from one's ancestors. The 1896 rebellions also took place in reaction to the Japanese assassination of Queen Min earlier on August 20, 1895. Kuksa p'yŏnch'an wiwŏnhoe, *Han'guk Sa*, vol. 19 (Seoul: Taehan min'guk mungyobu Kuksa p'yŏnch'an wiwŏnhoe, 1978), 369. For a study of peasant rebellion, cf. Sun Joo Kim, "Marginalized Elite, Regional Discrimination and the Tradition of Prophetic Belief in the Hong Kyŏng-nae Rebellion," (Ph.D. diss., University of Washington, 2000).
119. Karatani Kōjin has argued that modern Japanese literature began with the discovery of subjectivity, or "interiority," which made possible a discovery of the other, or "landscape," and that these discoveries were written in a language that equated writing with speech (*genbun itchi*). These discoveries were then naturalized, and their historicity forgotten, in a process that Karatani calls "inversion." Karatani Kōjin, *Origins of Modern Japanese Literature*, ed. Brett de Bary (Durham and London: Duke University Press, 1993). Michael Shin discusses Karatani Kōjin's theory of interiority, and Yi Kwang-su. Cf. Michael D. Shin, "Interior Landscapes: Yi Kwang-su's 'The Heartless,' and the Origins of Modern Literature," in *Colonial Modernity in Korea*, ed. Gi-Wook Shin and Michael Robinson (Cambridge: Harvard University Asia Center, 1999), 248–287.

significantly from classical Chinese.[120] Attempts were made to represent Korean with Chinese characters, through improvised practices known as *idu*, *kugyŏl* and *hyangch'al*.[121] Vernacular poetry from the Unified Silla era was recorded in *hyangch'al*.

The Korean alphabet, the *Hunmin Chŏngŭm* (Correct Sounds to Instruct the People), was invented by King Sejong, in 1443 or 1444.[122] The *Hunmin Chŏngŭm* was a phonemic alphabet designed to reflect the linguistic properties of the Korean language, though it evinced the influence of Chinese phonological theory and perhaps other foreign writing systems.[123] The alphabet was also designed to be used in spelling foreign loan words (i.e. Sino-Korean vocabulary) and phonetically transcribing foreign languages.[124] Korean was used to indicate pronunciation in Chinese character dictionaries, and used in *ŏnhae*, or "vulgate elucidations"[125] of Chinese poetry and fiction, Confucian classics, Buddhist texts, technical treatises and language books. Korean was used, moreover, in *naehun*, or books of moral instruction for women and family life.[126]

While Korean literature was primarily written in classical Chinese, there emerged a substantial tradition of poetry and fiction written in Korean. *Sijo*[127] and *kasa*[128] poetry were composed in a mixed style of Korean and Chinese.[129] Vernacular songs were recorded in Korean in anthologies like the

---

120. Yuen Ren Chao, *Language and Symbolic Systems* (Cambridge: Cambridge University Press, 1968), 87. For discussion of the Korean language, cf. Iksop Lee and S. Robert Ramsey, *The Korean Language* (State University of New York Press, 2001); Ho-min Sohn, *The Korean Language* (Honolulu: University of Hawaii Press, 1999).
121. Cf. Iksop Lee and S. Robert Ramsey, *The Korean Language* (State University of New York Press, 2001), 46–55.
122. Iksop Lee and S. Robert Ramsey, *The Korean Language*, 31–32.
123. Cf. theories of foreign influence evaluated in Gari Ledyard, "The Korean Language Reform of 1446: the Origin, Background and Early History of the Korean Alphabet," (Ph.D. diss., University of California, Berkeley, 1966). Gari Ledyard, "The International Linguistic Background of the Correct Sounds for the Instruction of the People," in *The Korean Alphabet: Its History and Structure*, ed. Young-key Kim-Renaud (Honolulu: University of Hawaii Press, 1997), 31–87.
124. Cf. The phonological analysis of the *Hunmin Chŏngŭm* in Lee Kimoon, *Kugŏ Ŏmunsa Yŏn'gu* (Studies in Korean Historical Phonology) (Seoul: T'ap ch'ulp'ansa, 1985).
125. I have used Edward Wagner's translation of the term. Cf. Lee Ki-baik, *A New History of Korea*, trans. Edward W. Wagner (Cambridge: Harvard University Press, 1984), 193.
126. Cf. John Duncan, "The *Naehun* and the Politics of Gender in Fifteenth-Century Korea," in *Creative Women of Korea: The Fifteenth through the Twentieth Centuries*, ed. Young-key Kim-Renaud (Armonk, New York: M.E. Sharpe, 2003), 26–57.
127. *Sijo* were songs that consisted of four lines, each line consisting of four rhythmic units and a caesura in the middle of the line. Cf. David R. McCann, *Form and Freedom in Korean Poetry*. (Leiden: Brill, 1989).
128. *Kasa* were songs and poetry composed in vernacular Korean, of varying length, each line consisting of four rhythmic units and a caesura in the middle of the line, like the *sijo*.
129. For research about Korean *sijo* and *kasa*, in English, and English translations, cf. Peter Lee, trans. *Pine River and Lone Peak: An Anthology of Three Chosŏn Dynasty Poets* (Honolulu:

Akchang Kasa (Music Texts and Songs), compiled in the fifteenth to sixteenth centuries and containing the lyrics of songs believed to date from the Koryŏ period and the early Chosŏn dynasty. Approximately five hundred thirty-one titles of traditional Korean vernacular novels (*kodae sosŏl*), moreover, remain extant in various editions. [130] These texts include handwritten manuscripts in palace-style script, [131] woodblock prints, and movable type editions. Chinese nevertheless continued to be the language of official and scholarly written discourse, and Korean was relegated to the status of an inferior language. The Korean alphabet was referred to as *ŏnmun* [132] or *ŏnsŏ*, meaning the "vulgar letters," terms used to contrast with the term *chinsŏ*, or "genuine letters," used to designate Chinese characters.

Koreans began to use the Korean language extensively as a literary medium in the nineteenth to early twentieth centuries. The combined use of the Korean alphabet and Chinese characters gained official sanction in the late nineteenth century when Korean came to be used in official documents and the civil service examination. [133] Under the reforms of 1894, the government sanctioned the use of Korean in legal and official documents. [134] Such texts could now be written in Korean, Chinese, or in *kukhanmun*, which was a mixed style combining Chinese characters and Korean. [135] The mixed style was used in nonfiction works such as a treatise on agriculture, entitled the *Nongjŏng Ch'waryo* (A Survey Study of Agriculture, 1886) by Chŏng Pyŏng-ha, a travelogue by Yu Kil-chun entitled *Sŏyu Kyŏnmun* (Things Seen and Heard While Traveling in the West, 1895), [136] and textbooks such as the *Simsang Sohak* (Elementary Textbook, 1896), published by the Department

University of Hawaii Press, 1990); David McCann, *Form and Freedom in Korean Poetry* (Leiden: E.J. Brill, 1988); Richard Rutt, *The Bamboo Grove* (Berkeley: University of California Press, 1971).
130. Cf. William Skillend, *Kodae sosŏl: A Survey of Korean Traditional Style Popular Novels* (London: School of Oriental and African Studies, 1968).
131. "Palace-style" Korean script changed gradually from a squarish style like that in which the *Hunmin Chŏngŭm* was printed, to styles used by various monarchs in their personal handwriting. Cf. Pak Pyŏng-ch'ŏn, *Han'gŭl Kungch'e Yŏn'gu* (Seoul: Ilchi sa, 1983), 116–117.
132. The term *ŏnmun* was first used by Ch'oe Sejin in the *Hunmong Cha Hoe* (Chungjong 22). Pak Pyŏng-ch'ŏn, *Han'gŭl Kungch'e Yŏn'gu*, 27.
133. For edicts pertaining to the use of Korean in official documents, cf. *Ilsŏngnok*, Kojong 31.7.8; *Kojong Sillok* Kojong 31.7.8; *Kwanbo* 503.7.8; *Ŭijong Chonan, cheil* 503.7.9. Cited in Yi Ŭngho, *Kaehwagi Han'gŭl Undongsa* (Seoul: Sŏngch'ŏngsa, 1975), 101.
134. The social and governmental reforms of 1894 were instituted by the Japanese-backed cabinet of Kim Hong-jip, after the ouster of pro-Chinese officials. The substitution of Korean for Chinese in government documents can be interpreted as part of Japanese efforts to reduce Chinese political and cultural influence in Korea in preparation for eventual Japanese occupation. For a concise and critical discussion of the Kabo reforms, see Carter Eckert, Ki-baik Lee, Young Ick Lew, Michael Robinson and Edward Wagner, *Korea Old and New: A History* (Seoul: Ilchogak, 1990), 222–230.
135. Yi Chae-sŏn, *Han'guk Kaehwagi Sosŏl Yŏn'gu* (Ilchogak, 1972), 16.
136. The manuscript had been completed earlier, in 1889.

of Education (*Hakpu*).[137] Korean became a central part of the curriculum, moreover, in the modern educational system established nationwide in 1895. Translations of foreign texts further promoted the use of written Korean as a literary and educational medium. *Pilgrim's Progress*, by Paul Bunyan, was translated into Korean in 1895 by James Scarth Gale. Vernacular Korean translations of Biblical texts began to be printed in large volume in 1882.[138] Eventually, the Korean language was no longer referred to as the "vulgar alphabet" (*ŏnmun*). In the preface to his 1811 Korean translation of the Chinese classic *Xi xiang ji*,[139] Kim Chŏng-hŭi (1786–1856) referred significantly to the Korean language as *chŏngŭm* or "correct sounds" (the original fifteenth-century name for the Korean alphabet).[140] Documents from the reforms of 1894 officially designated the Korean alphabet the "national script" (*kungmun*). Chu Si-gyŏng (1876–1914) gave the name han'gŭl to the Korean alphabet, a name which meant "Great Writing."[141] Ch'oe Nam-sŏn used the name *han'gŭl* in an article entitled "*Han'gŭl*," in the student journal *Aidŭl poi* (For the Children).[142] The word *han'gŭl* came into wider use in the 1920s with the activities of the Society for the Study of the Korean Language (Chosŏnŏ Yŏn'guhoe—later renamed the Han'gŭl Hakhoe).[143] Korean linguists made efforts to standardize spelling. The Society for the Study of the Korean language prepared the 1933 Proposals for the Standardization of Han'gŭl orthography (*Han'gŭl Mach'umpŏp T'ongiran*). The proposals included the elimination of several archaic letters from the alphabet, and the decision to use the alphabet morphophonemically—keeping a single, consistent shape for a morpheme (i.e. a meaningful unit of language); the older orthography was more of a phonemic orthography.[144]

Newspapers and journals[145] played a significant role in legitimizing the Korean alphabet as a literary medium. *Tongnip Sinmun* (The Independent),[146] first published in 1896, was written entirely in the Korean

---

137. Lee Ki-moon, "Kachwagi ŭi Kungmun Sayong e Kwanhan Yŏn'gu," *Han'guk Munhwa* 5 (1984), 70–71.
138. Cf. Ann Sung-hi Lee, "The Early Writings of Yi Gwang-su," *Korea Journal* 42, no. 2 (Summer 2002): 264–265.
139. Xi Xiangji, by Wang Shi-fu (fl. 1295-1307). Cf., Wang Shi-fu, *The Moon and the Zither: The Story of the Western Wing*, ed. and trans. Stephen West and Wilt L. Idema (Berkeley: University of California Press, 1991).
140. Ōtani Morishige, *Chosŏn Hugi Sosŏl Tokcha Yŏn'gu* (Seoul: Koryŏ Taehakkyo Minjok Munhwa sa, 1985), 116.
141. Ik-sŏp Lee and S. Robert Ramsey, *The Korean Language*, 13.
142. Yi Ŭng-ho, *Kaehwagi ŭi Han'gŭl Undong Sa* (Seoul: Sŏngch'ŏng sa, 1975), 21.
143. Ibid., 20.
144. Ik-sŏp Lee and S. Robert Ramsey, *The Korean Language*, 30, 22.
145. Andre Schmid has written about journalism in early modern Korea. Cf. *Korea Between Empires, 1895 to 1919* (New York: Columbia University Press, 2002). Kim Sang-t'ae is writing a book about journalism and the modern novel in Korea.
146. Cf. Vipan Chandra, *Imperialism, Resistance and Reform in Late Nineteenth-Century*

alphabet. Other nineteenth-century periodicals published in *han'gŭl* included the *Hyŏpsŏng Hoe Hoebo* (Magazine of the Society for Success Through Cooperative Effort, January 1898), which was published by the students in the Hyŏpsŏng Hoe (Society for Success Through Cooperative Effort) at Paejae Academy,[147] the *Kyŏngsŏng Sinmun* (Capital Newspaper, March 1898), published by the president of the Independence Club, Yun Ch'i-ho, and the *Cheguk Sinmun* (Imperial Newspaper, August 1898).[148] The *Taehan Maeil Sinbo* (Korea Daily News, July 1904–August 1910) was published at first in mixed *han'gŭl* and Chinese characters, but began publishing a separate *han'gŭl* edition on May 23, 1907.

YI'S EARLY WRITINGS AND LITERARY THOUGHT

From 1909 to 1917, Yi published several short stories, a prose poem and a play in various journals. He experimented with language, Naturalism, Romanticism and Christian Socialism in these works. Yi wrote in various literary styles, eventually developing a modern vernacular style. Autobiographical motifs appeared in many of these works, and would appear too in Yi's first novel *Mujŏng* (The Heartless, 1917).

Yi's earliest extant published literary work[149] is a short story written in Japanese, entitled "Ai ka" (Is This Love?), published in 1909 in the Meiji Gakuin newsletter, the *Shiragane Gakuhō*.[150] The story depicted homosexual love—a theme Yi also wrote about in the short story "Yun Gwang-ho" (written January 11, 1917).[151]

Korea: Enlightenment and the Independence Club (Berkeley: Center for Korean Studies, 1988).

147. Lee Ki-moon, "Kaehwagi ŭi Kungmun Sayong e Kwanhan Yŏn'gu," *Han'guk Munhwa* 5 (1984): 71.

148. The *Hyŏpsŏng Hoe Hoebo* became the *Maeil Sinmun* (Daily Newspaper) several months later (April 1898). The *Kyŏngsŏng Sinmun*, which appeared twice a week, later became the *Taehan Hwangsŏng Sinmun* (Newspaper of the Imperial Capital of Korea, April 1898), which in turn became the *Hwangsŏng Sinmun* (Newspaper of the Imperial Capital, 5 September 1898). Most articles in the *Hwangsŏng Sinmun* (5 September 1898–14 September 1910) were written in the *kukhanmun* style, though some were in pure *han'gŭl* or classical Chinese.

149. Before this, Yi published an article advocating the use of the Korean alphabet. "Kungmun kwa Hanmun ŭi Kwado sidae," *T'aegŭk Hakpo* (24 May 1908). Cited in Kim Yun-sik, *Yi Kwang-su wa Kŭ ŭi Sidae*, vol. 1 (Seoul: Han'gilsa, 1986), 215.

150. Yi Kwang-su, "Ai ka," *Shiragane Gakuhō* (1909); reprint, in Kurokawa Sō, ed., *Chōsen*, vol. 3 of "*Gaichi*" *no Nihon Bungaku Sen* (Tōkyō: Shinjuku Shobō, 1996), 21–26. I would like to thank Na Yŏng-gyun, and Yomota Gōki of Meiji Gakuin for this reference.

151. *Ch'ŏngchun* (Youth) 13, reprinted in Yi Kwang-su, *Yi Kwang-su Chŏnjip*, vol. 8 (1971), 96. Yi's contemporary, Kim Tong-in, noted that Yi wrote about homosexual love. Yi does not desire only a female, he desires males too—someone who will hold him in their arms, no matter what their gender, Kim commented with regard to Yi's story "Ŏrin Pŏt ege," which was published in *Ch'ŏngch'un* after Mujŏng was published. Kim Tong-in, "Ch'unwŏn Yŏn'gu," *Samch'ŏlli* 6, no. 12–7, no. 10 (December 1934–October 1935); reprint, *Kim Tong-in Munhak Chŏnjip*, vol. 12 (Seoul: Taejung Sŏgwan, 1983), 368, 369. Cf. Yi Kwang-su, "Ŏrin Pŏt ege," *Ch'ŏngch'un* 9–11;

The main character Mun-gil (pronounced Bunkichi in Japanese) meets Misao[152] in January of the year in which the story takes place. Mun-gil is eighteen years old in the story; Misao is described as a *shōnen*, or boy. Mun-gil has always felt different from other boys, and not accepted by his peers, because his parents died when he was only eleven years old (ten years old in Western age), and he believes that he acquired an adult maturity that set him apart from other boys his age. The text uses the "suffering passive" form of the verb *shinu* (to die), i.e. *shinareru*, to emphasize the effect that his parents' death had on Bunkichi: "Bunkichi wa zhūichi no toki ni chichi haha ni shinarete . . ."[153] In English, this sentence means "Bunkichi suffered the death of his father and mother when he was eleven years old." Mun-gil requires constant affirmations of love from Misao, and fears abandonment.

He told his feelings to Misao in a letter, and sought Misao's love. Then Misao sent Bunkichi a letter in which he said that he too was lonely, and that he loved Bunkichi too. One can imagine how Bunkichi must have felt when he received this letter. Bunkichi was happy, very happy. However, his suffering and anxiety were not ended. Rather, new anxieties had been added to the old. Misao tended to be very reticent. Bunkichi found this extremely painful. He felt as though Misao did not love him.[154]

Mun-gil fears rejection. However, this is not necessarily because he is Korean, though that is part of the reason; he also fears rejection because of his experiences of having lost his parents and having been rejected by other boys his age. Mun-gil is like the abandonment-neurotic Jean Veneuse, described by Frantz Fanon in *Black Skin, White Masks*—a neurotic whose color or ethnicity is "only an attempt to explain his psychic structure."[155]

Mun-gil's love for Bunkichi, however, has the same libidinal economy as that which characterizes woman as abjection.[156] Julia Kristeva defines abjection as a feeling that is "directed against a threat that seems to emanate from an exorbitant outside or inside, ejected beyond the scope of the possible, the tolerable, the thinkable . . . what disturbs identity, system, order." Refuse and corpses, for example, remind the self of what is set aside

reprint, *Yi Kwang-su Chŏnjip*, vol. 8 (1971), 66–90.

152. Yi's friend Yamazaki Nobuo wrote that Yamazaki and Yi had "special feelings" for a younger student at Meiji Gakuin named Kumagai Naomasa. Kim Yun-sik thinks Yi wrote "Ai ka" about Yi's love for Kumagai. Kim Yun-sik, *Yi Kwang-su wa Kŭ ŭi Sidae*, 220–1.

153. Yi Kwang-su, "Ai ka," 24.

154. Ibid., 25.

155. Frantz Fanon, *Black Skin, White Masks* (New York: Grove Press, 1967), 78. I would like to thank Andrew Jones for referring me to this book.

156. I discuss woman as abjection in the section about *Mujŏng*.

in order to live. "All abjection is in fact recognition of the want on which any being, meaning, language or desire is founded." Misao is like the mother, lost in the "immemorial violence with which a body becomes separated from another body in order to be";[157] death is projected onto the "others" of the maternal, and the same-sex lover, in order to define the modern, heterosexual state.[158] Modern language and the privileging of individual subjectivity make it possible for Bunkichi to fall in love, yet do not permit his love for Misao, a member of the same sex. The story does not specifically say whether or not Bunkichi and Misao have sex; however, their love is depicted as same-sex eroticism.

"Yun Kwang-ho," written January 11, 1917 and published in April 1918, portrayed a lonely college student struggling with poverty.[159] Kwang-ho is an orphan who, "in all of the twenty-four years of his life had never known the warmth of love." Yi's autobiographical writings dwell on a similar hunger for love, and describe love as the "fragrance of life."[160] Love and compassion would constitute central themes in Yi's first novel, *The Heartless*. Like Mun-gil in "Ai ka," Kwang-ho falls in love with another male student.

Yi wrote again about life as a Korean student in Tokyo, in the short story "Panghwang" (Wandering, 1918).[161] The first-person narrator lies ill in a dormitory room, shivering in the cold of the unheated room, and feeling oppressed by the winter sky outside. He contemplates the sound of his own heartbeat, and wonders why his heart goes on beating. Overwhelmed by a sense of life's futility, he tries to think of the things which have kept him alive. His friends' kindness seems only to bind him to life by creating a sense of duty. He has tried, unsuccessfully, to fill the emptiness in his life by serving the nation. The story ends with the narrator dreaming of becoming a monk. He thinks of an aunt who was married at age seventeen and widowed at eighteen, and who became a nun in a secluded mountain temple. He identifies with her loneliness.

Yi wrote an autobiographical short story entitled "Kim Kyŏng" (1915), about a Korean student who returns to Korea after studying in Japan. Like the

157. Julia Kristeva, *Powers of Horror*, trans. Leon Roudiez (New York: Columbia University Press, 1982), 1–3.
158. Ideologies were formed in Meiji Japan, to produce a modern, industrialized and patriarchal system of labor to support the state and complement the construction of a heterosexual modern subjectivity. Nina Cornyetz, *Dangerous Women, Deadly Words: Phallic Fantasy and Modernity in Three Japanese Writers* (Stanford: Stanford University Press, 1999), 23.
159. Yi Kwang-su, "Yun Kwang-ho," *Ch'ŏngchun* 13 (April 1918); reprint, *Yi Kwang-su Chŏnjip*, ed. Noh Yang-hwan, vol. 8 (Seoul: Samjungdang, 1971), 96–104.
160. Yi Kwang-su, *Insaeng ŭi Hyanggi* (Seoul: Hongji Ch'ulp'ansa, 1936); reprint, *Yi Kwang-su Chŏnjip*, ed. Noh Yang-hwan, vol. 8 (Seoul: Usinsa, 1978), 227–273.
161. Yi Kwang-su, "Panghwang," *Ch'ŏngch'un* 12 (March 1918); reprint in *Yi Kwang-su Chŏnjip*, vol. 8 (1971), 91–95.

main character Kim Kyŏng, Yi returned to Korea from Tokyo in 1910 when financial support for his studies was discontinued, and taught at Osan. Kim Kyŏng returns home, moreover, to care for his eighty-year-old grandfather. He wants to be a poet, and does not think he needs any further education.

Kim is like the character Hyŏng-sik, in *The Heartless*, in the way that he tries to live a meaningful life. He "had the habit of trying to give everything he did some noble meaning. He was fooling himself again this time, telling himself that he would stay at Osan to learn about self-sacrifice. He was not trying to defend his mistakes, though, but just pathetically trying to live a life of self-awareness and meaning."[162] The narrative is ironically distanced from Kim Kyŏng, commenting on his aspirations.

Most of the story is about Kim Kyŏng's life as a Korean student in Japan. The narrative writes Korean subjectivity into the context of Tokyo. In the story, we see how a Korean student responds to modern, foreign texts. Kim gives his own readings of texts such as the novel *Hi no Hashira* (Pillar of Fire, 1904) by Kinoshita Naoe (1869–1937), and the poetry of Byron and Milton. He also reads Tokutomi Rōka and Tolstoy. After trying to read the philosophy of Bergson, and not understanding any of it, he resolves to study psychology, logic, ethics, philosophy and math, in a methodical way. He feels that his reading has been too unorganized until then. He regrets that he has never had a mentor; he feels his intellectual growth has been haphazard, untrained. Kim Kyŏng attempts, moreover, to combine tradition and modernity in his life. He tries to follow some aspects of Confucian ethics in his life. For example, he quotes passages from the *Analects* and the *Doctrine of the Mean* that recommend dignity and silence. The narrative focuses on Kim Kyŏng's subjectivity to such an extent that any speech is mostly interior monologue; there is almost no dialogue.

Kim Kyŏng feels torn between "Byronism" and "Tolstoyism."[163] "Byronism" represents sexual emotion, freedom, Satanic defiance, evil, romantic angst and Naturalism.[164] "Tolstoyism" refers to selfless, altruistic emotion, chastity, moral restraint, Christian faith and humility, spiritual peace and idealism. Kim Kyŏng becomes influenced by the Christian Socialist literature of Kinoshita Naoe, and the religious writings of Tolstoy. His soul is "happy and at peace" until he reads the poetry of Byron, which "set his young soul in turmoil."[165]

---

162. Yi Kwang-su, "Kim Kyŏng," in *Yi Kwang-su Chŏnjip*, vol. 1 (1971), 571.

163. Kim Yun-sik thinks that Yi Kwang-su found his subjectivity in the process of thinking about "Tolstoyism" and "Byronism." Kim Yun-sik, *Yi Kwang-su wa Kŭ ŭi Sidae*, vol. 2, 211.

164. For a discussion of Japanese Romanticism and Japanese Naturalism, cf. William F. Sibley, "Naturalism in Japanese Literature," *Harvard Journal of Asiatic Studies*, vol. 28 (1968), 157–169.

165. "He borrowed a copy of the biography of the poet who was the 'satanic ruler of the literary world,' his heart aflame as it had been with Naoe's *Pillar of Fire*. . . Sometimes he would get drunk and seek woman's love, and this he called Byronism. His longing to be a warrior of justice

Yi wrote about Korean longing for national independence, in a style that was influenced by Romanticism. His prose poem "Okchung Hogŏl" (The Imprisoned Stalwart, 1909) described a caged bird.[166] The bird's spirit of defiance within captivity, and the images of soaring flight and great expanses of wilderness suggest the influence of poems like Byron's "Manfred" and "Childe Harold's Pilgrimage."

Yi also thought that sexual liberation was an important part of Byronic Romanticism. Byron's "Caine," "Childe Harold's Pilgrimage" and "Don Juan" "taught me the strength of evil and how thin and superficial the Puritanical life was."[167] Yi seems to have found different kinds of emotion represented in the literature of Byron and Tolstoy. He found sensuality in Byron, and Christian emotion in Tolstoy.

Yi saw in Tolstoy's writings a view of literature as a means of moral influence, and in Byron's poetry, a view of art for art's sake. Yi thought of Tolstoy as a philosopher-poet. He claimed to have been influenced by the literature, and religious and philosophical writings of Tolstoy. In "Tuong kwa na" (Tolstoy and I),[168] Yi wrote of having been drawn to Tolstoy's readings of the Bible, skepticism of organized religion, and opposition to war. Japanese writers similarly emphasized Tolstoy's religious and philosophical views. Writers of the Shirakaba (White Birch) school perceived Tolstoy primarily as a philosopher and moralist.[169] Ch'oe Nam-sŏn's introduction of Tolstoy to Korean readers in an article in Sonyŏn magazine in 1909 included a partial translation of a Japanese translation by Nakazato Yanosuke of one of Tolstoy's philosophical writings.[170] Yi found Tolstoy's "My Religion" and "The Kingdom of God is Within You" crucial to understanding Tolstoy's fiction. Tolstoy was both the artist and the moralist, concerned with the ideals of beauty (mi) and goodness (sŏn).[171] Art and religion, Yi observed, were inseparable in Tolstoy's work. "Tolstoy was

and righteousness, though, was Tolstoyism." Yi Kwang-su, "Kim Kyŏng," Yi Kwang-su Chŏnjip, vol. 1 (Seoul: Samjungdang, 1971), 570.

166. Yi Kwang-su, "Okchung Hogŏl," Taehan Hŭnghakpo, (January 1910); reprint, Yi Kwang-su Chŏnjip, vol. 1 (1971), 573–575. The Taehan Hŭnghakbo (Korean Journal for the Encouragement of Scholarship) was published by Korean students in Japan.

167. Yi Kwang-su, "Kŭ ŭi Chasŏjŏn," Chosŏn Ilbo 11 December 1936–1 May 1937; reprint, Yi Kwang-su Chŏnjip, vol. 6 (Seoul: Usinsa, 1978), 340.

168. Yi Kwang-su, "Tuong kwa Na," Chosŏn Ilbo 20 November 1935, reprint, Yi Kwang-su Chŏnjip, vol. 19 (1978), 590.

169. Kureno Toshio, "Torusutoi to Shirakaba Ha," in Nihon Kindai Bungaku no Hikaku Bungakuteki Kenkyū, ed. Yoshida Seiichi (Tokyo: Shimizu Kōbundō, Showa 46 [1971]), 306–329.

170. Ch'oe Nam-sŏn, "T'olsŭt'oi Sŏnsaeng ŭi Kyosi," Sonyŏn July 1909; reprint, Yuktang Ch'oe Nam-sŏn Chŏnjip, vol. 10, ed. Koryŏ Taehakkyo Asea Munje Yŏn'guso Yuktang Chŏnjip P'yŏnch'an Wiwŏnhoe (Seoul: Hyŏnamsa, 1973–1975), 142–145.

171. Yi Kwang-su, "Nae ka Sokhal Yuhyŏng," Munye Kongnon no. 1 (May 1929); reprint, Yi Kwang-su Chŏnjip, vol. 8 (1978), 400.

an artist, but one must understand his religious views in order to understand his art. For Tolstoy, life was religion and art its expression."[172] Yi's early works were also influenced by Naturalism. He said he was influenced by Naturalist art and the poetry of Byron. In 1910, at about the same time that he had been introduced to the poetry of Byron, Yi read Naturalist literary critic Hasegawa Tenkei's essay "Genjitsu Hakurō no Hiai" (The Sadness of the Exposure of Reality). The essay "destroyed the very foundation of the attitude of propriety I had maintained in matters of religion, morals and customs."[173] Tenkei wrote about his disillusionment with religion and idealism. Tenkei compared idealism to the garden of Eden—a home from which the modern intellectual had been banished. Tenkei said that Naturalist literature portrayed "the ugly, trivial, the un-ideal, the aesthetically unappealing, immoral, physical and sexual, not because they find these amusing, but because they find reality without artifice in these."[174]

Yi became more interested in science while he was a student at Waseda University from 1915 to 1918. Though he was a philosophy major, Yi began attending lectures on biology, astronomy and experimental psychology, and was "more interested in sociology, political science and economics than in philosophy."[175]

The theory of evolution increased Yi's skepticism of Christianity, and he became influenced by the application of the law of natural selection to ethics. "The foundation of my moral beliefs was undermined. My morals had rested on belief in the existence of a good God who ruled the world; without this belief, the system of morals I had followed collapsed. Where did good or bad lie?"[176] Truth was "the product of the times. It therefore passes with the times. The same may be said of ethics. The ethics of the first century were that century's ethics. They were no longer valid in the second century. . . . All we need are ethics appropriate to the present times."[177] New ethics would be based on life. Social ethics that harmed life would be set aside. "Ethics exist for the benefit of human beings; thus there are no ethics of death or harm to human beings."[178]

Yi was aware of the work of Herbert Spencer. In the article "Ahan ch'ŏngnyŏn tŭl kwa chŏngyuk non" (Korean Youth and the Nurturing of the

172. Yi Kwang-su, "Tuong kwa Na," *Chosŏn Ilbo* 20 November 1935; reprint, *Yi Kwang-su Chŏnjip*, vol. 10 (Seoul: Usinsa, 1978), 594–6.
173. Yi Kwang-su, "Kŭ ŭi Chasŏjŏn (An Autobiography)," *Chosŏn Ilbo* 11 December 1936–1 May 1937; reprint, *Yi Kwang-su Chŏnjip*, vol. 6, (1978), 340.
174. Hasegawa Tenkei, "Genjitsu no Hakurō no Hiai," *Taiyō* January Meiji 41 (1908); reprint, *Meiji Bungaku Zenshū*, vol. 43 (Tokyo: Chikuma Shobō, 1967), 180.
175. Yi Kwang-su, "Kŭ ŭi Chasŏjŏn," 422.
176. Ibid., 422.
177. Yi Kwang-su, "Chosŏn Saram in Ch'ŏngnyŏn ege," *Sonyŏn* June 1910; reprint, Yi Kwang-su, *Yi Kwang-su Chŏnjip*, vol. 1 (1978), 534.
178. Ibid., 534–535.

Emotions, February 1910), he referred to educational theories set forth in Spencer's *Education: Intellectual, Moral and Physical.*

Yi appears to have read a work on evolutionary theory, entitled *Shinkaron Kōwa* (Lectures on the Theory of Evolution), by Oka Asajirō, a work which Yi recommended in a 1916 article on education.[179] In memoirs from that time in his life, Yi wrote that he "recited phrases from evolutionary theory such as the 'struggle for life' and 'survival of the fittest.'" He began to interpret history in social Darwinist terms, despising the Korean people for having been weak.[180]

In the story "Hŏnsinja" (A Person of Dedication), the main character, Kim Kwang-ho, is a merchant who decides to use his money to start a modern school. He reaches this decision after hearing a speech at another school. The occupation of merchant is portrayed favorably, and the story criticizes traditional contempt for the merchant class; the narrative observes with irony the condescension of *yangban*, or the ruling class, [181] who comment, "There are decent human beings among the lowly classes after all!"[182]

Social Reform

The short story "Mujŏng" (The Heartless, March–April 1910), published in the *Taehan Hŭnghakpo* (Korean Journal for the Encouragement of Learning), criticized the customs of early marriage and concubinage. Yi would write a full-length novel with the same title in 1917. The short story depicts the suicide of a woman embittered by a marriage that is without love. She is many years older than her husband and was married to him when he was still a child, in keeping with certain traditional marriage customs. Now that he is older, her husband spends most nights away from home, leaving his wife to languish in loneliness and despair. When he decides to sleep with her one night, it is only in order to ask her to consent to his taking a concubine. Though shaken by her husband's decision, she is somewhat comforted later when she finds she has become pregnant. A shaman tells her, however, that the fetus is a girl, and the woman is plunged into despair at the thought of the sorrowful life which awaits the unborn girl. She commits suicide by swallowing poison; the story begins and ends at the scene of her suicide, as

179. Yi Kwang-su, "Ilban Insa ŭi P'iltok hal Sŏjŏk Sujong," *Maeil Sinbo* 9 November 1916; reprint, *Yi Kwang-su Chŏnjip*, ed. Noh Yang-hwan, vol. 10 (Seoul: Usinsa, 1978), 324.

180. Yi Kwang-su, "Kŭ ŭi Chasŏjŏn," *Chosŏn Ilbo* 11 December 1936–1 May 1937; reprint, *Yi Kwang-su Chŏnjip*, vol. 6 (1978), 423.

181. *Yangban* held ranked positions in government, and were, for the most part, from a hereditary aristocracy. Cf. Edward Willett Wagner, *The Literati Purges* (Cambridge: East Asian Research Center, 1974), 11–12.

182. Yi Kwang-su, "Hŏnsinja," *Sonyŏn* August 1910; reprint, *Yi Kwang-su Chŏnjip*, vol. 1 (Seoul: Samjungdang, 1971), 565, 567.

she lies writhing in a grove of trees, with her past recounted to the reader in retrospective flashbacks.[183] The reform of traditional marriage customs was a prominent theme in Yi's essays and autobiographical writings. Yi's own grandparents lived apart after his grandfather took a *kisaeng* concubine. Yi never met his grandmother, but wrote in his memoirs that he could not help but pity a woman who saw her husband only at ancestral memorial ceremonies. Yi's first marriage was an arranged marriage which he deeply regretted, and which eventually ended in divorce. He called for the reform of traditional marriage customs. In an article in the *Maeil Sinbo* entitled "Chohon ŭi Aksŭp" (The Evil Custom of Early Marriage) (23–26 November 1916), Yi argued that arranged marriage in early adolescence did not give the individual time to fully mature and develop goals and aspirations.[184]

The themes of marriage and concubinage had appeared in other works of fiction of the early twentieth century, but usually with stereotyped representations of the malicious concubine, or the jealous, vindictive wife, with the husband in most cases reduced to an object of manipulation. In the short story "Mujŏng," the omniscient narrative centers around the experiences and thoughts of the woman. There are no clear villains, for the husband is depicted as being as much a victim of the early marriage system as the woman. He is not in love with his wife, a woman married to him when he was twelve.

Criticism of traditional marriage customs was a theme of Naturalist literature in Japan. Naturalist writers attempted to depict in detail the biological, physiological aspects of life. In the story "Heartlessness," the woman's slow death through poisoning is portrayed in detail.

The two cups of poison she had drunk reached her head, passing through her blood vessels and capillaries and spreading to each of her organs and cells, until her heart grew more sluggish, her breathing more difficult, and her entire body was bathed in sweat. Her mind became more and more clouded, and her mental functions slowed, until she felt nothing but her bitter resentment and the pain that wracked her body. At first she lay down and closed her eyes expecting to die immediately, but the death that she wished for would not come, and instead there was only pain. Pain holds us in its grasp all our lives, then as if that were not enough, the moment we are dying, the unspent balance of pain in our lives sweeps over our body and minds all at once. "Ah, my stomach!"

183. Yi Kwang-su, "Mujŏng," *Taehan Hŭnghakpo* (March 1910–April 1910); reprint, *Yi Kwang-su Chŏnjip*, ed. Noh Yang-hwan, vol. 1 (Seoul: Usinsa, 1978), 561–565.
184. Yi Kwang-su, "Chohon ŭi Aksŭp," *Maeil Sinbo*, 23 November 1916–26 November 1916; reprint, *Yi Kwang-su Chŏnjip*, ed. Noh Yang-hwan, vol. 1 (Seoul: Samjungdang, 1971), 542–545.

Wrapped in cruel, heartless, excruciating pain, the woman tried to escape by screaming, but was as helpless in the throes of pain as a rabbit in the jaws of a tiger, and could only wait for her life to end.[185]

The passage emphasizes the heartless indifference of nature to human life. The woman is depicted as dying alone in a grove of trees, under an impassive sky. "The trees stood as before, the night was just as dark, and the universe was silent as always. Nature—all creatures in the universe except for humankind—was emotionless and cruel, indifferent as to whether we are happy or sad." Nature's only tie with humans is the unyielding rule of natural law. "Its laws are so strict that we cannot venture a single step beyond its limits. It will not comfort us when we are sad, and though we seek to live longer, will not grant us an extra minute or second more of life." Man's death is of no significance other than as the fulfillment of law. In the short story "Heartlessness," human beings are united with nature through natural laws which prevail over all nature. The tie is the unemotional, compulsory one of law; though humans may view the relationship with lyrical romanticism, nature remains indifferent. The contrast between the boundlessness of the universe, and the limited nature of human life corresponds to the world view expressed by Japanese Naturalist writer Kunikida Doppō in works such as "Gyūniku to Jagaimo," (Meat and Potatoes, 1901) and "Kami no Ko" (Child of God, 1903).[186]

Yi returned to the subject of marriage in two works written around the time he began publishing the novel *The Heartless*. One work was a play entitled "Kyuhan" (Sorrow of the Inner Room, January 1917). A woman receives an unexpected letter from her husband, who is a student in Tokyo. They have been apart for so long that she has been considering offering special prayers, as other students' wives have done, to bring him back home. The letter is thus a welcome surprise for her and since she does not know how to read, she has it read out loud. However, the voice of the absent husband declares his desire for a divorce: "It has been five years since you and I first met. You were seventeen, I was fourteen. But why do I bring this up? I was fourteen. At the time, I didn't even know what a wife was, nor what marriage meant. I did not marry you of my own free will, but was forced by my parents. Our marriage is therefore legally not binding. Since there is no such

185. Yi Kwang-su, "Mujŏng," *Taehan Hŭnghakpo* (March 1910–April 1910); reprint, *Yi Kwang-su Chŏnjip*, ed. Noh Yang-hwan, vol. 1 (Seoul: Usinsa, 1978), 562.

186. Chŏng Kwi-ryŏn, "Kankoku no Kindai Bungaku," 162. Chŏng notes that Yi's essay "Yŏ ŭi Chagak Han Insaeng" (*Sonyŏn* August 1910) expresses a world view similar to that in works of Doppō. Song Paek-hŏn discusses how Yi translated Doppō's reading of English Romanticism into the context of Korean nationalist, enlightenment literature. Song Paek-hŏn, "Ch'unwŏn 'Sonyŏn ŭi Piae' Yŏn'gu," in *Yi Kwang-su Yŏn'gu*, ed. Tongguk Taehakkyo Pusŏl Han'guk Munhwa Yŏn'guso, vol. 2 (Seoul: T'aehaksa, 1981), 174–188.

thing as marriage against one's will in today's civilized world, our marriage is null and void."[187] In the novel *The Heartless*, the character Kim Pyŏng-guk similarly wishes to end his marriage to a woman to whom he had been betrothed by his family in his early youth and whom he does not love. While studying in Tokyo, he had remained faithful to her though they were separated. Upon his return home, however, he becomes attracted to Yŏng-ch'ae, the friend of his sister.

At the end of the play "Kyuhan," the wife goes mad after hearing the letter read to her. She declares in strange, singsong phrases that she is "leaving—tying this ornament to my dress, and powdering my face." She speaks in a rhythmic speech that brings to mind the lyrics of one of the folksongs Yi learned in his childhood from his girl cousins: "The clouds are drifting away / The clouds are drifting away / And with them goes a fairy. / She has tied lily and tulip incense to the sash of her Korean blouse. / When she rides her horse amidst the flowers / there is an aroma of perfume from the horse's hoofs."[188] Characters in early-twentieth-century fiction often spoke in prosodic soliloquy when expressing intense emotion. Ok-nyŏ's mother in Yi In-jik's *Tears of Blood*, for example, laments aloud in *kasa* verse before attempting to commit suicide. The woman in "Kyuhan" similarly expresses anguish through poetry.

Yi wrote about marriage again in "Sonyŏn ŭi Piae" (A Boy's Sorrow, June 1917). The story depicts a young girl who is married off by her parents to a boy who is several years younger than she, and discovers on her wedding night that the boy is an idiot. Her cousin Mun-ho offers to take her to the capital with him and help her to get an education, but she refuses. When Mun-ho returns to the countryside a year later, he is saddened by the absence of his cousin, Nan-su, and the growing distance between himself and his other girl cousins as the girls grow closer to marriageable age. Himself the father of a three-year-old boy, he mourns the loss of youth to early marriage—an institution described in the story as *mujŏng hada*, or "heartless." The story criticized traditional marriage customs and the passivity of those who submitted to the dictates of custom.

Yi wrote an adapted translation of *Uncle Tom's Cabin*, by Harriet Beecher Stowe because he thought the work influential in its opposition to slavery. Ch'oe Nam-sŏn's publishing company, Sinmungwan, published the book in February in 1913.[189] Yi included passages that depicted the violence

187. "Kyuhan," *Hak chi Gwang* (January 1917); reprint, *Yi Kwang-su Chŏnjip*, ed. Noh Yang-hwan, vol. 8 (Seoul: Usinsa, 1978): 535.

188. Yi Kwang-su, "Tananhan Pansaeng ŭi Tojŏng," *Chogwang* April–June 1937; reprint, *Yi Kwang-su Chŏnjip*, ed. Noh Yang-hwan, vol. 8 (Seoul: Samjungdang, 1971), 446.

189. Cf. Yi Kwang-su, "Kŏmdungi ŭi Sŏrum," (Seoul: Sinmungwan, 1913), reprinted in *Yi Kwang-su Chŏnjip*, vol. 7 (1971), 601–644. Yi Kwang-su, ""Kŏmdungi ŭi Sŏrum Mŏri Mal," (Seoul: Sinmungwan, 1913); reprint, *Yi Kwang-su Chŏnjip*, vol. 10 (1971), 543–4.

of slavery, and the humanity of the main character Tom in the face of dehumanizing oppression.

Christianity

Yi translated Christian thought into Korean literature, as part of an ideology of nationalist reform. The story "Ŏrin Hŭisaeng" (The Young Sacrifice), published in the February and May issues of *Sonyŏn*, may have been an adaptation of a foreign work. Set in 1773, the short story takes place somewhere in Siberia or Manchuria. A young boy and his grandfather receive a telegram informing them that the boy's father has been killed in battle against the Russians. The boy vows to avenge his father's death.[190] When the boy is eventually killed by Russian soldiers, his grandfather avenges the deaths of his son and grandson by poisoning the soldiers as they drink in his home. Contemplating the corpses of the soldiers in the end, however, he is overcome with remorse.[191]

The story reflects in part the influence of Tolstoy, and Japanese Christian Socialist literature. Yi was introduced to Tolstoy's religious thought during his middle school days at Meiji Gakuin. A classmate named Yamazaki Nobuo[192] lent him a copy of a Japanese translation of Tolstoy's writings on religion, entitled "Waga Shūkyō" (My Religion).[193] Yi also read Tolstoy's *Resurrection* and *Anna Karenina*, according to a diary entry dated December 31, 1909.[194]

Yi joined his friend Yamazaki, who had introduced him to Tolstoy's writings, in condemning the Russo-Japanese war. Their stance aroused the enmity of some of their classmates.[195] Tolstoy had been associated with Japanese Socialist opposition to the Russo-Japanese War. A translation of an article by Tolstoy against the Russo-Japanese War had been translated in the socialist newspaper, the *Heimin Shimbun* (Commoners' Newspaper) in 1904. Yi also appears to have read Tolstoy's essay "The Kingdom of God is Within You," which included a criticism of political justifications of violence, and expressed hope in the progress of humankind towards the universal renunciation of violence.[196] He read in particular a Japanese translation,

190. Yi Kwang-su, "Ŏrin Hŭisaeng," *Sonyŏn* 5 February 1910; reprint, *Yi Kwang-su Chŏnjip*, ed. Noh Yang-hwan, vol. 1 (Seoul: Samjungdang, 1971), 558.

191. Ibid., 560–561.

192. Kim Yun-sik discusses Yi Kwang-su's friendship with Yamazaki Nobuo, in Kim Yun-sik, *Yi Kwang-su wa Kŭ ŭi Sidae*, vol. 1: 194–201.

193. Yi Kwang-su, "Tuong kwa Na," *Chosŏn Ilbo* 20 November 1935; reprint, *Yi Kwang-su Chŏnjip*, ed. Noh Yang-hwan, vol. 10 (Seoul: Usinsa, 1978), 594.

194. Yi Kwang-su, "Ilgi: Na ŭi Sonyŏn Sidae," in *Yi Kwang-su Chŏnjip*, vol. 9 (1978), 332.

195. "Kŭ ŭi Chasŏjŏn," *Chosŏn Ilbo* 22 December 1936–1 May 1937; reprint, *Yi Kwang-su Chŏnjip*, vol. 6 (1978), 329.

196. Cf. Leo Tolstoy, "The Kingdom of God is Within You. What is Art? What is Religion?" trans. Aline Delano (N.Y.: Crowell, 1899). "That action of violence actually weakens and

entitled "Kami no Kuni wa Nanjira no Naka ni Ari" (The Kingdom of God is Within You); he recommended this translation later in one of his essays on Tolstoy.[197] Yi admired the work for its "criticism and elucidation of basic principles of life, religion, the nation, economics and society." In the novel *The Heartless*, Yi expressed skepticism of institutional religion; he was influenced by a similar skepticism in Tolstoy's writings. Yi was eventually expelled from Osan Hakkyo and the school church for having encouraged heretical thought among the students by teaching the religious views of Tolstoy.

Yi said that he was also influenced by Socialist writer Kinoshita Naoe, who had opposed the Russo-Japanese war. In the autobiographical short story "Kim Kyŏng," published in *Ch'ŏngch'un* (Youth) magazine (March 1915), the main character gains inspiration from Kinoshita Naoe's *Hi no Hashira* (Pillar of Fire), *Otto no Jihaku* (A Husband's Confession), *Rei ka Kiku ka* (Spirit or Flesh?), and *Kikatsu* (Hunger and Thirst).[198] Yi wrote about love and nonviolence, moreover, in his commentary on Kim Ŏk's translation of Rabindranath Tagore's *Gardenisto*. He interpreted the "beloved" of *Gardenisto* to be "all things that possess life."[199]

Comparison of Yi's 1908–1917 works with the sinsosŏl

The *sinsosŏl* and Yi's literary works were in some ways just as didactic as traditional fiction, but advocated enlightenment ideology instead of Neo-Confucianism. Yi tried, however, to narrate individual subjectivity with more depth than the *sinsosŏl*. The depiction of Kim Kyŏng's thoughts in the short story "Kim Kyŏng," and the woman's feelings in the short story "Mujŏng," attempted more narrative verisimilitude and psychological depth than the *sinsosŏl*, although it could be said that Yi In-jik portrayed characters with complexity. Yi's writing style was linguistically different from that of the *sinsosŏl*. Yi's stories were written in contemporary vernacular Korean, unlike the traditional vernacular of the *sinsosŏl*. Like Japanese Christian Socialism, though, Yi's literature has been criticized as elitist in its depiction of the masses as objects of enlightenment rather than active subjects of change.[200] Yi's writings, moreover, did not specifically identify Japanese

destroys that which it wishes to support. . . . Violence, which men regard as an instrument for the support of Christian life, on the contrary, prevents the social system from reaching its full and perfect development. The social system is such as it is, not because of violence, but in spite of it."
197. "Tuong kwa Na," 596.
198. "Kim Kyŏng," *Ch'ŏngch'un* no. 3 (1 March 1915); reprint, *Yi Kwang-su Chŏnjip*, ed. Noh Yang-hwan, vol. 1 (Seoul: Usinsa, 1978), 569.
199. "T'agorŭ ŭi Wŏnjŏng e Taehayŏ," *Tonga Ilbo* 20 January 1925; reprint, *Yi Kwang-su Chŏnjip*, vol. 10 (1978), 560.
200. For a discussion of Japanese Christian Socialism, cf. Peter Duus and Irwin Scheiner, "Socialism, Liberalism and Marxism, 1901–31," in ed. Bob Tadashi Wakabayashi, *Modern Japanese Thought* (Cambridge: Cambridge University Press, 1998), 162, 166.

imperialism as the structural cause of the oppressions depicted therein. Yi's literature can thus be characterized as representative of the bourgeois nationalism of cultural nationalists.

Yi Kwang-su's literary thought

When Yi discovered notions of literature in Japanese and Western literature, these concepts had already been accepted as "universal," and their historicity forgotten. In the very moment when one becomes capable of perceiving the notion of literature, it appears to have always been there.[201] Michael Shin has discussed Yi Kwang-su's literature in terms of Karatani's concept of interiority. I would like to continue that discussion here, further tracing Yi's narratives of literature, and make more transparent the workings of that ideology.

Yi Kwang-su translated expressive views of literature into Korean. In his first novel, *The Heartless*, he depicted gendered subjectivity using an epistolary style similar to that in Kunikida Doppō's *Otozure*.[202] Doppō's work had been the first to embody the concept of "expression" in Japanese literature; "for Doppō, the 'inner' was the word (the voice), and expression was the projection outward of that voice."[203]

Yi defined literature as texts that move the reader emotionally and that imaginatively express human thoughts and emotions through artistic form.[204] Yi cited Tolstoy in particular, as having said that "art is a kind of language that is a means by which one can convey to one's countrymen what one has felt."[205] Yi translated Tolstoy's view that literature conveys or transmits emotions. Tolstoy's view resonated with the expressive theory of literary value set forth by Coleridge; descriptions of the natural world were of literary value only when "modified by a predominant passion."[206] Moreover, such a poetics of emotion was similar to premodern Korean literary thought about emotion and poetry. Yi's literary thought thus represented a hybrid of premodern and modern theory.

---

201. Karatani Kōjin, 29. Michael Shin discusses Yi's discovery of landscape, in "Interior Landscapes: Yi Kwangsu's *The Heartless* a nd the Origins of Modern Literature," in ed. Gi-wook Shin and Michael Robinson, *Colonial Modernity in Korea* (Cambridge: Harvard University Asia Center, 1999), 248–287.

202. Chŏng Kwi-ryŏn, "Kankoku no Kindai Bungaku," 169. Cf. discussion later in this introduction.

203. Karatani Kōjin, 40.

204. Yi Kwang-su, "Munhak Kanghwa," *Chosŏn Mundan* (October 1924–February 1925); reprint, *Yi Kwang-su Chŏnjip*, ed. Noh Yang-hwan, vol. 10 (Seoul: Samjungdang, 1971), 381.

205. Yi Kwang-su, "Munhak kwa Munsa wa Munjang," *Han'gŭl* (June–October 1935); reprint in *Yi Kwang-su Chŏnjip*, vol. 10 (1971), 472.

206. Raymond Williams, *Marxism and Literature* (New York: Oxford University Press, 1977), 43.

Yi's poetics of emotion had continuities with premodern Neo-Confucian thought. Literary thought of the eighteenth and nineteenth centuries set forth a poetics that recognized artistic expression by singers and writers of nonelite social status.[207] The Book of Odes, one of the classics of Neo-Confucian thought, had described poetry as the expression of emotion. Eighteenth- and nineteenth-century Korean literary thought used the commonality of emotion in all humans to recognize the work of singers and poets of all backgrounds.

This poetics maintained continuities with earlier Neo-Confucian literary thought, and yet had populist implications. Kim Man-jung (1637–1692) had praised the songs of "wood gathering children and women drawing water" for their naturalness and sincerity of emotion, and their moving qualities. Kim thought that such songs were better than Korean poetry written in Chinese. Kim Man-jung was writing in the context of commenting on the *kasa* of Songgang Chŏng Ch'ŏl (1536–1593), a *yangban* writer. *Kasa* were a genre of vernacular Korean poetry. Literary historian Ko Mi-suk sees in Kim Man-jung's comments a populist element. Kim referred to the songs of nonelite women and children, and thus alluded to a populist dimension in literary thought. Kim Man-jung used traditional poetics of emotion to bring the artistic expression of nonelite poets and singers into literary discourse, and to recognize the merit of these vernacular works of nonelite artists.

Hong Tae-yong (1731–1783), a scholar of Sirhak or "Practical Learning," compiled an anthology of vernacular Korean songs, entitled *Taedong P'ungyo* (Korean Folk Songs), and set forth a poetics of emotion similar to that of Kim Man-jung. Hong too thought the vernacular songs of nonelite Korean singers were to be preferred to poetry by elite Koreans who were trying to write in classical Chinese. Songs were the expression of emotion, and the best songs were those that emerged naturally and without artifice or pretension, from one's heaven-endowed material force (*ch'ŏn'gi*).[208] Singers of nonelite status too compiled song anthologies in the eighteenth and nineteenth centuries, and their commentary shared sentiments similar to those of Kim Man-jung.[209]

Yi Kwang-su would eventually write a novel entitled *Hŏ Saeng Chŏn*, or "The Story of Mr. Hŏ," based on the work by Sirhak scholar Pak Chi-wŏn (1737–1805). Yi's literary thought was a hybrid of his interest in premodern, Sirhak Neo-Confucian thought, and modern practices.

---

207. Ko Mi-suk, *Sipp'al Segi esŏ Isip Segi Ch'o Han'guk Sigasa ŭi Kudo* (Seoul: Somyŏng, 1998), 45–53.
208. Kim T'ae-jun, "Hong Tae-yong," in *Han'guk Munhak Chakkaron* 3, ed. Hwang P'ae-gang et al. (Seoul: Chimmundang, 2000), 170. I would like to thank Professor Young-key Kim-Renaud for referring me to this book.
209. Ko Mi-suk, *Sipp'al Segi esŏ Isip Segi Ch'o Han'guk Sigasa ŭi Kudo* (Seoul: Somyŏng, 1998), 53.

Yi thought that literary value was determined in part by the kind of emotions a work inspired in the reader.[210] Yi was preoccupied with reader reception of art, or the moral effect that literature might have on the reader. He argued that literature ought not to harm human life, since it was a part of life.[211] The Psalms of David in the Old Testament, for example, inspired in the reader emotions such as reverence, loyalty, submission and thankfulness; therein was the literary effectiveness of the work. Yi thought that what made works of literature such as the *Classic of Poetry* (Shi Jing) endure was that the emotions expressed in such literature could still move readers.[212]

Because of Yi's view of literature as a means of enlightenment, literary critics have identified Yi with the enlightenment and cultural nationalist projects in early-twentieth-century Korean culture. Cultural nationalists sought to achieve national independence through gradual cultural reform, and national self-strengthening. Chu Yo-han, Yi's contemporary, characterized Yi's writing as "enlightenment" (*kyemong*) literature.[213] Writing in 1977, literary critic Kim Hyŏn described Yi as belonging to the "enlightenment generation."[214] In a 1987 article, Cho Nam-hyŏn wrote that Yi's fiction used literature as a means of enlightenment, and was thus like literature of the enlightenment period (*kaehwagi*). Yi's enlightenment view of literature has also been characterized as "utilitarian." Yi Chae-sŏn has described Yi's literature as more utilitarian than art-for-art's sake; Yi wrote about the same issues as *sinsosŏl* writers, but in a more modern literary way, Yi Chae-sŏn concludes.[215] Kwŏn Yŏng-min writes that Yi Kwang-su and Kim Tong-in represented opposing views in early modern Korean literature: those of enlightenment literature and art-for-art's sake literature. Early

210. Recent literary criticism has returned to questions of reader-response, in refutation of the theory of the "affective fallacy" set forth by William Wimsatt and Monroe Beardsley. Wimsatt and Beardsley hypothesized that the affective fallacy was a confusion between the poem and its results. Critics of Wimsatt and Beardsley have argued that the "objectivity of the text is an illusion" and that it is illusory to think of the text as somehow self-sufficient. Cf. Stanley E. Fish, "Literature in the Reader: Affective Stylistics," in Jane P. Tompkins ed., *Reader-Response Criticism* (Baltimore: Johns Hopkins University Press, 1980), 70–100. Kim Yong-jik discusses the affective fallacy and Korean literary criticism, in *Han'guk Kŭndae Munhak ŭi Sajŏk Ihae* (Seoul: Samyŏngsa, 1977), 148–166.
211. Yi Kwang-su, "Uri Munye ŭi Panghyang," *Chosŏn Mundan* (November 1925), no. 13; reprint, *Yi Kwang-su Chŏnjip*, ed. Noh Yang-hwan, vol. 10 (Seoul: Samjungdang, 1971), 430.
212. Yi Kwang-su, "Munhak kwa Munsa wa Munjang," 475.
213. Chu Yo-han, "Ch'unwŏn ŭi In'gan kwa Saengae," *Sasanggye* February 1958, cited in Kwŏn Yŏng-min, "Ch'unwŏn Munhak ŭl Hyang Han Yŏrahop Kae ŭi Hwasal," *Munhak Sasang* 232 (1992): 118.
214. Kim Hyŏn, "Yi Kwang-su Munhak ŭi Chŏnbanjŏk Kŏmt'o," *Yi Kwang-su* (1977), cited in Kwŏn Yŏng-min, "Ch'unwŏn Munhak ŭl Hyang Han Yŏrahop Kae ŭi Hwasal," *Munhak Sasang* 232 (1992): 111–127.
215. Yi Chae-sŏn, *Han'guk Hyŏndae Sosŏlsa* (1979), cited in Kwŏn Yŏng-min, "Ch'unwŏn Munhak ŭl Hyang Han Yŏrahop Kae ŭi Hwasal": 123.

modern Korean literature emerged from this debate, Kwŏn says.[216] In colonial Korea, though, even a decision to write art-for-art's sake literature had political significance. One's literary practice reflected one's ideological views.

Yi was also interested in Japanese Christian Socialism. As a student in Japan, Yi read the novel *Hi no Hashira* (Pillar of Fire, 1904) by Christian Socialist writer Kinoshita Naoe. Yi admired the novel's idealism. The novel *The Heartless* took up the theme of the abolition of prostitution, a theme in *Hi no Hashira*. Naoe was among Japanese leftists who opposed militarism, and sought a more democratic society. Like Japanese Christian Socialists, however, Yi has been criticized as being elitist and more interested in intellectuals' subjectivity than that of the masses; critics have said that Yi depicts the masses as depending on the guidance of intellectuals in order to recognize their own subjectivity.

Yi made a distinction between the emotive value of a literary work, and didacticism. To Yi Kwang-su, didacticism meant Neo-Confucian moralism in fiction, poetry or drama, and the use of a contrived plot and stereotyped characters. Literature is not the slave of politics, morality or science, he wrote; it is their equal.[217] Modern Korean literature had to set aside traditional views of literature, and take as its subject matter all kinds of thought and emotion. Literature should not be didactic, but "realistically" portray human thought and emotion.

When adjudicating works in a modern Korean literature competition in 1918, for example, Yi observed that the stories had artistic merit and were not didactic like traditional Korean literature.[218] The works in the competition were "realistic" and avoided the stereotypical characters and situations of traditional literature. Yi thought that literature should be about daily life and everyday emotions. Yi cited the Neo-Confucian text, *The Doctrine of the Mean* (Zhong Yong), and its ethos of not going to extremes.[219] To Yi, realism meant a plausible plot and characters. He expressed admiration, moreover, for another work in the same competition, entitled "Ŭisim ŭi sonyŏ" (The Suspicious Girl), by Kim Myŏng-sun. There was not a trace of didacticism in the work. Yi thought this was one of the only

216. Kwŏn Yŏng-min, "Ch'unwŏn ŭi Munhak kwa Kim Tong-in ŭi Pip'an," *Han'guk Kŭndae Munhak kwa Sidae Chŏngsin* (1983), cited in Kwŏn Yŏng-min, "Ch'unwŏn Munhak ŭl Hyang Han Yŏrahop Kae ŭi Hwasal": 124.
217. Yi Kwang-su, "Munhak iran Hao," *Maeil Sinbo* (10 November 1916–23 November 1916); reprint, *Yi Kwang-su Chŏnjip*, ed. Noh Yang-hwan, vol. 1 (Seoul: Samjungdang, 1971), 549.
218. Yi Kwang-su, "Hyŏnsang Sosŏl Kosŏn Yŏŏn," *Ch'ŏngch'un* no. 12 (March 1918); reprint, Kwŏn Yŏng-min, ed., *Han'guk Hyŏndae Munhak Pip'yŏngsa Charyo* I (Seoul: Tandae Ch'ulp'ansa, 1981), 97–8.
219. Ku In-hwan, "Yi Kwang-su ŭi Munhak Sasang," *Hyŏndae Sahoe* no. 2 (1981); reprint, *Yi Kwang-su Yŏn'gu*, vol. 1, ed. Tongguk Taehakkyo Pusŏl Han'guk Munhak Yŏn'guso (Seoul: T'aehaksa, 1984), 551–2.

works of modern Korean literature so far that were free of didacticism: the other two were Yi's own novel *The Heartless*, and "Purŭjijŭm" (A Cry), by Chin Sun-sŏng.[220] In another competition, Yi praised the writing of Pak Hwa-sŏng for its realism: "'Ch'usŏk chŏnya' (The Eve of the Autumn Festival) by Pak Hwa-sŏng . . . makes us forget that we are reading a work of fiction, and overwhelms us with the reality of tragic human life. The writing is so skillful that it reminds me of Jack London's writing."[221]

Yi translated European concepts of "imagination," "art" and "creativity" into Korean. Yi cited Kant's *Critique of Reason* as the foundation of modern philosophy about art, and said that according to Kant, humans need art and that this need was separate from the need for religion and philosophy.[222] Art was the product of human emotion, and was necessary to human existence. Humans had a need to be creative. There were artifacts excavated from Paekche tombs in Puyŏ, for example, that were not tools but art objects. Yi compared the theories of Herbert Spencer (1820–1903) and Friedrich Wilhelm Joseph von Schelling (1775–1854).[223] Spencer thought art emerged from the instinct for play. Schelling thought that art combined the "objective and the subjective, nature and reason, the conscious and the subconscious," and was the highest means to attain knowledge. Yi thought Spencer's view too cynical, but also criticized Schelling's view as elitist. "Literature belongs to all people," and not to an elite few, he wrote.

Yi translated imagination as *sangsangnyŏk*. This word appears frequently in his writings about literature. "A minor writer cannot see beyond the surface or the outer garments of life, but an artist who possesses great imagination can perceive the inner workings of life and write great songs and stories that move the depths of the soul."[224] Truth could be found in the "imaginary world of the poet."[225]

The writer's imagination had to be free from material constraints such as commercial considerations and political censorship. "We cannot restrict the free flight of the writer's imagination—which is none other than creativity."[226] "Literature ought to rely only on the free imagination, that is, the creativity of the writer, and not be limited by standards imposed from

220. Yi Kwang-su, "Hyŏnsang Sosŏl Kosŏn Yŏŏn," 97.
221. Yi Kwang-su, "Sosŏl Sŏnhuŏn," *Chosŏn Mundan* no. 3 (December 1924); *Yi Kwang-su Chŏnjip*, ed. Noh Yang-hwan, vol. 10 (Seoul: Samjungdang, 1971), 573.
222. Yi Kwang-su, "Munhak kwa Munsa wa Munjang," *Han'gŭl* (June 1935–October 1935); reprint, *Yi Kwang-su Chŏnjip*, vol. 10 (1971), 478.
223. Yi Kwang-su, "Munhak Kanghwa," *Chosŏn Mundan* (October 1924–February 1925); reprint, *Yi Kwang-su Chŏnjip*, vol. 10 (1971), 382.
224. Yi Kwang-su, "Munhak e Taehan Sogyŏn," *Tonga Ilbo* (23 July 1929–1 August 1929); reprint, *Yi Kwang-su Chŏnjip*, vol. 10 (1971), 453.
225. Yi Kwang-su, "Yesul P'yŏngga ŭi P'yojun," *Tonggwang* (1926 May); reprint, *Yi Kwang-su Chŏnjip*, vol. 10 (1971), 442.
226. Yi Kwang-su, "Munhak e Taehan Sogyŏn," 453.

outside. This is indeed how literature usually is, and not just my saying how it ought to be. No writer writes poetry or fiction according to a certain law, or specific articles of a moral code. If there are such writers, they would be writers who enter contests to write songs or scenarios for promoting savings or to advertise an exhibit."[227] Yi apparently thought literature could be separate from material conditions. He accepted a view of literature as produced by an individual imagination that is somehow outside of society. Imagination provided the unity that privileged a genuinely "literary" work.[228] This view of literature concealed European and Japanese ideological hegemony; however, it was also a view that colonial authorities might not censor, and that would give Korean writers a space in which to write.

According to Yi, the "new art" of modern literature began to reach the Korean public at a popular level in 1920. Before that, the readership for modern literature was limited to students and a small number of intellectuals comprising a "newly emerging class" (*sinjin kyegŭp*).[229] Readers could have access to the "new art" through journals such as *Ch'angjo* (Creation), *P'yehŏ* (Ruins), *Paekcho* (White Tide), *Kaebyŏk* (Creation) and *Chosŏn Mundan* (The Korean Literary World). Daily newspapers published serialized fiction, and had arts columns, though the latter were sometimes combined with the "women's and family column." Every day, such arts columns would publish "new poetry" (*sinsi*), *sijo* and essays. Writing in 1925, Yi estimated that the Korean media published over a dozen works of fiction each month, many more works than that in poetry, and a few works of literary criticism. These reached hundreds of thousands of Korean readers. Yi estimated that all men and women aged thirty-four or five and under, who had received a modern education, had read the works of new Korean writers. The most enthusiastic readers of the "new arts" were students, male and female. These students could not study their own language or culture at school.

Modern literature did not yet have an established importance in Korean society, Yi observed. As Yi's contemporary Kim Tong-in wrote, *yangban*, scholars and gentlemen (*sinsa*) thought that fiction was something that was read only by dissipated, good-for-nothing laggards.[230] It was not self-evident to Koreans why there had to be any literature in their lives. Western overviews of literary theory always assumed the reader understood the significance of literature, and therefore did not bother to explain why

227. Ibid.
228. Anthony Easthope, *Literary into Cultural Studies* (London and New York: Routledge, 1991), 12.
229. Yi Kwang-su, "Uri Munye ŭi Panghyang," *Chosŏn Mundan* no. 13 (November 1925); reprint, *Yi Kwang-su Chŏnjip*, ed. Noh Yang-hwan, vol. 10 (Seoul: Samjungdang, 1971), 428.
230. Kim Tong-in, "Sosŏl e Taehan Chosŏn Saram ŭi Sasang ŭl," *Hak Chi Kwang* 18 (August 1918); reprint, Kwŏn Yŏng-min, ed., *Han'guk Hyŏndae Munhak Pip'yŏngsa (charyo I)* (Seoul: Tongguk Taehakkyo Ch'ulp'anbu, 1981), 135–138.

literature mattered in the first place. Yi thought that Koreans, however, needed such an explanation and introduction.

Koreans showed little interest in literature, Yi noted. "It is strange that Koreans should be so indifferent about literature, since Korea is a nation of literature," Yi added. He attributed this indifference to several factors. These included recent historical circumstances in Korea. This was a reference to the Japanese colonial occupation of Korea. Koreans were preoccupied with matters other than literature.

First of all, Koreans have not had the leisure to peacefully enjoy literature or the arts in the last thirty years. They have been compelled to focus their attention on politics, in response to the rapid decline in their national destiny. Koreans have always been political, but now that they find themselves under the present circumstances and are unable to participate in politics, it is only natural that they would take a deep interest in politics. Those with ambition regard literature as a pursuit indulged in by idle people, or a pastime or trivial skill used to relieve boredom. Thus, there are no people who think of the literary arts as a lifetime occupation. Literature is nothing more than a kind of easy side job.[231]

Poverty was another factor in Korean indifference to literature. "The Korean people keep growing poorer every day," Yi said. "Koreans do not have the mental or the economic leisure to enjoy literature or art. They do not have the money to buy so much as a single magazine or a single book, nor do they have the strength to motivate themselves to buy these things. Even if poets or writers produce works, there is thus no one to buy them. Then the writer is unable to eat. A writer must become a clerk in a financial cooperative or local administrative office and earn a monthly salary of twenty to thirty wŏn in order to live." Colonial censorship presented a further obstacle to the flourishing of literature in Korea, Yi added.

The practice of literary criticism would be necessary for the establishment of modern Korean literature, Yi argued, but there were not enough Koreans who had studied literature or literary criticism seriously, and literary criticism was not recognized as a discipline. Korean literary criticism was still just "impressionistic."[232] Yi considered modern literary criticism a new genre of literature. Literature included "art," or creative works, and "science," or literary theory, literary history and literary criticism.[233] Yi

231. Yi Kwang-su, "Chosŏn ŭi Munhak," *Samch'ŏlli* (March 1933); reprint, *Yi Kwang-su Chŏnjip*, ed. Noh Yang-hwan, vol. 10 (Seoul: Samjungdang, 1971), 468.

232. Yi Kwang-su, "Chosŏn Mundan ŭi Hyŏnhwang kwa Changnae," *Tonga Ilbo* 1 January 1925; reprint, *Yi Kwang-su Chŏnjip*, vol. 10 (1971), 400.

233. Yi Kwang-su, "Chosŏn Munhak ŭi Kaenyŏm," *Sinsaeng* 2, no. 1 (January 1929); reprint,

translated concepts of literary criticism from European hegemonic discourse.[234] In translating concepts of literary criticism into Korean, however, Yi engaged Koreans in the discussion of modernity.

Yi's thought on language and Korean literature

Yi advocated writing in contemporary vernacular Korean in order to make literature accessible to as many readers as possible. At first, he wrote in a mixed script that used both Chinese characters and the Korean alphabet, but he tried to use Korean vernacular diction. In an article in the *Hwangsŏng Sinmun* (The Hwangsŏng News) in 1910, Yi criticized the use of obscure classical Chinese diction in Korean mixed script texts: "If one looks at the use of (Chinese and Korean scripts) in contemporary Korean newspapers and magazines, it is evident that the style used is "mixed script" in name only; in actuality, it is nothing more than pure classical Chinese with Korean particles added. . . . Newspapers and magazines compete with one another to use difficult, dense classical Chinese diction that only someone with decades of study in classical Chinese would understand. Perhaps it would be all right if all Koreans had such training, but in reality, most Koreans do not."[235] Yi observed that Korean newspapers and journals were written in mixed script that used Chinese characters that most Koreans could not read. This limited the accessibility of Korean newspapers and journals.

He recommended the continued use of mixed script, which he referred to as *kukhanmun pyŏngyong*, or "using both the Korean alphabet and Chinese characters," but recommended using more Korean vernacular language instead of Chinese characters and diction. He thought using only the Korean alphabet would make it difficult to introduce "new knowledge" (*sin chisik*), or modernity, from Japan and China; many neologisms in Chinese and Japanese discourse were written in Chinese characters, and were introduced in Korean discourse using the same Chinese characters. The use of more vernacular Korean diction in mixed script, however, would be beneficial for readers and writers, and the Korean language would gain prestige. This would be good for the nation, Yi wrote. He was advocating a more vernacular style in order to make newspapers and journals more accessible to Korean readers.

Yi defined Korean literature as "literature written in Korean."[236] Yi cited the precedent of Japanese poet Yamada Bimyō, who wrote in the

Yi Kwang-su Chŏnjip, ed. Noh Yang-hwan, vol. 10 (Seoul: Samjungdang, 1971), 449–450.

234. Raymond Williams discusses the social history of literary criticism, in *Marxism and Literature*, 48–49.

235. 24 July 1910. This article is cited in Ch'oe Ki-yŏng, "Yi Kwang-su ŭi Rŏsia Ch'eryu wa Munp'il Hwaltong," *Minjok Munhaksa Yŏn'gu* 9 (1996), 378.

236. Yi Kwang-su, "Munhak iran Hao," *Maeil Sinbo* 10 November 1916–23 November 1916; reprint, *Yi Kwang-su Chŏnjip*, vol. 1, (1971), 554.

gembunitchi style, or a style that "unified" literary and vernacular language. "There can be no literature apart from a national language, and a national language, moreover, is preserved, refined and developed through literature. It goes without saying that Korean literature must be established on the foundation of Korean language," Yi wrote.[237] Yi's use of modern vernacular Korean in literature can be seen as a hybrid of modern literary practice, and Korean vernacular literary modes. In his autobiographical writing, Yi described how his interest in literature arose from reading vernacular stories to his grandmother, listening to his cousin read stories, and from songs he heard as a child.

In the article *Chosŏn Sosŏlsa* (A History of Korean Fiction, 1935), Yi defined Korean literature as literature written in Korean, but included works written in classical Chinese anyway. The latter included *Kŭmŏ sinhwa* (New Tales from Golden Turtle Mountain) by Kim Si-sŭp (1435–1493),[238] *Kuunmong* (The Nine Cloud Dream) by Kim Man-jung (1637–1692),[239] and *Sa ssi Nam Chŏnggi* (The Story of Madame Sa's Righteous Expedition to the South), also by Kim Man-jung. In other articles, he included only works written in Korean. Yi usually began Korean literary history with Silla *hyangga* as the earliest extant examples of Korean literature. These poems were written in *hyangch'al*, or the Sillan practice of using Chinese characters for phonetic or semantic value or both, and with Korean syntax. Although the poems used Chinese characters, Yi considered this to be Korean writing. Yi postulated that there may have been a flourishing tradition of literature written with such a Korean practice of using Chinese characters, but that such literature had been lost.[240] All that remained were the *hyangga* in the *Samguk Yusa* (Memorabilia of the Three Kingdoms, 1285) by Iryŏn. In one article, Yi chose to selectively trace Korean literary history through shaman song, and included *hyangga* as shaman song. "Shamans, and not the ancestors who left us poetry collections written in Chinese, must be credited with the achievement of having transmitted the sensibilities of Korean literature. The lyrics of shamans are for the most part ancient Korean poetry."[241] Yi here constituted a "tradition" of Korean literature that emphasized shaman songs, and privileged the Korean language, rather than

237. Yi Kwang-su, "Chosŏn Munhak ŭi Kaenyŏm," 459.
238. Part of this work has been translated by Peter H. Lee, in *Anthology of Korean Literature: From Early Times to the Nineteenth Century* (Honolulu: University of Hawaii Press, 1981), 79–91.
239. Part of this work has been translated by Peter H. Lee, in *Anthology of Korean Literature: From Early Times to the Nineteenth Century*, 161–176. Richard Rutt and Kim Chong-un translated the entire work, in *Virtuous Women: Three Classic Korean Novels* (Seoul: Royal Asiatic Society, 1974), 1–177.
240. Yi Kwang-su, "Puhwal ŭi Sŏgwang," *Ch'ŏngch'un* no. 12 (March 1918); reprint, *Yi Kwang-su Chŏnjip*, ed. Noh Yang-hwan, vol. 10 (Seoul: Samjungdang, 1971), 26–7.
241. Yi Kwang-su, "Chosŏn Munhak ŭi Kaenyŏm," 451.

classical Chinese. The idea of "tradition" could be used as by subaltern subjects to resist the contemporary Japanese colonial policy of obliterating the Korean language.

Korean literature did not flourish, Yi wrote, because of Korean worship of Chinese culture and the Chinese language. "The Korean alphabet became the slave of classical Chinese."[242] The civil service examination system contributed to the privileging of Chinese, and the devaluing of the Korean alphabet. Koreans nevertheless wrote *sijo* poetry in a mixed script of Korean and Chinese characters. "The several dozen Silla *hyanga* recorded in *idu* (i.e. *hyangch'al*) and thousands of *sijo* written in Korean are truly the origins and the essence of Korean literature. The form, prosody, thought, sensibility and life found therein make these poems genuine classics, the only records left to us of the Korean soul."[243] Yi also mentioned as Korean literature several songs by T'aejong and Chŏng Po-ŭn that were written in Chinese characters but with what Yi described as Korean syntax.[244] Yi included in Korean literary history vernacular fiction such as *Hong Kil-tong Chŏn* (The Story of Hong Kil-tong), attributed to Hŏ Kyun (1569–1618), and *Chŏn Uch'i Chŏn* (The Story of Chŏn Uch'i); *kasa* or songs; and *p'ansori*, or Korean sung narrative.

Yi used Western theories of character portrayal in writing about *p'ansori*. Character portrayal in the *p'ansori* work *Simch'ŏng Chŏn* (The Story of Simch'ŏng) was acceptable by modern standards because the depiction of character "types" such as Old Man Sim and Ppaengdŏk's mother could be found in the works of Shakespeare as well, and that a character such as Simch'ŏng corresponded to what Plato called an "ideal." "Types" appeared in Greek and Shakespearian works, Yi argued, and thus "one could hardly find fault with such portrayal." Yi's description of Simch'ŏng as an ideal character alluded to European concepts of "typicality." This engaged Korean literature with Western texts and theory. In the literary thought of Taine in the nineteenth century, typicality was associated with the hero who embodied Aristotelian "universals." "Typicality" in the theory of Belinsky, Chernyshevsky and Dobrolyubov, became the idea of the representative character or situation.[245]

The translation of Chinese classics and fiction into Korean, moreover, had contributed to Korean literature.[246] Yi included such translations, and

242. Yi Kwang-su, "Munhak iran Hao," 554.
243. Yi Kwang-su, "Chosŏn Munhak ŭi Kaenyŏm," 451.
244. Yi Kwang-su, "Munhak iran Hao," 554.
245. Raymond Williams, *Marxism and Literature* (Oxford and New York: Oxford University Press, 1977), 101. I audited a class at Seoul National University, taught by Professor Kim Yun-sik, in which Professor Kim discussed literary thought about typicality, or character "types."
246. Yi Kwang-su, "Munhak iran Hao," 555.

Korean translations of fiction written in Chinese by Korean writers, as Korean literature.[247] Yi thought that translation contributed to the vitality of a language. Koreans had a responsibility to translate foreign works, and Korean classics written in Chinese, into Korean. The translation of world classics into Korean was an urgent task, he believed, for the ongoing development of the Korean language. According to Yi, Chinese character neologisms that were translations of European words became a part of the Korean language and enriched the Korean language. He considered these neologisms a part of the Korean language. In *Na ŭi kobaek*, Yi discussed how Koreans in the Soviet Union responded to the Russian language, inventing Korean vernacular neologisms for Russian words, using loan words, and even translating Korean vernacular neologisms for Russian words into Chinese characters.[248] In an article published in 1916, Yi wrote, moreover, that the translation of the Bible and hymns had contributed significantly to the promotion of the Korean alphabet and had provided a great stimulus to the development of Korean literature.[249]

Yi criticized contemporary Koreans' neglect of the Korean language. Koreans had devalued the Korean language. "The Korean language has shared a common destiny with the Korean people," Yi wrote. "It cannot be destroyed unless the Korean people themselves abandon their own language and writing."[250] Writing in 1929, Yi observed that the Korean language was "deteriorating and falling into further disorder with every day that passes."[251] This decline was attributed to several factors. "Some of the reasons for this are that there are not enough hours of Korean language instruction in elementary Korean education, teaching materials are inappropriate, and teaching methodology is bad. Another reason is that we seem to have an inborn habit of worshiping the foreign, and we lack an adequate attachment to and respect for the Korean language. The biggest reason is that newspaper managers are ruining the Korean language. Writers, who ought to be devotees of the Korean language, do not study Korean, and produce mediocre, confused writing."[252] Yi added that Korean language instructors usually just focused on correcting spelling, or teaching grammar at a specialized level, but did not know how to teach "living, breathing Korean language." Koreans, moreover, did not have the linguistic consciousness to appreciate the Korean language. There were many Koreans who "will not

247. Yi Kwang-su, "Chosŏn Munhak ŭi Kaenyŏm," 451.
248. Yi Kwang-su, *Na ŭi Kobaek* (Seoul: Ch'unch'usa, 1948); reprint, *Yi Kwang-su Chŏnjip*, ed. Noh Yang-hwan, vol. 7 (Seoul: Samjungdang, 1971), 244.
249. Yi Kwang-su, "Munhak iran Hao," 555.
250. Yi Kwang-su, "Chosŏnŏ," *Chosŏn Ilbo* 11 October 1935; reprint, *Yi Kwang-su Chŏnjip*, ed. Noh Yang-hwan, vol. 9 (Seoul: Samjungdang, 1971), 455.
251. Yi Kwang-su, "Chosŏn Munhak e taehan Sogyŏn," *Tonga Ilbo* 23 July 1929–1 August, 458.
252. Ibid., 458.

give Korean literature a second glance and despise it because they think it is inferior to foreign language; but that is like spitting at and despising your appearance because you think it is inferior to those of foreigners."[253] The first duty of Koreans, Yi said, was to be fluent in Korean. "Anyone who does not diligently read Korean language newspapers and journals, or books, given our situation today, is not a Korean."[254] Yi criticized, moreover, colonial policy on Korean language. "It is common sense to teach children in primary school in the language that they use at home," Yi wrote in 1933. Nevertheless, Korean children were prohibited from using Korean.[255] Korean language was eventually banned from schools in Korea in October 1937, and all instruction was required to be in Japanese.[256]

Language and literary style in Yi's early writings
    Yi experimented with different writing styles between 1910, the year of his earliest published work, and 1917, when he wrote his first novel, *The Heartless*. He eventually wrote in a modern vernacular style that did not use the *-tŏ-ra* sentence ending that was characteristic of traditional vernacular fiction. He wrote in comparatively simple sentences, vernacular diction, and a neutral politeness level. The modern Korean writer sought verisimilitude, or a mimetic semblance of reality. The use of modern vernacular would contribute to the credibility of a literary representation of reality.
    Yi experimented, moreover, with various politeness styles for modern fiction. He tried writing in the somewhat pompous literary *ha-no-ra* style,[257] the archaic *ha-na-i-da* style,[258] and the epistolary *ha-o* style.[259] Yi eventually

253. Yi Kwang-su, "Chosŏn Ŏmun yech'an," *Chosŏn Ilbo* 29 October 1935–3 November 1935; reprint, *Yi Kwang-su Chŏnjip*, ed. Noh Yang-hwan, vol. 9 (Seoul: Samjungdang, 1971), 459.
254. Yi Kwang-su, "Chosŏn Munhak ŭi Kaenyŏm," 459.
255. Yi Kwang-su, "Chosŏnŏ ŭi Pin'gon," *Chosŏn Ilbo* 3 October 1933; reprint, *Yi Kwang-su Chŏnjip*, vol. 9 (1971), 353. With the annexation of Korea in 1910, the Japanese colonial government carried out a policy of assimilation (*dōka seisaku*) through promotion of the Japanese language and eventual banning of the Korean language in government, education and publication. Cf. Dong Wonmo, "Assimilation and Social Mobilization in Korea," in Andrew Nahm, ed., *Korea Under Japanese Colonial Rule* (Western Michigan University Center for Korean Studies, Institute of International and Area Studies, 1973). Michael Robinson discusses the response of the Korean language movement to Japanese colonial policy, in *Cultural Nationalism in Colonial Korea*, 82–92.
256. Wonmo Dong, 160.
257. Cf. Yi Kwang-su, "Okchung Hogŏl," *Taehan Hŭnghakpo* January 1910, in Yi Kwang-su, *Yi Kwang-su Chŏnjip*, ed. Noh Yang-hwan, vol. 1 (Seoul: Usinsa, 1978), 573–575.
258. Yi Kwang-su, "Sanghae Sŏ," *Ch'ŏngch'un* no. 3–4 (1 December 1914–1 January 1915); reprint, *Yi Kwang-su Chŏnjip*, vol. 9 (1978) 130–134. "Taegu esŏ," *Maeil Sinbo* 22–23 September 1916; reprint, *Yi Kwang-su Chŏnjip*, vol. 9 (1978), 137–139.
259. Yi Kwang-su, "Hŏnsinja," *Sonyŏn* August 1910; reprint, *Yi Kwang-su Chŏnjip*, vol. 1 (1978), 565–568. "Taegu esŏ," *Yi Kwang-su Chŏnjip*, vol. 9 (1978), 134–137; "Nongch'on Kyebal," in *Maeil Sinbo* (November 26, 1916–February 18, 1917); reprint, *Yi Kwang-su*

chose the neutral *hae-ra* style.[260] Yi also went from writing in a *kukhanmun* style which combined literary Chinese and Korean, to a demotic style written only in the Korean alphabet and with vernacular diction. Yi considered the novel *The Heartless* to be the first work he wrote completely in the Korean alphabet, in a vernacular style.

Yi's short story "Hŏnsinja" (A Person of Dedication, August 1910) was written in the *ha-o* style, which resulted in an informal, conversational tone.[261] Narrated in the first-person voice by a narrator who knows the main character, "Hŏnsinja" depicts a businessman who dedicated his wealth to education. The story was written in *kukhanmun*, or the Chinese characters and the Korean alphabet, and used the *ha-o* style, a conversational and epistolary style slightly less formal than the most formal style, the *hap-si-o* style. Writing in the *ha-o* style tacitly established the relationship of narrator to reader as that of a speaker addressing one who is either his junior or his peer, with polite deference.

Ch'oe Nam-sŏn had also experimented with narrative tone, using verb endings in the *ha-o* style instead of the *hae-ra* style of traditional vernacular fiction. Nonfiction articles in *Sonyŏn* had, for the most part, been written in the plain *hae-ra* style, but the *ha-o* style had been used in editorials and articles on science. Yi Kwang-su assisted Ch'oe in writing and editing *Sonyŏn* magazine, and his remarks elsewhere on the various levels of politeness offer insight into early-twentieth-century perceptions of the various styles. In *Ch'unwŏn sŏgan munbŏm* (Examples for Letter Writing),[262]

Chŏnjip, ed. Noh Yang-hwan, vol. 10 (Seoul: Usinsa, 1978), 62–97.

260. "The style is the part of the honorific system that depends upon the person listening to the sentence . . . the style is finely differentiated according to the degree of respect to be given to the listener." Iksop Lee and S. Robert Ramsey, *The Korean Language* (Albany: State University of New York Press, 2000), 249. The *hae-ra* style or "plain style" shows familiarity, and "is used with close friends, by parents to their children, or by a relatively older speaker to a child of up to high school age. . . . In written Korean, the plain style is ordinarily used when writing for a general audience." Iksop Lee and S. Robert Ramsey, *The Korean Language*, 253. Yi experimented with various levels of honorifics before adopting the plain style in his fiction writing.

The *ha-o* style or "semiformal style" is "used with someone in an inferior position, but in this case the person is treated with a greater degree of reserve than is the case with the familiar [*ha-ge*] style. It is a style a husband could use with his wife; an older man would use with a younger, former schoolmate *Kim-hyeng* or the like; a superior at a workplace with *Kim kwa-cang*. It is the appropriate style for a former superior officer in the military to use when he sees again the men who were once under his command. It is also a style sometimes used with strangers whose social rank is clear but not considered particularly high. Letters written in this style are often used among friends to show reserve." Iksop Lee and S. Robert Ramsey, *The Korean Language*, 256.

Shin Ji-weon has written about politeness strategies used by Korean women in nontraditional positions of authority, in *Acta Koreana*, 6:2 (July 2003).

261. Yi Kwang-su, "Hŏnsinja," *Sonyŏn* no. 8 (August 1910); reprint, *Yi Kwang-su chŏnjip*, ed. Noh Yang-hwan, vol. 1 (Seoul: Samjungdang, 1971), 565–568.

262. Yi Kwang-su, *Ch'unwŏn Sŏgan Munbŏm* (Seoul: Samjungdang, 1939); reprint, *Yi Kwang-su Chŏnjip*, ed. Noh Yang-hwan, vol. 9 (Seoul: Usinsa, 1978), 212.

Yi described the *ha-so* style (that is, the *ha-o* style, using the *-so* variant after verb stems ending in a consonant)[263] as one that could be used in written correspondence "between friends and to distant relatives who are one's inferior, and in writing to those with whom one is in a position to use the *ha-ge* style in conversation."[264] According to Yi, "one uses the *ha-ge* and *hae-ra* styles in written correspondence with relatives who are one's inferiors, or between teacher and pupil." In spite of Ch'oe Nam-sŏn's experimentation with the style in *Sonyŏn* magazine, however, the *ha-o* style was rarely used in fiction, though it found wide application in the grammatical examples given in early modern grammar books, and in the expository text of Korean textbooks during the Japanese occupation period.[265] The story "Hŏnsinja" may have used the *ha-o* style in the same way that it was used in the context of advertisements and public speech, in order to speak to a large audience. In "Hŏnsinja," the reader is addressed as *tokcha* (reader) and *tokcha chessi* (readers). The narrative tone was therefore not necessarily that of a conversation between two people or letter-writing, but that of one speaker addressing an audience of more than one listener.

"Hŏnsinja" also used the formal polite ending *-p-nida* occasionally, and the honorific affix *si* with verbs for which the reader was the implied subject. The narrator nevertheless uses the non-deferential first-person pronoun *na* to refer to himself. This is consistent with the somewhat elevated position given the narrator in the text. Some uses of the *hae* style, the most informal of styles, occur within the narrative, but in answer to rhetorical questions raised by the narrator to no one in particular. The narrative also used the informal *ha-ge* style interrogative *-n-ga* ending occasionally. The narrator does not directly address the reader; the question is rhetorical, and raised by the narrator for the sake of introducing the explanation that follows. Ko Yŏng-gŭn has pointed out that *-n-ga* appeared often in soliloquys and poetry up to the 1930s.[266]

With the novel *The Heartless*, Yi's style would change from a *kukhanmun* style using Chinese characters and Korean, traditional sentence structure, and the *-tŏ-ra* style, to a modern vernacular style that used vernacular diction, concise sentences, and the *hae-ra* politeness style. This is the style he would continue to use in his fiction.

---

263. In "Hŏnsinja," the narrator uses the *-so* affix in indicate statements after verb stems ending in a consonant, instead of the *-ŭ-o* ending that is the form that should follow a verb stem ending in a consonant in a *ha-o* style indicative sentence. Ko Yŏng-gŭn has noted that it was more common in early modern texts to use the *-so* variant than the *-ŭ-o* when using the *hao* style in a declarative sentence. Ko Yŏng-gŭn, "Hyŏndae Kugŏ ŭi Chonggyŏl Ŏmi e Taehan Kugŏjŏk Yŏn'gu," *Ŏhak ŏn'gu* 10.1 (1974): 124.

264. Yi Kwang-su, *Ch'unwŏn Sŏgan Munbŏm*, 212.

265. Ko Yŏng-gŭn, "Hyŏndae Kugŏ ŭi Munch'epŏp e Taehan Yŏn'gu: Sŏbŏp Ch'egye," 20.

266. Ibid., 25.

Writing for Korean newspapers in Russia
     While in Russia,[267] Yi Kwang-su wrote articles for the *Kwŏnŏp Sinmun*,
which was published in Vladivostok, and the *Taehanin Chyŏnggyobo*, which
was published in Chita. The *Kwŏnŏp Sinmun* was the official newspaper of
the Kwŏnŏphoe, and was published from May 5, 1912 to September 1,
1914.[268] Sin Ch'ae-ho, Yi Sang-sŏl and Kim Ha-gu wrote editorials for the
paper.[269] It was published completely in the Korean language, once a week
on Sunday, until the paper was closed. In 1912, seven hundred to eight
hundred copies were published; in 1913: 1,000–1,500; and in 1914: 2,000.[270]
The *Taehanin Chyŏnggyobo* was the official newspaper of the Taehanin
kungminhoe Siberia chibang ch'onghoe (Korean National Association,
Siberia Regional Assembly),[271] and was published from January 2, 1912 to
1913, when it was shut down because of Russian compliance with Japanese
opposition to the paper, and because the printer broke down.[272]
     Yi's articles for the *Kwŏnŏp Sinmun* were published March 1, 8, 15, and
22, 1914 (nos. 100–103). The *Kwŏnŏp Sinmun* was published entirely in
Korean, with no Chinese characters.[273] Writing under the literary name
Oebae or "solitary boat," Yi advocated the development of commerce, and
tried to find Korean precedents for such development.[274]
     It is likely that Yi began writing for the *Taehanin Chyŏnggyobo* with
volume ten, published May 1, 1914. Editor Yi Kang[275] had introduced Yi to

267. Yi later wrote about his experiences in Russia, in his 1948 memoir *Na ŭi Kobaek*. He wrote
in particular about the language and culture of Koreans in Russia. For a study of Koreans in
Russia, cf. Ross King, *Koryŏ Saram: Koreans in the Former USSR*, special issue of *Korean and
Korean American Studies Bulletin*, (New Haven, Connecticut: East Rock Institute, 2001).
268. Ch'oe Ki-yŏng, "Yi Kwang-su ŭi Rŏsia Ch'eryu wa Munp'il Hwaltong," *Minjok Munhaksa
Yŏn'gu* 9 (1996): 382.
269. Pak Hwan, *Rŏsia Hanin Minjok Undongsa* (Seoul: T'amgudang, 1995), 143.
270. "Kwŏnŏp Hoe Sinnyŏn Ch'onghoe," 1914 February 8; and "Ponbo Ch'anggan Che 2
Chunyŏn Kinyŏm," cited in Ch'oe Ki-yŏng, 382.
271. Pak Hwan, 112. The Taehanin Kungminhoe (Korean National Association) was based in
the United States. It was originally organized as the Kongnip Hyŏphoe, in San Francisco on
April 5, 1905, by An Ch'ang-ho. In February 20, 1908, a decision was reached to organize
branches in Vladivostok and Hawaii. The Vladivostok branch of the KH started a company
called the Asea Sirŏp Chusik Hoesa (Asia Manufacturing Company), to finance armed
resistance to Japan. Pak Hwan, 185–189.
272. Ch'oe Ki-yŏng, 384.
273. The newspaper used *arae a*, and a "conservative orthography" that Ross King has observed
in another Korean newspaper in Russia, the *Taehanin Chŏnggyobo*, i.e. spelling that preserves
/t(h)yV, c(h)V, c(h)yV, sV, syV/. (V stands for vowel.) Ross King, "Experimentation with
Han'gŭl in Russia and the USSR, 1914–1937," in ed. Young-key Kim-Renaud, *The Korean
Alphabet: Its History and Structure* (Honolulu: University of Hawaii Press, 1997), 231.
274. Ch'oe Ki-yŏng, 359. Yi later wrote for the journal *Ch'ŏngch'un*, using the pen name Oebae.
Cf. *Ch'ŏngch'un* nos. 3, 7, 10, 11 (1914–1917).
275. Yi Kang (1878–1964) was from South P'yŏngan Province. He studied classical Chinese
from age seven to seventeen. He joined the Methodist church. In 1902, he went to Hawaii. In
1907, An Ch'ang-ho's Kongnip Hyŏphoe in San Francisco sent Yi Kang to Vladivostok. Yi

readers in an earlier issue (March 1, 1914), saying that Yi would be presenting writings with "end rhyme" (*kkŭt sori nanŭn kŭl*).[276] Volume ten of the newspaper published several poems, including one original poem written with end rhyme and, moreover, rhymes at the beginning of each line.[277] The poems in volume ten were printed with the Korean letters written horizontally, side by side. This differed from the traditional practice of writing *han'gŭl* letters in syllable blocks (*moa ssŭgi*): "gather together and write."[278] According to Ross King, the idea of *karo p'urŏssŭgi*, or "linearly take apart and write," is attributed to Chu Si-gyŏng (1876–1914).[279] Yi's literary name Oebae, or "solitary boat," appeared as the byline for an article explaining the experimental horizontal orthography, in volume eleven of the newspaper.

Volume eleven of the *Taehanin Chyŏnggyobo* included several poems written by Yi Kwang-su. "Nara lŭl Ttŏnanŭn Sŏrum" (Sorrow Upon Leaving One's Country) consists of two *sijo* poems. It was written in the tradition of *sijo* poetry about parting from a place. The narrator is leaving Korea to seek freedom. The poem uses traditional *sijo* prosody and motifs to write about nation.

MUJŎNG

The title of the novel *Mujŏng* resembles that of Kuroiwa Ruikō's 1902 Japanese adaptation of Victor Hugo's novel *Les Misérables*, entitled "A Mujō."[280] "When I first read Kuroiwa Ruikō's adaptation of *Les Misérables*, entitled 'A Mujō,' in the *Yorozu chohō*, I resolved, though young and immature as I was, to write like that, if I were to write," Yi wrote. "After that, I read an English translation of *Les Misérables*, and a complete translation in Japanese, entitled *Aishi* (Sorrowful History); and I read the work in French

Kang began working for the *Haejo Sinmun*.
276. Ch'oe Ki-yŏng, 384.
277. Yi used a plus (+) sign over a word to indicate a rhyming word at the beginning of a sentence. An "x" over a word indicated a rhyming word at the end of a sentence. Although the poem was published anonymously, it is likely that it was written by Yi Kwang-su, since Yi Kang had said in the March 1 issue that Yi would be writing with end-rhyme. Yi Kwang-su experimented with end-rhyme, moreover, in several poems published in *Ch'ŏngch'un*, i.e. in five poems in no. 6 (January 1915), one poem in no. 7 (May 1917), and three poems in no. 8 (June 1917). *Yi Kwang-su chŏnjip*, ed. Noh Yang-hwan, vol. 9 (Seoul: Samjungdang, 1971), 467–470. The poem with rhyme in the *Taehanin Chyŏnggyobo*, moreover, uses the word *arinari* for Amnokkang; Yi Kwang-su used the word *arinari* in another poem entitled "Amnokkang esŏ," dated June 5, 1933, published in *Tonggwang Ch'ongsŏ* (1933).
278. Ross King, "Experimentation," 222.
279. Ibid., 222.
280. Kuroiwa Ruikō (given name Shūroku) (1862–1920) was a journalist and celebrated author of detective stories. Kuroiwa Ruikō, "A Mujō," *Yorozu Chohō* (8 October Meiji 35 [1902]–2 August Meiji 36 [1903]). The novel was also published separately in two volumes. *A Mujō*, vol. 1 (Tokyo: Fusōdō, January 1906); vol. 2 (Tokyo: Fusōdō, 25 April 1906). Cited in Kim Pyŏng-ch'ŏl, *Han'guk Kŭndae Pŏnyŏk Munhaksa Yŏn'gu* (Seoul: Ŭryu Munhwasa, 1975), 362.

once, in order to study French. I respected *Les Misérables* even more when I read that Tolstoy, whom I worshipped, praised *Les Misérables* as one of the greatest works of literature."[281] Yi characterized Hugo's work as "believing in human emotion (*injŏng chuŭi*)."[282]

The title *Mujŏng* means to be without emotion, without love, unfeeling, uncaring, lacking in compassion, heartless, and may also refer to the state of insentience.[283] The indifferent individual or society lacks compassion. Moreover, heartlessness may be sexual repression.

The two main protagonists of the omniscient narrative of *The Heartless* are a middle school English teacher named Yi Hyŏng-sik, and a woman named Pak Yŏng-ch'ae. Hyŏng-sik and Yŏng-ch'ae encounter one another at the beginning of the novel after having been apart for eight years. Yŏng-ch'ae's father, Scholar Pak, had been a second father to Hyŏng-sik when the latter lost his parents to cholera. Scholar Pak told Yŏng-ch'ae to marry Hyŏng-sik. Yŏng-ch'ae and Hyŏng-sik were separated, though, when Yŏng-ch'ae's father and brothers went to jail because of a crime committed by one of Scholar Pak's students. Yŏng-ch'ae then sold herself as a *kisaeng*, in order to acquire money to free her father and brothers. When Yŏng-ch'ae finds Hyŏng-sik in Seoul later, at the beginning of the novel, she leaves his presence in silence, ashamed that she has become a *kisaeng*. Although she is a *kisaeng*, she has kept her virginity, in hopes of marrying Hyŏng-sik. Yŏng-ch'ae is eventually sold, however, to a patron who rapes her when she resists his advances. She then resolves to commit suicide. Hyŏng-sik abandons all hope of finding Yŏng-ch'ae after he reads a suicide note from her; he then marries a woman named Sŏn-hyŏng, only to realize later that Yŏng-ch'ae is still alive.

281. "Wigo ŭi Sahu Osimnyŏn Che e," *Chosŏn Ilbo* 23 May 1935; reprint, *Yi Kwang-su Chŏnjip*, ed. Noh Yang-hwan, vol. 10 (Seoul: Usinsa, 1978), 591. Tokuda Shusei wrote a translation of *Les Misérables* entitled *Aishi*, which was published by Shinchosha in 1914 (Taishō 3), as part of the *Seiyō Daicho Monogatari Sōsho*, vol. 3. Nihon Kokuritsu Kokkai Toshokan, *Meiji-Taishō-Shōwa Honyaku Bungaku Mokuroku* (Tokyo: Fukan shobō, 1972), 648. Another translation entitled "Aishi," by Togawa Shukotsu, was published in 1914–15 (Taishō 3–4) by the Kokumin Bunkō Kankōkai, as part of its *Taisei Meicho Bunkō* series.

282. Ibid., 592. Yi said, moreover, that a movie version of *Les Misérables* was shown in Seoul. "Wigo ŭi Sahu Osimnyŏn Che e," *Chosŏn Ilbo* 23 May 1935; reprint, *Yi Kwang-su Chŏnjip*, vol. 10 (1978), 591. Yi cited, too, a translation of part of a work by Hugo, in the journal *Sonyŏn*. Ch'oe Nam-sŏn translated part of *Les Misérables*; the translation appears to have been based on a Japanese translation by Hara Yogorō, published 3 Feb. 1902 (Meiji 35), as "ABC Kumiai," (The ABC Fraternal League) (Naigai Shuppan Kyōkai, Bunkō Han) (Kim Pyŏng-ch'ŏl, 291). Cf. Ch'oe Nam-sŏn, trans., "ABC kye" (The ABC Cooperative), *Sonyŏn* 17 July 1910: 1–60. Hara acknowledged having translated from an English translation. Korean writer Hong Myŏng-hŭi wrote a partial translation of *Les Misérables* in 1914 entitled "Nŏ Ch'am Pulsangt'a," (How Pitiful You Are). Yi Chae-sŏn, *Han'guk Kaehwagi Sosŏl Yŏn'gu* (Seoul: Ilchogak, 1972), 320, no. 17.

283. *Mujō* and *mujŏng* are the Japanese and Korean readings of the Chinese *wu qing*.

Plot in *The Heartless* differs from that in the *sinsosŏl*, which usually ends with lovers happily joined in marriage. Instead of joining Hyŏng-sik and Yŏng-ch'ae in marriage, *The Heartless* narrates their separate journeys—paths converging momentarily, only to separate. When Yŏng-ch'ae attempts suicide, the narrative cautions readers not to expect a miraculous delivery and reunion typical of traditional fiction.

Let us now say something about Yŏng-ch'ae. Had she indeed descended through the blue waters of the Taedong River, and become a denizen of the Dragon King's palace? Some of you readers may have wept in sadness that Yŏng-ch'ae has died. Then again, there may be other readers who laughed to themselves, thinking that they saw past the meager skills of the novelist. They may have thought that just as Yŏng-ch'ae was about to drown in the Taedong River, she would be saved by some noble person, and become a nun in a hermitage, until she met Hyŏng-sik again and they were joyfully married, and enjoyed long life, wealth and prestige, and had many sons. It would be just as it had been since antiquity in all storybooks, in which women who were childless until late in life inevitably gave birth to a son, and that son always became a great man.

There may be readers who praised Yŏng-ch'ae's decision to go to P'yŏngyang, and thought it was right of Yŏng-ch'ae to drown herself. Some readers may have thought there was no reason for Yŏng-ch'ae to end her life, and may have thought her actions regrettable and a waste of a precious life. I do not know how the various thoughts of you, my readers, may differ or agree with what I am about to write with regard to Yŏng-ch'ae, but it will be interesting to compare your thoughts and mine.[284]

Yŏng-ch'ae escapes death and eventually meets Hyŏng-sik again, but only after Hyŏng-sik has married another woman and Yŏng-ch'ae has renounced her Confucian obligation to marry Hyŏng-sik.

The double plot resembles the plot structure of Tolstoy's *Resurrection*, a work mentioned in chapter fifty-seven of *The Heartless*.[285] Hyŏng-sik, like the character of Nekhlyudov, wavers between a socially and financially advantageous marriage, and marriage with a woman to whom he feels

284. *Mujŏng*, chapter 86, *Maeil Sinbo* 22 April 1917.
285. Hyŏng-sik thinks of scenes from *Resurrection* when he goes to a P'yŏngyang police station to search for Yŏng-ch'ae. *Mujŏng*, Chapter 57, *Maeil Sinbo* 13 March 1917. Paik Nak-chung discusses Yi Kwang-su and Tolstoy's novel *Resurrection*, in "Sŏyang Myŏngjak Sosŏl ŭi Chuch'ejŏk Ihae lŭl Wihae: Tolsŭttoi ŭi *Puhwal* ŭl Chungsim ŭro," *Wŏrha Yi Tonmyŏng Sŏnsaeng Hwan'gap Kinyŏm Munjip*, 1982; reprint, Paik Nak-chung, *Minjok Munhak kwa Segye Munhak*, II (Seoul: Ch'angbisa, 1985), 176–203.

obligated by the past and a sense of moral duty. Sŏn-hyŏng has graduated from a modern girls' school, and is the daughter of a wealthy church elder named Kim. Sŏn-hyŏng's father is a *yangban*, or Korean aristocrat. Her father, Elder Kim, is a wealthy former consul to the United States, and Elder in a Presbyterian church. Sŏn-hyŏng's mother had formerly been a *kisaeng*, and had been elevated from the status of concubine to that of wife when Elder Kim's first wife died. Pak Yŏng-ch'ae corresponds to Tolstoy's Katyusha, the orphaned servant whom Nekhlyudov seduces and who eventually becomes a prostitute.

Both works introduce the male main character and the woman from his past in a scene involving a sudden, startling recognition of one character by the other, or revelation of a character's identity to another character. Nekhlyudov is accidentally reunited with Katyusha after a period of several years, in the courtroom scene in which she appears as a defendant in a murder trial in which Nekhlyudov is participating as a juror. He recognizes her as she appears before the court, and is shocked at her altered appearance and situation. In *The Heartless*, Hyŏng-sik and Yŏng-ch'ae meet after a period of eight years, when Yŏng-ch'ae seeks him out in Seoul. He does not recognize her until she identifies herself, and he is deeply moved when he realizes that she is Yŏng-ch'ae.

Emotion, and gendered subjectivity

Yŏng-ch'ae is the main character of the novel at first. Yi had started writing *Mujŏng* based on a manuscript he had written about a character named Yŏng-ch'ae.[286] "I began writing out of the impulse to depict the unforgettable and dear memories I had of my poor parents' lives, my siblings, and my own unfortunate childhood. The first part of *Mujŏng* depicting Yŏng-ch'ae's childhood consisted of none other than my own childhood memories, both the fond and the bitter."[287]

The narrative portrays Yŏng-ch'ae's thoughts and feelings through dialogue and first-person monologue, as well as third-person omniscient narrative. Almost all of chapters nine and ten of the novel consist of Yŏng-ch'ae speaking in the first-person voice, telling Hyŏng-sik and his landlady about her life over the past eight years. Narrative perspective often modulates into the first-person voice, moreover, when depicting Yŏng-ch'ae's thoughts. In chapter fifteen, for example, the perspective

---

286. Yi Kwang-su, "Tananhan Pansaeng ŭi Tojŏng," 452.
287. Ibid. Kim Yun-sik has suggested that the character Yŏng-ch'ae was based on Pak Ye-ok and Siltan, two actual women whom Yi knew. Ye-ok was the daughter of Pak Tae-ryŏng, the Tonghak leader for whom Yi worked. Ye-ok married, but her husband left her. Kim Yun-sik, *Yi Kwang-su wa kŭ ŭi sidae*, vol. 1 (Seoul: Han'gilsa, 1976), 89. Siltan was Yi's first love, the girl he met in 1907 in Chŏngju.

changes to the first-person voice when Yŏng-ch'ae contemplates telling Hyŏng-sik that she has become a *kisaeng*.[288]

> She had become a *kisaeng* not because she wanted to, but only in an effort to help her aged father and her brothers. Who would understand, though? Heaven and God knew, but what human being would understand? If I tell Hyŏng-sik what has happened, will he believe me? she thought. Might he not despise me, and think that I have become a *kisaeng* because I have been unchaste, and that I am trying to seduce him now that I am getting old and, no doubt, sick and tired of life as a *kisaeng*? I went to see my father in jail about two or three months after I became a *kisaeng*. My father lost his temper when he heard that I had become a *kisaeng*. "Foolish girl! You have ruined our glorious family reputation. Have you defiled your body already, a young girl fallen prey to someone's schemes?" He thought I had become a *kisaeng* through immoral conduct, and he ended up committing suicide. If my own father reacted that way, then how can Hyŏng-sik believe in me?[289]

In this passage, the first-person narrative is not set off in the Korean text with quotation marks, or quotative markers such as "she said" or "she thought." Yŏng-ch'ae narrates her own identity, moreover, in chapters nine and ten of the novel, when she tells her life story directly, in the first-person voice. The reader often sees Hyŏng-sik, moreover, from Yŏng-ch'ae's perspective. When Yŏng-ch'ae sees Hyŏng-sik for the first time in eight years, Yŏng-ch'ae observes that "his face looked a little longer than before, and he had a mustache, but his appearance overall was the same."[290]

Although the novel *The Heartless* was written from the third-person perspective, it occasionally used epistolary style narrative to present the first-person voice. Yŏng-ch'ae, for example, writes a letter to Hyŏng-sik to let him know that she has decided to die. As Hyŏng-sik reads the letter out loud to Sin U-sŏn and Yŏng-ch'ae's proprietress, the narrative becomes centered on Yŏng-ch'ae's first-person voice. Yŏng-ch'ae becomes just as important a character as Hyŏng-sik, the male protagonist whose thoughts are conveyed through third-person narrative, first-person monologues and dialogue. Yi later used epistolary style narrative in the story "Ŏrin Pŏt ege" (July 1917).

---

288. Chŏng Sun-jin comments on the use of first-person monologue in the short story "Kyŏng-hŭi" (1918) by woman writer Na Hye-sŏk. Chŏng Sun-jin, *Han'guk Munhak kwa Yŏsŏng Chuŭi Pip'yŏng* (Seoul: Kukhak Charyowŏn, 1993), 264.
289. *Mujŏng*, chapter 15, *Maeil Sinbo*, 21 January 1917.
290. *Mujŏng*, chapter 6, *Maeil Sinbo*, 10 January 1917.

Chŏng Kwi-ryŏn believes this story was influenced by Kunikida epistolary style work "Otozure."[291]

Yŏng-ch'ae tries to emulate the virtuous women of Confucian text. When her father and brothers are jailed unjustly, she remembers the stories of virgins who sold themselves to deliver their parents from difficulty, and decides to do the same for her father and brothers. "She thought that if she sold herself like the virtuous virgins of former times, her father and brothers would be freed with the money. They would praise her when they were freed from jail. Others would call her a filial daughter, and record her deed in books. She would be like the virtuous women of the past, and young girls who read about her would weep and praise her, just as she had done when she had read such stories."[292]

Yŏng-ch'ae befriends Wŏr-hwa, a *kisaeng* slightly older than Yŏng-ch'ae. Wŏr-hwa admires Tang dynasty poets, and regrets not having been born in China during that time. She dreams of meeting men like heroes from traditional Korean fiction. The men who patronize the establishment where she is a *kisaeng*, however, disgust her, convincing her of the ignorance and coarseness of the Korean people. She tells Yŏng-ch'ae that there is not a poet or man of culture to be found in the city of P'yŏngyang. Then one night she overhears the melancholy song of a poet singing from atop a cliff overlooking the Taedong River. Wŏr-hwa falls in love with the unknown singer, and later recognizes his voice when she hears him speak to an assembly held at P'aesŏng Hakkyo,[293] where he is principal. After hearing his speech, she feels that he possesses the visionary idealism she has long sought. Convinced of the futility of her love for him, Wŏr-hwa then commits suicide by drowning herself in the Taedong River.

There is a lesbian eroticism in the scene in which Yŏng-ch'ae and Wŏr-hwa sleep together, and Yŏng-ch'ae, in her sleep, kisses Wŏr-hwa.

> Yŏng-ch'ae had also begun to feel a longing for the male sex. Her face grew hot when she faced a strange man, and when she lay down alone at night, she wished that there was someone who would hold her. Once, when Yŏng-ch'ae and Wŏr-hwa came back from a party late at night, and had gone to bed together in the same bed, Yŏng-ch'ae put her arms around Wŏr-hwa in her sleep, and kissed her on the mouth. Wŏr-hwa laughed to herself. "So you have awakened as well," she thought. "Sadness and suffering lie ahead of you." She woke Yŏng-ch'ae.

291. Chŏng Kwi-ryŏn, 169.
292. *Mujŏng*, chapter 15, *Maeil Sinbo*, 21 January 1917.
293. The name P'aesŏng alludes to the Taesŏng School, founded by Tosan An Ch'ang-ho. The principal of P'aesŏng School in *Mujŏng* resembles Tosan, and a character in the novel *Hi no Hashira*, by Kinoshita Naoe.

"Yŏng-ch'ae, you just put your arms around me and kissed me on the mouth." Yŏng-ch'ae buried her face in Wŏr-hwa's breasts, as she though were ashamed, and bit her white breasts. "I did it because it was you," she said.[294]

Wŏr-hwa thinks to herself that Yŏng-ch'ae has begun to think about sex. Yŏng-ch'ae becomes embarrassed, and says that it wasn't that she was thinking of men, but that she kissed Wŏr-hwa because "it was you." Yŏng-ch'ae seems to be ashamed of her sexual desire for men. There is a complete acceptance of same-sex eroticism.

The story of Wŏr-hwa and the school teacher resembles a similar subplot in the Japanese novel *Hi no hashira* (Pillar of Fire, 1904) by Kinoshita Naoe. Yi read the work in middle school, and liked its idealism.[295] In *Pillar of Fire*, the geisha Hanakichi admires Shinoda Chōji, a Christian Socialist. Shinoda advocates the abolition of prostitution. His sympathy and encouragement help Hanakichi regain her self-respect, and dispel the hatred in her heart towards men. Yŏng-ch'ae attempts suicide later, under Wŏr-hwa's influence, but is prevented by the young woman student Pyŏng-uk, who convinces her that the moral ideals for which she wishes to sacrifice herself are only a part of her life and not its entirety.

As Kim Mi-hyun[296] has noted, Korean literature of the colonial period depicted woman's body as a site where oppressive power has its effects, and as a point where resistance originates.[297] Yŏng-ch'ae is eventually raped by Kim Hyŏn-su and Pae Myŏng-sik, who believe that *kisaeng* are less human than other women, and that it is "all right to rape a *kisaeng* who does not do as she is told." They consider it "wrong for a woman from a respectable family to have illicit relations with a man, but a *kisaeng* was by definition an object available for any man to amuse himself with. Only women of good background could be chaste, not *kisaeng*."[298] Hyŏng-sik's friend, the journalist Sin Wu-sŏn, has the same double standard in his treatment of Yŏng-ch'ae, whom he tries to seduce at first because she is "only a *kisaeng*," but whom he later praises as a virtuous woman once he realizes that she is the daughter of Hyŏng-sik's former teacher.

---

294. *Mujŏng*, chapter 32, *Maeil Sinbo*, 10 February 1917.

295. "Kim Kyŏng," *Ch'ŏngch'un* (1915), reprinted in *Yi Kwang-su Chŏnjip*, ed. Noh Yang-hwan, vol. 1 (Seoul: Usinsa, 1978), 569. Yi Sŏn-yŏng examines the influence of Kinoshita Naoe on Yi Kwang-su, in "Ch'unwŏn ŭi Pigyo Munhakjŏk Koch'al," in Kim Hyŏn, ed., *Yi Kwang-su* (Seoul: Munhak kwa Chisŏngsa, 1977), 121–57.

296. Kim Mi-Hyun spells her name this way. The McCune-Reischauer romanization for her name is Kim Mi-hyŏn.

297. Kim invokes Michel Foucault's theory of the body. Kim Mi-hyun, "'Sai' e chip chitko salgi: Paek Sin-ae ron," in *P'eminijŭm kwa sosŏl pip'yŏng* (Seoul: Han'gilsa, 1995), 223.

298. Yi Kwang-su, "Mujŏng," chapter 40, *Maeil Sinbo* 21 February 1917.

Pyŏng-uk teaches Yŏng-ch'ae to be more like a "new woman."[299] Playing the violin, studying in Tokyo and pursuing free love, Pyŏng-uk exemplifies the "new woman." Yŏng-ch'ae eventually goes to Tokyo with Pyŏng-uk, to study music.

Hyŏng-sik identifies with the female characters Yŏng-ch'ae and Sun-ae. When Yŏng-ch'ae tells Hyŏng-sik that she had almost been sexually assaulted when she was ten (Western age, nine), Hyŏng-sik thinks of how he too had barely escaped sexual assault when he was eleven (Western age, ten). When he looks at Sŏn-hyŏng's friend Sun-ae, who has lost her parents, moreover, he sees the same look of having suffered from an early age that he sees in himself.

Hyŏng-sik has never been in a sexual relationship with a woman, and either idealizes them, or thinks of them as prostitutes. He has unrealistic perceptions of Yŏng-ch'ae, whom he sees as a virtuous Confucian woman one moment, and a prostitute the next. He has remained unmarried in deference to Yŏng-ch'ae's father's wish that Hyŏng-sik marry Yŏng-ch'ae. Yŏng-ch'ae's father, Scholar Pak, had been a friend of Hyŏng-sik's father, and had taken care of Hyŏng-sik after Hyŏng-sik lost his parents. Hyŏng-sik feels obligated to marry Yŏng-ch'ae because he feels indebted to Scholar Pak.[300] When Hyŏng-sik meets Yŏng-ch'ae in Seoul, he is preoccupied with whether or not she is a virgin. He remembers her from the past with affection but regards her present appearance with misgivings because she seems to have become a *kisaeng*, though he is not certain. Woman embodies abjection, which includes the maternal, death, transgression—all that the rational male subject rejects in order to define himself. The male subject of modernity depends on othering woman as abjection.[301]

Yŏng-ch'ae and Wŏr-hwa embody "spillages" and fluidity; Wŏr-hwa drowns herself in the Taedong River, and Yŏng-ch'ae tries to do the same. Hyŏng-sik has nightmarish visions in which he sees Yŏng-ch'ae as she

---

299. Yung-hee Kim has written about the depiction of feminist sisterhood in *Mujŏng*. "Re-visioning Gender and Womanhood in Colonial Korea: Yi Kwang-su's *Mujŏng* (The Heartless)." *The Review of Korean Studies* 6, no. 1 (2003): 187–219. For an article about feminist issues during the Japanese colonial occupation of Korea, cf. Yung-hee Kim, "Women's Issues in 1920s Korea," *Korean Culture* 15, no. 2 (Summer 1994): 26–33. Kyeong-Hee Choi has written about the "new woman" (*sin yŏsŏng*) and Pak Wan-sŏ's writing. Choi Kyeong-Hee, "Neither Colonial nor National: The Making of the 'New Woman' in Pak Wansŏ's 'Mother's Stake 1,'" in ed. Gi-Wook Shin and Michael Robinson, *Colonial Modernity in Korea* (Cambridge and London: Harvard University Asia Center, 1999), 221–247. Jina Kim is writing about how early modern Korean woman writers Na Hye-sŏk and Kang Kyŏng-ae depicted the modern girl. Jina is a graduate student at the University of Washington.

300. The late Professor Bill McCullough commented that the conflict between duty and emotion in *Mujŏng* is similar to that between *giri* and *ninjō* in Japanese literature. Graduate colloquium, Asian Languages Department, University of California, Berkeley, November 1988.

301. Nina Cornyetz, *Dangerous Women, Deadly Words: Phallic Fantasy and Modernity in Three Japanese Writers* (Stanford: Stanford University Press, 1999), 40.

looked the night he found her at Ch'ŏngnyangni after she had been raped. He sees Yŏng-ch'ae spraying him with blood from her mouth, her clothes torn and stained with blood. In terms of the "romantic triangle," the process of elimination of Yŏng-ch'ae in favor of Sŏn-hyŏng indicates what the author tries to "rebel against or suppress."[302] The male subject feels threatened by woman's "bodily seepage" into "uncanny topographies (*ikai*) reminiscent of either a premodern past or an amorphous, primordial . . . supernatural" world.[303] Hyŏng-sik objectifies Yŏng-ch'ae as abjection, and at the same time identifies with her; abjection threatens the boundedness of the male subject.

Modernity and language

The ideological construct of literature as expressive of interiority required that language be equivalent with speech.[304] Dialogue in the novel *The Heartless* shows changing social practices of language.[305] Hyŏng-sik is uncertain as to how he should speak towards Sŏn-hyŏng. He is not sure whether he should speak to her as if to a man, using formal sentential endings and a humble pronoun to refer to himself, or whether his speech ought to indicate distinctions in their status of teacher and pupil.

Hyŏng-sik addresses Yŏng-ch'ae with the respectful term *ssi* (Miss, Mr.), even though most men at the time did not show respect towards women, let alone towards a *kisaeng*. Language indicated attitudes towards gender. Hyŏng-sik's choice of language expresses his belief that social reform ought to include language practices. Us-ŏn, in contrast, does not speak respectfully towards Yŏng-ch'ae until he learns from Hyŏng-sik that she is the daughter of Hyŏng-sik's former mentor, and is from a good family. Until then, U-sŏn had spoken informally towards her because he thought *kisaeng* do not deserve respectful speech. His attitude indicates the discrimination between women of different classes that was used to perpetuate social divisions in Chosŏn dynasty society and reinforce the privileges of the *yangban* aristocracy.[306]

302. Kyoko Kurita, "The Romantic Triangle in Meiji Literature," in *New Directions in the Study of Meiji Japan*, ed. Helen Hardacre with Adam L. Kern (Leiden, New York, Köln: Brill, 1997), 230.
303. Nina Cornyetz, 14. Cf. Christine L. Marran, "The Allure of the Poison-Woman in Modern Japanese Literature," (Ph.D. diss., University of Washington, 1998).
304. Karatani Kōjin, 39.
305. Kim Kichung has written about Yi In-jik's novel *Hyŏl ŭi Nu*, early modern Korean language, and gender, in *The Rise of the Modern Korean Novel* (unpublished manuscript). As Kim observes, the characters Ok-nyŏ and Ku Wan-sŏ negotiate what honorific levels of speech to use towards one another.
306. Martina Deuchler, *The Confucian Transformation of Korea: A Study of Society and Ideology* (Cambridge: Council on East Asian Studies, Harvard University, 1992), 231–281.

The *kisaeng* Kye-hyang is unsure of how to speak with Hyŏng-sik. Her proprietress uses the traditional honorific terms *nari*, *chusa* (similar to *nari*), and *haksa* (scholar) to address men. Hyŏng-sik is a friend of Yŏng-ch'ae's, and not a patron. How could a *kisaeng* address a man she had met as an acquaintance, and not a patron? She has never known any men other than the men who visit the *kisaeng* house as patrons. She is also uncertain about how to address him because she doesn't know his occupation. Kye-hyang decides to use the preposition *yŏgi* (here) to mean "you" when speaking to Hyŏng-sik, using his location as a metonymic form of address. In the relationship between Kye-hyang and Hyŏng-sik, the narrative portrays modern love as including both sexual and spiritual emotion. New ideologies of gender rewrite social practices of language.

The novel was written, moreover, in a modern vernacular style. Whereas earlier fiction such as the *sinsosŏl* had been written in a traditional vernacular style, or literary styles that used classical Chinese vocabulary, *The Heartless* was written in modern vernacular Korean.[307]

Irony and character development in The Heartless

Song Ha-ch'un has noted the disappearance of the heroic subject in the novel *The Heartless*.[308] The subjectivities of the main characters are no longer completely those of Neo-Confucian heroes and heroines. The text resists its own didacticism with an irony that distances the reader from the characters' pretensions.

Irony may be a disparity between the apparent, propositional content of a statement, and an unexpected, different meaning which arises from the statement within a particular context. It may be a dislocation of perception arising between the postures and perceptions of characters, and how those characters' actions and thoughts are interpreted by others, whether by other characters, the author and/or the reader. Earlier Korean fiction depicted "evil" adversaries of main characters with irony. *The Heartless*, however, depicts main characters with irony.

Narrative irony reveals Hyŏng-sik's hypocrisies, conceits and doubts. Hyŏng-sik has bouts of self-recrimination and introspection that are followed by hypocrisy evident only to the reader and not to Hyŏng-sik himself. His sexual anxiety becomes the subject of irony in the monologic passage in

307. Kim U-jong describes Yi as arguably having been the first to write literature in contemporary Korean vernacular. Kim U-jong, "Minjok Munhak kwa Hwejŏl: Yi Kwang-su Ron"; reprint, Tongguk Taehakkyo Pusŏl Han'guk Munhak Yŏn'guso, ed., *Yi Kwang-su Yŏn'gu*, vol. 1 (Seoul: T'aehaksa, 1984), 488–513. Originally in *Singminji Sidae ŭi Munhak Yŏn'gu* (Seoul: Kip'ŭn Saem, 1980), 511.
308. Song Ha-ch'un, "'Mujŏng' ŭi Hyŏndae Sosŏljŏk Ŭiŭi," *Inmun Nonjip* no. 28, (December 1983): 3. For a discussion of the superfluous hero in Meiji literature, cf. Marleigh Grayer Ryan, *Japan's First Modern Novel: Ukigumo* (New York: Columbia University Press, 1967).

which Hyŏng-sik worries about bad breath and how to behave with his pupil, Sŏn-hyŏng.

> Shall I place a desk between us and sit face-to-face with her as I teach? Then our breaths would meet. Her upswept hair would occasionally brush against my forehead. Our knees would touch ever so lightly beneath the desk. Hyŏng-sik blushed and smiled at the thought. No, no, he thought. What if I should sin, if only in my thoughts? I know what I will do!—I will sit as far as possible from the desk, and if her knees touch mine, I will move away with a start. It would be rude to a woman for me to have bad breath, though. I have not yet had a cigarette since lunch, but just in case, he thought, and breathed against the palm of his hand.[309] He could test for bad odors by smelling his breath as it reflected against his hand and into his nose.[310]

The monologue reveals the incongruity between Hyŏng-sik's thoughts and his pretensions of decorum. Modern irony disregards the former sanctity of the hero or heroine.

Ironic perspective reduces Hyŏng-sik's moments of spiritual insight to the level of the pseudo-epiphany. For example, the implicit sentiments of the text differ from the thoughts that Hyŏng-sik has when he meets the *kisaeng* Kye-hyang. There is an ironic distance between Hyŏng-sik's confidence in his feelings, and the reader's awareness; the text reveals his selfishness as he forgets about Yŏng-ch'ae completely when he is with Kye-hyang.

> "Please do whatever you can to find Yŏng-ch'ae," she said. Hyŏng-sik, however, only regretted that he was leaving Kye-hyang. He did not think about Yŏng-ch'ae much at all. "I have awakened from a dream," he thought on the train, and smiled several times.[311]

---

309. His cigarette habit indicates the degree to which the modern tobacco industry had infiltrated the market in Asia; the earliest films shown in Korea were used as a marketing tool to sell Western cigarettes. An Englishman who screened a film in a warehouse in Korea in 1898 offered free admission to anyone who brought ten empty cigarette boxes. Yi Hyoin, *Han'guk Yŏnghwasa* (A History of Korean Film), 16–17. I would like to thank Michael Shin for referring me to this book. United States and English tobacco companies used the Yoshizawa touring movie company to sell and advertise their products in 1904. No Man, "Han'guk Yŏnghwa ŭi Chogamdo" (A Bird's Eye View of Korean Film), *Sasanggye* (World of Thought) May 1962. Cited in Yang Yunmo, "Han'guk Yŏnghwasa Yŏn'gu Sŏsŏl" (Preface to a Study of the History of Korean Film), *Ch'angjo* (Creation) (Sŏul Yesul Chŏnmun Taehak Yŏnghwakkwa, 1985), 32. Cited in Yi Hyoin, *Han'guk Yŏnghwasa*, 18.
310. *Mujŏng*, chapter 1, *Maeil Sinbo*, 1 January 1917.
311. *Mujŏng*, chapter 64, *Maeil Sinbo*, 24 March 1917.

Hyŏng-sik's thoughts about himself and Kye-hyang are subverted by the reader's awareness of his abandonment of Yŏng-ch'ae. Moreover, his recollections of his sorrow over Yŏng-ch'ae appear self-serving.

> He imagined her corpse floating down the Taedong River. He did not feel sad, though, but felt a boundless happiness when he looked at Kye-hyang standing beside him.
> This surprised him. "Have I changed that much?" he wondered.[312]

He cannot restrain his happiness the next day when he returns to Seoul and receives a marriage offer from Sŏn-hyŏng's family. The narrative observes with irony that "it occurred to him that Yŏng-ch'ae had died at an opportune moment for him."[313] The narrative contrasts, moreover, Yŏng-ch'ae's suffering, and Hyŏng-sik's unawareness of her pain. The day after she has been raped, Yŏng-ch'ae sits in her room contemplating suicide, even as Hyŏng-sik tutors Sŏn-hyŏng in English, oblivious of Yŏng-ch'ae's sorrow.

Yi's contemporary, writer Kim Tong-in, thought *Mujŏng* significant as a work that realistically documented conditions in early modern Korean and brought the author, Yi Kwang-su, popular recognition; however, Kim complained about the character, Yi Hyŏng-sik. Kim thought Hyŏng-sik, like most of Yi Kwang-su's male main characters, was pretentious, had delusions of grandeur, thought himself a tragic hero or a leader, was emotionally irresolute, given to daydreaming and idle speculation, and masochistic. Kim criticized in particular the chapters about Hyŏng-sik and Kye-hyang, and Hyŏng-sik's abandonment of Yŏng-ch'ae. Kim thought these chapters were unnecessary to the novel, and interpreted Hyŏng-sik's behavior as out of character.

> Why doesn't Hyŏng-sik look for Yŏng-ch'ae's body, if not determine her whereabouts? In order to cover up Hyŏng-sik's peculiar and contradictory behavior, the author talks about the sweat on the back of the *kisaeng* Kye-hyang's blouse.
> He should have . . . gone to the police station three or four times, and paced the banks of the Taedong River.[314]

Kim does not quite understand the deliberate irony of the narrative. Hyŏng-sik thinks he has attained increased awareness of his emotions, but he remains unaware of his cruelty to Yŏng-ch'ae. Irony deliberately distances the reader from Hyŏng-sik. Moreover, Hyŏng-sik behaves in contradictory

312. Ibid.
313. *Mujŏng*, chapter 76, *Maeil Sinbo*, 11 April 1917.
314. Kim Tong-in, "Ch'unwŏn Yŏn'gu," in *Kim Tong-in Munhak Chŏnjip*, vol. 12 (Seoul: Taejung Sŏgwan, 1983), 430, 372.

ways, but this inconsistency is within the range of his personality. Such inner contradiction, or "consistent inconsistency" makes Hyŏng-sik a character that we can recognize as "belonging to the contradictory human race."[315]

Yŏng-ch'ae is eventually raped because Hyŏng-sik lacks the money to redeem her from the *kisaeng* house. He does not have such money because he has spent his money helping indigent students and buying books which he wants to read in order to better educate Korean youths for the future. The wealthy Kim Hyŏn-su, in contrast, possesses the financial means with which to purchase Yŏng-ch'ae as concubine and possess her physically. Irony results from the juxtaposition of the poverty of a teacher who spends his money in order to serve his nation, and the wealth of the Japanese collaborator. The narrative depicts the cruelty of the exploitation and objectification of women through concubinage and prostitution.

Narrative tone modulates occasionally between oblique irony and direct commentary. When Hyŏng-sik declares that he plans to major in biology, the narrative observes that "none of those present, however, knew what biology was. Hyŏng-sik, of course, did not really know what biology was either."[316]

Dean Pae Myŏng-sik is caricatured with comic irony. When Hyŏng-sik asks him whether his educational philosophy is influenced by Pestalozzi or Ellen Key,[317] Pae says, "I have read the theories of P'usŭt'ŏl and Ŏllŭnk'ŏ. But those are all *passé.*" A geography and history major, Pae decides to alter the curriculum to suit his tastes.

> He doubled the number of hours spent on geography and history, saying that it was in these subjects that all of the various disciplines converged. He reduced the hours for math and natural history by twenty or thirty per cent, saying that these subjects were not that necessary for a middle school education.[318]

Pae is known among his students as "tigress," "fox" and "dog," referring to his "fierce ruthlessness," his scheming and deceitfulness, and finally, the way he "would prostrate himself on the ground before someone who was one level his superior, like a dog that wags its tail and licks the heels of the master who has fed it for some time."[319] The students' nicknames for the dean bring to mind the nicknames given by Natsume Sōseki's Botchan to the faculty of the provincial elementary school where he teaches, i.e. art teacher Red Shirt, drawing instructor Clown, head math teacher Porcupine, principal Badger,

---

315. Janet Burroway, *Writing Fiction* (New York: Longman, 2003), 124.
316. *Mujŏng*, chapter 125, *Maeil Sinbo*, 13 June 1917.
317. Theresa Hyun discusses the translation of Ellen Key's work into Japanese and Korean. Theresa Hyun, *Writing Women in Korea* (Honolulu: University of Hawaii Press, 2004), 53–4.
318. *Mujŏng*, chapter 20, *Maeil Sinbo*, 27 January 1917.
319. *Mujŏng*, chapter 21, *Maeil Sinbo*, 28 January 1917.

and English teacher Green Pumpkin.[320] Pae's infatuation with the *kisaeng* Wŏr-hyang and his attempts to secure her as his mistress, though he realizes she is devoted to Hyŏng-sik, correspond to Red Shirt's dalliance with geisha at the hot springs, and his schemes to win another man's fiancée for himself. Comic irony is used, moreover, in the passage in which Pae lectures to a diminishing audience of teachers. After his appointment to the post of dean, Pae formulates two hundred new rules which he forces the faculty to accept.

> One day he assembled all of the instructors at a staff meeting, and read each of the articles of the new regulations out loud himself, and explained the spirit behind each of the regulations. The meeting began at one o'clock. At four o'clock, it still was not over. Pae's forehead and nose were all sweaty, and his voice was hoarse. The staff squirmed in their seats, with sore buttocks and aching backs. Some lowered their heads and snored, only to be awakened from their deep sleep by Dean Pae's loud exclamations. The door slammed shut abruptly as one instructor left to go to the out-house; the instructor did not return to the meeting.[321]

Pae is depicted with comic irony. The incongruity between his self-importance and righteousness, and the reader's perception of his postures renders him the subject of ironic laughter. It becomes apparent that he cares little for the students or for education, but revels in his own esteem of himself.

Modernity and Korean culture: marriage

In the novel *The Heartless*, Yi wrote about emerging and changing practices of modernity. The narrative examines characters' perceptions of modernity, and portrays characters creating their own narratives of sexuality, social relations, and self realization.

Sŏn-hyŏng's engagement to Hyŏng-sik is a hybrid of traditional and modern marriage. The marriage has been arranged by her parents, and is not something she herself has determined. She gives her consent when asked, but it is still an arranged marriage. When Sŏn-hyŏng, Hyŏng-sik, Elder Kim, Mrs. Kim and the pastor meet to discuss the engagement, no one seems to know how to proceed. The characters seem to be creating new practices for marriage, drawing on their own interpretations of modernity.

The character Pyŏng-uk tells Yŏng-ch'ae that she does not have to feel obligated to marry Hyŏng-sik just because she thinks her father had approved of Hyŏng-sik or just because traditional morality requires her to be chaste and devoted to a man whom she once thought of marrying. As Kim Sang-t'ae

---

320. Natsume Sōseki, *Botchan*, transl. Alan Turney (London: P. Owen, 1973).
321. *Mujŏng*, chapter 20, *Maeil Sinbo*, 27 January 1917.

has observed, the "new morality" breaks with Confucianism; women do not have to obey men, and "free love is predicated on equality between man and woman."[322] Moreover, the idea of subjectivity in marriage was part of Yi's view of the importance of subjectivity in national reconstruction. Influenced by the Buddhist concept of karma, in which one's actions are the cause of karmic effect,[323] Yi criticized beliefs in fate and destiny, which he perceived as part of Neo-Confucian beliefs expounded in the *Zhou I* (Book of Changes) and its subsequent interpretations.[324] "We must apply our creativity, and try to create new conditions for happiness," he would write in 1918.[325]

Education

Like the character Mun-gil in the story "Ai ka," Hyŏng-sik has always felt different from other boys because his parents died when he was just a boy, and he has had to mature more quickly than most children.

> Hyŏng-sik, however, had suffered through difficulties in life since an early age, and he had lost the lovely, boyish looks of childhood; instead, there was a mature, adult aspect to his face and mind. Thus boys his own age would not befriend him, no matter how Hyŏng-sik tried to be close to them. There was also a big difference between Hyŏng-sik and the other boys in the extent of their learning, and because of this, the other boys respected Hyŏng-sik as their senior, but they would not walk shoulder to shoulder with him or hold his hand and try to be his friend.[326]

Hyŏng-sik has what Kim Yun-sik has described as an orphan complex, or *koa ŭisik* (orphan consciousness).[327] Hyŏng-sik's orphan complex becomes emotionally indistinguishable, moreover, from his "modernizer complex." He feels different because he lost his parents at an early age, and because he has studied modernity to a greater extent than most other youths his age. His

322. Kim Sang-t'ae, "Challenge to Confucian Values," *Tamkang Review* 18, nos. 1, 2, 3, 4: 346. Yi may have been influenced by Swedish feminist Ellen Key's theories of motherhood and marriage. Key's work had been introduced into Japan by the 1910s. Cf. Theresa Hyun, *Writing Women in Korea* (Honolulu: University of Hawaii Press, 2004), 53–4.
323. Kim Yŏng-dŏk has observed that Yi took a class in Buddhism while enrolled in the philosophy department at Waseda University in 1915. As Kim notes, Yi refers to this class in the novel *Kŭ ŭi Chasŏjŏn*. Although the latter was a work of fiction, narrated in the first-person perspective, parts of the novel correspond to Yi's own life and are considered autobiographical. Kim Yŏng-dŏk, "Ch'unwŏn ŭi Insaeng Ch'ŏrhakkwan Ko: Ki, Pulgyo Sasang ŭl Chungsim ŭro," *Han'guk Munhwa Yŏn'guso Nonch'ŏng* 26 (1975): 12.
324. Kim Yŏng-dŏk, 5.
325. "Sungmyŏngnonjŏk Insaenggwan esŏ Charyŏkchŏk Insaenggwan e," *Hak Chi Kwang* no. 17 (August 1918); reprint, *Yi Kwang-su Chŏnjip*, vol. 10 (1971), 47–49.
326. *Mujŏng*, chapter 67, *Maeil Sinbo*, 27 March 1917.
327. Kim Yun-sik, *Yi Kwang-su wa Kŭ ŭi Sidae*, vol. 1: 38, 217, 221, 222, 225.

self-image of modernizer is emotionally similar to his self-image as an orphan. As Kim Yun-sik has observed, Hyŏng-sik's identity as modernizer is a defense mechanism to compensate for the lack of self-esteem he feels as a result of having lost his parents and having been rejected by his peers.

Hyŏng-sik believes that education is necessary to change the Korean people into a "new Korean people," and to make a "new Korea" transformed by "modern civilization." His own education is a combination of traditional Chinese education, Japanese education and Korean practices of modern education.

His teacher and mentor, Scholar Pak, belonged to a generation that was educated in classical Chinese. Pak thus sought access to modernity through texts written in Chinese. Pak studied Western and Japanese culture through books published in Shanghai. He travelled to China and purchased several dozens of books published in Shanghai. He realized that "Korea could not go on as it was, and he began a movement to teach about modern civilization."[328]

Hyŏng-sik later studies in Tokyo. He thinks that the Japanese are among the most civilized peoples in the world. Koreans, he thinks, need to reach a level of civilization like that of the Japanese. He advocates national self-strengthening through "modernization."[329] Hyŏng-sik buys books at "Japan-Korea" bookstore and Tokyo Maruzen.[330] The books he buys there include books written in English and German, apparently imported by Japanese bookstores. Hyŏng-sik wishes to teach his students what he learns. Hyŏng-sik's emphasis on transforming Korea represents an ideology of nationalist reform.

There is an elitist emphasis, however, on the subjectivity of educated youth. Korean peasants are seen as lacking subjectivity. Towards the end of *Mujŏng*, the characters Hyŏng-sik, Sŏn-hyŏng, Yŏng-ch'ae and Pyŏng-uk watch as peasants are caught in heavy rains that deluge the countryside. The educated youths decide to have a fundraiser to help the flood victims, and resolve to return to Korea after their studies overseas, and teach Koreans. The educated youths see the peasants as part of a landscape of inundation. Bodies of water transgress boundaries. This abjection threatens "modern" subjectivity. The peasants themselves lack interiority; they are phallus, or lack, an empty sign.[331] Because the colonial origins of landscape have been suppressed, the narrative cannot question the contradictions of writing about nation from the perspective of colonial interiority.

328. *Mujŏng*, chapter 5, *Maeil Sinbo*, 9 January 1917.
329. Shin Yong-ha argues that "modernization" without civil rights is not really modernization. Shin Yong-ha, Fourth Pacific and Asia Conference on Korean Studies: "Korea Between Tradition and Modernity," University of British Columbia, Vancouver, May 11, 1998.
330. *Mujŏng*, chapter 24, *Maeil Sinbo*, 1 February 1917.
331. Nina Cornyetz, 5.

Korean practices of modernity and Christianity

The novel *The Heartless* depicts the character Elder Kim as a wealthy, upper-class Korean practitioner of Christianity and modernity. Yi ascribed to Christianity the introduction of modern civilization (*sin munmyŏng*), but criticized Christianity, nevertheless, for reinforcing elitism and social hierarchies, and criticized certain aspects of the church. Yi's views of Christianity as practiced by Koreans are evident in the character of Elder Kim. The narrative ironically portrays Elder Kim's hypocrisy and the shallowness of his Christian faith and knowledge of Western civilization. Elder Kim "was a disciple of Christ, who instructed his followers not to own as much as two sets of garments.[332] Nevertheless, once Kim had been enlightened in the ways of modern civilization, he too purchased land, saved money in the bank, bought stocks and a spacious house, and kept dozens of servants."[333]

The narrative criticizes the superficiality of Elder Kim's understanding of Western culture. Elder Kim "believes" that Koreans had to follow Western examples simply because the West is superior. The narrative emphasizes that this is a "belief," and not a carefully thought out view. Elder Kim sends his daughter to school, for example, not because he understands feminist thought but only because Westerners send their daughters to school. The Elder himself has no particular consciousness of feminism or oppressions of gender, class and nation.

Yi Kwang-su thought that Christianity had indeed improved women's status in Korea.[334] Eastern ethics, Yi said, were guilty of the crime of male chauvinism. Korean women had no right to an education, and could not assert their individuality or lead an independent life. A strength of Christianity was that women could attend church along with men. In the register of church members, both women and men were qualified to count as individuals (*il kaein*). Yi noted that women were eligible to be church workers, though they could not be pastor or elder. The church, moreover, established the first girls' school in Korea. Yi noted that the church recognized remarriage for women. Neo-Confucianism had not allowed this. Christianity thus gave women an important freedom. Christianity contributed to the abolition of the traditional custom of marriage at an early age.

Christianity helped Koreans become aware of individualism and of individual consciousness, Yi thought. He said that Neo-Confucianism obliterated individualism because it emphasized the formulation of ritual by

---

332. "These twelve Jesus sent out, charging them, 'Take no bag for your journey, nor two tunics, nor sandals, nor a staff; for the laborer deserves his food.'" Matthew 10:10.
333. *Mujŏng*, chapter 2, ed. Ch'oe Nam-sŏn (Seoul: Sinmungwan, 1918), 7.
334. Yi Kwang-su, "Yasogyo ŭi Chosŏn e Chun Ŭnhye," in *Ch'ŏngch'un* 9 (July 1917); reprint, *Yi Kwangsu Chŏnjip*, ed. Noh Yang-hwan, vol. 10 (Seoul: Samjungdang, 1971), 17.

"sages." In Christianity, however, each person had an individual soul, and sought the Lord directly through prayer. Yi thought, moreover, that the concept of the individual in modern ethics and political thought was centered on a concept of the "people" as derived from Christianity. Christianity taught people to love and respect one another, and that all were equal. Belief in the equality of all people derived from this belief in the individual soul. Yi used he word *hyŏndae* (modern) to describe ethics based on Christian belief in the individual soul, love and respect for all people, and the equality of all people.

Yi criticized certain aspects of Christian practice in Korea, though.[335] Yi thought that one flaw of the church was that it was hierarchical. Asian society—Korean society in particular—was hierarchical, and Christianity seemed to have been unable to change this. Sŏn-hyŏng is portrayed as a member of a church elite. Her father is elected Elder, and is wealthy and powerful.

Yi also criticized the Korean church for insisting on its own preeminence and authority. "True" Christians considered scholarship to be "secular knowledge," and they thought such knowledge weakened faith. Yi thought that church officials opposed "secular knowledge" because they did not understand science or modern civilization. Elder Kim, for example, thinks he understands Western civilization, but has never studied "science, philosophy, religion, art, politics, economics, industry or social systems. Even the most talented, diligent and perceptive of people would only begin to understand a different civilization after decades of reading, and learning from a teacher. How could Elder Kim, no matter how bright he was, understand the true meaning of modern civilization in all its complexity, without having read a single book on the subject?"[336]

Yi's writing was often quite didactic and political. "I cannot help grimacing now . . . when I think of how the author stepped forth from time to time in the novel [*Mujŏng*], and engaged in crude theorizing," Yi once wrote. "I thought I was doing it out of a duty to 'enlighten.'"[337]

Yi depicted the oppressive effects of aspects of patriarchal culture on human feelings,[338] and perceived of subjectivity as part of an ideology of nationalist reform. Images of woman and the same-sex lover as abjection, however, reveal the constructed nature of the male subject and what dominant ideology rejected in order to define subjectivity.[339] Yi's writing

335. Yi Kwang-su, "Kŭmil Chosŏn Yaso Kyohoe ŭi Kyŏlchŏm," *Ch'ŏngch'un* 11 (October 1917); reprint, *Yi Kwang-su Chŏnjip*, ed. Noh Yang-hwan, vol. 10 (Seoul: Samjungdang, 1971), 20–24.

336. *Mujŏng*, chapter 79, *Maeil Sinbo*, 14 April 1917.

337. Yi Kwang-su, "Tananhan Pansaeng ŭi Tojŏng," 452.

338. Cf. Kim Mi-hyun, "'Sai' e Chip Chitko Salgi: Paek Sin-ae Ron," in *P'eminijŭm kwa sosŏl pip'yŏng* (Seoul: Han'gilsa, 1995), 223.

339. Nina Cornyetz, *Dangerous Women, Deadly Words: Phallic Fantasy and Modernity in Three Japanese Writers*, 14.

reveals an unresolved tension between the appropriation of dominant colonial narratives of subjectivity, and the effort to write from the perspectives of those whose voices had been suppressed[340] and characterized as abject.

---

340. For research on marginalized subjectivities in Chosŏn dynasty society, cf. Sun Joo Kim, "Marginalized Elite, Regional Discrimination, and the Tradition of Prophetic Belief in the Hong Kyŏngnae Rebellion," (Ph.D. diss., University of Washington, 2000).

Left to right: Chin-gŭn; Yi Kwang-su; Pong-gŭn, holding Chin-gŭn's hand; Hŏ Yŏng-suk, holding Yung-keun, 1929. The family lived in Sungsam-dong, Seoul at the time.

Left to right: Hŏ Yŏng-suk, Chung Wha, Chung-nan, Yung-keun, and Yi Kwang-su. This picture was taken at home in Hyoja-dong, Seoul, around 1941–1942.

The Heartless

Note on Translation

My translation of the novel *Mujŏng* is based on the *Maeil Sinbo* text, which was published January 1 to June 14, 1917.[1] The novel was published in installments which were called *hoe* (for example, *cheil hoe*, "the first installment"). I have also referred to a 1985 facsimile reprint (*yŏnginbon*) of an edition published by Ch'oe Nam-sŏn's publishing company Sinmungwan in July 20, 1918.[2] I have noted textual variants in footnotes. I have followed the punctuation and paragraph format of the original *Maeil Sinbo* text; for example, interior monologue is often not punctuated with quotation marks.

1. Yi Kwang-su, *Mujŏng*, *Maeil Sinbo* (1 January–14 June 1917), facsimile reprint (Seoul: Kyŏngin Munhwasa, 1984).
2. Yi Kwang-su, *Mujŏng* (Seoul: Sinmungwan, 1918); facsimile reprint, *Han'guk Hyŏndae Sosŏl Ch'ongsŏ*, vol. 1 (Seoul: T'aeyŏngsa, 1985). Some scholars think that the Sinmungwan edition appears to have been edited by Yi Kwang-su, since meaningful revisions were made such as editing out sentences, and adding new sentences. Cf. Kim Ch'ŏl, Yi Kyŏng-hun, Sŏ Ŭn-ju and Im Chin-yŏng, "*Mujŏng* ŭi Kyebo: *Mujŏng* ŭi Chŏngbon Hwakchŏng ŭl Wihan P'anbon ŭi Pigyo Yŏn'gu," *Minjok Munhaksa Yŏn'gu* 20 (2002): 62–90. Kim Ch'ŏl et al. discuss nine extant editions of *Mujŏng*.

English instructor Yi Hyŏng-sik finished teaching his two o'clock fourth-year English class at the Kyŏngsŏng School, and set out for the home of Elder Kim in the Andong District of Seoul. He was sweating in the June sunshine as he walked. The Elder had hired him as a private tutor to teach English for an hour every day to his daughter Sŏn-hyŏng, who would be going to study in the United States the following year. They would begin their lessons that day at three o'clock. Hyŏng-sik was still single and had never socialized with women other than his female relatives. Like many an inexperienced, chaste young man, he was shy in front of young women, and blushed and hung his head bashfully. Such behavior could be considered foolish in a man, but better such a man than those sophisticated fellows who will find any excuse to approach a woman and have a word with her. He was now preoccupied with several thoughts. How should he greet her when they first met? Should he speak to her as if to a man? "Pleased to meet you. My name is Yi Hyŏng-sik." But for now, I am the one who is teaching, and you are the one who is learning, he thought. Surely a distinction should be made between the two. Perhaps he ought to wait for her to greet him first. So much for that problem. Ever since he had received Elder Kim's invitation the day before, he had been thinking about how to conduct the lesson, but no brilliant thought occurred to him. Shall I place a desk between us and sit face-to-face with her as I teach? Then our breaths would meet. Her upswept hair[1] would occasionally brush against my forehead. Our knees would touch ever so lightly beneath the desk. Hyŏng-sik blushed and smiled at the thought. No, no, he thought. What if I should sin, if only in my thoughts? I know what I will do!—I will sit as far as possible from the desk, and if her knees touch mine, I will move away with a start. It would be rude to a woman for me to have bad breath, though. I have not yet had a cigarette since lunch, but just in case, he thought, and breathed against the palm of his hand. He could test for

1. The word *hisashigami* refers to a Japanese style of putting up a woman's hair. The front of the upswept hairdo is full.

bad odors by smelling his breath as it reflected against his hand and into his nose. Alas, he thought, why am I having such thoughts? Am I that weak? He clenched his fists and tried with all his might to rid himself of these feeble thoughts, but strange flames began to rise in his breast.

"*Mr. Lee!*[2] Where are you going?" Startled, Hyŏng-sik raised his head. It was Sin U-sŏn,[3] striding down the street, wearing a straw hat[4] pushed back on his head. He was known among his friends for his happy-go-lucky cheerfulness. Worried that U-sŏn might read his thoughts, Hyŏng-sik assumed a glad expression as he tried to keep from blushing again.

"It has been quite some time," Hyŏng-sik said stiffly and shook Sin U-sŏn's hand.

"What do you mean, 'it has been quite some time'? I thought we agreed to use informal speech with each other the other day."

Hyŏng-sik felt embarrassed and turned his head away. "Perhaps it is because I am not yet used to using informal speech with you, but—" Hyŏng-sik said and could not finish his sentence.

"Where on earth are you going? If it isn't urgent, have lunch with me."

"I have already eaten."

"Then have a beer."

"Me, drink?"

"Nonsense. How can a man not drink? Now then, enough of the small talk, and let's get going." Sin pulled him by the hand to a Chinese restaurant in front of the Andong District Police Station.

"No, really. Any other day I would not refuse your offer, but not today." Hyŏng-sik's heart pounded as he wondered whether or not his words sounded suspicious. "You see, I have some business to take care of today."

"Business? What kind of business? What would keep you from having a drink?"

Anyone else would simply say that they had urgent business to attend to, and thereby have put an end to the matter. However, Hyŏng-sik, who was honest and weak-willed by nature, could not tell even the slightest lie. He hesitated, then said, "I have to give a private lesson at three o'clock."

"English?"

"Yes.

"Who is this person who gets their own private lessons?"

Hyŏng-sik could not speak. U-sŏn peered curiously into Hyŏng-sik's face with eyes that seemed to pierce all the way to his lungs and heart. Hyŏng-sik lowered his head as if dazzled by U-sŏn's gaze.

"Who is it, that you cannot speak, and are blushing?"

---

2. "*Misŭt'ŏ ri.*" Sin U-sŏn is speaking English here.
3. U-sŏn's name means "a good friend."
4. A *taep'aepap moja* is a straw hat woven of thin pieces of planed wood.

Flustered and nervous, Hyŏng-sik rubbed at his throat and laughed vaguely. "It's a woman."

"What do you know! *Omedetō!*[5] It seems that you have an *iinazuke.*[6] Hm, *naruhodo.*[7] And you haven't said a word to me about this? Now see here!" U-sŏn slapped Hyŏng-sik on the hand.

Hyŏng-sik felt so disconcerted that he dug at the ground with his shoe. "It is no one you would know! You see, there is this Elder Kim—"

"Of course, it's the daughter of Elder Kim. Wasn't it last year? She graduated first in her class from Chŏngsin Girls' School, and will be going to the United States next year. So that is who it is. *'Very good'.*"[8]

"How do you know about her?"

"Did you think I wouldn't know a thing like that? It is the least that one would expect[9] of a newspaper reporter. So when were you engaged?"[10]

"No, I am on my way there today for the first time because they asked me to teach her English for an hour every day, since she is preparing to go to the United States."

"Don't try to fool me!"

Hyŏng-sik scoffed at U-sŏn's words.

U-sŏn laughed. "She is known to be a beautiful woman. Try your best to please her, though knowing you, that isn't saying much. Well then, see you later." Sin doffed his straw hat and fanned himself briskly as he headed down Kyodong Street. Hyŏng-sik had always found fault with his friend's reckless ways, but today he rather envied him for his untrammeled spirit and cheerful personality.

2

The words "beautiful woman" did not displease Hyŏng-sik, but the words *iinazuke* and "engagement" made Hyŏng-sik particularly happy for some reason. Then Sin had gone on to say, "Try your best to please her, though knowing you, that isn't saying much." It was true. Hyŏng-sik was powerless. He did not have the power of money, in a world dominated by

---

5. *Omedetō* is Japanese for "congratulations." The word is transliterated in the text in Korean. Sin uses codeswitching here, modulating between Korean and Japanese. The narrative thereby suggests that U-sŏn has studied in Japan. U-sŏn uses codeswitching when speaking to Hyŏng-sik because Hyŏng-sik too has studied in Japan. I discuss codeswitching in Yi Kwang-su's letters to Hŏ Yŏng-suk, in the article, "Writing for a Woman Reader: Gender, Modernity and Language in the Multilingual Letters of Yi Kwang-su to Hŏ Yŏng-suk," *Acta Koreana* vol. 6, no. 1 (January 2003): 1–22.

6. *Iinazuke* means the arranged betrothal of a couple in childhood, through their parents' agreement, and can refer to either one of the betrothed couple. It can just mean a fiancé(e) too.

7. *Naruhodo* means "I see," in Japanese.

8. Sin uses the English words "very good," transliterated in Korean.

9. Here, Sin U-sŏn says in Japanese, *iyashikumo*: "it is the least that one would expect."

10. Sin U-sŏn uses the English word "engagement," transliterated in Korean.

money. Nor did he have the power of knowledge that people would look up to in an era of knowledge. He had believed in Jesus for some time, but since he had never had much interest in church, he was not particularly well regarded there either. He felt nauseated when he saw youths who lacked any knowledge or virtue frequent the homes of the pastor or the elders, showing off and thereby becoming deacons and stewards, and putting on airs in church. Hyŏng-sik had absolutely nothing with which to attract the affection of a fashionable young woman. The thought made Hyŏng-sik depressed and pessimistic. Just then, Hyŏng-sik arrived at a residential front door that had a nameplate that read "Kim Kwang-hyŏn." The Elder was a disciple of Christ, who had taught his followers not to own so much as two sets of clothing. Nevertheless, once Kim had been enlightened in the ways of modern civilization, he too purchased land, and kept dozens of servants.[11] He was considered the second or third wealthiest man in the Seoul Presbyterian Church,[12] and, moreover, a *yangban*.[13] His home was quite large, with more than ten rooms sprawled about on either side of the front door, for servants' quarters. Intimidated by such status and wealth, Hyŏng-sik felt frightened on the one hand, and had unpleasant qualms on the other. He cleared his throat and called out for a servant to answer the door. "Is anyone home?" No matter how hard he tried, though, his voice did not sound authoritative, but young and quavering, exactly like the voice of a person who has just come to Seoul from the countryside for the first time and is calling out for a servant to answer the door.

A maidservant answered and said, "You are invited to please enter." Hyŏng-sik passed through an inner door in yet another layer of wall, his heart pounding again, and stepped up into the living room. In former times, a guest would never have been allowed past the inner door; just being allowed to enter the inner door was a big change from the old ways. The living room was decorated partially in Western style, with glass doors, a table covered with a patterned cloth in the middle of the room, four or five chairs upholstered in red wool,[14] and piles of traditional and modern books in a shelf that extended along the length of the northern wall.[15] Elder Kim came out onto the veranda of the living room smiling, and waited for Hyŏng-sik to untie his shoes, then took him by the hand and led him inside. Hyŏng-sik bowed politely to the

11. The 1918 Sinmungwan edition revised this sentence: "Nevertheless, once Kim had been enlightened in the ways of modern civilization, he too purchased land, saved money in the bank, bought stocks and a spacious house, and kept dozens of servants." *Mujŏng*, ed. Ch'oe Nam-sŏn (Seoul: Sinmungwan, 1918), 7.
12. Sŏul Yesu Kyohoe.
13. *Yangban*: the educated elite.
14. *Mojŏn*: fabric made with animal hair (such as sheep's wool) that is processed with heat, or crushed; or rugs woven from animal hair and other fiber such as *ramie*.
15. The verb used in the text is *ssahyŏtta*, or "were piled up." Traditional books would have been piled one on top of the other.

Elder in the traditional manner—kneeling and touching his head to the floor—before seating himself in a chair that was offered him. Elder Kim was a clean-cut, middle-aged man of forty-five or six. A *yangban* who had held the official posts of bureau chief (*kukchang*) and provincial governor (*kamsa*), he had joined the church a little over ten years ago, and last year he had become a church elder. He offered Hyŏng-sik a fan.

"It's very hot. Please use this fan."

"Yes, it seems to be the first hot weather we've had this year." Hyŏng-sik took the fan and fanned himself twice, then put the fan down on a desk. The Elder rang a bell on the desk twice. "Yes?" A voice answered from a room that was off of the living room, and a pretty fourteen- or fifteen-year-old girl set a glass bowl and a silver, Western-style spoon on a tray, and placed the tray before Hyŏng-sik. It was a bowl of *omija* tea,[16] with peaches, honey, and pine nuts, and a handful of ice. The mere sight of it was refreshing. It seemed to have been prepared ahead of time in expectation of a visitor.

"It's hot. Please, have some of this." The Elder picked up the spoon himself and gave it to Hyŏng-sik. Hyŏng-sik saw no reason to decline, and drank a dozen spoonfuls one after the other. He wanted to take the bowl in both hands and gulp the drink down all at once, but he thought it might seem disgraceful, so he held back his thirst and stopped and put the spoon down. Just that much was enough to chill his stomach, stop the sweat and make his mind feel weak.

"I mentioned this to you the other day. I would like you to help my daughter. I know how busy you are, but there is no one else I can ask! There are many who know English. However, uh, that is to say, there aren't many people like you." The Elder paused for a moment and looked at Hyŏng-sik as if to say, "You are someone I can trust." Hyŏng-sik was happy and proud that someone would believe in his character enough to entrust him with their young daughter, but he felt shame and guilt surging up within him when he thought of how he had put his hand near his mouth and checked his breath earlier. Actually, though, the Elder had contracted this arrangement because he completely trusted Hyŏng-sik's character, having heard other people's opinions about Hyŏng-sik and having seen Hyŏng-sik himself. Otherwise, he would not have trusted a young instructor for an hour every day with his precious daughter, whom he was sending all the way to the United States.

"Please take on the responsibility of teaching her for a year, so that she knows something," the Elder said.

"I feel distressed by your request, since I don't know anything," replied Hyŏng-sik.

---

16. The fruit of the *Maximowiczia chinensis* is used to brew a tea that is consumed cold. It is believed to be good for the lungs, and for stopping perspiration and diarrhea.

"Not at all. I have heard of your learning in other subjects besides English, and am well aware of your sagacity." The Elder rang the bell again, and the same girl appeared. "Take these dishes, and tell my wife to come here with my daughter." "Yes sir." The girl took the tray and went into another room. The sound of whispering could be heard from the other room. Hyŏng-sik felt agitated, his heart pounded and his cheeks were flushed, as though he were awaiting an important first-time experience in his life. He straightened his collar, trying not to attract the Elder's notice, corrected his posture, and tried as much as possible to have the dignity of an older person.

After awhile, a sliding door was lifted and slid open in the doorway of the room adjoining the living room,[17] and a woman who seemed to be about forty approached the table in the living room, wearing a pale jade-colored Korean blouse and skirt of ramie. Behind her was a young woman student dressed the same way. Hyŏng-sik lowered his head, stood up and bowed politely. The woman and girl bowed and sat down on the chairs that the Elder pointed out to them. Hyŏng-sik sat down as well.

3

"This is Yi Hyŏng-sik, the man I have always been talking about," the Elder said, motioning towards Hyŏng-sik. "He is young, but very learned, and well-known for his writing. When I asked him to teach Sŏn-hyŏng English, he thought nothing of how busy he is, but gave his consent. He will be coming here every day from now on, so if I am not here, I want you to take good care of him, dear."

"This is my wife," he said to Hyŏng-sik. "And that is my daughter. Her name is Sŏn-hyŏng. She graduated last year from a place called the Chŏngsin School, but she is just a child who doesn't know anything."

Hyŏng-sik nodded his head towards no one in particular. Mrs. Kim and Sŏn-hyŏng nodded in return.

"Thank you for helping my daughter," said Mrs. Kim. "When could such a young man have learned so much. You are truly blessed."

"You are too kind," said Hyŏng-sik. He raised his head as if to look at Mrs. Kim, but looked at Sŏn-hyŏng instead. Sŏn-hyŏng sat about a pace behind her mother, so that half of her body was hidden from sight. Her head was lowered, so he could not see her eyes, but her black, natural eyebrows were like the contours of spring mountains drawn distinctly across her broad, white forehead. She had not pomaded her black hair, and it seemed to have been combed some time ago, for two loose strands fell against her red, peach

---

17. "The room adjoining the living room": The *kŏnnŏnpang* was a room across from the room traditionally occupied by the wife (*anpang*). Between the *anpang* and the *kŏnnŏnpang* was the *taech'ŏng*, or main hall, here used as a living room.

blossom-like cheeks, and, wafted by a breeze, struck against her tightly pursed lips. Her skin, which was of a healthy complexion, glowed through her thin ramie Korean blouse with its closely fitting neckline. The hands that lay on her lap seemed to be made of jade, and seemed as though they would be transparent if held up to a light. Mrs. Kim had been a famous *kisaeng* named Pu-yong in P'yŏngyang. She was beautiful, could write well, was outstanding in singing and dancing, and had been known as the Ch'un-hyang of P'yŏngyang.[18] She had been Elder Kim's concubine for over a decade, having found favor in his eyes when he was in P'yŏngyang while his father was provincial governor there; Kim had been a student in his twenties—a connoisseur of wine, women and song—preparing for the civil service examination. Then, when his first wife died, she had become his wife. Some might consider him to be in his dotage, having a *kisaeng* as his wife, and ever since he had begun to believe in Christ, he had come to regret having a concubine; yet he thought it would be wrong to abandon a woman with whom he had had a child, and with whom he had lived for many years. Then, as luck or misfortune would have it, his first wife had died, and he resolutely made this woman his wife, casting aside his relatives' and friends' pleas for him to take a new wife. Mrs. Kim was over forty now and had fine wrinkles at the corners of her eyes, but one could still see the lovely, gentle beauty that had melted her husband's heart. Sŏn-hyŏng's eyebrows, and the area around her mouth[19] were exactly like her mother's, and these alone would have been enough to qualify her as a beauty. Hyŏng-sik thought of Sŏn-hyŏng as a younger sister. This was how he always thought towards young women who were not his relatives. He did not know any other way to think of them. What he could not understand, though, were the strange flames that rose within his breast. These were inevitable when a young man and woman came into close contact, like the sparks that fly when positive and negative charges react—something that had been ordained when heaven created the universe. These feelings were restrained only by the strength of morals and cultivation, for the sake of maintaining social order.

"Why don't you start your lesson now," the Elder said to his daughter when he saw Hyŏng-sik sitting speechlessly. "Where did Sun-ae go? Let her study with you. I would like to learn some English too whenever I have the time."

"All right," said Sŏn-hyŏng. She went to the adjoining room and returned with a book and a pencil. Behind her came a young girl the same age as Sŏn-hyŏng, carrying a book and a pencil. The girl bowed politely. "This is

18. Ch'un-hyang was the heroine of the Korean sung narrative *Ch'un-hyang Ka* (Song of Ch'un-hyang), the love story of a beautiful young woman, Ch'un-hyang, who is the daughter of a *kisaeng*, and a handsome young man named Yi Mong-nyong.
19. The 1917 *Maeil Sinbo* text uses the words *ip ŏlle* (area around the mouth), whereas the 1918 Sinmungwan edition uses the words *ip ŏnjŏri* (area around the mouth).

Sun-ae, my daughter's friend," said the Elder. "She is a pitiful child with no parents and no home." Hyŏng-sik thought of himself and his younger sister, and looked at Sun-ae's face again. She wore her hair and clothes the same way as Sŏn-hyŏng, so it was obvious that the two were very close. Her face, however, bore the unmistakable signs of having encountered the turmoil and commotion of the outside world from an early age. It was the same look that Hyŏng-sik saw when he looked at his face in the mirror, and when he looked at his pitiful younger sister. As he looked at Sun-ae, the pounding in his chest subsided, and a feeling of fear came over him instead. Unconsciously, he heaved a sigh of pity, and looked at Sun-ae again. Sun-ae looked at Hyŏng-sik, too.

The Elder and his wife went to the adjoining room, and Hyŏng-sik and the two girls sat facing each other.

"Have you ever studied any English before?" he asked as calmly as he could, and expected to hear the two girls' voices for the first time. The two girls hung their heads down, however, and said nothing.

Hyŏng-sik too sat dumbfounded for a few moments, then repeated the question. "Have you ever studied any English before?"

Only then did Sŏn-hyŏng lift her head and look at Hyŏng-sik with eyes as clear as water in autumn.

"This is the first time for me. Sun-ae knows some English, though."

"No, I don't. This is the first time for me too."

"Then what about the alphabet?" Hyŏng-sik asked. "Of course, I'm sure you must know the alphabet."

A woman is always embarrassed to admit that she does not know something, and Sŏn-hyŏng's already red cheeks grew even redder.[20]

"I memorized it before, but I have forgotten it."

"Shall we begin with the alphabet, then?"

"Yes," the two girls answered together.

"Then give me those notebooks and pencils. I will write down the alphabet for you."

Son-hyŏng put her pencil on her notebook and handed the notebook to Hyŏng-sik with both hands. Hyŏng-sik opened the notebook and, after checking the pencil point, wrote the letters of the English alphabet "A, B, C, D . . . "[21] clearly and the pronunciation in Korean underneath the letters. Then he returned the notebook to Sŏn-hyŏng with both hands, and took Sun-ae's notebook and did the same.

---

20. The 1917 *Maeil Sinbo* and the 1918 Sinmungwan editions use the words *kajina pulgŭn* (red to begin with; already red); in the 1971 Samjungdang edition, this is written *kattŭgina pulgŭn* (very red).

21. Both the *Maeil Sinbo* and the 1918 Sinmungwan editions transliterate the letters in Korean.

"Let's just memorize the letters today, and study reading and writing beginning tomorrow. Now, let's pronounce the letters out loud: 'A.'"

The two students said nothing.

"Repeat after me: 'A.' Read it out loud: 'A.'"

Hyŏng-sik was taken aback and sat dumbfounded. Sŏn-hyŏng was biting her lips trying to hold back her laughter, and Sun-ae was looking at Sŏn-hyŏng and also trying not to laugh. Hyŏng-sik felt embarrassed and frustrated, and felt like getting up and leaving right then and there. Just then the Elder emerged from the next room.

"Read, you stupid things," he said. "Why don't you read like the teacher told you."

Only then did the girls stop laughing and look at their notebooks.

Hyŏng-sik had no choice but to try again.

"A."

"A."

"B."

"B."

"C."

"C."

They read through the alphabet together three or four times, and the girls agreed to memorize the letters and pronunciation by the next day. Then they bid one another goodbye, and ended the lesson.

4

Hyŏng-sik left Elder Kim's house and returned directly to his boarding house on Kyodong Street. He walked like a drunkard, aimlessly, unaware of where he was going, and found his way home out of mere force of habit formed while he had been living there for over a year. In other words, it was not Hyŏng-sik who went home but his feet that dragged him home. The landlady was preparing his dinner table, but paused and wiped her hands on her skirt.

"What's new, Mr. Yi?" she said and smiled at him in a strange way.

Hyŏng-sik's eyes grew wide. "Why do you ask?"

"Oh, it's nothing to be shocked about."

"Why, has something happened?"

Hyŏng-sik stood still and stared at the landlady.

The landlady laughed to herself, amused at the way Hyŏng-sik was pretending not to know what she was talking about and was acting surprised.

"A pretty young woman came to see you at about three o'clock. She wore her hair like a student, but no matter how I looked at her, I could not help but feel that she looked like a *kisaeng*. I didn't know you had friends like that."

"A young woman? A *kisaeng*?" Hyŏng-sik shook his head in bewilderment as he untied his shoes and stepped up onto the veranda. "There isn't a single woman in the entire city of Seoul who would come to see me. She must have been mistaken."

"Listen to you, pretending that you do not know her. She clearly asked for Mr. Yi Hyŏng-sik of P'yŏngyang."

Hyŏng-sik sat as if oblivious to what she was saying, and looked up at the sky.

"I just can't think of whom it might be. Did she say anything else?"

"She said she would come again in the evening, and she seemed to be very disappointed when she left."

"Did she say she knows me?"

"Why would she come looking for someone she doesn't know? Why don't you go to your room and eat your dinner, and wait for her. Your dinner will taste different tonight."

Hyŏng-sik could not comprehend the landlady's teasing. He really did not know any women who would come to see him. Kim Sŏn-hyŏng or Yun Sun-ae might visit him in the future, but what woman would seek him out at present? Let alone a *kisaeng*. Hyŏng-sik put the dinner table before him. No matter how hard he tried, he could not think of whom the woman might be. The landlady said she would come again soon, so he would know then. He began to eat his dinner. When he had finished his dinner and was reading the newspaper, someone came to the front door. "Now you just watch and see what I mean," the landlady said and winked at him as she went to the door. "Is Mr. Yi back yet?" A young woman followed the landlady into the courtyard. Just as the old woman had described her, she was dressed in a Korean blouse and skirt of ramie, and wore her hair braided and pinned up like a student. Hyŏng-sik and the young woman said nothing, and the landlady stood still with a befuddled expression, wondering why they said nothing. The young woman looked at Hyŏng-sik for a moment, then asked the landlady, "Is Mr. Yi at home?"

"That is Mr. Yi," the landlady said, finding it all rather odd.

"Yes, I am Yi Hyŏng-sik. Who are you?"

The young woman winced as though surprised, then stepped back and lowered her head. The sun was already setting, and, in all the houses, lamps began to blink their eyes open. Hyŏng-sik realized that the woman had a reason for coming to see him, and he stood up quickly, lit a lamp and spread a quilt on the veranda.

"Please come in. I hear you came by earlier. I'm sorry I wasn't in then."

The woman raised her head. There were tears in her eyes.

"Won't it affect your reputation for a woman like me to visit you?"

"Not at all. Please, come in. What brings you here?"

The woman bowed gently, and stepped up onto the veranda. The girl she had brought with her also stepped up onto the veranda and took a seat. Hyŏng-sik sat down too. The landlady watched the scene from the *kŏnnŏnpang*, smoking a pipe and not even bothering to light a lamp.

Hyŏng-sik looked for some time at the woman's face, which appeared pale in the lamplight, then bowed his head and closed his eyes, as if reminded of something.

"Do you not recognize me?"

"Well, your face seems familiar."

"Do you remember Pak Ŭng-jin?"

"Pak Ŭng-jin?" Hyŏng-sik's eyes widened, and he was at a loss for words. The woman collapsed on the desk before her and wept. Tears fell profusely from Hyŏng-sik's eyes.

"Ah, it is you, Yŏng-ch'ae, it is you," Hyŏng-sik said in a tragic voice. "Thank you. Thank you for coming to see an ungrateful scoundrel like me."

Neither of them said anything for some time, and there was only the sound of the young woman weeping. The girl who had come with her clung to her hand and cried too.

5

It had already been over ten years ago. A man named Scholar Pak had lived in a neighborhood a little over ten *li*[22] to the south of the town of Anju in South P'yŏngan Province. He had spent over forty years as a scholar, and everyone in nearby towns knew his name. His relatives had once numbered dozens of households, and the family had been very powerful in the town of Anju for generations as wealthy *yangban*. Then in 1871, when foreign ships arrived at Kanghwa Island and caused a disturbance, his relatives were cruelly purged as enemy sympathizers, and only Scholar Pak's household had somehow survived. About fifteen years ago, Scholar Pak then traveled to the state of Qing and brought back dozens of different kinds of new books published in Shanghai. He got an idea of what the situation was like in the West, and conditions in Japan, and realized that Korea could not go on as it was at present; thereupon, he tried to begin a "new civilization" movement. First, he gathered youths in his study, had them read the books he had bought in Shanghai, and lectured occasionally on new thought. People at the time, however, refused to listen to talk of "railroads" and "steamships," and they said that Scholar Pak was crazy. One by one, the students who had gathered in his study left. Scholar Pak then took in needy children who wanted to study but had no teacher, and began to teach them. After about three years, twenty to thirty students had received an education from Scholar Pak, and he had personally paid for all of their clothing, food, writing paper, writing

---

22. One *li* is a measure of distance equivalent to 3.9273 kilometers.

brushes and ink. Just then, a new movement arose in P'yŏngan Province, new schools emerged everywhere, and there were many people who wept.[23] Scholar Pak immediately cut his hair short and put on black clothes, and he had his two sons do the same. At the time, cutting one's hair and wearing black clothing was a very courageous decision. It symbolized the shattering of established customs that had been followed for over four thousand years, and adopting completely new ways. Then he built a school next to his home, went to Seoul and recruited instructors, and obtained school equipment. He urged neighborhood adults, and children and youths to come and study at his school. After a year, there were about thirty students at the school, and he hired two more instructors. The students were ages seven to thirty years old. In addition to being personally responsible for the costs of running the school, Scholar Pak continued to nurture and raise about a dozen youths. Yi Hyŏng-sik had been one of those youths. Hyŏng-sik had lost his parents at the time, and had been drifting about with no one to turn to when he heard that Scholar Pak was offering youths an education, and went to see him. Scholar Pak particularly loved Hyŏng-sik since Hyŏng-sik was intelligent, had good character, and was talented, and Hyŏng-sik's father and Scholar Pak had been friends of the same age. Scholar Pak's sons were four or five years older than Hyŏng-sik, but they were behind him in scholarly ability and, moreover, had to learn math and Japanese language from Hyŏng-sik. Several of Hyŏng-sik's classmates therefore teased Hyŏng-sik both jokingly and in jealousy, saying that Hyŏng-sik would become Scholar Pak's son-in-law in the future. In their opinion, Scholar Pak was the greatest teacher in Korea. Scholar Pak's daughter, Yŏng-ch'ae, had been ten years old at the time, so she would be nineteen now. Though others laughed at him, Scholar Pak ignored them and sent his daughter to school. When she returned from school, he would teach her texts such as the *Elementary Learning*[24] and *Biographies of Virtuous Women*, and the summer she turned twelve years old, he taught her the *Classic of Poetry* too. Scholar Pak was dignified, compassionate, serious, yet cheerful, so that youths and children thought of him as both an awe-inspiring teacher and a good friend. He tried to devote his personal wealth, his home, his body, his heart and even his life to serving others. The neighborhood people, however, did not feel grateful for his heartfelt efforts, but scorned him as a crazy man. After about seven years, his

---

23. The "new movement" refers to cultural nationalism. The phrase "and many people wept" could refer to nationalists weeping for the nation.
24. *Xiao-xue* (Elementary Learning) was a primer compiled by Zhu Xi in 1189. It contained the elementary rules of personal conduct and interpersonal relationships, and served as an introduction to the Four Books: the *Analects of Confucius* (Lun yu), the *Works of Mencius* (Meng zi), the *Greater Learning* (Da xue), and the *Doctrine of the Mean* (Zhung Yung). Martina Deuchler, *The Confucian Transformation of Korea: A Study of Society and Ideology* (Cambridge: Harvard-Yenching Institute Monograph Series, 1992), 21.

wealth, which had not been substantial to begin with, was completely gone, and he had to go without eating breakfast. Thus, there was no way he could go on operating the school. Scholar Pak then visited wealthy men in town, or sent others, to ask them to take on the responsibility of funding the school he was running. He had devoted all of his personal wealth, his heart and his strength to the school, for the sake of others, and now he was willing to entrust it to someone else, but no one stepped forward to take on the responsibility. On the contrary, people sneered at him, thinking he was only making the offer because he had nothing to eat. Scholar Pak's hair turned completely white, though he was not yet sixty years old. The students in his study scattered because there was nothing to eat, and the only ones left were the oldest student, who had the surname Hong, and Yi Hyŏng-sik, who was the youngest. Hyŏng-sik was sixteen years old at the time.

In the autumn of that year, a robber broke into the house of a wealthy man who lived about ten *li* from the school, stabbed the master of the house in the side, and stole over five hundred wŏn. The robber was the student named Hong who was living in Pak's study. Unable to bear the sight of his benefactor's poverty, Hong said he had at first intended to just threaten the wealthy man into giving him money. He said had killed him, however, because the wealthy man had been so rude and had said that he would report the incident to the military gendarmes. Hong set the five hundred wŏn before Pak. The latter was startled.

"Why have you done this? Heaven feeds and clothes those who work hard. Ah, why have you done this?" Pak told him to return the money immediately and plead for forgiveness. Hong was arrested on his way back to the wealthy man's house, and Pak and his two sons were arrested that morning on suspicion of instigating and conspiring to commit robbery and murder. The only people left in Scholar Pak's household were his two daughters-in-law, and Yŏng-ch'ae and Hyŏng-sik. Yŏng-ch'ae's mother had died less than two months after she gave birth to Yŏng-ch'ae.

Several of the students from Pak's study were taken in for questioning, and Hyŏng-sik was summoned as a witness, but was released after two days of questioning.

Two months later, Hong and Scholar Pak went to P'yŏngyang jail on life sentences. Pak's two sons were each sentenced to fifteen years in jail, and the others received five- to seven-year-sentences.

As a consequence, the two daughters-in-law had no choice but to return to their maternal homes. Yŏng-ch'ae went to live with relatives on her mother's side. Hyŏng-sik once again lost his sense of purpose, and drifted through a quiet, lonely world, like a floating weed. He sent letters twice to the prison in P'yŏngyang, but received no reply, nor were the letters returned. When he visited Anju last summer, strangers were laughing and playing

Korean chess[25] in Scholar Pak's house. Now he and Yŏng-ch'ae had met again for the first time in seven years.

6

The memories flashed through Hyŏng-sik's mind like lightning, and he wiped his tears away and looked at Yŏng-ch'ae, who had put her head down on the desk and was weeping. The girl who, ten years ago, had clung to his shoulder, smiling, and pulled at his hand, calling him "older brother," had become an adult. What kind of hardships had she endured over the past seven or eight years?

If Hyŏng-sik, who was a man, had spent the years in suffering and tears, how much more painful and bitter must it have been for a frail, young girl? He wanted to know what had happened to her during that time. He shook her by the shoulder.

"Please don't cry. Let me hear what you have to say. Please sit up." Hyŏng-sik himself could not keep himself from crying, so it was understandable that Yŏng-ch'ae would weep. "Please, sit up."

"I could not help crying."

Hyŏng-sik was silent.

"Seeing you again is like seeing my late father and brothers," Yŏng-ch'ae said. She started to cry again, and lay her head down on the desk again. Her late father and brothers? Had Scholar Pak and his sons passed away? Pak had lost his home and all his wealth. Had he finally lost his life as well? Yŏng-ch'ae had been the daughter of a well-to-do family that had rescued impoverished, needy Hyŏng-sik. Yet, in less than five years, had she too become a needy person as he had been? How could one believe in anything? If one could not have confidence in a young person's life, how much less so could one believe in money or status, which were like bubbles on the water. If Scholar Pak had passed away, he would have died in prison. Had he met his sons while staying in the same prison, then? Who would have given him a last spoonful of water, or closed his eyelids for him? Alone in death, had his body been wrapped in a straw mat and been given as food to the crows? Who would have mourned for him? Who would have wept for him when he set out alone for the nether world? The world for which he had wept did not think about him any more, but rather, oppressed and abused his only living flesh and blood. If there was a will to heaven, then one could only resent its heartlessness. If heaven had no will, then there was nothing in life[26] in which to believe.

---

25. Korean chess (*changgi*) is a variant of Chinese chess (*jiang qi*), but there are important differences between the games. Cf. Stewart Culin, *Korean Games: With Notes on the Corresponding Games of China and Japan* (New York: Dover Publications, Inc., 1991), 82–91.
26. The 1917 *Maeil Sinbo* and 1918 Sinmungwan editions use the word *insŏng* (human character), whereas the 1971 Samjungdang edition uses the word *insaeng* (life).

"Has Scholar Pak passed away?"

"Yes, Father passed away two years after he went to prison. My two older brothers passed away two weeks after father died."

"But how . . . how could they both have died two weeks after your father died?"

"I don't know the details. The authorities told me they died of illness. But one of the prison guards told me that father starved himself to death. Then my eldest brother starved himself to death too. The day that my eldest brother died, my other brother hung himself." Yŏng-ch'ae sobbed. Before he knew it, Hyŏng-sik was sobbing too.

The landlady had first thought Yŏng-ch'ae was a vulgar woman who had come to try to seduce Hyŏng-sik, but after hearing her story, it seemed to the landlady that Yŏng-ch'ae was from a good family and, moreover, had a truly pitiable life. The landlady went out to the street and bought shaved ice and some pears. She shook Yŏng-ch'ae gently. "There, there now. Have a bowl of shaved ice. You will feel refreshed. What is the use of crying now? One must think of all this as fate, and endure. I became a widow when I was young, and lost a fully grown child, but I am still alive. To be without parents is nothing compared to being without a husband. You have your whole life ahead of you, why worry? Now then, stop crying and have some shaved ice. Eat some pear too." The landlady hurried to the kitchen and fetched a rusty knife, and began peeling a pear. "Why Mr. Yi, you are crying more than she is, instead of making her feel better."

"I cannot help crying when my heart is breaking. This is the daughter of the benefactor who raised me for five years. But he died in jail on unjust charges, and his two sons died too. Between heaven and earth, this woman is his only living flesh and blood. For eight years I scarcely knew whether she was alive or dead. And now that I see her again, how can I help but feel sad?"

"But what is the use crying, no matter how sad you feel?" The landlady cut a piece of pear, and put an arm around Yŏng-ch'ae to pull her up from the desk. "Suffering in youth leads to happiness later. Don't be too sad. Here, have a piece of pear."

Yŏng-ch'ae was moved by the landlady's kind words, and wiped her tears away and accepted the piece of pear. Hyŏng-sik looked at Yŏng-ch'ae's face again. She still looked the same as before. Her large eyes, moreover, reminded him of Scholar Pak. Yŏng-ch'ae too regarded Hyŏng-sik's face. His face seemed longer than before, and he had a mustache, but his face as a whole looked the same. As the two of them looked at each other, events from over ten years ago flashed through their minds like a motion picture. The events appeared vividly before their eyes as though it were yesterday. The happy times they had spent together. How the household had lamented when Scholar Pak was arrested. How the family had scattered one by one. How generations of the Pak family had come to ruin. The day Hyŏng-sik left, he had said to Yŏng-ch'ae, "Who knows when we will see each other again. I will not be able to hear you call me 'older brother.'"[27] "Don't go. Take me with you," Yŏng-ch'ae had said, falling into his arms and weeping. Hyŏng-sik wanted to hear about what had happened to her over the years, and began to ask her about her life.

7

Hyŏng-sik and the landlady pleaded with her so much that Yŏng-ch'ae finally wiped her tears away, sat up, and ate some of the pear and shaved ice. Her eyes, red from weeping, and her flushed cheeks looked even more pathetic and lovely. Hyŏng-sik thought of Sŏn-hyŏng. She and Yŏng-ch'ae were both beautiful and had been adored by their parents, but why were their fates so different? One of them had parents, a home, and wealth, and could attend school in peace and ease, and was even going to the United States the next year, whereas the other had no parents or siblings, no home, and no one to rely on, and spent her days in tears. If Sŏn-hyŏng had been shown Yŏng-ch'ae's plight, she would most certainly have considered her a person from a different world. She would have thought that she was someone who could never become like Yŏng-ch'ae, and that Yŏng-ch'ae could never become like herself. She was someone who had been especially favored by heaven, whereas Yŏng-ch'ae had incurred heaven's divine wrath and punishment. Rich people thus ignored the poor and treated them with contempt. They considered the poor as unworthy of their notice. When people who lived by what was called their "own means" saw beggars on the street who were shivering from starvation,[28] they would treat them with contempt, as if the beggars were dogs or pigs, and make fun of them, and spit at them, and kick them. But where is the beggar who does not have a rich ancestor, or a rich person who does not have a beggar for an ancestor? Looking at a rich person, one would think they had been rich since creation, and would be rich until the end of the universe. But one of their ancestors once fought over cold, leftover rice with the dogs at the front door of another rich man's house, and before long there would come a day when their own descendants would do the same. Looking at Scholar Pak eight years ago, who would have thought that Scholar Pak's daughter would come to this?

All people were human beings alike; how much richer or nobler could one person be than others? It was like climbing onto a small rock and looking down at other people and saying, "You there, I am above you." How much higher could a person be than others? Someone else, moreover, had stood upon that very rock the day before, and someone else would be there the next

27. The word *oppa* means "older brother," but can mean an older male friend.
28. Whereas the 1917 *Maeil Sinbo* text uses the words *kulmŏttanŭn kŏji* (beggars said to be starving), the 1918 Sinmungwan edition changed this to *kulmŏ ttŏnŭn kŏji* (beggars shivering from starvation).

day. To feed a cold spoonful of rice to a beggar today was to ask that beggar's descendants to do the same favor to one's own descendants; and likewise, to mistreat and ridicule a beggar today was to ask that beggar's descendants to do the same to one's own descendants. Who knew how wealthy and noble Yŏng-ch'ae might be in the future, and how poor and lowly Sŏn-hyŏng might become? These were Hyŏng-sik's thoughts as he opened his mouth to speak. "Please tell me how you have been since we parted," he said.

"About two or three days after you left, I went to stay with my mother's relatives," said Yŏng-ch'ae, and began her story.

Her maternal grandparents were dead, and her maternal uncle had died before that. The only ones left in her mother's home were her maternal uncle's wife, and Yŏng-ch'ae's two older cousins and their children. With her mother and her loving grandparents gone, there was no one there who would look after her with affectionate attention. Relatives would only treat one as a relative if one was well off. When one was wealthy and powerful, even distant relatives would seek one out as though full of affection. Even a small child from one's house would be treated as an important visitor. If one became poor and powerless, though, the relatives would gradually stop visiting, and if one went to see them oneself, they would frown as though thinking, "Has (he or she) come to ask for something again?"

"My maternal uncle's wife liked me, and would comb my hair and give me things to eat, but my eldest cousin's wife was mean, and would yell at me and hit me for the slightest reason. I could put up with that, but the children imitated their mother and regarded me with contempt. When they were eating something delicious, they would just eat amongst themselves, and not ask me to eat too. The thirteen-year-old who had just been married (a son of one of my cousins) was the worst. He would berate me rudely, for no reason. 'I am his aunt, and he talks to me that way?' I thought, though I was just a young girl." Yŏng-ch'ae laughed. "It made me very upset, and I thought he was very rude.

"I had taken about four outfits of clothing with me from home, but they all got filthy because I was always drawing water from the well and lighting the fireplace. Since there was no one to wash my clothes for me, I had to wash my clothes myself and just wear them without ironing or starching them. My biggest worry was that I would wear one outfit so long that it would become full of lice, and I would feel unbearably itchy. I couldn't scratch in front of others, so when it became unbearable, I would go to the fenced enclosure behind the house where no one would watch, and scratch myself and remove lice from my body. I got caught once by my eldest cousin's wife and she scolded me severely. 'The children will get lice. Go sleep in the storage shed,' she said."

"When there was meat or rice cakes for an ancestral ceremony or holiday, they would just give me inedible things, and even then I would be told that all I did was eat and never work.

"Once a pair of silver rings disappeared from a chest. It looks as though I am going to get in trouble again, I thought, and sure enough, as I sat in the kitchen, my eldest cousin's wife ran into the kitchen angrily and started jabbing and hitting me with a poker, and yelling at me to give the rings back. I got indignant and answered back. Then my eldest cousin's wife hit me, saying, 'You wench! Daughter of a thief! If you didn't steal them, who did?' Since my father was jailed as a thief, she would always call me the daughter of a thief, and that hurt most of all."

"That is terrible. What an awful woman." The old woman clucked her tongue. Hyŏng-sik sat listening quietly, without saying anything.

Yŏng-ch'ae sighed deeply, and continued.

8

"Just as she was beating me, a girl who lived nearby came and said, 'A prostitute in that wine shop is wearing a large silver ring. When I asked her where it came from, the prostitute said that the recently married young man in the tiled roof house had given it to her. He has apparently been visiting the prostitute often.' I was thus cleared of suspicion, but my older cousin's wife and the girl in the wine shop got into a big fight. 'You have a man, but you had to sleep with a young man who belongs to someone else. You told him to bring you the rings, didn't you, wench.' Then the wine shop prostitute said, 'You should teach your son to know better, and you should not blame others.' That was what they said as they fought."

"Instead of educating a boy, people marry him off at an early age and make him learn nothing but bad habits," lamented Hyŏng-sik.

"Is that why you aren't getting married, Mr. Yi?"

Yŏng-ch'ae was surprised when she heard the old woman say that Hyŏng-sik had not yet taken a wife. She looked at Hyŏng-sik. She wanted to know why he hadn't gotten married. She wondered if it might not have to do with herself. She remembered her father jokingly asking her, "Would you like to be Hyŏng-sik's wife?" Even then she had thought Hyŏng-sik was a very good person and liked him best of all the students gathered in her father's study. She had never once forgotten Hyŏng-sik during the eight years or so that she had drifted far and wide like a willow leaf on the Han River, experiencing all kinds of suffering and joy. The older she became, the more she would think of his face with affection. She had even spent entire nights thinking about Hyŏng-sik and crying. She didn't know whether he was alone somewhere, or whether he was dead or alive. It had been seven years since she had sold herself and become a *kisaeng*, but she had never yielded her body to any man, though she had received such requests from many men.

Part of the reason that she refused to yield herself was that she had read the *Elementary Learning* and *Biographies of Virtuous Women* when she was a girl. The most important reason, however, was that she had been unable to forget Hyŏng-sik. Now that she was grown, it seemed that her father had not been joking when he told her to marry Hyŏng-sik, but that he had truly intended for the marriage to take place. She vowed not to violate her father's will, though her body turn to dust. But was Hyŏng-sik still alive, or had he died? If he were alive, he would already be married and have a family, she would think to herself and lose hope. She firmly resolved, nevertheless, that even if Hyŏng-sik were married, she would devote her life to him and not see any other men. She was happy now that she had found him by chance, but she was prepared to spend the rest of her life unmarried. When she heard that he had not yet married, she was both surprised and happy. She despaired again, however, upon further thought. Hyŏng-sik worked in academe, and his conduct and reputation were his very life. How would society regard him if he took a *kisaeng* for a wife?

As for Hyŏng-sik, he had been studying in Tokyo and had not had time to get married, but he had not been without offers. He had not accepted any offers, however, using his studies as an excuse, because deep in his heart he still thought of Yŏng-ch'ae. Hyŏng-sik had guessed that Scholar Pak wanted him to be his son-in-law from the way Pak had favored him in particular and from what others said, though Pak had never said so directly to Hyŏng-sik. When he left Pak's house, it was with many profound sorrows that he had held Yŏng-ch'ae's hand and said, "I may never see you again." After that, he had had no way of hearing news about Yŏng-ch'ae. She would have reached marriageable age, moreover, and was probably someone's wife and may even have given birth to children, he thought. He could not bring himself to cast aside the wishes of his former teacher, though, and marry someone else, so he had waited until now, hoping to hear word of Yŏng-ch'ae. Today they had met again, but he could not help but think that there was something in her appearance that suggested that she was a *kisaeng*. Then several men would have slept with her already. The reason he had wept aloud sadly a few moments ago was not so much that he was bitter thinking that she could not be his wife, but that he lamented that the flesh and blood of his benefactor Scholar Pak, who had exerted himself for the sake of others, had fallen to such a state. He had wanted to listen to her talk about her life, hoping that she had not become a *kisaeng*, or if she had, that she had followed the examples of women of olden times and had stayed a virgin. By now, both of them wanted to know how the other was feeling.

"Then what happened?"

"I cried and did not eat all day. I knew I could not stay in that house. All of a sudden I wanted to run away somewhere. But where could a thirteen-year-old girl go? I had heard that my paternal aunt lived in

Yŏngbyŏn, but I did not know where, and besides, she was said to have passed away, so even if I went there, would it be any different from being at my maternal relatives' home? I had heard that my father and two brothers were in P'yŏngyang, so I thought it would be better to go there. Even if he was in jail, I thought surely they would not keep his own daughter from being with him. I decided to run away to P'yŏngyang that night, so I ate plenty of food at dinner and waited for the rest of the household to fall asleep."

9

"I slept next to my maternal uncle's wife. She was an old lady, and no matter how long I waited, she just kept turning over in bed and would not fall asleep. Finally, I pretended I had to go to the outhouse, and got up and put my clothes on. My aunt got suspicious and asked me why I was getting dressed. I said I had to go to the outhouse, and quickly stepped outside. I knew I could not run away alone in girls' clothing, so I thought of stealing my nephew's clothes. I ended up actually stealing something," Yŏng-ch'ae said and laughed. "I knew that the clothes had been ironed[29] that evening and laid out on the veranda, so I sneaked to the veranda, took off my clothes, and changed into my nephew's clothes. It was the thirteenth of August, so the moon was bright though not quite a full moon yet, and there was a gentle evening breeze. When I stepped outside the front door, it was very bright outside. I wondered how I could just go without knowing whether P'yŏngyang was to the east or the west, and without any money. I thought about my parents, and myself, and tears came to my eyes. I knew with certainty that I could not stay in that house any longer, though, so I walked with heavy steps toward the road outside the village. The dog that had been sleeping near the front door, in the area between the front door and the inner door, stood still when it saw me, then followed me, wagging its tail. After I had walked a while, I sat down under a large ash tree that stood on the side of the road. I cried for awhile there, then embraced the dog, which was standing next to me, and said, 'I am going far away. I may never see you again. You have been a friend to me for a year. But I am leaving you behind and going far away. When you go home, if someone asks where I am, tell them that I have gone to P'yŏngyang to find my father.' Then I got up and went on. It is amazing how dogs seem to know people's feelings. The dog clung to my clothes with its teeth, and barked and motioned to me to go back home. 'But I cannot go home. You go home,' I said to the dog and slapped it on the head with my hand. The dog would not leave me, though, and kept

---

29. The text uses the verb *tarida*, which means to iron clothes using a *tarimi*, a utensil in which coals were placed. Koryŏ Taehakkyo Minjok Munhwa Yŏn'guso, *Han'guk Minsok Taegwan*, vol. 2 (Seoul: Koryŏ Taehakkyo Minjok Munhwa Yŏn'guso, 1982), 384–5.

following me. I did not slap it any more or chase it away. I thought it might be a companion to me on the lonely night road."

"Would you look at that! Dogs are better than human beings!" The landlady wiped her tears away.

Yŏng-ch'ae smiled. "However, one has to know where one is going. When I went gathering greens the spring before, I had seen a wide road and heard that the road led to Ŭiju and China to the west, and P'yŏngyang and Seoul to the east. So I hurried off in the direction of the wide road. Every time I passed a village, dogs would bark. Whenever I heard the sound of dogs barking, I would rejoice, but also feel afraid. The dog that was following me did not bark but quietly lowered its head and just followed me.

"After walking a while, roosters began to crow in a village, and, on the other side of the village, a road was visible, white in the moonlight. That is the road! I thought, and ran onto it with eager strides. Once I was on the road, I looked around me in all four directions. The moon sets in the west, I thought, so I put the moon at my back and walked on without stopping.

"The next day I went without breakfast, and kept walking until late in the day, then stopped at a village becaused I was hungry and my legs ached. The sound of rice cake dough being pounded could be heard in the houses, and children were wearing new clothes and going about in groups. I went to the largest house in the village. Adults were sitting in the study, drinking, laughing and talking. I said I was traveling, and had stopped in the village because I was hungry. They filled a bowl with rice cakes, and handed it to me. Since I was hungry, I ate three or four of the rice cakes all at once. One of the adults in the study, a man with a beard and a plump[30] face, drew near me. 'Who is your family?' he asked, stroking me on the head. 'You are very well behaved.' He asked me my name, where I lived, who my father was, and how old I was. I said whatever I could think of—that I was Kim so-and-so from Sukch'ŏn, and that I was on my way home from visiting my maternal relatives in Anju. There must have been something strange about the expression on my face and the way I spoke, though, because several of the adults stopped talking and just looked at me. My heart started pounding and my face grew red. I stood up without eating all of the rice cakes, bowed and ran out the door. When I got outside, bratty children gathered and teased me. 'Hey, where are you from? Where are you going?' 'I am from Sukch'ŏn. I am on my way home from visiting my maternal relatives in Anju,' I said and ducked my head down and ran away. Why run away when someone is asking you a question, the children said, and followed me, trying to pick a fight. I was just a kid, and had been walking all night, and my legs hurt. I knew I

---

30. Although the 1917 *Maeil Sinbo* text uses the words "*t'udom t'udom han*," which seems to be a variant of *tut'um han* (plump), the 1918 Sinmungwan edition revised this to "*ut'ul tut'ul han*" (coarse, rough).

could not run, so I stopped. The children then gathered around me, and the biggest one of them put his hand on my neck and asked me all kinds of questions with his stinking breath.When I answered, he would ask me another question. The other children laughed, and pinched me and poked me. They would not let me go no matter how I pleaded. After being tormented like this for awhile, I sobbed out loud. Just then, there was the loud sound of a man clearing his throat. A man who seemed to be a teacher in a Confucian academy approached wearing a horsehair hat pushed back on his head and waving a long pipe. 'Stop that, you kids!' he said reprimandingly. The children scattered. I ran away from the village, completely forgetting about how my legs ached. Behind me, I could hear children cursing me and making a racket. I did not look back, though. When I got to the big road, the dog showed up and followed me. It was bleeding beneath one ear, as though one of the children had struck it with a rock. I cried, and blew gently on the wound. Then I kept walking east, resting as I went.

"My body was weary and the sun had set. When I thought about what an ordeal I had gone through in the village, I shuddered and had no intention of stopping in another village. I had gone without food, though, and I could not sleep out in the open. I wondered what to do. After some hesitation, I stopped at an inn on the roadside. My teeth chatter even now when I think of what I endured that night." Yŏng-ch'ae wrung her hands and sighed.

10

"Without any money?" the landlady asked worriedly.

"I would not have suffered the way I did if I had had money," Yŏng-ch'ae said and continued.

"When I went into the inn, there were already six or seven guests there. The inn keeper was sitting in the warmest corner of the room, near the heating flue under the floor. Who are you, the inn keeper asked, looking at me. I said that I was traveling, and since it was dark, I wanted to stay there for the night and be on my way. Then you will need to eat dinner, the inn keeper said. I said I could not pay for dinner since I had no money, and asked if I could just sleep there. The inn keeper told me to go find a house in Andong where I could sleep in the study. There are already many guests here and there is nowhere for you to sleep, he said. Where can the young one go at this hour, said one of the guests, a very dignified-looking man with short hair. The man said he would pay for my food, and asked the inn keeper to give me dinner and breakfast and let me stay the night. I was so thankful I wanted to call the man my uncle,[31] and kneel on the floor and bow before him in

---

31. The term *ajŏssi* can be used in various situations. It can be used to address a man who is of one's parent's generation; it can be used by a female to address her older sister's husband; and it can be used to address an adult male who is no relation to oneself.

gratitude. After eating dinner, I listened to the guests talk, and then eventually lay down on the coldest part of the floor and fell asleep.

"I had a frightening dream in which I was being kidnapped by a robber. When I awoke from the dream, I heard the guests in the room discussing something. No, it is a boy, one of them said. Then another said how could it be a boy. She definitely has a girl's face and a girl's voice. Would a girl have reason to dress up as a boy and travel alone, said another. It was clear that they were talking about me. I lay there with my teeth chattering, and I wondered what to do. The men argued for awhile until one man said there is nothing to argue about, we will know for certain if we just look, and started moving towards me. I was terrified and clung to the wall. But my strength was no match for a man. Eventually, my true gender was exposed. I was so embarrassed and outraged that I started to cry."

"How awful! Those bad men couldn't just go to sleep, but had to stay up talking about that sort of thing." The landlady was furious.

"After I cried awhile, the man who had looked at my body said, 'I will take the girl, just as we wagered,' and he patted me on the back. I pleaded with him desperately, saying that I was on my way to look for my father who was in P'yŏngyang. 'Go look for your father next month,' he said. 'Let's go to my house first.' And he put his arm under my neck where I lay, and pulled me up. 'Let's get going,' he said. I looked at the other people's faces. I wondered if perhaps someone might help me."

"Where was the man who said he would pay for your food?" Hyŏng-sik asked with clenched fists.

"Well, please hear me out. That was the very man who was now trying to take me away. The others just smiled and did not say a word, as though they were afraid of that man. I cried and pleaded, until finally I screamed out with all my might for someone to save me. Dogs started barking when I screamed, and I could hear the dog I had brought with me barking too. The man gagged me with a cloth, and carried me out on his back. The others did not even look out, but just shut the door." Yŏng-ch'ae paused for a moment.

Hearing about Yŏng-ch'ae's arduous fate, Hyŏng-sik compared her life with what he had suffered in his youth, and he became lost in thought. What had happened to Yŏng-ch'ae after she was taken away by that wicked man? Had the man lusted after her pretty looks, and tried to satisfy a vile desire? Or had he tried to sell her for money to spend on wine and gambling? Whatever the case, Hyŏng-sik hoped that Yŏng-ch'ae's body had not been defiled by that bad man. Hyŏng-sik looked carefully at Yŏng-ch'ae's face and body again. He knew that a woman's face and body changed after relations with a man. She seemed to be a virgin still, and yet seemed to have given her body to a man. Her shaped brows and the perfume from her body, moreover, did not seem to be those of a guileless virgin. Hyŏng-sik suddenly disliked her. Had she not perhaps given her body to countless other men? Had she not kissed the mouths of all kinds of disgusting men and uttered seductive words with the very lips that now spoke of her woes? Perhaps the reason she was here saying these things and crying and acting meek was that it was some kind of plot to fool him, taking advantage of the affection of seven years ago. He thought of Sŏn-hyŏng. The latter was a very beautiful young woman. Her face was beautiful and her mind was beautiful too. If one compared Sŏn-hyŏng with Yŏng-ch'ae, it was like the difference between a divine being and a prostitute. He looked at Yŏng-ch'ae. Sparkling tears filled her eyes, and there was a sadness in her face that made one feel reverential towards her. Moreover, Hyŏng-sik felt swayed when he saw how the old landlady who had absolutely no relation to Yŏng-ch'ae was holding her hand and weeping honest tears down her wrinkled cheeks. No, no, he thought. I am wrong. Yŏng-ch'ae never forgot me, but came to see me and is telling me about her life as eagerly as though she had just been reunited with her parents or siblings. Since this is the case, it is terribly wrong towards Yŏng-ch'ae for me to have these disgusting thoughts. Surely she would not have defiled her body—not the daughter of a noble person such as Scholar Pak, not the Yŏng-ch'ae who had been as pretty as a flower. She would have been as unchanging and exemplary as the pine and bamboo in the midst of all her ordeals. But what had happened to her since then? Yŏng-ch'ae went on with her story, telling of what happened to her after she was abducted by that man, and up to the present.

11

　　　Yŏng-ch'ae was eventually taken away by that evil man. He lived in a small house at the foot of a mountain. One could tell at a glance that it was the house of a lazy man. Though he was committing this sordid deed now, he had once been known as a rich man in the neighborhood. He was from a lowly family, however, and was treated with contempt by others. Then in 1894, the Tonghak movement became rampant, and even ignorant farmers cut their hair, and wore horsehair caps. The local chiefs who had once been as feared as tigers could do nothing to stop them. The evil man who kidnapped Yŏng-ch'ae joined the Tonghak movement, admiring and coveting its power. He sold the few fields and rice paddies that had been handed down in his family, donated them to the movement, and became a poor man without clothing or food. His hopes of becoming a provincial governor, county magistrate or local chief, however, all came to nothing, and he was now a beggar without a patch of farm land. Had he been a good, morally cultivated man, his behavior would not have changed no matter how poor he became. However, since he had joined the Tonghak movement in order to become a *yangban* overnight, though he affected the outer deportment of a *yangban* or a gentlemen, as he lost the formal outer robe, horsehair cap and leather shoes necessary to keep up appearances, his pretenses at being a *yangban* and a gentleman gradually fell away as well. Now all he wanted was to do anything he could to get money and to drink. He became known in the neighborhood as a swindler and a no-good scoundrel. Some of his former pretenses of being a gentleman had returned to him when he offered to pay for Yŏng-ch'ae's meals at the inn; but it was an indication of the putrid state of his mind at present, that he carried Yŏng-ch'ae away on his back once he knew that she was a girl.

He had two sons. The eldest son was twenty-two years old and still unmarried. The second son was now a tow-headed youth of fifteen or sixteen. At first, when he carried Yŏng-ch'ae away, he had been thinking of giving her to his unmarried eldest son. Even someone whose heart and mind had become so depraved that he was almost a beast, was still able to think of his children. As he walked through the dark night with Yŏng-ch'ae on his back and no one else around, though, he became uncontrollably aroused by the sensation of Yŏng-ch'ae's warm flesh against his back and hands. It may sound strange that he felt sexually drawn to a girl who was barely thirteen years old and young enough to be his granddaughter, but it was not strange for him, since he had a healthy body, and all trace of morality and ethics had disappeared from his heart. He had a wife at home, but she was old, and had aged considerably after years of hardship, and she had no appealing warmth. Now that he had the flowerlike Yŏng-ch'ae in his hands, all thought of making her his daughter-in-law disappeared, and, unable to restrain the flames of sexual desire aroused within him, he stopped and set Yŏng-ch'ae by the side of an isolated road that was on the spur of a mountain. Since she was but a child, Yŏng-ch'ae did not know what kind of evil intentions the man had towards her. She just felt frightened, and pleaded for mercy, rubbing her hands together. He would not listen to her, but lay her on the ground as though he had gone mad.

Hyŏng-sik shuddered when he heard these words. Then Yŏng-ch'ae had not been a virgin for quite some time. Even if Yŏng-ch'ae said she had not been raped, Hyŏng-sik did not think he would believe her. When he thought of that man laying Yŏng-ch'ae on the ground, Hyŏng-sik felt sorry for Yŏng-ch'ae, and yet also felt that she was somehow unclean. The landlady hardly breathed as she watched Yŏng-ch'ae's lips move wearily. "Did you ever hear of such a thing!" she would say from time to time, and heave a sigh.

When the man lay Yŏng-ch'ae on the ground, for some reason Yŏng-ch'ae was seized with a tremendous fear, and kicked the man in the chest with all her might and screamed aloud. The man fell over backwards. Though Yŏng-ch'ae was young and weak, since she had kicked the man in the chest with all her might as he jumped at her, she had knocked the breath out of him. When Yŏng-ch'ae saw the man fall over, she jumped up and threw dirt and sand in his face when he tried to get up, and ran away as fast as she could. After running madly for awhile, she stopped and listened. She heard no noises, though. There was only a morning breeze grazing against her sweaty face. Yŏng-ch'ae seemed to see the shadow of the man running after her, and the flash of a knife dripping with blood, and she screamed and started running again. After she had run for some time, she looked behind her and saw the dog, about whom she had forgotten, following her and holding something white in its mouth. Yŏng-ch'ae was glad to see the dog, and embraced it. The dog's body, however, was covered with blood. When she held its head, she realized that her hands had become wet with blood from the dog's neck. Yŏng-ch'ae stepped back in shock. The dog barked twice, then staggered and fell to the ground. Yŏng-ch'ae stood in a daze, then picked up the white thing that the dog had held in its mouth. Though the early light of dawn was faint, Yŏng-ch'ae could see that it was part of the hem on the man's shirt. The dog had fought with the man for a long time, then finally had bitten the man and knocked him over, and brought a piece of the man's shirt in order to let Yŏng-ch'ae know what it had done. The dog, however, had been kicked by the man, struck with his fists, and bitten, so that flesh was gone in several places on the dog's body and the dog was bleeding. Two of the dog's left ribs were broken and had punctured the lungs and heart. Not knowing how much longer it had to live, the dog had wanted to die at the feet of its pitiful, beloved owner, after catching up with her and letting her know that it had avenged her enemy.

"I cried for a long time, holding the dog's body." Tears fell again from Yŏng-ch'ae's eyes.

12

Hyŏng-sik felt somewhat relieved when he heard what Yŏng-ch'ae said. He felt affectionate and loving towards her once more when he looked at her face again. He was sorry for having doubted her chastity. Yŏng-ch'ae was pure as jade or snow in every way. Hyŏng-sik could clearly see the image of Yŏng-ch'ae as he had known her in Anju, young and pretty. That image became one with the Yŏng-ch'ae who now sat before him telling him her life story. I will obey the wishes of the teacher to whom I owe so much, and marry Yŏng-ch'ae and happily spend my life with her, Hyŏng-sik thought. He could see the things they would do after he and Yŏng-ch'ae became husband and wife. First they would get dressed in nice clothes and stand before the pastor and exchange their vows. I will squeeze Yŏng-ch'ae's hand and look through the corner of my eye at her blushing cheeks. Then Yŏng-ch'ae will be so happy and embarrassed she will lower her head even further. That night we will lie together in the same bed, and embrace one another tightly, and talk about how we have suffered the past seven or eight years, and how we have thought about and missed one another. Yŏng-ch'ae will wet the pillow with tears of happiness as she opens her heart and expresses all the thoughts and feelings that she has been storing up inside. I will be overwhelmed with emotion, and take her in my arms, my whole body trembling, Hyŏng-sik thought. Then Yŏng-ch'ae will put her forehead on my chest, and tremble, and say, "Oh! Is this a dream?" Then I will make money writing and working as an instructor, and we will build a clean house and have fun starting a family and raising children. When I finish working and go home in the evening, Yŏng-ch'ae will be waiting for me, and come running into my arms when she sees me approach. As is the custom in the West, we will embrace and kiss each other on the lips. In awhile, we will have a son. He will have big eyes and a round face like Yŏng-ch'ae, and a strong physique like me, Hyŏng-sik thought. Then we will have a daughter. And then we will have another son. Ah, what a happy family ours will be.

However, what if Yŏng-ch'ae had not studied anything at all over the years? What if she did not have the learning to appreciate his mind and his love? She had done some studying as a child, but if she had not studied during the eight years since then, she would have forgotten everything. What if she were that ignorant? Could he have a happy family with her if she were that ignorant? Everything he had been thinking of seemed futile, and he somehow felt wistful and sad.[32] Thus, he looked at Yŏng-ch'ae's face again. Her bearing and the expression on her face did not seem to be those of a woman without education. Judging from her hands and clothes, moreover, she did not seem to have suffered hardship. She seemed to have lived in an upper-class family, and received a higher education. Otherwise, she would not have been able to bear herself with such accustomed poise, or speak with such well-mannered and practiced ease. There was a literary tone to her words, moreover, so that he could not help but think that she must have received a higher education.

Perhaps someone had helped her out and she had lived comfortably and graduated from a school somewhere, just as Hyŏng-sik himself had attained some success with the help of others. Perhaps she had lived and studied in the home of an aristocratic family or a gentleman enlightened in the ways of modern civilization, just as Yun Sun-ae lived in Elder Kim's house. Maybe she had graduated that year from a girls' high school. Wouldn't that be great, he thought. Of course, he thought. He convinced himself that this was indeed the case, and he rejoiced to himself. He wanted to hear about what had happened to Yŏng-ch'ae after that. He was sure that what she would tell him would be just what he had been thinking.

Yŏng-ch'ae ate a piece of pear that the landlady had peeled with heartfelt effort, and sighed deeply as she thought of past events. It was not that what she had spoken of thus far had not been hardship and cause for tears; but what

---

32. Whereas the word "somehow" (*ŏtchi*) is used in the 1917 *Maeil Sinbo* text, this was changed to "suddenly" (*puryŏndŭt*—now spelled *purhyŏndŭt* in standard Korean) in the 1918 Sinmungwan edition.

she was about to speak of was even sadder than what had gone before. Yŏng-ch'ae would shudder just thinking about the events from time to time, but she felt sadder and even more ashamed now that she had to tell others about what had happened. She had met many people over the past five years, and had many friends with whom she was as close as siblings. Sometimes when she and her friends were gathered together and talking about their lives, she would confide to them matters that she would not share with other people; but she had never told anyone what she was about to tell Hyŏng-sik. She knew that even if she had told someone, they just would have said that's a shame, but would not sympathize with her. Yŏng-ch'ae never told even her closest friends about her personal background, but just said that she had lost both her parents at an early age and had been raised by neighbors. She could not bring herself to talk about her father and her actual past. Thus she had kept her sad history to herself, deep within her heart. Had she never met Hyŏng-sik again, the thoughts and painful, bitter feelings that had accumulated inside of her never would have been revealed to the world.[33] There were many people in the world, but how many of them could understand the thoughts she kept deep within her heart? Sometimes when she was very distressed, she thought of seeking out the kindest of her friends and confiding everything. She thought her body would feel relieved of the weight of her sorrow. All of the people she met, though, wanted to exploit her, and catch her and devour her. The people who passed her indifferently on the street, and even people who approached her with smiling, affectionate faces and gentle words did not actually love her and take pity on her, but wanted to deceive her and seduce her to satisfy their greedy desires.

13

Yŏng-ch'ae thought she would confide all the thoughts she had been saving up within her heart, now that she had found Hyŏng-sik again—the man she had been unable to forget all her life and had thought of and longed for all this time. She was unspeakably happy that there was someone in the world who would listen to her thoughts. However, she had second thoughts. Yŏng-ch'ae could tell from the expression on Hyŏng-sik's face that Hyŏng-sik was glad to see her and took pity on her, and that he had a warm affection for her. How disappointed and sad he would be, though, if he knew that she had sold herself to become a *kisaeng*, and had been a plaything for dissolute men over the past six years. Moreover, Hyŏng-sik had a reputation for morally impeccable behavior. Wouldn't he dislike her if he knew that she had become a woman of such base status in life as that of a *kisaeng*? Now he

---

33. Part of this sentence seems to have been omitted in the 1917 *Maeil Sinbo* edition, and the sentence as such is incomplete and ungrammatical; the 1918 Sinmungwan edition completed the sentence. I have thus used the 1918 Sinmungwan edition to translate this sentence.

is weeping for me and showing affection towards me, but wouldn't he dislike me and have feelings of revulsion if he knew that I have become a *kisaeng*? Wouldn't he frown, and think "You are a vile person. You are not someone with whom I should associate." With these thoughts, Yŏng-ch'ae lost the courage to say anything more. She had felt as happy as though she had been reunited with her deceased parents and brothers. Those feelings now gave way to new sorrow and shame. Ah, he is just another stranger after all. Hyŏng-sik is just another stranger. I will not be able to put down my guard, and share all the secrets in my heart after all. Fresh tears rose in her eyes, and she lowered her head. Why did I become a *kisaeng*? she thought. Why did I become a *kisaeng* instead of becoming someone's servant? I would not be this ashamed in front of Hyŏng-sik and unable to speak my thoughts had I become a servant, or a nanny, or a seamstress. Why, oh why did I become a kisaeng? Yŏng-ch'ae had not, of course, become a *kisaeng* because she wanted to become a *kisaeng*. She had become a *kisaeng* in order to save her father and her two brothers. The first time Yŏng-ch'ae was granted an interview with her father after she arrived at the jail in P'yŏngyang, seeing her father both shocked and saddened her. Just a young child, her heart ached when she saw how her father had changed. Through a small hole in the door, her father's face could be seen wrinkled and gaunt with sunken eyes. The beard that had once been so fine to see and white as snow, was now unkempt and straggly. Most painful of all for her to see was the vile clothing stained with yellow mud. When she reached the jail door, she saw the prisoners wearing vile, mud-stained clothing, with strange straw hats, and thick chains that dragged behind them on the ground. They carried on their shoulders buckets full of something that smelled like feces. Yŏng-ch'ae's teeth chattered with fright as though she were seeing ghosts, or monsters,[34] of which she had been afraid as a child. Were those beings humans like herself? They must have committed terrible crimes. When she walked past them, those monstrous people cast strange glances at her, so that she shivered and felt afraid. Naively, however, she did not expect her own father to look like that. She thought he would be seated at a desk teaching young people and be dressed in a clean outer robe and clean Korean-style socks, just as he used to when he sat in his study in their home back in the old days. She had been through terrible suffering until she reached P'yŏngyang, but once she saw her father, she would stay at his side all her life, and run errands for him, wash and iron his clothes, and for the first time in a long time study interesting things like the *Elementary Learning, Biographies of Virtuous Women*, and the *Classic of Poetry*, just as she had done before. Father's face would always

---

34. *Ŏbwi.* This is pronounced *ebi* in standard Korean. It is childish language used to warn children. It means something frightening or monstrous. "If you cry, a monster (*ebi*) will catch you and take you away." It can be used to tell children not to touch something or eat something: "*Ebi!*"

be smiling, and there would always be a light in his eyes, his words would always be affectionate, and he would always be strong. When the prison guard took her into the meeting area after she had waited for over two hours, Yŏng-ch'ae was so happy she almost wept. Now that she was going to see her father, only happy thoughts filled her heart, and she forgot all about having been tormented by the children in that village in Sukch'ŏn, having been abducted the next day by that evil man and almost suffering a terrible disaster, and having been attacked by a miner near Sŏgamni, Sunan. When she went into the meeting room, her father would say, "Have you come to see me?" and run towards her and embrace her. When she went into the meeting room, she saw that there were thick planks on all the walls, and prison guards wearing long swords and looking at her with cold, heartless eyes walked by, their heavy footsteps echoing loudly. Her father was nowhere in sight, only a thickly bearded policeman who held some kind of rope in his hands. He was a prison guard, but Yŏng-ch'ae thought he was a policeman. "Do not cry. If you cry, I will not let you see your father," he ordered. Yŏng-ch'ae was disappointed, and felt afraid and sad. After awhile, the policeman pulled the rope he held, and a piece of wood on the plank-covered wall was raised with a clunking noise, uncovering a small, square hole where Yŏng-ch'ae's father's drastically altered face could be seen. He was visible only from the shoulders to his eyes; his head above his forehead was covered by the wall and could not be seen. Her father did not smile, but just stood still and looked out at Yŏng-ch'ae. The calm, gentle look that she used to see on his face had disappeared, and the laughter and light were gone from his eyes. Before, whenever he saw Yŏng-ch'ae, his face would become all smiles; but now his face had no expression, as though it were carved of wood. Is that my father, Yŏng-ch'ae wondered, and was so stricken with bitter grief[35] that she just stared at his face for some time. Her blood seemed to grow cold, and her limbs seemed to stiffen. In the sunken eyes on that wooden face, though, she saw tears, and only then did she realize that it was her father. "Father!" she cried. "What has happened to you?" she sobbed.

14

After meeting her father, Yŏng-ch'ae was taken by a prison guard back to the reception area. Unlike the guard holding the rope, this guard kindly tried to console Yŏng-ch'ae. He sat her down on a chair in the reception area. "Do not cry," he said in earnest. "Your father will be out of jail in no time at all." Yŏng-ch'ae was not that naive, though, and knew that he was only saying that to console her. She cried aloud for some time. Unable to keep

---

35. This sentence in the 1917 *Maeil Sinbo* edition seems to be incomplete: the 1918 Sinmungwan edition uses the words *ŏksaek hayŏ* (stricken with bitter grief), whereas the *Maeil Sinbo* edition uses the words *ŏk hayŏ*, omitting a syllable.

Yŏng-ch'ae from crying, the jailer said, "Stop crying, and go home." Then he left. "Why are you crying? Are you looking for someone who is locked up here?" asked a man next to her kindly. He had short hair, and was wearing a woolen outer robe. Yŏng-ch'ae told him that her father and brothers were in jail, that they were actually innocent of any crime, and that she had come from afar, alone, in order to see her father. Yŏng-ch'ae thought that if she told him these things, he might feel sorry for her, and help her to see her father often, and provide her with food for awhile. When the man heard what she said, he comforted her with solicitous, sympathetic words. "That's too bad! Why don't you stay at my house until your next interview with your father. Since they only grant interviews once a month, why don't you stay at my house for a month and see your father one more time before you go home," he said. Yŏng-ch'ae felt impatient when she heard that she would not be able to see her father again until a month later, but she was overwhelmed with gratitude for the man's kindness. She had thought that once she got to P'yŏngyang and saw her father, she would be able to stay with him for the rest of her life, but now that she was there she realized she could only see him once a month. She had no money, moreover, and did not know anyone in P'yŏngyang, so she would have to worry about what she was going to eat that evening and where she would sleep. Since it was past the twentieth day of the eighth month, moreover, there was a chilly wind at night, and she felt cold in just her traditional cotton summer pants and and ramie shirt. If she tried to sleep at night without anything to cover herself with, her limbs became cramped with the cold, and she could not fall asleep. She had spent the night before on the cold spot of the floor in a house just outside Ch'ilsŏng gate. She had been so cold that she could not fall asleep all night. In the morning, her stomach started to hurt, and she had diarrhea three times before she saw her father at the jail. She had no strength left in her body what with the fatigue of several days' strenuous travel and travails, and the sadness and disappointment she felt after seeing her father. She could not even think of taking another step. In the midst of her sorrows, Yŏng-ch'ae felt relieved that someone was so kindly offering to help her just then. She thought of how she had been deceived by the man with the short hair at the inn in Sukch'ŏn, though, and she wondered if this man might be like that other man. She examined his words and behavior carefully. However, unlike the man at Sukch'ŏn, this man wore nice clothes, had a dignified face, and did not seem to be a bad man. And if he does try to deceive me, she thought, all I have to do is bite his nose and run away. First she wanted to eat hot food, and sleep in a well-heated room, covering herself with a quilt. If she went to this man's house, they would give her tasty food and a quilt to cover herself with when she slept, she thought. He must be well off if he dresses like that, she thought. Yŏng-ch'ae thus did as he said, and followed him. On the way, he held her hand and kindly asked her various questions. Yŏng-ch'ae weakly answered his questions. The man lived in the city, near Namdaemun (South Gate). They reached his house just as Yŏng-ch'ae was getting so tired she thought she could not walk any further. His house was not very large, but she could see at a glance that it was clean. There was a name plate on the gate that said Kim Un-yong (Cloud Dragon Kim). Yŏng-ch'ae thought the letters were beautifully written. When they went in, she saw that the yard and the rooms were very clean and neat. A pretty young woman and a young girl were there. Yŏng-ch'ae thought the woman must be the man's wife, and the girl must be his sister. Why is the man's mother not here, she wondered. His mother must still be alive, she thought. Perhaps, like Yŏng-ch'ae's grandmother, she had gotten old and died. Everything was just as Yŏng-ch'ae had imagined it would be, so she set her mind to rest. It was even better that there was a girl who seemed to be the man's sister, and there were no other men. The members of the household all loved Yŏng-ch'ae. That evening, just as Yŏng-ch'ae had expected, she ate meat soup with delicious rice for the first time in a long time. After dinner, the man went out somewhere, and Yŏng-ch'ae and the woman and girl lit a lamp and started talking. The girl thought Yŏng-ch'ae was a boy, and did not say much, but the woman asked questions about Yŏng-ch'ae's life. The woman affectionately stroked Yŏng-ch'ae on the head, and rubbed Yŏng-ch'ae's hands. This moved Yŏng-ch'ae to tears, and she told them about her life. She told them in detail about how she had disguised herself as a boy and run away from her maternal relatives' home in order to come and see her father and brothers, and how she had gone through various ordeals on her way here. The girl's eyes grew wide, and the woman rubbed Yŏng-ch'ae's back and put her arm around her neck and cried. After hearing Yŏng-ch'ae's story, the woman wiped her eyes with her skirt sash and said, "I thought it was strange that your face looked so much like a girl's." She opened her clothes chest, and brought out a set of new clothes which she gave to Yŏng-ch'ae. Yŏng-ch'ae refused twice, but eventually put on the clothes. Then the three became even closer, and laughed and talked. The girl, who had been pretending to ignore them until then, suddenly smiled and held Yŏng-ch'ae's hand and spoke to her affectionately. Yŏng-ch'ae forgot about her father and brothers for awhile and felt as happy as though she had returned to the home she had lost. The man returned late at night, and was startled when he heard the woman tell him what Yŏng-ch'ae had said. They all laughed together. After spending a few days in this manner, Yŏng-ch'ae wished a month would pass quickly so that she could see her father again and tell him about her wonderful benefactor.

15

A month was a long time to wait. Yŏng-ch'ae began to think about her father again. She began to remember her father's frighteningly gaunt and emaciated face, his sunken eyes and his mud-stained clothes, the jailkeeper with the big beard, and the men who wore chains at their waist and carried buckets of feces. Every time Yŏng-ch'ae looked at the warm, pretty clothes she was wearing, and the delicious food she had in the morning and evening, she could see her father's pitiful image before her. She gradually lost her cheerful expression, and would not eat much. Sometimes she would sit alone and cry. The woman and girl consoled her sympathetically as always, but the solace was only for a moment; when she sat alone, she would cry. Could she not save her father and brothers somehow? Could she not help them get out of prison? Even if she could not get them out of jail, could she not get them clean clothes to wear and good food to eat? She heard that in jail the prisoners ate rice mixed with beans. Perhaps her father was so emaciated because he was not eating enough for a man his age. In old books, there was a girl who sold her body to save her parents, who had fallen into sin. I want to do the same, Yŏng-ch'ae thought. One day she told the man her intentions. The man praised her. "With money, you would be able to give your father food, and perhaps help him get out of jail." He looked at Yŏng-ch'ae's face. Yŏng-ch'ae thought about the stories of old. She remembered how her father had told her stories about women who sold themselves in order to redeem their father's sins. Though she had not been more than ten years old at the time, she had wept and thought, "I want to be like those women." "Shall I do what those women did?" thought Yŏng-ch'ae when she heard the man say that she would be able to give her father food and help him get out of jail if she had money. "But you have to have money," the man had said and smiled, looking at Yŏng-ch'ae's face. Of course! He is encouraging me to do as the women of the past did, thought Yŏng-ch'ae. Her father and brothers would get out of jail if she followed the example of women of long ago and sold her body. People would praise her as a filial daughter, and record her deed in books, just as had been done for women of long ago. And girls would read about her, and weep and praise her, as she had done when she had read such books. If she did not sell herself and save her father and brothers, though, this man and the rest of the world would scorn her as an unfilial girl. After staying at that house for awhile, moreover, Yŏng-ch'ae had learned that the woman had once been a *kisaeng*, and that the girl was studying to be a *kisaeng*. All the *kisaeng* who came to visit them were pretty and well dressed, and were good people. All *kisaeng* must be nice young women, thought Yŏng-ch'ae. They all wrote calligraphy well, moreover, and knew a lot about reading and writing, so that Yŏng-ch'ae thought all *kisaeng* were well educated. Yŏng-ch'ae thus made up her mind. "I have made up my mind," she said to the man. "I too want to be a *kisaeng*. I have studied reading and writing a little bit. I want to save my father with the money." Yŏng-ch'ae felt an inexplicable happiness and a kind of pride. "I admire your decision!" the man said, patting Yŏng-ch'ae on the back. "You are a filial daughter! I will help you do as you wish."

That was how Yŏng-ch'ae became a *kisaeng*. She had by no means become a *kisaeng* because she wanted to but because she thought she might be able to help her old father. In actuality, not only was she unable to save her father and brothers with the money for which she sold herself, but the man who had said he would help her took the money that was paid for Yŏng-ch'ae, and ran off somewhere, abandoning his wife and home. Yŏng-ch'ae's father, moreover, starved himself to death in prison after he heard that Yŏng-ch'ae had sold herself and become a *kisaeng* in order to save her father. However, she had become a *kisaeng* not because she wanted to, but only in an effort to help her aged father and her brothers.

Who would understand, though? Heaven and God knew, but what human being would understand? If I tell Hyŏng-sik what has happened, will he believe me? she thought. Might he not despise me, and think that I have become a *kisaeng* because I have been unchaste, and that I am trying to seduce him now that I am getting old and, no doubt, sick and tired of life as a *kisaeng*? I went to see my father in jail about two or three months after I became a *kisaeng*. My father lost his temper when he heard that I had become a *kisaeng*. "Foolish girl! You have ruined our glorious family reputation. Have you defiled your body already, a young girl fallen prey to someone's schemes?" He thought I had become a *kisaeng* through immoral conduct, and he ended up committing suicide. If my own father reacted that way, then how can Hyŏng-sik believe in me? That morning, when she decided to go and see Hyŏng-sik, Yŏng-ch'ae had intended to tell him all about her life since they had last seen each other. But now, with these other thoughts, she lost the resolve to tell him, and only sad and bitter thoughts came surging up in her heart. Will there never again be someone who will listen to and believe in what I have to say? she thought.

Yŏng-ch'ae sighed and wiped her eyes, then looked at Hyŏng-sik and the old woman. Hyŏng-sik was regarding her with affectionate eyes and waiting for her to talk about what happened next. The old woman rubbed Yŏng-ch'ae's back gently and blew her nose.

"What happened after you got away from that evil man?" Hyŏng-sik asked, encouraging Yŏng-ch'ae to continue her story. After awhile, Yŏng-ch'ae wiped her eyes, and stood up.[36]

"I will tell you some other day."

"Why?" asked Hyŏng-sik, trying to make her stay. She would not hear of it, though. "Where do you live?" he asked. She did not answer, but left,

---

36. The 1918 Sinmungwan edition adds the words "looked at Hyŏng-sik" (*Hyŏng-sik ŭl podŏni*): "After awhile, Yŏng-ch'ae looked at Hyŏng-sik, then wiped her eyes and stood up."

taking the girl with her. Hyŏng-sik and the old woman looked at one another and wondered why she had left.

16

Hyŏng-sik stood dumbfounded for some time after he watched Yŏng-ch'ae stop talking and suddenly get up and leave. Then he ran outside without even putting on a hat. However, he could not find Yŏng-ch'ae among the many passersby in the street. Hyŏng-sik regretted not having gone after Yŏng-ch'ae when she left. He walked up and down the street for awhile, then returned home disappointed. The old woman was still sitting in the same place crying.

Hyŏng-sik sat alone at his desk and thought about Yŏng-ch'ae. Why had she stopped in the middle of her story and left in such a hurry? Why had she stopped talking, and cried so sadly? No matter how he tried, he could not understand. Perhaps I acted displeased towards her. But no, I listened to her with only the greatest sympathy and care. When Yŏng-ch'ae looked at my face intently and I saw those clear eyes filled with tears, I felt an incredible love for her. Surely Yŏng-ch'ae must have seen this in my face. Then why did she stop talking and leave so quickly? The more I think about it, the more it seems as though there is some serious situation that she cannot tell me about. What could it be? When she came to see me, she probably wanted to tell me everything, but why did she interrupt herself and run away? The old woman had said, "She wore her hair like a student, but no matter how I looked at her, I could not help but feel that she looked like a *kisaeng*." What the old woman had said must be right, he thought. She may have come to P'yŏngyang alone, and been misled by some bad woman or man into becoming a *kisaeng*. While she was a *kisaeng* in Seoul, she must have heard that I was here, and come to see me. If that was the case, then why did she come to see me? Did she want to see me because she missed me as a childhood friend who used to play with her? When she saw me, she may have been reminded of the past, and her parents and brothers, and then cried and started telling me about her life. She may have hesitated to tell me that she had become a *kisaeng* because she was afraid that I would disapprove of her, and that was why she had abruptly stopped talking, and left. Had she indeed become a *kisaeng*? Had the daughter of Scholar Pak, to whom I owe so much, become a *kisaeng*? Scholar Pak had devoted his mind and body to serving others, and had had such passionate fervor. Had the world lured her into becoming the plaything of dissipated men? Maybe she had an appointment to meet some good-for-nothing man tonight, and had come to see me before the appointment. Perhaps she stopped by my house on her way to see that man. It seems quite likely now that I think about it. When I went out on the street, I saw a woman and a tall man walking with their arms around each other, side by side, past the Kyodong Police Station. Could that have been Yŏng-ch'ae?

Yŏng-ch'ae must be sitting in some restaurant now, holding hands with some sleazy man, accepting his embraces and embracing him in return, sharing wine from the same cup, and taking up the wanton pleasures of lewd songs and lewd words. Those eyes from which teardrops had fallen would now be casting flirtatious glances at men, and the lips that had spoken of such sorrows would now be making unspeakably obscene sounds. Perhaps at this very moment she was enjoying sordid pleasures in the arms of another man. With these thoughts, Hyŏng-sik's heart was filled with disagreeable feelings. Yŏng-ch'ae's pitiful appearance before me was just a momentary pretense. She must have been laughing at me and the old woman when we listened to her story and wept. What a disgusting woman, he thought. Ah, Yŏng-ch'ae has become a fallen woman. She has become a filthy, rotten whore. She has forgotten her parents and her brothers, given in to temptation, and gotten her body as soiled as dog feces. Scholar Pak's household has been ruined, he thought. Hyŏng-sik lifted his head and looked around the room absentmindedly. He picked up a fan from his desk, and fanned his burning face. Then he went out on the veranda and sat down. He could hear the sound of a motion picture orchestra, and the bells of rickshaw cars that were passing by on Kyodong Street. Unable to collect his scattered thoughts, Hyŏng-sik walked around the small yard for a few moments, then went to his room and lay down, still in his clothes. He closed his eyes. He could clearly see Yŏng-ch'ae crying in front of him, though. The events she had talked about appeared all around Yŏng-ch'ae, flashing by in quick succession, like images from a magic lantern[37] or a motion picture. Hyŏng-sik saw himself when he had left Pak's house for the last time, embracing Yŏng-ch'ae and saying, "I may never see you again." He saw Yŏng-ch'ae running out of her maternal relatives' home, and running away on a moonlit night, alone except for the dog that she took with her. He saw her being carried away from an inn in Sukch'ŏn by that evil man. And he saw her disguised in boy's clothes, sitting on some remote and desolate road at dawn, crying and holding the dog after it had died and collapsed on the ground. The motion picture stopped suddenly, however, and everything grew dark. Then he could see Yŏng-ch'ae sitting with a *changgo* drum[38] on her lap, entertaining some dissipated men, and singing vulgar songs with a vulgar expression on her face. He saw her asleep, sharing a pillow with another man.

He saw the married life that he had imagined for himself and Yŏng-ch'ae. He could see their wedding at a church, their happy family, their sons and daughter, as clearly as though he were looking back on an actual past.

---

37. A *hwandŭng* (magic lantern) was an early modern device that projected images, in much the same way that a slide projector does.
38. The *changgo* is a drum shaped like an hourglass, and struck on the left side of the drum with the hand, and on the right side with a stick.

"Yŏng-ch'ae has become a *kisaeng!*" he thought, and sighed and turned over in bed. He shuddered and shook his head, trying not to have these thoughts. He breathed loudly, hoping to fall asleep. Soon, though, the thoughts started bursting forth in his mind again. There leapt before his eyes the image of Yŏng-ch'ae speaking of her sorrowful life and gazing at Hyŏng-sik with tearful eyes.

17

Tears fell from Yŏng-ch'ae's eyes. Her pretty fingers trembled where they lay listlessly on her knees. Perhaps Yŏng-ch'ae had come to see Hyŏng-sik because she trusted him, and wanted to rely on his help. Perhaps when she heard that Hyŏng-sik lived in Seoul, she had come to see him in order to ask him to save her from her terrible situation. Maybe she thought that there was no one else in the entire world with whom she could talk, and no one she could trust, and no one on whom she could rely, and she had sought him out in the same way one might seek out one's parents or siblings. He could tell that Yŏng-ch'ae trusted in him and wanted his sympathy, and was asking him to take her in his arms and save her. It was obvious from the way that she had been startled and had stepped back and burst into tears when he said that he was Yi Hyŏng-sik, and from the way that she kept looking at his face while she talked about her life. Yŏng-ch'ae came to see me because she trusts me and wants to ask me to protect and help her. After having been tossed about in life's cold, painful sea of troubles for six or seven years, she had been happy and overjoyed when she heard that someone who would love her was in Seoul, and that was why she had come to see me. I have a responsibility to save her, Hyŏng-sik thought. Yŏng-ch'ae is the daughter of my benefactor and teacher, and he had given me approval to make her my wife. Even though she has momentarily fallen into dishonorable circumstances because of bad luck, I have the responsibility of saving her. I regret that I did not seek her out first, and I feel sorry towards her about that. How can I just ignore her now that she is here? I will save her. I will save her, and love her. If possible, I will make her my wife, just as I first intended. Even if she has become a *kisaeng*, she is from a *yangban* family, and received much instruction at home when she was little, so that I am sure she possesses all the lovely virtues that a woman ought to have. If she is a *kisaeng*, moreover, she must have learned much about human nature and the world, and must be good at poetry and singing. She would be the perfect woman for me, since I intend to spend my life writing, Hyŏng-sik thought, and opened his eyes. He stared vacantly through the mosquito netting over his bed, and listened to the mosquitoes buzzing outside the netting, then closed his eyes again and smiled to himself. Yŏng-ch'ae had looked beautiful today. Her complexion, her eyes and the way she looked when she was sitting there were all lovely, though Hyŏng-sik was somewhat put off by her plucked, shaped eyebrows and the smell of perfume. When she spoke, her white teeth could be glimpsed. When she sighed, she turned away for a moment and frowned ever so slightly. Hyŏng-sik had been so moved that he had not had the presence of mind to evaluate her face and manner, but now that he thought about it, Yŏng-ch'ae's every word and gesture, and even the way she tied the sash on her Korean blouse, were irresistibly lovely. Hyŏng-sik closed his eyes and smiled as he drew Yŏng-ch'ae's image once again in his mind. Even Sŏn-hyŏng, the Elder's daughter, could not compete when it came to the gentle, modest way that Yŏng-ch'ae carried herself. It was not that Sŏn-hyŏng's face and behavior were not gentle or modest, but there was less movement and vitality about her when compared with Yŏng-ch'ae. If Sŏn-hyŏng was like a seated Buddha, Yŏng-ch'ae was like a fairy dancing and singing above the clouds. Sŏn-hyŏng's face and bearing were like a painting, whereas Yŏng-ch'ae seemed to be in movement. Yŏng-ch'ae's appearance was never still, but like a thin fog that passes quickly, her face and her eyes were always full of change. This movement was unspeakably beautiful and gentle. Her voice also modulated in pitch and timbre, depending on her emotions. It was like listening to a wondrous music. Hyŏng-sik and the old woman had been moved to sorrow and tears by Yŏng-ch'ae's beautiful speaking abilities, and not just the events of her pitiful past. Hyŏng-sik forgot all the unpleasant feelings he had had towards Yŏng-ch'ae, and was dazzled by the image of her that he saw before his eyes. The Yŏng-ch'ae before him seemed to be looking at him with tears in her eyes, and saying, "Hyŏng-sik, you are the only one I can trust. Please love me." Yŏng-ch'ae, beautiful Yŏng-ch'ae, Hyŏng-sik thought. Scholar Pak's daughter. I love you, Yŏng-ch'ae. I love you this much. If he loved her like that, how her father would rejoice, where he lay at rest in the ground.[39] Later, we will have a joyful wedding in a church, and she will give birth to a son and a daughter, and we will be a happy family.

But where was Yŏng-ch'ae? Where was she now? Hyŏng-sik had unpleasant feelings again. He could see Yŏng-ch'ae joking around with another man.

"What is going on here, Yŏng-ch'ae?" he imagined himself saying and kicking Yŏng-ch'ae in the head. Then he lifted his leg and actually kicked the mosquito netting over his bed. The string from which the netting hung broke, and the netting fell on Hyŏng-sik's face. Hyŏng-sik got up, threw the netting aside and lit a cigarette. The old woman seemed to have gone to bed, and there was a cool breeze on which was wafted some indeterminate smell. Hyŏng-sik stared vacantly at the courtyard, unaware that his cigarette was

---

39. The 1918 Sinmungwan edition removed this sentence ("If he loved her . . . ") and added the following sentences: "Hyŏng-sik held out his arms as if in an embrace. Yŏng-ch'ae's warm cheek brushed against his cheek, and her breath met his lips. His heart leapt and his breathing grew louder. Yes, dear Yŏng-ch'ae is my wife, he thought."

burning up. Then he jumped out into the courtyard, as if he had thought of something. On Kyodong Street could be heard the footsteps of people returning home late at night. Stars shone in the clear summer sky. Hyŏng-sik gazed at the sky, then turned around.

"Life is strange," he said out loud to himself.

18

The next day, because he had not fallen asleep until late the night before, Hyŏng-sik did not get up until after eight o'clock. He washed his face, then ate breakfast, thinking about Yŏng-ch'ae. Just then, two of his students from the Kyŏngsŏng School came to his house. Hyŏng-sik was polite and kind to all students, so there were many students who liked him. Hyŏng-sik expressed sympathy in particular for impoverished students, remembering his own past circumstances, and there were two or three students whom he helped financially from his meager income. However, Hyŏng-sik had the habit of preferring students who were talented and well behaved. Everyone prefers people who are talented and well behaved, but most people do not let on that they feel this way. Hyŏng-sik, however, was so affectionate that he could not conceal his feelings when he particularly liked someone. "You are guilty of favoritism," one of his friends thus said to him reprimandingly.

"What is wrong with loving people who are more loveable?" Hyŏng-sik asked, smiling.

"A teacher should love all students equally."

"But what is wrong with particularly loving and teaching those who will some day grow up to be of great benefit to society?" Among colleagues and students, Hyŏng-sik thus got a reputation for favoritism. Some people who disliked Hyŏng-sik said that he only liked students with pretty faces. Some ill-natured, mischievous third- and fourth-year bullies heaped unpleasant calumny upon Hyŏng-sik's favorite students to their face, saying that Hyŏng-sik only liked students with pretty faces, and gave them extra points on tests, and taught them especially well when they asked questions. Hyŏng-sik's favorite students would defend him, but the ill-natured students would just scoff in contempt. One of the two students who had come to see Hyŏng-sik that day was a student whom he favored, a well behaved-looking student who was seventeen or eighteen years old. The tall, swarthy student who accompanied the latter was one of the students who hated Hyŏng-sik. The student who liked Hyŏng-sik was Yi Hŭi-gyŏng. He was the first-place student in the fourth-year level at the Kyŏngsŏng School. The other student was Kim Chong-nyŏl. He had barely kept from flunking out, and had moved up to the fourth-year class at the Kyŏngsŏng School along with Yi Hŭi-gyŏng. Kim Chong-nyŏl was older than most of the students and had no talent for studying, but he was good at getting things done, so that ever since the second year, he had assumed responsibility for all matters pertaining to his class, and, moreover, if he put forth an opinion, nine out of ten students in his class agreed with him. The other students did not necessarily respect or like Kim Chong-nyŏl. They rather disliked him and looked down on him because his grades were bad, he did not behave himself with propriety, had a vicious and unjust nature, and was sadistic and perverse. When it came to getting something done, though, all the students trusted in him and obeyed him without hesitation. He was of course honest. He spoke his thoughts without hesitation, and had the courage to express his opinions freely in front of any adult. In any case, he had a certain special ability. Now that he was a senior, he did not just have power over the fourth-year class, but wielded great power over all the students in the school. Even young, first-year students who had just entered the school knew his name, and bowed when they saw him. If a younger student did not bow to him, he would reprimand them immediately, with a stern voice and manner: "You, there, why don't you bow to an upper-classman?" Younger students thus politely bowed when they faced him, but stuck their tongue out and laughed when they turned their back. There was a fourth-year student named Kim Kye-do who was similar to Kim Chong-nyŏl. He was somewhat gentler and more polite than Kim Chong-nyŏl, and a bit more the kind of person one might want to befriend, but the two were the same in the way they liked to work and act like adults. They were both the same age, moreover, and had similar interests, so Kim Chong-nyŏl and Kim Kye-do became best friends. Kim Chong-nyŏl felt that the only people he could confide in and with whom he could discuss anything in the universe, were Napoleon and Kim Kye-do. He had never so much as read a biography of Napoleon, but based on what he had heard of Western history, he instantly concluded that Napoleon was such-and-such a person, and he made him the sole object of his veneration. He spoke of Napoleon when he talked with his friends, and when he gave speeches at alumni gatherings. Because he was always quoting Napoleon, the students nicknamed him "Napoleon." Since his face was swarthy, they added the adjective "swarthy" to his nickname, and called him the "swarthy Napoleon." Some smart alecks, including Yi Hŭi-gyŏng, shortened the nickname to "Swar-Na" for "Swarthy Napoleon," for the sake of convenience. Kim Chong-nyŏl knew that Napoleon was the emperor of France, but he did not know that Napoleon was originally from the Mediterranean island of Corsica. He heard from his history teacher that Napoleon was defeated at Waterloo by the English general Wellington, and died on a lonely island called Saint Helena in the Atlantic Ocean. He had forgotten words like "Waterloo" and "Saint Helena," though, which were difficult to memorize, and only remembered that Napoleon had been defeated and had died somewhere in the Atlantic Ocean. Napoleon was nevertheless the only person he worshipped. That is to say, Kim Chong-nyŏl's Napoleon was not the Napoleon who was born in Corsica and became emperor of France, but was the Napoleon that Kim had created after his own image, just as God had created Adam. This Napoleon worshiper knelt solemnly before Hyŏng-sik after greeting him, and began to speak. "The reason we have come to see you today is . . . "

19

Hyŏng-sik lit a cigarette, put it in his mouth, and greeted Kim Chong-nyŏl and Yi Hŭi-gyŏng with a smiling face. He did not know why they had come, but he knew that if Kim Chong-nyŏl and Yi Hŭi-gyŏng had come together, it must be a matter that concerned all the students, or all the fourth-year students. He knew that these two acted as student representatives for matters concerning all the students or all the fourth-year students. In terms of procedure, Yi Hŭi-gyŏng was senior class president and should have been the representative for all the students, but he was young, and did not enjoy taking action as much as Kim Chong-nyŏl, nor did he have Chong-nyŏl's skill in getting things done, so he was always subject to Kim's control. Sometimes, when there was a function for Yi Hŭi-gyŏng to attend, Kim Chong-nyŏl would go along as though unable to put his mind at rest over sending such a youngster alone. He would then speak before Hŭi-gyŏng had a chance to utter a word, so that Hŭi-gyŏng would step back and just smile as though he were only there because he had tagged along with Kim Chong-nyŏl. As Kim Chong-nyŏl encroached upon Hŭi-gyŏng's authority, at first Hŭi-gyŏng felt offended because he thought Kim was showing disrespect for his character, but as he became accustomed to Chong-nyŏl's intervention, he felt lucky that Kim was taking care of things for him, and whenever he was busy with his studies or did not feel like working, he would go to Kim Chong-nyŏl and ask him to take care of the work that he had taken on. Kim would agree immediately and set aside whatever he was doing and get involved. Yi Hŭi-gyŏng would laugh to himself every time this happened. On this particular occasion, Hyŏng-sik knew that Yi Hŭi-gyŏng was probably the official spokesperson, and Kim Chong-nyŏl was an assistant. The spokesperson, however, just sat smiling while the assistant opened his mouth and talked. It was so absurd that Hyŏng-sik laughed inside. Society could use someone like Kim Chong-nyŏl, he thought. Though a person like Kim had no particular talent, Kim was a man of action, and, if put to good use, would be effective in accomplishing a great deal of good. When Kim took on a small project, he spoke of it as though it were an important one; if he had a small success, he spoke as though it were a great one, of great benefit to society. If someone entrusted him with a task and told him that he was the only person for the job, he would go through hell or high water to take on the responsibility. Though now he thought of Yi Hŭi-gyŏng as naive and foolish, soon Hŭi-gyŏng would become someone who could order him around, and would be more respected by society than Chong-nyŏl.

Chong-nyŏl did not realize this, though, and Hyŏng-sik thought that Chong-nyŏl was happier not knowing this. Hyŏng-sik wondered what it was that the students had been discussing, for them to have sent Kim Chong-nyŏl. "Is something wrong?" Hyŏng-sik asked politely.

"There has been a controversy of the utmost significance at school." Kim Chong-nyŏl liked to use legal and political terminology concerning even trifling matters. He was extraordinarily good at memorizing legal and political terminology, though he was no good at memorizing other things, and could not even memorize the word "Bonaparte," surname of Napoleon, who was the only person whom he venerated. If he heard a legal or political term once, he always tried to use it in an actual situation. Sometimes he used these terms incorrectly, but five times out of ten he used the terms correctly. This time, when he told Hyŏng-sik that "there has been a controversy of the utmost significance," his use of terminology was correct.

"What controversy?"

"The fourth-year class intends to withdraw from school. We have joined in alliance because we are dissatisfied with the school's 'policy-rights' towards students." Chong-nyŏl gave Hyŏng-sik the petition. Chong-nyŏl had used two expressions incorrectly. The word "rights" was used ungrammatically, and the expression "we have joined in alliance" was too grandiose. Hyŏng-sik was startled, nevertheless, when he saw that over two hundred students had signed the petition; the entire document was about twelve feet long. It was indeed a "controversy of the utmost significance" after all, he thought, and the students had indeed grandiosely "joined in alliance." Kim Chong-nyŏl gave the document to Hyŏng-sik, and moved closer to Hyŏng-sik, as if to begin reciting the document out loud. Chong-nyŏl's rudeness made Hyŏng-sik uncomfortable, and Hyŏng-sik quickly put the petition on his desk and began to read it silently by himself. Chong-nyŏl made as if to move towards Hyŏng-sik's desk, but Yi Hŭi-gyŏng smiled and pulled him by the arm as if trying to tell him to sit still. "What's the matter with you?" Chong-nyŏl asked and glared at Hŭi-gyŏng, not understanding what Hŭi-gyŏng was trying to tell him. Hŭi-gyŏng's face grew red, and he turned his head and pretended to blow his nose while he laughed. Chong-nyŏl eventually went to the other side of Hyŏng-sik's desk and sat facing Hyŏng-sik. Hyŏng-sik was going to turn away from him but could not quite bring himself to do so. He gave the petition back to Chong-nyŏl.

"This is not good, Chong-nyŏl," he said. "It is wrong for students to have a 'strike' against their school, whatever the reason."

Kim Chong-nyŏl did not know exactly what "strike" meant, but he knew that the word "strike" was used in baseball, so he thought that it must mean attacking the school somehow.

He picked up the petition, and said in a somber voice, "Our school administration has reached a state of extreme corruption. Alas! The school will perish if we brave youths do not start a revolution at this time." His words indicated an unyielding determination. Hyŏng-sik realized there was nothing he could do to stop them. He turned to look at Yi Hŭi-gyŏng.

"Are you of the same opinion, Hŭi-gyŏng?"

"Yes. The third- and fourth-year classes met yesterday after school and decided to withdraw from school."

"Do you have definite evidence?"

"Yes," said Kim Chong-nyŏl, raising his voice. "Several of the students are direct witnesses." He shook his fists. "We have definite evidence. We cannot overlook the situation."

20

The dean (hakkam) at the Kyŏngsŏng School was Pae Myŏng-sik. He was also responsible for teaching geography and history. Since he drank a lot and frequented kisaeng houses, the students felt that he was unqualified to be the dean or an instructor, both of which were positions involving the education of youths. The students also said that he always ignored the opinions of the students as a whole, and made decisions about the distribution of courses in the curriculum and other matters according to his own whims. He was unfair and capricious in his decisions about disciplining and rewarding students. Dean Pae Myŏng-sik had graduated from a program of study in the geography and history department at the Tokyo School of Education. Three years ago, he had returned to Korea and, upon the invitation of Baron Kim, had obtained the important post of Dean at the Kyŏngsŏng School. While the other instructors had no legally recognized qualifications to be middle school level faculty, he prided himself on having graduated from no less than the Tokyo School of Education, and felt justified to follow his own dictates in all matters at the Kyŏngsŏng School. According to Pae, the Tokyo School of Education was the greatest school in the world, and, since he was a graduate of that school, he was therefore the greatest educator in Korea. He knew everything there was to know about education, and everything that he tried to do was in accordance with basic principles of education, and appropriate to conditions in Korea at the time. In actuality, though, he was not any better than the instructors who had not graduated from a college of education. When he had just started his job, he insisted on revising the curriculum. He doubled the number of hours spent on geography and history, saying that it was in these subjects that all of the various disciplines converged. He reduced the hours for math and natural history by twenty or thirty per cent, saying that these subjects were not that necessary for a middle school education. He said that he believed in an education centered on history and geography. He told students that history and geography were the most necessary and important subjects of all, and that history and geography instructors were therefore the most important instructors of all and had the most demanding jobs. Other instructors opposed Pae's assertions. They based their opposition on the Government General's Directives for Korean Secondary and Primary Education, and on the Japanese Middle School system. Dean Pae laughed. "Do you now know the basic principles of education?" He insisted that his theory of education was right.

"But this is how courses are distributed in the curriculum in Japanese middle schools," someone would argue back.

"Are there any great educators in Japan? Japanese education is very incomplete, I tell you." Pae thought he was the proverbial pupil who was better than his teacher. Though he had studied in Japan, he thought he had new theories and educational ideals that were better than those of all the first-rate educators in Japan. Pae's revised curriculum was eventually rejected by the department in the Ministry of Education that oversaw the Kyŏngsŏng School, and the curriculum returned to the way it had been before, so that instructors at the school laughed at Pae. They rejoiced over their victory. Pae, however, felt indignant, thinking that the world was still too simple-minded to carry out his advanced theories.

Hyŏng-sik once asked him half jokingly, "On whose theories do you base your theory? That of Pestalozzi? Ellen Key?"

Dean Pae vaguely recalled having heard of Pestalozzi and Ellen Key, but he could not remember who they were. It would be a disgrace, though, for a first-rate educator such as himself not to know some names that a third- or fourth-rate educator knew, so he laughed and said, "I have read the theories of P'usŭt'ŏl and Ŏllŭnk'ŏ. But those are all *passé*."[40] Hyŏng-sik felt pity for Pae, who was so ignorant that he forgot what he had just heard and called Pestalozzi "P'usŭt'ŏl," and Ellen Key "Ŏllŭnk'ŏ,", and still claimed that he had read their work. One had to praise Pae for having the courage to add without hesitation that "those are all outdated theories." With this thought, Hyŏng-sik laughed to himself. In reality, Pae spoke often of new theory, but he did not seem to know what theory really meant. He may have studied extensively when he was at the Tokyo School of Education; he had taken taken five years to graduate, whereas others took four years, so perhaps he had studied prodigiously and read all of the works of the "hundred philosophers"[41] of education. After he returned to Korea, though, he might glance at articles on page three of the newspaper from day to day, but Hyŏng-sik had never seen him reading, nor had he heard any rumors of him reading.

40. In the 1917 *Maeil Sinbo* text, the words for *passé*, or "out-of-date," are written in Japanese, transliterated into Korean: *jidai okure*.

41. *Cheja paekka* usually refers to the "hundred philosophers" of the Eastern Zhou period in China. Wm. Theodore de Bary, Wing-tsit Chan, and Burton Watson, comp., *Sources of Chinese Tradition* (New York and London: Columbia University Press, 1960), xx.

A teacher who worked with Hyŏng-sik at the Kyŏngsŏng School once said to Hyŏng-sik, "Pae is white paper."

"What do you mean by 'white paper'?"

"There is nothing written on it. He is ignorant."

Hyŏng-sik had laughed.

"You are wrong. He is black paper."

"Why is that?"

"White paper may have nothing written on it, but can be written on in the future. But nothing can be written on black paper." Hyŏng-sik and the other teacher laughed.

Pae liked rules and regulations. His favorite words were "regular" and "strict." He revised school regulations personally soon after he assumed his post at the Kyŏngsŏng School. He abolished existing rules, saying that they were not in accordance with basic principles of education, and he formulated over two hundred grand regulations that were based on his own new theories. One day he assembled all of the instructors at a staff meeting, and read each of the articles of the new regulations out loud himself, and explained the spirit behind each of the regulations. The meeting began at one o'clock. At four o'clock, it still was not over. Pae's forehead and nose were all sweaty, and his voice was hoarse. The staff squirmed in their seats, with sore buttocks and aching backs. Some lowered their heads and snored, only to be awakened from their deep sleep by Dean Pae's loud exclamations. The door slammed shut abruptly as one instructor left to go to the out-house; the instructor did not return to the meeting.

Hyŏng-sik could not stand any more of Pae's rules, and protested the excessive number of regulations. "Those aren't school regulations, they're laws for an entire nation." The five or six instructors who were left in the room (after those who had gone to the outhouse had left) all expressed agreement with Hyŏng-sik's words. The regulations were finalized through Dean Pae's authority. It was at this time that conflict between Pae, the faculty and students grew serious.

21

"Will it help to do what is not right, though?[42] You must exercise restraint," Hyŏng-sik said to an enraged Kim Chong-nyŏl.

"I have put up with this for three years," said Kim. He was determined to oust Dean Pae.

"Over one hundred courageous students have formed an alliance. We cannot yield a single step."

"What will you do if the Superintendent does not approve?"

42. This sentence was edited out of the 1918 Sinmungwan edition.

Kim Chong-nyŏl became somewhat subdued when he heard the word "Superintendent." He thought for awhile. "That is why we are withdrawing from school. Are there no other schools besides the Kyŏngsŏng School?" "It is wrong to withdraw from school, even if only temporarily. And wouldn't it be difficult to leave your alma mater?" "What alma mater? It was an alma mater when Teacher Pak was principal and Teacher Yun was dean, but now I have no affection whatsoever for the school. The principal knows nothing at all, and the man who is called the dean frequents *kisaeng* houses." Anger rose in Kim Chong-nyŏl's eyes.

Yi Hŭi-gyŏng poked Kim Chong-nyŏl with his elbow when Kim said "the man who is called the dean." "How can you say that?"

"Why not? What else can I call such a dean?"

"Are you going to go to the principal's home now?" Hyŏng-sik asked with a worried expression.

"Yes, we will go to the principal's home, and then at around ten o'clock, we will go to the Superintendent's house. They say the Superintendent does not wake up until around ten o'clock. Do you sympathize with us, though?"

"I am an instructor and cannot say whether or not I sympathize. Think it over, though, and do not do this." With this, Hyŏng-sik sent the two youths off. Hyŏng-sik agreed with the ousting of Pae. He had spoken to that effect several times in class, at the close of other remarks. No one among the four hundred students and dozen or so faculty liked Pae. The faculty made efforts not to talk with Pae, and the students pretended not to see him if they met him on the street. Someone using a pseudonym wrote a letter to Pae urging him to resign. Someone else wrote satirically on the blackboard during one of Pae's history or geography classes, "Pae for principal! Pae is the greatest history and geography teacher in the world!" And the words "Dean Pae's restaurant" written in pencil on the outhouse were probably written in anger by some first- or second-year students to whom Pae had said reprimandingly, "You call yourself a human being?" All the teachers had nicknames, but Pae had the most. The other teachers were given nicknames for fun, but Pae was given nicknames out of hatred and resentment. The younger students were unable to reply immediately when they were scolded harshly by a red-faced Pae who shouted, "You call yourself a human being?!" Once they stepped outside of his office, though, they would vent their anger by sticking their tongue out and calling him a new nickname, invented especially for the occasion, several times. The younger students used his nicknames as a kind of medicine for venting their anger at him. When a group of students had been reprimanded by Pae with the words, "You call yourself a human being?" they would gather afterwards and call him by all of his nicknames, as though they were monks assembled at a temple in the morning, reciting incantations. After having vented their anger by fervidly calling him names for awhile, they would then cry out, "Hurrah!" Then they would call him by the nickname that best fitted the situation, and everyone would applaud. The three most popular nicknames for Bae were "lioness," "fox" and "dog." "Lioness" referred to Pae's ferocity. "Fox" referred to his cunning. "Dog," however, had a more complex meaning. It referred to the way Pae licked the feet of the Superintendent, Baron Kim, and ate his crap, and acted as a German-style sleuthing dog. He was ferocious towards those who were below him in rank. Towards those who were one level his superior, however, he would prostrate himself on the ground, like a dog that wags its tail and licks the heels of the owner who has fed it for some time. When he saw someone who was the slightest bit his subordinate, he would draw himself upright, and his tongue would crawl back inside his mouth. In front of someone who was a level of authority above him, though, the muscles of his tongue, neck and waist would be unloosened, and he would bow and scrape, and use all kinds of honorific language. Impressively enough, he thus obtained the trust of Baron Kim, and he became the Baron's only youthful friend. Thus, although Pae had a very bad reputation among teachers and students, he was esteemed among persons of the so-called elite class, beginning with Baron Kim. Therefore no matter how his colleagues or students might agitate against him, Pae's position was as secure as a foundation stone. If any colleague disobeyed Pae, or criticized him, or if Pae just disliked someone for no reason, Pae would speak to the Superintendent, and within several days an order would be issued for that person's dismissal. Pae drove out former principal Pak and former dean Yun, the two teachers Kim Chong-nyŏl admired so much, and appointed as principal a foolish old man who could not tell the difference between beans and barley. Pae himself assumed the important position of dean. He thus came to have his way in all affairs within the school. Any teachers who had the slightest devotion to education thus fled the school, and there remained only those who had nowhere else to go or those who did not mind putting up with Pae's control, so that the school gradually fell into disarray. Pae did not subject Hyŏng-sik to much contempt, simply because Hyŏng-sik had studied in Tokyo. Hyŏng-sik stayed at the school because he thought that if he left, the school would decline even further.

The entire school denounced Pae, and moreover, the present uproar had resulted when it was discovered that Pae had lately taken to visiting *kisaeng* houses near Kurigae in Tadong as if to assuage some anxiety that he had.

"I cannot just stand to the side and watch!" Hyŏng-sik thought, and went to school immediately.

22

I must see to it that this matter is resolved without incident, Hyŏng-sik thought as he went to school. Since Dean Pae is the cause of the controversy,

I will meet with him and let him know what is going on, and then advise him to observe discretion and restraint in his behavior. Pae had always resented the fact that Hyŏng-sik had not joined his side, so outwardly he pretended to be close to Hyŏng-sik and to respect him, but inwardly he thought of Hyŏng-sik as dirt in his eyelid,[43] and he vowed to drive Hyŏng-sik out of the school. Hyŏng-sik was aware of this, but he nevertheless felt that he ought to exert his efforts because he loved the school, and for the sake of Pae Myŏng-sik, since they had been friends for the past five years, regardless of whether or not Pae's behavior was that befitting the name "human."

When Hyŏng-sik entered the school gate, some first- and second-year students were playing with a ball. They gathered around Hyŏng-sik and asked, "Is school cancelled today? Can we take the day off too?" They said the third- and fourth-year students were taking the day off, so they wanted to do the same. Hyŏng-sik went into the school office. Dean Pae seemed to be angry, for his sharp-looking face seemed even sharper, and he seemed not to notice when Hyŏng-sik walked in the office. Hyŏng-sik did not greet Pae, but greeted only the teachers who were sitting beside Pae. The teachers each had a box of chalk and some textbooks in front of them, but they had no intention of going to class, even though it was over ten minutes past nine. Hyŏng-sik knew that there had been a disturbance, but he pretended not to know. "It's time to begin. Why aren't you going to class?" he asked.

"None of the third- or fourth-year students showed up to class," said one instructor. They all looked at the dean.

Hyŏng-sik looked intently at Pae, then went and stood near him. "Superintendent Pae, something has happened here at school," he said.

"I don't know anything about it," said Pae, and averted his face.

"Shouldn't you think of a plan? How can you just sit there?" Hyŏng-sik said, lowering his voice.

"What's going on? Why aren't these miscreants—the third- and fourth-year laggards—coming to school?"

You haven't heard yet, Hyŏng-sik thought to himself. He hesitated, wondering whether or not he should tell Pae that the third- and fourth-year students had formed an alliance to withdraw from school. He thought it would be wrong of him, though, to say nothing when he already knew.

"Don't you know?"

"What?"

"The third- and fourth-year students have decided to form an alliance to withdraw from school, and they have presented a petition to the principal and the Superintendent stating the reasons for their withdrawal."

"What? Withdraw from school?" Even Pae seemed somewhat startled by the news. His version of education based on "new theories" had failed.

---

43. In the 1918 Sinmungwan edition, this was revised to "a nail in his eye" (*nun sok ŭi mot*).

Nearby instructors were also taken aback, and left their desks to gather around Pae. "How did you find out?" Pae asked, taken aback. "Some students just came to see me with a petition. They said they were on their way to the principal's house." Hyŏng-sik winced and was a little bit surprised after he said these words. I should not have spoken, he thought. Pae glared at Hyŏng-sik with eyes full of venom, and sprang to his feet. "You have done well. You have ruined the school, inciting innocent students!" Pae had always known that students respected Hyŏng-sik more than him, and that many students visited Hyŏng-sik, while none visited Pae. This made Pae jealous. He thought that the students liked Hyŏng-sik not because Hyŏng-sik had more integrity and was more affectionate than Pae, but because Hyŏng-sik must be using some means to lure them, and that the students were misled by Hyŏng-sik into liking him. Hyŏng-sik is ruining the students, Pae thought to himself, and he could not overcome his feelings of loathing when he saw students speaking politely and respectfully to Hyŏng-sik. Pae thought the students ought to respect himself, not Hyŏng-sik. The only reason they respected Hyŏng-sik and not himself was that they were foolish, he thought. When Pae saw that students were beginning to denounce him more and more, he thought this was because Hyŏng-sik was inciting naive students, and deliberately trying to oust Pae. Hyŏng-sik is making students denounce me so that he can be dean, Pae had once told someone. When Pae heard Hyŏng-sik say that some students had visited his home with a petition, Pae was sure that the whole matter was Hyŏng-sik's doing. "Well done, Mr. Yi," Pae said, clenching his fists.

Hyŏng-sik felt offended that his good intentions had been misunderstood. "You are judging others in terms of your own deceitful mind," he said angrily. "I mentioned this to you only because I wanted this matter to be resolved harmoniously and in the best interests of yourself and the school. But now you are accusing me of . . . "

Before Hyŏng-sik could finish speaking, Pae's face flushed even redder, and he stepped up to Hyŏng-sik and said, "You listen to me, Yi Hyŏng-sik. I've known all along about your tricks and schemes, and I just kept quiet. Students have rebelled against the school four or five times, and I know it was all your doing. Do you mean to destroy this school?" He emphasized the word "destroy," and pounded the desk with his fist.

Hyŏng-sik was at a loss for words, and laughed. "Pae Myŏng-sik. I thought you were a human being." Hyŏng-sik lost his temper, and his voice shook with anger. "You are incapable of recognizing the good intentions of a friend. Do you realize how often I have tried to mediate between the students and faculty on your behalf, and tried to defend you?"

"'Defend' me! That's what you say, but you made the students rebel against the school. We'll see how powerful you are." Pae took up his hat and left the room without taking his leave. "I'll bet he's going to the residence of-His Lordship,[44] the Superintendent again," said the teachers left standing in the room. They laughed. Hyŏng-sik paced back and forth, unable to contain his anger.

23

"I guess Hyŏng-sik too will be kicked out of the school now," thought the teachers.

One of the teachers looked at Hyŏng-sik pacing back and forth, and asked, "Why are the students withdrawing from school this time?"

Hyŏng-sik looked at the yard outside for awhile, and did not let on that he heard the question, as though he did not want to answer. Then he sat down at his desk all of a sudden, opened the drawer, and started pulling out various books and scraps of paper. "Why are the students withdrawing from school? It is because of you-know-what."

"One need not ask to know. It must be Dean Pae's affair with Wŏr-hyang," said another instructor. "That is it, right?" the instructor asked, looking at Hyŏng-sik as if seeking confirmation. Hyŏng-sik tore up some of the papers that he had taken out from the desk drawer, and folded up some of them after reading them.

"Pae's affair with Wŏr-hyang?" asked a third instructor.

"You did not know? It is quite a well-known affair. A *kisaeng* named Wŏr-hyang has become very famous in the 'world of flowers and willows'[45] recently. She is said to have arrived from P'yŏngyang two months ago. They say that she is pretty, articulate, and plays the *kŏmun'go* and sings the 'Susimga' (Song of Sorrow) beautifully. Perhaps that is why all of the pleasure-loving connoisseurs in the capital are jumping at her with their mouths drooling. There is one strange thing about her, though. It seems that no one has been able to make a conquest of her yet."

"A conquest?" asked an honest-looking teacher who seemed intoxicated by such talk.

The man laughed. "You are indeed a gentleman of morals. Many men have been trying frantically to make Wŏr-hyang their own. They say that she teases men unbearably by pretending to be half-listening to their pleas, but just when a man thinks he has won her over, she will abruptly say, 'I cannot do it.' She therefore has a reputation of being a woman who is impossible to understand."

"Why is she like that?" asked the honest-looking teacher.

"How would I know? That is just what others say!"

44. The Superintendent is a Baron, a title of nobility given by the Japanese colonial government to collaborators.
45. The "world of flowers and willows" means the world of *kisaeng*.

"It seems that you too have been rejected by her several times!" said a teacher with a Kaiser mustache. "Was it painful?" The teacher with the Kaiser mustache laughed.

"What? A man like me has nothing to do with the extravagant 'world of flowers and willows.' I'm clean." The man laughed.

"You never know," said another teacher. Several people laughed.

The honest-looking teacher laughed too, but kept asking questions, like a student questioning a teacher, as though he wanted to know more.

"And? How have things turned out?"

The teacher with the Kaiser mustache hit the honest-looking teacher on the shoulder. "You too are not indifferent when it comes to a beautiful woman!" he said, and laughed. The honest-looking teacher's face reddened. The teacher who had been talking about Wŏr-hyang lit a cigarette and continued.

"Dean Pae has become a prisoner of Wŏr-hyang. He has apparently propositioned her about a dozen times. But no matter how much he begs her, will she listen? She says no to him, and then seems to be listening to him. Then she kicks him away. Now Pae has a fever. Didn't he come to school in a bad mood today? (Here, the instructor winced.) That is a sign that he got kicked away again by Wŏr-hyang last night."

"Of course! Of course! I wondered why his expression was even more dour lately. But of course, it is because of that woman, right?" The teacher with the Kaiser mustache laughed. The honest-looking teacher wanted to ask more questions, but he stayed quiet because he was afraid others would laugh at him.

A teacher who had been listening quietly and smiling said, "Did the students know about this? Is this the reason the students are withdrawing from school?"

"I do not know," said the teacher, and looked at Hyŏng-sik as if to say "only you would know about that." Hyŏng-sik listened to the teachers' conversation as he went on pretending to examine pieces of paper. He wondered if Wŏr-hyang might not be Pak Yŏng-ch'ae. Noticing that Hyŏng-sik was quiet, the teacher who had been speaking continued. "I do not know the details, but that is probably the reason." The teacher who had been talking about Wŏr-hyang felt discomfited by Hyŏng-sik's silence, and stopped talking and just wrote letters in the air with his cigarette smoke.

"How could the students have known?" asked the honest-looking teacher, as though he could not keep from asking.

"How could the students not know?" said the teacher with the Kaiser mustache. "Don't you know how much they spy on teachers? They even know when a teacher has gone to the bathroom. They pretend to be docile and naive, but I hear they have their own police headquarters and their own detectives. A student must have observed the dean going into Wŏr-hyang's house."

"Caught at the scene of the crime!" said one teacher, laughing.

"Here is what happened," said the teacher with the Kaiser mustache. He had been drawing letters in the air with cigarette smoke, and listening to the teachers talk. As if unable to hold himself back any longer, he put his cigarette out in an ashtray and began to speak again. "It seems that the dean could not stand it any more, and decided to buy her and make her his own. He has many rivals, though. If A bids three hundred wŏn, then B bids four hundred wŏn, and C bids five hundred wŏn. The bidding has apparently gone up to one thousand wŏn. Even if the dean sold his house, it would only amount to about three hundred wŏn. He cannot compete financially. He therefore goes and prays to Wŏr-hyang every night, trying to win her over with his reputation and devotion. A mischievous student must have followed him last night." The teacher laughed. The other teachers looked at him with rapt attention, as though fascinated. They tried to imagine what would happen with the dean and Wŏr-hyang.

Hyŏng-sik stopped sorting through the scraps of paper spread out on his desk, and seemed to be thinking about something. As if some thought had occurred to him, he hurriedly put the scraps of paper back into his desk drawer, bid his colleagues good day, and left the room. They all watched Hyŏng-sik leave, then looked at their watches and yawned.

24

Hyŏng-sik walked out of the school gates and went home. Is Wŏr-hyang Pak Yŏng-ch'ae? he thought as he walked home. They say she is a *kisaeng* from P'yŏngyang, and that she is pretty, and that no one has ever slept with her. Could she indeed be Yŏng-ch'ae? Had Yŏng-ch'ae become a *kisaeng* named Wŏr-hyang, and come to Seoul two or three months ago and become famous in the world of *kisaeng*? They say that no one has ever slept with her. Is she is trying to stay chaste because of me? he thought.[46] Yes, that's it. She is keeping herself chaste because of me. Flamboyant, extravagant men were trying to make her their possession, though, because she would not let them have their way! And men like Dean Pae too were trying to make her their own! What would become of Yŏng-ch'ae's life if the unthinkable happened and she became the possession of a beastlike man such as Pae Myŏng-sik? Would such a man have any compassion? Pae was only temporarily infatuated, and wanted to make Yŏng-ch'ae his plaything in order to satisfy his sordid lust. Pae's wife had grown old waiting for him for about eight years while he was in Tokyo. When he returned from Tokyo three years ago,

---

46. A few words seem to have been omitted from this sentence in the 1917 *Maeil Sinbo* text; I have thus translated the sentence as written in the 1918 Sinmungwan edition.

he falsely accused her of adultery, and divorced her. Last year, he married a student. Now, less than a year after he had married, he was already trying to get his hands on another woman. How could Yŏng-ch'ae become the concubine of such a heartless scoundrel? Yŏng-ch'ae, the daughter of my benefactor! It must not happen. No. Four or five men were competing to make Yŏng-ch'ae their possession, and Pae Myŏng-sik was visiting her almost every night. How she must be suffering in the midst of those beastlike men who knew nothing but lust. Perhaps Yŏng-ch'ae had sought me out yesterday because she could not bear such suffering, and wanted to seek my help. Perhaps upon coming to my home, she had stopping talking and left because she had seen how wretched my clothes and dwelling were and had realized that it would be useless to ask me to help her. Hyŏng-sik felt even sadder and more ashamed of his poverty. Indeed, Hyŏng-sik really wasn't qualified to help her. If the *kisaeng* Wŏr-hyang were indeed Yŏng-ch'ae, Hyŏng-sik definitely did not have the means to save her. Hyŏng-sik sighed when he thought of how one of the teachers had said that "the bidding has apparently gone up to one thousand wŏn." A thousand wŏn! I must have one thousand wŏn if I want to save Yŏng-ch'ae—save her from those beastlike men and give her a life of human dignity. But do I have one thousand wŏn? Hyŏng-sik thought about his personal wealth. Hyŏng-sik's personal wealth consisted of nothing but the worn out wallet in his waistcoat vest. Even if one were to fill it with ten wŏn notes, it would barely contain three hundred wŏn. Hyŏng-sik's wallet had never even once contained a one hundred wŏn note. Once, when he graduated from school in Tokyo and was returning to Korea, he had put in his wallet eighty wŏn that a friend had given him for clothing and travel as a gesture of friendship. That was the first time Hyong-sik had ever had that much money. It had been four or five years since Hyŏng-sik had returned to Korea from Tokyo. Had he saved ten wŏn a month, he would have accumulated five or six hundred wŏn by now. Hyŏng-sik had thought of his present situation, however, as a provisional and preparatory one, not his true life, and whatever money he had left over, he would give to indigent students, without so much as a thought of saving any money from his trifling salary. He had a habit of buying books, though, and every month on payday he would go to Irhan bookstore or a bookstore such as Tokyo Maruzen, and spend five wŏn. His only pastime was watching gold-lettered books fill up his bookshelves. While others went to *kisaeng* houses and drank and played *paduk*,[47] Hyŏng-sik's only diversion was reading new books that he had just bought. He was thus praised by his colleagues as a diligent reader, and another reason that students respected him was that his shelves were filled with books with gold-lettered titles in English and German that they themselves could not read. He was always saying that the only way for

---

47. *Paduk* is the Korean name for go, a board game played with black and white stones.

Koreans to survive would be to bring the Korean people to the same level of civilization as that of all of the most civilized peoples in the world—that is, the same level of civilization as that of the Japanese people.[48] In order to do so, there needed to be many people in Korea who studied ambitiously. He thought that since he was aware of this need, his responsibility was therefore to study as much as possible, and thoroughly understand the civilizations of the world, and propagate civilization among the Korean people. This was why he did not spare any money buying books, and loved talented students and tried as much as he could to help them.

What would he do about the "thousand wŏn," though? he thought with pain in his heart. Of his last month's pay of thirty-five wŏn, he had sent five wŏn to a Tokyo bookstore for the collected works of Plato; ten wŏn he had divided up among several students; and he had given eight wŏn to the landlady for his meals. All that was left in his wallet was a five wŏn note and some silver coins. What shall I do about the thousand wŏn? he thought, and felt even more miserable. "Where can I get one thousand wŏn?" he exclaimed out loud, wiping the sweat from his face with a handkerchief. When he eventually reached his lodgings in Kyodong, three young men, each in a rickshaw, raced past him towards Ch'ŏlmulgyo, bells ringing. Each man was dressed in a flashy new Western suit, and leaned back in his rickshaw half-drunk, with a *kisaeng* in another rickshaw in front of him. Hyŏng-sik jumped out of the way and stood watching the six rickshaws race away in clouds of dust. There are people who have a thousand wŏn! he thought. Actually, the young men in the rickshaws with the *kisaeng* in front of them had access to not just a thousand wŏn, but to ten thousand wŏn. Hyŏng-sik stood there for a few moments. Deep in thought, he went into his lodgings, where not a breeze moved the air.

25

When he went in, the old woman was making lunch, and came out of the kitchen.

"Why are you home early? Is there no school today?" she asked.

Hyŏng-sik removed his hat and Korean-style outer coat, and tossed them into his room. Then he sat at the edge of the veranda, loosened the sash on his Korean-style shirt, and fanned himself.

"The third- and fourth-year students say that they have formed an alliance to withdraw from school," he said with exasperation.

48. The 1917 *Maeil Sinbo* text uses the words *uri naeji minjok*, or "the people of our inner land" to refer to Japan here. Japanese imperialist propaganda referred to Japan as *naichi*, or "inner land" (pronounced *naeji* in Korean) and Japanese colonies as *gaichi*, or "outer land." The 1918 Sinmungwan edition changed this reference to Japan to *Ilbon minjok*, "the Japanese people."

"Again? That Dean Pae, or whatever his name is, must have gone and done something again." She wiped the sweat from her face with her skirt, and looked at Hyŏng-sik's face. "What is the matter? Are you ill?"

"No."

"You seem worried about something. Please leave that school. There are constant disturbances at that school. Every time there is a commotion, you worry. Why do you stay there?" She sat in the shade of the veranda outside the *kŏnnŏnpang*, and smoked. Hyŏng-sik fanned himself for a few moments as though unable to overcome his anger.

"School is the same as always. I am not worried about that."

"Then is there something else that you are worried about?"

Hyŏng-sik sprawled out on the floor and shook his legs.

"I must have money," he said to himself.

The landlady laughed. "You have finally realized that. They say this is a world of money. I would not have to struggle like this if I had money."

"That kind of struggle is happiness."

"Ha! It may seem that way to other people. I am already sixty years old. Whenever I do anything, my back hurts, and the more my back hurts the more I suffer. Is there anyone to console me? Do I have so much as a son, even a son with a disability?[49] Why should a thing like me go on living? I am only alive because the life in me is tough and refuses to die." She struck her pipe against a stone so forcefully that it seemed as though the pipe would break, and shook the ashes from the bowl of the pipe. Then she filled her pipe again, and placed it against the ashes she had just emptied out, and took two deep puffs. "I cannot even light my pipe," she said in a burst of anger, and threw the pipe in her room. Then she went back to the kitchen to finish making lunch.

Hyŏng-sik laughed to himself when he heard what the old woman said and saw her actions. Everyone has their own worries, and everyone thinks their worries are the biggest worries in the world, he thought. Everyone had such anxieties, though. There were many different kinds of anxieties: anxiety because one had no son; anxiety because one could not hold office; anxiety because one could not get a wife; anxiety because one could not get a husband. Most of the worries of modern day people, however, had to do with not having money. It was no surprise that people valued money in a world in which one could purchase someone's body and even their soul if one had the money, thought Hyŏng-sik. Ah! One thousand wŏn! Where can I get one thousand wŏn? Hyŏng-sik stood up, went into his room, and sat down. Would this house be worth a thousand wŏn? he wondered. Would the hundred or so volumes of books, bound in Western-style binding, with

---

49. This sentence was not in the 1917 *Maeil Sinbo* text, and was added in the 1918 Sinmungwan edition.

leather or faux leather covers, on his shelves be worth a thousand wŏn? The author's rights for each book would be worth over one thousand wŏn. He would be able to make a thousand wŏn if he wrote such a book and sold it to a publisher. First, however, he would have to study writing in English. After that, it would take time for him to write. Then he would have to send the manuscript to the United States or England. Then the owner of a book company in the United States or England would have to read the manuscript and decide to publish the book at their company. Then the owner would send someone to the post office to send a bill of exchange for one thousand wŏn to Yi Hyŏng-sik. By the time the bill of exchange had crossed the Pacific Ocean by boat and arrived at the Kyŏngsŏng post office, it would be too late. When would he be able to make all of that come to pass?

It occurred to him that if he had not bought books and had not given money to students over the past five years, he would have saved twenty wŏn each month, or one thousand wŏn over fifty months. If only he had done that, he would not be worried now. It had been wasteful to give money to students. I gave them money with all my heart when I did not even have enough for myself, he thought, but the students seemed to feel entitled to the money, and even complained if the money was late. They were not the least bit grateful. His helping the students might prove to be meaningful if they grew up to be great people; but for now, they had no particularly outstanding genius or character. Helping them financially had been futile. If only he had saved the money, he would not be worried now. From this month on, I should refuse to give any more money to the students I have been helping out, he thought. Hyŏng-sik changed his mind, though, when the image came to his mind of those pitiful students calling out to him "Teacher!"

Ah, where could he get one thousand wŏn? What if someone went and purchased Yŏng-ch'ae with one thousand wŏn that very night? Maybe someone had already purchased her the night before, and taken her to his home. Then she would have given the chaste body she had protected for nineteen years, to some filthy, beastlike man last night. At first, she would have resisted, pushing the man away and crying and screaming, and then, finally, she would have yielded. Hyŏng-sik could see the beastlike man attacking poor, lovely Yŏng-ch'ae, the man's eyes red with lust. He could see Yŏng-ch'ae resisting him, crying and pushing him away, then finally collapsing with a sob, as if in despair. Hyŏng-sik's body grew rigid with outrage and sorrow, and he heaved a long sigh. Perhaps Yŏng-ch'ae had run away at night, knowing that she had been sold to someone. Where would she go? That pretty face! That lovely young nineteen-year-old girl who had no one to protect her! Everywhere she went there would be beastlike men with "one thousand wŏn." Would Yŏng-ch'ae run away?

Of course she would! Yŏng-ch'ae was fiercely chaste. She was so resolute that if she found out she had been sold to some man, she might even commit suicide. Suicide! Hyŏng-sik trembled at the thought.

26

What should I do? he thought. How can I get one thousand wŏn and save poor Yŏng-ch'ae—beloved Yŏng-ch'ae—the daughter of my benefactor? Shall I do this? Shall I do that? Still unable to reach a decision, he left for Elder Kim's house at one o'clock to teach English to Sŏn-hyŏng and Sun-ae. The Elder's wife came out and greeted Hyŏng-sik. The Elder had gone out somewhere and was not home. When the Elder's wife went to get Sŏn-hyŏng and Sun-ae, Hyŏng-sik sat alone in a corner room, which they used as their classroom, and waited for the two students. On one side of the room was a portrait of Christ on the crucifix. On the other side of the room was a photograph of Elder Kim. The flowers decorating the two pictures seemed to be the work of Sŏn-hyŏng and Sun-ae. The crucified Christ wore a crown of thorns, and blood flowed from his side, which had been pierced by a Roman soldier's spear. Christ's head leaned to the left, and his eyes were directed towards the sky. At the foot of the cross the painting depicted a person covering their face with the hem of their robe and weeping, someone looking on the scene indifferently, and, to one side of the cross, soldiers drawing lots for Jesus' clothes. Hyŏng-sik stared at the painting. The man on the cross was a human being. The men who put a crown of thorns on Christ's head and stabbed him in the side were human beings. The person beneath the cross wiping their tears with the hem of their robe, the person who looked upon the scene indifferently, the men who had killed a man and now drew lots for the dead man's clothes—all of these people were human beings. All of the comedies and tragedies that took place in the world of human life every hour of every day involved human beings. The students who were withdrawing from school and petitioning for Dean Pae's resignation, and the object of their attacks, Pae himself, were all human beings. I myself am a human being, for that matter, Hyŏng-sik thought. Poor Yŏng-ch'ae, the greedy old woman who tried to sell Yŏng-ch'ae, the beastly men who were trying to buy Yŏng-ch'ae, and I myself, who sorrow over Yŏng-ch'ae—all of us alike are human beings. It is only small differences in color and form that set us apart as "you" and "me," "wrong" and "right." Jesus could be the Roman soldiers who pierced his side, and the Roman soldiers could be Jesus. As though making a Korean singer of tales become characters such as Ch'un-hyang and Master Yi, some power inexplicably made someone to be Jesus, and others to be the Roman soldiers who pierced Jesus' side, and another to be someone who just watched indifferently. In light of this, all human beings seemed to Hyŏng-sik to be his brethren, and similar to himself. He felt sorry for them, moreover, since they could not help giving rise to tragedies and comedies that they had not intended, shackled by some unknown power. The evil actions of human beings were like the doings of a Korean singer of tales who played the part of the newly appointed prefect of Namwŏn and flogged the pitiful Ch'un-hyang. One could not help but forgive human beings for their actions. Pae could therefore not be hated all that much. The treacherous Jewish man who spat on Jesus' face and asked that Jesus be killed was not that hateful either.

He had to save Yŏng-ch'ae, though. He had to save her, even if this was only an incident in a play. This thought came to him out of the blue, and Hyŏng-sik looked away from the portrait of Jesus, and looked vacantly at the ceiling. There were four or five flies on the ceiling. Just as though they too were in a drama that was like that of human life, one of them chased another while the latter fled, one sat, and one rubbed its front feet together. Hyŏng-sik bowed his head and thought, This household would have one thousand wŏn.

"Teacher!"

Hyŏng-sik looked up. Sŏn-hyŏng and Sun-ae stood at the door holding books and pencils, and politely greeted him when he lifted his head and looked at them. Startled, Hyŏng-sik quickly stood up and greeted them in return.

He smiled and said cheerfully, "It is hotter today than it was yesterday." He motioned for Sŏn-hyŏng and Sun-ae to sit down, and sat across from them with a desk between himself and the two students. The two young women lowered their heads and opened their books. The agitated thoughts he had been having disappeared, and he felt somewhat mentally exhausted. As Sŏn-hyŏng and Sun-ae sat with their heads lowered, Hyŏng-sik looked at their black hair and the broad, jade-colored ribbons[50] on their Western-style chignons. He looked at their fingers on the desk. When a gentle breeze passed, a fragrance was lifted from the two young women's bodies and hair. The back of Sŏn-hyŏng's Korean blouse of ramie was wet with sweat, and adhered to the white skin of her back; whenever she moved, the area of her blouse that adhered to her skin grew larger or smaller. Sun-ae squirmed at her seat twice, pulling at her skirt in order to cover her feet. Beads of sweat formed on Sŏn-hyŏng's forehead, and she wiped her forehead from time to time with the hem of her skirt and fanned herself with her hand from beneath the desk. Hyŏng-sik felt a fragrant, cool breeze enter his heart, which had been full of pain and sadness all morning. Women were beautiful creatures, he thought. The roundness of their shoulders, the blush of their cheeks, their long, black hair, the way they sat, the way they tied the sash on their Korean blouse. Especially refined was the way the neck of the Korean blouse gradually narrowed, and was tied tightly at the center with a sash, the tip of

---

50. The text uses the foreign loan word "ribbon," transliterated in Korean as *ribon* in the 1917 *Maeil Sinbo* edition, and as *ribong* in the 1918 Sinmungwan edition.

the bow slanting towards the left breast and the length of the sash flowing past the sleeve, which was loose and full at the elbow. As he sat and watched the two young women, an indescribable, fragrant pleasure filled his body, and his blood seemed to circulate through his body smoothly and exhilaratingly. Life could be joyful if one wished it to be. If people sat facing each other without any objectives or schemes, then life could be loving and joyful. Intimacy, warm love and sweet pleasure could arise when women and men, or indeed any of the beings of the universe, just quietly beheld one another. The useless exercise of knowledge, moving one's mouth in speech, and motioning with one's hands only shattered this beautiful pleasure just when it had finally come into being. With these thoughts, Hyŏng-sik sat and watched the two young women recite the English alphabet.

27

Sŏn-hyŏng and Sun-ae did well at reciting and writing the English alphabet and memorizing it. They had practiced reading and writing the alphabet all day the previous day, and all morning today without stopping to rest. Sŏn-hyŏng did so with the thought of going to the United States. Sun-ae did so because she wanted to learn as much as the next person. They also felt a kind of exhilarating pride because their learning English for the first time seemed to be a sign that their scholarly knowledge had been significantly elevated. Sŏn-hyŏng imagined herself going to the United States dressed in a nice Western suit and a Western hat with a feather on it. She imagined herself speaking freely in English with young Western women similar to herself. Sŏn-hyŏng smiled to herself. If she learned English well, it would add to her accomplishments and qualifications, and others would love and respect her even more. After she graduated from an American college in the United States like young American women, and returned home, she was sure someone would accompany her.[51] That someone would be a man, a tall, good-looking man, a graduate of an American college. Sŏn-hyŏng had never met such a man, nor had she ever heard of such a man, but she nevertheless believed that after she graduated from college in the United States and returned to Korea, such a man would certainly become her companion. They would be standing on the deck of a ship on the Pacific Ocean, facing away from each other, and watching the sea. What would she do when the boat shook and she fell against his chest? That would be how they met. After she returned to Korea, she would probably start a loving family with that man. They would live in a two-story, brick house, and she would play the piano . . .

---

51. The words *tonghaeng hanŭn saram*, or "fellow traveler," are used here. Was this a Marxist allusion? A fellow traveler, in leftist thought, was someone sympathetic to Marxism. I would like to thank Professor Chŏng Sun-jin for explaining the concept of "fellow traveler" to me and my advanced Korean class at the University of Washington.

These were Sŏn-hyŏng's dreams as she began to study English. She had never been struck by Cupid's arrow. She had never thought much about life, and had never thought about woman and man. She thought the entire world would be like her family, and all people would be like herself. Actually, it would be more accurate to say that she had never even thought about whether the world was similar to or different from her family, or whether or not people were similar to or different from herself. If one were to liken her to a flower that has bloomed on a warm spring morning, she was a fresh flower that knew nothing yet of wind or rain, or old age, or fading and withering. No one had told her that there were such things as wind and rain, or that if the wind and rain came together, a freshly blossomed flower could fall, or that even a flower bud that had not completely blossomed could fall. She memorized lines from the Bible. She only knew them by rote, though. She believed that God made Adam and Eve, and she memorized word-for-word the passages about how all evils such as old age and death entered the world because Eve was seduced by the serpent into plucking and eating the forbidden fruit of knowledge. She memorized words about heaven and hell, and Jesus on the cross, exactly as they were written in the Bible. She knew what she read every day on the third page of the newspaper—reports of robbery, fraud, adultery, people who died of starvation, people who committed suicide by hanging. She even told her friends about these reports. However, she gave no further thought to such things. These matters had nothing to do with her, she thought. Actually, she never even tried to think about whether or not such matters had any relation to herself. She was the same as when she had been born—the same as when she had been organically and biologically produced. She was like a machine that had been kept in a storage shed and never actually been used. She was not yet a person. Since she had grown up in a Christian family, she had received the baptism of heaven. However, she had not yet received the fiery baptism of life. Had she been born in a "civilized" nation, she would have received the baptism of life through poetry, fiction, music, art and storytelling from the early ages of seven or eight, or perhaps four or five, and now that she was eighteen years old, she would have been a woman who was a real human being. Sŏn-hyŏng was not yet, however, a human being. The human being within Sŏn-hyŏng had not yet awakened. No one but God knew whether or not she would awaken.

One could say she was "virginal" and "pure of heart," but she was certainly not a human being. She was only potential material for a human being. She was like marble that was to become a sculpture. Marble became a sculpture with eyes and a nose only after it had been worked with a chisel. Similarly, someone like Sŏn-hyŏng would become a true human being only after she had received the fiery baptism of life and the "person" within her had awakened.

Unlike Sŏn-hyŏng, the "person" within Sun-ae had been somewhat awakened by the natural character-building through adversity that she had experienced since an early age. The "person" within her, however, had only rolled over inside its quilt, and had not yet fully awakened.

Hyŏng-sik considered himself an awakened human being, but he had not yet received the fiery baptism of life either. What paths would lead the three young men and women gathered there in the room to become human beings? The hearts of these three people were like an ocean that awaits an impending storm. The ocean was now smooth, without waves or whitecaps or currents. Soon a great wind would descend from the sky and shake the waters of the ocean, creating waves, whitecaps and currents. Only then would it be a real ocean. What was the nature of that wind, and who sent it? These matters could not be fathomed. Strange clouds wandered at the edge of the sky in Hyŏng-sik's heart, as though an augury of that very wind.

28

Hyŏng-sik left Elder Kim's house. Strange clouds circled Paegundae (White Cloud Platform Mountain),[52] and a cool breeze grazed Hyŏng-sik's burning face. Hyŏng-sik felt refreshed by the breeze. Perhaps a shower would be passing through. The weather would cool off after rain. He wished there would be a thunderstorm.

Hyŏng-sik felt that something was different from when he had entered Elder Kim's house just a while ago. He sensed in the heavens and earth the presence of something he had never known before. It flickered before his eyes, like lightning in a cloud. He thought it might be something of great significance to himself. An ineffable beauty and joy seemed to be hidden within the flickering light. Hyŏng-sik felt a vague new hope and happiness arise within his heart. The happiness was like that which he had experienced when he sat facing Sŏn-hyŏng and Sun-ae and observed the scent of their flesh, the contours of their blouse necklines and sashes, and their voices speaking. A side of life that he had never known before was revealed to him. There seemed to be more to life than what he had hitherto known, and this new aspect of life seemed to be much more important and meaningful than everything else he had known before. There seemed to be something else to life besides honor and fortune, law and morality, scholarship and success—things that Hyŏng-sik had valued the most until now. Hyŏng-sik could not yet name what it was, but could only be amazed at how strange it was.

---

52. Paegundae is the highest of the mountains that comprise Samgaksan (Three Corners Mountain), situated to the north of Seoul, and in Koyang County, Kyŏng-gi Province. The other two mountains are Kungmangbong (Nation Viewing Peak) and Insubong (Humanity and Long Life Peak).

He felt surprised when he walked down the Kyodong District, where he had walked every day for five years. Everything was the same—the street, the houses, the objects that were arrayed inside the houses, the people walking in the street, the telegraph poles, the mailbox that stood tall and straight, but Hyŏng-sik found in them colors and scents he had never noticed before. Everything seemed to have a new light and a new meaning. The people walking in the street were not just passersby, but seemed to contain within themselves something unknowable. There seemed to be a deeper meaning to the bean curd vendor's cries, than just "buy my bean curd and *piji*."[53] Hyŏng-sik felt that an outer skin or husk had been removed from his eyes.[54] Actually, it was not that a skin or husk had been removed from his eyes, but that one of his eyes, closed until now, had opened. The first stage of his awakening had taken place when he saw the portrait of Christ on the cross and saw Jesus not just as Christ on the cross but discovered a new meaning in the portrait. The second stage of his awakening had taken place when he looked at the two young girls Sŏn-hyŏng and Sun-ae and saw them as the expression of some mysterious power of life and the universe, and not just two young girls. A third stage in Hyŏng-sik's awakening took place now when he found a new, hitherto unnoticed light and scent in everything he saw in the Kyodong District. He could not clearly put a name to these experiences, though, but only thought that it was all very strange, and felt a vague happiness.

Hyŏng-sik returned to his room and reflected upon the new transformations that were taking place in his mind, forgetting all about Yŏng-ch'ae for awhile. If he sat and closed his eyes, poetry and fiction that he had read before rose in his mind with a different aspect than when he had first read them. Everything had a strong color and fragrance, and profound meaning. Until now, I have read books and life without understanding their meaning, he thought. He brought forth various memories, and looked at them with his newly opened eyes. He found new colors that he had never seen before, in all of his memories. Hyŏng-sik smiled, his eyes dazzled. He looked at the books, bound in Western-style binding, lined up on his shelves. He had thought that he had read them and understood them, but now he realized that he had actually not read with comprehension. Hyŏng-sik wanted to read all books, and all of life and the world, all over again. If he read everything over again from the first line of the first page, he was sure that each line and every word would shine with new meaning, as though he had never read them before. He took some books off the shelf, and tried reading several passages that he had read before. The results were just as he had expected.

---

53. *Piji* is the dregs left over after making bean curd. *Piji* can be used in soup.
54. This sentence was emphasized with circles beside each syllable in the 1918 Sinmungwan text.

The inner self within Hyŏng-sik had opened its eyes. He could now see the inner meaning of all existence with his inner eyes. The inner self within Hyŏng-sik had been liberated. A pine seedling hides within its shell, and is confined there, for a long time until, under the warmth of spring, it bursts with great strength through its shell and sprouts outward into the pitilessly wide world. Then it becomes tendrils, branches, leaves and flowers. The inner self within Hyŏng-sik similarly constituted the seed of the person named Hyŏng-sik. This inner self had broken through its shell, sprouted into the wide world, and started to grow endlessly in the sunshine and dew.

Hyŏng-sik's inner self had long been ripe for bursting from its shell. A grain seedling will swell as much as it can within its shell, inside the soil, and then sprout overnight after a light drizzle. Hyŏng-sik's inner self had grown, nourished by religion, literature, and Hyŏng-sik's actual social experiences, which were more abundant than those of most people. This "inner self" had then suddenly burst through its shell when it met with the two young women named Sŏn-hyŏng and Yŏng-ch'ae, and spring rain and breezes.

If someone were to ask "What is the inner self?" or "How does the inner self awaken?" the answer would be as follows: one cannot answer these questions, just as one cannot answer the questions "What is life?" and "What does it mean to say that 'I am life'?" Only one whose inner self has awakened can know their inner self and know what it is like for their inner self to be awakened.

What would happen to the newly awakened Hyŏng-sik? You must see how this story develops in order to know.

29

There was indeed a passing shower that day. Part of a lovely rainbow that arched between Tongdaemun (East Gate) and Namsan (South Mountain) could be seen from Hyŏng-sik's room. Hyŏng-sik sat looking at the rainbow in a daze for a long time. Then suddenly he thought of Yŏng-ch'ae. Her crisis seemed to be drawing nearer to her with every second. Hyŏng-sik put on his *turumagi*, and ran out. For awhile, though, he was at a loss as to where to go or what to do. Then suddenly he began to walk hastily towards Andong, as if having reached a decision. Hyŏng-sik stopped before a door with the words "Student dormitory" written on it. Soon, a boy appeared dragging his shoes, and greeted Hyŏng-sik. Hyŏng-sik shook the boy's hand. Then Hyŏng-sik asked hesitantly, "Who is the student who followed Dean Pae yesterday?"

The boy smiled and said, "I don't know." He looked at Hyŏng-sik's face as though he thought the question odd. Hyŏng-sik's face looked pale in the light of dusk.

"This is an urgent matter, Hŭi-gyŏng," said Hyŏng-sik. "Please tell me who followed Dean Pae."

Hŭi-gyŏng thought there was something strange about Hyŏng-sik's manner, so he held back his laughter and thought for a moment. Hyŏng-sik's voice was shaking. Finally Hŭi-gyŏng said, "Chong-nyŏl and I followed him." As if expecting a reprimand, Hŭi-gyŏng made an about-face turn away from Hyŏng-sik.

"*You* followed him?" Hyŏng-sik asked joyously. "That is just great!" Hŭi-gyŏng thought Hyŏng-sik's manner was even stranger. Surely Hyŏng-sik was not after Wŏr-hyang, no matter how famous a *kisaeng* she might be.

"Why do you ask?" said Hŭi-gyŏng, peering at Hyŏng-sik even more attentively.

Hyŏng-sik did not answer the question. "Do you know the street number? For the house that the dean visited?"

"No, I do not."

Hyŏng-sik was disappointed with the reply. Then he grabbed Hŭi-gyŏng's hand again and said, "I am sorry, but would you please show me where that house is?"

As though he saw no way out of the situation, Hŭi-gyŏng went and put on his hat and *turumagi* and came out. Perhaps Hyŏng-sik is investigating something about the dean, he thought, and walked ahead of Hyŏng-sik, towards Chongno. What shall I do when I get there, thought Hyŏng-sik as he followed Hŭi-gyŏng. Even if it is Yŏng-ch'ae, what shall I do since I do not have "one thousand wŏn"? If someone were to take a thousand wŏn and contract an agreement to purchase Yŏng-ch'ae then and there, Hyŏng-sik would be able to do nothing but gnash his teeth, since he did not have one thousand wŏn.

It was a chilly evening. One could hear from the Chongno evening market the sound of vendors shouting out how cheap their goods were, and advertising medicines as they wielded long knives. The places where dozens of people were gathered seemed to be places where cheap, useful goods were being sold. People wandered about aimlessly, intoxicated with the taste of the cool evening. Groups of students in twos and threes ran about between the people on the street, chattering amongst themselves, as though on some urgent business. There were some women who still covered their heads[55] when they left the house, and went about with a girl carrying a lantern to light their way, in traditional style. The noise of a Western orchestra could be heard from the Umigwan, where what was known as an "action movie" (*taehwalgŭk*) was probably showing. Through the windows of the second floor of the Youth Association building flickered the shadows

---

55. Korean women of the elite *yangban*, or educated elite class would traditionally cover their heads when they left the house.

of youths walking about energetically, perhaps playing billiards. Hŭi-gyŏng would stop wherever people were gathered, and watch for awhile, then move on when he heard Hyŏng-sik's footsteps. The rain had fallen after a dry spell, so the warm scent of earth would rise through the air every now and then.

Hyŏng-sik and Hŭi-gyŏng turned the corner at Chonggak, and went towards Kwangjunggyo.[56] An electric car going to Sinyongsan ran past them with its large eyes wide open. Hyŏng-sik and Hŭi-gyŏng stepped onto the dark banks of a stream in Tabang-gol.[57] Men and women sat together on straw mats spread on the banks of the stream, talking and laughing. They grew quiet when they saw Hyŏng-sik and Hŭi-gyŏng approach, and looked at them in the darkness. When the two were no longer in sight, they resumed their talking and laughing. The shiny, pomaded hair of a maid who lived in the servants' quarters in the outer wing of a large household could be seen as she peered out of a back window. Hŭi-gyŏng would sometimes stop and look around in all four directions, as though he had forgotten the way, and then move on. Sometimes he would say, "I have come the wrong way," and walk back a few paces and walk into a narrow alley. In front of one house were several rickshaws that had passenger seats with hooded shades. The rickshawmen sat on the footrests of the rickshaws, and talked in low voices among themselves. Lamps at front gates and beneath the eaves of houses could be seen, with pretty names such as Kye-ok (Cinnamon Jade) and Sŏl-mae (Snow Plum) written on them. The tremulous sound of the first line from a *sijo* song could be heard from somewhere. "This heart half-sick with sorrow . . . " What seemed to be several men laughing together could be heard after that. "This must be the 'flowers and willows' town—the *kisaeng* district!" Hyŏng-sik thought to himself. Hyŏng-sik's heart felt strangely chilled upon visiting the place for the first time. He even looked behind him to see if anyone might have seen him. At a street corner, two *kisaeng* dressed in indigo blue skirts walked past, looking at Hyŏng-sik and Hŭi-gyŏng and whispering to each other and laughing. Unbeknownst to others, Hyŏng-sik's heart leapt and his face burned. Hyŏng-sik and Hŭi-gyŏng walked onwards without a word. The sound of their shoes on the ground as they walked along confidently rang strangely against the walls. Hŭi-gyŏng lost his way several times, and then finally said, "Here it is." He pointed to a house with a lamp in front of it. Hyŏng-sik felt his heart grow even colder, and stood at the gate and looked at the lamp. The name "Kye Wŏr-hyang" was written on the lamp.

---

56. The 1918 Sinmungwan edition changed this to Kwangt'unggyo.
57. The name Tabang-gol means "tearoom village."

"Kye Wŏr-hyang!"[58] Hyŏng-sik shook his head. Perhaps Wŏr-hyang was not Yŏng-ch'ae. Even if she had become a *kisaeng* and changed her name, surely she would not have changed her surname as well. Maybe Wŏr-hyang was not Yŏng-ch'ae. And Yŏng-ch'ae had not become a *kisaeng*. Perhaps Yŏng-ch'ae had been taken care of by a good family, and was going to school and living happily, just as Hyŏng-sik had imagined. Hyŏng-sik was full of doubt. Hŭi-gyŏng stood to the side a few steps and looked at Hyŏng-sik's face, which looked pallid in the light of the lamps at the gate. "He is worried about something!" he thought.

30

When Yŏng-ch'ae saw Hyŏng-sik for the first time in seven years, she had been happy and had wept, unable to contain her happiness. She had tried to talk about the past seven years of her life, but had stopped suddenly, gotten up and left, crying, and gone home.

When she heard that Hyŏng-sik was in Seoul, her desire to see him had risen within her like flames, but she had been unable to resolve to seek him out, and so one month had passed. That morning she had thought, "Today I must go and see him," and she had gone to see him that afternoon. Unable to see him then because he was not at home, she had gone again in the evening.

Yŏng-ch'ae felt closest to Hyŏng-sik. She had no parents, no siblings, no relatives, only a man named Hyŏng-sik, with whom she had grown up together. Yŏng-ch'ae had lived only for her father and brothers, until they had died in the P'yŏngyang jail. After they died, Yŏng-ch'ae had lived only for Hyŏng-sik. As she grew older, moreover, and after she had become a *kisaeng* and been harassed by hundreds of beastlike men who knew nothing but lust, it seemed to her that Hyŏng-sik was the only man she could trust, and on whom she could rely. Yŏng-ch'ae was not worried about how Hyŏng-sik might have changed during the seven years since they had gone their separate ways, or what kind of person he might have become. Yŏng-ch'ae was sure that no matter how many years passed—a thousand years, ten thousand years—Hyŏng-sik would always be the same Hyŏng-sik she had known at her house in the town of Anju. Yŏng-ch'ae did not know that people who had once been good could change for the worse. She thought that a good person was good by nature, and would always be good. Similarly, she thought that an evil person was born that way, and would always be thus. Yŏng-ch'ae had never known any evil people in her childhood. Her father was a good person. Her brothers were good people. The students who lived in her father's study, and the students who visited there in order to learn, were also good people. Of course, Hyŏng-sik too was a good person. The people in books such as the *Elementary Learning* and *Biographies of Virtuous Women*,

---

58. Kye Wŏr-hyang means "Cinnamon Moon Fragrance."

which she had studied, were all good people too. In her childish mind, the characters in the books that she read, and the people in her family and around her, were all the same. She herself was good. She thought the women in the *Admonitions for Women* and *Biographies of Virtuous Women* were the same as herself. She also thought that since the world was like her home, all the people in the world would be like herself and the people around her. Kim Sŏn-hyŏng and Pak Yŏng-ch'ae were similar in this respect.

Yŏng-ch'ae's young mind was shocked, however, when her good father and the people around her became the object of people's contempt and ridicule for having committed wrongdoing. She was treated cruelly by her maternal cousin's wife and her nieces and nephews. After she ran away from that house, she was tormented by the children in another village. That very night, she had had that terrible experience at the inn in Sukch'ŏn. And eventually she had been sold in P'yŏngyang to become a *kisaeng*. She realized at a young age that the world was different from her family, and that the people of the world were different from herself and those she had known at home. In other words, she had realized that there was evil in the world, and that there were evil people. She thought that the world of evil, and evil people had nothing to do with herself, though. She could not in the least confuse her virtuous family with the evil world, or the good people she had known with the evil people whom she saw now. There was a good world and an evil world, she thought, and good people and evil people. These were different, and like oil and water, could not be merged. Yŏng-ch'ae realized another truth as she gained experience in life: the evil world was larger than the good world, and there were more evil people than there were good.

Since leaving home seven years ago, Yŏng-ch'ae had never even once seen the good world, nor met any good people. She had left the good world of her hometown, and become a sojourner in evil, unfamiliar lands. She had left her good relatives, and experienced all manner of humiliation and torture from evil people who were her enemies. She did not think, however, that there was no good world or that there were no good people at all; she had once witnessed such a world and such people seven years ago. She thought that she herself, moreover, was like one of the women in *Biographies of Virtuous Women*, the *Admonitions for Women* and the *Elementary Learning*, and that she was someone who would certainly not stay in the evil world for long. Her life was governed by *Biographies of Virtuous Women*, the *Admonitions for Women*, and the *Elementary Learning* that her father had taught her when she was a child.

Yŏng-ch'ae believed that there was indeed a good world and there were good people, but by some fate she had left that world and such people. She believed that she would find that good world and those good people again some day. When she looked at the myriad houses stretching from Namdaemun to Tongdaemun, she wondered which home was the one that would be like the one she had lived in seven years ago. And when she saw the tens of thousands of people walking about at the four-way intersection at Chongno, she wondered which one of them was the man who would be like the people she had known earlier in life.

Men in nice clothes and wearing fine watches tried to approach her, but she faced them with a kind of contempt, thinking to herself, "You are people of a different world from mine." Yŏng-ch'ae believed that there would be a good home and a good man in Seoul. She tried hard day and night to find that home and that man. The only good man in her thoughts, however, was Yi Hyŏng-sik. This was why she had single-mindedly looked for Hyŏng-sik for seven years, refusing to yield her body to anyone, even though she had met hundreds of men. Then she had heard that Hyŏng-sik was in Seoul, and she had come to see him.

31

Yŏng-ch'ae had met several *kisaeng* over the years. She had seen what kinds of people were among the ranks of *kisaeng*. There were dozens of *kisaeng* whom she affectionately called *hyŏngnim* (older sister), dozens of *kisaeng* who were her friends and with whom she used intimate speech, and there were several younger *kisaeng* who affectionately looked up to her as an older sister as well.

The first *kisaeng* she had grown close to and called "older sister" was Kye Wŏr-hwa,[59] who was pretty and had a good voice. Indeed, in the "world of flowers and willows" in P'yŏngyang at the time, all handsome, pleasure-loving men were drawn to Wŏr-hwa alone. Wŏr-hwa could compose *tanyul*[60] and paint in ink as well as anyone. She was therefore very proud, and very selective about the men she would allow near her. Men who had been rejected reproached her as an "arrogant, annoying wench," and the old woman who was her "mother" cautioned her to "be polite to the guests." Wŏr-hwa had great confidence, however, in her looks and talent. When faced with a guest whom she looked down upon, Wŏr-hwa would sing the following *sijo* by Sor-i:

Sing for us, Sor-i.[61]
My name, Sor-i, means pine tree
enduring strength
the pine that is always green
upon a steep cliff.

59. Kye Wŏr-hwa means "Cinnamon Moon Flower."
60. *Tanyul:* a short poem written in classical Chinese, in regulated verse style (*lü shi*), in either five- or seven-syllable lines.
61. Sor is homophonous with the Korean word for pine; and Sor-i is homophonous with the Korean word for singing.

The woodcutter boy down in the street
dares not try to take me.

Her friends therefore called Wŏr-hwa "Sor-i." The *kisaeng* Sor-i was
indeed Wŏr-hwa's ideal. This was why Yŏng-ch'ae came to love Wŏr-hwa.
Yŏng-ch'ae thought Wŏr-hwa worthy of being in *Biographies of Virtuous
Women*. Though Yŏng-ch'ae did not know what kind of *kisaeng* Sor-i had
been, since Wŏr-hwa took her as a role model, Yŏng-ch'ae did too. "Let us
be friends, you, me and Sor-i," Yŏng-ch'ae had once said in Wŏr-hwa's
embrace. Yŏng-ch'ae vowed to emulate Sor-i, just as her "older sister"
Wŏr-hwa did.

Many men were drooling over Wŏr-hwa because of her looks and her
talent. Some of the men were rich and some were handsome. They vied with
one another, dressing in fine clothes, wearing gold watches and gold rings, in
an effort to win Wŏr-hwa's love. The kind of man whom Wŏr-hwa dreamed
about, however, was not that sort of frivolous type. Wŏr-hwa was thinking of
Chinese poets of the High Tang period[62] such as Li Bo,[63] Gao Shi,[64] Wang
Chang-ling[65] and famous characters in Korean literature and song, such as
Yang Ch'ang-gok[66] and Yi To-ryŏng.[67] There were no men like that around
Wŏr-hwa, though; there were only men with money and lust. Wŏr-hwa
would often visit Yŏng-ch'ae late at night on her way home, after having
been summoned to a restaurant or some such place. Weeping, she would say,
"Why is the world such a lonely place, Yŏng-ch'ae? I can find no human
beings in P'yŏngyang."

Yŏng-ch'ae was not sure what Wŏr-hwa meant, but she guessed that it
meant that Wŏr-hwa could not find a man she liked. Young as she was, she
would think to herself, "I have Yi Hyŏng-sik, though."

62. High Tang (712 to 755). Cf. Stephen Owen, *An Anthology of Chinese Literature: Beginnings
to 1911* (New York: W. W. Norton and Co., 1996), 385.
63. Li Bo (701–762). Cf. Stephen Owen, *An Anthology of Chinese Literature*, 398–404.
64. Gao Shi. Cf. *Tang Shu* 143, *Jiu Tang Shu* 111. Cited in Morohashi Tetsuji, *Dai Kanwa Jiten*,
vol. 12 (Tokyo: Taishū Shokan, 1976), 612.
65. Wang Chang-ling. Cf. *Tang Shu* 203, *Jiu Tang Shu* 190. Cited in Morohashi Tetsuji, *Dai
Kanwa Jiten*, vol. 7, 876.
66. Yang Ch'ang-gok was a character in the Korean vernacular novel *Ongnyŏn Mong* (The Jade
Lotus Dream), by Nam Yŏng-no. A 1913 edition published by Pakhak Sŏwŏn includes a preface
which states that the text was based on a handwritten text written seventy years earlier by Nam
Yŏng-no, and was being published by Nam Yŏng-no's grandson Nam Chŏng-ŭi for the first
time. Yang Ch'ang-gok is also the main character in a very similar Korean vernacular novel
entitled *Ongnu Mong* (Dream of the Jade Pavilion); *Ongnyŏn Mong* seems to be a shorter
version of *Ongnu Mong*. Cf. W. E. Skillend, *Kodae Sosŏl: A Survey of Korean Traditional Style
Popular Novels* (London: School of Oriental and African Studies, University of London, 1968),
147. Kim Tong-ni et al., *Han'guk Munhak Tae Sajŏn* (Seoul: Munwŏn'gak, 1973), 749–750.
67. Yi To-ryŏng: Ch'un-hyang's lover in *Ch'un-hyang Ka* (The Song of Ch'un-hyang), a work
of *p'ansori*, or Korean sung and spoken narrative.

Wŏr-hwa came to look upon the world more and more tragically. While teaching Yŏng-ch'ae Tang poetry, she would often embrace her tightly and weep. "Why were you and I born in such a Korea, Yŏng-ch'ae?" she would say. Not knowing what she meant, Yŏng-ch'ae would ask, "Then where would you like to have been born?"

"You still don't understand," Wŏr-hwa would think, pitying Yŏng-ch'ae's youth. Wŏr-hwa regretted not having been born in Jiangnan[68] during the High Tang period. She lamented that she was Zhuo Wen-jun without Si-ma Xiang-ru[69] to seduce her with the "Song of the Phoenix." Heaven had created the Taedong River and Moranbong (Peony Mountain). If Kye Wŏr-hwa were the Taedong River, who would be Moranbong, and cast reflections of flowers in spring and foliage in autumn, on the waters before Pubyŏk Pavilion?

Wŏr-hwa resented the way the Korean people were ignorant and lacked compassion. She lamented, moreover, that there wasn't a single poet or writer among the men in P'yŏngyang. She was twenty years old, and had never met a man who fit her ideals. Full of sadness and contempt for the world, she found her only solace in reciting classical poems, and writing her own poetry and songs. She also loved and doted upon Yŏng-ch'ae as though she were her own younger sister, and taught her to read and write poetry. When Wŏr-hwa felt sad, she would confide her feelings to an uncomprehending Yŏng-ch'ae. "Sister!" Yŏng-ch'ae would say, and weep in Wŏr-hwa's embrace.

Once there was a party at which so-called first-class gentlemen and first-class *kisaeng* of P'yŏngyang were gathered. The party took place at Pubyŏk Pavilion, at the foot of Moranbong, in the gentle breezes of early summer. "Look, Yŏng-ch'ae," said Wŏr-hwa, pulling Yŏng-ch'ae aside and whispering. "What?" asked Yŏng-ch'ae, looking at the people seated at the party. "Those people are considered first-class gentlemen of P'yŏngyang," whispered Wŏr-hwa. "But those ostensibly first-class men are just scarecrows." Wŏr-hwa pointed to the *kisaeng*. "Those are all disgusting women who sell their singing and their bodies." Yŏng-ch'ae was fifteen years old[70] at the time, and could understand more clearly than before what Wŏr-hwa meant. "You are right," Yŏng-ch'ae said, and nodded her little head. Just then, a man in a Western-style suit approached Wŏr-hwa and put

68. Jiangnan refers to the region of China south of the Yangzi River, and, moreover, can be a metonymy for China.

69. Si-ma Xiang-ru (179–117 B.C.) was Emperor Wu's court poet. After hearing the Han writer Si-ma Xiang-ru play his harp, Zhuo Wen-jun ran off with him to Lin-qiong. Stephen Owen, *An Anthology of Chinese Literature: Beginnings to 1911* (New York: W. W. Norton and Company, 1996), 222, 903.

70. Yŏng-ch'ae was fifteen in Korean years, and fourteen in Western years.

his hand on her neck. "Why are you standing over here, Wŏr-hwa?" he asked and tried to pull her away with him. The man was the eldest son of Kim Yun-su of P'yŏngyang, who was crazy about Wŏr-hwa at the time. He was over thirty years old, but had done nothing up until now but fool around with *kisaeng*. Wŏr-hwa, of course, despised this man. That was why she had sung the "Sori, sori" song to him. Wŏr-hwa was disgusted, and brushed him off, saying, "Leave me alone." Yŏng-ch'ae later learned that there was one man there to whom Wŏr-hwa was attracted. What kind of man was he, and what would be the relationship between him and Wŏr-hwa?

32

On the way back from the party, Yŏng-ch'ae took a walk with Wŏr-hwa below Ch'ŏngnyu Cliff. A group of four or five students from P'aesŏng[71] Middle School in P'yŏngyang were standing on some rocks at Ch'ŏngnyu Cliff and singing cheerfully.

The Taedong River curves and wraps itself around Nŭngna Island.
Moranbong moves its contours in dance
I sit on Ch'ŏngnyu Cliff and say to the river:
Listen to me, departing waters—
I want to give you the hot blood of my youth.

Wŏr-hwa tugged at Yŏng-ch'ae's sleeve. "Do you hear that song?"
"It's very nice."
Wŏr-hwa sighed. "There, among them, is a poet after all," she said, and wept tears of wistful sadness. Yŏng-ch'ae did not understand what Wŏr-hwa meant, and just looked at the students who were singing on Ch'ŏngnyu Cliff. The students were still singing, and their *turumagi* were flapping in the wind. Yŏng-ch'ae felt an affection for the students, and yet an indefinable sadness seemed to rise in her breast, and she leaned against Wŏr-hwa's shoulder and wept with Wŏr-hwa. Wŏr-hwa put her arms around Yŏng-ch'ae.
"Yŏng-ch'ae, there is a real poet among them," she said. "The men we meet every day are dead men. They do not have anything in their lives but eating, dressing up and playing around with women. There is a true poet, however, in that group of students over there."
The students began singing another song.

Early morning lights the sky
The sun rises.
All things on earth

71. In the Samjungdang edition, this is misspelled as "Taesŏng." The 1917 *Maeil Sinbo* text and the 1918 Sinmungwan text spell the name "P'aesŏng."

dance for joy.

> While other people on earth dream,
> I alone am awake.
> I look up at the sky
> and sing a sad song.

Wŏr-hwa pounded her feet on the ground as though she could not endure it. "Let's go up there," she said.

Before she had finished speaking, though, the students had taken off their hats and walked away over a hill. Wŏr-hwa sat down on a rock beside the road, and sang the song that the students had sung, over a dozen times. Yŏng-ch'ae too liked the song, and sang along. Wŏr-hwa stared at where the students had been. The students did not appear again, though.

After that, there were more days when Wŏr-hwa cried. Yŏng-ch'ae would cry with Wŏr-hwa, and tried to be with her when she had the chance. Yŏng-ch'ae became fonder of Wŏr-hwa, and Wŏr-hwa loved Yŏng-ch'ae more too. Yŏng-ch'ae, who was now fifteen years old, gradually began to understand Wŏr-hwa better. The more she understood, the more she sympathized with Wŏr-hwa's tears. Yŏng-ch'ae became increasingly well known as a beauty, and for singing well and writing short Chinese poems in regulated verse style. Many men wanted to pluck this flower named Yŏng-ch'ae that had just bloomed this morning. Yŏng-ch'ae began to understand what Wŏr-hwa had said at Pubyŏk Pavilion.

When Yŏng-ch'ae saw how Wŏr-hwa had been suffering ever since the party at Pubyŏk Pavilion, though, Yŏng-ch'ae guessed that something had happened to Wŏr-hwa. Yŏng-ch'ae had also begun to feel a longing for the male sex. Her face grew hot when she faced a strange man, and when she lay down alone at night, she wished that there was someone who would hold her. Once, when Yŏng-ch'ae and Wŏr-hwa came back from a party late at night, and had gone to bed together in the same bed, Yŏng-ch'ae put her arms around Wŏr-hwa in her sleep, and kissed her on the mouth. Wŏr-hwa laughed to herself. "So you have awakened as well," she thought. "Sadness and suffering lie ahead of you." She woke Yŏng-ch'ae.

"Yŏng-ch'ae, you just put your arms around me and kissed me on the mouth." Yŏng-ch'ae buried her face in Wŏr-hwa's breasts, as she though were ashamed, and bit her white breasts. "I did it because it was you," she said. Since Yŏng-ch'ae had matured to this extent, she knew that there must be a certain reason for Wŏr-hwa's tears. She thought of asking Wŏr-hwa about it, but was too embarrassed. Wŏr-hwa must be thinking about the students who sang at Ch'ŏngnyu Cliff, she thought. Yŏng-ch'ae too had been unable to forget the image of the students who had sung at Ch'ŏngnyu Cliff.

Of course, looking at people on Ch'ŏngnyu Cliff from the street, one could see the contours of their faces, but could not clearly see their eyes or noses. Their sublime appearance, clear voices, and meaningful and beautiful songs, though, had brought chills to the women's hearts. The students had probably sung at the spur of the moment, without any particular intention in mind, but the two young women had never met any "genuine" or "sincere" people, or people with aspirations and hope, or human beings worthy of the name. The students and their songs, therefore, left a very clear and bright impression with the two young women. Yŏng-ch'ae could not help but grow fond of the students, when she compared them with the so-called gentlemen whom she had spent time with. Lately, there was a chill in her heart, her body felt restless, and she felt lonely. When Wŏr-hwa gazed at her, Yŏng-ch'ae would lower her head, afraid that Wŏr-hwa might see into her thoughts. Wŏr-hwa too realized that Yŏng-ch'ae was maturing. Yŏng-ch'ae would have much sorrow in her future, Wŏr-hwa thought, remembering her own past. As if fearing that Yŏng-ch'ae might make a mistake and become mixed up with the outside world, Wŏr-hwa always encouraged her to make classical poetry her lifelong companion. "There is no one on whom we can rely, Yŏng-ch'ae," she would say.

Yŏng-ch'ae wanted to know the meaning of Wŏr-hwa's tears. She eventually had a chance to find out.

33

One evening, Wŏr-hwa sought out Yŏng-ch'ae and asked her to go with her to hear a speech. A new school called P'aesŏng had been started in P'yŏngyang, and hundreds of students were gathered there from all directions. The principal of the school, Ham Sang-mo, was truly admired by the students. Principal Ham gave a speech every Sunday, and invited the public to come and listen. People from P'yŏngyang filled the auditorium to overflowing. Some went to hear something new, some went to watch out of curiosity. The principal had enthusiasm and eloquence. When he said something sad, the audience would weep. When he said something happy, the audience would clap and shout for joy. When he reproached something evil, the audience would narrow their eyes and foam at the mouth. He said that the Korean people must cast aside their old ways and bring in new civilization. The Korean people were now lazy and lacked energy and vigor. In order to become a new, prosperous people, they needed to have a new spirit and new courage. Education was of the utmost importance. Daughters and sons must receive a new education, he said.

Yŏng-ch'ae went with Wŏr-hwa to the P'aesŏng School because she too had heard of Principal Ham, and had heard that he gave good speeches. Yŏng-ch'ae and Wŏr-hwa tried to dress in clothes that were as simple as possible, but their faces and demeanor gave away the fact that they were *kisaeng*. They were well-known *kisaeng* in P'yŏngyang, moreover, and people at the assembly pointed at them and whispered. Wŏr-hwa and Yŏng-ch'ae went through the crowds, and sat together in a corner of the auditorium. Some people deliberately pushed them on the back, stepped on their feet, or brushed against their hands. Someone put his hand under Wŏr-hwa's arm, beside her breast. "All you see is two *kisaeng*, you do not see us as human beings," thought Wŏr-hwa. She put her arms around Yŏng-ch'ae and led the way through the crowd. Since there were no women from women's circles who were expected to attend or who even wished to attend, there was no women's seating section. Yŏng-ch'ae and Wŏr-hwa thus sat at one end of a bench where some men were sitting. Principal Ham noticed that some women were present, and called a student over to him and said something. The student put two chairs at the left end of the front row, then went over to the two women. He bowed politely.

"Please sit over there," he said, and led them to the seats. The two women felt as though they had been treated like human beings for the first time since they had become *kisaeng*. After some time, students entered the auditorium and sat down. Wŏr-hwa watched the students to see if they were looking at her. The students just sat facing the front of the auditorium without so much as a glance at her.

Wŏr-hwa said to Yŏng-ch'ae quietly, "Those students are people of a different world from that of the people we have known, aren't they?" Principal Ham indeed taught young people very well. Although he still had traces about him of the traditional kind of educator who has the same expectations of everyone without taking individuality into consideration, he was nevertheless the only educator in Korea at the time who was progressive and enthusiastic. P'aesŏng School youths were the only men within the walls of P'yŏngyang who would look at Wŏr-hwa without salacious grins. When the students saw Wŏr-hwa they might think, "She is pretty," or "Let's have another look at her," but they certainly did not think, like other men, "I wish I could sleep with her for one night." Even if they thought of making her their own, they would not, like other men, obtain her in order to play around with her.[72] Instead, they would make her their wife, and love and respect her. Other men thought of Wŏr-hwa as a plaything. The students thought *kisaeng* were of lowly status, but nevertheless thought that Wŏr-hwa too was a fellow Korean and their sister.

After awhile Principal Ham stepped up to the podium. The whole room burst into applause, and Wŏr-hwa too applauded twice. That is the man who sang near Pubyŏk Pavilion! thought Yŏng-ch'ae. Principal Ham looked at the

---

72. The 1918 Sinmungwan edition revised this sentence to: ". . . they would not, like other men, obtain her in order to put her on their lap and play around with her."

audience solemnly for a few moments, and then opened his mouth and began to speak.

"Your ancestors did not have rotted, deteriorated minds and hearts and were not lazy and listless like you. Our ancestors who built P'yŏngyang Fortress had grandeur of character. Our ancestors who built Ŭlmil Look-out and Pubyŏk Pavilion had great ambition." He bowed his head down for a long time, as though in awe. "The waters of the Taedong River flow away continuously. Gone are the waters that once reflected the images of the ancestors who built P'yŏngyang Fortress and Ŭlmil Look-out. Only Moranbong, with its distinct contours, has retained our ancestors' footsteps since antiquity. Have you dedicated the spirit that is your legacy from the great ancestors, to the flowing Taedong River and to Moranbong, which has stood tall since antiquity?" He stopped for a moment in tears. Everyone in the audience lowered their heads solemnly. Principal Ham lamented the ways in which the Korean people had become degenerate. He raised his voice somewhat and said, "Let us tear down the deteriorating ruins of P'yŏngyang Fortress and Ŭlmil Look-out, and send them down the Taedong River, and build a new P'yŏngyang Fortress and Ŭlmil Platform, with a new spirit and new strength!" He stepped calmly down from the podium, and the room shook with applause and cheers for quite some time. Wŏr-hwa grasped Yŏng-ch'ae's hand tightly, and her body trembled. Yŏng-ch'ae looked at Wŏr-hwa in surprise, and saw large teardrops falling onto the hem of Wŏr-hwa's skirt where it lay on Wŏr-hwa's lap.

Yŏng-ch'ae thought of her late father when she saw Principal Ham's presence and heard his speech. She followed Wŏr-hwa home, weeping. Wŏr-hwa's tears were different from those of Yŏng-ch'ae, though. What was the nature of Wŏr-hwa's tears?

34

When Wŏr-hwa got home, she sat down and said to Yŏng-ch'ae, "I have found the man I sought. I was enraptured when I saw Principal Ham's presence and heard his words, at Pubyŏk Pavilion. And I fell completely in love with him tonight when I saw his appearance and presence, and heard him again. I have finally met the man for whom I was looking all over Korea." Yŏng-ch'ae now understood why Wŏr-hwa had wept. Yŏng-ch'ae had thought of Principal Ham as being like her father, but Wŏr-hwa had thought of Ham as a cherished love. Yŏng-ch'ae looked at Wŏr-hwa's face again. Clear tears hung from her eyelashes.

"Yŏng-ch'ae, do you understand the song that he sang at Pubyŏk Pavilion?

"'While other people on earth dream,
I alone am awake.
Looking up to heaven,

I sing a sad song.'
"Do you understand this song?"
Yŏng-ch'ae thought she understood, but could not express what she felt, and sat quietly.
After some time, Wŏr-hwa looked at Yŏng-ch'ae. "The Korean people are asleep, dreaming, and only Principal Ham is awake. The so-called first-class gentlemen who come to see us are all asleep. Principal Ham is the only one awake among them all."
This made sense to Yŏng-ch'ae. "Then why is he looking up at heaven and singing a sad song?" she asked.
"When he awoke, he saw that everyone else was still dreaming. No matter how he tries to wake them, they will not awaken, but only talk in their sleep. How could he help but feel lonely and sad? That is why he looks up to heaven and sings a sad song." Wŏr-hwa took Yŏng-ch'ae by the hand, and made her lie across her lap. "I too look up to heaven and sing."
"Why?" asked Yŏng-ch'ae. She thought she understood Wŏr-hwa, but asked nonetheless. "Why do you sing a sad song?"
"Who else but I among the sixty *kisaeng* within the walls of P'yŏngyang, has awakened? They don't know what a human being is, or what heaven is. I am the only one who is awake. And I am lonely and sad. You are the only one who will listen to my feelings." Wŏr-hwa rubbed her forehead on Yŏng-ch'ae's back, and hugged her tightly at the waist. Now Yŏng-ch'ae understood all of what Wŏr-hwa was saying.
"I am now twenty years old," continued Wŏr-hwa. "I have finally met the friend I sought for twenty years. But I know he is someone I can only meet in passing, and not someone I can talk with at length. That is why I want to leave." Wŏr-hwa made Yŏng-ch'ae sit up. Her voice grew even more affectionate. "You and I have been like sisters for three years. It must have been fate. You were born in Anju, and I was born in P'yŏngyang. Who would have known that we would meet like this and become such good friends? Don't forget me, and always call me 'older sister.'" Wŏr-hwa collapsed, weeping. Wŏr-hwa's words sounded strange, and gave Yŏng-ch'ae gooseflesh.
"Why are you saying things like that tonight, older sister?"
Wŏr-hwa sat up, wiped away her tears, and sat staring vacantly. "I want you to live alone, and not be seduced by people of the world! If you do not meet the right man, make people of the past your companions." After this conversation, they slept together that night. They slept face-to-face, and embraced one another. Yŏng-ch'ae, who was young, fell asleep, though. Wŏr-hwa watched Yŏng-ch'ae's face for awhile as she slept, breathing peacefully. Then she kissed Yŏng-ch'ae's lips with all her might. Yŏng-ch'ae put her lovely arm around Wŏr-hwa's neck and held her close without waking. Wŏr-hwa trembled. Wŏr-hwa sat up, opened a cabinet door,

and removed from a drawer her jade ring. She put the ring on Yŏng-ch'ae's hand, and hugged Yŏng-ch'ae again. The short summer night came to an end. Yŏng-ch'ae half awoke from her sleep, and reached for Wŏr-hwa with one arm. The bed was empty where Wŏr-hwa had been. Surprised, Yŏng-ch'ae sat up. "Sister! Sister!" she called out. There was no answer. Nor would there ever be an answer. Yŏng-ch'ae saw the jade ring on her finger, and wept. That evening, a fishing boat found a corpse in the Taedong River. It was Wŏr-hwa. Since she had left no suicide note, no one knew why she had died. Only Yŏng-ch'ae, who wore the jade ring that Wŏr-hwa had slipped on her finger, knew, and wept hot tears. Wŏr-hwa's "mother" called Wŏr-hwa "no good," and resented the loss of a money-making investment. The son of Kim Yun-su of P'yŏngyang called Wŏr-hwa a "crazy wench," and regretted the loss of a plaything. Wŏr-hwa's corpse was wrapped in thick hemp, and carried on the shoulders of three water bearers to Pungmang Mountain, outside North Gate. The body was buried there. That evening, the hand that wore the jade ring scattered a handful of flowers and a handful of tears on the grave. No marker was placed on the grave, so there is no way to know which one of the graves is that of the acclaimed *kisaeng* Kye Wŏr-hwa. One cannot help wondering if Principal Ham knew what had happened. Kye Wŏr-hwa was indeed an older sister and a friend to Yŏng-ch'ae. She truly loved Yŏng-ch'ae. Yŏng-ch'ae was very much influenced by Wŏr-hwa.

It was Wŏr-hwa who had given Yŏng-ch'ae half the strength to think of Hyŏng-sik as her partner in life and to remain chaste for seven years. If she were unable to find Hyŏng-sik, Yŏng-ch'ae had vowed to follow Wŏr-hwa's example and throw herself in the Taedong River. Then she had happened to learn about Hyŏng-sik's whereabouts, and thought that her wish had been fulfilled. What would she do if he were already married, though? And even if he was not married, what if he refused to give her a second glance once he found out that she was a *kisaeng*? That was why she had not gone to see Hyŏng-sik for over a month after she had found out where he lived. That was also why she had stopped talking about her life the day before when she went to see him, and had come home instead. What happened to Yŏng-ch'ae after she left Hyŏng-sik's home and went back to her dwelling?

35

As she faced Hyŏng-sik and told him about her life, Yŏng-ch'ae had been momentarily happy when she heard that Hyŏng-sik was not yet married. She was a *kisaeng*, though. It occurred to her that Hyŏng-sik would not give her a second glance once he knew that she was a *kisaeng*. Even if he did give her a second glance, she needed money in order to be freed. She saw from Hyŏng-sik's living conditions that he would not be able to help her. If she told him she were a *kisaeng*, the man she had longed for all her life might reject her in his mind and heart. Even if he did not abandon her, she might cause her beloved Hyŏng-sik needless suffering because he did not have the power to help her. Instead of either of these things happening, she would rather throw herself into the waters of the Taedong River, following after Wŏr-hwa, who had died five years earlier, and live with Wŏr-hwa in the netherworld. She could see Wŏr-hwa's face. "Come with me, Yŏng-ch'ae," she seemed to be saying. That was why Yŏng-ch'ae had looked at the jade ring on her finger, and stopped in the middle of telling Hyŏng-sik about her life, and gone home.

Yŏng-ch'ae resolved to go to P'yŏngyang. If she was going to drown herself, she wanted to do it in the Taedong River, where her beloved sister Wŏr-hwa had drowned. She wanted to go to P'yŏngyang and, first of all, visit the graves of her father and Wŏr-hwa at Pungmang Mountain, and tell them all about how she had been. Her father had died because he had heard that she had become a *kisaeng*. She wanted to tell him that she had sold herself to become a *kisaeng* in order to rescue her father and brothers from jail. She wanted to tell him that she had not soiled the flesh and blood that she had received from her father, in the seven years since she had become a *kisaeng*. She also wanted to tell him that she had guarded her chastity for the sake of Yi Hyŏng-sik, to whom her father had tacitly betrothed her. If there was a soul after death, she wanted to relieve her father of the bitter sorrow that she had caused him while he had been alive. If he had gone to heaven, she would look for him in heaven. If he had gone to hell, she would look for him in hell.

I did what Wŏr-hwa asked me to do, she thought. I did not intermingle with the people of the world, but protected my chastity for seven years, for the sake of the man I love. I have taken up the life that Wŏr-hwa had left behind her when she died. I am going to be with you, Wŏr-hwa, she thought.

Yŏng-ch'ae felt as though she were standing on Ch'ŏngnyu Cliff, where those students had sung the words, "While other people on earth dream, I alone am awake. I look up at the sky, and sing a sad song." She thought about the ill-fated nineteen years of her life. The memories that she had told Hyŏng-sik about in particular flashed before her eyes as vividly as though they had happened only yesterday. Sometimes it felt as though the scenes were stabbing her heart and ripping her guts out. She felt bitter, and sorry for herself, and resentful, when she thought of how she would have to die in the indifferent waters of the Taedong River, in the flower of her youth, without ever having known any happiness. After having been tormented and harassed half her life by a heartless world and heartless people, she had finally found Hyŏng-sik again, the man for whom she had longed and hoped. Now that she had found him, though, it did not seem likely that he would try to help her. What kind of fate is this? she wondered, and spent the night crying alone in her room, unable to sleep. Why will these arms never embrace the man I love? Why will these breasts never suckle adorable sons and daughters? My heart is full of love, but will I never be able to give that love to the man of whom I have been thinking? I have been called a *kisaeng*. Why shall I never be called by the affectionate and hallowed names of wife, mother, aunt? A *kisaeng*! How she hated to hear the word. Her teeth chattered at the mere thought of the word.

There were reportedly four or five men who were now trying to purchase her body. She had earned tens of thousands of wŏn for her owner over the past seven years, with her singing and dancing. The old woman who owned Yŏng-ch'ae had thus bought rice fields and dry fields, a large house, and silk clothes. After all the money that Yŏng-ch'ae had made for the old woman, one would think that she would release Yŏng-ch'ae. The old woman's greed had not been satisfied, though, and now she was trying to sell Yŏng-ch'ae for thousands of wŏn. The old woman was bad enough, but what about the men who were trying to buy Yŏng-ch'ae? Yŏng-ch'ae had somehow protected her chastity until now, but what good would it be to save herself for Hyŏng-sik once she was sold to become someone else's concubine? There is nothing for me to do but to die, she thought.

She was happy that she had found her beloved Hyŏng-sik, but it pained her that not even Hyŏng-sik, in whom she had put such hopes, could save her.

Yŏng-ch'ae despaired. Until now, she had thought that she had temporarily lost her way in a strange land, and that she would return to the good world, her hometown, where good people lived, and live as happily as she had with her family seven years ago. But now all her hopes seemed to have been in vain. Hyŏng-sik had been the only man she had thought of as good, and the only man whom she thought she could rely on. Now that she had seen him again, though, he seemed to be just an ordinary man. After having been stuck in the midst of evil people for seven years, Yŏng-ch'ae had thought that a man as good as Hyŏng-sik would most certainly have a face, and presence, and way of speaking that were different from those of all average people. Now that she had seen his face, though, he seemed to be just average. Right, she thought, there is nothing for me to do but die. I have to go to the Taedong River. I could never bring myself to mingle with the sordid world, and let my days drag on in humiliation. I must rejoin my beloved Wŏr-hwa as soon as possible beneath the clear waves of the Taedong River, where we will embrace one another and talk.

Yŏng-ch'ae had no money, though. The next morning, she got up and tried to get five wŏn from several of her friends. In the end, however, she was unable to obtain any money, and sat in her room until after lunchtime, crying. Meanwhile, at the very same time that Yŏng-ch'ae sat in her room crying and grieving, Hyŏng-sik was at Elder Kim's house, intoxicated with happy fantasies as he looked at Sŏn-hyŏng and Sun-ae. Did Hyŏng-sik ever meet up with Yŏng-ch'ae when he went to look for her that evening?

36

Hyŏng-sik stood for a long time looking at a lamp with the name Kye Wŏr-hyang written on it. Then he sent Hŭi-gyŏng away, and stepped through the door resolutely. There seemed to be no guests, for it was very quiet. He walked into the courtyard without hesitation. Lamps were lit in several rooms, but there was no trace of any people around. Hyŏng-sik's heart was pounding. Unsure of how to inquire about Yŏng-ch'ae, he made shuffling noises with his feet and cleared his throat. When he saw a fat old woman emerge from a room across the courtyard, Hyŏng-sik took a step towards the room. There were iridescent chests and armoires[73] inlaid with mother of pearl, and designed for use by a *kisaeng*. Pink mosquito netting was hung over the warmest spot on the floor, closest to the stone heating flu that was beneath the floor.[74] A *kayako*[75] in a bag made of shimmering, iridescent fabric was propped up against the wall in a corner to the right. Is this Yŏng-ch'ae's room? Hyŏng-sik thought. He had inexplicable feelings of sadness and revlusion. Had Yŏng-ch'ae played the *kayako*, and sung and danced for various men in this room? And every night with a different man within that mosquito netting, had she . . . Hyŏng-sik could not bear to think further. But where had she gone? Had she been sold to someone already for one thousand wŏn? Had she been sold even as she walked back home from my place? If she was chaste, might she not have gone somewhere and committed suicide? Thousands of thoughts crowded Hyŏng-sik's head one after another. That must be her so-called mother, Hyŏng-sik thought when he saw a fat old woman (old, though she was only about forty or fifty years old) emerging from the room. The old woman held a round fan with the red, yellow and blue Daoist image of the "Great Origin" (*Tai ji*), and was smoking a traditional Korean long-stemmed pipe. She came out tying the sash of her silk gauze Korean blouse, as though she had been sitting around without wearing a blouse. Disgusting old woman, thought Hyŏng-sik and felt repulsed. The old woman saw that Hyŏng-sik's appearance was extremely shabby, and she asked contemptuously, "For whom are you looking?" No one with such a shabby appearance ever came to see Wŏr-hyang. The old woman thought that Hyŏng-sik must be someone who ran errands for some rich man's son. That was why she could be so cold to a man who had come to a *kisaeng* house. Hyŏng-sik knew that the old woman looked down on

---

73. *Hamnong:* chests (*ham*) and wardrobes (*nong*) used for storing clothing and sewing supplies in a woman's room. *Nong* could consist of two or three tiers. Cf. Koryŏ Taehakkyo Minjok Munhwa Yŏn'guso, *Han'guk Minsok Taegwan*, vol. 2 (Seoul: Kodae Minjok Munhwa Yŏn'guso, 1982), 638, 718–9.
74. Traditional Korean homes were heated by *ondol*, a radiant heating system. Heat circulated in stone flues beneath floors that were covered with oiled paper. Koreans slept on bedding that was spread on the floor.
75. A *kayako* is a twelve-stringed Korean zither.

him. He felt even more repulsed. I am very widely recognized in the world of education, he thought to himself. The old woman's eyes saw only rich men and playboys, though, not men recognized in the world of education. Had Hyŏng-sik dressed in a fine, Western-style three-piece suit, with a pink necktie, and flourished a walking stick and been drunk, and come in saying, "You there!" the old woman would have hurriedly put aside her pipe and come running into the courtyard, and greeted him with an ingratiating smile. Hyŏng-sik, though, wore a coarse *turumagi* of ramie and a straw hat[76] covered with fly droppings, and he was not drunk, did not wield a walking stick, and, moreover, did not say "You there!" Someone like Hyŏng-sik therefore seemed very lower class in the old woman's eyes.

Hyŏng-sik could hardly open his mouth. "Where is Miss Wŏr-hyang?" he asked. He immediately regretted saying "Miss." He had never omitted a "Mr.," "Miss" or "Mrs." before someone's name, though. He thought it only proper, moreover, always to use the respectful title "Miss" before the name of a woman who was not a relative. Men who are supposedly sophisticated know to use "Miss" for woman students, and no polite title at all for *kisaeng*; however, Hyŏng-sik did not know that he was supposed to make such distinctions between woman students and *kisaeng*. Hyŏng-sik thought that people were people, whether woman students or *kisaeng*. He thought it would be right to use the word "Miss" before Wŏr-hyang's name. After some consideration, he thus summoned up all his courage and said, "Where is Miss Wŏr-hyang?" After having spoken, though, he thought about it and felt somewhat embarrassed. He looked at the old woman's face.

The old woman's lips were twitching, as though she were trying not to laugh. "Wŏr-hyang went somewhere with a guest," she said. "Why?"

"Where did she go?"

This fellow is a real country bumpkin, the old woman thought to herself. "She went to Ch'ŏngnyangni this afternoon. She said she would be back at six o'clock. She is not back yet." As though annoyed, the old woman disappeared into a room without so much as bidding Hyŏng-sik good day. "Who is it?" asked a man's voice. "I do not know," the old woman could be heard saying in P'yŏngyang dialect. "Some beggar." Hyŏng-sik turned away. He felt disappointed. He also felt ashamed and angry that the old woman had shown contempt for him. "Kye Wŏr-hyang! Did Pak Yŏng-ch'ae change her name to Kye Wŏr-hyang?" Hyŏng-sik wanted to ask about Kye Wŏr-hyang's background, but after having been treated with such contempt by the old woman, he lacked the courage to ask any further questions, and just went out the door. Hyŏng-sik lowered his head and left the way he had come. The same voice that had sung "This heart sick with sorrow" could now be heard singing "I am leaving . . ." Several people could be heard laughing together,

---

76. Hyŏng-sik's hat is a *maekkomoja*, a straw hat woven of stalks of barley or wheat.

just as before. Hyŏng-sik wondered what to do. "Ch'ŏngnyangni! She left in the afternoon, and said she would be back by six, but she still is not back yet!" These words assumed an ominous significance, and gave Hyŏng-sik gooseflesh. "Yŏng-ch'ae is in Ch'ŏngnyangni, alone with some man! And it is past eight o'clock[77] in the evening!" He clenched his fists. Hyŏng-sik ran as fast as he could down to the banks of the stream in Tabang-gol. I must go to Ch'ŏngnyangni, he thought. He could hear Yŏng-ch'ae's weeping voice saying, "Save me, Hyŏng-sik! I am in trouble right now!" Hyŏng-sik ran towards Chonggak, [78] in order to catch a trolley that was now crossing Kwangch'ung Bridge and was headed for Tongdaemun. However, the trolley turned the corner at Chonggak with a screech, let off two people, and went on. Hyŏng-sik ran after the trolley about ten paces, but it raced past the Youth Association building, completely oblivious to Hyŏng-sik. There were more people gathered at the night market than earlier that evening. The voice of what seemed to be an old bachelor could be heard from the corner at Chonggak calling out in the darkness, "Ice cream! Ice cream!"

37

Hyŏng-sik took the next trolley. A signal worker waved a blue light,[79] and the trolley went around a bend, screeching again. In his anxious haste, Hyŏng-sik had mistakenly taken a trolley going from Kurigae to Sŏdaemun (West Gate). Hyŏng-sik jumped off and caught a trolley for Tongdaemun immediately afterwards. He wiped the sweat from his forehead and neck with a handkerchief. The conductor took Hyŏng-sik's money and rang a bell, peering at Hyŏng-sik's face all the while. Hyŏng-sik's face was very red. Hyŏng-sik looked around the inside of the trolley, then sank his head down and closed his eyes. The trolley seemed to be going too slow deliberately. There were so many people walking about in the night market that the driver had to drive very slowly, ringing the bells continuously with both feet. Flames rose in Hyŏng-sik's breast. He thought of how Westerners in motion pictures rode cars that traveled fast as the wind, and he wished that he too could ride a car at a time like this. Hyŏng-sik imagined himself getting in a car at Chongno, and going across Ch'ŏlmul Bridge, then passing Paeogae and Tongdaemun, then going through the willow trees in front of the Mulberry Garden where the Royal Household cultivated silkworms, then passing Ch'ŏngnyangni, and racing towards a forest of pines in Hongnŭng. He imagined himself sweating as he went from door to door at the secluded Buddhist hermitage that Kim Hyŏn-su frequented, looking for Yŏng-ch'ae, worried that someone might be inflicting suffering on Yŏng-ch'ae at that

---

77. The 1918 Sinmungwan edition changed this to six o'clock.
78. Chonggak means "Bell Pavilion."
79. *P'urŭn tŭng.* This was changed to *p'urŭn ki* (a blue flag) in the 1918 Sinmungwan edition.

very moment. He imagined himself asking Buddhist nuns, and getting even more anxious when they smiled and said, "I do not know." Just then, someone hit Hyŏng-sik on the shoulder.

"Hey, where are you going?" Hyŏng-sik turned his head in surprise. It was Sin U-sŏn, the newspaper reporter. He sat next to Hyŏng-sik, and fanned himself with his straw hat. "So how did it go? Did Elder Kim's daughter fall in love with you?" He spoke loudly, as though he did not care whether or not people nearby overheard him. Hyŏng-sik thought for a moment about how he had seen Sŏn-hyŏng and Sun-ae at Elder Kim's house earlier that day. It occurred to him that U-sŏn would be able to help him with the matter that he was on his way to try to resolve. He moved closer to U-sŏn and spoke into his ear. "Something terrible has happened," he said.

U-sŏn laughed. "Well, well, something is always happening to you! What is it this time?" Hyŏng-sik grasped U-sŏn's arm and motioned to him not to speak loudly. Then he went on, telling him how the daughter of someone who had helped him was a *kisaeng* here in Seoul, and that she was protecting her virtue for Hyŏng-sik's sake, and that several powerful men were now trying to get their hands on her, and that she was now in danger in Ch'ŏngnyangni and he was on his way to save her.

"You must help me," Hyŏng-sik said. As he spoke, Hyŏng-sik could see Yŏng-ch'ae in a crisis situation, being threatened by some man at that very moment.

U-sŏn listened attentively to Hyŏng-sik's words as he spoke in a subdued voice. "Hm. I see. And what is her name?"

"Her original name is Pak Yŏng-ch'ae, but they say that she is called Kye Wŏr-hyang." Hyŏng-sik wondered whether or not Kye Wŏr-hyang was indeed Pak Yŏng-ch'ae.

U-sŏn was taken aback when he heard the name Kye Wŏr-hyang and then heard that Wŏr-hyang was protecting her virtue for the sake of Hyŏng-sik. [80] U-sŏn's eyes widened. "Really?" He looked at Hyŏng-sik.

Hyŏng-sik's breathing grew labored, as though he could not overcome his anxiety. "Really!" He told U-sŏn about how Yŏng-ch'ae had visited him last night and talked about her life, and that he had just been to Wŏr-hyang's house in Tabang-gol. "You must help me," he said.

"*Tōdaimon shūten*[81]—this is the last stop, Tongdaemun," the conductor announced. Hyŏng-sik and U-sŏn stopped talking and got off the trolley. The trolley for Ch'ŏngnyangni had not yet arrived.

---

80. The 1918 Sinmungwan edition added a few words to this sentence, i.e. "U-sŏn was taken aback when he heard the name Kye Wŏr-hyang and then heard that Wŏr-hyang was the daughter of someone who had been a benefactor to Hyŏng-sik, and that Wŏr-hyang was protecting her virtue for the sake of Hyŏng-sik."

81. The Japanese words *Tōdaimon shūten* are transliterated in *han'gŭl*.

U-sŏn had reason to be taken aback when he heard Hyŏng-sik's words. U-sŏn himself was one of the men who had gone crazy over Yŏng-ch'ae at first sight. U-sŏn was a handsome, cheerful, manly, one-in-a-million kind of fellow. He had a fine presence, was articulate, wrote prose and poetry well though he was only twenty-six years old, was the son of a respectable family and was well connected with the scions of the rich and famous, and, moreover, was a reporter at a large, influential newspaper. He had all the right qualifications for charming women. He was on friendly terms with several *kisaeng*, frequented "music rooms" (*aksil*) run by theatrical professionals, and had trysts with *samp'ae*[82] and *p'ansori* singers. It may sound as though Sin U-sŏn was a prodigal son who did nothing but chase women, but he had the depth and sensitivity of a poet, the bearing of a gentleman, warmth, and a sense of right and wrong. His friends reproached him for his profligate ways, but they loved him for his talent and his friendly, cheerful nature. Hyŏng-sik said of U-sŏn, "He is a pleasure-loving connoisseur right out of Chinese fiction." U-sŏn did indeed have the ways of a heroic young man of Suzhou or Hangzhou in the Tang dynasty.

Sin had set his heart on Kye Wŏr-hyang about a month ago. U-sŏn had confidence in his charms, and believed that Wŏr-hyang would fall for him just like other women. He thought Wŏr-hyang had rejected various sons of wealthy households because she sought a heroic, talented man to whom she could entrust her life, and U-sŏn thought that himself a qualified candidate. While other men tried to win over Wŏr-hyang with money and lust, he thus thought he would win her with his character, talent and personality. U-sŏn could not compete with the others financially, of course. That was why he wrote poetry every night and sent it to Wŏr-hyang through the mail or gave it to her directly. He thought Wŏr-hyang would recognize his character and genius, and think, "At last, I have met my partner," and open her arms to his embrace. Then he heard what Hyŏng-sik told him, and was understandably taken aback.

38

While U-sŏn waited for the trolley to arrive, he looked at Hyŏng-sik's anguished face. The generator at the trolley station power plant made a thundering noise, and conductors and drivers in yellow uniforms walked about beneath the electric lights. "That must be why Wŏr-hyang asked me whether I had any friends from P'yŏngyang," U-sŏn thought.

Once when U-sŏn had gone to see Wŏr-hyang, he had talked about several things when Wŏr-hyang asked him casually, "Do you have any friends from P'yŏngyang?" U-sŏn thought she probably wanted to meet people from P'yŏngyang since she was from P'yŏngyang.

---

82. *Samp'ae* were low-ranking *kisaeng*.

"I have two or three friends from P'yŏngyang," he said.

"What do they do?" Wŏr-hyang asked. She wanted to find out about Hyŏng-sik's whereabouts, and also learn about how people from P'yŏngyang fared in Seoul. Wŏr-hyang knew that there were many students from P'yŏngan Province in Seoul, but since she was a *kisaeng*, she had no way of knowing about the lives of those students or the lives of men from P'yŏngan Province. Wŏr-hyang's visitors included a few men from P'yŏngan Province. They all wore flashy Western-style suits, conversed in Japanese, spoke of how they had gone to college in Tokyo, and were pretentious. Wŏr-hyang, however, remembered what Wŏr-hwa had said four years ago at Pubyŏk Pavilion: "Those men are scarecrows." These men are like that too, thought Wŏr-hyang. Were they the best among the men from P'yŏngyan Province who are in Seoul? Wŏr-hyang felt sad for her home province. When U-sŏn said that he had several friends from P'yŏngan Province, Wŏr-hyang wondered whether or not there were any among them who were like Wŏr-hwa's ideal. Might one of those men be Hyŏng-sik, whom she had been waiting for? Wŏr-hyang thought there not many men like U-sŏn in Korea. He was like a man in the poems of antiquity. She loved his heroic, fearless way of thinking.[83] "I wish I could show him to Wŏr-hwa," she thought. Any man who was a friend of U-sŏn's must be quite a man, she thought.

"What do your friends do?" she asked.

"One of them is a teacher, one is a writer, one is a businessman."

"Who is the best among them?" she asked with even greater interest. "Who is the most famous?"

"This woman is seeking a spouse who is from her home province" thought U-sŏn. He felt somewhat jealous.

"A man named Yi Hyŏng-sik is the most promising of them all; however—" He emphasized the "however" in order to lower Hyŏng-sik's worth.

Wŏr-hyang's heart leapt. She hid her feelings, though, and asked in a flirtatious voice, "He is the most promising. However?"

U-sŏn felt a bit ashamed that he seemed to have spoken poorly of his friend. "He is a good man! Very promising." Afraid of losing Wŏr-hyang to Hyŏng-sik, he added, "He is still a little naive. Wet behind the ears." He spoke as though Hyŏng-sik were far beneath him. This was not a lie, of course. U-sŏn most certainly did not think that Hyŏng-sik surpassed him in character, learning or writing ability. He did not even consider Hyŏng-sik his equal. "Hyŏng-sik is lacking in scholarly knowledge," he thought. He overlooked the fact that Hyŏng-sik knew more Japanese and English than he

---

83. While the 1917 *Maeil Sinbo* text used the word *ŭisik* (consciousness, way of thinking) here, the 1918 Sinmungwan edition revised this to *inmul* (character): "She loved his heroic, fearless character."

did. He considered himself Hyŏng-sik's superior in every way. Nor did Hyŏng-sik insist on being considered his equal. If U-sŏn considered himself Hyŏng-sik's superior, then Hyŏng-sik treated him that way. When U-sŏn suggested the other day that they speak to one another in informal language, Hyŏng-sik agreed very politely and modestly, as though U-sŏn were a superior who were granting him permission to speak with him informally. U-sŏn definitely did not hate or despise Hyŏng-sik, though. U-sŏn truly believed that Hyŏng-sik had great potential. When he said to Wŏr-hyang, "Hyŏng-sik is promising, but he is still wet behind the ears," he had not been speaking ill of Hyŏng-sik, but was expressing a sincere criticism he had of Hyŏng-sik.

"Is this why we ended up talking about Hyŏng-sik that day?" U-sŏn wondered. He looked again at Hyŏng-sik, who stood waiting for the trolley.

Hyŏng-sik paced back and forth anxiously, and kept looking eastward. "Why isn't the trolley coming?"

"It's late at night, so perhaps the train only runs once every thirty minutes." U-sŏn sympathized with Hyŏng-sik's suffering.

Overcome with pity and sorrow for Yŏng-ch'ae, Hyŏng-sik seized U-sŏn's hand. "Please help me tonight." All alone in the world, Hyŏng-sik had no one else whom he could trust besides U-sŏn in circumstances like this. If only U-sŏn helps me, I will be able to save Yŏng-ch'ae, Hyŏng-sik thought. "Do not worry," said U-sŏn, and laughed as he turned the other way. He had reason to laugh.

U-sŏn had heard at Wŏr-hyang's house that Kim Hyŏn-su, the son of the Kyŏngsŏng School's Superintendent Baron Kim, and Pae Myŏng-sik had taken Wŏr-hyang to Ch'ŏngnyangni. U-sŏn thought that Kim Hyŏn-su would have his way with Wŏr-hyang that night. U-sŏn had therefore gone to the Police Station and asked a detective for help.[84] He wanted to defeat Kim Hyŏn-su's scheme. Even if he could not take Wŏr-hyang away from Kim Hyŏn-su, he wanted to report the facts of the incident in the newspaper and vent his frustrations, and maybe even get money for a beer out of Kim Hyŏn-su. He had just left the Police Station when he got on the trolley at Ch'ŏlmulgyo. Now it seemed that Wŏr-hyang was devoted to Hyŏng-sik. He was not without jealousy, but he thought that helping Hyŏng-sik was the proper thing to do.

---

84. In the 1918 edition published by Sinmungwan, this passage was revised: "U-sŏn had therefore gone to the *Chongno* Police Station and asked *Detective Yi* for help." (Italics added for changes.) Ono Nōmi thinks that Yi Kwang-su may have realized that a police station would not have dispatched a detective to accompany U-sŏn just because Kim Hyŏn-su had taken Yŏng-ch'ae to a house in Ch'ŏngnyangni; U-sŏn would have had to use a personal connection. Thus, the revised passage specifically refers to a "Detective Yi" of the "Chongno Police Station." Kim Ch'ŏl, Yi Kyŏng-hun, Sŏ Ŭn-ju and Im Chin-yŏng, "*Mujŏng* ŭi Kyebo," *Minjok Munhaksa Yŏn'gu* no. 20 (2002): 70.

39

The two men arrived at the house in Ch'ŏngnyangni. A detective from the Police Station followed after them. U-sŏn knew the secluded house that Kim Hyŏn-su frequented. It was a small house to the north of a well, and was the cleanest and quietest of several houses that were supposed to be used for meditation. U-sŏn walked quietly through the front door, and motioned to Hyŏng-sik to stay outside. Could Yŏng-ch'ae be here? wondered Hyŏng-sik. He listened, his legs shaking. There seemed to be the sound of a woman in distress, though it could not be heard clearly. Hyŏng-sik walked a step closer and listened, rubbing his chest with one hand. There was indeed the sound of a woman in distress. Unable to pull himself together, Hyŏng-sik ran through the front door. A light was lit outside the house, and the door panels were closed, but the silhouettes of men with short, Western-style hair could be seen moving about. Hyŏng-sik began to breathe more rapidly. U-sŏn peered in through the windows, then sneaked out the front door surreptitiously like a cat. He put a hand on Hyŏng-sik's shoulder and said in Japanese, "We can be of no use now."[85]

Hyŏng-sik's eyes flashed with rage, and he jumped up onto the veranda of the house and kicked at the door panel.[86] The door panel collapsed inward into the room with a loud crash. The men in the room struggled to get up from under the door. Hyŏng-sik kicked the men over without even seeing their faces. Someone grabbed Hyŏng-sik's arm.

"Pae Myŏng-sik, you scoundrel!" shouted Hyŏng-sik, foaming at the mouth. Hyŏng-sik was speechless with rage, and could say no more. He punched Pae in the face with his free arm, and kicked the other man with all his might several times where he lay fallen on the ground. The man opened another door and ran out.

"Kim Hyŏn-su, you wretch!" shouted Hyŏng-sik. Hyŏng-sik picked up the collapsed door. The woman covered her face with both hands and sobbed. Her hands and feet were tied. Her Korean skirt and trousers were torn. Her hair had come undone and flowed down her back. Blood flowed from her lower lip. Beer bottles—some of them broken—and a bowl of ice were spread out in one corner of the room. Hyŏng-sik covered the woman with her skirt, and helped her to sit up. The woman just kept crying, covering her face with her two bound hands. U-sŏn came into the room. He began to untie the woman's hands and feet.

"Those two have been arrested," U-sŏn said to Hyŏng-sik, and laughed. Hyŏng-sik resented U-sŏn for laughing at a time like this. U-sŏn, however, did not think this incident was as serious as Hyŏng-sik thought it was. U-sŏn

---

85. Sin speaks in Japanese (*Mō dame da*) transliterated in Korean as "Mo—ttametta" (it's no use now).
86. *Yŏngch'ang*: door panels that slide open sideways, installed between a room and the veranda of a traditional Korean house.

was the kind of person who tries to laugh at everything. Hyŏng-sik untied the woman's wrists. The woman kept her hands on her face and wept. Hyŏng-sik's rage subsided somewhat, and he was able to think more dispassionately. From where he stood, he could see that the woman's sashes had been undone, and her skirt had slipped down, so that a hand's width of her white waist was visible. Hyŏng-sik sorrowed anew at the sight. "Is this Yŏng-ch'ae after all?" he wondered. "I wish it were not," he thought. He looked at the woman's clothes and head. She was not wearing a skirt of fine ramie, of course, nor was she wearing her hair in a Western-style chignon. Hyŏng-sik did not know of what kind of fabric the skirt was made. He just thought it must be some kind of silk. The woman wore a blood red ribbon in her hair, and a yellowish jade ring. Hyŏng-sik wanted to see the woman's face. He could not bring himself to look at her face, though. He was afraid she might be Yŏng-ch'ae.

U-sŏn knew that the woman was Wŏr-hyang. After he had heard that Wŏr-hyang was the daughter of someone who had been kind to his friend Hyŏng-sik, and that Wŏr-hyang had been saving herself for Hyŏng-sik, U-sŏn felt bad that he had said rudely, "Hey, Wŏr-hyang" when addressing her, and he felt sorry that he had tried to get near to her. U-sŏn therefore stood one step behind Hyŏng-sik now, and just watched him. The woman kept crying, with her hands covering her face. Hyŏng-sik stood helpless for awhile unsure of how to address the woman.

"Excuse me," he said. "Please do not worry. Those beasts have been arrested." Hyŏng-sik himself was not sure what he meant when he said "please do not worry." How could the arrest of those two beasts have anything to do with whether or not she found peace of mind? Was it not as U-sŏn had said? "It is no good. We are too late."

"Miss Pak Yŏng-ch'ae!" said U-sŏn, unable to hold back any longer. U-sŏn knew that the woman was Wŏr-hyang, and that Wŏr-hyang was Pak Yŏng-ch'ae. He had therefore stopped saying "Hey, Wŏr-hyang" to her and said, "Excuse me, Miss Pak Yŏng-ch'ae" for the past month or so. That would have been difficult for most men to do, but it was not all that difficult for U-sŏn.

"Excuse me, Miss Pak!" he said again. "Mr. Yi Hyŏng-sik is here." The woman started and suddenly removed her hands from her face. She looked at Hyŏng-sik with dazed and bewildered eyes. Hyŏng-sik looked at her face. It was Wŏr-hyang. Pak Yŏng-ch'ae. Yŏng-ch'ae looked at Hyŏng-sik. It was him. Yi Hyŏng-sik. Hyŏng-sik and Yŏng-ch'ae looked at one another for a long time, both as still as though they were made of wood. U-sŏn looked at each of them by turns, without a word. The three people looked at one another like this for awhile. Eventually tears rose in U-sŏn's eyes, then in Hyŏng-sik and Yŏng-ch'ae's eyes. Yŏng-ch'ae bit her bleeding lips again. Her jadelike front tooth became stained with red. Hyŏng-sik folded his arms over his chest and averted his head. U-sŏn looked away too. Hyŏng-sik wept aloud. Yŏng-ch'ae fell forward again and wept. U-sŏn bit his lip, and wiped his tears away with his sleeve. A bell chimed three or four times.

40

The detective tied up Kim Hyŏn-su and Pae Myŏng-sik with rope, and brought them into the courtyard. Hyŏng-sik wanted then and there to go and chew off their flesh, and grind their bones and eat them.[87] The two men sank their heads down, as though ashamed. They were not contrite, though. They thought it was all right to rape a kisaeng if she did not do as she was told. They thought it was a sin for a woman of a good family to have illicit relations with a man; but a kisaeng was a woman with whom any man could fool around. They thought that the virtue of chastity was for women of good family, not kisaeng. They were right. According to law, a kisaeng entertained guests with singing and dancing. In reality, however, all kisaeng slept with "guests" every night. Kim Hyŏn-su and Pae Myŏng-sik thus thought that women known as kisaeng were a special kind of creature that was beyond morality and ethics. They therefore thought that what they had done that night did not go against their morals or conscience. They were only afraid that because there were inconvenient laws, having sexual relations with a woman against her will was considered rape. They thought that if they could just get away from the scene, then the next morning they would be entirely innocent of any wrongdoing. As a so-called educator, Pae was worried that his position as dean at the Kyŏngsŏng School might be endangered if he were arrested on such charges.

Hyŏng-sik looked angrily at the two men who hung their heads low. One might expect as much from a man like Kim Hyŏn-su, but it angered Hyŏng-sik that Pae, who was what is called an educator, would commit such a serious crime. Hyŏng-sik stood next to Pae and asked in a derisive voice, "What kind of behavior is this, Mr. Pae? How can an educator commit rape?"

Pae had nothing to say. "Why is Yi Hyŏng-sik getting involved in this?" he thought, and found it rather strange. He felt annoyed at Hyŏng-sik for interfering in a matter that was none of Hyŏng-sik's business. Pae thought it appropriate to be arrested by the detective, since he had committed rape, but he wondered why he was being reprimanded by Yi Hyŏng-sik, who had nothing to do with the matter. Yi Hyŏng-sik pretended outwardly to be a righteous, decent man, thought Pae, but actually frequented kisaeng houses and must have grown close to Wŏr-hyang. Pae thought that Hyŏng-sik must have brought the detective because Hyŏng-sik was jealous that Pae was trying to have his way with Wŏr-hyang. Why else would Hyŏng-sik have brought a detective and gotten so angry over something that had nothing to

87. The 1918 Sinmungwan edition revised this to: "grind their bones and drink them down."

do with him? Pae Myŏng-sik was incapable of feeling sadness or pain over anything that was not relevant to his own self interest. He could be sad if he saw his own child get cut a little on the finger with a knife; but if someone else's son died, he would say, "I am very sad for you," as though he meant it more than anyone else, but could not be sad in his heart.

Had Yŏng-ch'ae been his sister or daughter and someone had raped her, he would have been even more furious than Hyŏng-sik and would have attacked the perpetrator with a knife. Since Yŏng-ch'ae was not his sister and not his daughter, though, he did not care if Yŏng-ch'ae was raped. He would not care if she died, even.

"You are from the nobility!" Hyŏng-sik said to Kim Hyŏn-su. "The title 'nobility' does not refer to people who commit evil deeds. You studied in Tokyo for five years. Do you remember what you once said at a meeting? You said you were devoting your life to education." Hyŏng-sik stomped his feet in outrage. Hyŏn-su thought he was being insulted by a lowly fellow from the countryside. I am a baron, a rich man who owns hundreds of thousands of wŏn. You are an impecunious scholar. You are insulting me now, but someday you will bow at my feet, he thought. Even if I am arrested, I will be released tomorrow morning, but once you go to jail, you will easily spend the rest of your life there, until you rot and die in there. No matter how decent you may be, you will make a mistake someday, and when that happens, I will take revenge on you for all of my humiliation today. When he thought of the pleasure he had had holding Yŏng-ch'ae earlier, he detested Hyŏng-sik for interrupting. It was not the time or place for him to speak, though, and he could not wield his authority as baron, or the power of his wealth, in the midst of an isolated forest of pines in Ch'ŏngnyangni.

U-sŏn expected Hyŏng-sik to reprimand the two men harshly, but when he saw Hyŏng-sik speak to them as though teaching students in a classroom how to behave, it seemed to him that Hyŏng-sik was still a very naive young man who knew little about the world. "If I had been Hyŏng-sik and been in such a situation, I would reprimand them quite severely and vent my anger," U-sŏn thought. Hyŏng-sik, however, did not know how to reprimand someone any more severely than that.

Thus, Hyŏng-sik stomped his feet on the ground again and said, "Please become human beings!" Hyŏng-sik believed that if he said this, the two men would feel guilty, and would regret what they had done, and would vow never to do such a thing again. He thought the two men hung down their heads because they had felt shame and remorse upon hearing what he said. In fact, however, the two men were embarrassed but not repentant.

U-sŏn could not stand any more of this. "You take Miss Yŏng-ch'ae home," U-sŏn said to Hyŏng-sik. "I will take care of these two."

41

Yŏng-ch'ae got home a little after eleven o'clock. Hyŏng-sik accompanied her to the front door of her house, and then went back to his lodgings. Neither of them spoke on the way from Ch'ŏngnyangni to Tabang-gol, and they did not look at each other. They could not bring themselves to speak or to look at one another's face. They felt neither happy nor sad, and they gave no thought to what might happen in the future. It was as though they had no thoughts at all. In short, the two went home in a state of mental oblivion.

Yŏng-ch'ae staggered to her room. As soon as she reached it, she cried out and collapsed in tears. The old woman had fallen asleep in the other room, and came running out without even putting on a skirt when she heard the sound of weeping. She stood outside of Yŏng-ch'ae's room, and saw Yŏng-ch'ae collapsed on the floor, crying.

"Why are you late?" she asked. "Why are you crying?" The old woman looked at Yŏng-ch'ae's torn clothes. "Yŏng-ch'ae had a man tonight," the old woman thought, nodding. She remembered how she too had been saving herself for someone—no one in particular, just some special person—when she was fifteen or sixteen years old.[88] She remembered pushing away Governor Min's son with her arms when he attacked her, and how he had cursed her for resisting. "Bitch!" he had said. She cried when she heard him say that. She remembered, however, that she had gladly started sleeping with men after that. She remembered that she enjoyed sleeping with a new man now and then, rather than with the same man for a long time. "I had slept with over a hundred men by the time I was nineteen years old," she thought. She felt sorry for Yŏng-ch'ae, who had only today begun sleeping with men. Yŏng-ch'ae had been arrogant until now because she had never been with a man, and had seemed to look down on the old woman. Now Yŏng-ch'ae will not be able to put on such airs any more, the old woman thought, and laughed.

"Why get your skirt torn? Why put up such a struggle that you get your skirt torn?" thought the old woman, looking at Yŏng-ch'ae's back as she shook with sobs. The old woman thought of the grotesque-looking Kim Hyŏn-su being pushed away by Yŏng-ch'ae, and the even more grotesque-looking Pae Myŏng-sik grabbing hold of Yŏng-ch'ae's arms as she struggled and screamed. She thought of Yŏng-ch'ae grinding her teeth. The old woman laughed again. "Stupid wench," she thought. "It happens to everyone." Yŏng-ch'ae was just reacting that way because she was still immature, the old woman thought derisively. "The son of a baron! And in such a nice setting!" thought the old woman. She both pitied and resented

88. Here, the 1918 Sinmungwan edition adds the following sentence: "Then she remembered losing her virginity when she was raped by Governor Min's son."

Yŏng-ch'ae for being too immature to appreciate a good situation. She even felt envious of Yŏng-ch'ae. "If only I were younger," she thought. She felt angry about being old. "Who would look at me now?" she thought. "I have to make do with an ugly old husband. How could Yŏng-ch'ae turn down a young man—and the son of a baron, at that!" The old woman hated Yŏng-ch'ae. If Yŏng-ch'ae had slept with guests over the past five years at the rate of one hundred guests per year, or a total of five hundred guests, charging five wŏn per guest, the old woman would have made at least two thousand five hundred wŏn. I was weak, though, and gave in to Yŏng-ch'ae's stupid stubbornness. The old woman wanted to kick Yŏng-ch'ae. She regretted feeding and clothing Yŏng-ch'ae in vain all that time. "She has started sleeping with guests now, though," the old woman thought, and felt loath to sell Yŏng-ch'ae to Kim Hyŏn-su for one thousand wŏn. If she kept her another three years, she would be able to recover all of her investment. "That would be the best plan," she thought, and laughed again. If she did sell Yŏng-ch'ae to Kim Hyŏn-su as a concubine, this time she would ask for two thousand wŏn. By now, he would not hesitate at paying even twenty thousand wŏn, let alone two thousand wŏn. Yes, of course. If she kept Yŏng-ch'ae a long time, Yŏng-ch'ae could get sick eventually. It would be better to sell Yŏng-ch'ae now for two thousand wŏn, and be spared medical bills and the cost of disposing of the corpse. Kim Hyŏn-su would be there the next morning, before breakfast. She would settle a deal with him to sell Yŏng-ch'ae for two thousand wŏn, she thought, and laughed.

The old woman noticed that Yŏng-ch'ae was sobbing even more violently than before. She frowned. Then she felt frightened. She remembered that once, in P'yŏngyang, when the son of Kim Yun-su had tried to attack Yŏng-ch'ae, Yŏng-ch'ae had taken a knife out from where she kept it hidden against her breast, and had tried to slit her own throat. "Evil woman!" he said, and never came to see Yŏng-ch'ae any more after that. The old woman looked around Yŏng-ch'ae's room, and looked at Yŏng-ch'ae's hands again. She wondered whether or not Yŏng-ch'ae had a knife. Various thoughts flashed through the old woman's mind: a knife, opium, a well, the Han River. It gave the old woman gooseflesh. She looked at Yŏng-ch'ae. Yŏng-ch'ae had both hands wound around her braid. Her back heaved with sobs. The old woman's eyes grew wide. She could see Yŏng-ch'ae pulling out a sharp knife and running towards her screaming, "Wretched woman! Thief!" then stabbing the old woman in the chest and twisting the knife as the old woman's ribs made a crunching noise. Then she could see Yŏng-ch'ae removing the knife and slitting her own throat. The blood gushed out and sprayed her face and arm. The old woman winced, and sighed deeply.

The old woman stepped quietly inside the doorway to Yŏng-ch'ae's room. "Wŏr-hwa! Wŏr-hwa!" Yŏng-ch'ae said to herself, gnashing her teeth, unaware that the old woman was there. The old woman winced and left Yŏng-ch'ae's room.

"I should soothe Yŏng-ch'ae," she thought. "I feel sorry for her. I will give her a hug. She is the daughter I have raised for seven years," she thought. "Wŏr-hyang!" she said smiling, and stepped into Yŏng-ch'ae's room.

42

"Wŏr-hyang!" When she got no answer from Yŏng-ch'ae, the old woman squatted next to Yŏng-ch'ae and shook her by the back. "Wŏr-hyang! Why are you crying?" Yŏng-ch'ae lifted her head and looked at the old woman. The old woman was not wearing a skirt, and her two legs and fat body looked nauseatingly repulsive to Yŏng-ch'ae. The old woman's wicked, deceitful eyes were even more disgusting. That old woman has grown fat sucking my blood, Yŏng-ch'ae thought. Everything I have been through for the past seven years has been because of that old woman. And I have soiled the virtue that I guarded for nineteen years, because of that old woman. I want to chew this bitch of an old woman to pieces. It was the old woman's plan to send me to Ch'ŏngnyangni. She sent me there knowing that this would happen to me. She looked bitterly at the old woman. The old woman saw Yŏng-ch'ae looking at her with bloodshot eyes.

"What is wrong?" the old woman asked in an even more affectionate voice, trying to hold back her fright. "You have blood on your lip. Did you cut your lip?"

It is all because of you, thought Yŏng-ch'ae.

"I bit my lip! I wanted to bite my lips off! Other people want to eat my flesh, so I wanted to eat my flesh too!" As she said this, Yŏng-ch'ae felt like biting off the old woman's thick lips. The old woman picked up a cloth that was next to her, and put her arm around Yŏng-ch'ae's neck.

"That must hurt. Let me wipe the blood off," said the old woman. In her heart, the old woman truly began to feel pity for Yŏng-ch'ae. Yŏng-ch'ae saw tears welling in the old woman's eyes. "At least she still has the heart of a human being!" she thought. She let the old woman wipe her blood off with a cloth. She thought it strange that there were tears in the old woman's eyes. She had lived with the old woman for seven years and had never once seen the old woman cry. Once the old woman had cried for three days because she had a cavity in her molar, but Yŏng-ch'ae had never seen her cry about her life, or because she felt sorry for someone. Those must be bitter-tasting, cold tears, Yŏng-ch'ae thought as she looked at the old woman's tears. Yŏng-ch'ae felt no pain in her bit lip. The old woman wiped the blood carefully from Yŏng-ch'ae's lip with a soft silk cloth, afraid that it might hurt. The lip kept bleeding the more she wiped it. Red drops of blood kept rising from the deep tooth marks left by Yŏng-ch'ae's two front teeth. The silk cloth became mottled with blood. The old woman sighed and looked at the cloth in the light.[89] Yŏng-ch'ae looked too. "That is my blood! The blood I received from my parents!" she thought. Yŏng-ch'ae looked at the torn front of her skirt and thought of what had happened at Ch'ŏngnyangni.

"This blood has become tainted blood," she thought. She took the cloth from the old woman, and put it between her teeth and tore it to pieces. "My blood is tainted blood!" she cried, and trembled. The scene at Ch'ŏngnyangni appeared even more clearly before Yŏng-ch'ae's eyes. She could see Kim Hyŏn-su's beastlike eyes, and Pae Myŏng-sik standing next to him and gagging her mouth with a handkerchief that smelled of sweat. While Pae Myŏng-sik grabbed hold of her arms, Kim Hyŏn-su, as though he had gone mad, grasped her ears and put his stinking mouth against hers. "Let's tie this girl up," Kim Hyŏn-su had said. Kim held her two feet, and Pae winked at him and tied Yŏng-ch'ae's wrists together with a silk sash used to tie the end of a trouser leg. "Bitch!" said Kim after that. "I should give you a good kick. You still won't listen, eh?" He laughed. Yŏng-ch'ae pounded her chest with her fists and thrashed her legs.

"Give me a knife! Give me a knife!" she cried. "I want to cut my lips off! Give me a knife!" she wept.

The old woman hugged Yŏng-ch'ae.

"Wŏr-hyang! Pull yourself together!" The tears that had welled in the old woman's eyes fell on Yŏng-ch'ae's head. "Try not to cry, Wŏr-hyang!" Yŏng-ch'ae's body shook like a person shivering with cold. She bit her lower lip again. Warm drops of blood fell onto the back of the old woman's hand where it lay on Yŏng-ch'ae's breast. The old woman looked up from Yŏng-ch'ae's shoulder at her face. Blood rose from her lip like water from a spring. Her front teeth were stained red, and bubbles of blood flowed through her teeth and dripped down. Her dishevelled hair covered her eyes and cheeks, and, shadowed by her hair, her face looked like that of a dead person. The old woman released the arm that was wrapped around Yŏng-ch'ae's breast, and put it around Yŏng-ch'ae's neck. She rubbed her cheek against Yŏng-ch'ae's cheek. Yŏng-ch'ae's cheek was as hot as fire. The old woman sobbed.

"I was wrong, Wŏr-hyang, I was wrong. Please stop crying. I deserve to be killed." The old woman cried out loud. "I did not know that Wŏr-hyang was so strong willed," thought the old woman. "I did wrong, and now I have made poor Wŏr-hyang shed her blood. Pretty Wŏr-hyang! My daughter," the old woman thought, and inwardly brought her hands together and bowed before Yŏng-ch'ae. The old woman cried even louder, and rubbed her cheek

---

89. The phrase "in the light" was added to this sentence in the 1918 Sinmungwan edition.

against Yŏng-ch'ae's cheek. She chewed strands of Yŏng-ch'ae's fragrant hair. Bright red blood dripped onto the front of Yŏng-ch'ae's torn, wrinkled skirt. The silk cloth stained with the blood from Yŏng-ch'ae's lips lay crumpled before Yŏng-ch'ae's feet, and glittered in the light from the electric lamps. The strings of the *kayako* propped against the wall in a bag made of shimmering fabric sobbed twice for some reason. The old woman's husband, who had been waiting for his wife in the other room, walked over and stood outside Yŏng-ch'ae's door without even bothering to tie the sashes on his Korean trousers.

"Why is everyone crying?" he asked.

43

Hyŏng-sik arrived at his home. He had never gotten home this late before, the landlady thought. "Why are you so late?" she asked as she lay in her room. Hyŏng-sik did not answer, but went to his room, turned on the light, and sat down at his desk still wearing his hat and *turumagi*. The landlady locked the front door, then quietly went to Hyŏng-sik's door and looked at his face. Hyŏng-sik sat with his eyes closed. The landlady wondered what Hyŏng-sik was so worried about lately. Hyŏng-sik had lived there for three years. The landlady thus felt as though he were her son or younger brother. She felt that he was not just a guest who was staying in her house, but a member of her family. When she prepared his meals in the kitchen, she did not think of the food as something purchased by a guest in her house, but prepared the food with the same care that she had used to prepare her husband's meals decades ago. The landlady had no friends and no relatives. Hyŏng-sik was the only friend she had in the world. Hyŏng-sik for his part loved and respected the old woman very much. Hyŏng-sik used very polite and respectful language and behavior towards the landlady, but was also warm and affectionate, as though she were his mother. Whenever Hyŏng-sik saw that the old woman was worried about something, he would go to her room with tobacco, or invite her to his room, and comfort her with various entertaining stories. Then the landlady would say, "You are right, the world is like that," and her worries would go away, and she would laugh. Then she would buy him fruits or rice cakes. The landlady's worries would completely disappear whenever she heard Hyŏng-sik speak, and Hyŏng-sik himself would feel a strange happiness after comforting the old woman. Sometimes Hyŏng-sik would pretend that something unpleasant had happened, or that he was angry about something. Then the landlady would go to Hyŏng-sik's room with tobacco, and try diligently to console him. She would say the same things that Hyŏng-sik said when he tried to make her feel better. The old woman had no friends, and could not read. She had nowhere to obtain knowledge except from Hyŏng-sik. She had obtained most of her present knowledge from the things that Hyŏng-sik told her to boost her spirits. His words were philosophy and religion to the old woman. She did not think of these words as something she had obtained from Hyŏng-sik, though; she thought they were words of wisdom that came from herself. She was not being ungrateful. She just did not realize that she had heard these things from Hyŏng-sik. When the landlady tried to comfort Hyŏng-sik, he thus could pretty much guess from her very first words the rest of what she was going to say, and he would smile to himself. One in ten times, though, or perhaps one in twenty times, the landlady had her own unique thoughts. She was very dull-witted, but had powers of deduction. She could think up new theses from the material that she heard from Hyŏng-sik.

Hyŏng-sik knew that what she talked about was what she had heard from Hyŏng-sik himself, but the words had a new meaning when they came from her. Words such as "The world is like that," had a different meaning and flavor when they came from the old woman's mouth. Hyŏng-sik therefore took great solace in hearing anew the words he had said to the landlady. He could not suppress a smile, though, when he heard the landlady reciting the words he had said to her as though they were some truth that she in particular had discovered. In any case, the landlady liked Hyŏng-sik, and he liked her too. He felt sorry for her, though, and she felt sorry for him. The landlady had been a servant in a *yangban* household when she was young. Then she had gotten pregnant with the seed of the man of the house, who was a government official of rank, and she was quite powerful for awhile. The government official loved her very much, and her friends looked up to her, and she boasted to her friends. She was not satisfied with just the man of the house, though, who was an old man, and she had a secret affair with a cute young man who often visited the house. The old man learned about it, though. After that, the young man disappeared, and her genitals were mutilated with a hot iron. Her five months of glory ended in one day, and became nothing more than a dream. The old woman had thus been well acquainted with the power of the office-holding aristocracy. She thought any man who could not hold office was a pathetic man. She had therefore been urging Hyŏng-sik for three years to hold office. Hyŏng-sik laughed and said, "Who would appoint someone like me to office?" The landlady knew that Hyŏng-sik had talent and was a good person. That was why she thought he should hold office. Whenever she saw the men who came to see Hyŏng-sik, with their uniforms trimmed in gold and their swords, she lamented on Hyŏng-sik's behalf, thinking, "Why doesn't our Hyŏng-sik hold office?" After the guests in gold-trimmed uniforms and swords left, she would ask Hyŏng-sik, "Why don't you hold office?" Then Hyŏng-sik would say, "Who would appoint someone like me?" Eventually she realized that he would not budge on this matter no matter how much she tried to persuade him, and since a year and a half ago, she had stopped talking about it altogether. Whenever she saw his office-holding friends visit, or saw people call him "Mr. Lee," she would take solace in the thought that even if he would not hold office, he was just as good as any of the people who did hold office. She therefore addressed him these days with the word "Teacher" or "Mister" instead of "Your honor." She nevertheless deeply cherished within her breast the thought that he should hold office.

The landlady stood outside of Hyŏng-sik's room for a long time watching him. She was going to speak, but thought, "He must be thinking about something," and went quietly back to her room. She could not fall asleep even after she went to bed, though. Several times she lit her pipe and stuck her head out of her door to look over at Hyŏng-sik's room. Even when she woke after sleeping for awhile, and looked out, the light was still on in Hyŏng-sik's room.

44

Hyŏng-sik thought about Yŏng-ch'ae, and was unaware that the landlady had been standing outside his door. He thought about the scene that he had witnessed at Ch'ŏngnyangni. He remembered how Kim Hyŏn-su had pushed the window aside and gotten up from where he lay. He remembered how Yŏng-ch'ae's lip had been bleeding, and her clothes had slipped down so that her white waist was showing. He remembered how U-sŏn had said, "It is no use. We are too late." Had her body indeed been soiled by Kim Hyŏn-su? What had U-sŏn meant when he looked through the window and said, "It is no use. We are too late"? Had he meant that Yŏng-ch'ae's body had already been soiled; or had U-sŏn spoken because he had seen Yŏng-ch'ae about to have her body defiled? Hyŏng-sik wished that he had looked through the window once before he had kicked it in. He was loath to interpret U-sŏn's remark as meaning that Yŏng-ch'ae's virtue had indeed been stained. Was it not the case that through divine intervention, he and U-sŏn had rescued her just as she was about to be raped? Yes, that is it, he thought, and sighed as though relieved.

What was the significance of her bound wrists and feet, though? Her torn skirt and trousers, and exposed legs? What was the significance of the fact that Yŏng-ch'ae had covered her face with her two hands, and bitten her lip? Why had she not said anything to Hyŏng-sik? Was it true that they had been "too late"? Yes, of course, Yŏng-ch'ae had been defiled. Her body had been soiled by Kim Hyŏn-su. Hyŏng-sik clenched his fists and swung them twice in the air. He lit a cigarette and puffed at it without even bothering to breathe in the smoke deeply. The cigarette smoke would not spread through the humid, windless air, but circled Hyŏng-sik's burning head in waves. Hyŏng-sik threw his cigarette into the courtyard before he had finished even half of it, and waved away the billows of smoke that circled his head. The smoke dispersed in all directions, some of it quickly, some of it slowly, as though having lost its sense of direction. A fly that had fallen asleep on the ceiling was surprised out of sleep, and began buzzing, then was silent again. Hyŏng-sik lowered his head, and sat as still as though he were a drawn image. Had Yŏng-ch'ae been a virgin until now? Was it possible to be a *kisaeng* for eight years and still be a virgin? Was it possible to be a *kisaeng* and not be a prostitute? When men propositioned her with lust and money ten times, twenty times, could Yŏng-ch'ae have kept her virginity? Though she was of good family, and had studied the *Admonitions for Women*, and *Biographies of Virtuous Women*, could she have overcome temptation on hundreds of occasions over eight years? Hyŏng-sik thought about the female heroines in the fiction he had read, and the women he had read about in the newspapers or heard about. In Chinese fiction and Korean storybooks of antiquity, there were indeed women who protected their chastity with the constancy of pine and bamboo.[90] That was in fiction, though. Could there be such instances in reality? In the fiction of antiquity, there were women who had not had to shed their red blood[91] even though they became *kisaeng*. Could such people exist in reality, though? Could a nineteen-year-old girl refuse the men who were always propositioning her? Even if Yŏng-ch'ae had been exceptionally strong willed, and been able to overcome all temptation, would there not have been other men like Kim Hyŏn-su? Men like Kim Hyŏn-su did not exist only in Seoul, and there would be more than one like him in Seoul. Perhaps what had happened to Yŏng-ch'ae at Ch'ŏngnyangni had happened to her several times before. Yŏng-ch'ae could not possibly be a virgin, Hyŏng-sik thought. He jumped to his feet, and paced back and forth in his room.

Hyŏng-sik sat down and started smoking again. He thought about his past. He had never seen a woman's body exposed until today. One could say that a young man who had never seen a woman's unclothed body until he was twenty-five years old was a very chaste young man. Had he been chaste because he was strong willed and had a clean mind? Hyŏng-sik shook his head. Once when he was in Tokyo, a woman had sought Hyŏng-sik's love, with the landlady as a go-between. Hyŏng-sik had refused without hesitation. He received two or three such requests afterwards, but he refused. Had he been all that pure at heart though? Had his conscience been all that strong? "How can one speak of such a thing? I could never go through with it!" he had said, and refused. Afterwards, though, he regretted turning down the offer. "I am a fool. Why did I refuse?" If the girl asked him again, he would act as though he could not help but give in to the girl's request. It was Hyŏng-sik's lips that had refused the requests, not his heart. When the old

90. The pine represented constant virtue because it was always green. The bamboo set an example of constant virtue because of the even, regular spacing of its joints.
91. Neo-Confucianism required a woman to take her own life if she lost her virtue. Hyŏng-sik is thinking of women of fiction who kept their virtue even though they were *kisaeng*, and never had to take their own life.

landlady smiled at him and said, "How about it?" Hyŏng-sik had said no simply because he was too embarrassed to say yes. Would he have been displeased with the landlady, though, if she had taken his "no" for a "yes," and put the girl in his room one night? Hyŏng-sik shook his head. After he turned down the offer, the woman came one evening and spent the night in the landlady's room. The old woman winked furtively at Hyŏng-sik that day when he spread out his bedding. Hyŏng-sik cleared his throat and firmly said no. Then he laughed suggestively, so that the landlady would take his no for a yes. The old woman laughed too. Then Hyŏng-sik lay down and waited for the woman to come to his room, thinking that she would be there any moment now. He coughed loudly for no reason on his way to and from the bathroom. The next morning, Hyŏng-sik thought regretfully that the landlady was honest to a fault. Hyŏng-sik shook his head. It was impossible for Yŏng-ch'ae to be a virgin still, he thought once again.

45

Hyŏng-sik heard the old woman tapping ashes from her pipe. She was sitting in the *anpang*. Hyŏng-sik lit another cigarette. What should he do? What should he do about Yŏng-ch'ae?

Should he make her his wife because she was the daughter of his benefactor, Scholar Pak? Would that be the proper thing for him to do? Hyŏng-sik could see Yŏng-ch'ae sitting in his room the night before. "Father starved to death in prison," she had said. Her face, with the tears falling from her eyes, was beautiful. Hyŏng-sik had been dazzled by her beauty. He had imagined them getting married in church, and had imagined the many cute, healthy sons and daughters they would have. Hyŏng-sik looked at where Yŏng-ch'ae had sat the night before, and he thought of the scene that night and the fantasies that he had imagined. He felt dazed for awhile.

"And yet," he thought, and opened his eyes. "Yŏng-ch'ae is not a virgin. Even if she had been a virgin until yesterday, she is not a virgin tonight." He thought of the scene at the house in Ch'ŏngnyangni. Last night, Hyŏng-sik had been thinking hopefully that perhaps Yŏng-ch'ae had been taken care of by a good family, and had graduated from a girls' school like Sŏn-hyŏng and Sun-ae, and was still a virgin. Even if she had become a *kisaeng*, she would certainly have kept her virginity for Hyŏng-sik's sake. Now, however, Hyŏng-sik thought she was not a virgin. He lowered his head, and sat that way for a long time.

The old woman could be heard in the room off of the veranda, tapping ashes from her pipe again. Hyŏng-sik lifted his head. He looked around the room. He thought of how he had sat facing Sŏn-hyŏng and Sun-ae at Elder Kim's house. The fragrance from their hair, the white, almost translucent fingers pressed against the desk, the jade-colored ramie skirts that were slightly wrinkled and soiled, the wide, jade-colored ribbons, the way their soft, lovely skin glowed through the back of their blouses, which were damp with perspiration—all this stimulated Hyŏng-sik's weary nerves, with an inexpressible fragrance and pleasure. He remembered vividly, too, that when he met with these sensations, his whole body seemed to melt with happiness, and all the universe seemed to be shining with happiness and singing for joy. Sŏn-hyŏng was like an immortal, he thought. She was completely free of the slightest particle of unclean behavior or unclean thought. She was clear and pure, like snow or white jade, or crystal. Hyŏng-sik smiled. He closed his eyes. He could see Sŏn-hyŏng and Yŏng-ch'ae side by side. At first they were both dressed in garments white as snow, and each held a flower in one hand, and held one hand open towards Hyŏng-sik, as though asking him to clasp their hand. "Take my hand, Hyŏng-sik! Please!" they said, smiling and holding their head slightly to one side coquettishly. Shall I take this hand, or that one? Hyŏng-sik thought, and reached both of his hands into the air, then hesitated. Then Yŏng-ch'ae's appearance began to change. The white, snowlike dress gave way to a bloody, torn skirt of some nameless kind of silk, and her bloodied legs showed through the torn skirt. Tears fell from her eyes, and her lip was bleeding. The flower in her hand disappeared, and she held instead a fistful of soil. He shook his head and opened his eyes. Sŏn-hyŏng still stood before him, dressed in white, and smiling. "Please take my hand, Hyŏng-sik!" she said, reaching her hand out to him, and bowing her head. When Hyŏng-sik reached for Sŏn-hyŏng's hand in a daze, Yŏng-ch'ae's face as she stood beside Sŏn-hyŏng, was hideously transformed like that of a ghost. She bit her lip and sprayed blood over Hyŏng-sik. Hyŏng-sik started with terror.

Hyŏng-sik stood up again, and walked around the room. Trying to rid himself of the thoughts he had been having, he went out to the yard, singing a *ch'angga*[92] that students had been singing recently. The sky was perfectly clear, without a trace of clouds or the rain that had passed. The freshly watered stars blinked as though drowsy. The brightness in the south was the lights on Chin Pass.

Hyŏng-sik gazed at the sky. A cool breeze that seemed to descend from the twinkling stars brushed against Hyŏng-sik's hot face from time to time, like someone's breath against his face. His seething breast grew cooler.

When had those stars first shone? Why did they shine?[93] Who had placed the stars where they were, deciding where each star should be? If one were to fly into the black space that could be seen between the stars, where

---

92. The *Ch'angga* was a genre of poetry popular during the early modern period in Korea. It made nationalism and the independence movement its themes, and was often sung to a Western-style melody. The term *ch'angga* could also refer to "new style" songs learned in school.
93. The 1918 Sinmungwan edition added this latter sentence, "Why did they shine?" which is not in the 1917 *Maeil Sinbo* text.

would one be? Hyŏng-sik remembered studying astronomy when he was in Tokyo, with a teacher who had tuberculosis. "I am not saying that you should all be astronomers, but I do hope that you will look at the sky every night," the teacher had said. Then the teacher had coughed up blood into a spittoon. Hyŏng-sik too always said that whenever one was troubled with thoughts of the chaotic world, just looking at the boundless sky and the countless stars would make all worries disappear like spring snow. He himself, however, had never been so upset that he had to look at the sky. Now, however, he understood deep within his heart what his astronomy teacher had been saying.

"We occupy only a moment in infinite time, and a point in infinite space. How significant could any of our 'significant matters' be? Or how painful any of our sorrows?" He looked up at the sky again, then bowed his head in prayer.

46

Hyŏng-sik did not fall asleep until after three in the morning, and slept until nine o'clock the next morning. He was very tired mentally and physically, and even after he was half-asleep, he had various agitated dreams. The old woman had already prepared breakfast, and had looked into his room four or five times. She had wondered what was wrong with him when he went to sleep still wearing his *turumagi* and without even bothering to spread his bedding. She did not try to wake him, though, since she knew that he had gone to bed late the night before. She worried that the bean paste soup she had taken such care to make would get cold. Just then, Sin U-sŏn came by wearing a straw hat pushed back on his head, and carrying a walking stick.

"How are you? Is Mr. Yi home?" he asked cheerfully, yet politely.

The old woman knew Sin U-sŏn well. "He is a very cheerful, pleasant man," she had once said to Hyŏng-sik, voicing her opinion of Sin. She smiled and went forward to greet Sin U-sŏn.

"Mr. Lee came home late last night, and sat up till dawn thinking about something," she said. "He is still asleep. His breakfast is getting cold." The old woman thought about the bean paste soup. She did not make a very good bean paste soup. She thought she was very good at making bean paste soup, though, and she boasted about it to Hyŏng-sik. Hyŏng-sik often found maggots in the bean paste soup that the old woman made.[94] He did not want to hurt her pride, though, or seem ungrateful for her effort, so he always said, "It's very good." However, he had never said that her soup was delicious. The old woman was nevertheless satisfied with "very good." Sin U-sŏn had once eaten over at Hyŏng-sik's place when the old woman made bean paste

---

94. Maggots could get into *toenjang* (bean paste), which was stored in earthenware jars. That is why they might have appeared in the soup.

soup. There happened to be a large maggot in the soup that day. Because of that, Sin U-sŏn made fun of what a terrible bean paste soup the old woman made. Hyŏng-sik, who was sitting next to U-sŏn, hurriedly tried to cover U-sŏn's mouth, but Sin U-sŏn smiled and, in a loud voice, went on to protest his dismay at the old woman's lousy soup-making ability.

"It is because I am old," the old woman said, sitting on the veranda outside her room and puffing away indignantly at her pipe. She meant to imply that she used to make good bean paste soup when she was young. After that, she never said Sin U-sŏn was a "cheerful, pleasant man" any more. She was still as polite to him as ever, though. She was afraid that otherwise he might further criticize her bean paste soup. U-sŏn heard all about this from Hyŏng-sik.

"Any maggots in your bean paste soup lately?" he said to the old woman. He went into Hyŏng-sik's room. "Get out of bed! What are you doing sleeping?" he said. Hyŏng-sik had vaguely heard U-sŏn and the old woman's conversation, but had not been completely awake. When he heard Sin U-sŏn's loud voice talking to him, he got up, rubbing his eyes, and looked at the round alarm clock on his desk.

"What are you looking at the clock for? It's ten o'clock! Ten o'clock! Wash up and get dressed. Eat your breakfast."

The clock said nine o'clock.[95] Only when Hyŏng-sik heard U-sŏn tell him to get dressed did he remember what had happened the night before. He thought of Yŏng-ch'ae. Looking at the expression on U-sŏn's face, he knew that something had happened, and that it had to do with Yŏng-ch'ae. He remembered how he had stayed awake thinking last night, unable to sleep.

"Has something happened?"

"Just wash up and eat your breakfast! Do I have to do your thinking for you?" U-sŏn went to the shelf and took out a book that was written in English, and began reading, syllable by syllable, a few words at a time, in English that was about the level of volume three of the book, *Choice Readings.*[96] Hyŏng-sik did not know what had happened, but from the expression on Sin U-sŏn's face and the way he was speaking, Hyŏng-sik knew that U-sŏn was there because of Yŏng-ch'ae. He put his toothbrush in his mouth, picked up a towel and left the room. "I am worried about you too," U-sŏn thought as he saw Hyŏng-sik going out to wash up. Sin U-sŏn believed that Hyŏng-sik was a man of such character that Hyŏng-sik would marry Yŏng-ch'ae. However, if Hyŏng-sik made Yŏng-ch'ae his wife, the scene at the house in Ch'ŏngnyangni would always remain in Hyŏng-sik's mind and

---

95. In the 1917 *Maeil Sinbo* edition, it is "half past nine." The 1918 Sinmungwan edition changed this to "nine o'clock."
96. There were several books published in the late nineteenth to early twentieth century with the title *Choice Readings.* These were compilations of selections from literary texts, and were intended for use in teaching elocution.

would cause him much pain and suffering. It was within Sin's power to decide whether or not Hyŏng-sik would suffer. For only he, Kim Hyŏn-su and Pae Myŏng-sik knew whether or not Yŏng-ch'ae was still a virgin. Sin wanted to torment Hyŏng-sik for a long time by withholding this secret. How else could U-sŏn take out his frustration at having been interested in Yŏng-ch'ae too but having been rejected? He had no malicious intentions. Sin U-sŏn thought of life as a game, and this was nothing more than his way of being mischievous. Hyŏng-sik, however, did not think of life as a game. Hyŏng-sik was completely seriously about life. U-sŏn went through life laughing, no matter what happened, but Hyŏng-sik tried to find meaning, and wanted to contribute to the world somehow, to the best of his ability. Hyŏng-sik thought even the most minute phenomena and even the smallest incidents in life were material for research and study. He could not go through life laughing as U-sŏn did. U-sŏn said that Hyŏng-sik had not yet been able to transcend conventionality. Hyŏng-sik said that U-sŏn was a man of neither harm nor benefit to the world. U-sŏn was not indifferent to promoting world civilization and the well-being of others, though. U-sŏn tried his best to do work that would benefit the world. He just did not have Hyŏng-sik's passion for dedicating his life to serving the world. In Hyŏng-sik's words, U-sŏn had received a Chinese education that was centered on the self, whereas Hyŏng-sik had received a Greek education that was centered on society. U-sŏn had been educated in classical Chinese writings, and Hyŏng-sik had been educated in English and German writings.

Hyŏng-sik ran his toothbrush over his teeth twice, then washed his face and hands and returned to his room. He looked at himself in the mirror, and parted his hair. For some reason, U-sŏn hated the way Hyŏng-sik parted his hair. He was always telling Hyŏng-sik to get his hair cut short. "Men who part their hair are weak men," he would say sometimes, though he would not say on what premise he had based this conclusion.

"What has happened?" Hyŏng-sik asked pleadingly, picking maggots from the bean paste soup. U-sŏn did not answer, but walked back and forth in the room, smiling and waiting as Hyŏng-sik ate his breakfast in a hurry. When Hyŏng-sik finished eating, U-sŏn dragged him out of the house. The old woman began clearing the breakfast dishes, and peered into the two men's faces as they left. She put the breakfast table on the veranda and stood up to straighten her back.

"I wonder what is going on," she thought.

47

Thinking of how happy Hyŏng-sik would be, U-sŏn took Hyŏng-sik to Kye Wŏr-hyang's house in Tabang-gol as though he were introducing someone to a new sight worth seeing. As soon as they had turned the corner at Chonggak, Hyŏng-sik knew that U-sŏn was taking him to Yŏng-ch'ae's house. When Hyŏng-sik saw U-sŏn taking him in this direction, and saw how happy U-sŏn was, Hyŏng-sik sensed that there was something to rejoice about, something that would save Yŏng-ch'ae. But it is too late, he thought. She was not a virgin any more. He remembered how Yŏng-ch'ae and Sŏn-hyŏng had stood dressed in white last night, and reached their hands out to him, smiling, and said, "Take my hand, Hyŏng-sik." Then Yŏng-ch'ae's body had changed suddenly. He remembered how her face had become ghastly as a ghost, and how she had sprayed him with blood from her lips. Hyŏng-sik and U-sŏn arrived at the door.

"This will be the last day for that lamp with the name 'Kye Wŏr-hyang' written on it," said U-sŏn, grinning at Hyŏng-sik. U-sŏn struck the lamp several times with his walking stick.

"Someone will come looking for Kye Wŏr-hyang again tonight, and they will be in for a surprise. I would like to see the look on their face when they can't find her, and leave." U-sŏn struck the roof over the lamp with his walking stick as forcefully as if he were trying to break the tiles. Then he laughed. The lamp squeaked as if in pain, and danced about.

"What if something breaks?" Hyŏng-sik thought. He said nothing, and would not smile. U-sŏn was disappointed when he saw that Hyŏng-sik did not look happy. He pretended not to notice, however. "Answer the door!" he called out loudly. A housemaid came out of the gatehouse, adjusting her clothes as though she had just been nursing a child.

"Please come in. No need for you to announce yourself. Just come right in."

"He has been here often," thought Hyŏng-sik. He wondered whether or not U-sŏn might have been one of the men who had taken Yŏng-ch'ae's virginity. He immediately retracted the thought, though.

U-sŏn made as if to strike the housemaid with his walking stick. "Are you still calling me 'sir,' and not 'old man'?" U-sŏn laughed, baring his broad front teeth.

"Is the young miss at home?" he asked.

"She took the train to P'yŏngyang this morning."

U-sŏn and Hyŏng-sik were both taken aback. U-sŏn, moreover, shook his head dejectedly.

"Why?"

"I don't know. How should I know? Last night she came home after eleven o'clock, and I could hear her crying for awhile. Then I fell asleep, and I don't know what happened after that. This morning, before breakfast, the master's wife told me to summon a cart.[97] I thought the young miss was going to a party. But it was awfully early for a party. Maybe there is a boating party at Nodŭl Crossing, I thought. Then the master's wife said that the

---

97. The text uses the Japanese word *kuruma*, transliterated in Korean.

young miss was taking a nine-thirty train to P'yŏngyang." The housemaid spoke volubly.

"She isn't lying," thought Hyŏng-sik in shock. He looked carefully at the housemaid. There was a look of doubt on her face. "Why would Yŏng-ch'ae go to P'yŏngyang?" thought Hyŏng-sik. A baby started to cry in the gatehouse. As the maid turned to go back in, U-sŏn lowered his voice and asked, "Did anyone visit this morning?"

"No, there were no visitors this morning. However . . . " The woman pointed to a house across the street and two houses down. "The young miss from that house came and asked our young miss to go to the bathhouse with her." The maid went back inside. She could be heard spanking the baby and saying "Don't cry!" How could she speak so politely to them, yet be so harsh towards a baby, Hyŏng-sik wondered.

U-sŏn wrote some letters on the ground with his walking stick, then said to Hyŏng-sik, "Go inside anyway. We can find out what happened from the old woman." U-sŏn took off his hat and went in first. The mirth was gone from U-sŏn's voice. Hyŏng-sik followed him. Hyŏng-sik remembered how he had been there the night before and had been treated with contempt by the old woman. He smiled. That was how dispassionate and cold Hyŏng-sik's emotions were right now. However, U-sŏn was very anxious, more anxious than Hyŏng-sik.

There was no one in Wŏr-hyang's room. The old woman's "stupid husband," as she called him, had fallen asleep on the veranda reading a storybook, and was snoring, his head on a wooden pillow. U-sŏn knew the old man well. The old man was the son of a rich man who had lived just outside the P'yŏngyang city walls. He was good at composing poetry, and singing. Thirty or forty years ago he had been a famous playboy, known to everyone in P'yŏngyang. After over a decade of life in dissipation, however, he had used up all of his wealth, and had nothing left. He had nothing left but style, as the saying goes. Over a decade ago, he had become an inhabitant of sorts—not quite husband, not quite visitor—in the old woman's house. She had once been a *kisaeng* who sat on his lap and entertained him. At first he fought with the old woman from time to time. "Insolent bitch!" he would shout at her when he was angry. He had been unable to do that for the last two or three years, though. Instead, every few days or so, the old woman would tell him to "go drop dead." He would just laugh and say, "It is a sin to say that to someone." He would not even think of putting up a fight. For the most part, though, the old woman was kind to her husband. What was even more amazing was that every night, she would spread his bedding with her own hands, and let him sleep on the warmest part of the floor, nearest the heating furnace.

U-sŏn stepped onto the veranda without removing his shoes. "Hello?" he called out, tapping the veranda with his walking stick. Hyŏng-sik stood as he had stood there the night before, and looked at Yŏng-ch'ae's room, just as he had done then. Everything in the room was exactly as it had been that night, he noticed. Hyŏng-sik, however, was no longer as anguished as he had been then.

48

When there was no reply, U-sŏn stomped his feet on the veranda and struck the floor with his walking stick all at once, as though angry. "Hello!" he said again, raising his voice. "Old woman!" Hyŏng-sik laughed at the sound of U-sŏn calling the old woman. After awhile, the old woman appeared at a corner of the courtyard, tying the sash of her Korean skirt.

"It's Mr. Sin! Why are you making such a fuss? I was in the outhouse." She looked at Hyŏng-sik momentarily. He is the man who was here last night, asking if "Miss Wŏr-hyang" was home. Then he must be an errand boy for Mr. Sin, she thought. She ignored Hyŏng-sik, as though he were a person of no particular importance, and stepped up on the veranda.

"Why are you here this early?" she asked U-sŏn with familiarity. She kicked her husband. "Wake up, dear! We have a visitor. If you want that much to lie down, why don't you just crawl into the ground," she said, and kicked the wooden pillow out from under the old man's head. The wooden pillow hit a storybook that had been on the floor nearby, sending the book flying, then rolled across the floor, hit the wall, and came to a stop lying on its side, straight up in the air. The old man's balding head,[98] on which remained nothing but a few strands of grey, hit the wooden floor. He sat up suddenly. "What kind of behavior is that?" he said, and stood up and went to his room without acknowledging U-sŏn's presence. The old man reminded Hyŏng-sik of his late grandfather. Hyŏng-sik's late grandfather had once been wealthy, but eventually sold off all his possessions and lived in a small hovel, treated with contempt by his concubine, who had been a *kisaeng*. His sons all died before him. His grandson, Hyŏng-sik, went to Japan. Hyŏng-sik thought his grandfather had been a better person than this old man, though.

"Has the young miss gone to P'yŏngyang?" U-sŏn asked. The old woman did not reply, and went to Yŏng-ch'ae's room. "Come in," she said to U-sŏn. "Are you afraid the house will collapse?"

"Go in," U-sŏn said to Hyŏng-sik with an attentive smile, then removed his shoes and went into the room. Hyŏng-sik took a step towards the room, then felt repulsed when he saw the chests and armoires inlaid with mother-of-pearl, and the shimmering bag that contained a *kayako*, and the pink mosquito netting over the warmest part of the floor. He was going to

---

98. In the 1917 *Maeil Sinbo* edition, the old man's head is "red" (*ppalgan*); the 1918 Sinmungwan edition changed this to "balding" (*maengsung maengsung han*).

take off his shoes, but decided not to, and sat down on the edge of the veranda.

"I will sit here," he said, smiling.

"Come in," said U-sŏn. "From today, you are the master of this room." He stood up and pulled Hyŏng-sik by the arm. Hyŏng-sik's face suddenly grew red. "He is still a child," thought U-sŏn, and pulled at Hyŏng-sik's arm. The old woman was surprised to see U-sŏn treating Hyŏng-sik like a friend, and her eyes widened when she heard U-sŏn say, "From today, you are the master of this room." She was good at being obsequious, though, and forced a smile at Hyŏng-sik.

"Please come in. I didn't know who you were. I was rude to you last night. You were dressed so modestly." Hyŏng-sik was embarrassed, and his heart pounded. "Now you know who I am," he thought nevertheless, and went into the room. He looked around the room again as he went in, avoiding the old woman's eyes. The mosquito netting had the same fold in it as yesterday, so Yŏng-ch'ae must have slept without the mosquito netting last night, he thought. Had Yŏng-ch'ae leaned against that wall in suffering, unable to sleep? he wondered. His heart grew sad. He looked away from the mosquito netting, and toward the wall where the door was. He winced. A torn skirt was hung there. He could see the scene at Ch'ŏngnyangni. The front hem of the skirt was stained with blood. Hyŏng-sik calmed his frantic breath, and bit his lips. "I am biting my lip, just like Yŏng-ch'ae!" he thought. He looked away from the torn skirt, unable to bear the sight.[99] On the electric car to Tongdaemun, Yŏng-ch'ae had tried to hide her bloodstained hem from sight. Women thought of appearances and propriety even at a time like that, he thought. Beneath the skirt that hung on the wall, Hyŏng-sik saw a bloodstained silk cloth. He did not know what it was. Hot waves began to rise in his breast, which had been cold until then. "Why did she go to P'yŏngyang?" he wondered. The question tormented him as though with an ominous significance. He wished U-sŏn would hurry up and ask the old woman why Yŏng-ch'ae had gone to P'yŏngyang.

U-sŏn lit a cigarette and put it in his mouth. "Where has the young miss gone?" U-sŏn felt too embarrassed to say "Wŏr-hyang," but if he said "Yŏng-ch'ae," the old woman would not know of whom he was talking. So he just said "young miss." The old woman thought U-sŏn was saying "young miss" as a joke, so she did not sneer when he used the respectful term.

"She left this morning all of a sudden, saying that she was going to visit P'yŏngyang. She said she wanted to visit her father's grave, since she had not been there in a long time." The old woman thought the two men did not know

---

99. This phrase "unable to bear the sight" appears to have been omitted in the 1917 *Maeil Sinbo* edition except for the first word in the phrase, "*ch'am*"; the mistake was corrected in the 1918 Sinmungwan edition.

about what had happened the night before. She thought U-sŏn had brought his friend to have a good time. She thought Hyŏng-sik had visited last night because he had heard about Wŏr-hyang and wanted to meet her; he must have thought the old woman refused to let him see Wŏr-hyang because of his shabby appearance, and therefore had returned today with U-sŏn, who was on close terms with Wŏr-hyang. How could such a pathetic man go around chasing *kisaeng*, she wondered.

When Hyŏng-sik heard that Yŏng-ch'ae had gone to P'yŏngyang to visit her father's grave, he thought of Scholar Pak, who Yŏng-ch'ae said had died in jail. Before he could finish imagining Scholar Pak's face, however, the words "visit her father's grave" overwhelmed Hyŏng-sik's heart with unspeakable fear. "Visit her father's grave?" Hyŏng-sik exclaimed out loud, unawares. U-sŏn and the old woman looked at Hyŏng-sik's face. Shock and sorrow could be seen clearly in his eyes. The old woman stood up, as though she had thought of something, and went to another room.

49

U-sŏn too thought there was something significant about word that Yŏng-ch'ae had gone suddenly to P'yŏngyang. He looked at the old woman as she stood up and went to her room. The old woman would be able to explain the mystery behind the grave visit. The fact that the old woman had stood up and gone to her room, moreover, was of the utmost importance in explaining the mystery of the grave visit, he thought. Hyŏng-sik and U-sŏn both looked at the door that the old woman had disappeared through. They both lowered their breath, as though waiting for some important incident to take place. The summer sun burned like fire in the courtyard, and it seemed as though flames would rise from the soil. The sun shone on the roof tiles, and steam descended from the ceiling. The ramie *turumagi* that Hyŏng-sik had changed into that morning was stuck to his back in two places with sweat. There were drops of sweat on U-sŏn's forehead too, but he did not try to wipe his forehead, nor did he try to fan himself with his straw hat. Several flies had fallen into a glass container of water placed at the foot of the clothes chests to catch flies. The flies tried to swim over to the walls of the container and crawl out, but kept falling in again. A cat with patches of varicolored fur jumped out from where it had been taking a nap, and stopped in front of Yŏng-ch'ae's room. It yawned and stretched as it looked at Hyŏng-sik and U-sŏn.

After some time, the old woman came out of her room with a letter in an envelope, and said to U-sŏn, "Wŏr-hyang gave this to me at the station just as the train was to leave, and told me to give it to a Mr. Yi Hyŏng-sik, whoever he is." She gave the letter to U-sŏn, and looked quickly at Hyŏng-sik. Yi Hyŏng-sik must be one of the men who visit Wŏr-hyang, the old woman had thought when she received the letter at the train station. But I would know anyone who was close enough to Wŏr-hyang that she would write a letter especially for him, she had thought perplexedly. She could not ask Wŏr-hyang further about the man, though, since the train was about to leave. I can always ask someone else, the old woman thought. Then she saw that U-sŏn and Hyŏng-sik were worried about Yŏng-ch'ae, and that Hyŏng-sik looked strangely anguished. "She went to visit her father's grave?" he had said in shock. Perhaps this man was Yi Hyŏng-sik. That was why she had brought out the letter, and why she had looked at Hyŏng-sik when she gave the letter to U-sŏn. Hyŏng-sik gasped when he saw written on the envelope in familiar handwriting the words "To Mr. Yi Hyŏng-sik." He grabbed the letter from U-sŏn and looked at the back of the envelope. Nothing was written on the back except the date "June 29, morning" written to one side. Hyŏng-sik's hand shook as he held the envelope. There must be some reason for Wŏr-hyang's visit to her father's grave, and Hyŏng-sik knows what it is, U-sŏn thought, and quieted his breathing. The old woman looked at the two men's faces and was taken aback, wondering what was wrong. There seemed to be some meaning behind Wŏr-hyang's decision to go to P'yŏngyang, she thought. That morning, the sadness had disappeared from Wŏr-hyang's face, and she had gotten up early, washed up, powdered her face, put on perfume and dressed like a student, in a ramie skirt and blouse. Then she had gone to the old woman's room. The old woman had not yet gotten out of bed.

"Mother," she had said smiling, as though feeling very cheerful. "I am sorry about last night. I was wrong. It all seemed so absurd when I thought about it this morning after getting some sleep." The old woman, who had gone to bed worried, had grasped Wŏr-hyang's hand joyfully.

"You are right," she said. "That is the right attitude. I am glad." Then she had put her mind at ease. She had been twice as happy when she thought of how Wŏr-hyang would now have guests at night too. Then Yŏng-ch'ae had paused, as if sorry about what she had to say next.

"Mother," she said. "I am going to visit P'yŏngyang. I want to visit my father's grave for the first time in awhile, and get some fresh air." The old woman was glad that Wŏr-hyang had stopped being sad and stubborn. She had come to feel some affection for Wŏr-hyang when she had held Wŏr-hyang in her arms the night before and wept (though three-fourths of that affection had cooled off overnight). She thought it would be good to let Wŏr-hyang do as she wished if it were something small.

"Do that. It has been three months since you were in P'yŏngyang. It is only natural that you would want to go. Go and see your friends to your heart's content. Stay for three or four days," the old woman said. She went to the station herself, and bought Wŏr-hyang a second-class ticket, something to eat for lunch, and plenty of "K'al" brand cigarettes too. The old woman even went so far as to request a few favors of Yŏng-ch'ae. "Give my best to so-and-so," she said. "Tell them I have been too busy to write." She had been sure that Wŏr-hyang would return within a few days, smiling, but now that she saw how shocked U-sŏn and Hyŏng-sik were by the letter, it seemed as though Wŏr-hyang had gone to P'yŏngyang for some profound, fearful reason, and her heart stung. She suddenly thought of the death of Wŏr-hwa five years ago. She thought of how Yŏng-ch'ae always wore the yellow jade ring that Wŏr-hwa had given her. Then the old woman thought about what had happened at Ch'ŏngnyangni the night before, and her eyes widened.

"Why did Wŏr-hyang go to P'yŏngyang?" she asked. She was asking them the very question that they had wanted to ask her.

When U-sŏn saw Hyŏng-sik sitting vacantly with the letter in his hand, he could not overcome his anxiety.

"Open the letter," he said.

With a trembling hand, Hyŏng-sik took hold of one end of the envelope. He could not, however, bring himself to open it. His hand trembled more and more, and the muscles in his face grew more tense. "Open it! Open it!" U-sŏn said, urging Hyŏng-sik to open the envelope. The old woman watched Hyŏng-sik's hand as it grasped one end of the envelope. What message would emerge from the letter, she wondered. The hearts of the three people there beat quickly beneath their summer clothing, and their backs were wet with sweat. The cat that had stopped in front of the door and stood looking into the room, meowed and leapt after a sparrow that it saw on the roof. Hyŏng-sik finally tore open one end of the envelope with a trembling hand. The sound of the envelope being torn open reverberated in the hearts of all three like the rumbling of a cannon.

50

Hyŏng-sik held the letter in his trembling hand. The envelope, open at one end, fell into his lap. The old woman squinched closer to Hyŏng-sik's side from where she was sitting. U-sŏn leaned over Hyŏng-sik's shoulder. Hyŏng-sik's heart was racing. U-sŏn and the old woman stared, as though their eyes were made of glass, at each letter that was revealed as Hyŏng-sik slowly spread the letter open. Hyŏng-sik shrugged his shoulders as though trying to force back his sorrow, then began to read. The letter was written in flowing, palace-style Korean script. U-sŏn and the old woman were all eyes and ears. Hyŏng-sik skipped over the words "To Mr. Yi Hyŏng-sik," and began to read.

"Seeing you last night was like seeing my late father. It made me very happy. I have missed you these seven years that we have been apart. When I saw you, I thought of how you held me beneath the willow tree in front of our house and said goodbye seven years ago when you were leaving Anju. You said we would never see each other again, and you wept. I was a silly twelve year old then. I clung to you and begged you not to go, and asked you where you were going, and pleaded with you to take me with you. When I remembered all that, I could not help feeling sad, and wept aloud.

"I have cried many tears, and sighed countless times over the last seven years since we parted. Young and lonely, with no one on whom to rely, I drifted whichever way the wind blew or the waters carried me, like a water weed, experiencing all kinds of suffering, and wandering east and west.

"The only thing I lived for was to see my father, who was suffering in jail in P'yŏngyang. Just thirteen years old, I drifted here and there, like a leaf tossed about in the wind. When I eventually saw my father, he was wearing clothes covered with mud, and his face was frighteningly emaciated. I felt a stabbing pain in my heart.

"I naively decided to follow the example of virtuous women of antiquity, and sell myself to be a *kisaeng*, in order to get money to free my father from jail. In the autumn of the year that I turned thirteen, I sold myself to be a *kisaeng*, with the help of someone who acted as a go-between. The go-between absconded with the two hundred wŏn that were paid for me. I had sold the flesh and blood that I received from my parents, in hopes of freeing my father from jail. But I was not able to do that after all. I could not even offer my old father who was suffering in jail a single meal of delicious food. I regret this bitterly, to the marrow of my bones. Instead, my father and two brothers died within five days because I had sold myself to become a *kisaeng*. My life has been a disaster. What sins must I have committed in a former life, for my father and brothers to be jailed when I was still so young, and then for them to die, choking up the blood of bitter resentment, because of me? When I think about it my heart could just break, and the marrow of my bones freezes. If only I had had the slightest bit of wisdom, I would have followed my father and brothers in death, but alas! This obdurate, evil breath of life within me has not died out, but continues to endure.

"Whom could I trust in after I lost my father and brothers? I have no one to whom I can turn. You would understand what I mean, Mr. Yi. You know there is no one to whom I can turn for help. Only heaven. And earth. And, in all the world, there is only you.

"After that, I lived only for you. I hoped that perhaps in the course of my wanderings, I might see you again. This hope was what sustained my life, which otherwise might have perished like dew. I have deliberately kept my virginity for you, since you were the man my father approved of as my betrothed when he was alive. In this, I have observed the teachings of the sages of antiquity and the teachings of my father. I am enclosing the knife that I carried with me at all times in order to defend my chastity.

"My body is now unclean, though. Alas, Mr. Yi, my body is unclean. The virginity that I tried so hard to defend on my own, weak as I am, disappeared last night.

"I am now a terrible, evil sinner who cannot remain on earth, and whom God will not allow to continue living. I am a sinner who hurt my father and brothers, and lost the virginity that I was saving for my husband. "Mr. Yi! I am leaving. I have lived my short life of nineteen years in sad tears and vile sin. I am too ashamed to behold the birds and the beasts, and the grasses and trees, and fear punishment from heaven if I allow this body to remain in the world another day. I am going to cast myself into the blue waters of the Taedong River, waters full of lingering resentment and bitterness, and let the waves wash my unclean body. I want the heartless fishes of the water to tear this body to pieces.

"Mr. Yi! My immense sorrow has been assuaged now that I have seen your kind face again during this life. Whenever rain falls on you near the Taedong River, think of it as the tears of this unfortunate sinner, Pak Yŏng-ch'ae. Hot tears blur my vision now as I finish this letter and lift my brush from the paper. Mr. Yi! May you always be well, and may you become a pillar of the nation." The letter was dated and signed in shaky handwriting: "In the *pyŏngjin* year,[100] June 29, 2 a.m. Weeping tears of blood and bowing one hundred times, the sinner Pak Yŏng-ch'ae." Hyŏng-sik's hand trembled more and more violently, until he dropped the letter in his lap. He sobbed and wept, his large tears drenching the letter. The tears made the writing in the letter even more distinct. U-sŏn wiped tears away with his sleeve. The old woman covered her face with her skirt, and lay prostrate on the floor. No one said anything for a long time. Steam rose in increasing amounts from the courtyard.

51

Hyŏng-sik wiped his tears away with his sleeve, and randomly read parts of the tear-drenched letter over again. He could not see the letters in the words very clearly, though. He rolled the letter up, put it on the floor, and opened the small envelope that had been enclosed with the letter. U-sŏn and the old woman looked with teary eyes at the small envelope in Hyŏng-sik's hand. Hyŏng-sik noticed that there was something heavy in the envelope, and he turned the envelope upside down and emptied the contents in his lap. Something long, wrapped in a red silk cloth, fell out. Hyŏng-sik severed the thread that tied the bundle, and opened the silk cloth. Inside the cloth was a wad of old, thick Korean paper. Hyŏng-sik picked up the wad of paper. A thought seemed to occur to him, and he spread out the wad of paper. Then he gasped. U-sŏn and the old woman looked from the wad of paper to Hyŏng-sik's face. They saw that fresh tears had risen in his widened eyes. U-sŏn and the old woman looked again at the piece of thick Korean paper in Hyŏng-sik's trembling hand. Written on the piece of paper were the Korean

100. The *pyŏngjin* year would be 1916.

letters *kiŭk, niŭn,* and *riŭl,* and the syllables *ka, na,* and *ta.* This was what children wrote when first learning the Korean alphabet. The handwriting was childish. Hyŏng-sik rubbed his forehead on the piece of paper and sobbed, heedless of the fact that others were watching him. U-sŏn and the old woman just looked at Hyŏng-sik as he sobbed. Hyŏng-sik rubbed his face on the piece of paper in distress, and sobbed even louder. Tears rose in U-sŏn's eyes again. Hyŏng-sik is such a child, he thought.

Hyŏng-sik thought back to over a decade ago. Yŏng-ch'ae had been eight years old when Hyŏng-sik first went to Scholar Pak's house. She was reading the *Ch'ŏnchamun* (Thousand Character Classic), the *Tongmong sŏnsŭp* (Preliminary Studies for Children), [101] the *Kyemong p'yŏn* (Enlightenment Book), and untitled Chinese *shi* poems. She had not yet learned the Korean alphabet, though. "You should learn the Korean alphabet," Scholar Pak said once, and wrote out syllables using the Korean alphabet, on a piece of fine paper. Yŏng-ch'ae took the paper outside, however, and lost it while playing. Afraid of being scolded by her father, she was on the verge of tears, and secretly asked Hyŏng-sik to help her. He was thirteen years old at the time.

"Please write the letters of the Korean alphabet for me," she said, wiping the tears from her eyes with her fists and averting her face. Hyŏng-sik and Yŏng-ch'ae had not yet spoken to one another, so she was embarrassed. To Hyŏng-sik Yŏng-ch'ae's face and manner were unsurpassably beautiful. What a pretty girl, he thought. He grew shy. "All right," he said. "I will write it out for you tomorrow morning." Then he went to a paper store that was five *li* away, and bought some paper (this was the very paper that he had bought), and, with painstaking effort and the utmost care, wrote out the Korean alphabet on these four pieces of paper. He put the papers between some books, and wished it would be morning soon. He could not fall asleep. The image of Yŏng-ch'ae standing half turned away from him, rubbing her teary eyes with her fists, and asking him to write the letters of the Korean alphabet for her, left a deep impression on Hyŏng-sik. The next morning, Hyŏng-sik brushed his teeth and washed his face and hands more attentively than usual, carefully put on a long Korean outer coat, then folded the papers (these very ones!), put them in his shirt, and waited for Yŏng-ch'ae outside the front door of Scholar Pak's house. He was just like a man in love, waiting for the woman he loved, in a place where they could be alone together. Yŏng-ch'ae came out of the front door after some time, looking carefully in all directions as though trying to avoid being seen. She went over to Hyŏng-sik. Blushing

---

101. Written during the reign of Chungjong, in the Chosŏn dynasty, by Pak Se-mu, the *Tongmong sŏnsŭp* summarized the essence of the "five relationships" of Neo-Confucianism, and added a brief history of China and the Chosŏn dynasty. It was used as a textbook for children after they had studied the *Thousand Character Classic* and before they studied the *Elementary Learning* (Sohak).

furiously, she hugged him at the waist, as though overjoyed to see him. Her hair brushed against his breast. Hyŏng-sik touched her hair for a moment. It was damp, as though she had just washed her face. He took the papers out of his shirt and gave them to Yŏng-ch'ae. The papers were warm from being placed against his breast. Yŏng-ch'ae stepped back as though she had noticed the warmth, then looked at Hyŏng-sik. She blushed and ran away. These are the papers I gave her! Hyŏng-sik lifted his head, and looked again at the papers and the Korean letters that were written on them. Each of the letters seemed to be telling a story of the past. Images from the past flashed through Hyŏng-sik's mind: images of events in Anju, how Hyŏng-sik had lived since then, and Yŏng-ch'ae's life as he had seen it through her stories, her letter, and in his imagination. Hyŏng-sik bit his lip again. "I have unconsciously learned from Yŏng-ch'ae to bite my lip!" he thought. He unfurled the letter to the very end. At the end of the letter were several lines written in vertical columns: "This is a memento of you that I have kept with me all my life."

When U-sŏn and the old woman saw these words, they guessed why Hyŏng-sik had cried. U-sŏn pulled the papers from Hyŏng-sik's hand and looked at them again. The old woman looked at the papers with U-sŏn. Hyŏng-sik opened a package wrapped in paper that had also fallen into his lap. It contained one yellow jade ring—the other ring was missing[102]—and a small knife. When light glinted off the blade of the knife, the hearts of the three onlookers twinged with pain. That's the knife she pulled out from her blouse two years ago in front of Kim Yun-su's son, thought the old woman. Hyŏng-sik picked up the knife and looked at both sides of the knife. The words "an unchanging heart" were engraved on the inside of the knife, in the *haengsŏ*[103] style of calligraphy. Hyŏng-sik and U-sŏn understood the meaning of the knife. Hyŏng-sik picked up the ring again. "Why is there only one ring?" the old woman asked. Hyŏng-sik saw that there was no engraving on the ring. He picked up the paper wrapping. The following words were written there in tiny letters.

"These are the rings of Kye Wŏr-hwa, a *kisaeng* of P'yŏngyang. If you wish to know what kind of a person she was, ask anyone in P'yŏngyang. Wŏr-hwa gave me these rings as a way of telling me not to be tainted by a corrupt world. I have tried my best to live by this teaching. I am going to return one of the rings to Wŏr-hwa, who became an embittered spirit in the Taedong River. I would like to give the other ring to Mr. Yi, for reasons of my own." The note ended with the same words as the letter: "the Pyŏngjin year, June 29, 2 a.m. Weeping tears of blood and bowing one hundred times, the sinner Pak Yŏng-ch'ae."

---

102. A complete pair of jade rings consists of two rings.
103. The *xingshu* style of calligraphy is more flowing than the *kaishu* or "standard" style, and somewhat less flowing than the *caoshu* or "grass" style.

52

Hyŏng-sik, U-sŏn and the old woman bowed their heads without a word. Each had their own thoughts. Finally the old woman spoke up. "What shall we do?" she asked, short of breath with anxiety. She looked back and forth at Hyŏng-sik and U-sŏn. This was the first time the old woman had ever truly felt sorry for someone else, and worried and agonized about them. The old woman thought of how she had held Yŏng-ch'ae the night before and cried with sincerity. What Yŏng-ch'ae had thought was true: it was indeed the first time the old woman had ever honestly wept for someone else. The old woman's mind had been in a sanctified state when the warm blood from Yŏng-ch'ae's lip fell on the back of the old woman's hand, and when Yŏng-ch'ae kept biting at her bleeding lip, saying, "Everyone else wants to consume my flesh, why shouldn't I do the same?" The old woman put her cheek against Yŏng-ch'ae's cheek, and sobbed. At that moment, the old woman's mind was that of a genuine human being. When the old woman mentally put her hands together in prayer and bowed before Yŏng-ch'ae, her soul cast aside its foul sins, and caught a distinct glimpse of the pure, clear image of God, of Buddha. She had paid two hundred wŏn to acquire the *kisaeng* Kye Wŏr-hyang, and had used her as a money-making machine. However, now she saw in Wŏr-hyang something before which she could bow and which she could look up to with reverence. She resolved to set Yŏng-ch'ae free the next day. The old woman would herself become a new person. Together, the two of them would live as loving mother and daughter, and hold each other and comfort one another, and live happy, moral lives. When she went back to her room, she saw her old husband asleep already and snoring. Filthy beast, she thought and went to sleep alone at the far end of the room, still dressed in her clothes. When she thought of him as a "filthy beast," she did not just mean that he was physically dirty. She could not help feeling nauseated when she saw his vile self with the same eyes that had just seen Yŏng-ch'ae's soul, and her own soul, and God, and Buddha. She was like a person who has lived in a filthy house all their life and been unaware that their house was filthy. Once they had seen a clean house, they realized how dirty their own house was. The old woman had never before seen a pure soul or genuine human being. With the touch of Yŏng-ch'ae's hot blood on her hand, however, the old woman's soul, pure in nature, awoke from over fifty years of sleep buried in sin. She beheld Yŏng-ch'ae's soul, pure as snow or crystal, and, with the same eyes, then saw her own soul. When she saw her "old husband," she finally realized how filthy he was. But when Yŏng-ch'ae came into her room in the morning powdered, perfumed and smiling, the old woman's soul had closed its eyes, and she saw only Yŏng-ch'ae's body, not the inner being that she had glimpsed the night before. Last night seemed to have been decades ago. She was glad when Yŏng-ch'ae told her that "it all seemed so absurd." "That is the right attitude," the old woman had said, and had become greedy again at the thought of using Yŏng-ch'ae as a money-making machine. From the time that she had sent Yŏng-ch'ae to P'yŏngyang, till now, when she read Yŏng-ch'ae's letter, the old woman had been busy thinking only of forcing Yŏng-ch'ae to take guests at night, and of selling Yŏng-ch'ae to Kim Hyŏn-su for two thousand wŏn. However, those thoughts disappeared after the old woman read Yŏng-ch'ae's letter; and when she saw the knife, the ring and Hyŏng-sik's tears, her soul could see again just as it had the night before. She felt ashamed, and sorry towards Yŏng-ch'ae's inner being, when she thought of how she had said to Yŏng-ch'ae, "That is the right attitude!" Yŏng-ch'ae seemed to be standing before her and saying derisively, "That is the right attitude."

The old woman could see the surging waters of the Taedong River. Yŏng-ch'ae stood on a small rock, then held the edge of her skirt with both hands, weeping, and was about to jump into the water. The old woman ran towards the water, trying to grab her. "I am sorry, Wŏr-hyang! I should die for what I did to you!" Yŏng-ch'ae, however, turned her head and laughed. "It is no use. My body is unclean!" Then she jumped into the water. The old woman stood on the small rock and stomped her feet. "I'm sorry, Wŏr-hyang! I am the one who made your body unclean! Forgive me, Wŏr-hyang!"

"There is nothing I can do," Kim Hyŏn-su had said in disappointment the day before. "She keeps trying to kill herself."

"A man shouldn't be so weak," the old woman had said. "Once the deed is done, that is the end of that!" she had said, and winked, encouraging Kim Hyŏn-su to take Yŏng-ch'ae by force. I am the one who ruined Wŏr-hyang's chastity, she thought. I am the one who killed her. The old woman's breast was on fire, and she had to breathe through her mouth.

"What shall we do?" she said, and pounded her knees against the floor. Hyŏng-sik had been glaring at the old woman with loathing until then, his heart aching and his resentment growing deeper as he thought, That fat, filthy old woman is the person who has caused this tragedy. When he saw her worrying about Yŏng-ch'ae, though, he thought, The soul that was asleep within you has awakened! He thought of the robbers who were crucified with Christ. That old woman is a human being just like me, he thought. She is a human being just like Yŏng-ch'ae. He pitied the old woman's anguish. When he remembered how the old woman had said, "I didn't realize who you were," however, his pity for her disappeared, and he disliked her even more. Hyŏng-sik glared at the old woman again.

The old woman saw Hyŏng-sik glaring at her. "What shall we do?" she said again, pounding her knees against the floor. U-sŏn sat in silence.

Then he said to Hyŏng-sik, "Send a telegram to the police in P'yŏngyang right away, and take a night train to P'yŏngyang."

53

U-sŏn thought that what Yŏng-ch'ae had done was right. A woman's virginity was her life. If she lost her virginity, it was right for her to kill herself. This was the only thing Yŏng-ch'ae could do after the incident at the house in Ch'ŏngnyangni, he thought. Yŏng-ch'ae is a good woman after all, he thought. He began to respect her, and felt ashamed of having tried to seduce her. He was unaware, however, of any contradictions in his way of thinking. When Yŏng-ch'ae was the *kisaeng* Wŏr-hyang, U-sŏn thought it was all right for her to lose her virginity, but when he realized that Wŏr-hyang was Yŏng-ch'ae, he thought she should remain chaste. This was obviously contradictory, but U-sŏn did not notice it. If one followed the implications of this line of thought, one could say that U-sŏn believed that it was a sin for a "virtuous woman" to be unchaste, but not a sin for a woman who was not a "virtuous woman" to be unchaste. This was a reversal of premise and conclusion. In actuality one did not remain chaste because one was a virtuous woman; one was a virtuous woman because one was chaste. But U-sŏn thought that a woman ought to be chaste only if she was a "virtuous woman," and if she was not a virtuous woman, then it was all right for her not to be chaste. That was why U-sŏn had tried to seduce Yŏng-ch'ae when he did not know she was a virtuous woman, and regretted his actions and felt ashamed after he realized that she was a virtuous woman. In any case, U-sŏn thought that Yŏng-ch'ae had done the best thing she could have done under the circumstances. Hyŏng-sik thought differently, though. He was moved by Yŏng-ch'ae's chasteness. He even respected the pure, sanctified spirit with which she wanted to take her own life. However, he did not think that what she had done was right. Human life was like the life of the universe. Just as the universe contained all things, human life too encompassed all existence. The universe did not just contain the sun and the North Pole, but also included all of the stars, and all things on earth. Even tiny stars in the sky were a part of all life in the universe. The smallest leaf of grass or particle was a part of the life of the universe. One might say that the sun had a larger role in the life of the universe than the earth because it was greater than the earth. Nevertheless, one could not say that the sun comprised all the life of the universe, or that the earth had nothing to do with the life of the universe. The sun was the center of the solar system, but the sun itself was no more than a particle when compared with the limitless vastness of the entire universe. Similarly, human life did not exist for the sake of one particular responsibility or one moral law, but existed for all the myriad responsibilities in human life, and all the myriad responsibilities towards the universe. Loyalty, filial piety, chastity, honor—these were not the center of human life. Human life was not contained within concepts such as loyalty or filial piety, but rather, loyalty and filial piety derived from human life. Human life was not fixed to concepts such as "loyalty," or "filial piety," but embraced concepts such as loyalty, filial piety, chastity and honor. It was like the way the life of the universe did not consist only of the North Star (Polaris), or the White Wolf Star (Sirius), or the sun, but included them along with other larger stars and smaller stars, and all microscopic things on earth. Human life manifested itself in diverse ways, sometimes as loyalty, sometimes as filial piety, sometimes as chastity, or any of the countless other phenomena of human life. Human life would, of necessity, choose a few of these phenomena from among the myriad human phenomena, depending on ethnicity, conditions in a specific nation, and era, and would make these the center of human activity. These are what are known as belief, morality, law and ethics. In order for the life of a society to be complete, each of its members must observe the moral rules and laws of that society. This was not, however, the entirety of life. Human life was more important than any moral rules or laws. Life was absolute, morality and laws were relative. Life could endlessly create new moral rules and laws that were different from those of the present. This was the view of life that Hyŏng-sik had learned. For Yŏng-ch'ae to take her life because she had lost her virginity, was to confuse a few moral rules such as "filial piety" and "chastity" with the entirety of a woman's life.[104] Filial piety and chastity were morals that were at present the center of women's lives. Those morals were nevertheless things that emerged from a woman's life, and were only one part of human life. Yŏng-ch'ae had indeed been unfilial to her parents. Nor had she kept herself chaste for her future husband. She had not been that way intentionally, though. Heartless society had forced frail Yŏng-ch'ae to be unfilial and unchaste. Even if she had not carried out her responsibilities to be filial and chaste deliberately, that would still be no reason for her to end her life. Filial piety and chastity were only two of her responsibilities in life. Though they were important parts of her life, a part was smaller than the whole. Even if she had failed to carry out these two responsibilities, she still had countless other responsibilities in her life. There was still the responsibility of loyalty, and her responsibility to the world, and to animals, and to the mountains and streams, and stars, and to God,[105] and to Buddha. It was wrong for her to end a life with so many responsibilities, just for the sake of two duties (even if those two duties were important, and even if she had not succeeded in fulfilling those duties as she wished). It was nevertheless one of life's glories when a person who was passionate, and pure of mind and body, made their most important responsibilities their very life.

Hyŏng-sik thought that what Yŏng-ch'ae had done was wrong in theory, in terms of emotion, but he could not help crying for her. You are a woman,

104. The word "life" was written in the Korean alphabet, Chinese characters and in English in both the 1917 *Maeil Sinbo* and 1918 Sinmungwan editions.
105. The 1918 Sinmungwan edition added the words "and to God."

he thought nonetheless. A traditional woman, passionate, and pure of mind and body, he thought. U-sŏn, however, thought that what Yŏng-ch'ae had done was absolutely virtuous. One man had an English way of thought, the other had a classical Chinese way of thought.

54

Hyŏng-sik eventually fell asleep for awhile, but opened his eyes again with a start. Some passengers were leaning against the windows, some folded their arms over their chest, and some had fallen into an exhausted sleep, their heads thrown back. The only passenger awake was a man sitting in a seat across from Hyŏng-sik, four or five seats away. He looked like a labor supervisor. He sat blinking his eyes and smoking. Eventually the light of dawn began to shine through the train windows. Hyŏng-sik looked at the old woman, who sat in the seat opposite from him. She was drooling as she slept. Disgusting woman, he thought, and frowned. He thought about the old woman's life. She had probably grown up in a lowly household, and had never seen good deeds or heard good words. After she was sold to be a *kisaeng*, she met no one but beastlike playboys, or beastlike *kisaeng*. All her life she had heard and spoken nothing but lascivious, vile language. If the old woman had learned to read and write, and had heard the wise teachings of the sages of antiquity, she might have had thoughts worthy of a human being. Judging from her face, though, she was dull by nature, and seemed as though she would be sadistic and perverse, greedy and capricious. Her long, black eyelashes, moreover, suggested that she was by nature a dissolute, sensuous woman. Such a woman could easily become an evil person, even if one taught her from an early age. Since she had spent her entire life in a sordid world of sin, her beastlike mind had flourished, while her human mind had not had a chance to open its eyes. She had never heard of goodness or virtue, and had never met a good person or a virtuous person. She therefore thought the whole world was like the society she knew, and that all people were like herself. Thus, she certainly did not think she was more evil than anyone else,[106] let alone more stupid than anyone else. On the contrary, she would sometimes look at others and think, What an evil person! She was no different from most people who consider themselves good. She had never had a chance to meet a "true human being," nor did she try to meet such a person. She had likewise never tried to become a "true human being." She thought she was a "true human being." She had seen Yŏng-ch'ae morning and night for seven years, but had never seen the true human being that was Yŏng-ch'ae, only the flesh and bones of a *kisaeng* named Wŏr-hyang. When Yŏng-ch'ae tried to protect her chastity, the old woman thought she was

106. The 1918 Sinmungwan edition changed the word "nicer" to "more evil."

foolish, naive and stubborn. The old woman thought it was a good thing for a *kisaeng* to give herself to any man. She therefore thought it was evil for Yŏng-ch'ae to try to stay a virgin. Hyŏng-sik looked at the old woman's face again. This time he felt sorry for her instead of hating her and thinking of her as disgusting. If he had been in her circumstances, he would have turned out the same as the old woman. And if she had received about fifteen years of education as had Hyŏng-sik, she would have been like Hyŏng-sik himself. He looked at the various individuals who were fast asleep in the train car. There were laborers, gentlemen, greedy-looking types and evil-looking characters. There were Koreans, Japanese and Chinese. If they had awoken and looked at one another, some might regard the others with contempt. Some might regard the others with envy. They might consider one another evil, or ignorant, or rude. Had they grown up under the same circumstances, with the same education, the same moral influences, the same blessings, then, in spite of differences in heredity, they all would have turned out to be equally good people. Hyŏng-sik looked at the old woman's face again as she slept. Hyŏng-sik felt a kind of affection for the old woman this time. She too was a human being, just like Hyŏng-sik and Yŏng-ch'ae. He remembered what he had thought the day before at Elder Kim's house when he saw the portrait of Christ on the crucifix. People were all the same human beings. A person could be Ch'un-hyang, or Yi To-ryŏng. One could be Ch'un-hyang's mother, or the governor of Namwŏn City. Some people loved, some hated. Some hit others, some were beaten. Some became *yangban*, some became lowly people. Some were good, some were evil. They were all human beings to begin with, though. When Hyŏng-sik looked at the old woman, he felt the affection one feels for one's mother or sister. Hyŏng-sik was happy and thankful that the old woman had discovered her true self for the first time and her soul had awakened, when she saw Yŏng-ch'ae's resolve to die. She had wept real tears for the first time in her life, and was going all the way to P'yŏngyang to save Yŏng-ch'ae. Unable to contain his feelings of affection for the old woman, Hyŏng-sik pulled the old woman's blanket up over her stomach.

He looked out the window, wondering where they were. After awhile, there was the sound of the train whistle, and then the train could be heard crossing a bridge. Suddenly, he thought of the Taedong River. What had happened to Yŏng-ch'ae? Had she drowned in the blue waters of the Taedong River? Had she been stopped by a policeman, and was she now in a detention room at a police station, weeping? "Wake up!" he said, shaking the old woman's shoulders gently. "We are at the Taedong River." This was the first time Hyŏng-sik had spoken so warmly to the old woman. Obnoxious woman, he had thought the day before at the old woman's house. He had hated and despised her as he sat across from her on the train for eight hours, and had not said a word to her. The old woman opened her eyes and sat up.

"What? The Taedong River?" She looked out the window. The Taedong River flowed silently in the faint light of dawn, and the sound of a train whistle traveled far into the distance towards P'yŏngyang Station. Hyŏng-sik and the old woman thought of Yŏng-ch'ae.

55

Hyŏng-sik opened the window and looked in the direction of Nŭngna Island. Nothing could be seen distinctly in the early morning haze, but Hyŏng-sik had seen P'yŏngyang several times and could place the general terrain. "That must be Nŭngna Island," he thought. "That would be Moranbong, and that must be Ch'ŏngnyu Cliff." He thought of the letter from Yŏng-ch'ae that he had read the day before. "I am going to throw myself into the blue waters of the Taedong River," she had written. He sighed. He could see Yŏng-ch'ae in the darkness near Nŭngna Island. "I want to let the waves wash my unclean body. I want the heartless creatures of the water to tear this body to pieces." Hyŏng-sik could almost see Yŏng-ch'ae's body floating beneath the steel bridge. He stuck his head out the window and looked down at the waters. He could see the waves flowing in round currents against the pillars of the bridge. He felt something fall on his neck. He lifted his head and looked up at the sky. The sky was covered with dark clouds that would not move, and there was a fine drizzle mixed with a few large raindrops. A cool breeze passed, lifting Hyŏng-sik's long, parted hair. Hyŏng-sik winced as though he had seen something dreadful, and pulled his head back inside the train. "Whenever you see rain that drenches your sleeves near the Taedong River, think of it as the tears of this unfortunate sinner, Pak Yŏng-ch'ae." This sentence from Yŏng-ch'ae's letter flashed before Hyŏng-sik's eyes. He took out from his bag Yŏng-ch'ae's letter, the pieces of paper with the Korean alphabet written on them, and the paper bundle that contained the knife and the ring. He began to look at them, but then put them away again. The train finished passing over the bridge. To the left and right were empty freight cars, and small look-out sheds for keeping watch. The old woman looked vacantly out the window, then turned her eyes to Hyŏng-sik.

"I wonder what has happened to Yŏng-ch'ae," she said. There was still a look of genuine worry on her face. The old woman's soul is still awake! thought Hyŏng-sik. The old woman had had a frightening dream. In the dream, she was on the train to P'yŏngyang, but when the train reached the steel bridge over the Taedong River, the bridge collapsed, and the train car in which she was a passenger fell into the Taedong River. The old woman barely kept herself afloat. "Save me!" she cried. It was the rainy season, though, and large muddy waves covered the old woman's head several times. "I am going to die!" sobbed the old woman, as she was repeatedly submerged in the water, then struggled to the surface. Then Yŏng-ch'ae appeared, dressed in white. "It is absurd now that I think about it," she said smiling, just as she had done when she had gone to the old woman's room the previous morning. The old woman reached out her hand and said, "I am sorry. Please forgive me. Take hold of my hand." Yŏng-ch'ae would not take the old woman's hand, though, but instead her face turned pale and she bit her lips with her white teeth, and sprayed blood on the old woman's face. The old woman felt drops of blood, hot as boiling water, strike her forehead and cheeks. "Help me, Yŏng-ch'ae," she said, flailing about in the water. Then she woke up. As soon as she awoke, she looked down at the Taedong River. There had been a drought for quite some time, though, and the Taedong River was not the way it had been in her dream. She worried, however, that the bridge might collapse the way it had in her dream, and her teeth chattered with fear until the train had finished crossing the bridge and reached land. Then she sighed with relief, and said to Hyŏng-sik, "I wonder what has happened to Yŏng-ch'ae."

Hyŏng-sik smiled and said, "We sent a telegram yesterday, so she must be at the police station now." His words and attitude indicated that there was nothing to worry about. The old woman felt somewhat reassured by what Hyŏng-sik said. She had never made use of the services of a telegram or the police, though, and she found it difficult to be completely reassured. She knew that a telegram was much faster than a train, but how would the police know who Yŏng-ch'ae was among so many people? The old woman had lived her whole life in the world of *kisaeng*, moreover, and thought of the police as people who disliked her and pestered her. When Hyŏng-sik said that Yŏng-ch'ae was probably at the police station, the old woman remembered how she had once been arrested in P'yŏngyang for unlicensed prostitution, and had spent three days shivering in a detention room. It is now summer, though, she thought, and felt somewhat reassured that Yŏng-ch'ae would not have shivered as she had, even if she had spent the night at the police station.

Their train arrived at P'yŏngyang Station. Before the train had come to a complete stop, the voice of a station employee crying "*Heijō*" (the Japanese pronunciation of P'yŏngyang) could be heard, and there was the sound of wooden shoes [107] clattering on the platform. Some of the passengers who had tied their luggage together and put on their wraps, pushed others out of their way in order to get off first. Some of them just let others off ahead of them, smiling broadly with the politest of airs. Hyŏng-sik and the fat old woman stepped out of the train and onto the platform. Young army officers stood by the first-class car and saluted and bowed several times, apparently to a high-ranking army official. Two fat Westerners paced back and forth, hands in their pockets, oblivious to the

---

107. *Namaksin*: Korean shoes made of wood, and worn in muddy conditions.

people around them. A Japanese woman carrying a *shingenbukuro*[108] ran quickly, as if trying not to miss her train. Passengers who were continuing northward came out and stood absentmindedly on the platform, bareheaded, faces unwashed. They watched the station entrance as though looking for someone they knew. The conductor stood clicking his ticket puncher without any tickets to punch. Hyŏng-sik and the old woman left the station. A policeman who was watching the station cast a sharp glance at the two as they walked away. Their two rickshaws wove through a crowd of other rickshaws, running past the pointed steles outside the city of P'yŏngyang and into the city streets, which were still glittering at that hour with electric lamps. There was still a fine drizzle.

56

Sitting in his rickshaw, Hyŏng-sik remembered the first time he had come to P'yŏngyang. He had arrived one morning in early spring through Ch'ilsŏngmun (Seven Star Gate), his feet wrapped in cotton cloth,[109] his hair still in a long braid, with a white ribbon because he was in mourning for his parents. It certainly is a big city, he had thought, looking down at the city streets from just inside Ch'ilsŏngmun. Hyŏng-sik had been eleven years old at the time. He had heard the name P'yŏngyang, and that P'yŏngyang was nice, but he did not know what kind of a city it was, or that Moranbang and Ch'ŏngnyu Cliff were there. He had read the *Four Classics* (Sasŏ), the *Outline History* (Saryak),[110] and the *Elementary Learning*. Since there were no modern schools at the time, however, he had never studied Korean geography or read Korean history. If he were like children in enlightened countries, he thought, he would have known about P'yŏngyang history, the famous sites there, its population, and its products. Just then, Hyŏng-sik saw, for the first time, a Japanese store on a street near Taedongmun (the Great Eastern Gate). He thought the large glass windows and the strange clothes that the people wore were interesting. When Hyŏng-sik saw the Japanese soldiers who came to Korea in 1904, he thought all Japanese people wore black clothes, and hats with red lines on the edges. He walked up and down the streets near Taedongmun and peered into the Japanese stores. Some of the stores had boxes of matches and kerosene. He had never seen so many matches. "I guess matches are all

---

108. The Japanese word *shingenbukuro*, transliterated in Korean, means a bag made of thick cloth.
109. Hyŏng-sik has his feet wrapped in Korean leggings, which could be worn instead of *pŏsŏn* (socks).
110. *Saryak* could refer to the Korean translation of the *Shijiu Shi Lue Tong Kao* (Comprehensive Investigation of the Nineteen Outline Histories), a Ming dynasty work by Yu Jin. The Korean translation was entitled *Sipku Saryak Ŏnhae* (Vulgate Elucidation of the Nineteen Outline Histories), and published in the Chosŏn dynasty in the 48th reign year of Yŏngjo (1772).

made here," he thought, nodding. When he saw Japanese people sitting facing each other and talking, he wondered, "How can they understand one another?" All the words seemed to sound the same to him. Even more interesting to Hyŏng-sik were the Japanese women's hair and that thing that they carried on their back.[111] He wondered what they carried inside that thing on their back. He was unable to solve this question for quite some time.

He went outside Taedongmun and looked at the Taedong River. It seemed to be a little larger than the Ch'ŏngchŏn River.[112] He saw steamboats, too. The steamboats were very strange, blowing black smoke through a black smokestack, and moving about without a sail, the paddle wheel turning with a strange noise. When he saw people walking to and fro on the steamboats, he wished he could go for a ride on a steamboat too.

There sure are a lot of water bearers here, he thought. The only water bearer in the village where Hyŏng-sik grew up was at a small tavern where wine was brewed, and where noodles were made in winter. He therefore thought all water bearers usually worked at small taverns. There must be many taverns in P'yŏngyang, he thought when he saw countless water bearers going back and forth through Taedongmun. Moreover, he heard mention of the governor of P'yŏngyang, and spent some time looking for the governor's house, wondering where the governor was, but gave up after awhile. Hyŏng-sik looked out at the streets through an opening in the rickshaw cover, and smiled to himself. A hand-propelled trolley full of people clattered past Hyŏng-sik's rickshaw on tracks that ran alongside the road.

Hyŏng-sik continued his thoughts. That day, after sightseeing in P'yŏngyang all day, he had gone into an inn in front of state-run lodgings for travelers. The innkeeper was a man wearing a horsehair hat over his topknot. "Do you have any money?" the innkeeper asked. Hyŏng-sik thought of his money bag. I have twenty *nyang*,[113] he thought. "Why wouldn't I have money?" Hyŏng-sik said to the innkeeper and, without hesitation,[114] he went and sat down on the coldest part of the floor, furthest from the furnace. I too am a guest, he thought.[115] The next day, about a dozen itinerant peddlers entered the inn. Their feet wrapped in leggings, they were in town for the P'yŏngyang market. Hyŏng-sik was somewhat frightened, but he pretended to be calm, and just read the letters that were written on the paper that was plastered to the wall. When he tried to go to sleep that night, however, three

111. Hyŏng-sik is referring to an *obi*, a broad sash worn with a Japanese *kimono*.
112. The Ch'ŏngch'ŏn River is in North P'yŏngan Province.
113. The *nyang* was a unit of Korean currency.
114. The 1918 Sinmungwan edition added the words "without hesitation."
115. The 1918 Sinmungwan edition added the words "I too am a guest, he thought."

men argued with one another over who would get to sleep next t⌐
Hyŏng-sik. Terrified, Hyŏng-sik sat silently in a corner of the room and
watched the men. He grasped a wooden pillow in his hand. After the three
men had argued for awhile, the darkest, most fearsome-looking one smiled
and put his arms around Hyŏng-sik. "Let's sleep together tonight. I will pay
you," he said, and put his arm around Hyŏng-sik's neck and tried to kiss
Hyŏng-sik. Hyŏng-sik started to cry, and looked at the dozen or so men
seated around the room. They all just smiled, though. One of the men said
"Sleep with me," and took out a handful of coins from his purse and held
them out to Hyŏng-sik. Hyŏng-sik fought back, but the dark man's stinking
mouth touched Hyŏng-sik's mouth. Hyŏng-sik hit the man's face forcefully
with his head, and when the man's head fell back, Hyŏng-sik hit him in the
chest with the wooden pillow. The man dodged the wooden pillow, stood
up, grabbed Hyŏng-sik's head by the hair, and smashed his head into the
wall. Hyŏng-sik cried, gnashing his teeth. Just then, a tall man who sat
quietly in another corner of the room, jumped up and ran over. He grabbed
Hyŏng-sik's aggressor by the topknot, and pounded his fist on the man's
ears[116] several times, then dropped the man on the floor. "Beast!" he said,
and kicked the man. The others were shocked, and stood up. No one dared
attack, though.

Hyŏng-sik thought of Yŏng-ch'ae. He and Yŏng-ch'ae seemed to have
strangely similar destinies. He realized that his affection for Yŏng-ch'ae was
growing even stronger. I must marry Yŏng-ch'ae, and we must spend our
lives together, loving each other, he thought.

Was Yŏng-ch'ae still alive, though? Was she alive, and at the police
station? He thought of Yŏng-ch'ae's letter, and what he had thought about as
the train crossed the Taedong River. He saw on his lap the briefcase that held
Yŏng-ch'ae's letter and the pieces of paper with the Korean alphabet written
out. He imagined the building in which the Chongno Police Station was
located, and the door to the building, and the people sitting there doing office
work, the detention room where Yŏng-ch'ae sat alone crying, and the old
woman and himself going into Yŏng-ch'ae's room.

The rickshaw stopped, and the rickshawman removed the hood. A
Western-style house painted with lime stood before Hyŏng-sik. The words
"P'yŏngyang Police Station" were written in large letters over the door.

57

Hyŏng-sik's heart beat rapidly as he walked through the door of the
police station. He could see desks and chairs where office work was done. A
policeman in a white uniform and no sword, and a towel around his

---

116. The 1917 *Maeil Sinbo* edition used the word "chest"; the 1918 Sinmungwan edition
changed this to "ears."

shoulders, sat reading a newspaper beneath a glass window. Hyŏng-sik had never been to a police station on Korean soil. He once had been summoned to a police station in Tokyo, and had a cup of tea and smoked a cigarette there, and talked with the chief of police, but he had never been to a police station as a citizen going to a government office. When he read "Resurrection" by Tolstoy, he had tried to imagine what a Russian police station would look like. It was with some uneasiness and revulsion that Hyŏng-sik removed his hat and said, "Excuse me, I would like to make an inquiry." His face grew red. The old woman stood next to Hyŏng-sik, her teeth chattering with fear and pain. The policeman, however, appeared not to have heard Hyŏng-sik.

"Excuse me," Hyŏng-sik said in a slightly louder voice. Only then did the policeman turn his head and look at Hyŏng-sik and the old woman intently.

"What is it?" he said.

"I sent a telegram yesterday, asking that you look after a certain woman. The telegram was sent from Seoul to the P'yŏngyang Police Station." I probably won't be able to know anything in detail until I talk to the police chief, Hyŏng-sik thought to himself.

"A woman?" asked the policeman before Hyŏng-sik finished speaking.

Yŏng-ch'ae is here after all! Hyŏng-sik and the old woman thought.

"Yes, I sent a telegram asking you to look after a certain woman . . . We just got here on a night train. Is the woman here in the station, by chance?" Hyŏng-sik looked at the policeman's face.

The policeman said nothing, lifted the newspaper again, and read two more lines. Then he got up from his chair, and walked over to Hyŏng-sik and the old woman. "You sent a telegram to the P'yŏngyang Police Station asking us to look after a woman?" he asked loudly, as though he could not quite understand what Hyŏng-sik had said. Hyŏng-sik felt somewhat disappointed. That policeman would have known if Yŏng-ch'ae had been taken into the police station.

The old woman's eyes grew wide. "She is nineteen years old, and was wearing a Korean blouse and skirt of ramie, with her hair put up in Western style. Has she been here?" the old woman asked, tears flowing from her eyes. The policeman held his head to one side for awhile as if in thought, then put one hand in his pants pocket, and passed between a desk and chair and went to another room. Hyŏng-sik and the old woman were disappointed. Yŏng-ch'ae is not here at the P'yŏngyang Police Station, they thought. If she wasn't there, where might she be? Had she arrived in P'yŏngyang the day before at four o'clock, visited the graves of her father and Wŏr-hwa, then gone to Ch'ŏngnyu Cliff and jumped into the water below Yŏn'gwang Pavilion? That must be what happened. Yŏng-ch'ae is dead, they thought. The old woman took hold of Hyŏng-sik's arm, and said, "What has happened to Yŏng-ch'ae?" Hyŏng-sik bit his lip, trying to keep from crying.

"I am sure she is not dead. We can ask the police chief when he comes out," Hyŏng-sik said, comforting the old woman, but he did not think that Yŏng-ch'ae was still alive. "Why die?" he thought. The *Elementary Learning* and *Biographies of Virtuous Women* have killed Yŏng-ch'ae! he thought. If he had had the chance to talk with Yŏng-ch'ae for just one more hour, she would not be dead, he thought. "Why die?" he said out loud. The old woman had been relieved when Hyŏng-sik said, "I'm sure she isn't dead." When she heard him exclaim "Why die?" though, she despaired once again. She seized his hand.

"What shall we do?" she said, and cried. Her heart stung with the thought that Yŏng-ch'ae had died because of her. I had such a terrible dream, she thought, and remembered what she had dreamed. She remembered how Yŏng-ch'ae had stood over the water, dressed in white, and said, "How absurd it is when I think about it." Then her face had changed, and she had bit her lip and sprayed hot blood on the old woman's face. Had that not been Yŏng-ch'ae's soul? the old woman thought. Had Yŏng-ch'ae drowned in the Taedong River at sunset, and her soul then entered the old woman's dreams? The old woman covered her face with her hands. Alas, wouldn't Yŏng-ch'ae's bitter spirit follow the old woman day and night, and torment her in the form of illness during the day, and nightmares at night? Wouldn't the old woman fall ill that day, and, after suffering for awhile, eventually be taken away by Yŏng-ch'ae? Or when the old woman went back to Seoul, wouldn't Yŏng-ch'ae tear the steel bridge apart with her teeth, just as she had bitten her lips, and wouldn't the old woman's train fall into the Taedong River? Yŏng-ch'ae seemed to stand before the old woman that very moment, frighteningly transformed. The old woman buried her face on Hyŏng-sik's shoulder, weeping.

"Don't cry," Hyŏng-sik said, rubbing the old woman's back as she sobbed. He tried not to cry himself. "We can ask the police chief when he comes out."

After awhile, another policeman came out of the room that the first policeman had gone into. The police chief also looked at Hyŏng-sik and the old woman carefully, then took out a telegram from a desk drawer. "Are you Yi Hyŏng-sik?" he said, looking at Hyŏng-sik.

"Yes, I am," said Hyŏng-sik, glancing at the telegram in the policeman's hand.

"Have you seen the woman?" the old woman asked the police officer in a tearful voice.

The policeman did not answer the old woman. "I received the telegram and went to the train station, but how could I find her when the telegram did not say what she looked like, or what she was wearing?" The policeman put the telegram on a desk.

"Was she running away?" he asked.

Hyŏng-sik was disappointed. Yŏng-ch'ae must be dead, Hyŏng-sik thought. "No, we are worried that she might try to commit suicide," he said. He regretted not having described her appearance in detail when he sent the telegram. The policeman they had seen first came out of the other room and looked at the telegram on the desk.

"Do you know how many people come to P'yŏngyang?" he said. "How can we know who is who among that many people?"

58

Hyŏng-sik and the old woman left the police station in utter despair. The streets were damp from drizzle. There were more people and more cars than before. The outer shutters of the stores had been opened. Someone sat on the side of the street washing their face and hands. Another person sat inside and read a newspaper out loud. Water bearers carrying buckets of water slung on a pole across their shoulders, turned sideways to carry their creaking loads through narrow streets. A mailman carrying a black leather bag and a bunch of keys sprinted towards them. The old woman clung to Hyŏng-sik's hand, and could not walk very well. Hyŏng-sik began to feel hungry.

"Let's stop somewhere and eat breakfast, and then look. I am sure she is not dead," he said to the old woman.

"I wish I could go drown in the Taedong River," the old woman said to Hyŏng-sik, and wiped tears from her eyes. Hyŏng-sik remembered the old woman as he had seen her the day before when he went to her house with U-sŏn. She had been tying the sash on her skirt, and saying, "I was in the bathroom. Why are you making such a fuss?"

"Don't be too sad," Hyŏng-sik said. "Who knows, but Yŏng-ch'ae might not have died, and might still be alive. Let's go somewhere and have breakfast."

"I wonder if we can get any beef soup with rice around here," he added as though to himself, looking around in all directions.

The old woman found solace in the words "who knows, but Yŏng-ch'ae might not have died, and might still be alive." "How can we go to a beef-soup-and-rice place? You must go to a place I know," she said. Any place the old woman knew would be a *kisaeng* house, Hyŏng-sik thought. He momentarily visualized young, pretty *kisaeng*. He suddenly wanted to go along with the old woman. What's wrong with just looking at beautiful women? he thought. It's like looking at beautiful scenery, or lovely flowers. He reflected upon his mind, though. I would be making excuses to myself to go there, he thought. But no, my mind is chaste, he thought.

"Where is this place you know? Let's go there," he said. Nevertheless, he thought it would be unseemly to follow the old woman to a *kisaeng* house. He decided to take the old woman to the *kisaeng* house, and then go somewhere else on his own.

Hyŏng-sik followed the old woman to the front door of a tidy-looking *kisaeng* house with clay roof tiles. The words "peace for the nation and the people" were written on the front door, which was not yet open. "Hey, everyone!" the old woman called out. "Are you asleep? Open the door!" She spoke as though she were talking to her own servants. She knocked on the door three or four times, then looked back at Hyŏng-sik. "Wouldn't it be nice if Yŏng-ch'ae were here?" she said, and smiled for no reason.

But Yŏng-ch'ae is already dead, Hyŏng-sik thought to himself and said nothing. A door could be heard opening, and shoes shuffling across the ground.

"Who is it?" a voice asked and opened the door. Hyŏng-sik stepped aside. A thirteen- or fourteen-year-old girl with traces of powder on her face joyfully clasped the old woman's hand and clung to her.

"Mother has come to visit!" she exclaimed in a lilting voice. Her hair and clothes look like she just jumped out of bed, thought Hyŏng-sik as he watched the two greet each other joyously. She was a pretty young woman. She looked as though she would be talented and passionate, Hyŏng-sik thought. She was a *kisaeng*, though. He pitied her. She was dressed like a young, unmarried woman, but she was probably no longer a virgin, he thought. Perhaps a man had exploited her as a plaything the night before. The old woman stepped through the door, then looked out again.

"Please come in," the old woman said to Hyŏng-sik. "It's just like my own home." Only then did the young *kisaeng* realize that there was someone else outside the door. She leaned her head to one side and looked at Hyŏng-sik. Hyŏng-sik thought her thick eyelids were pretty.

"I am going to meet a friend," Hyŏng-sik said. "I will come back here after I have eaten breakfast." He took off his hat. The old woman stepped outside the door again.

"There's no need to do that. Please come in. This is my younger sister's house." She pulled Hyŏng-sik by the sleeve. When Hyŏng-sik nevertheless insisted on leaving, the young *kisaeng* came outside and pushed him towards the house with her lovely hands.

"Please go in," she said flirtatiously. It seemed to Hyŏng-sik that the young *kisaeng's* mind was completely free of impurity. She was a pure young woman like Yŏng-ch'ae or Sŏn-hyŏng. A warmth seemed to flow, moreover, from her lovely hands when she touched him. Hyŏng-sik tried to think of young women to whom he was not related, as younger sisters. After trying to refuse several times, he reluctantly went into the house. It was pleasant, though, to be going in with the old woman holding one of his arms, and the pretty *kisaeng* holding the other. The room he was taken to was not much different in size from Yŏng-ch'ae's room. The young *kisaeng* ran into the room and began folding up the bedding. Hyŏng-sik saw silk quilts with red borders shimmering in the young *kisaeng's* hands. The *kisaeng* went to another room and said in a happy voice, "Mother! Mother from Seoul is here!" The room seemed to Hyŏng-sik to give off a certain fragrance. His hands touching the floor felt a warmth. This was the warmth flowing from the *kisaeng's* body, he thought. After awhile, the *kisaeng* came running into the room again like a child. "Mother is coming. Did you arrive on a morning train?" She could not conceal the happiness in her voice and face. People are all the same, Hyŏng-sik thought. One will find warm affection wherever one finds human beings. When Hyŏng-sik took out a cigarette and looked for a match in his vest, the *kisaeng* quickly picked up a match, lit the match, and offered it to him, steadying herself with one hand on his knee.

"Please, light your cigarette," she said. She was like an innocent child, thought Hyŏng-sik.

59

Hyŏng-sik felt too embarrassed and shy to let a woman light his cigarette.

"Here, I will take it," he said. The *kisaeng* giggled at the way Hyŏng-sik was using honorific language towards her. A large, gold front tooth glinted when she smiled. She pressed down on his knee with her hand, and fretted flirtatiously.

"Now then, light your cigarette," she said, taking care to use honorific language towards Hyŏng-sik. The old woman smiled, remembering how she had thought it funny when Hyŏng-sik asked for "Miss Wŏr-hyang," using the honorific term "Miss." The match that the *kisaeng* held almost burned down to the end of the matchstick while Hyŏng-sik kept refusing.

"Ouch! That is hot!" the *kisaeng* said, and dropped the match on the floor. She fell to her knees and blew on her hand, then grabbed her ear with the same hand. Hyŏng-sik felt apologetic, and his face grew red. He wanted to take her hand and blow on it.

"It must have been hot!" he said. The *kisaeng* put her finger against her ear, glanced at Hyŏng-sik, then lit another match and put one hand on Hyŏng-sik's knee to steady herself, as she had done before.

"Light your cigarette quickly this time," she said. When she saw the match burning halfway down, she made frantic motions with her body, and said, "Hurry! Hurry!" Hyŏng-sik lowered his head, lit his cigarette, and exhaled the first breath of smoke to his side so that it would not go in the *kisaeng's* face. The *kisaeng* kept watching Hyŏng-sik's face even after he had finished lighting his cigarette. Hyŏng-sik lifted his head and looked out at the yard, as though dazzled by her gaze. She has dreamy eyes, he thought. The *kisaeng* turned the match around with her fingers, as though waiting for it to burn out. Hyŏng-sik looked at her hair and back. Her black hair was loosely plaited, and she wore a bright red, silk ribbon at the end of her braid. Her braid hung down her back, and the ribbon was tied in a half-bow that lay horizontally near the waist of her Korean skirt. The ribbon was blood red, Hyŏng-sik thought. The *kisaeng* twirled the match around between her fingers, then accidentally dropped it on Hyŏng-sik's leg. "Oh my goodness!" she exclaimed, and brushed off his leg with both of her hands. The embers, however, got caught in a fold of Hyŏng-sik's silk summer trousers, and burned a hole. Hyŏng-sik felt a burning sensation on his thigh. Afraid that the *kisaeng* would feel bad, he covered his trouser leg with his *turumagi*.

"The fire went out," he said.

The *kisaeng* removed her hand from his knee and cringed with remorse. "Oh, no! Your trousers got burned, didn't they? It must have been hot!" She turned her head and looked at the old woman.

The old woman smiled. "You are just a child after all, Kye-hyang!" she said. The old woman saw in the *kisaeng* a pure soul that was not visible to the eye. There was no impure lust in Hyŏng-sik's eyes, moreover, as he looked at the *kisaeng*, the old woman thought. She did not meet that kind of person often, she thought. Now she thought he was well mannered and worthy of respect for having used honorifics towards the young *kisaeng*, even though she had first thought him rustic and ignorant.

Listening to the young *kisaeng* talk, and looking at her, Hyŏng-sik felt a pleasure like that of being tipsy from a fine, delicious wine. His body felt ticklish. When the *kisaeng* put her hand on his knee, moreover, and dropped the match and brushed off his thigh gently with her small hands, his whole body tingled, as though a current of electricity had passed through his body. This was the first time he had ever known such a delicate, enthralling pleasure, he thought. Her eyes shone with a wondrous light that brought one's entire body into ecstasy, and her skin gave off mysterious emanations that made one's muscles tingle.

Hyŏng-sik thought about Sŏn-hyŏng, and the joy that he had felt the other day when he sat across from her. He thought about the sweet happiness that he felt whenever he was with Hŭi-gyŏng, and the happiness he had known when he was with other dear friends. He thought how there were certain strangers who gave him an unspeakable joy when he saw them on a train, or a boat, or on the street. This was the first time, however, that he had experienced the happiness that the young *kisaeng* now seemed to give him. This happiness arose from the beauty of the young *kisaeng's* face, manner and mind, and from the fact that neither Hyŏng-sik nor the *kisaeng* had any feelings of greed towards one another, or manipulative schemes on one another, or any suspicions towards one another; their naked souls had cast aside all man-made externals, and had merged together. This was the most sacred of all happiness given to human beings by heaven, thought Hyŏng-sik.

Everyone had something about them that could make others happy, but people covered it up with various outer layers, so that it could not show through. A world that should have been rejoicing was, instead, a cold, dreary and lonely place, Hyŏng-sik thought. People with beautiful faces and minds, people who drew beautiful drawings and made beautiful sculptures, or wrote poetry: these people were destined to make life joyful.

After awhile, the *kisaeng's* "mother" appeared. "Oh my goodness! Older sister is here!" she said. They were human beings too, Hyŏng-sik thought. They too had a "true human being" within them. They too were red-blooded, and possessed the warm affection of human beings. The *kisaeng's* "mother" promptly exchanged introductory greetings with Hyŏng-sik, then sat beside the old woman.

"How is Wŏr-hyang?" she asked.

"I forgot to ask about Wŏr-hyang!" exclaimed the *kisaeng*. She fluttered her thick eyelids, and looked at Hyŏng-sik. It is not that you forgot, but that you are such an affectionate and caring person that you were busy taking care of others, thought Hyŏng-sik.

60

The old woman told them about Yŏng-ch'ae, tears flowing from her eyes again. She told them about how Yŏng-ch'ae had almost been raped at a house in Ch'ŏngnyangni, how Yŏng-ch'ae had come home that day and bit her own lip and wept, and how Yŏng-ch'ae had come to her room the next morning when she was still sleeping, and told her that she was going to P'yŏngyang. When Yŏng-ch'ae was getting on the train, she had given the old woman a letter. The old woman told them what was written in the letter, and told them about how she and Hyŏng-sik had gone to the P'yŏngyang Police Station that morning and asked about Yŏng-ch'ae.

"This man is none other than Yi Hyŏng-sik!" the old woman said pointing to Hyŏng-sik. Then she collapsed in tears on the shoulder of the *kisaeng's* "mother." Tears rose in the eyes of Kye-hyang and her "mother" as they listened to the old woman talk about Yŏng-ch'ae; then, when the old woman finished her story, Kye-hyang and her mother wept, and looked at Hyŏng-sik, their eyes blurred with tears. Hyŏng-sik was surprised. He had thought Kye-hyang's "mother" would get angry when she heard about Yŏng-ch'ae, and say, "Crazy bitch! Why did she have to go and die?" When he saw her crying sadly after she heard that Yŏng-ch'ae had died, he realized that her warm compassion was no different from his own. He was ashamed that he had thought of *kisaeng* as inferior human beings, no better than beasts, who had nothing in common with him spiritually. Kye-hyang's "mother" cried a while, then blew her nose.

"Wŏr-hyang was honest, naive and obstinate. She was also close to Wŏr-hwa, and after listening to Wŏr-hwa night and day, she became just like her. It was wrong of you not to see that, and to force her to take a client. What's past is past. Don't cry." Kye-hyang's "mother" looked at Hyŏng-sik. He averted his head, trying not to show his tears, and smoked a cigarette. The old woman blew her nose. "It was not that I hated her. I raised her for ten years, as though she were my daughter. She was getting older, and she couldn't be a *kisaeng* all her life. I thought I would find her a nice place where she could spend the rest of her life in ease. Kim Hyŏn-su is wealthy, and the son of a baron. I thought it would be best for her if I sent her off to him." The old woman wiped tears from her eyes. Hyŏng-sik was startled. Had the old woman tried to force Yŏng-ch'ae to be with Kim Hyŏn-su out of consideration for Yŏng-ch'ae's well being? Had she made Yŏng-ch'ae die out of good intentions, rather than just the evil intention of obtaining one thousand wŏn? Then were Hyŏng-sik and the old woman of the same mind, she who had caused Yŏng-ch'ae to commit suicide, and he who had tried to save Yŏng-ch'ae? Had this incident occurred because there were different moral standards and ways of thinking in the world?

"You must be in sorrow, Mr. Yi," Mother said to him gently. "However, it is the karma from a former life. It is beyond our control. That is life." She turned to the old woman.

"Please stop crying. It is the karma from a former life, and beyond our control. You must be hungry. Let's have breakfast." Then she said to herself, Shall I order in beef soup with rice, or tell my servants to prepare something? She hesitated, then hurriedly left the room. These are their life views, thought Hyŏng-sik. They think that all sad events that arise in society are the karma of a former lifetime, and are beyond our control. They cry for awhile, then dry their eyes and give up. They think that only fools spend too much time weeping; better to wipe the tears away, and stop crying as soon as possible. They put the responsibility for everything on "karma from a former life," and "destiny," and not human beings. Karma is responsible (and not the old woman, Yŏng-ch'ae or Kim Hyŏn-su) for Yŏng-ch'ae having become a *kisaeng*, and having been raped by Kim Hyŏn-su, and drowning in the Taedong River. Yŏng-ch'ae had guarded her virginity not because she as a person wanted to, but because of her karma from a former life. In their view, there are no particularly good or bad people. Everyone just lives according to their karma from a former life, and their destiny. In this their views were somewhat similar to those of Hyŏng-sik. There was a fundamental difference, however, in their views of life. Hyŏng-sik believed that while all human beings were the same by nature, an individual or a society could be improved and uplifted with the effort of that society or individual. The women, however, believed that humans had no responsibility for what happened in life. Human beings just lived life as it happened, with no improvement or reform through human will. This is how Koreans view life! thought Hyŏng-sik. Kye-hyang's "mother" wept momentarily, then stopped.

Yŏng-ch'ae's proprietress, however, did not stop weeping as easily. The old woman saw human beings, in addition to life in general. When Yŏng-ch'ae's hot blood had fallen on the back of her hand, the old woman had seen a "human being." The old woman could not put complete responsibility for what had happened to Yŏng-ch'ae on karma and destiny. She knew that she and Kim Hyŏn-su were responsible for Yŏng-ch'ae's death, and that Yŏng-ch'ae had guarded her virginity with the strength of her true self. The old woman realized now that human beings were responsible for what had happened. That was why she could not weep for just a few moments. She would shed these tears for the rest of her life. Kye-hyang leaned against Hyŏng-sik's knee and gazed at him with eyes reddened from weeping. "Do you think Yŏng-ch'ae is dead?" she asked.

61

Hyŏng-sik ate breakfast there, then stepped outside the front door. He had eaten more than usual because the three women took turns urging him to eat. The rice, soup and *chŏn'gol,*[117] moreover, were exceedingly delicious to Hyŏng-sik, who had eaten his meals at boarding houses all his life. He had never sat at table, moreover, with so many people warmly offering him food. Never had he been urged to "please have some more," with such kindness, by such a beautiful young woman as Kye-hyang. Kye-hyang sat next to Hyŏng-sik's table, and cut the broiled croaker fish into small pieces for him. There were yellowish burn marks on the fingers with which she had held the match. She took Hyŏng-sik's spoon from him, and put rice in his bowl of soup for him. "I can't eat that much," Hyŏng-sik said, but he ate all of it. Kye-hyang smiled happily when she saw Hyŏng-sik eat all of his rice. There were still tears on her lashes as she smiled. The three women were warm and sincere as they urged him to eat. They earnestly fed him spoonfuls of hot rice and delicious side dishes, just as though he were their son or brother. He felt as affectionate towards them as though they were his mother or sister. When they apologized for having nothing for him to eat, it did not sound like the usual formality that people always used, but rather sounded as though they were sincerely lamenting their lack of good side dishes to offer him. Hyŏng-sik felt an unutterable happiness when he stepped outside the front door. He had almost forgotten his feelings of worry, sadness and anxiety over Yŏng-ch'ae, and had discovered a new happiness. It had stopped drizzling; mist lingered in the air, and one began to sweat just looking at the sun that filled the sky.[118] Hyŏng-sik had walked a few steps when someone called out to him. "Let me go with you." That is Kye-hyang's voice, thought

---

117. *Chŏn'gol* is thinly sliced beef or pork mixed with seasonings and vegetables, and cooked in a broth.
118. In the 1917 *Maeil Sinbo* edition, this sentence is incoherent because of a few missing words. The 1918 Sinmungwan edition completed the sentence.

Hyŏng-sik, and stopped and turned his head. Kye-hyang ran to Hyŏng-sik's side, and reached for his hand, but decided not to. She looked at him and said, "Let me go with you." Hyŏng-sik thought of how he was going to be walking to the graveyard for criminals, which was outside Ch'ilsŏng Gate, and to Ch'ŏngnyu Cliff, crossing over Pungmang Mountain, which was on the other side of Kija's tomb,[119] and over Moranbong.

"Your legs will ache if you go with me," he said, dissuading her, even as he looked down into her eyes and thought, I wish you would go with me.

"My legs won't ache!" she said, shrugging her body impetuously and indicating her determination to go.

"It's hot too," Hyŏng-sik said. Then he walked towards Chongno with Kye-hyang following behind him. Steam rose gently from the thatched roofs of the houses on the street. People were already using fans to shade their faces from the sun as they walked about. A glimmering beaded curtain hung heavily in a shop that served shaved ice. The shop was empty, with no customers. The beaded curtain would make a clicking noise when there was a breeze, thought Hyŏng-sik to no purpose. Kye-hyang would peek into the shops on the street, then pick up the hem of her skirt and follow after Hyŏng-sik. She looked at his yellowed straw hat, and wondered what he did for a living, and what kind of person he was. She thought about the people she met every day, and compared them to Hyŏng-sik. She did not yet know how to judge the character of those whom she saw every day, though. She just thought that if someone dressed poorly, they must be poor. She looked at Hyŏng-sik's wrinkled *turumagi*. He must have gotten it wrinkled on the train last night, she thought. Why hadn't he taken it off and hung it up? she wondered. She looked at his feet. New shoes! she thought. She thought of how she had lit his cigarette. She looked at her fingers. My fingers still hurt, she thought. She remembered how Hyŏng-sik had looked at the burning match and said, "Please give me the match." That was the first time anyone had used honorifics towards her, she thought. She stepped aside to let an ox-drawn cart pass, then followed after Hyŏng-sik, and took hold of his hand. Hyŏng-sik turned his head for a moment and looked at Kye-hyang. Smiling, he did not brush her hand away. The two of them went around the corner of a noodle shop that was in an octagonal-shaped building, then went up a steep slope. Drops of sweat rose on Kye-hyang's forehead. Hyŏng-sik saw this, and stopped walking for awhile.

"There is sweat on your forehead," he said.

119. Kija founded Kija Chosŏn, according to legend, and was a member of the House of Yin. For a study of Kija worship in Korea, cf. Han Young-woo, "Kija Worship in the Koryŏ and Early Yi Dynasties: A Cultural Symbol in the Relationship Between Korea and China," in Wm. Theodore de Bary and JaHyun Kim Haboush, *The Rise of Neo-Confucianism in Korea* (New York: Columbia University Press, 1985) 349–374.

Kye-hyang wiped her forehead with the hand that had held Hyŏng-sik's hand. "I am not hot," she said, and took Hyŏng-sik's hand again. Hyŏng-sik deliberately slowed his pace. Dirty, naked children stood scratching their heads and watching Hyŏng-sik and Yŏng-ch'ae. A woman wearing only her underclothes and no skirt or blouse ran out of a steamy kitchen, tears streaming from her face, and struck one of the children, a boy, on the head with a wooden poker from which smoke was still rising. The boy started crying, and picked up a handful of dirt from the street and threw it at the woman's face. Hyŏng-sik thought of how some man had carried Yŏng-ch'ae out of an inn in Sukch'ŏn, and how Yŏng-ch'ae had thrown a handful of dirt in his face. Kye-hyang stopped and looked back at the crying boy, then squeezed Hyŏng-sik's hand with both of her hands. Hyŏng-sik and Kye-hyang walked on.

Kye-hyang thought about the child who had just been beaten. After awhile, she stopped thinking about the child, and started wondering about the relationship between Hyŏng-sik and Wŏr-hyang. When had Yŏng-ch'ae known this man? If Yŏng-ch'ae had known him in P'yŏngyang, then I would have known about him too, she thought. Why, however, had Hyŏng-sik abandoned Yŏng-ch'ae and made her die? She hated him, and scrutinized his face. Then she saw his worried expression, and realized that he was sorrowing over Yŏng-ch'ae.

Just then a young man riding a bicycle passed by in front of Hyŏng-sik and Kye-hyang, then suddenly looked back, got off his bike, and went towards the two. Kye-hyang dropped Hyŏng-sik's hand, stepped back and looked at the man who was approaching.

62

The man leaned against his bicycle, and said cheerfully, "What are you doing here? When did you get here?" He took out some cigarettes, offered one to Hyŏng-sik and lit one for himself.

"I got here this morning on a train," Hyŏng-sik said, exhaling smoke through his nose and mouth. He looked at the glistening bell on the bicycle as though reluctant to speak. The man stared at Kye-hyang, who stood a step away from Hyŏng-sik's side. Is Hyŏng-sik going somewhere with a *kisaeng*? he wondered to himself, unable to believe his eyes.

"Where are you staying?" he said. "Why didn't you come right to my home?" He looked at Hyŏng-sik's face. Hyŏng-sik is preoccupied with something, he thought.

"I am here for only a short while. There was a matter that I had to attend to here," Hyŏng-sik replied. He lifted his head and looked at the Taedong River, which looked white in the distance.

"Who is that woman?" the man asked, looking at Kye-hyang again.

Hyŏng-sik's face reddened, and he did not know what to say. Kye-hyang bowed her head, as if she too were embarrassed. The man held his head to one side, as though having grown suspicious when Hyŏng-sik could not readily answer. "She is my younger sister," Hyŏng-sik said, smiling. Good answer, he thought, and was satisfied with what he had said. He gained new courage, and looked at the man face-to-face. The man stood with a blank look on his face, a cigarette hanging out of his mouth. He did not understand what Hyŏng-sik meant when Hyŏng-sik referred to Kye-hyang as his younger sister. He knew Hyŏng-sik had only one younger sister, and that younger sister was already married.

After standing vacantly for a few moments, the man rubbed out his cigarette stub with his foot and said, "Where are you going?"

"I am going to see the grave of Kija," Hyŏng-sik said. The man thought Hyŏng-sik's actions and appearance were strange. "Then come to my place in the evening," he said. "Let's spend the night talking." Then he got on his bike and went away. After he had gone a distance, he turned his head and watched Hyŏng-sik and Kye-hyang slowly walking along, then he went around a bend in the road. The tip of his Napoleon hat kept reappearing and disappearing, until finally it could no longer be seen. Kye-hyang took hold of Hyŏng-sik's hand, as though relieved.

"Who is that man?" she asked.

"He is my friend. We were at the same school when I was in Tokyo."

"Is Hyŏng-sik a student in Tokyo?" Kye-hyang wondered to herself. She thought of several Tokyo students who visited her house. One of them could paint very well. She thought of how the man who could paint well was always drunk. When he held her close, his mouth smelled like alcohol. Once he said that he would paint her portrait, and told her to pose nude for him, but she said no, and ran to the *kŏnnŏnpang*.

Hyŏng-sik and Kye-hyang reached Ch'ilsŏngmun and paused. A cool breeze blew through the gate. Hyŏng-sik loosened the sash of his *turumagi*, looked at his Korean shirt, which was damp with sweat, then held open his *turumagi* as though trying to air out his clothes in the wind. Kye-hyang let out a long, deep breath, and fanned herself beneath her ears. Hyŏng-sik looked at Kye-hyang's face. She had a round face. Her cheeks were red, as though intoxicated with the hot weather. She had not put on any powder that morning, but there were still traces of powder beneath her ears from the day before. The back of Kye-hyang's blouse was also damp with sweat. Hyŏng-sik remembered how Sŏn-hyŏng's blouse had been damp with sweat, and how the wet spot kept growing large, then small, large, then small. He smiled.

"Why are you smiling?" Kye-hyang asked.

"The back of your blouse is damp with sweat," Hyŏng-sik said touching her shoulder.

Kye-hyang turned around quickly, touched Hyŏng-sik's back, then hesitated. "Your shirt is damp with sweat, too," she said. Kye-hyang was not sure how to address Hyŏng-sik. Her "mother" called the Tokyo students *chusa* (Mr.), or *nari* (Sir). [120] Her "mother" called the tall man who worked in the inn that was in front of the state travel lodgings "Student Kim." Kye-hyang did not know what to call Hyŏng-sik. When she saw that his shirt was damp with sweat, she had paused, wondering whether to call him "nari" or "Student Yi." Then she had just said, "Your shirt is damp with sweat, too." Hyŏng-sik understood this.

He smiled again and said, "Your face is red, as though you were drunk, Miss Kye-hyang!" Kye-hyang became embarrassed when she realized that Hyŏng-sik had noticed her hesitation over how to address him.

"Older brother's face too is . . . is . . . " Kye-hyang bowed her head down as though embarrassed, and could not finish what she was saying. Kye-hyang thought of how Hyŏng-sik had said, "She is my younger sister." Hyŏng-sik wanted to hear her call him "older brother." When he heard her say "older brother," though, he felt somewhat embarrassed. Hyŏng-sik had one younger sister, and three female cousins. His sister had gone to live in Hamgyŏng Province, though, with her husband's family, and Hyŏng-sik had not seen her for the last four or five years. Whenever he went to his hometown on vacations, Hyŏng-sik would go to see his three cousins first of all. His cousins were very fond of him, and were glad to see him. Two of his female cousins were younger than Hyŏng-sik, and always cried when they welcomed him and when he was leaving. They could not freely express their gladness in front of their mother-in-law and father-in-law; however, he got a sufficient idea of their affection from the way they said "older brother!" when he arrived, and from the generous amounts of chicken they put in the soup on his dinner table. Indeed, Hyŏng-sik went to his hometown on school vacations just to hear those two cousins calling him "older brother." It gave him tremendous happiness when he heard Kye-hyang say the simple words "older brother's face." Hyŏng-sik and Kye-hyang began walking again. Kye-hyang did not, however, take Hyŏng-sik's hand in hers.

63

The two of them walked through Ch'ilsŏng Gate. The streets were lined with deteriorating houses. There used to be passersby before the railroad was built, and shops would sell wine and rice cakes. Nowadays, though, there was not so much as the shadow of a person, except on market days. Outside the

---

120. The word *nari* was used as an honorific way of addressing someone. It was used for royal princes, and officials of certain ranks.

gate was a wooden platform bed made of a piece of wood that looked like a door. A straw mat was spread over the piece of wood. An old man sat idly on the bed, swaying his body back and forth, and watched them walk by. He wore an old *t'anggŏn*, or hat made of horsehair that was worn over his topknot, and dirty cotton clothing that seemed too heavy for the hot summer weather. His face was red, and there was a light in his eyes. There was something very righteous and dignified about him. Hyŏng-sik recognized the old man as one of the men who used to disport themselves joyfully in the provincial governor's offices, when Korea was still the Korea of old. Hyŏng-sik thought of men in his hometown who had acted as though they owned the world. Then the world had changed abruptly ever since the Sino-Japanese war of 1894, and the Kabo reforms, and many old men had fallen behind the times, and now passed their days in desolate loneliness. Hyŏng-sik stopped and looked at the old man again. The old man looked at Hyŏng-sik and Kye-hyang.

Before 1894, when the old man was in his prime, he must have thought the rivers and mountains of P'yŏngyang, and all the people in the world, existed for him. With the cannonfire from Ŭlmil Pavilion in 1894, though, the peaceful times he had dreamed of were shattered, and a new age began, like a flash of lightning in the darkness. He became a person abandoned by the world, and young people whom he did not know and had never seen before, took over. He knew nothing about railroads, telegraphs, telephones, submarines or torpedo boats. He lived outside Ch'ilsŏngmun, less than five *li* away from Taedongmun Street, and yet he knew nothing about what took place every day and every night within the city of P'yŏngyang. There was nothing in his head but the traditional provincial governor's hall of office (*Sŏnhwadang*); he knew nothing about the modern provincial government's offices (*toch'ŏng*). Since he would never realize what this new world was like, it was as though he were living outside of the world, even though he dwelled within it. Hyŏng-sik and the old man were people of different countries, who did not speak or write the same language, thought Hyŏng-sik. He is a man behind the times, a man living in the past. Hyŏng-sik thought of his late, paternal grand-uncle, who passed away never having understood the new world, no matter how Hyŏng-sik tried to talk to him about it. Hyŏng-sik felt an unspeakable sadness for the old man. When Kye-hyang saw Hyŏng-sik standing for a long time and thinking, she pulled at his sleeve. "Come on!" she said. Hyŏng-sik looked back at the old man and thought, He is made of stone . . . No, he is a petrified man. The old man looked at Hyŏng-sik for awhile, then closed his eyes, as if upon some thought, and swayed back and forth.

"Do you know that old man?" Kye-hyang asked. Hyŏng-sik put his hand on Kye-hyang's shoulder and began walking again.

"Yes, I knew him before, but now I don't know him any more." He smiled and looked at Kye-hyang. You will never know that old man, Kye-hyang, Hyŏng-sik thought. Hyŏng-sik thought of how he had passed this way when he first came to P'yŏngyang. He thought of himself as a boy walking this very path, wearing leggings, and a white Korean ribbon on his braid. The boy knew the old man, he thought. The boy who wondered at the large glass windows on Taedongmun Street and the steamboats that clanged on the Taedong River—he knew the old man. The boy had long since died, though. He had died when he saw the steamboats with the paddle wheel that turned and the horn that tooted. A new Yi Hyŏng-sik took his place, in the same way that the traditional provincial governor's hall of office had given way to the offices of the provincial government, and the provincial governor had become a provincial minister. Hyŏng-sik looked at Kye-hyang as she walked beside him. He thought of the distance between Kye-hyang and the old man. That distance was infinite. Hyŏng-sik looked at the old man again as he was about to turn the corner at a house. The old man was still swaying back and forth. Kye-hyang looked at the old man.

"Who is he?" she asked.

"You wouldn't know him," Hyŏng-sik said, and smiled. Kye-hyang looked at Hyŏng-sik's face, as though suspicious. She took Hyŏng-sik's hand in hers.

They walked southward along a sloping path at the foot of the city walls. Small leaves of grass hung limply, slightly wilted in the hot sun. Hyŏng-sik looked at the crumbling city walls, and thought about the ancestors who had built those walls, and the prosperity of the ancestors, witnessed by the walls. He wondered how many times those walls had been struck by bullets and cannonballs. The walls that stood above the sloping path seemed to have emotions and tears, like a human being. They looked sad, as though they had much to say but no one to listen to them.

Kye-hyang followed behind Hyŏng-sik, sweating. She thought of how she had called Hyŏng-sik "older brother" just then. She had never known anyone she could call "older brother." Kye-hyang was an only child. She did not know who her father was, so she had no paternal relatives whom she knew. She knew about three women whom she called "older sister," but she had no one to call "older brother." Nor was she the only one like that. There weren't any other women around her who used the term "older brother," nor were there any men who used the term "older sister." Kye-hyang's society was a society of women. The men she met were men who came to visit a *kisaeng* house. She was very happy that she had called someone "older brother" for the first time. She felt even more affectionately towards Hyŏng-sik now than she had when she lit his cigarette. She wanted to call him "older brother" again. Hyŏng-sik and Kye-hyang reached the graveyard for criminals.

64

Kye-hyang went ahead of Hyŏng-sik and sought out three graves that were side by side. The grave mounds which had been small to begin with had become almost level ground, after having been washed with rain for years. Wooden grave markers seemed to have been placed there once; rotting pieces of wood lay on the ground before the graves. There were dozens of similar graves around those three graves. Some of the graves still had new wooden markers that were about four *ch'i*[121] in width. Kye-hyang pointed to three graves that stood side by side.

"This is the grave of Wŏr-hyang's father, and these are the graves of her two brothers," she said. She thought of how she had been there before with Wŏr-hyang. Kye-hyang had visited these graves several times with Wŏr-hyang. Last spring, when Wŏr-hyang was about to go to Seoul, Wŏr-hyang had visited the graves with Kye-hyang, bringing a bottle of wine. It had been a warm spring day, and small nameless flowers blossomed beside the graves of those pitiful human beings. In the fields, waves of newly sprouted sorghum and millet moved in the gentle breeze. Wŏr-hyang poured a cup of wine and set it before her father's grave. Then she wept for a long time. Afterwards, she rubbed Kye-hyang's back and asked her to visit the graves and look after them twice a year after she went to Seoul.

"Your father is my father," Kye-hyang had said. "And your brothers are my brothers." Kye-hyang wept at these thoughts, and looked at Hyŏng-sik. Hyŏng-sik stood without a word, looking at the three graves. He thought of Scholar Pak, with his large eyes and his high nose. Scholar Pak had been a tall man, and always sat with his back straight. Hyŏng-sik remembered how Scholar Pak had gathered youths in his study and taught them with the lithographed books he had brought from Shanghai. When Scholar Pak was arrested, he had wept and said, "I do not lament being taken away, but that the school will be closed." He thought of how Yŏng-ch'ae had said that her father had starved himself to death in prison when he heard that she had become a *kisaeng*. Hyŏng-sik thought of the tragic destiny of one who is ahead of their time. Scholar Pak had awakened too early. Actually, it was not that he had awakened too early, but that his countrymen had awakened too late. The kind of school that Pak had tried to start could now be found everywhere, and men all wore their hair short now, just as Pak had done. If Pak had tried to start an enlightenment movement now, he would have been praised and respected instead of persecuted. There are always people whose lives are sacrificed when the times change, but none whose lives were as tragically sacrificed as Pak's. What had happened to Pak's two daughters-in-law? If Yŏng-ch'ae were dead, that would mean that Pak's entire family had perished. Everyone in Hyŏng-sik's own family had died

121. One *ch'i* = 3.03 cm.

except for Hyŏng-sik, and Yŏng-ch'ae had been the only survivor in her family. If Yŏng-ch'ae were dead, though, that would mean that her family had perished without any living descendants in the world. Pak had once had dozens of households of relatives, but they had all perished in the *Sinmi* incident,[122] leaving only Scholar Pak's household. Now even Scholar Pak's family had perished, a sacrificial victim of the "new civilization" movement. The fate of Scholar Pak's family and his relatives was incomprehensible, Hyŏng-sik thought. One could never predict the fate of a family or a clan.

Hyŏng-sik did not feel sad as he looked at the graves, though. He was too happy to be sad about anything. Hyŏng-sik thought it was better to rejoice over the living, than to mourn the dead. Rather than think about his pitiful benefactor's body, which had rotted away leaving nothing but bones, Hyŏng-sik preferred to rejoice over the flowers on the grave, that were fed by the decaying flesh. Hyŏng-sik thought about Yŏng-ch'ae. He imagined her corpse floating down the Taedong River. He did not feel sad, though, but felt a boundless happiness when he looked at Kye-hyang standing beside him.

This surprised him. "Have I changed that much?" he wondered. Hyŏng-sik was so surprised that he opened his eyes wide and clenched his fists. He had wept when he read Yŏng-ch'ae's letter the day before. He had been so sad that he thought his heart would break. While on the night train to P'yŏngyang, his heart had ached, and he had surreptitiously wiped away his tears. At the police station, when he realized that Yŏng-ch'ae was dead, Hyŏng-sik had felt as though his body were being immersed in scalding hot water. After he left Kye-hyang's house and was on his way to Scholar Pak's grave, he had intended to throw himself before the grave and sob aloud to his heart's content. Then why did he feel the way he felt now? He tried to force himself to weep before his benefactor's grave, but he couldn't feel sad at all. Could a person change so suddenly? he wondered and smiled to himself.

Kye-hyang thought Hyŏng-sik was acting strangely, but she did not try to find out why.

Hyŏng-sik thought it would be better to converse pleasantly with Kye-hyang while walking hand-in-hand, than remain in that morbid place.

"Let's go," Hyŏng-sik said.

"Where?" Kye-hyang asked, as though she thought it strange that he wanted to leave already.

"Home."

122. The text uses the term *Sinmi hyŏngmyŏng*, which means "the revolution of 1871." American warships arrived at Kanghwa Island in 1871 (the year *sinmi*, according to the traditional system of naming calendar years by using combinations of the twelve branches and ten stems), and demanded trade relations; when the Koreans refused, the Americans advanced to Kwangsŏng fortress on Kanghwa Island, provoking military conflict with the Koreans. Pak's relatives were executed as "enemy sympathizers," apparently because of their openness to Western culture.

"And not go to Pungmang Mountain?"

"Why go there? Let's talk on our way back. There are no signs of Yŏng-ch'ae having been here, so she must not have come here at all." Hyŏng-sik took Kye-hyang's hand in his.

Hyŏng-sik went back to Kye-hyang's house, having made up his mind that Yŏng-ch'ae must be dead. The old woman said that she would stay in P'yŏngyang for two or three more days. Hyŏng-sik returned to Seoul alone that evening on a train. When he left P'yŏngyang, the old woman walked out of the front door of Kye-hyang's house with him, and clasped his hands and wept.

"Please do whatever you can to find Yŏng-ch'ae," she said. Hyŏng-sik, however, only regretted that he was leaving Kye-hyang. He did not think about Yŏng-ch'ae much at all. "I have awakened from a dream," he thought on the train, and smiled several times.

65

Hyŏng-sik felt a boundless happiness on his way from P'yŏngyang to Seoul. He felt drawn by love to all of the people on the train, and everyone seemed to give him an unspeakable happiness. The sound of the train wheels on the tracks was like cheerful music, and the roaring noise that was heard whenever the train crossed a bridge or passed a cave sounded like glorious military music. Too excited to sleep, Hyŏng-sik opened a window and let a cool breeze blow against his face. He looked at the mountain ranges of Hwanghae Province that were vaguely visible in the faint moonlight. The mountains were one color, without valleys, trees or stones,[123] like an ink painting. It was as though the moonlight, and the color of the clouds and the night had been mixed together and painted on paper, in geomantically auspicious formation,[124] using a giant brush. Hyŏng-sik's mind was in a similar state. Sorrow, pain, greed, happiness, love, hatred and all other workings of the spirit had gathered together, and melted and become amassed as one, so that he could not distinguish one from the other. It was as though all of these spiritual workings had been put into a pot, and then clear water had been added and a fire lit beneath the pot, and the contents of the pot stirred until it melted together and became like taffy or rice porridge. To put it in a positive way, one could say that the workings of Hyŏng-sik's mind were in a condition of utmost harmony; or, to put it in a negative way, one could say that the workings of his mind were in a condition of utter chaos. The light of the moon, which was hidden behind a thin layer of clouds, made

123. In the 1971 Samjungdang edition, the word *tol* (stone) is mistakenly printed as *tŭl* (field). In the 1917 *Maeil Sinbo* and 1918 Sinmungwan editions, it is written as *tol* (stone).
124. According to geomancy, or the theory of *feng shui*, the natural features of a land area affect a country's or an individual's fate. Cf. Ki-baik Lee, *A New History of Korea* (Cambridge, MA and London: Harvard University Press, 1984), 107–108.

the mountains and fields blurred and indistinct, as though in a dream. The moonlight shone on Hyŏng-sik's mind, and melted and colored his thoughts and emotions, until they too were vague and indistinct as if in a dream. Hyŏng-sik's eyes sparkled vacantly, and his mind was all in a muddle. His body swayed with the train, and his ears took in whatever could be heard. He did not try to think of anything in particular. He did not try to see or hear anything in particular either. He heard the wheels of the train moving, the earth rotating, stars colliding with one another in infinitely distant space, and the flowing of infinitesimally minute molecules of ether. He heard the rustling of grass and trees growing at night in the mountains and fields, and the blood circulating in his body, and the whispering of his cells as they joyfully received his blood.

His mind was in the chaotic state in which the universe had been at creation, and in which the universe would be when it declined and perished. He could see God, head poised in thought as he tried to create light, stars, the sky and the earth. He saw God rolling up his sleeves and starting to create the universe, having finished his deliberations. After making light, darkness, grass, trees, birds and beasts, God smiled with joy. God then dug some earth, brought water and added it to the earth, kneaded the mixture into clay, and made it into the form of a human being. Then God breathed into the nostrils of the human being, and the clay human being came to life. Blood circulated in the human being's veins, and the person began to sing. Although the person had been only a motionless lump of clay at first, it began to breathe, and utter sounds, and blood began to circulate in the person's body. When Hyŏng-sik saw this happen, it seemed to him that the human being was none other than himself. Hyŏng-sik smiled. Of course, he thought. He had been a lifeless lump of clay. A lump of clay that could not breathe, move or sing. He had been unable to see the myriad entities around him, or hear the sounds from those entities. Even when the light and sound of other beings around him entered his eyes and ears, to him it had been no more than waves of ether. He had not known how to find happiness, sadness or meaning in the light or sound of other beings. Though he had laughed and cried before then, he had been like a rubber doll that laughs and cries automatically when you press its belly. He had laughed and cried not of his own volition, but involuntarily.

He had not used his intelligence, or personal judgment, or emotions to decide for himself what was right or wrong, sad or happy, but had completely followed tradition and social custom. If something had been said to be right since antiquity, he too thought it was right. If others liked something, he too liked it. It had been as simple as that. What power, though, could something that had been considered right since antiquity, have over him? And of what relevance was it to him if others liked something? He had his own intelligence, and will. The only thing that mattered was judging for himself what was right, or good, happy or sad, using his own intelligence and will. He used to abandon without further thought what he considered to be right, just because it had been considered wrong since the olden days, or because others thought it wasn't right. This had been a mistake. He had killed himself, and abandoned himself.

Only now had he become aware of his life. He had realized that he had a self. The North Star was not Cygnus or Canopus, but was only the North Star. It did not have the exact same size, color, position, composition, history and mission in the universe as Cygnus and Canopus, but had its own unique characteristics. Similarly, Hyŏng-sik had a self, and an intelligence, will, location, mission and appearance of his own that were not necessarily the same as those of other people. Hyŏng-sik felt a tremendous happiness.

He looked out the train window, smiling.

66

The train now passed Namch'ŏn Station in Sinmak, and raced towards the vicinity of former Kŭmch'ŏn Mountain, the most mountainous part of the Kyŏngŭi Railroad.[125] The crescent moon had already disappeared from the sky, and it was dark outside the train windows. The absence of moonlight made it easier to see the mountains. The boundary between sky and mountains could be seen clearly like a twisting, curving line painted with a thick brush. Through the clacking of the train wheels, a mountain stream could be heard, rushing through rapids filled with stones. Two thatched huts in a small mountain ravine appeared for a moment in the light of the fire from the engine smokestack, and a small stream that had been reduced to a trickle in the long drought, could be glimpsed, flowing reluctantly. When the train turned the spur of the mountain, a small light could be seen twinkling in the darkness. The light stayed in Hyŏng-sik's window for quite some time, flickering on and off as the train progressed, as though occasionally obscured by thick foliage. Hyŏng-sik stared at the light. Who was sitting beside that light, and what were they doing? Was an impoverished mother sitting mending her husband and children's ragged clothing after having put her children to bed? Did she have difficulty threading her needle because her eyesight was bad? Did she then turn the flame up on her lamp several times, and rub her eyes? "I have grown old!" she would exclaim, and thick tears would fall on the rags that she had been mending. Did her sick baby son, who was asleep on the warmest part of the floor, wake from a dream, crying? Did she embrace him, and give him her breast, even though her breast had no milk since she herself had nothing to eat? Or did an old couple stand on either

---

125. The Kyŏngŭi Railroad ran between Seoul and Sinŭiji (in North P'yŏngan Province). It opened in 1906.

side of their only child, a son, as he lay in his bed, sick, and take turns stroking his body and weeping and trying to soothe him, while they prayed inwardly for God to look down upon them? Hyŏng-sik thought of his parents, who had passed away over a decade ago. His mother had still been young, but his father had been over fifty years old. Whenever Hyŏng-sik was even the slightest bit ill, his father would bathe and perform ablutions, and stay by his side all night. When Hyŏng-sik eventually opened his eyes, his father would smile broadly, as if overjoyed that his son had opened his eyes, and would clasp his hand. Hyŏng-sik remembered his mother, who was not yet thirty years old, dozing where she sat, overcome by fatigue. Hyŏng-sik felt saddened for a moment, then looked at the light again. He thought of that one solitary light blinking in the darkness, and of someone sitting awake beside that light when everyone else was fast asleep. These images seemed to represent his own plight. The train turned the spur of a mountain, and the light could no longer be seen. Hyŏng-sik turned away from the window somewhat wistfully. The people in the same train car with him were all fast asleep. A boy who looked like a laborer sat across from Hyŏng-sik, huddled up as though cold. Hyŏng-sik quickly shut the train window, and covered the boy with the blanket that Hyŏng-sik had been using. The boy wore muddy, cotton Korean trousers and a rag tied around his head. He seemed to be on his way to work in a mine. His hair was dishevelled, and his neck and the skin beneath his ears were filthy. His head was pillowed on a mud-stained sack. The sack was tied with a string made of twined paper. The string dangled beneath the bench where the boy slept. Hyŏng-sik picked up the end of the string beneath the sack, and tucked it beneath the sack. A pack of Kuksu, or "Chrysanthemum Waters" brand cigarettes was sticking out of the pocket of the boy's Korean vest, which was made of thick ramie. Inside the pack of cigarettes were about four cigarettes which had become flattened at the end that one puts in one's mouth. He's saving those cigarettes, Hyŏng-sik thought. He smiled, and touched his own pack of Choil[126] cigarettes. He suddenly wanted to light a cigarette, and took one out. Hyŏng-sik lit the cigarette and drew a deep breathful.[127] The cigarette had a special taste just then.

Hyŏng-sik looked around the train car again. A Japanese woman woke from her sleep and looked around herself in a daze. She rubbed the top of her head, then her neck, and looked this way and that as if trying to find something. Then she lay back down on a *shingenbukuro*,[128] and fell asleep. Hyŏng-sik decided to get some sleep so that he would not be tired the next

---

126. The word *Choil* is written in the text in the Korean alphabet, and then in Chinese characters in parentheses. The Japanese pronunciation for the Chinese characters is *Asahi*.
127. Cigarette smoking can cause cancer.
128. The word for "Japanese cloth bag" was written in the text using the Korean alphabet, as *sinhyŏndae*, and then in Chinese characters, which are pronounced *shingenbukuro* in Japanese.

day. He folded a towel, and placed it against the edge of the window. Then he pillowed his head on the towel, and closed his eyes. Hyŏng-sik felt even more tired mentally, but could not fall asleep. He kept his eyes closed, though, hoping to fall asleep, and counted the noises made by the train wheels turning. He became as calm as an ocean where waves have subsided. Various images flashed through his mind in no particular order: images of Yŏng-ch'ae, Sŏn-hyŏng, the old woman, Dean Pae, Yi Hŭi-gyŏng, the old man he had seen outside Ch'ilsŏngmun, Scholar Pak's grave, Kye-hyang. Hyŏng-sik looked at their faces with his eyes closed. Some of them were smiling, some were crying. Some thrust their mouth forward as though angry. Some glared through the corner of their eyes. Some feigned indifference, their face as motionless as though carved in wood. Yŏng-ch'ae's face appeared the most often, and for the longest time. Hyong-sik thought of the briefcase beside him. He visualized Yŏng-ch'ae's letter, the ring, and the knife. Hyŏng-sik shivered and opened his eyes.

Have I been wrong? he wondered. Have I not been too heartless? Shouldn't I have spent more time looking for Yŏng-ch'ae? If Yŏng-ch'ae was dead, shouldn't I at least have looked for her body? Shouldn't I have stood by the Taedong River and wept hot tears into the waters? Yŏng-ch'ae took her life, thinking of me. I shed no tears for Yŏng-ch'ae, though. Ah, how cruel I am. I am not a human being. The train raced towards Namdaemun. Hyŏng-sik wanted to turn the train around and go to P'yŏngyang. Hyŏng-sik arrived nevertheless at Namdaemun and got off the train, though his mind was drawn towards P'yŏngyang.

67

Hyŏng-sik returned to his lodgings, ate breakfast, and went right to school. "You look very tired. You should take the day off," the old woman said. Hyŏng-sik would not listen to the old woman, though. Hyŏng-sik was exhausted from the last four days of mental exertion and lack of sleep. The fatigue showed in his face. He had to teach fourth-year English that morning during the first hour of school, though. He had taken yesterday off. If he took another day off, that would be two days in a row. This pained Hyŏng-sik. Hyŏng-sik had never taken time off from school. Even if he caught a cold and his head ached and he had a fever, he would still force himself to go to school. Then he would come home content that he had fulfilled his responsibility, even if it meant that his cold got worse. Hyŏng-sik thought it would be a serious wrong for him to take so much as an hour off so that he could rest in ease, and make over a hundred students waste an hour. There was another reason, however, besides a sense of responsibility, that made Hyŏng-sik go to school so diligently.

Hyŏng-sik had been lonely growing up. He had grown up never knowing the love of parents or brothers or sisters. He had no beloved friends, moreover. The love of friends who are one's own age and of similar personality and interests can be just as important as the love of brothers and sisters. Hyŏng-sik never had the chance to make such friends, though, since he was never in one fixed place, and in the days when he was wandering about in poverty, kids who could have been his friends slighted him, and would not befriend him. When Hyŏng-sik was twelve, he had been very fond of one of his cousins. The cousin was the same age as Hyŏng-sik, and they had once read books together. Once Hyŏng-sik went to play at his cousin's house until late at night. Hyŏng-sik was very happy at the thought of being able to sleep over at his cousin's house and share the same bed with his cousin. Although he could have gone back to his paternal uncle's house, where he was staying, he insisted that it was too dark outside for him to go, and he asked his cousin if he could sleep with him.

"Your clothes are full of lice," his cousin said loudly, though, so that everyone in the house could hear. Hyŏng-sik felt humiliated and aggrieved, but there was nothing he could do but run out of the house, crying. His clothes and hair were indeed full of lice. Twelve-year old Hyŏng-sik thus could not even know what it was like to have a friend's love. Afterwards, Hyŏng-sik went to live at Scholar Pak's house, where he was with youths over ten years older than himself. It was the same when he went to Kyŏngsŏng later. If there ever was a time when Hyŏng-sik could have learned what it was like to have a friend, it would have been when he was studying in Tokyo. There were many boys his age in Tokyo. Hungry for friendship, Hyŏng-sik tried his best to befriend the boys he met there. Hyŏng-sik, however, had suffered through difficulties in life since an early age, and he had lost the pretty, boyish looks of childhood; instead, there was a mature, adult aspect to his face and mind. Thus boys his own age would not befriend him, no matter how Hyŏng-sik tried to be close to them. There was also a big difference between Hyŏng-sik and the other boys in the extent of their learning, and because of this, the other boys respected Hyŏng-sik as their senior, but they would not walk shoulder to shoulder with him or hold his hand and try to be his friend. When they played hide and seek, they would stop when they saw Hyŏng-sik, and bow their head and respectfully say, "How are you." Then Hyŏng-sik could do nothing but reply, "How are you."

Once, Hyŏng-sik grabbed hold of a boy two years younger than he was, and said, "Let's be friends. You and me." The boy thought it was a joke and said, "Yes," then took off his hat, bowed respectfully, and ran away. Hyŏng-sik kept trying every chance he had to try and make friends with other boys, but they would just laugh, then bow politely and run away. In the end, Hyŏng-sik was never able to make any friends among boys his age. All his life, he made friends only with those over ten years older than he.

"I skipped my boyhood years," he once lamented. He felt lonely because he had never had a boyhood. "I have been robbed of one of my rights in life," he always said. "That right is one of the greatest, most joyful rights one can have." Whenever Hyŏng-sik said this, he would sigh, overwhelmed with loneliness.

When he was twenty-one years old, he became an instructor at the Kyŏngsŏng School, and worked closely with many young boys. When the boys called him "teacher," and avoided him, Hyŏng-sik felt as lonely as ever. He even wanted to be admitted to a middle school, and play together with those boys.

Hyŏng-sik loved his students very much. All of his words and actions towards the students were inspired by a warm affection. Hyŏng-sik wiped the noses of the younger students, and even tied their shoes and Korean sashes for them. One of the instructors made fun of Hyŏng-sik, and negatively interpreted Hyŏng-sik's devoted love for his students. The instructor said that Hyŏng-sik loved Yi Hŭi-gyŏng in particular for his face; someone else said that he knew for certain that Hyŏng-sik and Hŭi-gyŏng were involved in an improper relationship. A friend had thus tried to admonish Hyŏng-sik, and Hŭi-gyŏng had been teased with insinuating comments by his classmates. Someone alleged that Hyŏng-sik had arranged to have Hŭi-gyŏng graduate first in his class.

Hyŏng-sik, however, continued to love his students. Hyŏng-sik would have severed his own artery if his blood were needed to cure an ill student. He felt towards a few students like Hŭi-gyŏng, moreover, the kind of very passionate love that a man feels for a woman.

68

We diverge from our story momentarily here, but there is a need to discuss Hyŏng-sik's life as a teacher. Hyŏng-sik's life as a teacher at the Kyŏngsŏng School over the past four years could be summarized as a life of love and anguish.

When Hyŏng-sik became a teacher and began to interact with the boys at school, the love that had been trapped inside of him, starving, for over twenty years, began to emerge. His love was like a bud of grass that sprouts in a spring breeze, after having been covered with snow. Hyŏng-sik had never known the love of parents, siblings or friends, let alone even dreamed of a woman's love. Now his love swept over the four hundred young students like high tide on the fifteenth and the last day of the month on the lunar calendar.

"You are my parents, siblings, wife, friend, son," he once wrote in his diary. "You alone take up all of my love, and all my mind. I will work for you, and love you until my blood runs dry, my flesh is all spent, and my bones break." These words expressed Hyŏng-sik's genuine emotions. Hyŏng-sik felt happy every morning when he walked through the school gate and saw the students playing. It gave him great happiness every hour to stand at the lectern and see the students looking at him and listening to him. At night when he lay alone in his bed, it made him happy to think of the students playing and learning. He tried to speak of everything he knew, and tried all methods that he could, in order to teach the students as much as possible, impart goodness and beauty to their behavior, and enlighten their minds. Hyŏng-sik was therefore overjoyed when, during a debate contest, students used words he had taught them, or when students working on a project used a method he had taught them.

Hyŏng-sik had used most of his time and experience over the past four years, working for the students. As a result, his nerves had grown frazzled, and his body weak. He himself knew this. Nevertheless, when Hyŏng-sik saw the fourth-year students whom he had educated, he felt the happiness and satisfaction that a farmer who has sweated and suffered from spring through summer feels when seeing drooping heads of golden, ripening grain in paddies and fields in autumn. He thought that the fourth-year students' knowledge, and their beautiful thoughts, words and actions were mostly the result of his devoted efforts. Hyŏng-sik in fact never lost the least chance to tell students about what he knew, his experiences, his thoughts, and interesting stories. He told the fourth-year students everything, so that now he did not have much more to say to them. After teaching from the textbook, Hyŏng-sik would use the rest of the class time to tell the students about things that he thought were new and beneficial. One of the reasons that Hyŏng-sik read books was because of his desire to teach his students. The students, moreover, enjoyed listening to him. "Tell us some more," the students would say to him. Hyŏng-sik would feel even more gratified when he heard this. Of course, there were some students who thought Hyŏng-sik's stories were annoying, and some students would deliberately look away and scribble in their notebooks when Hyŏng-sik was speaking in earnest. Most of the students, however, seemed to Hyŏng-sik to be listening with interest. The students thus received a considerable amount of influence, knowledge and amusement from Hyŏng-sik. Others too acknowledged that Hyŏng-sik had influenced the students the most, among all the instructors. Hyŏng-sik himself was certain of this.

The instructors did not think, however, that Hyŏng-sik had been a very good influence on the students. Some instructors criticized Hyŏng-sik for having made the students arrogant, or confusing the students by reading them bad novels.

These criticisms were not entirely without cause. Hyŏng-sik always insisted on giving the students as much freedom as possible, and advocated that the school administration also respect the students' opinions as much as possible. When Hyŏng-sik first came to the Kyŏngsŏng School as an instructor, the principal and dean were adherents of dictatorship, and would not permit the students to express their opinions. If a student so much as uttered a single word that was critical of school orders or what teachers said, the student would be firmly reprimanded in front of all of the other students, and then suspended, or, in the worst cases, expelled from school. Hyŏng-sik, with his belief in liberty, had thus had several conflicts of opinion with the school administration.

Hyŏng-sik would say such dangerous things as, "It is right for you students to openly speak out when you have a grievance, and it is right for you to oppose the school if the school is against a just cause." When Dean Pae said that the recent unrest at school had been incited by Hyŏng-sik, the accusation thus was not entirely unfounded.

Hyŏng-sik encouraged the third- and fourth-year students, moreover, to take an interest in literature. Some of the students thus began to read novels, philosophy books, and magazines, and a few of these students began to walk around with their heads lowered, as if in profound thought, as though they were the greatest of writers, or thinkers, or philosophers. Such students scorned the other instructors as simpletons who did not understand what it was to have an intellectual life. Hyŏng-sik thought this meant that the students had progressed, and that this was therefore something to be happy about, but the other teachers thought the students had gone astray and become impudent. Students as well as instructors ridiculed Yi Hŭi-gyŏng and his friends for carrying around books full of text that was difficult to understand, and magazines that had been published that month.

69

Yi Hŭi-gyŏng and his friends could not, of course, understand those difficult books. After reading ten or twenty pages, they could not systematically understand what they had read. They were content if there were a few phrases here and there that they could understand. They were proud of reading several pages a day, even though they could not understand what they were reading, and they considered it the one glory of their life to memorize and recite the names they had heard from Hyŏng-sik, of famous Western writers, philosophers, and religious thinkers, and the names of their writings. They memorized from the books they read, phrases such as "What is life?" or "What is the universe?" and used these quotes in debate contests, and among friends. Sometimes they would quote sayings from Tolstoy or Shakespeare, or memorize and recite such sayings verbatim in English. They thought they could present their message better if they used such quotes, even if they themselves did not understand what the quotes meant. The students who heard them would sneer, but inwardly envy them for having so much knowledge. They would then secretly buy old magazines; in quiet moments, they would remember what Yi Hŭi-gyŏng and his friends said, and use those words elsewhere to show off.

Yi Hŭi-gyŏng had very good powers of comprehension. Hyŏng-sik thought Hŭi-gyŏng had the most mature thinking among all of the students, and Hŭi-gyŏng himself thought he had a good understanding of whatever Hyŏng-sik said. When Hyŏng-sik and Hŭi-gyŏng sat together, all kinds of subjects emerged, one after the other, in their conversation, concerning life and the universe. It was as if they were two thinkers who thought alike and were meeting again for the first time in a long time. Hyŏng-sik, however, felt that he still had certain refined, high-minded thoughts that he could not discuss with Hŭi-gyŏng. This was true. Sometimes Hyŏng-sik would talk about his thoughts, and then notice a vacant look on Hŭi-gyŏng's face. Then Hyŏng-sik would smile and stop talking. You don't understand yet, he would think. Then Hŭi-gyŏng's face would get red, as if Hyŏng-sik had insulted him. Hŭi-gyŏng recognized, of course, that Hyŏng-sik knew more than he did and had more profound thoughts. Hŭi-gyŏng did not think that Hyŏng-sik was dozens of *li* ahead of him, though. He therefore felt displeased and resentful when Hyŏng-sik treated him condescendingly. Until Hŭi-gyŏng was a second-year student, Hyŏng-sik had seemed to him to be several thousand *li* ahead of him. There was nothing that Hyŏng-sik did not know, and everything he said seemed to have deep meaning. He thought Hyŏng-sik was the most knowledgeable and most profound person in Korea. Halfway through his third year, though, Hŭi-gyŏng began to see Hyŏng-sik as someone who was not very different from himself. Hyŏng-sik did not know all that much, and even Hŭi-gyŏng could have the thoughts that Hyŏng-sik had. The things that Hyŏng-sik said at the lectern, moreover, were not particularly impressive. Hŭi-gyŏng too could easily do as well if he were to step up to the lectern. Nevertheless, when he tried to speak at debates, he just did not seem to do as well as Hyŏng-sik, no matter how he tried. He thought this was not because he was not as good a speaker as Hyŏng-sik but that Hyŏng-sik's speaking skills had matured as a result of being a teacher for several years; Hŭi-gyŏng felt that he himself would speak even better than Hyŏng-sik once he had had as much practice. Hŭi-gyŏng thought that within only three years, he would surpass Hyŏng-sik in thought, knowledge and speaking. Once Hŭi-gyŏng had become a fourth-year student and began studying the fourth-year reader, there were words that even Hyŏng-sik did not know, and grammar that even Hyŏng-sik could not clearly explain. Hŭi-gyŏng thus no longer looked up to Hyŏng-sik all that much in the subject of English as well. To Hŭi-gyŏng, it seemed as though Hyŏng-sik were no more than two steps ahead of him, and that Hŭi-gyŏng would in the future be ten or twenty times better than Hyŏng-sik. Hŭi-gyŏng began to look down on middle school teachers. He had long thought of middle school teachers as empty-headed types who knew nothing, but now he realized that even Hyŏng-sik, who seemed to know more than any of the other teachers, was not that impressive once you got to know him well. He himself would never be a middle school teacher, he thought. He would be a great scholar, or a Ph.D. If he were ever to work at a middle school, it would be as a principal.

Hŭi-gyŏng thought middle school teachers were trifling characters who had gone as far as they were going to go in life, whereas he himself had the potential for limitless success. Hŭi-gyŏng did not know that Hyŏng-sik had thought just like him about seven years ago. Hŭi-gyŏng thought that Hyŏng-sik had been a middle school teacher for four years, and, moreover, would be a middle school teacher for the rest of his life because he was of meager abilities and did not know how to set higher aspirations. Hŭi-gyŏng felt both contempt and pity for Hyŏng-sik. Hŭi-gyŏng was not the only student who thought this way. All of the students who, like Hŭi-gyŏng, tried to read difficult books thought that way too. The rest of the students had never had any respect for Hyŏng-sik to begin with, but just thought he was a very kind teacher. They ridiculed the way Hyŏng-sik favored Hŭi-gyŏng and his friends and particularly loved Hŭi-gyŏng. They even began to dislike Hyŏng-sik.

The students had gone from being children to becoming adults. They had gone from the first year to the fourth year. They had known nothing, and now they had the knowledge expected of an average person. The students felt that they had made progress and had grown over the past four years. It seemed to them, however, that Hyŏng-sik had not changed at all between the time they were first-year students and now, when they were in their fourth year. Since Hyŏng-sik had given almost all of his knowledge to the students, he did not seem to them to have any particular qualifications that set him above the students. Although the students outwardly continued to behave the same as they always had towards Hyŏng-sik, inwardly they thus considered him to be at their level or beneath them.

70

Hyŏng-sik had a habit of lamenting that he did not have enough knowledge and cultivation. He sincerely meant it, but the students had thought he was only being modest. Recently, however, the students realized it was the truth. They therefore would not trust what Hyŏng-sik said any more. When he said he was lacking in knowledge and cultivation, he seemed to be apologizing to them out of fear of them. That was not Hyŏng-sik's intent, though. Even if he was indeed deficient in knowledge and cultivation, it was not to the extent that he feared falling behind Hŭi-gyŏng and his friends. To Hyŏng-sik, Hŭi-gyŏng and his friends were still children. Even if they were to run after him with all their might, fists clenched, it would take them seven years to catch up with him. Hyŏng-sik believed that he was a pioneer with the most advanced thinking in Korea. Within his modesty was a pride and arrogance towards Korean society. He had read Western philosophy and Western literature. He had read Rousseau's *Confessions* and

Émile, Shakespeare's *Hamlet,* Goethe's *Faust,* and Kropotkin's *The Conquest for Bread.*[129] He read political theory and literary criticism in newly published journals, and had once won a prize in a fiction contest sponsored by a Japanese journal. He knew the name Tagore, and had read a biography of Ellen Kay. He thought about the universe and about life. He took confidence in having his own views about life, the universe, religion, and art, and his own opinions on education. When he rode a full train and saw the people jostling about, he thought of how he knew many words and had many thoughts that they did not, and he felt a proud happiness. At the same time, he felt the responsibility of one who is ahead of his time, wondering to himself when those people would ever be taught to know as much as he did. He felt the loneliness and sorrow of the pioneer, thinking of how there were few people among twenty million Koreans who would understand his words and intentions. He tried to think of friends who would understand what he said. He could count them on less than ten fingers. These individuals, moreover, were themselves pioneers of Korea who understood modern civilization. They were individuals who could teach and guide the Korean people. He felt very content that he had over the past four years brought Hŭi-gyŏng and about four other students up to his own level. They were still children compared to himself, but compared to others, they were adults and pioneers, thought Hyŏng-sik. There were many schools in Korea, and many students, but no students who could rival Hŭi-gyŏng and his friends, he thought. Hyŏng-sik therefore thought that he was the only Korean educator who understood modern civilization and could see Korea's future path. The hundreds of teachers in Seoul did not understand the significance of educating Koreans, and taught math and Japanese by rote, like machines. Hyŏng-sik was thus always dissatisfied with Korean educators' circles. Hyŏng-sik had once worked busily for two months trying to establish the Kyŏngsŏng Educational Association, in order to promote his educational ideals. Other teachers, however, did not recognize Hyŏng-sik as having advanced knowledge or thought, and some did not even consider him their equal. There was, indeed, nothing exceptional about what Hyŏng-sik said or did. The things that Hyŏng-sik said so fervently as though they were great truths did not particularly move others. The only unique characteristic he had was the way he used a lot of English, referred to the names of famous

---

129. *La Conquête du Pain* (1892) by Petr A. Kropotkin (1842–1921). Kropotkin, son of Prince Aleksei Petrovich Kropotkin, was a geographer and revolutionary who supported anarchism. He thought that the savage laws of Social Darwinism could be refuted by evidence of mutual aid practiced among certain animals. He declined an official appointment in 1871 because he thought he had no right to "those higher joys, when all around me was misery, and the struggle for a moldy piece of bread." He thought the nation-state was an anachronism, and that voluntary societies would transform the state. Cf. G. Woodcock and I. Avakumovic, *The Anarchist Prince* (London, New York: T.V. Boardman, 1950).

Westerners, quoted famous sayings, and spoke at length using incomprehensible words. His speeches and writings seemed to be literal translations of Western texts. According to Hyŏng-sik, it was impossible to express deep, detailed thought without such speech or writing. He thought the reason that others did not follow his opinions was that they could not understand his thought, and this made him upset. In all fairness to Hyŏng-sik, he was somewhat ahead of the instructors in certain ways, and had the enthusiasm and sincerity to put into practice what he believed. He was not very good, however, at understanding others. He thought others were of the same mind as he, and that others too would recognize as good whatever he thought was good. To put it simply, Hyŏng-sik was subjective and idealistic, not practical or pragmatic.

His four years as a teacher had been a failure. He had set forth his ideas on several matters, but none of his ideas had been used. He had taught many things to his students and made various recommendations to them, but the students did not welcome any of this, nor did they carry out what he told them to do. This made Hyŏng-sik furious and pessimistic on several occasions. He did not think that others rejected his ideas because he was somehow deficient, though, but thought it was because others could not yet understand his high-minded thought. This was the sorrow of the pioneer, he thought, and felt reassured. Others, however, did not think they had rejected Hyŏng-sik's ideas because they could not understand his thought. They thought Hyŏng-sik's ideas could not be put into practice, or, if put into practice, would not be effective. Several people, however, eventually recognized that Hyŏng-sik was very knowledgeable, read many difficult books, and was quite a profound thinker. They therefore called him "The Thinker" and "The Philosopher," both jokingly and in praise. The meaning behind these nicknames was mostly derisive: "Go ahead and think all you want. You cannot do anything in reality." When Hyŏng-sik heard these nicknames, though, he felt contemptuous. You do not even understand what a thinker or a philosopher is, he thought. Nonetheless, the nicknames did not entirely displease him.

71

Hyŏng-sik went to the office. The bell signaling the beginning of class had already rung, and the teachers were all in class. Dean Pae sat at his desk smoking a cigarette. He glanced at Hyŏng-sik, then turned his head away. Hyŏng-sik had an unpleasant feeling when he saw Pae, but kept quiet and got a box of chalk and his books, and went to his classroom on the second floor.

"I am sorry that I am late," Hyŏng-sik said, and looked around the classroom gladly. Hŭi-gyŏng looked at Hyŏng-sik and smiled, then lowered his head. The other students were smiling too as they looked at Hyŏng-sik or at each other. Only Kim Chong-nyŏl sat in a dignified manner, without smiling.

Hyŏng-sik opened his book and put it on his desk, then sat in his chair and looked at everyone as though he thought they were behaving strangely. An unpleasant feeling that he could not quite express arose in his heart. The students' behavior was definitely odd, he thought. This had never happened before. There was something derisive in the students' attitude towards him today. "Why are you all looking at me and smiling? Let's begin class. Lesson eighteen. Please read for us, Mr. Kim."

As if they could not hold it back any longer, the students all burst into laughter. Some of them put their foreheads on their desks and laughed. Their backs shook with laughter. Hyŏng-sik's face grew red. He felt embarrassed, angry and sad. He wanted to stomp his feet on the ground, and scold them, but he also wanted to cry. Hyŏng-sik stood up.

"What is going on? What kind of behavior is this?" he said in a stern voice. He opened his eyes wide. His voice, however, was shaking. The students stopped laughing and sat up straight. Hŭi-gyŏng lowered his head and wrote something on his desk with a pencil. Kim Chong-nyŏl still sat with an indifferent expression. Hyŏng-sik could not bring himself to teach the lesson. His heart was racing and he was out of breath. He was angry because he felt that he had been insulted by students whom he had taught with all his mind and heart for the past four years or so. A teacher was lecturing on math in the classroom across the hall, but stopped talking when laughter broke out in Hyŏng-sik's class and Hyŏng-sik began speaking in a loud voice. The other teacher seemed to be listening to what was going on in Hyŏng-sik's classroom.

"What is the matter? Someone tell me. What kind of behavior is this for students? Speak up!"

The students turned their eyes to Kim Chong-nyŏl. Hŭi-gyŏng lowered his head further and wrote something with his pencil, his legs twitching nervously. Kim Chong-nyŏl stood up. The students looked back and forth at Hyŏng-sik and Chong-nyŏl, and smiled and nudged each other. Some students whispered. Hyŏng-sik's hair seemed to stand on end.

Chong-nyŏl coughed once like an orator, then said, "I have a question to ask you, sir." He glared at Hyŏng-sik. Hyŏng-sik started at the word "question." He felt confident, however, that he would be able to cope regardless of what question he was asked.

"What question?" he said, looking at Chong-nyŏl.

"Where have you been, sir? That is what I would like to ask you." Chong-nyŏl sat down again. Everyone looked at Hyŏng-sik's lips.

"I have been to P'yŏngyang. So what? What about it?"

"Why did you go to P'yŏngyang?" a student asked as if thinking aloud to himself.

"With whom did you go?" asked another student. The students laughed again.

"Whom were you following?"

Hyŏng-sik now understood what this was all about.

Chong-nyŏl stood up again, and said, "Why did you go to P'yŏngyang? It is not difficult to surmise that something serious must have happened, since you took time off from teaching."

Hyŏng-sik could not speak. He bowed his head and closed his eyes. He stood still for a long time, unaware himself of what he was thinking. The students laughed again. "He was following Kye Wŏr-hyang," a student said, and laughed.

Just then Dean Pae walked abruptly into the room.

"Why is this classroom so noisy, Mr. Yi?" he asked. "Teachers and students in other classrooms cannot have class with this noise." Pae looked around at the students. "What is the meaning of this ruckus?" he asked.

"It is because of Kye Wŏr-hyang!" cried out one student. Pae glared at Hyŏng-sik, then left the room and closed the door. Hyŏng-sik lifted his head and looked at the students.

"My four years of instruction with you have now come to an end. I am leaving," he said in a trembling voice. Then he left the classroom. Laughter and chatter could be heard coming from the classroom. Tears rose in Hyŏng-sik's eyes.

He went to his office and picked up his hat. He wanted to run away somewhere. Pae, however, was there and began to talk to him.

"Have a seat." Pae offered him a seat. Hyŏng-sik sat down without further thought, and took out a cigarette and lit up.

"Where have you been?" Pae asked him.

"I went to P'yŏngyang."

"I am sure you had a good time. The scenery in P'yŏngyang is very nice, isn't it?"

"Are you ridiculing me?" asked Hyŏng-sik, casting a sidelong glance at Pae.

"Now, now, there's no need to get angry. There is nothing wrong with a man having some fun with a *kisaeng*. I just thought you were so virtuous that you would never do something like that. I did not know that you loved Kye Wŏr-hyang. I would not have committed such an affront to your dignity if I had known. Why were you keeping Kye Wŏr-hyang all to yourself? You should let even men like me see her face and listen to her singing. You're a lucky man."

"You are assuming that others think the same way you do! You think that I am just like you!"

"No, not you, you are a virtuous man! A sage! Just like Bo Yi and Shu Qi!"[130]

Hyŏng-sik struck a desk with his fist, and walked out of the front gate of the school.

72

Hyŏng-sik went to the outdoor gymnasium. The first-year students looked at Hyŏng-sik as they did their calisthenics. The fat physical education teacher wiped sweat from his forehead with a cloth and greeted Hyŏng-sik. They all seemed to Hyŏng-sik to be laughing at him. He thought there seemed to be a derisive look in the eyes of the physical education teacher in particular; the latter had been a lifelong sycophant of Dean Pae, and was always aligned against Hyŏng-sik. I will never set foot in this school again, thought Hyŏng-sik as he walked out of the school gate. Once he had stepped out of the gate, however, he stood and hesitated for awhile. He did, after all, feel sad leaving forever the school that he had considered his home for about four years, and his loved ones, the students, whom he had loved as his own siblings, children, or spouse. He had grown to love every clump of grass and every branch of every tree in the outdoor gymnasium. During his first year at the school, Hyŏng-sik had planted with his own hands the poplar tree behind the chin-up bar, and had taken care of it, watering it every day and eliminating pests. It was now over ten *kil*[131] in height. The branches of the poplar had spread, and the leaves had grown luxuriant, so that it was a fine shade tree and gathering place. Hyŏng-sik always felt happy when he saw students sitting adorably in the shade of the tree during the day in happy conversation. He thought it was as though his heart had become that poplar, and was providing shade for the young students. He too would walk beneath the tree during his break, and touch the tree as if glad to see it. Now, however, he was leaving. The tree would grow even more, and countless young students would joyfully disport themselves in the shade, but no one would ever think of Hyŏng-sik. Hyŏng-sik turned his head and looked at the tree for awhile. He wept sad tears. He could not bear to stand outside the school gate for long, though, and hung his head down and walked towards the Andong District four-way intersection. The weather grew warmer every day and there were clouds in the sky, but it did not seem as though it would rain any time soon. People fanned themselves, and men who pulled carts could hardly open their eyes because they were sweating so much. A policeman dressed in

---

130. Bo Yi and Shu Qi were outraged by the conquest of the Yin dynasty by King Wu of Zhou, and starved to death on Shou-yang Mountain rather than eat the grain of Zhou. Ssu-ma Ch'ien, *Records of the Historian: Chapters from the Shih Chi of Ssu-ma Ch'ien*, translated by Burton Watson (New York: Columbia University Press, 1969), 12–15.
131. *Kil.* Unit of measure for height or distance. 1 *kil* = eight to ten *cha*. 1 *cha* = .33 m. The tree is therefore over thirty meters in height.

white stood in the shade beneath the eaves of the police station, panting in the heat. Hyŏng-sik was unaware of the heat, though, as he walked through the streets of Andong, moving aside occasionally for an approaching cart. Hyŏng-sik felt confused. Should he submit his resignation? He wasn't sure what else he should do. His head was seething like boiling water. In addition to several days of mental and physical exhaustion, his senses had been severely agitated at school, so that he was like a man sick with fever. His head felt weighed down with a sorrow of ten thousand *kŭn*.[132]

The incident in the classroom was of the most dire significance to Hyŏng-sik, and a terrible misfortune to him. All of his hopes and all of his happiness had been centered on the fourth-year class. Because of his fourth year-class, he had not been lonely, and had been able to find joy even in his plain, monotonous life. The fourth-year class had been, in a sense, his wealth and his life for the past four or five years. They were his work, to which he devoted all of his strength and energies. He thought the thirty-some students in the fourth-year class would always be his spiritual brothers and sons, and that they would never forget him, just as he could not forget them whether he was awake or asleep. He thought they would love him just as he loved them.

That, however, was a dream. Hyŏng-sik loved them that much because he had no parents or brothers or sisters, and almost no close friends. They, however, had parents, siblings and beloved friends besides Hyŏng-sik. There had been some students who liked Hyŏng-sik and emulated him over the past five years. Hŭi-gyŏng liked Hyŏng-sik the most of all the students. Not even Hŭi-gyŏng, though, considered Hyŏng-sik an important, beloved person in his life. Hyŏng-sik had been unaware of this, and had only today realized it. Only today had he clearly seen the way the fourth-year students saw him.

How sad one must feel when one realizes one morning that someone whom one has loved with all one's heart and whom one believes loves oneself with all their heart too, in fact does not love one at all. There is probably no greater sadness in life than that caused by disappointment in love.

This was precisely the state in which Hyŏng-sik was. Hyŏng-sik now had nothing left. He could have explained his trip to P'yŏngyang, but he did not see the need. Even if he were to explain his trip to P'yŏngyang, that would not change the fact that the fourth-year students did not love him. Hyŏng-sik did not feel sad about the damage to his reputation. Reputation ranks only third or fourth among the things that are most important to human beings. Hyŏng-sik had now lost the very roots of his life. It was as though he had lost his footing in life, and was floating in midair. Whether Hyŏng-sik

132. A *kŭn* is a unit of measure for weight, approximately equivalent to 600 g. It is also used as 375 grams.

would shrivel up and die, or put down roots again somewhere and live, remained to be seen.

73

Hyŏng-sik returned home in a daze. The old woman sat on the veranda in her underwear, without wearing a blouse, smoking her pipe. Her shoulders and elbows were bony, and her two breasts were stuck to her chest as though they had dried up and adhered to the surface. Two streams of sweat that flowed from beneath her ears gave the impression of fluid from a rotting corpse. She had lost most of her hair, and only a few strands remained. Her cheeks were sunken and wrinkled. Her flesh was like grass that has withered in the hot sun. She sat hunched over, smoking. The sight made one unspeakably sad. She had once been a young, beautiful woman who had dazzled several men. She had thought that all men lost their minds when they saw her. She had thought that the beauty of her face and body would last forever. That was how she had thought only twenty or thirty years ago. The beauty of her face and body, however, eventually disappeared. Her sweat seemed to be fluid from her beauty as it melted away.

Why had she been born? What had she done with her life? What happiness had she known? The old woman went on living, though. She took medicine if she got sick. She wore clothes padded with cotton in the winter. She did not seem to be thinking of dying yet. When night was over and it was morning, she would rise from her bed once more, and cook, and wash the laundry. Perhaps she was waiting for some new happiness the next day or the next year.

Once when Hyŏng-sik had seen the old woman pause while doing laundry, to hit her back and take a smoke, he had said, "You seem to live for the pleasure of smoking." The old woman smiled. Hyŏng-sik did not know what the smile meant. He did not know if it meant "yes" or "no." No one knew, not even the old woman herself. Anyone who saw her, though, would think that the old woman lived to smoke. All of her happiness and work seemed to be in the smoke from her tobacco pipe. The old woman spent almost half of the twenty-four hours in a day looking at tobacco smoke. Her life was centered around staring unblinkingly at the poisonous fumes from her pipe. To take tobacco away from the old woman would be to take away her life. Her bamboo pipe, which she propped up at one end of the room, near the warmest part of the floor, was stained with bamboo resin and was wrapped in three places with pieces of cloth; that pipe was her life. If smoke were ever to cease issuing from her mouth, that would mean that her blood no longer circulated. The old woman herself may not have thought that way, but any bystander could not help but get that impression. It did not seem as though the old woman had any purpose in life other than to smoke. When Hyŏng-sik came home in a daze, he did not know what the old woman was thinking. She was probably just looking at the billowing smoke from her pipe and not thinking anything in particular. If she had been thinking of something, it probably would have been memories of her youth, glimpsed as though through a thin mist. She might have been thinking of how she had once seized power in the household of a high ranking official; or being embraced by a young, handsome visitor; having her plump breast grasped by a baby's chubby hand; her grown-up son writhing as he died; wearing beautiful clothes and eating delicious food. She probably saw such memories floating up through the smoke from her pipe several times every day. There was no telling what memory had emerged just now. The old woman looked at Hyŏng-sik and quickly put on her sweat-stained Korean blouse, which was next to her.

"Back so soon?" she asked.

Hyŏng-sik took off his hat and Korean outer coat, and tossed them in his room.

"I am finished with school," he said.

"You mean you are not working there any more?"

"I am going to quit teaching." Hyŏng-sik sat himself down on the veranda with a thud. "Please give me a drink of water. My insides are all on fire. It is unbearable."

The old woman went to the kitchen, filled a brass bowl with cold water, and gave it to Hyŏng-sik. He drank the water all at once.

"That was refreshing. There is nothing like cold water." He smacked his lips, then licked the water from his lips, as though he had just drunk water sweetened with honey. The old woman stared at him as though puzzled, then went to her room and got her tobacco pouch and pipe, and went back to Hyŏng-sik. Looks like the old woman is going to try to cheer me up again, Hyŏng-sik thought, and smiled inwardly, in spite of his pain. He was afraid, though, that listening to her try to cheer him up would make him feel even worse, so he tried to change the subject.

"Did Mr. Sin come by yesterday?"

"No."

"You do not like Mr. Sin these days. You liked him very much for awhile."

"I do not dislike Mr. Sin. He is just too careless with his words, that is all." The old woman laughed.

"You are saying that because he said there were maggots in your bean paste soup." Hyŏng-sik laughed too.

As if trying to take advantage of this moment in the conversation, the old woman asked, "Are you going to quit working at the school? Did you have an argument with that Dean Pae or whatever his name is?"

"It was not an argument. I have been teaching for too long. It is time to try something else."

"Something else? What? Of course, now you can hold office. You are so skinny because you work for someone like Dean Pae. It would be great if you got an official post. The woman across the street, her son was once a *chusa*[133] or something."

"I would rather be a monk than work for the government. I would like a small hermitage, deep in the mountains. I would wear robes of arrowroot and hemp, and recite the name of Amitābha.[134] Yes, that is what I want most." Hyŏng-sik laughed and looked at the old woman. The old woman's eyes widened.

"That is awful! You can do other work, why be a monk?"

"What else can I do, if not be a monk?" Hyŏng-sik said.

Both were quiet for some time.

74

Hyŏng-sik had not been thinking about what he was saying when he said he wanted to be a monk. Now that he had said it, though, it did indeed seem to be the best thing to do. He seemed to have no alternative. He seemed to have lost all at once the will to exert himself for both Korean civilization and his own reputation. He was full of the sadness and despair of one who has been bereaved of wife and children, and lost all his property. Yŏng-ch'ae's death, the obliteration of her family, and the humiliation to which Hyŏng-sik had been subjected by his fourth-year students seemed to join forces to drag Hyŏng-sik's mind into the deep, dark ground. The life he had led until then seemed to be meaningless and bland, and he felt a sense of aversion, as though he had just awakened from a long, unpleasant dream. Everything he had done seemed shameful and ineffective: teaching for five years, chalk in hand; reading and memorizing foreign vocabulary until late at night; teaching English to Sŏn-hyŏng and Sun-ae; seeing Yŏng-ch'ae again; what he had done at Ch'ŏngnyangni; and going to P'yŏngyang. Even the old woman, whom he had thought of with affection until now, seemed like a filthy, smelly object. Everything seemed shameful, unpleasant and irritating. Why have I been living like this? he thought. Of what value and meaning has my life been thus far? He wanted to cast aside his present way of living, and

---

133. A *chusa* was a government official.
134. The teachings of Pure Land Buddhism claim that a disciple can gain entrance into the Pure Land by recollecting the name of the Buddha Amitābha. "The Pure Land, a transcendental sphere of existence created through a Buddha's vows, was said to offer ideal conditions for spiritual development; consequently, by recollecting the Buddha's name and gaining rebirth in that Buddha's Pure Land, great efforts to cultivate the path in this lifetime would be unnecessary." Koryŏ dynasty monk Chinul interpreted Pure Land practice in such a way that it too could lead to the same goal as other forms of Buddhist practice. Robert E. Buswell, Jr., *Tracing Back the Radiance: Chinul's Korean Way of Zen* (Honolulu: University of Hawaii, 1991), 72.

go into hiding somewhere isolated where there were no people. He hated to stay as much as another hour in Seoul, in the old woman's house.

"It is best to be a monk," Hyŏng-sik said to the old woman. "What fun could it be to stay in the real world?"

"Why wouldn't someone like you have fun? You are young. You are talented. You could enjoy life in the real world."

"You must have had a good time when you were young."

The old woman smiled.

"When I was young, I was happy every day. I cried sometimes, but crying when you are young is more pleasurable than smiling when you are old."

The old woman speaks well, Hyŏng-sik thought, and looked at her face. A tranquil look passed over the old woman's face, as though just thinking about her youth made her happy.

"I do not know what pleasures you live for, Mr. Yi. You do not have a good government post, you do not have a beautiful woman." The old woman laughed. "You always frown whenever I say things like that. I am right, though. Why sit alone in your room, staring at the walls, while you are still in the flower of your youth? That is why you talk of the world being no fun, and of becoming a monk. When I was young . . . But what is the use of talking about it. It is no use once you are old." The old woman said these things to Hyŏng-sik almost once every month. Hyŏng-sik would just smile and listen. Today, though, the old woman's words seemed to have a new meaning and force. Hyŏng-sik thought of how happy he had been when he was with Sŏn-hyŏng and Yŏng-ch'ae. He thought of how foreign books praised the joys of love. Was romantic love indeed the greatest happiness in life? The old woman at least spoke as though romantic love were the only joy in life. Hyŏng-sik wondered if he had been lonely all his life and unable to enjoy life because he had never tasted romantic love.

He smiled and said, "Could I too have fun?" He felt embarrassed, as though he had asked a foolish question.

"Of course!" the old woman said. "Any beautiful woman in the city would desire you. You are handsome, you have a nice personality. Things are different now that the world is coming to an end, but in the old days, someone like you would have passed the higher civil service examination, and have so many beautiful women swarming around you that you would not be able to stand up."

"You mean I am useless now. Since there is no civil service examination."

"It is not like the old days, but there are hundreds of first rate *kisaeng* in the capital." The old woman lowered her voice, and moved her head to one side, as though trying to remember something.

"But speaking of *kisaeng* . . . Who was it? Yŏng-ch'ae? What happened with her? Have you seen her since then?"

Hyŏng-sik felt a twinge in his heart when he heard the old woman mention Yŏng-ch'ae. He dropped his cigarette on the ground, startled.

"She drowned herself."

"Drowned herself? When?"

"Probably yesterday."

"What? Why would she drown herself? That is terrible."

Hyŏng-sik put his arms around his neck and lowered his head. Scenes from the last three or four days flashed before his eyes. Tears welled in the old woman's eyes.

"What was wrong?"

"Perhaps she found the world as unamusing as I do."

"That is awful. Why die in the flower of your youth? It is sad enough to die when one has reached the end of one's life, but why drown oneself?" The old woman sat in silence for a long time, then wiped her tears away with the back of her hand. "It is your fault that she died."

"Why?"

"You were so heartless to her when she came looking for you. She had been thinking about you for over ten years."

Hyŏng-sik was taken aback when the old woman used the word "heartless."

"Heartless? How was I heartless?"

"You were heartless! You should have been kind enough to hold her hand in yours, but you did not."

"How could I hold her hand?"

"Why not? The way I see it, Myŏng-ch'ae—"

"Her name is Yŏng-ch'ae, not Myŏng-ch'ae."

"Right, the way I see it, Yŏng-ch'ae was in love with you. How could you have been so heartless? When she was leaving, you should have held onto her and told her not to go, or followed after her. But you did not." The old woman resented Hyŏng-sik.

75

Hyŏng-sik was further taken aback with what the old woman said. Had he indeed been heartless to Yŏng-ch'ae? Should he have taken her hand and told her that he too had thought of her and missed her while they had been apart? When she got up to leave, shouldn't he have held onto her and asked her about her plans for the future? Shouldn't he have said right then and there that he would take care of her, and then gone with her to where she lived, and spoken with her proprietress? Then Yŏng-ch'ae would not have gone to Ch'ŏngnyangni the next day, and would not have been attacked. When they were walking back together from Ch'ŏngnyangni to Tabang-gol, shouldn't he have offered then to take care of her? Shouldn't he have taken her to other lodgings, or his own lodgings, instead of taking her back to Tabang-gol? Then she would not have thought of going to P'yŏngyang, and would not have drowned herself. The old woman was right. He had indeed killed Yŏng-ch'ae. Yŏng-ch'ae had gone to see him hoping to hear him say that he too had been waiting for her. She wanted to hear him say how happy he was to see her again. She wanted to hear him say that she would be his wife from that moment on. What had he been thinking at the time? He had been hoping that she had been taken in by an upper-class family and had attended a girls' school. That was what he had been thinking. In his heart, he had wondered why Yŏng-ch'ae had to show up just when there was Sŏn-hyŏng. Then he had wished that Yŏng-ch'ae had become a *kisaeng* or concubine. Now that he thought about it, though, he wondered why he had been preoccupied with whether or not Yŏng-ch'e had been living with an "upper-class family," or whether or not Yŏng-ch'ae was a *kisaeng*.

Why hadn't he gone to see Yŏng-ch'ae early the next morning? Because of school? Because of his reputation as an educator?

The old woman was right. He had killed Yŏng-ch'ae. He had, moreover, gone to P'yŏngyang in pursuit of Yŏng-ch'ae, but had returned without even looking for her body. He had even been happy while he was walking around outside Ch'ilsŏngmun. He had not thought of Yŏng-ch'ae all night while on the train back to Seoul. Indeed, he had felt as though Yŏng-ch'ae's death had lightened his burden.

Hyŏng-sik shook his head.

"You are right. I killed Yŏng-ch'ae. I killed her. I killed her with my own hands, the woman who had been living for only me." Hyŏng-sik's breathing grew labored, as though he were in great pain.

"It was her destiny."

"No. I killed her."

Just then, Sin U-sŏn came in swinging his straw hat.

"When did you get back? Did you find her?" he asked without any greeting.

Hyŏng-sik did not even look at U-sŏn.

"I killed her. I killed Yŏng-ch'ae," he said.

"What? She's dead? Didn't your telegram get through?"

"I killed her! And I came back without even looking for her body. I guess I was worried about canceling class."

"It was because you missed Elder Kim's daughter, right?" U-sŏn did not forget to be humorous even in a situation like this. "What on earth happened to her?"

"She died." Hyŏng-sik jumped up. "Do you have any money? Could you lend me five wŏn?" Hyŏng-sik now had no source of income. The school would pay him his salary for the month of June, but he could not go there to get it. He would have no income at all beginning with the month of July. "What do you want the money for?" "I want to go and look for Yŏng-ch'ae's body. I want to give her a proper burial, even if I have to carry the body on my back." Hyŏng-sik paced back and forth in the courtyard as if unbearably tormented. The back of his Korean shirt was damp with sweat. U-sŏn leaned against his walking stick, and looked at Hyŏng-sik. "The body has probably floated away by now. It must be somewhere in the Yellow Sea." "Why would that be?" asked the old woman, looking at U-sŏn. "They say that drowned bodies stay in the same place for three days." "If the body has floated away, I will go after it. I will follow it to wherever it has gone." Hyŏng-sik closed his eyes and stood still. Then he opened his eyes as if having reached a decision, and went over to U-sŏn and held out his hand.

"Hurry up and give me five wŏn."

"Are you going to leave right now?"

"I am going to the station and take whatever train I can get."

As if unable to refuse the request, U-sŏn reluctantly gave Hyŏng-sik a five wŏn note. U-sŏn himself was sorrowful when he heard that Yŏng-ch'ae had died. He felt as though he had lost something very precious to him.

Hyŏng-sik took the money, went to his room, put on his Korean outer coat, picked up a book to take with him, and went out to put his shoes on. At that moment, a man wearing a panama hat came to see Hyŏng-sik. Hyŏng-sik frowned and went reluctantly to the door. It was the pastor at Elder Kim's church. The pastor had a youthful face with no facial hair, and his cheeks were furrowed with a few wrinkles. He was an honest-looking middle-aged man. U-sŏn and the old woman went to the veranda outside the old woman's room, and watched the two men in a stupefied daze. Hyŏng-sik put his book down and invited the pastor in and had him take a seat.

"Were you on your way out?"

"Yes, I was going for a walk. What brings you here in this hot weather?"

"I was thinking that it has been a long time since I saw you, and there was something I wanted to talk to you about."

"You wanted to talk to me?" Hyŏng-sik looked at the pastor. The pastor smiled meaningfully.

"You aren't too busy right now, are you?"

"No, not at all. Please speak."

"You will be very happy to hear what I have to tell you." The pastor smiled again and looked around Hyŏng-sik's room. The old woman and U-sŏn looked at one another and whispered. The old woman did not seem to dislike U-sŏn very much that day.

The pastor fanned himself for awhile, then looked attentively at Hyŏng-sik, and began to speak. "The reason I came to see you is . . ." He seemed to be having difficulty trying to say what he had to say. Hyŏng-sik had no idea what this could be about, and thought the pastor's behavior strange. He wished the pastor would hurry up and finish speaking so that he could run to the train station.

76

The pastor began to speak. The old woman and U-sŏn listened attentively, though pretending not to. "Elder Kim says that he is sending his daughter Sŏn-hyŏng to the United States this autumn."

"Yes," said Hyŏng-sik politely, trying to keep in pace with the conversation.

"Before Sŏn-hyŏng goes to the United States, though, she will have to, uh . . . get engaged. It would be difficult, moreover, for Elder Kim to send his daughter overseas alone. Therefore," (the pastor said "uh" and "therefore" frequently), "Elder Kim has expressed his wish that Sŏn-hyŏng be engaged, and has expressed his intention to send the bride and groom together to the United States." The pastor stopped speaking, and smiled as he looked at Hyŏng-sik. The latter turned his head away as though embarrassed.

"Yes," Hyŏng-sik said. He did not know what else to say.

"The Elder was hoping that if you would, uh, give your consent . . . the Elder would like you to go and study in the United States too. In any event, Elder Kim and his wife seem to be very fond of you. That is why they asked me to ask you about how you feel. And so . . . "

"How I feel?"

"Yes."

"What do you mean?"

U-sŏn turned to the old woman and smiled. The old woman smiled too. The pastor looked at Hyŏng-sik, whose eyes were wide with bewilderment.

"I think I have said enough for you to know what I mean," the pastor said somewhat condescendingly.

Hyŏng-sik said nothing.

"Then let me explain it to you again. Elder Kim would like you and Sŏn-hyŏng to be engaged to be married. You have no doubt received other marriage offers; however, Elder Kim and his wife seem to like you very much."

Only now did Hyŏng-sik clearly understand what the pastor was trying to say. His heart twinged with pain.

"What do you think?" the pastor asked.

Hyŏng-sik did not know what to think. He sat quietly.

"You have been teaching Sŏn-hyŏng English, have you not?"

"Yes, since a few days ago."

"Were you aware of the significance of those English lessons?"

"Significance?"

The pastor laughed. "Yes, were you aware of what Elder Kim's intentions were in asking you to teach Sŏn-hyŏng English?"

Hyŏng-sik said nothing.

"Times have changed, and marriage can no longer be carried out strictly in accordance with parents' wishes. The Elder wanted you and Sŏn-hyŏng to meet each other first, and get to know each other. So what do you think?"

"I dare not accept. How can I get married when I am having difficulty supporting just myself?"

"That is not an issue."

"But it is a most important issue! How can there be marriage without an economic foundation? It is a very important problem."

"It is an important problem. However, after you have studied in the United States for three or four years, you will not have anything to worry about. You will not, moreover, easily find another girl like Sŏn-hyŏng. You are very fortunate. Now then, tell me what you think."

Even after this reassurance, Hyŏng-sik just lowered his head, and sat quietly. The pastor smiled and fanned himself. Though it was none of her business, the old woman wondered anxiously why Hyŏng-sik would not say "yes." U-sŏn remembered the conversation he had had with Hyŏng-sik the other day in Andong, and smiled. While everyone else was rejoicing, Hyŏng-sik, unbeknownst to the others, was in anguish.

"Surely there is no need for further thought. Please give me your answer."

"I will give you my answer later. I am humbly grateful that you would consider someone like me."

"Is there any need to wait until later? Why don't you go with me to Elder Kim's house this afternoon. He said he would like to have dinner with you."

Hyŏng-sik did not know what to do. He had to go to P'yŏngyang, but going to dinner at Elder Kim's house seemed more important. He was too ashamed, though, to say "yes" to the pastor, and abandon his resolve to find Yŏng-ch'ae's body just because he was suddenly intoxicated with Sŏn-hyŏng. The mere mention of getting engaged to Sŏn-hyŏng made him happy. He even thought he was lucky that Yŏng-ch'ae had happened to die just then. In addition to that, he would be going to study in the United States! He could not help but feel drawn to the offer. To study in the West, just as he had wanted to all his life, and with a beautiful woman whom he loved! Either one of these would have been compelling offers to Hyŏng-sik, but to have both! A voice within him could not help but say that Hyŏng-sik had received a great blessing. If one had looked carefully at Hyŏng-sik's face as he sat with his head lowered as if in pain, one would have clearly seen a look of irrepressible happiness. His face had been unhappy when he had first seen the pastor. One by one, though, the pastor's words did away with the sad expression on his face, and imbued instead a happy expression. It was like the way snow melts all at once in the warm spring sunshine, and the mountains and fields are suddenly suffused with spring colors. Hyŏng-sik therefore could not bring himself to lift his head. He was ashamed to show others how happy he was. Hyŏng-sik tried to wear a sad expression. He deliberately tried, moreover, to make himself feel sad.

At times like this, Hyŏng-sik's mind was so confused he did not know what to do. There were times when he would make hasty decisions without considering the results. Then again, there were times when he was hesitant and could not make up his mind. Sometimes he would be walking somewhere, and stop and hesitate dozens of times. This is characteristic of a weak-willed person. It was weakness that made him make hasty decisions, and weakness that made him indecisive. Right now he did not know how he should answer the pastor, and pondered what to say. He wished there were someone beside him who would answer for him. Hyŏng-sik lifted his head and looked at the room on the other side of the main hallway. He knew that U-sŏn would have been decisive in such a situation. U-sŏn smiled and looked back at Hyŏng-sik.

77

U-sŏn winked at Hyŏng-sik. Hyŏng-sik deliberately pretended not to notice. U-sŏn winked at him again. Hyŏng-sik saw him but pretended that he had not. Hyŏng-sik lowered his head. He felt even more embarrassed and confused. He tried to interpret the meaning of U-sŏn's winks. He was not sure whether U-sŏn meant "hurry up and accept the proposal," or "why are you just sitting here instead of going to P'yŏngyang?"

The old woman poked U-sŏn impatiently with her elbow. "Why isn't Mr. Yi accepting the proposal? Doesn't he like the girl?"

"She is a well-known beauty in Seoul."

"And rich?"

"It is because she is rich that they are sending the son-in-law to the United States too."

The old woman did not understand what sending the son-in-law to the United States had to do with being rich.

"Then why is he just sitting there?" the old woman asked. She smacked her lips and put tobacco in her pipe.

"Please accept the invitation," the pastor said, trying again to persuade Hyŏng-sik.

"I will go to dinner," Hyŏng-sik barely managed to say. "But I will talk about the engagement some other time."

"I will stop by here on my way back from church," the pastor said, smiling, and left. Hyŏng-sik saw the pastor to the front door, then went back in the house. He looked like someone who had just awoken from a light sleep.

U-sŏn ran over to him. "This is your lucky break! You've gotten a beautiful woman, and you're going to study in the United States!" He shook Yi's hand. Hyŏng-sik avoided U-sŏn's eyes, and averted his head. There was a smile, however, in Hyŏng-sik's eyes.

"You have a way with women! You got Sŏn-hyŏng in only two or three days."

"I knew it," the old woman said, smiling. "When Yŏng-ch'ae visited, you did not try to stop her from leaving. Poor Yŏng-ch'ae. It was no use for her to come and see you when you already had someone else in mind—"

"Shh!" said U-sŏn, looking back at the old woman and winking. Hyŏng-sik pretended not to hear the old woman.

"I have resigned from Kyŏngsŏng."

"Why resign now? You should get engaged first, then resign. Heh-heh."

"That is not what I mean. I do not want to be a schoolteacher any more."

"Of course. When you return from studying in the United States, you can become a professor."

Hyŏng-sik turned towards U-sŏn suddenly, as if annoyed.

"All you want to do is make fun of what other people say, even when others are in pain."

"I sympathize with you. You must be in great pain."

The old woman walked over and stood next to U-sŏn.

"I am so happy. To hear that Mr. Yi is getting married reminds me of when my son . . . " The old woman paused. It made her sad to think of her son, and it seemed, moreover, rude to compare Hyŏng-sik to her son. "When you go there tonight, give them a definite 'yes.' Why did you just sit there when the pastor was talking to you?" The old woman laughed. "It must be because you are still a young, unmarried man, and shy."

Hyŏng-sik did not know what to do. He raised his head, then lowered it again. He clenched his left hand into a fist, then unclenched his hand again. He cracked his knuckles.

"Listen. I am going to P'yŏngyang. No matter how I think about it, it seems as though that is what I must do."

U-sŏn glared at Hyŏng-sik as though threatening him.

"You fool. No one should give their daughter to a man like you. She would just waste away."

Hyŏng-sik himself laughed. He too thought he was a fool.

"Try to be strong from now on. What do you mean by such talk. You are not a girl. Say no more, just go to Elder Kim's house tonight. They will bring up the subject of marriage again. Don't be a coward like you were just now, but say yes. Then go to the United States. I heard about what happened at the

Kyŏngsŏng School. You probably would have been kicked out even if you hadn't resigned."

"Kicked out? Why?"

"Because you followed a *kisaeng* to P'yŏngyang. Pae is taking revenge on you for what happened at Ch'ŏngnyangni. Just get engaged and go to the United States."

"What shall I do about Yŏng-ch'ae?"

"What can you do for her now that she is dead? Do you want to die too? Like a 'virtuous man'? Don't say such foolish things, just do as I say."

Hyŏng-sik felt somewhat reassured when he heard U-sŏn's words. It was not that he was incapable of such thoughts himself, but his thoughts alone were not enough to reassure him. He had to hear U-sŏn's brisk words before he could feel reassured. Hyŏng-sik decided to do as U-sŏn told him. He felt more content to do as U-sŏn told him than obey his own thoughts.

Hyŏng-sik smiled. "I don't know," he said. The old woman was happy for no particular reason.

"Shall I make lunch? You should have a bite to eat too, Mr. Sin."

"Are you going to give me bean paste soup again?" U-sŏn took a cigarette out of Hyŏng-sik's vest, as though the cigarettes were his own, and tapped the cigarette on the palm of his hand.

"Stop that. What do you mean 'bean paste soup again'?"

"I will go order some noodles in cold broth," Hyŏng-sik said, standing up.

"Are you treating us to lunch? Then get some beer."

"I don't have money."

"You're a wealthy man's son-in-law. What do you have to worry about?"

"Even if that happens later, I still don't have any money right now."

"Where is the five wŏn I gave you?"

"I have to go to P'yŏngyang."

"You're still going to P'yŏngyang again?"

"I have to find Yŏng-ch'ae's body."

"It must be in the Yellow Sea by now! Did you think it would still be at the foot of Ch'ŏngnyu Cliff, waiting for a heartless man like you? Let's go to a Chinese restaurant."

"Would the body have already reached the Yellow Sea?" Hyŏng-sik looked at the sky. The morning sun had risen over the center of Seoul, and deluged the city with a fiery light, as if trying to burn all living things to death. Hyŏng-sik became aware again of how hot it was.

78

The sun was setting over the ridge of Inwang Mountain. Telegraph poles on Chongno Avenue cast long shadows. The windows of the cathedral tower in the Chonghyŏn District shone like fire, reflecting the setting sun. The bean curd vender could no longer be heard crying, "Bean curd! Bean curd dregs!" The front and back doors of the houses were thrown open, and everyone was eating dinner, wiping the sweat from their brow. The yellow earth of Pugaksan (North Summit Mountain) gave off a red light in the slanting rays of the sun, and the evening chatter of magpies could be heard in groves of old trees in the gardens of Kyŏngbok Palace.

Clay roof tiles that had been heated red hot all day long, now seemed to be breathing warm gusts of air into the gentle breezes from the Han River. The faces of all the people walking the streets were red.

People who had been sitting inside the houses stepped out into the streets and walked around, wiping sweat from their tired faces. "Cool evening is approaching," they seemed to be thinking.

The setting sun that lay lightly over the pine forests on Namsan gradually disappeared, as though being obliterated somehow, and purplish dusk crept through the luxuriant branches and needles of the forest like strands of a cobweb.

The wheel of the sun fell from the top of Inwangsan. Sunlight lingered over Pugaksan in the shape of a Buddhist nun's hood. A dark blue curtain fell over the myriad houses in the city. One edge of the curtain began to move steadily over Pugaksan, until eventually the nun's hood too was dyed blue.

A mountain of clouds rose in the direction of Kangwŏn Province. It looked like flames of fire at first, then gradually cooled and blackened. As the mountain of clouds grew black, the curtain over the city darkened and turned purple, then finally gray. Small electric lights blinked in the darkness like fireflies. The noise of bands playing at theaters and film houses began to be heard.

There were more and more people walking on Chongno and on the banks of streams, with cigarettes in their mouths, and holding fans in their hands. Merchants set up a night market, bringing in small carts, driving horse posts into the ground, and setting up canopies.

People's stomachs were full of food, their bodies felt cool, and their minds were refreshed. Even people who had been sleeping during the day began to come to life, and talked and laughed.

Lights were lit in all the rooms at Elder Kim's house in Andong. The yard had been sprinkled with water, and the smell of earth and flowers in the garden entered the house and aroused the senses of the people who were joyfully eating and drinking. Elder Kim dabbed at his mustache with a napkin. [135] Pastor Han put his arms out behind him and leaned back.

---

135. Elder Kim's mustache is described as *yŏdŏl p'alcha suyŏm*, or shaped like the Chinese character for "eight." The Chinese considered this a lucky number because it was homophonous with the character for "fortune."

Hyŏng-sik took a mouthful of rice water,[136] and quietly rinsed his teeth. The three men ate their dinner with gusto and in good spirits.

Mrs. Kim, Sŏn-hyong, Sun-ae and a maidservant ate their dinner in another room. They too enjoyed their meal, and when they had finished, they looked at one another and smiled. Perhaps it was only in the eyes of the beholders, but to the people who saw her that night, Sŏn-hyŏng's cheeks seemed to be blushing with a rosy hue. Mrs. Kim gazed at her daughter as if entranced. Sŏn-hyŏng glanced at her mother, then turned to Sun-ae.

"Sun-ae!" she said. "Let's play the piano! You haven't forgotten what we learned the other day, have you?"

"No, I still remember."[137]

"Go play the piano," Mrs. Kim said, and was the first to rise to her feet. Sŏn-hyŏng and Sun-ae went to the room where the piano was kept.

Sŏn-hyŏng sat on a wicker chair, gathered her skirts, opened the piano lid, and wiped off the keyboard twice, from one end of the keyboard to the other. The clear sounds floated into the evening air. Sun-ae stood idly with one hand on the piano and watched Sŏn-hyŏng's white hand moving up and down the keyboard. Sŏn-hyŏng opened a large musical score, and, her head nodding, opened her mouth and began to sing. "La la la la." Then she found the first notes on the keyboard, and began to play. Her eyes followed the notes on the score, and her hands moved over the keyboard. Her movements grew rapid or slow, according to the score. Beautiful sounds filled the room. The sounds spilled out from the room, and were carried by the evening breeze, across the yard and over the wall, then spread like waves in all directions. How many people would lean their head to one side to hear the sound, or pause while walking in the street?

Sŏn-hyŏng's hands moved up and down the keyboard in accordance with the music, and her body moved along with her hands. Finally, the clear sound of her singing broke forth from between her soft lips.

"O cloud, floating there in the sky,
Where are you going, taking the rain?"

Sun-ae sang along with her in a thin voice. Hyŏng-sik heard the singing. His mind floated into the air together with the singing. It was as though his

---

136. *Sungnyung*, or rice water, is made by adding water to the pot in which rice has been cooked; this creates a broth that is then served at the end of the meal.
137. In the 1917 *Maeil Sinbo* and 1918 Sinmungwan editions, this line is written, "'No, I still remember. Go play the piano,' Mrs. Kim said . . . " A 1992 edition edited by Noh Yang-hwan, and published by Usinsa revised this so that the words "No, I still remember" are a separate quote (implicitly spoken by Sun-ae), and Mrs. Kim then tells them to play. Cf. Kim Ch'ŏl, Yi Kyŏng-hun, Sŏ Ŭn-ju and Im Chin-yŏng, "*Mujŏng* ŭi Kyebo: *Mujŏng* ŭi Chŏngbon Hwakchŏng ŭl Wihan P'anbon ŭi Pigyo Yŏn'gu," *Minjok Munhaksa Yŏn'gu* 20 (2002): 87.

spirit had grown wings and was flying amidst the clouds. An indefinable happiness that was both cool and warm at the same time filled his breast.

Elder Kim turned to the pastor and said, "Let's go to my study, and talk." The three of them stood up.

79

Elder Kim's study was furnished in Western style. Ever since he had been to the United States as consul, he had tried to live in Western style.

A red carpet with peony patterns was spread on the floor, and there were framed paintings on the walls. Most of the paintings were religious. On the northern wall, in the largest frame, was a portrait of Jesus praying in Gethsemane. Several feet away to the east, in a slightly smaller frame, was a painting of Jesus in the manger. On the western wall was a half-length portrait of Elder Kim himself. If he had been like gentlemen of other nations, Elder Kim would have hung several world famous masterpieces, in addition to religious paintings, on his walls. Elder Kim, however, had no interest in art as of yet, and did not appreciate its worth. Elder Kim thought that religious paintings were the only paintings of any worth. He somewhat valued traditional Chinese-style landscapes and paintings of fungi, orchids, plums and bamboos. He thought such paintings would be inappropriate, though, in a Western-style room. He had never seen Western portrait paintings, or Western paintings of women and nudes, nor did he make an effort to see them. Even if he had seen them, he would not have recognized their worth. He did not know the word "art," and, moreover, did not see the need for such things as paintings. He had probably never thought about sculpture in all his fifty years of life. Art, which Westerners deemed as precious as religion, would have been practically worthless to Elder Kim. Westerners would wonder, "How can one be a civilized person and not understand art?" All civilized people understood art.

Elder Kim not only furnished his study in Western style, but also wore Western-style suits often, and slept in a Western-style bed. He respected the United States in particular, among Western nations. He tried to follow Western examples as much as possible. Indeed, he had been following Western examples now for over twenty years. He may have started believing in Christ in order to be like Westerners. He thought he knew the West very well, and had done a good job of modeling himself after the West. He had been a diplomat, moreover, stationed in the United States, in the city of Washington. He was sure that no one understood conditions in the West better than he. He thought there was no need for him to hear anything more, or learn anything more, about the West. He prided himself on being the most advanced, civilized person in Korea. Others at church and throughout the world thought the same. There were some, however, who did not share this opinion. They were Western missionaries.

Missionaries knew that Elder Kim did not understand Western civilization with any depth. They knew that he did not understand science, philosophy, art, economics and industry. Elder Kim thought he understood religion, but he only knew the beliefs of Korean Christianity. He had never, of course, thought about what the true nature of Christianity might be, or the relationship between Christianity and all humanity, or the relationship between Christ and the Korean people.

Civilization includes science, philosophy, religion, art, politics, economics, industry, and social systems. To understand western civilization is to understand all of this. Then how could Elder Kim say that he understood western civilization? Western missionaries knew this. They therefore said he was just imitating Western civilization. This was not calumny, but an accurate description of Elder Kim's condition. What else could it be called but imitation, when one wore Western clothes, built a Western-style house, and observed Western customs, while not thoroughly understanding Westerners' civilization? Perhaps Elder Kim could be forgiven such imitative behavior, though, since he did not imitate the West frivolously or without any opinion, or out of vanity, but from the belief (not a realization) that the West was superior to Koreans and that Koreans therefore had to follow Western example. Thus, one could not find fault with him for imitating the West out of ignorance. Kim was, indeed, ignorant. He would be angry if he heard this, but he was ignorant. He thought he had grasped Western civilization with one glance. He knew no better way to learn about the West. Could one, though, understand Western civilization at a glance? Even the most talented, diligent and perceptive of people would only begin to understand a different civilization after decades of reading, and learning from a teacher. How could Elder Kim, no matter how bright he was, understand the true meaning of modern civilization in all its complexity, without having read a single book on the subject?

Elder Kim sent his children to school, though. He did not know what they were learning at school, but he thought it was right to send them to school since Westerners all sent their children to school. Actually, it would be more accurate to say that Kim believed, rather than thought, it was the correct thing to do. His children would then learn about civilization. In this way, Koreans would eventually completely absorb modern civilization.

There was only one danger, and that was that people like Elder Kim might believe in their own knowledge so much that they might try to interfere in the way their children thought, as the children studied at school and began to understand modern civilization. When their children talked about modern civilization, they knew what they were talking about; but parents felt it was some sort of heresy for their children to think things that the parents themselves had never thought, and the parents would inevitably try to suppress their childrens' thoughts. This was the clash of modern and traditional thought—a tragedy that often arose when modern civilization was introduced to a culture. Old-fashioned people thought it was heresy to think things they had never thought, but it was actually the comprehension of new truths that the old-fashioned people had never known before. A son must always be better than his father. Otherwise there were would be no such thing as progress. People who are behind the times, however, dislike it when newcomers know more than they do. Old-fashioned people are thus often responsible for the tragedy that results from the clash of modern and traditional thought.

80

Elder Kim had not hung paintings inside his house for the sake of art. His children, however, saw the paintings, and the paintings indirectly motivated the children to love art. Elder Kim had put the paintings up because they were portraits of Christ, and not because they were paintings. Kim's children, however, came to take an interest in the paintings as paintings, rather than for the depictions of Christ. How could a particular painting have been so exquisitely painted? There was happiness in the faces of people who were rejoicing, and anguish in the faces of those who suffered. Grass looked just like grass, and flowers like flowers. How could this have been done? This was what interested Elder Kim's children. This was a pleasure that Elder Kim was unaware of and that only his children understood.

Elder Kim looked around the room once as though proud and satisfied that it was modern and flashy, then offered chairs to the pastor and Hyŏng-sik. The three of them sat around a circular table, like three handles on a pot. Hyŏng-sik held back the urge to smoke a cigarette. He looked around the room. A cool evening breeze gently lifted the lace curtains. The delicate leaves of a potted laurel tree at the window trembled in the breeze. Hyŏng-sik's heart leapt when he thought of the conversation that was about to take place. He was ready to answer without hesitation, whatever was said. He was determined to answer as U-sŏn had told him. The piano and the singing could still be heard. Hyŏng-sik was happy. He looked at the pastor and the Elder's lips, and wished they would begin talking.

"I talked about this with Hyŏng-sik earlier," the pastor said. "Why don't you speak with him now directly." The pastor looked at Hyŏng-sik.

"Yes, thank you," said Elder Kim. "My daughter is unexceptional, but if you would see fit to keep her . . ."

The pastor laughed. "The Elder is too modest. The two are very well suited for each other." The pastor alone was effusive.

"I will not try to persuade you if you are not interested. I spoke of this only because I have much affection for you."

Hyŏng-sik answered quickly, determined not to waver as he had before. "I don't know what to say to such a kind offer. However, I dare not accept."

Hyŏng-sik's face reddened nonetheless. The Elder leaned back in his chair as if pleased.

"You are too modest. Then you accept the proposal?" He looked Hyŏng-sik over intently. Hyŏng-sik lowered his head for a moment, then remembered what U-sŏn had said about not being a coward. He lifted his head, thrust out his chest, and assumed a dignified look on his face. No matter how hard he tried, though, the word "yes" would not come out of his mouth. His mind was in a turmoil.

"Hurry up and give us your answer," the pastor said.

"Yes. What reason is there to hesitate?" Hyŏng-sik summoned all of his strength and said, "Yes." Then he turned his head away because he thought he sounded ridiculous, and felt embarrassed.

"You accept?" The Elder leaned forward, as though exacting a vow.

"Yes, I will do as you say," Hyŏng-sik said, imitating U-sŏn's cheerful manner. Then he breathed a sigh of relief, as though he had just completed a difficult task. His heart felt light, as though he had been freed of a heavy burden. A new happiness filled his breast, and he felt a new affection for Elder Kim's well-groomed face. Hyŏng-sik felt as though he were in a dream.

"This is cause for rejoicing," the pastor said, and shrugged his shoulders as if relieved.

"This makes me very happy," the Elder said. "I will ask my wife to join us, and then we can conclude the discussion." The Elder looked towards the pastor as if seeking his approval.

"Yes, of course," the pastor said. "Ask Sŏn-hyŏng to join us too, since nowadays the consent of the bride and groom themselves is important in marriage." The pastor acted as though he thought himself quite the modern man who had set aside old customs.

The Elder rang a bell that was on the table, twice. A maidservant appeared.

"Tell my wife to come here with my daughter."

The maidservant glanced at Hyŏng-sik and smiled, as though she had guessed what was going on, then left the room. The three men sat wordlessly. The smile in their eyes, however, spoke of their happiness. Hyŏng-sik thought of how he would soon be seeing Sŏn-hyŏng. He remembered the thoughts he had had when he first met her, and when he had taught her English the other day. Hyŏng-sik felt as though he were drunk. He was so happy that his entire body ached.

Elder Kim's wife entered the room, with Sŏn-hyŏng behind her. Hyŏng-sik arose from his chair and greeted Mrs. Kim. She smiled and greeted him in return. From where she stood behind her mother, Sŏn-hyŏng greeted the pastor and then Hyŏng-sik. Sŏn-hyŏng was blushing, and so was

Hyŏng-sik. Hyŏng-sik wiped sweat from his forehead with a handkerchief. Mrs. Kim sat dọwn beside Elder Kim, and Sŏn-hyŏng sat between her mother and the pastor. Hyŏng-sik sat across from Mrs. Kim.

81

Sŏn-hyŏng sat with her head lowered. Until then, she had never thought Hyŏng-sik would become her husband.

"Is Mr. Yi a good teacher?" Elder Kim had asked her that morning for the first time, smiling and looking at her intently.

"Yes, he is very kind," she said lackadaisically.

"Do you think he is a good man?"

Only then did Sŏn-hyŏng realize that her father had a particular reason in mind for asking her about Hyŏng-sik. She hesitated, but had no choice but to reply.

"Yes," she said, and looked away. She thought about Hyŏng-sik all day after that. She thought about whether or not she really liked Hyŏng-sik, and whether or not she wanted to become his wife. She was not sure about either question, though. She liked him somewhat, and yet did not.

"Hey, Sun-ae," she said. "It looks as though my parents are trying to marry me off. What should I do?"

Sun-ae did not seem particularly surprised. "To whom?"

"I am not exactly sure, but I think they want me to get married to Mr. Yi."

"Mr. Yi?" Sun-ae looked startled. "What did they say?"

"My father just asked me whether I think Mr. Yi is a good man, and he looked at me kind of strangely."

Sun-ae thought for a moment. "So what do you think?"

"I don't know. I just don't know! What should I do?"

"It depends on what you think. If you like him, marry him. If you don't like him, then don't. That is all."

"I have to marry him if my father tells me to."

"Why? You don't have to marry him if you don't like him. Your parents wouldn't force you to get married against your will, especially nowadays."

"Do you think so?" Sŏn-hyŏng sat quietly, holding her head at different angles, as though unable to decide. "What do you think, Sun-ae?"

"About what?"

"About me getting married . . . to Mr. Yi."

"How should I know?"

"Stop that, and answer me. Whom else can I talk with? I was going to talk about this with my mother, but I felt too embarrassed."

"How should I know when you yourself don't know? This sort of thing depends on your own heart. Who cares what anyone else says."

"Then what do you think of Mr. Yi as a person? Do you think he is a good man?"

"Of course."

"No, really, tell me what you think of him."

"How should I know what kind of man he is when I have only studied with him for an hour a day, over two or three days? What do you think?"

"I don't know either. What should I do?"

Such was the conversation between Sŏn-hyŏng and Sun-ae. As evident from their conversation, Sŏn-hyŏng did not know what to do about Hyŏng-sik. She was an eighteen-year-old girl, though, and did not dislike any man as long as he was not terribly evil, base or ugly. Nor did Sŏn-hyŏng dislike Hyŏng-sik. He was a man whom others praised. She was somewhat fond of him, and felt even fonder of him after the discussion with her father that morning. Sŏn-hyŏng did not love Hyŏng-sik, though, needless to say. There was no reason for love to form within the space of two or three days. There was no love between them now, though there might be in the future.

Neither knew each other's personality. Hyŏng-sik's love for Sŏn-hyŏng was like love for a beautiful flower. He loved her because she was lovable to the sight. It was a very superficial love. A love between two pairs of eyes, and two faces. Their spirits had not yet met even once. As Hyŏng-sik and Sŏn-yŏng looked at one another, each was probably wondering what the other was like. They were probably thinking that it would take some time to get to know one another. Elder Kim, his wife and Pastor Han thought they knew Sŏn-hyŏng and Hyŏng-sik very well. They did not, of course, know as much as Sŏn-hyŏng and Hyŏng-sik themselves knew, but they still thought they knew them very well. They were certain that Sŏn-hyŏng and Hyŏng-sik would be happy after they became husband and wife. That was why they were putting them together. They were joining them together simply because in their foolishly shallow opinion, it seemed like a good thing to do. If the couple somehow became unhappy, moreover, the Kims and the pastor would not share the responsibility, but would blame Sŏn-hyŏng and Hyŏng-sik, fate, or the will of God. This was how thousands of couples were formed each day.

82

Elder Kim looked back and forth at Hyŏng-sik and Sŏn-hyŏng.

"How shall we proceed?" Elder Kim asked the pastor. Elder Kim had never had any experience with the new style of marriage, and genuinely did not know how to proceed. The pastor himself had no idea, but could not admit it now that he was in this situation.

"We are about to discuss one of the most important matters in human relations, so let us pray." The pastor bowed his head in prayer. Everyone else lowered their heads too and put their hands on their knees. The pastor was silent for a few moments, as though concentrating, then began to speak in a very earnest and reverential voice, barely audible at first, then louder as he continued.

"Our heavenly Father, Lord Jehovah omnipotent, you love us always, even though we are sinners. We are immature, unwise, ignorant, foolish sinners. Yet we seek to engage your beloved Hyŏng-sik and Sŏn-hyŏng in vows of marriage, as you have ordained through the ages. May the Holy Spirit be with us ignorant sinners, like a dove, and watch over these proceedings. We ignorant sinners have done nothing to deserve to be able to pray to you, Oh Holy God, Jehovah. We pray only in the name of our Redeemer, Jesus Christ, who shed his precious blood for us and who sits at the right hand of God. Amen." The pastor kept his head lowered for quite some time, and lifted his head slowly only after everyone else had done so. The pastor had prayed with all his heart for Hyŏng-sik and Sŏn-hyŏng. The others too said an earnest "amen."

"Now then, everyone should, uh, formally speak with one another," the pastor said in a dignified voice. He looked at Elder Kim and his wife, and then at Sŏn-hyong. The Elder seemed uncertain as to what to say, and pounded on the table twice with his right hand. He thought it might be right for him to speak first, to his wife.

"Darling," he said slowly, as befit a man of upper-class status in Korean society. "I asked Hyŏng-sik to become engaged to Sŏn-hyŏng, and he said yes. What do you think?" Satisfied that he had spoken with good judgment and in a modern way, Elder Kim looked at his wife. Mrs. Kim thought it was silly for him to ask her about the matter again, since they had discussed it together earlier. This must be what the new ways are like, she thought, and shifted her body and lowered her head, as if embarrassed.

"Thank you," she said.

"Then you agree," the Elder said.

"Yes," she said, and lifted her head and looked at a painting on the opposite wall.

"Then the engagement has been finalized," the Elder said, and looked at the pastor. The pastor looked up towards the sky, as though in prayer.

"We must hear from the bride and bridegroom themselves," the pastor said. He seemed pleased with himself, thinking that he knew more than the Elder about the new ways. "They have both agreed to the marriage, but we must hear their thoughts nevertheless." The pastor looked at Hyŏng-sik. Am I right? he seemed to be asking Hyŏng-sik. Hyŏng-sik only glanced at the pastor and lowered his head again.

"Then let us ask them what they think," said the Elder. He assumed a solemn, imposing manner, as though he were a judge making interrogations. He thought it would be correct to ask Hyŏng-sik about his thoughts first since Hyŏng-sik was a man, and ask Sŏn-hyŏng after that.

"Do you too agree with this marriage?"

The pastor seemed to be dissatisfied with the way the question was put, and looked at Hyŏng-sik and said, "Nowadays marriage can take place only after hearing from the bride and bridegroom themselves. Please make it clear . . . do you want to marry Sŏn-hyŏng?" Hyŏng-sik held back the urge to laugh. He was too embarrassed, though, to answer.

Then he remembered U-sŏn, and quickly lifted his head, assumed an air of dignity, and said, "Yes." His own reply seemed ridiculous too.

"Now we must ask Sŏn-hyŏng." The pastor looked at Sŏn-hyŏng's lowered face from the side. "Tell us what you think. There is nothing to be embarrassed about," the Elder said.

Sŏn-hyŏng thought it was funny, and felt embarrassed. She thus did not answer when the Elder asked her what she thought. The Elder turned to the pastor and smiled. Mrs. Kim smiled too.

"Mrs. Kim, why don't you ask her," the pastor said, as dignified as ever.

"Answer him, dear," Mrs. Kim said.

"That is the new way. Please answer," the pastor rejoined.

"Answer him," Mrs. Kim said again. This time her voice was somewhat sharper. Seeing that she had no alternative, Sŏn-hyŏng said quietly, "Yes." No one heard her voice, though.

"Hurry up and answer," the Elder said. After this repeated urging, Sŏn-hyŏng said again, "Yes." Neither the Elder nor the pastor heard her this time either. Mrs. Kim, however, heard her. Hyŏng-sik too heard her.

"Hurry up and answer," the pastor said.

"She has given her answer," Mrs. Kim said on behalf of her daughter. Sŏn-hyŏng had lowered her head so far that her face was practically touching her knees.

83

"Then it is settled. The engagement has been formally concluded, now that we have the approval of the parents, and the consent of the bride and groom." The pastor finally seemed satisfied, and smiled. He thought these conditions should be sufficient for a modern marriage. The Elder thought it would be proper to formally declare the engagement.

"The engagement has been finalized," he said. Looking at Hyŏng-sik, he said, "I know my daughter is rather mediocre, but just the same I ask you to please take good care of her for the rest of her life," the Elder said. Then the Elder looked at Sŏn-hyŏng, and was about to say something to her, but stopped. Hyŏng-sik was as happy as if he were in a dream. All the blood in his body seemed to have risen to his head, and he could not see anything. He tried to control his breathing, afraid that others might hear his belabored breathing. The pastor and Elder Kim looked at Hyŏng-sik's red face and smiled. Sŏn-hyŏng too was happy though she was not quite sure why. She was happy that she had said yes, but she also thought it was funny. She wiped sweat from her forehead and nose with her skirt sash, as she had done the other day when she was studying with Hyŏng-sik.

Everyone sat looking at one another for awhile.

"Should the wedding take place before we send them to America, or after they have finished their studies?" Elder Kim asked the pastor.

"That's a good question," the pastor said. "How many years will it take for them to graduate?"

"It will take at least five years for Sŏn-hyŏng," said Elder Kim. "You said that you will graduate in five years, right?" Elder Kim said to Sŏn-hyŏng.

"Yes, if I start college in the spring of next year." This time she replied promptly, and lifted her head. Hyŏng-sik and Sŏn-hyŏng's eyes met briefly, then parted. It happened in an instant, like a flash of lightning, and the looks they exchanged had as much powerful energy as lightning.

"How about you, Hyŏng-sik?" the pastor asked. "How many years will it take for you to graduate?"

Hyŏng-sik did not know what to say. He had heard from the pastor that Elder Kim would be sending him to the United States, but he felt too embarrassed to talk as though it were definite.

"What?" Hyŏng-sik said.

"If you go to the United States this autumn, when will you graduate?" the pastor asked.

"If I enter school this year, I will graduate in four years."

"Will you be a Ph.D. then?"

"Of course not!" said Elder Kim. He thought it was a good time to show off how knowledgeable he was. "It takes more time after graduation from college to get a Ph.D." Elder Kim did not, however, know how many more years were required. Hyŏng-sik realized this, and laughed inwardly. Elder Kim, however, was now the father of the woman whom Hyŏng-sik loved. He was Hyŏng-sik's father-in-law. Hyŏng-sik stopped laughing.

"After graduating from college, if one goes to graduate school for two years, one receives a master's degree. One has to study three or four years more after that in order to qualify for the doctoral exam." Hyŏng-sik felt less shy after having said that.

"Then you should get a Ph.D., Mr. Yi. Are there women Ph.D.s?"

"Yes, of course, there are women Ph.D.s in the west. There was a Japanese woman who got a Ph.D. in the United States. She passed away several years ago." Hyŏng-sik looked at Sŏn-hyŏng.

"There are women Ph.D.s?" Mrs. Kim asked with surprise, and laughed. Elder Kim himself had not known there were women Ph.D.s. He too was surprised, but pretended not to be.

"There are even women monarchs," Elder Kim said, trying to demonstrate his sagacity.

"Then Sŏn-hyŏng should get a Ph.D. too," the pastor said. "That is amazing. Both husband and wife will be getting Ph.D.s." He smiled happily, as though Sŏn-hyŏng and Hyŏng-sik had already gotten their Ph.D.s. Hyŏng-sik and Sŏn-hyŏng smiled too. Everyone smiled. It was as though Hyŏng-sik and Sŏn-hyŏng were already getting their Ph.D.s. Mrs. Kim too thought of Hyŏng-sik and Sŏn-hyŏng getting their Ph.D.s, and was happy. The pastor continued the discussion.

"Then it would be best to have the wedding before they leave. Especially if it will take as many as five years."

"They should nevertheless finish their studies first, and then get married," Elder Kim said.

"How can they do that!" Mrs. Kim said, sympathizing with her daughter.

"No, they should get married now."

"Then how can they study? They should get married after they finish their studies."

"Let's ask Sŏn-hyŏng and Hyŏng-sik themselves," the pastor said, insisting again on modern ways. "What do you think, Hyŏng-sik?"

"How should I know?"

"Who would know if not you?"

Hyŏng-sik laughed.

"What do you think?" the pastor asked Sŏn-hyŏng.

Sŏn-hyŏng laughed inwardly, and said nothing. The pastor felt somewhat chagrined. There were no reasons for them to be married now, and no reasons for them not to be married now. If the marriage were arranged without any particular reason or conviction, then how could there be any reason or conviction in carrying out the wedding? The betrothal had been carried out as though it were child's play, and in a similar manner, it was decided that the two would be married after they finished their studies. Everyone nevertheless thought they had carried out the proceedings most rationally. They believed they had been guided by the Holy Spirit. It was dangerous business.

84

Hyŏng-sik stepped outside of the front door of Elder Kim's house. The humid air of the summer evening flowed past Hyŏng-sik's sweaty body like waves of water. It was very cool and refreshing to Hyŏng-sik. Hyŏng-sik returned home in a joyous mood, glancing at the stars that twinkled in the sky, the lights in the houses, and the faces of passersby. Spring seemed to have returned to his personal fortunes. Sŏn-hyŏng had become his wife. She was his, to love to his heart's desire. It had become possible, moreover, for him to go to the United States, enter college, and become a scholar and get a

Ph.D. He would be able to take a train and a boat with his beloved Sŏn-hyŏng, and go to the United States with her, and stay with her, together, in the same house and the same school. How happy they would be. After they finished their studies they would return to Korea, arm in arm, together on a boat and train, to the envy and congratulations of all. He and Sŏn-hyŏng would be so happy. Then he would live with Sŏn-hyŏng in a clean house, with nice scenery; they would put a piano in the house, and hang a violin on the wall. They would always love one another, and live happily ever after. What a joy it would be. Hyŏng-sik was as happy as a child. Whatever happiness the future might bring, he was elated just having these thoughts at present. In order to give himself more time to dwell on these thoughts, he deliberately took a detour, walking by Kwanghwamun, then along Chongno Avenue, and through Pagoda Park. Even then he felt sorry to arrive at home. The image of Sŏn-hyŏng sitting before him with her head lowered, had left a deep impression on him. The more he thought of that image, the more lovable and the prettier she became.

Hyŏng-sik paused for awhile outside his front door. I will no longer walk through this door, he thought. He thought himself suddenly enobled, and elevated in stature. He thus knocked on the front door once, then walked into the yard, smiling to himself.

The old woman and U-sŏn were sitting on the veranda talking. They stood up when they saw Hyŏng-sik. U-sŏn hit Hyŏng-sik on the shoulder.

"Hey. How did it go?" he said, smiling.

Hyŏng-sik pretended not to know what he meant. "What do you mean?"

"You know what I mean."

"What did you do?" asked the old woman. "Did everything work out?" she smiled.

"What do you mean?" Hyŏng-sik said, and smiled too.

"Tell me everything, from beginning to end. You went and ate dinner. What happened after that?"

"I drank water."

"And after that?"

"We talked."

"And after that?"

"I came home, of course."

"Don't want to tell us what happened, eh?" U-sŏn grabbed Hyŏng-sik's arm with both hands, and began to twist it behind his back. "Do you still not want to tell us what happened?"

"Ow! Okay, I will talk!"

U-sŏn let go of Hyŏng-sik's arm.

"What did you want me to tell you about?"

"Do you have to have your arm twisted before you will talk?" U-sŏn twisted Hyŏng-sik's arm again firmly.

"Ow! All right, all right. I will talk."

"Good! Let's hear you." U-sŏn would not let go of Hyŏng-sik's arm, but waited for Hyŏng-sik to keep his word. "Wait a minute. Let's turn on the light, and sit down and talk." Hyŏng-sik lit the lamp on the veranda outside his room, and took off his hat and *turumagi*, and tossed them in his room. The motion with which he tossed his hat and *turumagi* had a different significance now, however, than it had had that morning. The old woman went over to Hyŏng-sik's room with her tobacco pouch and pipe. U-sŏn too lit a cigarette and put it in his mouth, and fanned his chest, legs and back with his straw hat as he waited for Hyŏng-sik to speak.

"I got engaged," Hyŏng-sik said, smiling.

"When will you be getting married?"

"After graduation."

"After graduation? You mean, in the United States?"

"Yes. In five years."

"Five years?" Startled, the old woman took the pipe from her mouth. "In five years, when you're all old? What kind of silliness is that?"

"I will not be old in five years," Hyŏng-sik said, and smiled at the old woman.

"Are you just going to stare at each other, when you could be having the time of your life? Hurry up and get married! What's this talk of getting married five years from now?" The old woman expressed her vehement opposition, as though the matter directly concerned her. Hyŏng-sik thought the old woman was right.

"It will be good for us to spend some time looking at each other," Hyŏng-sik said. "We will be leaving at the end of July," Hyŏng-sik said to U-sŏn, "so that we can be admitted to school in September."

85

"The end of July?" U-sŏn was startled. "That soon?"

"If we aren't admitted to school in September, we will lose a year."

"What are you going to study?"

"I will have to go there to know for certain, but I would like to study education. All of my experience until now has been in education, and, moreover, education seems to be the most important thing for Korea now. I want to study modern education as best I can, and spend my life in education."

"Education?"

"By education, of course, I mean elementary and middle school education. Korea is waiting for a Pestalozzi. With what else but education can we make the Korean people into an entirely new people? Everyone must exert efforts for the sake of education. This would be true for any nation in any time, but it is particularly the case in a Korea where we urgently need to cast aside the old Korea, and make a new Korea, transformed by modern civilization. You are a writer, U-sŏn. Please, by all means, do advocate interest in education. The present state of education is indeed lamentable."

"Then you intend to study only education for four years?"

"Does four years seem like a long time to you? Ten years would not be enough to study it adequately."

"I too am aware of that, but is that all you are going to study?"

"I will study other subjects relevant to education, but I will center my studies on education. I would like to make a particular effort to study social systems and ethics." Hyŏng-sik looked at U-sŏn as though it occurred to him that U-sŏn did not understand what he was saying. It was true that U-sŏn did not understand. He had his own guesses, though, as to what Hyŏng-sik might be talking about.

"And what about your wife? Or, um, what shall I call her? Your sweetheart?" U-sŏn asked, smiling.

Hyŏng-sik smiled and turned red in the face. "How should I know?"

"Who else would know, if not her husband?"

"She herself would know. Nowadays a husband cannot restrict his wife's freedom."

"Then you won't have a say in what she studies?"

"Of course I won't. There is such a thing as the 'self,' you see. Everyone has the right to do what they want to do. How can one control another person's 'self'? One can advise others and tell them 'I think it would be good to do this or that,' but it is interfering in others' lives to tell them 'do this because I think you should do it.'"

U-sŏn was quite surprised. It made sense, he thought. Yet surely Hyŏng-sik did not intend to live that way, he thought. He gave no thought to discussing the matter further, though. He simply thought that Hyŏng-sik's ways of thinking were different from his own, and nodded his head this way and that in bewilderment. Hyŏng-sik looked at U-sŏn's forehead and mouth, and grinned. I have won the argument, Hyŏng-sik's happy expression said. The old woman had no idea what the two men were talking about. She only knew that Hyŏng-sik was going somewhere. The three of them each lived in different worlds. U-sŏn and Hyŏng-sik might eventually come to inhabit the same world, but the old woman would never be able to be in the same world as Hyŏng-sik. The three of them sat together in the same room, at the same moment, yet belonged to different worlds. They only spoke of things that the others could understand. That was why the old woman thought they all belonged to the same world. Then by chance the conversation would turn to talk of a different world, and the old woman's eyes would widen with surprise.

"Are you going away somewhere, Mr. Yi?" she said as if utterly surprised. Hyŏng-sik and U-sŏn laughed.

"Yes, I may be leaving at the end of next month . . . " Remembering that the old woman only knew the lunar calendar, Hyŏng-sik added, "I intend to go to the United States at about the time of the full moon next month."

"The United States! Do you mean the Western nation?"

"Yes, the Western nation."

"The nation where people with big noses and sunken eyes live," added U-sŏn, laughing. U-sŏn and Hyŏng-sik laughed. The old woman was surprised.

"How far away is the Western nation?"

"About thirty thousand *li*," said Hyŏng-sik.

"That's one hundred thousand *li* by sea," U-sŏn said, and laughed. The old woman did not know the difference between thirty thousand *li* and one hundred thousand *li*. She didn't know how far thirty thousand *li* might be to begin with. All she could do was gape.

"It's as far as going from here to Tongnae and back again fifteen times," said U-sŏn. "One takes a large iron boat that makes a pounding noise."

"Oh. One takes a steam boat. How many months does it take to get there?" The old woman even forgot to smoke her pipe.

"It takes a little over thirty months," said U-sŏn, then turned his head, and shut his mouth in a mischievous smile.

"Oh my."

"That is a lie. One can get there in about fifteen days," said Hyŏng-sik. The old woman looked resentfully at U-sŏn.

"Why are you going so far away?" she asked Hyŏng-sik. "What about your wife? My goodness!" The old woman shivered.

"His wife will go with him. Now that Mr. Yi is going to the Western nation with his wife, why don't you go too, ma'am? Get on a thundering iron boat, and go to the Western nation, where the sky meets the land."

The old woman pretended not to hear U-sŏn.

"When will you return?"

"I don't know. Probably in four or five years. I will come to see you when we get back." Hyŏng-sik smiled.

The old woman sighed. "Will I live another five years?" she said. Tears gathered in her eyes. Hyŏng-sik and U-sŏn stopped smiling, and looked at the old woman.

86

Let us now say something about Yŏng-ch'ae. Had she indeed descended through the blue waters of the Taedong River, and become a denizen of the Dragon King's palace? Some of you readers may have wept in sadness that Yŏng-ch'ae has died. Then again, there may be other readers who laughed to themselves, thinking that they saw past the meager skills of the novelist. They may have thought that just as Yŏng-ch'ae was about to drown in the Taedong River, she would be saved by some noble person, and become a nun in a hermitage, until she met Hyŏng-sik again and they were joyfully married, and enjoyed long life, wealth and prestige, and had many sons. It would be just as it had been since antiquity in all storybooks, in which women who were childless until late in life inevitably gave birth to a son, and that son always became a great man.

There may be readers who praised Yŏng-ch'ae's decision to go to P'yŏngyang, and thought it was right of Yŏng-ch'ae to drown herself. Some readers may have thought there was no reason for Yŏng-ch'ae to end her life, and may have thought her actions regrettable and a waste of a precious life. I do not know how the various thoughts of you, my readers, may differ or agree with what I am about to write with regard to Yŏng-ch'ae, but it will be interesting to compare your thoughts and mine.

The second-class train car from Pusan dropped off most of its passengers at Namdaemun, and there were only about five or six men and women in the car in which Yŏng-ch'ae sat. Yŏng-ch'ae had taken a seat in a corner of the car, and as soon as the car left the station, she stuck her head out the window, as though trying to hide her face from the other passengers. She gazed at the foot of Namsan, with a cool wind in her face. Nothing in particular drew her attention, though. She just kept watching the passing mountains and fields because she did not want to show her face to the others on the train. She was not particularly sad or in anguish. She was somewhat dazed, as though she had half awoken from a deep sleep. She felt as though she were in a dream.

She had indeed felt sad when her two friends and the old proprietress saw her off. She even felt sorry for herself. Her heart ached with the thought that she was on her way to die, leaving behind the world in which she had lived for over twenty years. She also felt relieved to be leaving a painful, miserable world that was not to her liking. Her mind was seething with all kinds of thoughts and feelings. After two hours, though, her mind grew calm. She seemed to have forgotten how she had managed to get to Namdaemun Station and board the train. It seemed to have been decades since she had left Namdaemun Station, and the faces of Yŏng-ch'ae's friends and the proprietress were indistinct, like those one tries to remember after many years.

Yŏng-ch'ae could see blue mountains in the summer sun, yellow waves of wheat and barley, and green waves of millet. A breeze that smelled of grass brushed against Yŏng-ch'ae's face and into her ramie blouse, cooling her perspiring flesh. All of these were pleasurable sensations to Yŏng-ch'ae. Like a person in a dream, Yŏng-ch'ae thus made no effort to see what was not readily visible, or disregard what was visible, but looked at whatever she saw, and listened to whatever she heard. She did not know where she was going, or what she was going to do.

Once in awhile she would think of how she was on her way to die. Then she would blink and shudder, as though she had died and come back to life. Then she would think about home, P'yŏngyang and Hyŏng-sik. She would start to come out of her dreamlike stupor, only to collapse again into the same condition.

She saw scenes from Ch'ŏngnyangni. She thought of how those beastlike men had grabbed her wrists, and she sucked at her lips. If she bit at her lips, she could taste the blood in her mouth. Then she would close her mouth, as if savoring the taste of her blood. After awhile, she would shake her head, as if trying to forget everything, and spit, and look at the mountains and fields as before. Her hair fluttered in the wind.

The train passed through Kaesŏng Tunnel, and raced towards the mountainous region of Hwanghae Province. The train would climb a mountain, then descend, then turn the spur of a mountain, whistle blowing again, and make a long descent for dozens of meters,[138] practically sliding down the mountain. When the train chugged up the mountains, mist rose from thickly wooded ravines on either side of the tracks. When the train made its descent, cool winds would blow briskly past the train, as though lying in wait. Weird, treacherous-looking rocks in the mountains seemed to be making whispering noises in the sunshine. A few lonely trees stood here and there dozing, without a leaf in motion. Now and then there would be a level clearing, and one could see an ox sleeping beside a stream, and a peasant woman with a small child, looking up at the train as she weeded a field where the barley had grown the span of a hand's width tall. Yŏng-ch'ae, however, still sat in a dreamlike stupor, her chin propped on the windowsill of the train window.

As the train passed a mountain bend, the whistle sounding long and loud, smoke from the engine car blew past Yŏng-ch'ae, and placed a piece of coal dust in her right eye. Yŏng-ch'ae closed her eyes and pulled her head inside the train. She wiped her eye with a cotton handkerchief that she had in her hand. The coal dust would not come out of her eye, though, and tears kept welling up in her eye. It was very painful.

87

Yŏng-ch'ae grimaced as she dabbed at her eye with her handkerchief. Ouch, that hurts! she thought. At first the piece of coal dust seemed to have gotten under her eyelid. After she rubbed her eye for awhile, she was not sure where the coal dust was, and her eye just hurt. Then she put her handkerchief in her eye and tried to wipe out the particle. When it still did not come out,

---

138 . The train descends for "tens of *kil*." 1 *kil* = eight to ten *cha*. 1 *cha* = .33 m.

she got upset, put her hand on the windowsill, and leaned her face against her hand and cried. Tears came gushing out, as though the sorrow that had been dozing had suddenly awakened. She just felt sad without knowing exactly why, and cried, trying to hold back the sound. Her mind, which had been in a dreamlike stupor, suddenly grew clear. All of the thoughts she had been having arose clearly in her mind, imbued with a sad light. Yŏng-ch'ae forgot about the bit of coal dust in her eye, and wept in sorrow, alone. Tonight I will die, she thought. I will drown in the Taedong River. My tears and the warmth in my body will disappear. This is the last time I will see the mountains, fields and people I have seen today. I will die within a few hours. The thought pained her body like the pricking of needles. Why was I born? Why have I lived? She had feelings of regret for her life.

Just then someone shook her gently.

"Are you all right? Please lift your head." Yŏng-ch'ae lifted her head in surprise, and squinted with one eye at the person who was speaking to her. It was a young woman dressed in Japanese clothing. She held a piece of cloth in her hand. "Here, turn towards me. Did you get some coal dust in your eye? I will get it out for you." She was smiled at Yŏng-ch'ae. When she saw Yŏng-ch'ae's sad expression, she opened her eyes wide and looked carefully at Yŏng-ch'ae's face. Feeling both grateful and embarrassed, Yŏng-ch'ae obliged the woman's request, and turned towards her.

"I am all right," Yŏng-ch'ae said, and lowered her head. The woman sat facing Yŏng-ch'ae, and practically embraced her.

"No, once coal dust gets in your eye, it is difficult to get it out." The woman wound the cloth around the tip of her finger, and put her other hand on Yŏng-ch'ae's brow.

"Is it this eye? Or this one?" she asked. Finally, she lifted Yŏng-ch'ae's right eyelid, looked carefully into the eye, then dabbed at the eye with the cloth. The woman's manner was very assured and calm. Yŏng-ch'ae sat still as the woman helped her. She felt the woman's warm, somewhat weary breathing touch her mouth and nose with a pleasant smell. The woman sat even closer to Yŏng-ch'ae, lifted Yŏng-ch'ae's eyelid, and, leaning forward, dabbed several times at her eye.

"Oh! If no one else was around, I would get it out with my tongue," the woman said as if exasperated. "There! It came out. Look at this. You had a piece of coal dust this large in your eye." She showed Yŏng-ch'ae the coal dust on the cloth. Yŏng-ch'ae could not see it very well, though, since her eyes stung and were full of tears. The woman stood up from the seat, and put her arm around Yŏng-ch'ae and helped her up.

"Now then, why don't you go to the faucet and wash up," the woman said, and led the way. The train was shaking, but the woman was steady on her feet as she led Yŏng-ch'ae to a wash stand at the other end of the train car. Halfway through the car, the woman got some soap and a towel from a suit-clad youth who had been sitting with her. Across the aisle, a man in a suit watched Yŏng-ch'ae and the woman vacantly, then resumed reading a book. Yŏng-ch'ae followed with faltering steps to the washroom. On a marble counter was a white porcelain wash basin. The woman washed the basin out once with water, swirling it around with her hand, then filled it with clean water. Then she opened the container of soap, and covered Yŏng-ch'ae's shoulders and neckline with a towel that had a red stripe. Putting her arm around Yŏng-ch'ae's waist, she propped Yŏng-ch'ae's body against hers for support.

"Now then, wash yourself up with soap." The woman looked at Yŏng-ch'ae's glossy hair, the Korean hairpin ornamented with flowers that was in her chignon, her white neck, and back, and wondered who she was. From time to time, she would adjust the towel over Yŏng-ch'ae's shoulders to keep it from slipping, and would tuck tendrils of hair behind Yŏng-ch'ae's ear. Anyone looking at them might think they were sisters—an older sister helping her younger sister. Indeed, the woman thought of Yŏng-ch'ae as a younger sister. What a gentle, well-behaved young woman, she thought. She looks as though she would be talented. And educated. She thought of how Yŏng-ch'ae had cried when she got coal dust in her eye. She is young and adorable, the woman thought.

In the midst of her sorrow, Yŏng-ch'ae felt thankful and happy for the woman's affection, and washed her face diligently. When she felt the woman's hand on her back, she remembered being embraced by Wŏr-hwa. She thought the woman's face somehow resembled that of Wŏr-hwa. I am going to die, though, she thought. She finished washing, and straightened her back. The woman gave Yŏng-ch'ae a towel. Yŏng-ch'ae wiped her face and hands. The woman asked for the towel, then gently wiped Yŏng-ch'ae's neck and behind her ears. Yŏng-ch'ae opened her eyes, and looked at the woman, face-to-face. Yŏng-ch'ae's eyes were red. There were still a few tearlike droplets of water on her lashes. The woman smiled at Yŏng-ch'ae. The expression in her eyes was that of a mother looking at her daughter.

Then she put her arm around Yŏng-ch'ae's waist and said, "Let's go have lunch."

88

They went back to Yŏng-ch'ae's seat. Only then did Yŏng-ch'ae manage to thank the woman.

"Thank you," she said. The woman was about to sit down, but then thought of something, and went to where she had sat earlier, spoke with the youth, and took out a four-cornered paper box from a travel bag. She brought the box over, and sat across from Yŏng-ch'ae.

"Please have some of this," she said, and removed the lid from the paper box. Yŏng-ch'ae did not know what it was. There was a thin piece of cold meat between two pieces of what seemed to be some kind of rice cake with large holes scattered throughout it. Too embarrassed to ask what it was, Yŏng-ch'ae just sat quietly. The woman glanced at Yŏng-ch'ae's eyes. You don't know what this food is! she thought. She offered some to Yŏng-ch'ae. "Where are you going?" the woman asked, and helped herself to some of the food first. "Please, have some," she said to Yŏng-ch'ae.

"I am going to P'yŏngyang," Yŏng-ch'ae said, and picked up a piece of the food, and ate it the same way the woman was eating. She did not know how to eat the food at first.

"Is your home in P'yŏngyang?" the woman asked, and helped herself to another piece of food. Yŏng-ch'ae did not know how to answer. Do I have a home, she wondered. If she had a home, it would be where her proprietress lived, she thought.

She turned her head and said, "Yes, I used to live in P'yŏngyang, but now I live in Seoul." She finished eating her piece of food, and sat quietly.

"Please, have another," the woman said, picking up another piece of food and giving it to Yŏng-ch'ae. Only then would Yŏng-ch'ae eat more. The food was not especially delicious, but the slightly salty meat between the pieces of cake was not bad. The food as a whole did not have a particular flavor, but nevertheless had a certain refined taste. The woman took another piece of the food and turned it over once.

"Are you on vacation now?" she asked Yŏng-ch'ae.

She thinks I am a student, Yŏng-ch'ae thought, and felt excruciatingly ashamed of herself. She wondered how a Japanese woman could speak Korean so well. She spoke Korean so well that Yŏng-ch'ae realized she must be a Korean woman studying in Japan.

"No, I am just going for a visit. I am not in school."

"Then you have already graduated. What school did you attend? Sungmyŏng? Chinmyŏng?"

"I have not attended any schools."

Upon these words, the woman stared at Yŏng-ch'ae blankly, forgetting to chew the food in her mouth. Then what kind of woman is she, the woman thought. It occurred to her that Yŏng-ch'ae might be a concubine. When Yŏng-ch'ae said that she had not attended school, the woman felt somewhat contemptuous of her, and yet was also curious as to what kind of woman Yŏng-ch'ae might be. The woman sat thinking for a few moments, not sure how to ask Yŏng-ch'ae more about herself.

"Do you have relatives in P'yŏngyang?" she asked finally.

Yŏng-ch'ae herself was not sure as to how to reply. She was going to die that evening. Since the woman had been so kind to her, Yŏng-ch'ae wanted to tell her about everything from beginning to end, but was nevertheless too embarrassed to speak, and did not know where to begin, or how to begin. She thus just sat quietly with her head lowered, the cake still in her hand. The woman sat in silence too. This woman has a secret, she thought, and became even more curious. Seeing that Yŏng-ch'ae was uncomfortable, though, she changed the subject. "My home is in Hwangju. I am studying in Tokyo. It is school break, so I am going home. That boy is my younger brother."[139] Yŏng-ch'ae just said, "Oh, really," and looked at the youth. The youth sat leaning back in his chair and blinking his eyes. He looked at Yŏng-ch'ae, and their eyes met. Then he looked away, out the window. She noticed that his face was round and plump, and his eyes large, with long lashes. What an adorable face, Yŏng-ch'ae thought. Brother and sister look alike, she thought. The woman and her brother did not say anything to each other, though, but only looked at one another from time to time. Yŏng-ch'ae wished she too had a younger brother like that. She envied the woman for studying in Tokyo. I am going to die, she thought. Why am I so unfortunate, she wondered. Why was I born to spend my life in tears, and then just die? The train moved on. The sun set. The hour of my death is growing nearer, she thought, and looked at her hands and body. Tears came to her eyes before she was aware of it. Yŏng-ch'ae tried to hide her tears, but began to sob, and her tears flowed even faster. Eventually, Yŏng-ch'ae put her forehead to her knees and cried. The woman student moved over and sat beside Yŏng-ch'ae, put her arms around her, and helped her to sit up.

"There, now. Why are you crying?"

Still bent over, Yŏng-ch'ae clasped one of the woman's hands tightly where it rested beneath her breast, and put her lips to the woman's hand.

"Thank you, friend," Yŏng-ch'ae said. "I am on my way to die. Oh thank you for your kindness." Yŏng-ch'ae sobbed harder.

"What?" said the woman student, taken aback. "What are you talking about? What is the matter? Please tell me. I will try my best to make you feel better. Why do you want to die? Now then, stop crying, and speak to me. You must live. You are in the flower of your youth. You should be happy, and live life to the fullest. Why do you want to die?" The woman wiped Yŏng-ch'ae's tears with a cloth. Yŏng-ch'ae opened her eyes wide and looked at the woman student. There were tears in the woman student's eyes. Yŏng-ch'ae thought it was strange for there to be tears in the eyes of such an energetic, manlike woman. Yŏng-ch'ae felt a strong affection for the woman student. The woman student's handkerchief was stained with blood from Yŏng-ch'ae's lip. The woman student looked at the blood, and at Yŏng-ch'ae's face. She felt an urgent sympathy for Yŏng-ch'ae.

---

139. The younger brother does not appear later in passages about Pyŏng-uk's family. Pyŏng-uk's parents are depicted as living with Pyŏng-uk's older brother and his wife, and there is no mention of a younger brother. This seems to be an inconsistency in the plot.

89

The woman student listened to Yŏng-ch'ae's life story.

"Do you still love Hyŏng-sik?" she asked.

Yŏng-ch'ae felt her heart ache at the words. Had she indeed loved Hyŏng-sik? She did not know. She had just thought Hyŏng-sik was someone she had to find and care for as her husband. In the past eight years, she had never asked herself whether or not she loved him, though. She had just wanted to find him as soon as possible. She had thought that once she saw him, her wishes would be fulfilled, and she would be happy. Yŏng-ch'ae looked into the distance, then at the woman student.

"I have never thought about it," she said. "We separated when we were very young, so I could not even remember his face very well."

"Then you have been looking for Hyŏng-sik all this time just because your father told you to marry Hyŏng-sik! Even though you were not particularly in love with him."

"Yes. I also remember that I was very fond of him when I was a child. I miss him very much when I think of those days."

"That is understandable. No one can forget childhood memories. You probably remember other kids from your childhood too, besides Hyŏng-sik."

Yŏng-ch'ae thought for awhile.

"Yes, I remember several friends. But my fondest memories are of Hyŏng-sik. Then when I actually saw his face the other day, everything felt different from what I had thought it would be like. My affection for him seemed to have fallen apart. I do not know why. That day, I went home and felt so sad that I cried."

The woman student nodded understandingly, and said somewhat hesitantly, "Then you don't particularly love him now."

Yŏng-ch'ae thought a while, as though uncertain of her own feelings. "I was happy to see him again, but he was not the man for whom I had been waiting and longing. He was different from the man I had pictured. I myself was taken aback. He did not seem very glad to see me, moreover."

"I think I understand," the woman student said, and closed her eyes. What does she mean? thought Yŏng-ch'ae, and closed her eyes too.

"Why did you decide to die, though?" asked the woman student.

"What else can I do? I have lived until now for him alone. In one day, I lost my virginity." A mournful look came over Yŏng-ch'ae's face. "I will never be able to be by his side as a wife. For what can I live?" Yŏng-ch'ae bowed her head as if in despair.

"I do not think that is a reason to die."

"Then what can I do?"

"Live! Why die?"

Yŏng-ch'ae looked at the woman in surprise. The woman spoke with strength in her voice.

"First of all, you have been living an illusion. You saved your virginity for a man named Yi Hyŏng-sik, even though you did not love him. You saved yourself for him for eight years, just because of something your father said once jokingly. Is it not futile to save oneself for someone whom one does not love, and with whom there has been no mutual discussion of feelings? Is it different from saving oneself for a dead person—someone who is no longer of this world? Your intentions are beautiful, Yŏng-ch'ae. You are chaste. But that is all that one can say for being chaste. Isn't there someone else to whom you could devote your beautiful spirit and chaste self? If you love Hyŏng-sik, then devote yourself mind and body to him from now on. If you do not love him, find another man."

"I have always thought of him as my intended, though. What about the teachings of the sages of antiquity?"

"No, you have been dreaming until now. How can you regard someone whose face you scarcely know and whose mind you do not know, as your intended? Such are the shackles of outdated thought. People live through the breath of life that is within them. A husband whom one does not love is not a husband. Your past is a dream. Your true life begins from now on."

Yŏng-ch'ae was surprised at these words. They seemed different from the concept of "virtuous woman." What the woman student said seemed to be right, though. She had indeed never loved Hyŏng-sik. She had created an illusion, a man to her liking, whom she named Hyŏng-sik, and had thought they were the same. Then she had gone looking for Hyŏng-sik, instead of looking for the man of her illusions. When she saw Hyŏng-sik, she had realized he was not the illusion she had created, and she had been disappointed. I will never see Hyŏng-sik, she had thought in despair. Yŏng-ch'ae realized that she had made a mistake in her way of thinking. Though still in despair, she seemed to see a new light.

"Will a true life open for me? Will I be able to live again?" Yŏng-ch'ae looked at the woman student.

90

"Yes, a true life will unfurl for you. You have lived a deception until now. Your real life begins now. Happiness awaits you. Why throw away the happiness that awaits you, and end your life?" The woman student felt sure that this would be enough to change Yŏng-ch'ae's resolve to die. "Stop crying, and smile. Let's smile." The woman student smiled. Then Yŏng-ch'ae smiled too.

"Could happiness await me? What about duty? Shall I neglect duty, and seek happiness? Would it be right?" Yŏng-ch'ae could not decide.

"Duty? Do you think it is your duty to die?"

"Isn't it?"

"How?"

"If one has thought of a man as one's husband, and then loses one's virginity before one can give her body to him, then is it not her duty to die?"

All right then, the woman student seemed to be thinking. "Then I will ask you a few questions," she said. "First of all, is it you who chose Hyŏng-sik as your intended? That is, did you yourself decide? Or did a few words from your father decide for you?"

"My father decided, of course."

"Then you decided your entire future because of a few words that your father said!"

"Yes. Is that not one of the 'three obediences'?"[140]

"Ha! The 'three obediences' have taken the lives of tens of millions of women for thousands of years, and made tens of millions of men miserable. Those accursed two words."

Yŏng-ch'ae was shocked. "Are you saying that the 'three obediences' are wrong?"

"It is the responsibility of sons and daughters to listen to their parents. It is the responsibility of a wife to listen to her husband. However, isn't the life of a son or daughter more important than the words of his or her parents? And isn't the life of a wife more important than the words of a husband? To decide one's life in accordance with what someone else thinks is to kill oneself. That is indeed a sin against humanity. 'A woman must obey her son if her husband dies.' These words express the capricious cruelty and violence of men. They show a disregard for woman's character. It is only right that a mother should teach her son and have authority. It is a grievous injustice for a parent to have to be submissive towards their son or daughter." The woman student forcefully attacked traditional morals, her face reddening. "You have been a slave of such outdated thought, and have tasted futile suffering. Free yourself from those shackles. Awake from your dream. Be a person who lives for herself. Attain freedom." The woman student had a very serious expression on her face.

"Then what should I do?" asked Yŏng-ch'ae. Her thoughts became confused. Yŏng-ch'ae seemed to have voluntarily entrusted her life to the woman student. It seemed as though her life would be decided by the words that came from the woman student's lips. Yŏng-ch'ae watched the woman student's eyes and mouth.

"A woman is a human being, too," the woman student said. "Since a woman is a human being, she has many roles. She can be a daughter, a wife, a mother. There are many ways she can fulfill her role in life, whether through religion, science or art; or work for society or the state. In the past, though, the only role for women has been that of wife, and even that was

---

140. Neo-Confucian ethics required a woman to obey her father; her husband, after she married; and her son, after her husband died.

decided by others' intentions and others' words. Until now, women
been nothing but an accoutrement for men, a possession. You were try
go from being a possession of your father, to being a possession of M
Just like an object being passed from one person to another. We too must be
human beings. We must be women, but we must first be human beings. There
are many things for you to do. You were not born only for the sake of your
father and Mr. Yi. You were born for the tens of millions of Koreans of past
generations, our 1.6 billion fellow countrymen in the present, and the tens of
millions of our descendants in future generations. You therefore have
responsibilities towards your ancestors, your fellow countrymen, and your
descendants, in addition to your responsibilities to your father and to Mr. Yi.
It is a sin for you to try to end your life, without fulfilling these responsibilities."

"Then what should I do?"

The woman student smiled.

"You must begin a new life from today."

"How?"

"You must begin everything anew. Forget the past, and start anew. You
lived following others' wishes in the past. From now on, though . . . " The
woman student paused and looked at Yŏng-ch'ae. Yŏng-ch'ae's face grew
flushed, and her breathing grew labored, her gaze clinging to the woman
student's eyes and mouth.

"Yes?" said Yŏng-ch'ae.

"From now on, you must live according to your own wishes."

The train emerged from the mountains, and headed towards the fields of
Sŏhŭng. A clear stream kept reappearing beside the train, now on the left,
now on the right. Yŏng-ch'ae and the woman student sat quietly and looked
outside.

91

When the woman student got off the train at Hwangju, she took
Yŏng-ch'ae with her. She thought of Yŏng-ch'ae as a friend, and wanted to
introduce her to her family, and let her stay with her in her own room. Living
at home were her parents, who were in their forties, a brother who was three
or four years older than she was, and her grandmother, who had a stooped
back. When her grandmother saw her, she said nothing, but was so happy that
tears flowed from her eyes. The woman student's mother was an affectionate,
gentle, good-natured woman. When the woman student bowed before her
father, his face showed no sign of gladness, and he turned his head away. The
woman student smiled to herself when she saw this. Her brother greeted her
with a smile.

"Why didn't you let us know what day you were coming?" he said,
patting her on the shoulder. He asked about Tokyo. The woman student's

sister-in-law just smiled quietly in front of her parents-in-law, but when she sat facing the woman student, she held her hand and rubbed her back, her expression full of happiness. What a fun family, Yŏng-ch'ae thought as she saw these scenes. She thought of her own family, now gone. That evening the entire family, except for the father, gathered and talked joyfully as they ate wheat noodles. Yŏng-ch'ae sat quietly next to the woman student. The woman student's brother seemed to feel uncomfortable around Yŏng-ch'ae, and got up and left after talking awhile. Only the women were left. The woman student cheerfully told her grandmother, mother and sister-in-law about her past year in Tokyo. Her grandmother nodded her head from time to time, smiling. Her sister-in-law showed the most interest in what she had to say. Her mother kept telling her to eat this and that, and now and then asked questions that were completely irrelevant to what her daughter was saying, as though she weren't listening. "You are not listening to me, mother," the daughter said. "I am listening," the mother said. "Keep talking." Then the mother would ask another irrelevant question, making the young women laugh. Yŏng-ch'ae laughed with them. Actually, the woman student's mother could not really understand what her daughter was talking about. The grandmother was even less able to understand; she stopped smiling, and started to yawn. Only the sister-in-law and Yŏng-ch'ae listened with interest, each with her chin propped on her hand as she listened intently. After awhile, the mother blinked her eyes as if tired, and her eyes watered. She got up and took down a pillow, then gave it to the grandmother.

"Go to sleep, mother," she said. "I don't know what these girls are talking about." She too lay down, pillowing her head on her arm. The two older women fell asleep, and the three young women talked until late at night. They were happy. Yŏng-ch'ae became good friends with the sister-in-law. That evening, the three of them slept together, side by side. Yŏng-ch'ae could not fall asleep until later. She eventually fell asleep, though, and in her dreams she saw Wŏr-hwa.

When she got up in the morning, she smiled to herself. It was strange to her that someone who had been on her way to die, someone who had almost died last night, was still alive. She was worried, though, about her future.

The woman student's name was Pyŏng-uk. According to Pyŏng-uk, her name had been Pyŏng-ok at first, but she had changed it to Pyŏng-mok because she thought Pyŏng-ok seemed too soft and feminine. "Pyŏng-mok," though, was a bit too strong and masculine, so she made her name Pyŏng-uk instead, which seemed to be somewhere in between the other two names.

"Pyŏng-uk is a lonely name, isn't it?" she said to Yŏng-ch'ae once. "I don't want to have to be quiet and soft as required of women by traditional thought. Nor do I want to be quite as strong and stiff as a man either. I think somewhere in between is just right."

"Yŏng-ch'ae," she said smiling. "Yŏng-ch'ae. That is a pretty name."[141] At home, though, she was called Pyŏng-ok, not Pyŏng-uk. She would still answer when they called her by the name Pyŏng-ok.

Pyŏng-uk thought Yŏng-ch'ae was a very talented, intelligent, well-educated woman. At first she had tried to use words that were easy to understand, since she thought Yŏng-ch'ae might not be able to understand what she said; but now she spoke as to an equal. Yŏng-ch'ae thought Pyŏng-uk had an infinite amount of strange knowledge and thoughts. She thus listened attentively to whatever words came from Pyŏng-uk's lips, and tried to understand their meaning. After about three days, Yŏng-ch'ae had an overall idea of Pyŏng-uk's thoughts, and realized that Pyŏng-uk's way of thinking was the opposite of the way Yŏng-ch'ae had thought until then. Pyŏng-uk's way of thinking, moreover, seemed to be more rational than that of Yŏng-ch'ae. Now Yŏng-ch'ae could understand very well what Pyŏng-uk had said on the train.

Pyŏng-uk and Yŏng-ch'ae became very fond of one another. When they sat together, they would become enraptured in conversation, and lose track of time. Yŏng-ch'ae learned new knowledge from Pyŏng-uk, and had a taste of Western emotions. Pyŏng-uk learned traditional knowledge from Yŏng-ch'ae, and had a taste of Eastern emotions. Pyŏng-uk had disliked anything that was outdated. After coming into contact with Yŏng-ch'ae's thorough understanding of traditional thought, though, Pyŏng-uk realized that there were appealing aspects to even traditional thought. She even thought of studying the *Elementary Learning*, *Biographies of Virtuous Women*, and classical Chinese poetry and prose. She took out dust-covered books at home, such as the *Komun Chinbo* (Genuine Treasures of Classical Literature),[142] and studied these books with Yŏng-ch'ae, and memorized what she learned. "This is such fun," she would exclaim, rejoicing like a child, and she would recite the texts out loud. "Hm," Pyŏng-uk's father would say when he heard his daughter reciting classical texts, though it was not clear whether he was praising her, or expressing ridicule.

92

Pyŏng-uk studied music. Once when she was playing the violin, she said to Yŏng-ch'ae, "My parents are upset because I study music. My parents say they won't give me money for tuition. They ask me if I intend to become a *kwangdae*[143] with that kind of training. I cried and made a fuss, so that they

---

141. The 1918 Sinmungwan edition adds the words, "It is not too feminine, either."

142. The *Komun Chinbo* is an anthology of Chinese poetry from the Zhou dynasty to the Later Song period. It is not known who compiled the anthology.

143. *Kwangdae* performed Korean sung and spoken narrative, known as *p'ansori*. Marshall Pihl discusses the history of the *kwangdae*, in *The Korean Singer of Tales* (Cambridge: Council on

would let me study music. They say I have gone wild. Older brother is more understanding, though." Pyŏng-uk smiled. Pyŏng-uk would be absorbed in playing the violin for awhile, then, smiling, would childishly feign a shudder of annoyance when she heard her father clear his throat outside. Yŏng-ch'ae liked the sound of the violin. She had not heard much Western music. The music that was played in Pagoda Park had therefore not particularly interested her. Now, however, she seemed to be gradually understanding more and more of the remarkable beauty of Western music.

Pyŏng-uk took great pleasure in playing the violin, reading classical Chinese poetry, and talking with Yŏng-ch'ae. She even forgot to play the violin sometimes, because of the pleasures of Chinese poetry, which she was tasting anew. She also went about busily helping her sister-in-law take care of the housework. One day she put on one of her grandmother's old, wrinkled skirts, rolled up her sleeves, took up a hoe, and weeded in the inner courtyard, the ground around the walls, and the outer yard enclosed by a wattle fence. Then she got flowers from a neighbor, and planted them at home. She wiped the sweat from her brow with her muddy hand, leaving yellow mud here and there on her face. Just as she was in the midst of digging at the tough soil, her father came into the yard and stood and watched. "We will have to marry Pyŏng-uk off to a farming household," he said, smiling.

"That is enough," Pyŏng-uk's mother said to her daughter when she was weeding. "Who told you to weed in this hot weather?" Her mother smiled nonetheless.

"Just wait and see," said Pyŏng-uk. "The whole house will be a flower garden," she said, and smiled. Pyŏng-uk saw, however, that her parents did not seem to think that planting flowers was very important. She looked at Yŏng-ch'ae, who was standing beside her.

"How could they like my studying music, when they do not appreciate flowers?" Pyŏng-uk said. "Next, I am going to get a live rooster and chicken somehow, and put them outside father's room. Surely he won't say that he dislikes the sound of a rooster crowing. What do you think? Wouldn't that be extraordinary?" Pyŏng-uk smiled.

"Yes, it would," said Yŏng-ch'ae, and smiled.

"Don't you pity those who don't appreciate the loveliness of flowers, or the crowing of a rooster?" Pyŏng-uk looked at Yŏng-ch'ae as though asking her to agree with her. Yŏng-ch'ae understood what she meant. Yŏng-ch'ae had learned the word "art" earlier, but only now realized the meaning of the word. *Kisaeng* were a kind of artist. They used their art, however, in a lowly way, Yŏng-ch'ae thought. The famous *kisaeng* of the past had all been artists. They sang, played musical instruments, danced, composed poetry and songs, and painted. They were what are now considered artists! Yŏng-ch'ae thought to herself. She too was an artist. She wondered if her heaven-ordained occupation might be that of becoming an artist. Shall I study music, just like Pyŏng-uk? she thought. She now realized that dancing and singing had meaning, though she had despised them until then. After awhile, Yŏng-ch'ae stopped thinking about dying, and resolved to exert herself to live joyously, like Pyŏng-uk. There came to be happiness in her heart.

Pyŏng-uk too knew that Yŏng-ch'ae was changing. Pyŏng-uk rejoiced. Pyŏng-uk encouraged Yŏng-ch'ae to study singing, and told her that there were schools in Tokyo that specialized in teaching voice, and that one could attain world renown if one learned singing and dancing well. Pyŏng-uk was intoxicated with Yŏng-ch'ae's voice, to the point of infatuation. If Yŏng-ch'ae's voice is that beautiful when she sings songs that she does not know very well, then how beautiful her voice must be when she sings songs that she does know, thought Pyŏng-uk.

Pyŏng-uk lived outside the western gate of the city of Hwangju. Her house was on a clean, quiet site. There were not many houses in the neighborhood, so Yŏng-ch'ae and Pyŏng-uk could take walks, hand in hand, in the setting sun. They would talk about their dreams for the future as they walked. They dipped their feet in a stream that flowed beneath ripened heads of grain, and sang songs together.

"My parents keep telling me to get married."

"With whom?"

"Who knows. Anyone of whom they approve, of course. This time they have given me strict orders to get married."

"What are you going to do?"

"I will get married whenever I want to," said Pyŏng-uk. She thought for awhile, as though hesitant to say something that she found difficult to talk about. Then she smiled and said, "I too have someone with whom I am in love." Her face reddened.

"Where? In Tokyo?" asked Yŏng-ch'ae.

"Yes. My parents are opposed, though. He is an illegitimate son. And poor. Heh-heh. He is a good man, though. He is handsome, well built, talented, with a kind, generous, good mind. Ah, I have boasted about him too much. I am not just boasting, though. You would probably love him too if you saw him. I will show him to you some day. You must not take him away from me, though," Pyŏng-uk said, and smiled at Yŏng-ch'ae. Yŏng-ch'ae smiled with her head lowered.

Four or five days went by like this. Yŏng-ch'ae did not let Hyŏng-sik or the old woman in Seoul know that she was alive. She hoped that there would be a day when they would know that she was alive. How would Yŏng-ch'ae live her life from now on, though?

93

Yŏng-ch'ae learned more and more about Pyŏng-uk's family. Yŏng-ch'ae had been without a family for a long time. Pyŏng-uk's family had parents and siblings, and seemed joyous and happy as heaven on earth. When Yŏng-ch'ae learned more about Pyŏng-uk's family, though, she realized that they too had their own sorrows and distress. First of all, father and son disagreed with one other about the son's idea of starting a business. Pyŏng-uk's brother, Pyŏng-guk, had studied economics in Tokyo, and wanted to invest capital to organize a company that he would manage. The father, however, thought it was risky, and was very much opposed to the idea. The son, moreover, was in favor of sending Pyŏng-uk to Tokyo to study, but their father was opposed, saying that there was no purpose for a girl to study that much, and that it would be best for her to just get married soon. Every time Pyŏng-uk came home for vacation, the father would express his opposition, but he would eventually give in to his son. Last summer the father's opposition had been severe, and he had said he would not give Pyŏng-uk money to travel to Tokyo. Pyŏng-uk cried for two days, and the son and mother secretly put together the money for Pyŏng-uk, so that she could go. Pyŏng-uk then left for Tokyo and could not even bid her father farewell. Her father was angry for a few days after that, and would not talk to the family. Not much later, though, he asked, "Have you sent Pyŏng-uk money for tuition this month? Send her some money for clothes." This time, too, father and son argued twice because the father said Pyŏng-uk had to get married, and the son said to wait until after Pyŏng-uk graduated. One of Pyŏng-uk's father's friends had a son who had graduated from Kyŏngsŏng Vocational School, and was now a court clerk. Pyŏng-uk's father liked the man, and since the man had been widowed last year, Pyŏng-uk's father thought it would be a good chance to make him his son-in-law. Pyŏng-guk, however, was opposed. The man was from a wealthy family, and had begun to live a dissipated life when he was sixteen, then decided that he wanted to get a government job, and went to a vocational school. Like many youths nowadays, he had no particularly high-minded ideals or great goals, but only took pride in wearing a uniform with gold trim, and a sword. He fooled around with *kisaeng* several times a month, and got several dozen wŏn from his parents each month in addition to his salary. He was a somewhat arrogant, frivolous, vain youth. No one knew what it was that Pyŏng-uk's father saw in the man, but he seemed to think the man was the only good man for Pyŏng-uk. Pyŏng-uk's brother, however, not only disliked the man, but had contempt for him. There was almost nothing that the father and son agreed about. The father thought his son was stubborn, immature, and disobedient towards his parents. The son thought his father was closed-minded, ignorant and unaware of how the world was changing. The father nevertheless knew that Pyŏng-guk was sincere and that Pyŏng-guk's friends respected

Pyŏng-guk. The son, moreover, knew that his father too was sincere and loving. Although father and son disagreed about everything, they thus were also somehow at one with each other. The mother did not have any particular opinions, but often agreed with her son. Whenever she did that, the father would glare at her, and she would glare back at him. They were like children glaring at each other, though, and they soon got over it.

Another worry in their household was the lack of affection between Pyŏng-guk and his wife. Even after Yŏng-ch'ae had been there for over ten days, she never saw Pyŏng-guk and his wife talk to each other. They would glance at each other like passersby, then turn their heads away, or leave. The wife nonetheless was always washing and ironing her husband's clothes. Ever since Yŏng-ch'ae had arrived, the daughter-in-law, Pyŏng-uk and Yŏng-ch'ae slept together every night in the same room. Pyŏng-guk apparently slept alone in the study. Yŏng-ch'ae felt apologetic, and asked Pyŏng-uk if they could stay in another room.

"Don't worry about it," Pyŏng-uk said smiling. "My brother doesn't sleep with his wife anyway."

"Why?"

"I don't know. He wasn't like that before, but he has grown more and more distant from his wife ever since he returned from Japan." Pyŏng-uk put her lips close to Yŏng-ch'ae's ear. "Sister-in-law cries to me about it," she said, and sighed as if in sympathy. Yŏng-ch'ae too felt sorry for the sister-in-law. How could he dislike a wife with such a lovely face and a beautiful heart, she thought.

"Is it because he thinks her lacking in some way?"

"I do not know. There is nothing wrong with her; he just does not love her. When I asked him about it, he said he just does not like the sight of her, though he himself does not know why. Perhaps it is because my sister-in-law is older than my brother. It is a worrisome matter." She shook her head.

"Is elder sister that old?" Yŏng-ch'ae asked in surprise. Yŏng-ch'ae too called Pyŏng-uk's sister-in-law "elder sister." There was no other appropriate word she could use, and Yŏng-ch'ae wanted to call her "elder sister" anyway.

"She is five years older than my brother," Pyŏng-uk said, smiling. "My brother was barely twelve years old when he and my sister-in-law were married. My sister-in-law was seventeen. How could there be any romantic feelings between them? My sister-in-law raised my brother. And now that he is an adult—" Pyŏng-uk laughed. "Brother is a very loving, gentle person, but love is not something one can control." Pyŏng-uk and Yŏng-ch'ae felt a boundless sympathy for the couple.

"What can they do? They cannot go on living this way."

"Most young couples are like that these days, I have heard. It is a serious problem, and it must be resolved." Pyŏng-uk and Yŏng-ch'ae looked at one another.

94

Differences of opinion between father and son can be tolerated; however, it must be quite unbearable for there to be no love between husband and wife, thought Yŏng-ch'ae. Though the matter of Pyŏng-uk's marriage did not directly affect Yŏng-ch'ae, Yŏng-ch'ae had developed an affection for Pyŏng-uk's family after having stayed with them for over a week, and she became worried about the young couple. Yŏng-ch'ae wanted to bring the couple closer together if at all possible. She was fond of both the husband and the wife. The more that Yŏng-ch'ae interacted with the wife, the more Yŏng-ch'ae liked her, and now she truly wanted to call her "sister." She felt an affection towards the wife that was similar to the affection she had felt for Wŏr-hwa. She did not, of course, have quite the same feelings of reverence and dependency as those she had had towards Wŏr-hwa, but she felt the utmost affection for the wife, and felt sorry for her with all her heart. She thus tried to be at the wife's side as much as possible, and talk with her, and take every chance to help her feel better. The wife grew close to Yŏng-ch'ae, and told her about her thoughts. Whereas Pyŏng-uk was affectionate but somewhat stiff, Yŏng-ch'ae was both affectionate and had a soft way about her. Talking with Yŏng-ch'ae was one of the only pleasures that the wife had. In some ways, the wife was even fonder of Yŏng-ch'ae than she was of her sister-in-law. "What shall I do?" she said once, squeezing Yŏng-ch'ae's hand.

Yŏng-ch'ae's own feelings were even more painful. For some reason, Yŏng-ch'ae began to have feelings for the wife's husband. At first she thought she felt affection for him because he was the older brother of a friend, but gradually she began to yearn passionately for his image, and every time she saw his image, her heart pounded and she blushed. It seemed to Yŏng-ch'ae that he too looked at her with affection in his eyes. Yŏng-ch'ae tried to hold back her feelings, but her feelings could not be controlled. When she lay down to sleep, his broad face would appear before her eyes, and she could not fall asleep. Whenever this happened, she would embrace Pyŏng-uk's sister-in-law, who lay beside her, and the sister-in-law would embrace her too. Yŏng-ch'ae felt apologetic towards the wife, and felt that she had wronged her. I must leave this house, she thought, and yet could not bring herself to leave. Yŏng-ch'ae thus had a new cause for sorrow. These days, Yŏng-ch'ae would often sit lost in thought. "What's the matter?" someone would ask her, and she would be startled from her thoughts.

From then on, she began to long for men more and more. She had lived in loneliness before then, but a different kind of loneliness now weighed more heavily upon her breast. She had used to feel as though she were alone in the world. Now, however, she felt as though she were missing half of herself. It seemed as though she would need this other half of herself in order to be complete. Her heart throbbed and her face felt hot for no reason. She felt tired, and as though she were drunk. She wanted to lean against something, and to be held in someone's arms.

Yŏng-ch'ae sat quietly and thought about several of the men she had known. She thought about men who had grabbed her by the wrist, men who had put their arm around her and drawn her into their embrace, men who had forced her to put her cheek against theirs, men who had tried to seduce her with lascivious looks, men who had threatened her with arrogant words. Those men had seemed to be her enemies, and had seemed hateful, yet gave her an indescribable sensation of warmth. She remembered with exhilaration the touch of a man's flesh against hers. She wished she had a man at her side just then. She wanted to give her hand to hold to any man who asked, and let herself be embraced.

She thought of Sin U-sŏn and Hyŏng-sik. Of all the men Yŏng-ch'ae had come in contact with over the past few years, Yŏng-ch'ae had felt the most attracted to Sin U-sŏn. He was handsome, had a cheerful personality, and had some kind of power that drew others to him. She had not been unmoved when they had sat face-to-face one evening, and U-sŏn had been trying to seduce her. She wanted to put her forehead against his chest then and there, and ask him to take care of her. She had restrained herself, though, because she was sure at the time that she was devoted body and soul to Hyŏng-sik. All this time, she had thought it was a great sin if the image of any other man appeared in her thoughts, and she would pinch herself and try to hold back such thoughts. She had thus been nothing more than a model of some moral rule, and had not been an independent person who thought for herself. Just as a silkworm forms a cocoon and goes inside it and lies down there, Yŏng-ch'ae too had built herself a home called chastity, and had thought of it as her world. The recent incident had shattered that house, and only then had Yŏng-ch'ae jumped out into the wide world. When she met Pyŏng-uk on the train, moreover, Yŏng-ch'ae realized that the world she had thought of until then as the only existing world was actually only a worthless illusion, and that there existed a free, joyous world. Only then did Yŏng-ch'ae become a free, youthful human being, and a beautiful young woman. The blood of a human being began to course through her body with warmth for the first time, and she began to burn with human emotion. Yŏng-ch'ae thought of how her mind and heart had been completely transformed. It was like emerging into a world of sunshine for the first time, where breezes blew, flowers bloomed, and birds sang, after one has been living in a dark, narrow, mud dugout. Yŏng-ch'ae played the *kŏmun'go* and the violin. The music assumed a new aspect. Tears of happiness and sorrow rose in her eyes.

95

Hyŏng-sik passed the time in dreamlike happiness. Every day, he taught Sŏn-hyŏng English, and afterwards, they would talk about various things. Sŏn-hyŏng began to feel familiar with Hyŏng-sik, and even began to joke little by little, though she was still shy. Sun-ae, however, was as unsmiling as ever, and did not say much. Hyŏng-sik would be talking happily with Sŏn-hyŏng, then suddenly stop when he noticed Sun-ae sitting silently. Then he would glance at her apologetically. Sun-ae would not try to avoid his eyes, but just sat looking at whatever it was that she had been looking at, indifferent to whether Hyŏng-sik was looking at her or not. Then Hyŏng-sik would feel his happy mood broken, and Sŏn-hyŏng would start rummaging through a bookshelf. Sometimes Sun-ae would get up and leave, as Hyŏng-sik and Sŏn-hyŏng sat and watched her. Her posture was somewhat slouched, and there was something sad about her appearance from the back. Then Hyŏng-sik and Yŏng-ch'ae would look at each other and smile, though they did not know why.

Hyŏng-sik seemed to have completely cut his ties with the world. He resigned from school, students stopped visiting him, and what few friends he had no longer came to see him these days. Even U-sŏn seemed to be busy, and did not show up. Hyŏng-sik thought only of Sŏn-hyŏng and the United States, from the moment he awoke to the time he went to sleep. He did not feel the slightest bit lonely; on the contrary, he could not have been happier. All of his hopes were on Sŏn-hyŏng and the United States. Even though others gossiped that he had gone to a *kisaeng* house, and criticized him for having married for money, he thought such talk was ridiculous. Even if all the people in the world were to hate and sneer at him, if Sŏn-hyŏng loved and praised him, that was all that mattered. The day he returned from the United States, everyone would look up to him and respect him. A person without hope for the future tries to value the present the most; Hyŏng-sik, however, was very hopeful about his future, and the present was worthless to him. Teaching as an instructor at the Kyŏngsŏng School, loving his students, thinking that his life and work had meaning—all of this now seemed ridiculous to Hyŏng-sik. His past self, moreover, seemed worthless and foolish. His past life had been a provisional life; it seemed as though his life from here onwards would be his real life. There seemed to be only happiness in his future; misfortune seemed unlikely. His body seemed to have left the painful, chaotic world, and ascended to another world far above. The people he met on the street seemed to be pitiful people of a kind different from himself. His landlady, whom he had thought of as a friend before, now looked very pathetic, and suddenly seemed older and more bent with age. A new worry, however, presented itself to the unfortunate Hyŏng-sik.

Someone told Elder Kim that Hyŏng-sik was not of proper moral character.

"You cannot trust anyone," said Elder Kim one day to his wife, a displeased expression on his face.

"Why?"

"Hyŏng-sik is said to frequent a *kisaeng* house."

Since Elder Kim's wife had been a *kisaeng*, such words were painful to her; however, since she was now a lady, she thought she need not take offense at such a remark.

"What do you mean?" she exclaimed.

"Someone says that Hyŏng-sik was infatuated with a *kisaeng* named Kye Wŏr-hyang, who lives in Tabang-gol, and that he went to see her every night. He supposedly got into a fight with another man over her somewhere—at a Buddhist residence in T'apkol, or some such place—and he kicked the man and hit him. Not only that, Wŏr-hyang supposedly got tired of him, and ran away to P'yŏngyang, and Hyŏng-sik went after her. When I expressed disbelief, this person said that they knew exact dates, and had definite evidence." Elder Kim sighed. "I have been too careless in this matter."

His wife looked startled.

"Who said this?" she asked. Her heart ached to think of giving her daughter, whom she loved so much, to such a man. Judging from Hyŏng-sik's appearance and speech, though, Hyŏng-sik did not seem to be such a man.

"It must be someone trying to slander Hyŏng-sik," Mrs. Kim said.

"I thought that too at first. After hearing more, it seems to be certain. The days he is said to have gone to P'yŏngyang are the exact two days he did not come to our house. They say he has apparently been kicked out of the Kyŏngsŏng School."

"Oh no!"

Then Sŏn-hyŏng came into the room, and they stopped talking. Sŏn-hyŏng, however, had heard most of what they had said. Elder Kim and his wife did not discuss the matter further after that, but there was an unspeakable anxiety in their hearts. Sŏn-hyŏng too felt displeased after having heard the conversation. When she saw Hyŏng-sik, she did not feel like smiling, but rather had feelings of dislike. Though she still had affection for him, she began to dislike and doubt him. She began to have feelings of pain and suffering in her heart. Unaware of this, Hyŏng-sik was as cheerful as ever; Elder Kim and his family, however, began to speak less and smile less, and when they faced Hyŏng-sik, they felt a kind of displeasure, contempt, and annoyance. Hyŏng-sik gradually became aware of this change. Sun-ae watched them all with her sad-looking eyes.

96

Sŏn-hyong thought that Hyŏng-sik was too unqualified to be her partner. Her ideal husband was the following: first of all, his face was round, and he had white skin with a rosy, glowing complexion; he was articulate and cheerful; he was sleek and trim, any way you looked at him; his hands were soft and white and talented; and he had graduated from college. It would be difficult to find such a man from any family but a wealthy one. At first Sŏn-hyŏng wanted her husband to be the son of a pastor or church elder, but she eventually realized that pastors and church elders were not particularly noble positions after all. She had then decided that her ideal husband would be a man who was studying in the United States.

When she met Hyŏng-sik, she had indeed felt the joy that a young woman feels when she meets a man for the first time; however, she had not thought of him as her partner. She had thought Hyŏng-sik must be someone who belonged to a class several ranks beneath her own. For one thing, his face did not fit her idea of the ideal face. His face was longish, and he had prominent cheekbones, his cheeks were somewhat sunken, the corners of his eyes drooped somewhat, and, moreover, there were several wrinkles on his forehead, the traces of having lived in poverty for quite some time. His hands were too large, and his fingers were shapeless. He was not an ugly man, but he was hopelessly different from the ideal man she had longed for. There was an unmistakable air of poverty about Hyŏng-sik's manner, and a melancholy tendency to be unable to release himself completely. His personal background, moreover, and his occupational position as an instructor at the Kyŏngsŏng School, moreover, appeared too shabby for Sŏn-hyŏng's tastes. She had thus never thought of him with any affection, let alone love. If she had any positive feelings toward him, it would be that of pity. Hyŏng-sik seemed pitiful in her eyes. After studying English with him for several hours, and after having heard him speak, she realized he had a certain hidden dignity and strength. However, these qualities were not very important to an eighteen-year-old woman. She had even hoped that Hyŏng-sik and Sun-ae might get married to each other.

When she heard that she herself would be engaged to Hyŏng-sik, she felt both surprised and disappointed. She resented her father for trying to make a man like Hyŏng-sik her spouse, and was very unhappy. Her ideals seemed to have been shattered, and her status seemed to have suddenly been lowered. She knew, however, that she could not disobey her parents. She thought one word from her father could decide her entire life.

Sŏn-hyŏng therefore tried to pick out Hyŏng-sik's good points. She tried to revise his face in several ways. She raised the corners of his long eyes, pushed in his cheekbones, made his hands somewhat smaller, pushed in his long chin to make his face round, added the right amount of flesh to his cheeks and forehead, and added some pink color to his face. After she had made these revisions, his face gradually came to fit her tastes. Sometimes, however, his cheekbones jutted out again, his cheeks became even more sunken, and his eyes became very narrow, or even became big as a cow's eyes. When this happened, she would get angry, and stomp out Hyŏng-sik's face with her feet, and sit with her eyes closed. She could find no peace of mind then, however, and would start to revise Hyŏng-sik's face again.

Sometimes his face would turn out the way she wanted it to, and she would be looking at it and enjoying the sight, alone, when the real Hyŏng-sik would walk in the room with a joyful face, and ruin the face she had taken such effort to create. While she was studying, occasionally she would look at Hyŏng-sik and try the face that she had created on him. The face did not fit very well, though. While Hyŏng-sik was trying his best to teach English to his beloved future wife, Sŏn-hyŏng would be diligently changing his face. Sun-ae sat beside them and looked back and forth at Hyŏng-sik and Sŏn-hyŏng, trying to figure out what they were thinking about.

Then Sŏn-hyŏng stopped trying to revise Hyŏng-sik's face. She realized that it was a venture that would simply not succeed. She tried to acquire an affection for his face. Until then, she had been trying to change Hyŏng-sik's face to fit her heart, but now she tried to change her heart to fit Hyŏng-sik's face. She tried to force herself to think of Hyŏng-sik's face as beautiful. She tried to feel affection for his protruding cheekbones and the way the outer corners of his eyelids slanted downwards. She tried to think of his large hands and long fingers as manly. Then his appearance would seem either lovable indeed, or even more loathsome.

As Sŏn-hyŏng spent more time with Hyŏng-sik, though, and heard what he said, and as they came to understand each other's thoughts, Sŏn-hyŏng gradually became fond of Hyŏng-sik. She began to think his lips were beautiful, and that he was a very lovable person with a very nice personality. When she went to bed she would always draw an image of his face in her mind, and make changes to his face. She liked his lips best, and after drawing his lips she would look at them and smile to herself, and say to herself, "These lips alone are good enough." Sŏn-hyŏng loved Hyŏng-sik's lips. Sometimes Hyŏng-sik's entire face would become nothing but lips.

97

Hyŏng-sik himself did not think Sŏn-hyŏng would be attracted to his appearance. After getting engaged to Sŏn-hyŏng, Hyŏng-sik had examined his face in the mirror and thought about which parts Sŏn-hyŏng would like and which parts she would not like, and, like Sŏn-hyŏng, had made imaginary changes to his face. He did not know that Sŏn-hyŏng had rubbed out his face with her feet, though. Nevertheless, Hyŏng-sik felt confident about his moral character and his knowledge. He thought that Sŏn-hyŏng would be won over by the strength of his moral character. Sŏn-hyŏng was still a child. She could not be his friend, someone with whom he could talk. She could not yet appreciate his character. This was painful to Hyŏng-sik. He wondered why he did not have the kind of face or body that would intoxicate women, or the wealth, status and reputation that the world envies. He now wished that he had looks, wealth and status, though he had scorned them all his life. He imagined that he was the son of a wealthy family, and an elegant, handsome youth, and then put Sŏn-hyŏng before him. After having done that, his actual circumstances seemed so pitifully shabby that it made sweat run down his spine. Did Sŏn-hyŏng love him? Would she not despise him or feel sorry for him? With these thoughts, Hyŏng-sik did not feel like seeing her again. In marrying Sŏn-hyŏng would he not be marrying above his status? The man he imagined had money, social status and looks, but what did Hyŏng-sik have? Hyŏng-sik felt ashamed. "Moreover, I am going to study in the United States using my wife's parents' money," he thought, and felt even more ashamed. The world seemed to scorn him for being that pathetic.

He had thought that there was no one else in Korea as passionately motivated or with as much character and learning as himself. He had taken pride in having set the foundation for modern Korean civilization. Now however his pride had completely disappeared. Actually, it had not disappeared, but was simply not very important to Hyŏng-sik at the moment. He had to win Sŏn-hyŏng's love. This was his only objective. He might not win her love. This was his only sadness. It even seemed right to him to go to the United States not for the sake of Korean civilization, but for the sake of winning Sŏn-hyŏng's love. All of his arrogance and pride disappeared in the presence of love.

Hyŏng-sik could not live without Sŏn-hyŏng. If Sŏn-hyŏng left him, he would have nothing left to look forward to in the world. If Sŏn-hyŏng left him, he would kill Sŏn-hyŏng and himself with a knife. Fortunately, Sŏn-hyŏng was not someone who would disobey her father, or leave Hyŏng-sik because she did not love him. Hyŏng-sik thought, however, that it would be shameful to have to rely on the strength of morals and laws in order to make Sŏn-hyŏng accept his love. He thus tried to believe firmly that Sŏn-hyŏng loved him.

Hyŏng-sik could not find peace of mind, though, and he thought of testing Sŏn-hyŏng's love. First he would ask to hold hands, and then he would ask for a kiss. If she said yes, that would be a sign that she loved him. If she said no, that would be a sign that she did not. Hyŏng-sik remembered how U-sŏn had told him to be manly and lively, and he resolved to put that advice into practice that day. In the end, though, he could not carry it out.

Elder Kim and his wife's feelings towards Hyŏng-sik seemed to have changed lately. Sŏn-hyŏng's feelings seemed the same, but there seemed to be some kind of worry in her eyes. Hyŏng-sik sensed what was on their minds, but could not bring himself to speak first, and just worried to himself.

He was certain that there would be a day when their misunderstandings would be cleared up, since he had done nothing wrong. Thus he spent his days just teaching English, and would go home afterwards and read. One day Hyŏng-sik received a letter. It was from Kim Pyŏng-guk in Hwangju.

"As you know, there is no love between me and my wife. It has gotten worse these days. There is nothing wrong with my wife, nor is it because I am dissipated at heart. I have come to feel an abiding sorrow these days, and my wife cannot help me.

"I am searching for something, or rather, someone, and I think that someone is a person of the opposite sex. I feel so lonely that I will die if I do not find this person. Therefore, I have tried to force myself to love my wife. The more I try, though, the more distant we become.

"My younger sister has returned. I am always happy to see her. My sister understands how I feel, and has been very reassuring. I have tried to seek the spiritual companionship I cannot get from my wife, from my sister. And I have found that companionship. However, I have discovered another fact. That is, there is a limit to my sister's love. I cannot get by with just my sister's love. I thought I was only looking for spiritual companionship, but now I realize that is not so. I realize that what I am seeking is not a partial love that it is just spiritual or physical, but a love that involves my entire self, and is both spiritual and physical.

"A woman has come into my life. I feel unbearably drawn to her. I am suffering, caught between responsibility and love."

Such were the contents of the long letter.

98

Hyŏng-sik was shocked when he read Pyŏng-guk's letter. Pyŏng-guk had been one of the Korean students in Japan with the most integrity. He did not drink, and he did not go anywhere near women. He had very firm beliefs about marriage. If anyone said they did not love their wife and wanted to get divorced, Pyŏng-guk would be vehemently opposed. Pyŏng-guk had a Christian view of marriage. He thought that once a couple were married, they had a responsibility to love one another until death. When notions of free love and divorce became popular among Korean students in Japan, Pyŏng-guk had been a persuasive advocate of the sanctity of marriage. Now he was saying something different, though. Hyŏng-sik read the letter again. He read the part about how Pyŏng-guk tried to love his wife, and how the more he tried the more distant they became. Hyŏng-sik thought about how Pyŏng-guk had written about searching for someone—a woman—and how he said he was so lonely he would die if he did not find her. Pyŏng-guk said he was looking for a love that was not a partial love that was only spiritual or physical, but a love that would involve his entire self. Hyŏng-sik could visualize Pyŏng-guk's anguish, and he had much sympathy for him. Hyŏng-sik thought of his own situation. Did Sŏn-hyŏng indeed love Hyŏng-sik? Did she love him with a love that was not a partial love but that involved her entire self? No matter how he looked at it, it seemed as though Sŏn-hyŏng's feelings towards him were cold. Was this engagement based on love after all?

Sŏn-hyŏng had answered "yes" that evening. However, what did that "yes" mean? Did it mean that she loved Hyŏng-sik? Or did it mean that her parents were ordering her to marry him and she was doing what her parents told her to do? Wasn't Sŏn-hyŏng's situation with Hyŏng-sik the same as Pyŏng-guk's situation with his wife? The thought was unpleasant to Hyŏng-sik. If Sŏn-hyŏng had answered "yes" only because she could not bring herself to disobey her parents, and if she did not love Hyŏng-sik, then poor Sŏn-hyŏng was sacrificing herself. Sŏn-hyŏng would inevitably spend her life in misery with a husband she did not love, and Hyŏng-sik himself would definitely not be happy. Was it not inhumane to satisfy one's desires at the cost of sacrificing someone else's life? Hyŏng-sik decided to ask Sŏn-hyŏng about her feelings and intentions.

The next day Sun-ae had a headache and had to stay in bed, so Hyŏng-sik had a chance to sit alone with Sŏn-hyŏng. After teaching Sŏn-hyŏng English, Hyŏng-sik summoned up his strength and said, "Sŏn-hyŏng, there is something I would like to ask you." Hyŏng-sik lowered his head, but Sŏn-hyŏng lifted hers and looked at his parted hair. She seemed to be full of misgivings.

"What is it?" she asked, and blushed.

"You must answer straightforwardly what I ask you. It is only right. What can lovers keep from one another?" Hyŏng-sik's heart pounded. It was as though a life-or-death verdict would be pronounced at any moment. Sŏn-hyŏng was frightened by what Hyŏng-sik said. She had never been asked a question of such serious responsibility. "All right," she said simply, not sure how to answer. She said it the same way she had said "yes" the day they got engaged. Hyŏng-sik found it difficult to say anything more. He was afraid of what her answer might be. However, he was even more afraid of not knowing Sŏn-hyŏng's true feelings, and living in doubt. He thought of how U-sŏn had told him to be manly, and gathered his strength and said in a trembling voice, "Do you love me?" He looked directly into Sŏn-hyŏng's eyes. Sŏn-hyŏng's eyes grew wide at the unexpected question. She felt even more frightened. She had never actually asked herself whether or not she loved Hyŏng-sik. She did not even know that she had the right to think about such things. She was already Hyŏng-sik's wife. Therefore, it was her duty to care for him. She tried to feel affection for Hyŏng-sik, but she had never in her dreams thought about what she might do if she could not feel affection for him. Hyŏng-sik's question caught her completely by surprise. She stared at Hyŏng-sik.

"Why are you asking me such a question?"

"I have to ask. We should have asked one another about this before getting engaged, but the order got reversed. I have to ask you, though, even if it's late."

Sŏn-hyŏng sat quietly.

"Please tell me clearly whether or not you love me."

Sŏn-hyŏng thought there was no need to ask or answer such a question. Were they not a couple already? What was the use of asking?

"Why are you asking me such a question?" she said, laughing.

"The sooner I know, the better for both of us. Before the marriage is finalized."

"What? What do you mean 'before the marriage is finalized'?"

"We are only engaged. We are not married yet. We still have time to correct any mistakes."

These words frightened Sŏn-hyŏng even more, and made her hair stand on end. She could not understand what Hyŏng-sik was talking about.

"You mean break off the engagement?" she asked. Inexplicable tears rose in her eyes. When Hyŏng-sik saw her tears, he regretted having spoken.

"Yes," he said.

"Why?"

"If you do not love me, then . . . "

"Even though we are already engaged?"

"An engagement is not that important."

"Then what is?"

"Love is."

"What if we aren't in love?"

"Then the engagement is null."

99

Sŏn-hyŏng thought for a few moments. "How do *you* feel?" she asked.

"I love you. I love you more than my own life."

"Isn't that enough?"

"No. You have to love me too."

"Would a wife not love her husband?"

Hyŏng-sik looked intently at Sŏn-hyŏng. She lowered her head.

"Whose words are those?" Hyŏng-sik asked.

"Aren't those words in the Bible?" Sŏn-hyŏng replied.

"But what do *you* think, Sŏn-hyŏng? What are your true feelings?"

"I agree with the Bible."

"That a wife loves her husband because she is a wife? Or that one becomes a wife because one loves?" Sŏn-hyŏng heard these words too for the first time. "Aren't they the same?" she said, bewildered. Hyŏng-sik was taken aback. How could they be the same thing? This woman does not yet know how to think about such matters, he thought to himself. "Please answer me yes or no. Do you love me?" There was a pleading tone to his voice. He thought he would die if she said no. Her tightly pursed lips seemed like those of a judge who was deciding whether or not Hyŏng-sik would live or die. Sŏn-hyŏng felt dazed and could not think any more. She just felt frightened when she looked at Hyŏng-sik's miserable face. That was why she simply answered, "Yes." Hyŏng-sik was going to ask one more time, but stopped himself, afraid that her answer might change to "no." He suddenly clasped Sŏn-hyŏng's hand. Her hand was soft and warm, and seemed to melt in his own. She sat still. He squeezed her hand. He waited for her to squeeze back, but she just hung her head and stayed still. Hyŏng-sik quickly put her hand down, and went home. He himself was not sure why he left so suddenly. Sŏn-hyŏng did not say goodbye, but just watched him leave.

Sŏn-hyŏng leaned on her desk, closed her eyes and thought. She remembered clearly what Hyŏng-sik had said. She did not know what any of it meant, though. How could he have asked her whether or not she loved him? Didn't he feel embarrassed? He did not seem like a decent man if he could say such things without embarrassment. Was it not something he said to *kisaeng* when he went to *kisaeng* houses? She felt as though Hyŏng-sik had insulted her. The word "love" seemed very sacred when speaking of love for God, or love for one's countrymen, or how husband and wife should love one another; but it seemed vulgar and undignified to ask someone to love oneself, or to tell someone that one loved them. According to what Sŏn-hyŏng had heard at home and at church, all other kinds of love were holy and clean, but the love between young men and women was impure and sinful. Sŏn-hyŏng did not know that the notion of love, and the very word "love" originated in love between the sexes. Hyŏng-sik's words were thus very unpleasant to her. Sŏn-hyŏng thought her husband ought to be a very clean, dignified man. Hyŏng-sik seemed like a sinner, saying such things without shame. He used the same behavior he uses with vile *kisaeng*, towards me, she thought, and grimaced. She looked at her hand, the one that Hyŏng-sik had held. She thought of how her hand had been buried in his big hand, and how he had squeezed her hand. She wrung her hand three or four times as though shaking off something, and wiped it with her skirt.

When she thought about it again, though, she did not completely dislike what he had said about loving her, and how he had held her hand. Moreover, when Hyŏng-sik had squeezed her hand, she had even been so happy that her entire body seemed to tremble. She held her hand out again and looked at it, then put it to her lips, smiling.

Do I love Hyŏng-sik, she wondered. She thought of how he had asked her whether she thought a wife loves her husband because she is a wife, or becomes a wife because she loves her husband. He had said that the engagement would be null if they were not in love. What about her parents' orders, though? If she did not love Hyŏng-sik, could she tell her parents that she was refusing this marriage that her parents had arranged because she was not in love? Would it be right to do that? No. Marriage was something sacred that God had ordained, and human beings could not tamper with it at will. What Hyŏng-sik had said was wrong. His words were impure. She was Hyŏng-sik's wife, though. She was his wife, and no human being could do anything about it.

She stood up and paced about the room. Unable to settle her thoughts, she leaned against her desk and prayed.

"Dear Lord. Please forgive your sinful daughter, and show me the way. Keep me from temptation." She paused a moment, then added, "Please help me to love my husband with all my heart."

100

One day Pyŏng-uk sat plucking the strings of the violin that lay on the floor beside her, and read the *Komun Chinbo* that she had studied with Yŏng-ch'ae. Just then her brother Pyŏng-guk came home, and sat down at the threshold of Pyŏng-uk's room, fanning himself with a panama hat.

"Looks like you're crazy about Chinese poetry these days. You should quit music and study Chinese poetry," he said and laughed.

"Why? I can play music with my hands like this, and read poetry with my eyes." Pyŏng-uk plucked the violin strings, and recited poetry aloud, swaying back and forth the way children do when reading out loud.[144]

Pyŏng-guk sat laughing as he watched Pyŏng-uk sway back and forth. "Where is our guest?"

Pyŏng-uk looked up and laughed. "You mean we have a guest? Where from?"

Pyŏng-guk knew that his sister was teasing him, but nevertheless said in earnest, "You know. Her."

"Whom do you mean by 'her'?"

Pyŏng-uk said this because she knew her brother was suffering over Yŏng-ch'ae.

---

144. A traditional way of reading in a Confucian Academy was to read aloud, while swaying back and forth.

"Forget it," said Pyŏng-guk, and turned around abruptly. He could not take any more, and stood up to leave. Pyŏng-uk ran out and grabbed his sleeve.

"Please come in, older brother. I am sorry."

"I don't want to. I have to go somewhere," he said, and pulled his sleeve loose.

Pyŏng-uk laughed. "I have something to ask you. Sit down," she said. Pyŏng-guk sat down again. Pyŏng-uk caught a fly that was sitting on Pyŏng-guk's back with her hand.

"Is something worrying you, older brother?" she asked. She stopped smiling and looked at her brother's face from the side. Pyŏng-guk turned his head and looked at Pyŏng-uk as if surprised.

"No, why? Do I look worried?"

"Yes. You look like something is bothering you." She smiled as though she knew what it was that was bothering him.

Pyŏng-guk scratched his head. "I want to start a silkworm factory, but father will not let me. I just got back from business about that. You play the violin. I have to make money."

Pyŏng-uk stepped back and looked away. "Is that what you have been worried about?" she said scornfully. "That I spend too much money? If that's the case, then I will quit. I will make money with my own two hands. Who says a woman cannot feed herself?"

Pyŏng-guk laughed. "I am sorry, sister," he said. "There is nothing to get upset about. You were teasing me, so I teased you."

Pyŏng-uk went over to Pyong-guk again. "I was joking," she said. She sat down, shrugged eagerly and lowered her voice. "Older brother, I am taking Yŏng-ch'ae with me to Tokyo. Don't you think it's a good idea?"

"Do whatever you want," Pyŏng-guk said. He pretended to be indifferent, but his heart was already aflutter. "Why are you telling me this?"

"Help me. I don't want to stay at home, and if I take Yŏng-ch'ae to Tokyo, she will have to make preparations in order to get into school. Help us so that we can leave right away." She peered at Pyŏng-guk. Pyŏng-guk understood his sister's intensions. He appreciated his sister's affection even more. He was not sure about what to do, though.

"There is still a month until school starts. Why are you in such a hurry?"

Pyŏng-uk looked into her older brother's eyes for awhile, then said gently, "We have to go. Don't you think so?" Pyŏng-guk felt his heart twinge at these words. It was true. He would suffer more if Yŏng-ch'ae stayed near him, and it might indeed be dangerous. He too had thought of this. He knew he ought to leave for travel somewhere, or send Yŏng-ch'ae away. He felt drawn to her, though, and could not put his thoughts into action. Pyŏng-guk thought for awhile, his head lowered.

"Yes, you are right. You must leave." He sighed. Pyǒng-uk rubbed her brother's shoulder.

"Yǒng-ch'ae loves you too. Think of her as a sister, and please love her always. I too will think of her as a sister, and stay with her always. We will go to Tokyo and stay in the same house, and cook our meals and study. It is good to help those in need, isn't it? With further study, Yǒng-ch'ae too will become a wonderful worker."

Pyǒng-guk listened to his sister with his head lowered, struck his knee with his hand, and stretched himself.

"I agree with you. What could I ever hide from you. I have suffered terribly all this time." He thought for a moment, then said with new resolve, "When will you leave?"

"We will leave whenever you tell us to leave."

"Then leave on a day train the day after tomorrow. I will get you travel money tomorrow."

Yǒng-ch'ae came running through the front door just then. When she saw Pyǒng-guk, she nodded her head in greeting. Pyǒng-guk hurriedly stood up and returned her greeting. Yǒng-ch'ae gave Pyǒng-uk some irises that she had picked on the mountain behind the house. Pyǒng-uk took the flowers and sorted through them, then divided them into two bunches.

"Put these on brother's desk. And these are for us."

101

They were going to leave the day after tomorrow, but Pyǒng-uk's mother was opposed, and so they left a week later.

"We miss you all year long, and now that we have seen you again, you are leaving after less than a month? You do not want to see me! Do not leave until you have eaten all of the honeydew and watermelons that I planted for you in the cotton field."

Pyǒng-uk could not oppose her mother's wishes.

"What do you think of my mother's love?" Pyǒng-uk said to Yǒng-ch'ae, tears welling in her eyes. Yǒng-ch'ae was reminded of her father, and wiped her eyes with her sleeve.

Every day after lunch, Pyǒng-uk and Yǒng-ch'ae would go to the family's cotton fields, which were on a sunny plot of land less than five *li* from Pyǒng-uk's house. They would pick honeydew and watermelons, and sit on a corner of the field and eat with gusto, while talking about their dreams for the future. Sometimes Pyǒng-uk's wife would go out to the field with them, and the three of them would sit together and talk, unaware of the sun setting. The field was surrounded by woods, so there were no passersby and it was very quiet. One day, Pyǒng-guk's wife said, "Father said not to plant honeydew or watermelons because they would be harmful to the cotton plants, but mother insisted, and mother and I planted these ourselves."

Pyŏng-uk walked through the field, in the furrows between the ridges of earth that separated various patches, and examined the honeydew and melons that dangled beautifully from the vines. She picked a spotted honeydew melon and emerged from the patch. "How did this one get so spotted? Why are some of them black, some white, and some spotted? I have never seen two that are the same." "What fun would it be if they were all the same? People are that way too," said Yŏng-ch'ae, smiling. "In any case, nature is very interesting. All kinds of grasses, trees and flowers grow from the same soil." "This too is soil transformed into a melon," Pyŏng-uk said, sniffing a honeydew melon she had plucked. "They say that people were created from earth,' said Pyŏng-guk's wife. "That's right," said Pyŏng-uk. "All creation came from the soil. The earth is the mother of all creation. It gave birth to all things, and embraces them. Rice, water, this honeydew melon: these are mother's milk." Pyŏng-uk caressed the honeydew melon lovingly and looked around in all directions. "Isn't it wonderful?" she said. "The sky is clear, the sun is warm, the mountains are green, the waters of a stream are flowing nearby, and those grasses are growing so vigorously. And we are sitting in the midst of all of this. It's wonderful!" Pyŏng-uk laughed and danced about.

Yŏng-ch'ae picked up a round stone, and tossed it up and down in her hands. "Maybe it is because I grew up in the countryside, but I like the countryside, where there are grass and trees," she said. "Living in a city like Seoul or P'yŏngyang is like being in prison."

"Absolutely. When one is in the midst of the vastness of nature, as we are now, one's mind and body feel free and relaxed. In the city, though, the dust! The stinking air! Even one's mind begins to stink." Pyŏng-uk grimaced as though at a bad odor. "Here, though, there are wide open spaces, and it is clean." She breathed deeply. The air was indeed clear. The intoxicating scent was carried on gusts of warm air.

After talking and having a good time, they went home, each carrying a watermelon. The watermelons were for Pyŏng-uk's parents and the other family members at home.

Pyŏng-uk cut the top off of a watermelon, put some honey in the melon, and gave it to her grandmother, who was lying on the warmest part of the floor. Her grandmother ate with pleasure, a childlike smile on her withered cheeks. Pyŏng-uk watched happily, occasionally helping her grandmother scoop out the melon with a spoon. When Pyŏng-uk's grandmother had eaten almost all of the melon, she gazed at Pyŏng-uk, smiling.

"How you have grown. Why does a big girl like you not want to get married?" She pulled herself closer to Pyŏng-uk, and patted her on the back. "After you leave, I may never see you again," she said, and sighed.

"What are you talking about, grandmother? You will have no problem living to be ninety," Pyŏng-uk said in a loud voice so that her grandmother could hear her. "Hm," said Pyŏng-uk's grandmother, acknowledging Pyŏng-uk's remark. "Ninety?" Pyŏng-uk's grandmother said. She was seventy-three now; there were still seventeen years before she would be ninety. Will I live that long? I hope so, she seemed to be thinking. Now and then, she would tell her granddaughter to play the violin. Pyŏng-uk would do as she was told. "You do the listening," Pyŏng-uk would say to Yŏng-ch'ae, who sat next to her. "Grandmother listens with her eyes." Pyŏng-uk and Yŏng-ch'ae would laugh. Pyŏng-uk's grandmother would laugh too, even though she did not know what they were laughing about. Pyŏng-uk would lower her head and start to play the violin, moving her bow over the strings. After watching intently, within less than five minutes, Pyŏng-uk's grandmother would always start to doze off. Then the two young women would look at one another and laugh, and go on having fun just amongst themselves.

102

Pyŏng-uk's mother prepared various delicious things to eat on the occasion of her daughter's departure for a faraway destination. She cooked rice, made rice cakes and slaughtered a chicken. Then she sat quietly and watched her daughter eat. Pyŏng-uk's father bought some ribs of beef, and Pyŏng-guk went into the city and bought some cakes, tangerines and soft drinks. Pyŏng-uk and Yŏng-ch'ae went to the cotton field, and picked Korean honeydew melons and watermelons. Then they put either sugar or honey in the melons, and let them sit overnight before serving them. Some of the melons they chilled in well water. Yŏng-ch'ae offered some watermelon that she had slathered with honey, to Pyŏng-uk's father. He took the melon as if somewhat surprised, and dug in with a spoon, eating with relish.

"Thank you," he said. Yŏng-ch'ae thought again about her late father.

Pyŏng-uk gave a watermelon to her brother, and said jokingly, "Yŏng-ch'ae prepared this especially for you." Standing next to Pyŏng-uk, Yŏng-ch'ae blushed.

Pyŏng-guk's wife was genuinely sorry that the two young women were leaving. Moreover, she was sad to be parting with her new friend Yŏng-ch'ae after less than a month. She wished that she too could fly away to Seoul or Tokyo like the other two young women, but she knew that she could not. She did envy them, but she was also cultivated enough to know how to be content with her situation in life. Those two young women were meant to live their lives, and she was meant to live her life. She was resigned to this fact, and did not trouble herself over it that much.

A week seemed as though it might be plenty of time, but it passed as quickly as a dream, with their busy festivities. When the day came for them to leave, the two young women packed their things and got dressed. Pyŏng-uk's family did not want them to leave, and Pyŏng-uk and Yŏng-ch'ae did not want to go. There was an unspeakable loneliness and sorrow in a corner of everyone's hearts. Pyŏng-uk's grandmother lay on the warmest part of the floor. Pyŏng-uk's father sat smoking his pipe, pretending he did not know they were leaving. Pyŏng-uk's mother wrapped red bean paste and salted, dried croaker. Pyŏng-uk's sister-in-law helped Pyŏng-uk's mother without saying a word. Pyŏng-guk had put on a panama hat, which he wore pushed back on his head, and a *turumagi*, and was busily helping to tie up bundles of luggage. Pyŏng-uk walked about to and fro laughing cheerfully. Yŏng-ch'ae stood and watched quietly.

Pyŏng-uk and Yŏng-ch'ae bowed deeply in farewell to Pyŏng-uk's grandmother, father, and mother each, in that order. "I will probably never see you again," her grandmother said. Leaning on Pyŏng-guk, she walked as far as the front door to see them off, tears in her weak eyes. Pyŏng-uk's father merely acknowledged their bows, and said nothing.

"Be good students," Pyŏng-guk's mother said. "Come home for winter break. You come next year too, Yŏng-ch'ae," she said, smoothing out the back of Yŏng-ch'ae's Korean blouse.

It was about one o'clock in the afternoon by the time they had finished exchanging farewells with people in the neighborhood, and reached the mouth of the village. The August sunshine seemed to be pouring fire over them.

The group walked along, trying to say all the loving words they wanted to say to each other. Sometimes they would gather in a group; sometimes they walked in pairs, a dozen steps apart from the others, or one of them would walk alone and stop to pick grasses on the side of the road, and look behind them. Pyŏng-uk and her mother would often form one pair, and Pyŏng-guk's wife and Yŏng-ch'ae another. Pyŏng-guk and his father would walk alone, silently. From time to time, the young man who was carrying the luggage would stop and stand, bracing the weight of the *chige*[145] on his back, and wait for the group. Then he would run ahead, anxious to get to the station and put the frame down and rest. A cart without any passengers and a rickshaw passed them from the opposite direction and from behind them on the road, clattering as they passed. The group's faces grew red in the heat, and drops of sweat fell from their foreheads. The men fanned themselves with fans, and the women wiped the sweat from their faces with cloths.

They had exhausted their seemingly endless supply of things to talk about, and now just walked along the sturdy-looking, newly paved road,

145. A *chige* is an A-shaped carrying rack used to carry loads on one's back.

looking at the sun. The "Song of Sorrow" and "Song of Debauchery" drifted sleepily from a shed in a melon field, then died away when the group passed.

A monk's head, a head wearing the horsehair hat of a government official, a head wrapped in a cloth, and the large head of an unmarried man who wore his hair in a long braid, emerged abruptly from the shed and mumbled amongst themselves. Laughter was heard once the group had passed. The group just walked silently towards the station.

Yŏng-ch'ae looked at the fields of newly sprouting millet and thought about the events of the past month. Her body had been still, but there had been much change and commotion in her mind. One could say she was a new person since she had changed so much. She had been on her way to commit suicide and had chanced to meet Pyŏng-uk. She had once again tasted the joys of family life for the first time in eight years, at Pyŏng-uk's home. She had realized that there was a wide, free, joyful world beyond the prisonlike world in which she had suffered until then. She had felt a burning passion for Pyŏng-guk. And now she was going to Tokyo to study. It seemed as though her destiny were unexpectedly changing. It was so wondrous that she smiled to herself.

Meanwhile, the group had reached the train station and took over one of the benches in the waiting room. In the last twenty minutes they had left, they tried to finish saying whatever had been left unsaid.

103

Pyŏng-uk and Yŏng-ch'ae got on the train, and looked out the train windows at the group that was sending them off. Pyŏng-guk had to go to Sariwŏn on business, and got on the train with them, but he just sat in his seat and did not bother to look outside since he would be returning home that evening. Pyŏng-uk's mother stood outside the window.

"Take care!" she said twice. "Be sure to write home twice a month!" she said repeatedly. Pyŏng-guk's wife stood next to her mother-in-law, and looked at Pyŏng-uk and Yŏng-ch'ae by turns. Her small face, with its distinct features and fresh, clear complexion, was flushed from the heat, and looked beautiful. A bell rang, and the conductor's whistle was heard.

Pyŏng-guk's wife pressed Yŏng-ch'ae's hand where it was on the edge of the train window, and said, "Please write to me when you get there." There were tears in her eyes, and tears in Yŏng-ch'ae's eyes too as she looked at Pyŏng-guk's wife. Military gendarmes kept glancing at them. As soon as the voice of a youth selling *bentō*[146] lunches faded away, the train's engine started up, and the train began to move.

---

146. The text uses the Japanese word *bentō*, transliterating the word in Korean as *bentto*. The Japanese word *bentō* means a box lunch.

"Take care!" Pyŏng-uk's mother said again and blinked. Pyŏng-uk and Yŏng-ch'ae put their heads out the window, and waved their handkerchiefs. Pyŏng-uk's mother waved a handkerchief too, but Pyŏng-guk's wife just stood still watching them. Pyŏng-uk's father lifted his arm and waved, then turned around and left the station. There was a creaking noise, and the train began to race away. Then the figures at the train station could no longer be seen. Pyŏng-uk and Yŏng-ch'ae nevertheless waved their handkerchiefs two more times, then sat down in their seats. Neither of them spoke for some time. As the train moved faster, a cool breeze blew into the train car. Pyŏng-guk sat at an angle, on a row of seats across from them, and looked over at them as he fanned himself. In the train car was an old Westerner who seemed to be a missionary, a fat official who wore two bands of gold trim, and three people in Japanese clothing. They were all looking at these second-class passengers dressed in white clothing, as though they thought them strange.

Pyŏng-guk leaned forward so that his sister could hear him, and said, "Thanks to you, I am riding second class for the first time." He laughed.

"If you are so envious of second class, take the second-class train on your way back," said Pyŏng-uk and laughed.

"Even third class is wasted on good-for-nothing people like me who do no work. How could I go second class? I would feel so guilty."

"Then why did you buy us second-class tickets? You should have just put us on a baggage train." Pyŏng-uk pretended to be angry. Yŏng-ch'ae thought it was funny, and lowered her head to hide her face.

After joking with Pyŏng-uk, as though they were children quarreling, Pyŏng-guk said, "Will you come back to Korea next year, Yŏng-ch'ae?"

"I don't know."

"Come home with me! Or should I come home alone? Sisters should go around together!" Pyŏng-uk looked at Yŏng-ch'ae, then looked at Pyŏngguk.

"I will come if Pyŏng-uk says she will bring me," Yŏng-ch'ae said and smiled.

"Yŏng-ch'ae and I will come home together next year, Pyŏng-guk," Pyŏng-uk said, as though in reply to Yŏng-ch'ae's question, and trying to persuade Pyŏng-guk. She writhed and pretended to throw a tantrum.

"Then please come back with Pyŏng-uk. Since you have no home, please think of our home as yours."

"Thank you," said Yŏng-ch'ae and looked down.

The train came to a stop even as they were speaking.

A porter's voice could be heard calling out the name of the station. "Shariin! Shariin!"[147]

147. "Shariin" is the Japanese pronunciation of the Korean place name Sariwŏn.

"Good-bye!" Pyŏng-guk said, doffing his hat and running to get off the train. After he had gotten off, he went and stood beneath the window where Pyŏng-uk and Yŏng-ch'ae were sitting. The two young women looked out. After several people had hurriedly gotten off and on the train, the conductor's whistle could be heard again. The train began to move. Pyŏng-guk lifted his hat. Pyŏng-uk and Yŏng-ch'ae waved their hands out the window, and lowered their heads. Pyŏng-guk watched their arms and heads grow smaller into the distance, and Pyŏng-uk and Yŏng-ch'ae watched Pyŏng-guk too grow smaller as he waved his hat at them.

Yŏng-ch'ae began to feel suffocated with anxiety and frustration. She became dazed. Pyŏng-uk glanced at Yŏng-ch'ae's face.

"Remember how you cried when you got a piece of soot in your eye?" she said, trying to brighten Yŏng-ch'ae's spirits. Pyŏng-uk laughed. Yŏng-ch'ae laughed too.

"Did it really hurt when the soot got in your eye?"

"I wasn't crying because it hurt. I was crying because I was angry." Yŏng-ch'ae closed her eyes, thinking about that time, then opened them again and laughed.

"You looked so pretty when you were crying. If I were a man, I would have been quite taken with you."

"Oh, is that all you talk about?" Yŏng-ch'ae slapped Pyŏng-uk on the knee.

"Let's stop by in Seoul."

"I don't want to. What if someone sees us?"

"Everyone in Seoul thinks you're dead. Even Yi Hyŏng-sik, or whatever his name is."

"You're probably right. I had in fact died."

"Who? You? Why?"

"Wasn't I dead then? When you washed my face for me."

"Then you were resurrected."

"Yes, I was resurrected. I would be dead if not for you. My body would have decayed by now."

"You think your flesh would have stayed intact long enough to decay?"

"Yes, why not?"

"The fish would have eaten your flesh."

"How could the fish eat something that big?" Yŏng-ch'ae covered her mouth with her hand and laughed.

"What did you think when you first saw me?"

"I wondered who this Japanese woman was who spoke Korean so well and was so kind."

"And?"

"I thought you were a very vivacious woman."

"Do you know what it was you ate then?"

"No. I did not know how to eat it, so I watched you."

"I knew it. It was a Western type of food called a sandwich. It's very delicious, isn't it?"

"Yes," Yŏng-ch'ae said, nodding her head. She pronounced the word "sandwich" carefully, trying to memorize it.

104

The train arrived at Namdaemun. It was not yet completely dark outside, but electric lights were twinkling in all directions. The sounds of the city—the train, the rickshaws—together with that of wooden shoes clattering on the wide station platform, were very unsettling to the ears of the two young women, who had been in the midst of quiet nature until then. The noises of the city were those of civilization. A nation prospered the louder those noises were. The sounds of wagon wheels, and steam and electric-powered engines combined to give rise to civilization in all its brilliance. Modern civilization was a civilization of noise. There was not yet enough noise in Seoul. It ought to be so noisy in Seoul that people could not hear one another speak if they stood on Chongno in the vicinity of Namdaemun. How pitiful, though. The three hundred thousand people who wore white clothes[148] and lived in Seoul did not know the meaning of this noise. Nor did they care about the noise. It was necessary, however, that they learn to appreciate this noise, and rejoice, and contribute to this noise with their own hands. How many of those who were hurrying over the platform understood the meaning of their busy activity? How many of them knew why so many of those electric lights were lit, and why telegraph machines and telephone equipment made such a cacophony day and night, and why those monstrous trains and electric cars were always running. How many people understood the significance of all of that?

In the midst of all this commotion, Yŏng-ch'ae sat with her head lowered, afraid that someone might see her face in the crowd. Pyŏng-uk went down to the platform and walked around, hoping that she might chance to see friends from her school. She did not see anyone she knew, though, and was getting back on the train when someone slapped her on the shoulder.

"Pyŏng-uk, is that you?"

Pyŏng-uk turned around in surprise, and saw a friend from school who was two years her junior.

"How long has it been?"

"Where are you going?"

"I am on my way to Tokyo."

---

148. Koreans traditionally wore white clothing.

"Already. And you weren't going to stop by and visit me? How heartless." The woman turned away from Pyŏng-uk, then said, "Anyway, you must get off the train. Let's go to my house."

"No thanks. I'm traveling with a friend. Did you come to see someone off?"

"Yes, don't you know?"

"What?"

"I can't believe you don't know. You know Sŏn-hyŏng, right? Sŏn-hyŏng is leaving for the United States today."

"Sŏn-hyŏng is going to the United States?" Pyŏng-uk was surprised. The student pointed to where people were standing gathered around a second-class car. "She is on that train. She got married, and husband and wife are going to the United States to study. Everyone is doing so well, going to the United States and Japan. I am the only one who is rotting away!"

Pyŏng-uk followed the student to Sŏn-hyŏng's car, but there were so many people there that she could not get very close. Sŏn-hyŏng was dressed in a white suit and her head was bare. She was standing beneath one of the train windows and replying to the greetings of those who had come to see her off. Beneath the next window stood a young man in a suit, nodding his head and exchanging greetings. The crowd of well-wishers stood in two lines, women on one side and men on the other. The men were all of a class in Seoul that professed itself to be enlightened. Pyŏng-uk stood watching for awhile, then went to her own train car, which was right behind Sŏn-hyŏng's car, to try and go see Sŏn-hyŏng. Yŏng-ch'ae still sat with her head lowered. Most of the people who had gotten on board earlier got off, and new passengers got on until the car was practically full. Some of the passengers took their coat or jacket off, and hung it up; others went to a window to bid their farewells; some passengers already sat reading a newspaper. Pyŏng-uk and Yŏng-ch'ae were the only ones wearing white clothes.

Pyŏng-uk sat down, looked around the car, then said to Yŏng-ch'ae, "Why were you sitting with your head down like that?"

"When I heard the name Namdaemun, my thoughts became strangely confused. I wish the train would leave soon." Just then the bell rang. Farewells rang out like a burst of rain. "*Sayōnara, gokigenyō!*"[149] Then the train began to move.

"Long live Yi Hyŏng-sik!" Pyŏng-uk and Yŏng-ch'ae were startled, and listened attentively.

"Long live Yi Hyŏng-sik!" The man who had said these words could be glimpsed outside Pyŏng-uk and Yŏng-ch'ae's window. He was wearing a long Korean overcoat of ramie, and a panama hat. Pyŏng-uk guessed that the

---

149. The words *sayōnara* and *gokigenyō*, which are farewell greetings in Japanese, are transliterated in the text in Korean.

man who had been standing beside Sŏn-hyŏng was Hyŏng-sik, and that Hyŏng-sik was Sŏn-hyŏng's husband. She said nothing, though.
Yŏng-ch'ae felt her heart leap when she heard the name Hyŏng-sik. She had tried to forget him until then, but when she realized that he was on the same train, tears fell from her eyes for reasons she could not explain.
Pyŏng-uk squeezed Yŏng-ch'ae's hand. "Don't cry," she said. "Why are you crying?"
"I don't know." Yŏng-ch'ae wiped her tears away, and tried to smile.
After they had passed Yongsan, Pyŏng-uk went to see Sŏn-hyŏng. Sŏn-hyŏng took Pyŏng-uk's hand in hers.
"What a surprise to see you!"
"I am on my way to Tokyo. I hear you are going to the United States."
"Yes, I wanted to write to you, but I didn't know whether you were in Tokyo, or somewhere else."
"I happened to see Kyŏng-ae at Namdaemun, and that is how I found out that you were on this train." Pyŏng-uk greeted the gentleman who sat across from her. He greeted her in return and offered her a seat. She inspected Hyŏng-sik whenever she could, wondering what kind of man he was that Yŏng-ch'ae had saved herself for him for over a decade.

105
Yŏng-ch'ae sat alone and thought. First of all, she wondered where Hyŏng-sik was going. He seemed to be going somewhere far away since someone had said, "Long live Hyŏng-sik!" I know that he is on this train, but he probably does not know that I am here, she thought. Memories of the past seven or eight years passed like a motion picture. Fortunate people do not think much about the past, but people with a sad past take every chance to look back and think about their past. Yŏng-ch'ae must have looked back on her sad past hundreds of times. She had looked back on it so often that it now had an order and plot like a novel, and if she pulled at the end of one thread, the entire story would unravel before her eyes. Eight years had seemed but a day as she longed for and cherished Hyŏng-sik. Finally, she had even tried to take her own life because of Hyŏng-sik. When she thought of this, the memory of Hyŏng-sik was renewed, and her affections for him grew. I want to see him again, she thought. The more she thought about it, the more she wanted to see him. He would be happy to see her, since he thought she was dead. It seemed that she would not find peace of mind until she had seen him and said all of the words she had kept in her heart. Why didn't I go to him back then and openly tell him that I had been thinking of him all that time? she thought. Why didn't I ask him whether or not he loved me? If I see him again, I will ask him without hesitation, she thought.

She wanted to run to his car right then and there. Strong flames of emotion rose in her heart. I should discuss this with Pyŏng-uk first, she thought, and held back her feelings.

Just then the train arrived at Suwŏn Station. It was dark outside. Pyŏng-uk came into the car bringing Sŏn-hyŏng with her, and sat her down beside her. "Yŏng-ch'ae, this is Kim Sŏn-hyŏng. She is a classmate of mine. She is on her way to the United States." Pyŏng-uk turned to Sŏn-hyŏng. "This is Pak Yŏng-ch'ae. She is my younger sister," she said. After being introduced, Sŏn-hyŏng and Yŏng-ch'ae nodded to one another. Sŏn-hyŏng wondered how Yŏng-ch'ae could be Pyŏng-uk's sister. Pyŏng-uk looked back and forth at Yŏng-ch'ae and Sŏn-hyŏng, and compared the two young women's faces and destinies. Yŏng-ch'ae did not know about Sŏn-hyŏng's relationship with Hyŏng-sik, and Sŏn-hyŏng of course had no way of knowing that Yŏng-ch'ae had saved herself for Hyŏng-sik for eight years, and finally had tried to give up her life for him. Sŏn-hyŏng had only heard that Hyŏng-sik had had sordid relations with a woman named Kye Wŏr-hyang; she did not know that Pak Yŏng-ch'ae was none other than Kye Wŏr-hyang. The three young women talked of how they would all study diligently and, sometime in their future, join together to enlighten the Korean women's world. They spoke of how one had to go to study in the United States or Japan if one wanted to get a good education, and that one had to learn English or German. Pyŏng-uk and Yŏng-ch'ae said they were going to study music. Sŏn-hyŏng said she had not yet decided, but would try to be admitted to a teachers' college. They wished one another much success. All eyes in the car were on these three young Korean women as they talked joyously.

When Sŏn-hyŏng returned to her seat, Hyŏng-sik straightened the blanket that was spread over her seat. "Who was her friend?"

"Someone named Pak Yŏng-ch'ae. She is a very nice person. Pyŏng-uk says Yŏng-ch'ae is her younger sister." Hyŏng-sik was so startled that he could not breathe, and his body trembled. His eyes widened.

"What? Who was that again?" He could hardly speak. Sŏn-hyŏng did not know why Hyŏng-sik was reacting this way, and looked at his face as though she thought his behavior strange.

"Pak Yŏng-ch'ae."

"Pak Yŏng-ch'ae! Pak Yŏng-ch'ae!" Hyŏng-sik could not speak for awhile. U-sŏn, who was sitting behind him, jumped up.

"What? Who? Pak Yŏng-ch'ae?" U-sŏn said.

The three of them fell mute.

U-sŏn sat beside Hyŏng-sik.

"What is the meaning of this?" said U-sŏn. "Then she is alive. Could there be someone with the same surname and given name?"

Hyŏng-sik covered his face with both hands.

"This is cause for rejoicing, in any event," he said. There was pain in his heart, though. It seemed as though he had committed a serious sin in not having followed Yŏng-ch'ae to P'yŏngyang and found out whether or not she was alive or dead. Moreover, he had hurried back to Seoul and gotten engaged to someone else the next day, and had forgotten all about Yŏng-ch'ae ever since then. He was indeed heartless, after all. Hyŏng-sik should have used the five wŏn he had borrowed from U-sŏn to go to P'yŏngyang. He should have found Yŏng-ch'ae's corpse, and done all he could to have a generous funeral for her. Moreover, he should have had the decency to wait at least a year before getting married. He should have wept sorrowfully, and mourned for her; she had saved herself for him for eight years, and had given her body and even her life for him.

Now that Hyŏng-sik heard that Yŏng-ch'ae was alive, his sinfulness in trying to forget her once she was gone from the world stabbed at his heart like a knife. He clenched his teeth and sobbed. He seemed to have forgotten that Sŏn-hyŏng was sitting next to him.

U-sŏn jumped up and went in the direction of Yŏng-ch'ae's car. He wanted to investigate whether or not it really was Yŏng-ch'ae.

106

"What's wrong?" Sŏn-hyŏng said after U-sŏn got up. "What kind of person is Pak Yŏng-ch'ae?"

Since Hyŏng-sik did not answer, Sŏn-hyŏng said, "Were there rumors that Pak Yŏng-ch'ae was dead?" Hyŏng-sik lowered his head and said nothing. Sŏn-hyŏng looked at Hyŏng-sik, and wondered aloud what was going on, then was quiet.

Hyŏng-sik lifted his head after awhile and said, "I have done wrong. I am a sinner, a terrible sinner." Then he could not speak. Sŏn-hyŏng was even more taken aback, and rolled her eyes in bewilderment. Hyŏng-sik continued.

"I should have told you before, but there was no chance. Actually, I was too weak of heart to tell you, and said nothing about it all this time. Pak Yŏng-ch'ae is the daughter of my former benefactor. Her father and two brothers died in prison of unjust charges. She was deceived by someone into selling her body to be a *kisaeng* in order to save her father."

"What? She became a *kisaeng*?" Sŏn-hyŏng was taken aback. The name Kye Wŏr-hyang flashed through her mind.

"Yes, she became a *kisaeng*. For eight years after that . . . " Hyŏng-sik paused as if he found it difficult to speak. "She saved herself for me. I did not know where she was, and she did not know where I was. Then by chance she happened to learn of my whereabouts, and came to see me." He was not sure what to say after that. Sŏn-hyŏng thought of Yŏng-ch'ae, whom she had just met. Had she become a *kisaeng* and saved herself for Hyŏng-sik for eight years? She had thought Kye Wŏr-hyang would be a seductive, dissolute woman, but now that she had met her, she saw that was she just a nice young woman no different from herself. Why had Hyŏng-sik abandoned Yŏng-ch'ae? she wondered.

"Then what happened?"

Hyŏng-sik heaved a sigh.

"She left a letter saying that she was going to commit suicide, and then went to P'yŏngyang. I went after her. I could not find her, though. I thought she must have drowned in the Taedong River as she had said she was going to do. However, she is alive and on the same train as we are!" He shook his head twice sadly.

"Is that why you went to P'yŏngyang that time?" Sŏn-hyŏng asked, looking Hyŏng-sik in the face. Her eyes looked threatening, and Hyŏng-sik averted his eyes.

"Yes," he said.

Then the day Yŏng-ch'ae was supposed to have died was none other than the day that Hyŏng-sik and Sŏn-hyŏng had gotten engaged. Sŏn-hyŏng's suspicions about Hyŏng-sik—that he had been crazy about a *kisaeng* named Kye Wŏr-hyang—were now resolved, but her heart grew heavy with a new, unspeakable pain. Her body seemed to have fallen into sin, and strange difficulties and suffering seemed to block her future.

U-sŏn came back just then with a serious expression on his face, and said in Japanese, "It is definitely her."[150] He sat down next to Hyŏng-sik. "It is incredible."

"Did you speak with her?"

"No, but I could see her from the door. She was talking with the woman who was just here." U-sŏn looked at Sŏn-hyŏng sitting near Hyŏng-sik, and stopped talking, as though he thought it were better not to talk about it.

"In any event, things have turned out well. She is apparently going to Tokyo with that student, probably to study."

Hyŏng-sik leaned back in his seat, and closed his eyes for no particular reason.

"My heart is aflutter somehow," Yŏng-ch'ae said after Sŏn-hyŏng left.

"Why, because you heard Hyŏng-sik's name?"

"Yes. Until now, I thought I had forgotten him, but I haven't. He was hidden deep in my heart. Then when I heard someone say, 'Long live Yi Hyŏng-sik!' it all came bursting forth. I cannot calm my feelings. It is unbearable."

---

150. U-sŏn speaks in Japanese here: "Tashika dayo." The text transliterates the Japanese words in Korean.

"How could you help but feel that way? One cannot easily forget someone whom one has thought about day and night for eight years. Though you may forget him after some time."

"Do I have to forget him?"

"Of course, what else can you do?"

"Couldn't I not forget him?"

Pyŏng-uk looked at Yŏng-ch'ae, then went and sat beside her and put her arm around her waist.

"Hyŏng-sik has already gotten married. I hear he is going to the United States with his wife."

"What? Married?" Yŏng-ch'ae grasped Pyŏng-uk's arm.

"The woman who was here—Sŏn-hyŏng—she is his wife," Pyŏng-uk said gently.

"Then was he already engaged when I went to see him?" Yŏng-ch'ae felt disappointed about the past. Her past life seemed even sadder and more grievous. It seemed as though she had been deceived by the world and lived a life that could hardly be called a life. Everything she had striven for until now seemed to be meaningless. Her heart burst with disappointment and sorrow all at once. Moreover, she had devoted her body and mind to Hyŏng-sik, but he seemed to give her no more thought than he would a wisp of straw.

"I don't know why, but I feel bitter," Yŏng-ch'ae said.

"You have the future, though, don't you?" Pyong-uk hugged Yŏng-ch'ae tightly.

107

Hyŏng-sik wanted to see Yŏng-ch'ae's face immediately. He seemed to have forgotten her face as he had seen it before, and thought he must see her face again. He wanted to see the face of the woman he had thought was dead. When he saw Sŏn-hyŏng sitting before him, though, he could not summon up the courage to go see Yŏng-ch'ae. He looked at Sŏn-hyŏng's face. She was sitting quietly with her eyes half-closed, as though disappointed over something. Once in awhile, she would glance at Hyŏng-sik, then close her eyes again as if displeased, or turn her head and look at her face reflected in the window. Whenever Sŏn-hyŏng and Hyŏng-sik's eyes met, Hyŏng-sik felt his body burn.

Most of the passengers in the car were asleep. Hyŏng-sik too leaned back and closed his eyes. He shook his body once as though determined not to think about anything, and clasped his hands and put them on his stomach. Hyŏng-sik's mind did not obey his intentions, though, and was like a surging ocean in a storm.

Yŏng-ch'ae was supposed to have died. Or if she were alive, he should not have found out. Or he should have seen her before he got engaged to

Sŏn-hyŏng. It was truly a joke of the Creator for him to see her after he had gotten engaged and was on his way to the United States. Hyŏng-sik had not intended to abandon Yŏng-ch'ae. He had been unable to forget her for a long time, and when he saw her again, his affection for her had been as strong as ever, and he had thought of how he would get married, and live happily ever after, and have beautiful children, and give them an ideal upbringing. When he found out that Yŏng-ch'ae was a *kisaeng*, he had been in anguish all day because he could not come up with one thousand wŏn. If Yŏng-ch'ae had not gone to P'yŏngyang—if she had not left a suicide note saying that she was on her way to die—he would have spent the rest of his life with her. Then he would have fulfilled his duties to his benefactor, and his duties to Yŏng-ch'ae.

Hyŏng-sik compared Yŏng-ch'ae and Sŏn-hyŏng again. Sŏn-hyŏng was the first young woman with whom he had come in contact. Her looks were such that anyone would be dazzled by her, and had left a very strong, profound impression on Hyŏng-sik. Like many a young man who encounters a young woman for the first time, Hyŏng-sik thus thought she was the most beautiful woman in the world. He was sure that not only was she beautiful in outward appearance, but her mind would be as beautiful as her looks. The first day Hyŏng-sik saw Sŏn-hyŏng, he had attributed to her all the beautiful virtues a woman could have. Sŏn-hyŏng had seemed to him to be perfectly complete and beautiful.

The evening of the day when he had received such a strong impression from Sŏn-hyŏng, he had seen Yŏng-ch'ae again. Yŏng-ch'ae had a beautiful appearance. To an impartial observer, Yŏng-ch'ae's face would seem even prettier than Sŏn-hyŏng's. Hyŏng-sik, however, believed that Sŏn-hyŏng was the best woman in the universe, and he could not think of Yŏng-ch'ae as anything but the second-best woman in the universe. Moreover, Sŏn-hyŏng had received a complete education, as the daughter of a rich family of good repute, whereas who knows where Yŏng-ch'ae had been over the years. Because of all of these factors, Yŏng-ch'ae did not seem to be Sŏn-hyŏng's equal. Sŏn-hyŏng was a branch of a cinnamon tree in the moon, and beyond Hyŏng-sik's reach, whereas Yŏng-ch'ae was a branch of plum blossom[151] by the roadside that he could pluck if he wanted. Hyŏng-sik had thus abandoned Sŏn-hyŏng, whom he thought of as number one, and tried to get Yŏng-ch'ae, whom he thought of as number two. Then Yŏng-ch'ae had jumped into the Taedong River, and, moreover, Elder Kim had asked him to marry his daughter. Hyŏng-sik had gotten engaged without much hesitation and, without much sorrow, had tried to forget Yŏng-ch'ae.

Hyŏng-sik had never really loved Sŏn-hyŏng or Yŏng-ch'ae. His love was all about looks. Hyŏng-sik thought he loved Sŏn-hyŏng as dearly as his

---

151. The 1918 Sinmungwan edition uses the word *haenghwa*, or apricot blossom.

own life, but he knew nothing about her personality. He did not know whether or not she was a cold, intellectual type of person, or a passionate, emotional type, or what her natural disposition was like, or her preferences, her strengths and weaknesses, what he had in common with her, what contradictions they might have between them, or in what direction her personality and abilities would develop in the future. He just blindly loved her. His love was a primitive love that had not yet evolved. His love was like that of children who grow fond of one another and do not want to be parted; or like that of uncivilized peoples who love only a pretty face. The only difference was that the love of uncivilized people was a physical love; Hyŏng-sik's love, though, had many spiritual elements. However, Hyŏng-sik knew only the concept of spiritual love, and did not know what it was really like. He did not know that true love arose from understanding one another spiritually. Hyŏng-sik's love was the kind of love that was common among youths—Korean youths—of the transitional period between the old era, an era that had not yet awakened, and a new era, an era of awakening. Once Hyŏng-sik realized this about his love, a great change would be inevitable in his future life.

As he sat still with his eyes closed, the things he had done over the past month rose before his eyes as clearly as though he were looking at them through a microscope.

108

The Elder and Mrs. Kim did not seem to believe Hyŏng-sik about his relationship with Yŏng-ch'ae.

Once, after Hyŏng-sik had talked about his relationship with Yŏng-ch'ae, the Elder had smiled and said, "It is common for most men to have an affair like this once or twice." Hyŏng-sik did not try to explain any further, but it bothered him that Elder Kim did not seem to trust his character. After that, Hyŏng-sik felt both vexed and embarrassed whenever he faced the Elder and Mrs. Kim. It seemed to Hyŏng-sik that the Elder and Mrs. Kim did not think that Hyŏng-sik was qualified to be Sŏn-hyŏng's mate. At first they had thought his character and behavior were irreproachable, and that he had great potential, but after they heard that he associated with *kisaeng* and had followed a *kisaeng* to P'yŏngyang, they suddenly seemed to think Hyŏng-sik could not be trusted. It bothered Hyŏng-sik that they would try to judge his worth by that one incident. It seemed to Hyŏng-sik that the Elder wanted to break off the engagement with Hyŏng-sik if at all possible but could not bring himself to break a promise without losing face. To Hyŏng-sik, the Elder seemed to think that even if Hyŏng-sik could not be trusted, it was just Sŏn-hyŏng's fate.

Moreover, Hyŏng-sik knew that a stylish young man who had returned from the United States was interested in Sŏn-hyŏng and was trying his best to get her. A powerful individual in the church had stepped forward as a go-between, and tried to bring about the marriage of Sŏn-hyŏng to this young man, praising the young man's wealth, his English ability, and his having studied in the United States. The go-between spoke ill of Hyŏng-sik, and tried to have the engagement between Hyŏng-sik and Sŏn-hyŏng broken off. Hyŏng-sik knew that the Elder and Mrs. Kim were sixty percent inclined to prefer that young man, and that Sŏn-hyŏng's attitude towards Hyŏng-sik had grown colder, and that she even seemed anxious at times. Hyŏng-sik knew too that Mrs. Kim was displeased with Hyŏng-sik, and that she was the one who was most in favor of marrying Sŏn-hyŏng to the young man who had returned from the United States. The matter was eventually dropped, though, because the Elder was a *yangban*,[152] and a church elder, and could not go back on his word, and would lose face if he did.

Hyŏng-sik knew that, for over ten days, he became an object of dislike in the Elder's house. At that time, Hyŏng-sik was so enfuriated that he did not go to the Elder's house for three or four days. He stayed at home and suffered alone, full of anger and shame. Today I will go and break off the engagement, Hyŏng-sik thought one day, and got dressed and was going to go out when Sŏn-hyŏng came to visit him for the first time.

"Are you unwell?" she asked politely. Sun-ae came in behind her, bringing a basket of fruit. She had apparently come to visit him because she thought he was sick.

"The passports arrived yesterday," Sŏn-hyŏng said. She looked happy, even. Hyŏng-sik's anger subsided.

"I am all right, I am not sick," he said.

Sŏn-hyŏng and Sun-ae stared at Hyŏng-sik. Sŏn-hyŏng for her part knew what problems had arisen at her house. She knew that her parents had ill feelings towards Hyŏng-sik. She herself did not feel favorably towards him. He seemed to have noticed her parents' feelings, because he had not visited for several days. When this happened, Sŏn-hyŏng began to feel sympathy for Hyŏng-sik, and thought of him with affection. That was why she had come to see him, bringing Sun-ae with her. Hyŏng-sik seemed very lovable to her just then. Hyŏng-sik could not have been happier when he saw the loving look in Sŏn-hyŏng's eyes.

However, this love was a sympathy like that of someone who jumps into the water to save someone who is drowning. It was effective for a moment, but would not last long. The love between husband and wife should not be like that. It should be such that one could only live if the other lived. One could only be happy if the other was happy. One became one body with the

---

152. The term *yangban* meant the "two orders" of officialdom, that is, the civil and military officials. The *yangban* class thus had a privileged social status. Cf. Lee Ki-baik, *A New History of Korea*, trans. Edward W. Wagner with Edward J. Shultz (Cambridge: Harvard University Press, 1984), 173–175.

other. Sŏn-hyŏng's love for Hyŏng-sik was like sympathy for a drowning person. Although Hyŏng-sik was not sure of how Sŏn-hyŏng felt towards him, he was aware to a certain extent that she felt this way. Hyŏng-sik, however, could not do without Sŏn-hyŏng. His whole life seemed to depend on Sŏn-hyŏng. Even if Sŏn-hyŏng were to say to him, "I don't like you, go away," and spit in his face and kick him, he would not be able to keep himself from clinging to the edge of her clothes for dear life. Even though it was unpleasant for him to go to Elder Kim's house or face Sŏn-hyŏng, such unpleasantness was better than the disappointment and sorrow of completely losing someone whom one loved. It was better to cut off an arm or a leg than have one's entire body go into a pit of fire.

Hyŏng-sik had thus spent the days in anguish. A few days before Sŏn-hyŏng and Hyŏng-sik left, though, the Elder and Mrs. Kim became very kind towards Hyŏng-sik, and even Sŏn-hyŏng treated Hyŏng-sik with more civility and warmth. Human emotions were inconstant, Hyŏng-sik thought, but he nonetheless felt as happy as though he had gone to heaven. Moreover, the day before Sŏn-hyŏng and Hyŏng-sik left, the Elder and Mrs. Kim called the two before them, and offered a fervent prayer for the two, then began to lecture the two of them. Hyŏng-sik experienced a happiness he had never known before. When the Elder and Mrs. Kim addressed them as "you two," it seemed to make Hyŏng-sik and his beloved Sŏn-hyŏng as one body. Sŏn-hyŏng glanced at Hyŏng-sik and smiled. The four of them prayed that the moment would last forever.

109

Hyŏng-sik thought that nothing but happiness awaited him. He felt nothing but happiness as he received his friend's farewells when leaving Namdaemun. His chest tightened with sorrow when he saw Hŭi-gyŏng and his friends standing behind the other well-wishers and looking at him. However, all of his sadness disappeared when he saw Sŏn-hyŏng standing beside him. Hyŏng-sik and Sŏn-hyŏng would be going to the other side of the earth, over twenty thousand *li* away, and when they had joyously finished their studies, they would return arm in arm to Namdaemun to cheering crowds. The people standing here would congratulate him with even greater emotion, and greet him with even more respect. The mere thought made him feel affectionately towards Seoul and Namdaemun for the first time. Namdaemun seemed to exist only for the purpose of sending off and greeting happy, fortunate Hyŏng-sik. There is scarcely any need to describe Hyŏng-sik's feelings as the conductor's whistle and his friends' cheers were heard.

Sŏn-hyŏng was a woman, and no matter how her ambition and pride as a "new woman" made her happy that she was going to study in the United States, when she saw her beloved father and mother, siblings and friends growing distant from her window, the tears that had been welling in her heart burst forth, and she collapsed on the train seat, sobbing in spite of herself. Hyŏng-sik tapped her gently on the shoulder. "Please sit up. And wipe away your tears," he said. Then he realized he need not be so timid, and, after some hesitation, he put his arm around Sŏn-hyŏng's chest and lifted her up. Her flesh where it touched his arm was soft and warm. Sŏn-hyŏng let him help her sit up, and took hold of his hand for a moment. Then she wiped away her tears with a kerchief.

"Oh look at me. The foreign[153] passengers must be laughing," she said and smiled. Her eyes and cheeks were red from weeping, and looked even lovelier. The foreign passengers were indeed laughing.

U-sŏn sat behind Hyŏng-sik, and read a newspaper and smiled as he listened to Hyŏng-sik and Sŏn-hyŏng talk nearby.

Then he turned his head and said, "Listen. Something has happened." Hyŏng-sik had forgotten about U-sŏn and sat looking at Sŏn-hyŏng. He turned around, startled.

"What is it?"

"Oh, it's nothing to be that alarmed about. It started raining this morning in North and South Kyŏng-sang, and North Chŏlla Province, and the Kŭm and Naktong Rivers have risen over ten feet."

"Let me see." Hyŏng-sik took the newspaper that U-sŏn had been reading. "Then won't the railroads be impassable?" he said.

Sŏn-hyŏng's eyes widened.

"Well, everyone has been using rainwater sparingly, but now . . . " said U-sŏn, and put his head out the window and looked around. It was dusk, and one could not see very clearly, but the sky was covered with dark clouds, and a chilly wind blew, bearing a few large drops of rain. Other passengers looked up from their newspapers and talked about how they were worried that the railroad tracks might be damaged. It was not very important to Hyŏng-sik and Sŏn-hyŏng, though. If the railroad tracks were damaged, they could stop over at an inn.

It was then that Pyŏng-uk had come to see Sŏn-hyŏng, and then Sŏn-hyŏng had gone to visit with Pyŏng-uk; then Sŏn-hyŏng had returned, and Hyŏng-sik had asked about Pyŏng-uk's friend, and Sŏn-hyŏng had said it was "a person named Pak Yŏng-ch'ae," and that she was a "very nice person." Then U-sŏn had gone to see, and had reported that it was indeed Yŏng-ch'ae.

After thinking about what had happened, Hyŏng-sik said to Sŏn-hyŏng, "I must go and see Pak Yŏng-ch'ae."

---

153. The 1918 Sinmungwan edition uses the word *oeguk* (foreign), whereas the 1917 *Maeil Sinbo* edition uses the word *naeji* (of the 'inner land'; Japanese).

"Of course," said Sŏn-hyŏng. Her reply seemed to have some kind of special meaning behind it. Sŏn-hyŏng had indeed been having misgivings. So was that the *kisaeng* Wŏr-hyang? she thought. He had said she was dead, but had that been a lie? Did he have all kinds of evil schemes inside him, but outwardly pretend to be decent? Pyŏng-uk was such a nice person that she may have fallen for that woman's wiles. Perhaps Yŏng-ch'ae had heard that Sŏn-hyŏng and Hyŏng-sik were leaving that day and had deliberately chosen to take this train. Or perhaps Hyŏng-sik had been unable to forget Yŏng-ch'ae, and had secretly told Yŏng-ch'ae the date of their departure, scheming to see Yŏng-ch'ae one more time before he went to the United States. Sŏn-hyŏng felt jealous at the thought, and turned her head away indignantly.

Hyŏng-sik stood looking at Sŏn-hyŏng's unhappy expression for awhile, then said defensively, "Now that I know she is on the same train, how can I pretend that I don't know?" He sat down again and waited for Sŏn-hyŏng's answer.

Sŏn-hyŏng sat quietly, then said, smiling, "Well then go. Who is telling you not to?" The last remark would have been better left unsaid. Hyŏng-sik lowered his head and sat listlessly, then jumped up.

"I'll be back," he said to Sŏn-hyŏng. "I am going to go see Yŏng-ch'ae," he said to U-sŏn.

"All right. Tell her I asked about her." U-sŏn glanced at Sŏn-hyŏng. U-sŏn wondered what relations would be like between these three people.

U-sŏn too felt uncomfortable after he had seen Yŏng-ch'ae. He wanted to know why Yŏng-ch'ae had changed her mind about dying, and how it was that she was going to Tokyo to study.

110

U-sŏn had loved Yŏng-ch'ae for her looks, but after he realized that she had saved herself for Hyŏng-sik all this time, and after he saw her resolve to die because of the incident at Ch'ŏngnyangni, he loved her because he thought she was an ideal woman who had beauty, talent and virtue. He would have gone mad over her if not for his feelings of friendship towards Hyŏng-sik.

U-sŏn had been quite heartbroken when he realized that Kye Wŏr-hyang, whom he was so crazy about, was really Pak Yŏng-ch'ae, who was keeping herself for Hyŏng-sik. U-sŏn placed much importance on friendship, though, and prided himself on being chivalrous. He thus resolved to try his best to suppress his own feelings, and help Hyŏng-sik and Yŏng-ch'ae. If Yŏng-ch'ae became Hyŏng-sik's wife, U-sŏn would be content to consider her his wife's friend for the rest of his life. However, U-sŏn felt a deep sadness and disappointment when she left that sad suicide note and went to P'yŏngyang. U-sŏn made it his life philosophy not to be moved by a woman, but now there was never a moment when he forgot about Yŏng-ch'ae. This was evident in the fact that U-sŏn wrote a few lines of Chinese *lü shi* poetry[154] in his diary, with Yŏng-ch'ae in mind, every day before he went to bed.

It was only natural that U-sŏn felt his heart pounding when he found out that Yŏng-ch'ae was alive and on the same train as he. Moreover, he became even more envious of Hyŏng-sik when he saw that Hyŏng-sik had exchanged the beautiful vows of marriage with the lovely Sŏn-hyŏng, and that the two of them were going away to learn beautiful things. U-sŏn thought about his wife wearing an apron and washing baby diapers. She was already thirty years old, and had given birth to a son and a daughter. She knew nothing but how to cook, make clothes and give birth to babies. In over ten years of marriage, U-sŏn had never sat with her and had an affectionate conversation, let alone told her his thoughts. They were only together when they slept. It was as though his wife existed only for him. He went to his wife's room like a widower goes to a brothel, overcome with lust.

Meanwhile, they called one another husband and wife, and had had a son and a daughter. It was a relationship in which neither one knew anything about the other's thoughts, and made no effort to learn about the other's thoughts, though they had been together for over ten years. One could say that such a relationship was indeed a mystery. However, U-sŏn thought it was inescapable destiny, and never tried to get out of the relationship. He thought this was what having a wife was like. It was enough to keep her at home, and feed her, and give her children, and visit her now and then. Whatever diversion he could not get from his wife, he would simply seek from *kisaeng*, he thought. Indeed, that was why the institution of *kisaeng* existed, he thought. When he was with Hyŏng-sik, the two of them often quarreled about this issue. Hyŏng-sik stubbornly insisted on strict monogamy, while U-sŏn did not think it was wrong for a man to have a concubine, or have affairs with *kisaeng*. U-sŏn did not think he would be able to live very long without a concubine or *kisaeng*. U-sŏn's polygamist beliefs, and Hyŏng-sik's monogamist beliefs partially emerged from Chosŏn dynasty morality and Western Christian morality, but also emerged from U-sŏn and Hyŏng-sik's situations in life. If U-sŏn were to be given Yŏng-ch'ae, and Yŏng-ch'ae loved him, then U-sŏn would probably stop going to *kisaeng* houses from that day on.

U-sŏn was very envious of Hyŏng-sik, and felt very sorry for himself. He too wanted to take a train together with a wife whom he loved, and travel and visit foreign countries. It was good to amuse oneself with *kisaeng*, but

---

154. *Lü shi*, Chinese regulated verse, is a song style using a seven-syllable line. Stephen Owen, ed. and transl., *An Anthology of Chinese Literature: Beginnings to 1911* (New York and London: W.W. Norton and Company, 1996) 415–416.

there was something missing from *kisaeng*, though he was not sure what it was. No matter how kind *kisaeng* acted towards him, and even if he liked a *kisaeng*, there was something missing nonetheless. It was not something trifling, but quite significant. First of all, there wasn't a feeling of spiritual union and involvement; moreover, one did not have the confidence that comes of "belonging to one another," which is the strongest element in love. If one paid money and obtained a *kisaeng's* release from a *kisaeng* house, that *kisaeng* would be one's possession; but spiritual union was something beyond human power to control. Love of looks was superficial. Therefore, it grew cold very quickly. Spiritual love was deep, and therefore lasted a long time. A love of looks was a beastly love, but love that was only spiritual was for ghosts. Only a love that combined the body and mind could be as wide as the universe, as deep as the sea, and have the infinite transformations of a spring day. People don't say it out loud, but this is the kind of love that everyone is always seeking. Such love is like gold or jade, though, and the right person is only one person in a thousand, and perhaps to be found only once in ten or a hundred years. Women thus envy Ch'un-hyang, and men envy Yi To-ryŏng. Since they cannot actually taste of such love, they behold it in fiction, drama, or poetry, and laugh and cry with pleasure. Ch'un-hyang and Yi To-ryŏng's love had been the greatest love in Korea since the creation of the universe. Everyone wanted to be Ch'un-hyang and Yi To-ryŏng, but no one could even approach them. The evil marriage system of the Chosŏn dynasty had killed within the loving heart the seeds of love received from heaven. U-sŏn was one of the victims of that marriage system.

It was therefore only natural that U-sŏn felt miserable when he saw Hyŏng-sik and Sŏn-hyŏng, and thought of how Yŏng-ch'ae was on the same train, being drawn by the same engine car. Moreover, Yŏng-ch'ae was neither a *kisaeng* nor Hyŏng-sik's wife. She was just a young woman. The thought occurred like a flash of lightning in U-sŏn's mind. U-sŏn thus followed after Hyŏng-sik, and stood outside the car door, taking in the breeze, and listening carefully. Hyŏng-sik was sitting next to Yŏng-ch'ae and talking. Pyŏng-uk spoke up too once in awhile. The faces of the three were very serious. U-sŏn wondered whether or not he should go in, then decided to wait for Hyŏng-sik. He folded his hands behind his back, leaned against a wall, and thought as he listened to the roaring of the train wheels.

111

Pyŏng-uk returned after seeing Sŏn-hyŏng back to her seat. When Yŏng-ch'ae saw Pyŏng-uk return, she took her by the hand and sat her down.

"What do you think?" Yŏng-ch'ae asked, not sure herself what she meant.

"What is there to say? He was well mannered, and just sat there, pretending that he did not know you. He said he knows my brother, and that they were in Tokyo together."

A sigh escaped from Yŏng-ch'ae.

"What is the matter? Do you miss Hyŏng-sik? I see you have not gotten over him yet!"

"No, it isn't that."

"Then why did you sigh?"

"I don't know." Yŏng-ch'ae slapped Pyŏng-uk on the knee and laughed. "Just the same, I suppose you are not feeling too good about all of this." Pyŏng-uk smiled too.

Yŏng-ch'ae thought for awhile, then squeezed Pyŏng-uk's hand. "You are right," she said, and smiled as though embarrassed. "I feel unhappy for some reason," she said, and blushed. Pyŏng-uk was astonished that a woman who had spent almost ten years as a *kisaeng* could be just like a woman who had grown up at home in the women's quarters. Pyŏng-uk wanted to know what Yŏng-ch'ae was thinking and feeling right now.

"What do you mean by unhappy?"

"I don't know."

"Stop being childish, and answer me. I will buy you something tasty to eat." They both laughed.

"I think Yi Hyŏng-sik is a very heartless person. When I said I was going to P'yŏngyang to die, he should have at least gone to look for me. However, in no time at all, he got married." Yŏng-ch'ae put her head on Pyŏng-uk's lap, and hid her face. "Oh, why am I saying things like this?"

Pyŏng-uk rubbed Yŏng-ch'ae's head, neck and back, and said, as if to a child, "So what if you say these things? Go on."

"He must know I am here, right?"

"I am sure he does. After Sŏn-hyŏng was here, she probably went and told him. So what if he knows?"

"Yes, but he would be shocked when he hears that someone who had supposedly died is still alive."

"Of course he would be shocked. That will teach him a lesson. I am sure he would not be cold-hearted enough to be unaffected."

"What if he comes to see me? Should I talk with him?"

"Of course. Why, do you have a grudge against him?"

"No, but somehow . . . "

"You feel outraged?"

The two of them looked at one another for awhile.

"It was wrong of you to save me. I should have died then. If I had died then, I would have rotted away by now. My bones would have scattered one by one. I should have died then." She shook her head regretfully. Pyŏng-uk was alarmed when she saw the sudden change in Yŏng-ch'ae's expression, and she grabbed Yŏng-ch'ae by both arms.

"Listen, Yŏng-ch'ae! Why are you talking that way? You and I are going to study music, and then travel through America and Europe, and do all the sightseeing we want. And then we will return to our nation, and start a new music, and live interesting lives." She shook Yŏng-ch'ae. Yŏng-ch'ae sat gazing absently at Pyŏng-uk's eyes. Then tears fell from Yŏng-ch'ae's eyes. "No, I am not someone who should live. I am someone who should die. When I think about my past life, it does not seem as though I were meant to live. My father and two brothers died in prison, and the last eight years of suffering I have endured have all been in vain." Yŏng-ch'ae sobbed.

"What are you saying? You have forgotten all that and were happy. Why this sudden outburst? What shall I do if you keep going on like this? Now, now, don't cry."

"No matter how I try, I cannot find the will to live."

"Why? You have not yet gotten over Yi Hyŏng-sik! Didn't you tell me back then that you did not actually love him?"

"No. It's not just that. The world is my enemy. It took away my parents, my brothers, tormented my young body. Finally, it took my virginity. And the man to whom I have devoted myself all my life doesn't even acknowledge me. Why should I hang on to a world that is deliberately trying to destroy me? If the world hates me, then I hate the world. If the world dislikes me, then I will leave the world and run away. I will go to the heavens." Pyŏng-uk too found herself weeping when she heard Yŏng-ch'ae's tearful words.

"Since you have lost so much to the world, you must find something to take for yourself. You keep giving away what belongs to you! Since you have suffered for twenty years, shouldn't you get something in return?"

"What do you mean? If I live another day, I will only have more taken away."

"No. Why do you say that? You must seek and find what is yours from now on. You have your future ahead of you. Why are you already despairing? You must live to the utmost, and seek and find as much as you can . . . through work, through happiness. Why die instead, without seeking?"

"Happiness? Happiness? Could there be happiness for me? Would this world give me happiness?" Yŏng-ch'ae looked at Pyŏng-uk's tearful eyes.

112

Pyŏng-uk wiped Yŏng-ch'ae's tears away with a cloth.

"The other passengers will think it strange. Stop crying. Why wouldn't this world give you happiness? If it doesn't, you should demand it. If it still doesn't give you happiness, then you should take it anyway. If you can't find a way to take it, then at least get even. Think about it. Are you the only person in the world who has suffered sorrow? There must be many people like you in Korea.[155] You and I should change this wrongful social system, and help our descendants to live in happiness. If we do not, who will? However if you die, unable to endure your suffering, you will be abandoning your responsibilities to our future descendants. Let's try to live as long as we can, and work as much as we can. Now stop crying and let's have some strawberries." Pyŏng-uk stood up and took down a small wicker basket.

"I could actually do something?"

"Of course, why not? The Lord gave you suffering in your early years in order to prepare you to be a great worker. We have each other, don't we? Forget about that Yi Hyŏng-sik. Let's rely on each other. Here, let's eat." Pyŏng-uk took out some ripe, red strawberries and ate one first. After she put the strawberry in her mouth and chewed it, a blood red color stained her teeth. They had picked the strawberries the morning before, as they plucked and ate melons in the cotton field with Pyŏng-guk's wife for their going-away party.

Yŏng-ch'ae knew it was useless to cry, and stopped weeping. There was affection, strength and wisdom in Pyŏng-uk's words, and she felt happy, though somewhat intimidated. Though her heart ached as though it would break, just hearing one word from Pyŏng-uk helped ease the pain. Yŏng-ch'ae knew that although Pyŏng-uk was as outgoing as a man, inwardly she had warm, sensitive feelings, and that when Pyŏng-uk comforted her, she genuinely put herself in Yŏng-ch'ae's position. If Yŏng-ch'ae were to attempt suicide, and stood at the water's edge or stood holding a knife, were she to hear Pyŏng-uk's voice, she would immediately cry out, "Sister!" and follow her. To Yŏng-ch'ae, Pyŏng-uk was more of a mother than a sister.

It was impossible to expect Yŏng-ch'ae's twenty years of accumulated sorrows to be dispelled by Pyŏng-uk's words. However, Yŏng-ch'ae felt too sorry towards Pyŏng-uk to insist on being stubborn, since Pyŏng-uk was being so kind. Thus Yŏng-ch'ae too ate some of the strawberries. The red strawberries passed through the two young women's lovely lips, and stained their white teeth red. Rain fell on the train windows. Tearlike drops rolled down the windows, flowing together with other droplets of water. Mayflies swarmed around the electric lamps, which shook with the movements of the train. Just when the two young women's lips and fingertips were red with strawberry juice, Hyŏng-sik arrived before them and stood there.

"Yŏng-ch'ae!" he said.

---

155. The narrative uses the word "uri nara" (our nation) for Korea. Japan had annexed Korea in 1910, and censored the concept of an independent Korean nation; the novel *Mujŏng* therefore could make only vague references to Korea as "our nation."

Hyŏng-sik had entered the train car a while ago, and had wanted to approach Yŏng-ch'ae, but when he saw that she seemed to be crying, he had sat down several seats away, and listened quietly to the two young women's conversation. He could not hear everything in detail because of the noise from the train wheels, but he was able to guess the general drift of their conversation, from the occasional word that he did hear. Hyŏng-sik felt sorry towards Yŏng-ch'ae, and could not help feeling ashamed of himself. He resolved to beg for her forgiveness with all his heart.

Yŏng-ch'ae and Pyŏng-uk were startled, and stood up. The two young women lowered their heads at the same time. Yŏng-ch'ae, however, quickly turned her face away to one side. Hyŏng-sik hung his head.

Pyŏng-uk looked up and said to Hyŏng-sik, "Please sit down." Hyŏng-sik took a seat.

"Sit down." Pyŏng-uk said to Yŏng-ch'ae. Yŏng-ch'ae too sat down. Hyŏng-sik felt shivers run down his body as though he were facing something fearful. He felt oppressed and threatened by the sight of Yŏng-ch'ae, whose back was turned to him. He wondered whether it was Yŏng-ch'ae's ghost that appeared before him now and was tormenting him—the ghost of Yŏng-ch'ae, who had drowned in the Taedong River. It seemed as though Yŏng-ch'ae would turn around any moment now and glare at him with a terrifying face, and spray a mouthful of hot blood at him. "You heartless scoundrel! May you be eternally cursed!" she would say, and come running towards him. Why hadn't he investigated further when he had gone to P'yŏngyang? And why hadn't he gone to P'yŏngyang again promptly, using the five wŏn that he had borrowed from U-sŏn? What would he do now if Yŏng-ch'ae turned her head and faced him? He wished he had not come to see her.

"Please have a strawberry," Pyŏng-uk said just then, and offered him the container of strawberries.

"Hey, Yŏng-ch'ae." Pyŏng-uk pressed down on Yŏng-ch'ae's foot with her own foot. Yŏng-ch'ae turned around. She would not look at Hyŏng-sik, though.

"Please forgive me, Yŏng-ch'ae," Hyŏng-sik said. "I have nothing to say for myself. I have sinned against you and Scholar Pak. If only you would reproach me."

"Not at all. I foolishly sought you out and caused you needless anxiety. How worried you must have been when I said I was going to die, even though I didn't die." Yŏng-ch'ae hung her head.

This won't do, Pyŏng-uk thought to herself.

113

Hyŏng-sik could not summon up the courage to say anything further to Yŏng-ch'ae, so he spoke to Pyŏng-uk. "How do you two know each other? Have you known Yŏng-ch'ae for a long time?"

Pyŏng-uk looked at Hyŏng-sik and laughed. Her laugh made him feel unspeakably ashamed. He thought she was making fun of him.

"No, I met Yŏng-ch'ae on the train when I was on my way home for vacation."

Hyŏng-sik's looked at Yŏng-ch'ae, his eyes widening. "Then you met her when she was on her way to P'yŏngyang?" he asked.

"Yes." Hyŏng-sik wanted to know more. He wanted to know in detail how Yŏng-ch'ae had given up her resolve to die, and how it had come about that she was going to Tokyo.

"Then what happened?" he asked.

Pyŏng-uk lowered her head and looked at Yŏng-ch'ae's face.

"'Why die?' I said to her. It is enough to worry about how to add so much as another day to our joyous lives. Why deliberately be in such a hurry to die, I said. You have been abused and treated cruelly by everyone until now . . . " Pyŏng-uk paused hesitantly and looked at Hyŏng-sik, then laughed again. "And been abandoned by the man you thought of and cherished all your life . . . " Before these words were over, Hyŏng-sik's chest felt as though he were being pricked with needles. Pyŏng-uk paused when she saw Hyŏng-sik's expression change.

"I said to her, 'Your life until now has been one of tears and bitterness; but now your future lies before you, vast and joyful.' And I pulled her off the train."

"Thank you very much. My sins seem to have grown lighter thanks to you. I thought for sure Yŏng-ch'ae had died."

(Hmph! thought Pyŏng-uk and Yŏng-ch'ae at these words.)

"I immediately sent a telegram to the P'yŏngyang Police Station, and went to P'yŏngyang on the next train . . . " (Hyŏng-sik was happy that he now had an opportunity to explain his actions.)[156] "The police told me that they went to the station and investigated, but could not find you. So I went to a household where people might know what had happened to you, and I went to Scholar Pak's grave too." Then Hyŏng-sik remembered how he had stopped in the midst of searching for Yŏng-ch'ae, and returned to Seoul. He stopped talking, and hung his head. If only he had gone as far as Pungmang Mountain, and spent at least two hours on the banks of the Taedong River looking for her body, he thought.

"Yes, I am sure you must have done that. Then you must have exerted great effort to find Yŏng-ch'ae's body."

---

156. These parentheses were in the original text.

This woman sure knows how to give a fellow a difficult time, thought Hyŏng-sik. He felt sweat trickling down his back.

Yŏng-ch'ae listened to everything that Hyŏng-sik was saying. Her bitterness towards Hyŏng-sik was somewhat dispelled. She felt thankful that he had followed her immediately to P'yŏngyang and had made an effort to find her body; however, her thankfulness was outweighed by the thought of how Hyŏng-sik had gotten married to Sŏn-hyŏng and was going to the United States with her, all in less than a month after Yŏng-ch'ae had supposedly died. To Yŏng-ch'ae, Hyŏng-sik was both someone she had much affection for, and a cold-hearted lover. It was all in the past, though. What was the use of lamenting, and airing one's anger now? It would be better to face Hyŏng-sik with a smiling face, and make him happy. She thus changed her mood somewhat, but she did not quite want to smile at Hyŏng-sik and give him peace of mind.

"I am very sorry," she said. "I was going to write to you after I got to Hwangju, but I thought why let you know that I was momentarily still alive, when I might die any day. I decided not to write to you because I thought you might have more peace of mind if you thought I was dead. Now I see that it was good that I did not let you know that I was alive." Yŏng-ch'ae herself thought she had said too much, and smiled.

"Why didn't you send at least a postcard?" Hyŏng-sik asked. "How could you put me through that?" he said in an irate voice. Hyŏng-sik truly resented Yŏng-ch'ae when he heard her words. If Yŏng-ch'ae had sent so much as a postcard, he would have gone to her and taken her hand, as he ought to have done. Pyŏng-uk and Yŏng-ch'ae looked at Hyŏng-sik's distraught face. Yŏng-ch'ae felt even sorrier towards Hyŏng-sik.

"I knew that if I let you know that I was alive, it would only give you more futile anxiety. It would be wrong of me to dishonor you and damage your reputation. That was why I held back and said nothing." Tears flowed from Yŏng-ch'ae's eyes.

Hyŏng-sik listened to Yŏng-ch'ae, and saw the tears falling from her eyes, then turned his head away. He was more grateful than ever towards Yŏng-ch'ae for the way she always thought of what was best for him. She had tried to die for his sake, and, for his sake, had not let him know she was alive. When Hyŏng-sik thought of this, he regretted that he had been so heartless towards Yŏng-ch'ae.

Hyŏng-sik's thoughts and feelings were very confused as he looked at Yŏng-ch'ae weeping across from him, and thought of Sŏn-hyŏng sitting in the other train car. Hyŏng-sik, Yŏng-ch'ae and Pyŏng-uk said nothing for awhile. The train roared as it crossed a steel bridge. It was still raining heavily, as one could tell from the rain falling on the windows, and the sound of flowing water. There might be a flood.

114

Hyŏng-sik left Yŏng-ch'ae's train car with his head full of seething thoughts and emotions.

U-sŏn stood by waiting, then hit Hyŏng-sik on the shoulder. "Miss Yŏng-ch'ae cried!"

Hyŏng-sik took U-sŏn's hand. "What should I do?"

"Why, has something happened? Miss Yŏng-ch'ae must have been nagging you. You ladies' man, you!"

"I am not joking. Really, what should I do?"

"You have so many worries! All you have to do is get on a boat at Pusan, then get on a train at Shimonoseki, then get on a boat at Yokohama, and get off at San Francisco. What are you worried about?"

Hyŏng-sik looked resentfully at U-sŏn, and stood thinking.

"I want to cancel my trip to the United States."

"What?" U-sŏn was shocked. "Why?"

"I want to cancel my trip. It is the correct thing to do. That is what I will do." Hyŏng-sik put down U-sŏn's hand, and tried to go back to his train car, but U-sŏn grabbed him by the hand again and pulled him back.

"Have you lost your mind? Get over here."

Hyŏng-sik stood lost in thought.

"You are confused right now. What do you mean you are canceling your trip to the United States?"

"She tried to take her own life for my sake. How can I go? I will tell Sŏn-hyŏng about my intentions, and call off the marriage. That is the correct thing to do."

"Then you are going to marry Yŏng-ch'ae?"

"Yes. That is what I should do."

"Did Yŏng-ch'ae say she would marry you?"

"No."

"What if Yŏng-ch'ae says she doesn't want to marry you?"

Hyŏng-sik thought for awhile.

"Then I will live the rest of my life without getting married. I will go to a temple and be a monk."

U-sŏn laughed. "You are feeling light-headed.[157] You're just a child. You don't know anything about the world. Don't have such thoughts, even in your dreams. Just go to the United States."

"And abandon Yŏng-ch'ae?"

"You are not abandoning her. Things have already turned out this way. What is the use of having such thoughts now? Moreover, Yŏng-ch'ae is going to Tokyo to study. You should both do well in your studies, and be as

---

157. The text uses the Japanese word *nobose* (to feel light-headed). The word is transliterated in Korean, then written in a Chinese character compound in parentheses.

brother and sister in the future. Stop saying such crazy things." U-sŏn hit
Hyŏng-sik on the back. The conductor passed by, wearing a red cloth tied
around his arm, and glanced at U-sŏn and Hyŏng-sik.

Hyŏng-sik went back to his seat, leaned back and closed his eyes slowly.
Sŏn-hyŏng seemed to be asleep, or thinking, leaning back in her chair, as still
as though she were a painting.

A new question arose in Hyŏng-sik's mind. Whom did he love? Sŏn-hyŏng? Or Yŏng-ch'ae? When he faced
Yŏng-ch'ae, he thought he loved Yŏng-ch'ae. When he faced Sŏn-hyŏng, he
thought he loved Sŏn-hyŏng. Until he had boarded the train at Namdaemun,
he had thought that his body and mind were devoted to Sŏn-hyŏng; but now
that he saw Yŏng-ch'ae, Sŏn-hyŏng became number two, and Yŏng-ch'ae
became the woman he loved most. Then he looked at Sŏn-hyŏng seated
before him, and thought, This is truly my wife, my beloved wife. Did he love
both Sŏn-hyŏng and Yŏng-ch'ae? Could he love both at the same time?
According to what others said and what he himself had always thought, one
could not be truly in love with more than one person at a time. In what
condition was his mind now? He needed to somehow set some standards, and
choose between Sŏn-hyŏng and Yŏng-ch'ae.

After thinking for some time, Hyŏng-sik reached the following
conclusions.

His love for Sŏn-hyŏng was not a very deeply rooted love after all. He
knew that Sŏn-hyŏng had a pretty face, was quiet and well mannered, had
graduated first in her class at school, and was the daughter of a wealthy
yangban family. However, he did not know much else about her. Even
though they were engaged, he still knew nothing about her personality.
Sŏn-hyŏng of course did not know anything about his personality either.
Could there be true love without mutual understanding? Did Hyŏng-sik's
soul desire Sŏn-hyŏng, and did Sŏn-hyŏng's soul desire his? Did their souls
merge, and their hearts become one whenever they met? Was there between
them an actual love that could not be severed with a knife or destroyed with
fire?

With these thoughts, Hyŏng-sik could not help but feel discouraged.
Even though he sought such love from Sŏn-hyŏng, she refused to reveal her
soul and mind to him. She might not even have a soul and mind to give him,
now that he thought about it. Perhaps she was just going along with him
because she had no choice, oppressed by her parents' orders and worldly
morality. Sŏn-hyŏng had said "yes," of course. However, had that reply
indeed emerged from self-awareness?

Was Hyŏng-sik's love any different from that commonly felt by men
who are infatuated with the looks of beautiful women such as *kisaeng*? Could
he say after all that his love was a love baptized by civilization and one that
involved all of his character?

115

Hyŏng-sik had certainly not wanted Sŏn-hyŏng merely as a plaything, or out of mere physical desire. He had a strong aversion to his fellow countrymen's attitude that love was just a diversion, an amusement. He thought it was a great sin to love the opposite sex just to satisfy a moment's desire. Hyŏng-sik believed that love was one of the most important and most sacred aspects of human spirituality. His love for Sŏn-hyŏng thus was very meaningful and sacred to him, and he thought it a great spiritual revolution in comparison to the attitudes of his fellow countrymen. His attitude towards love was religiously fervent and reverent. Though he did not think that love was all there was to life, he did think that one could decide one's views of life in accordance with one's attitude towards love. His love for Sŏn-hyŏng had been too naive, though, now that he thought about it. It had been too weak in its foundations, and had been insubstantial.

Hyŏng-sik had realized it this evening. He felt the disappointment that one feels when a project to which one has devoted all of one's experience in life, has come to nothing overnight. He realized that he was still very immature in terms of spiritual and emotional development. He realized that he did not yet understand life, and that therefore it was not yet time for him to talk of love. He realized it had been very presumptuous of him to teach about civilization and life to students. He was still a child. He had tried to take on the role of an adult because he was in a society where there were no adults. When he realized this he felt embarrassed.

His thoughts continued.

I thought I knew the road that Korea[158] should take, he thought. I thought I had a firm grasp of the ideals that Korean people and Korean educators should have. However this too was nothing more than childish thinking. I still do not know Korea's past or present, he thought. In order to learn about Korea's past, he would need to cultivate an expert understanding of history, and research Korean history in detail. Moreover, in order to learn about Korea's present, he would need to understand modern civilization, the world situation, and cultivate the judgment necessary to understand society and civilization. Only then could he research in detail Korea's present condition. He would have to have a sufficient understanding of Korea's past and present in order to know what direction Korea should take. Everything I have thought and advocated until now has been childish, he thought.

Moreover, I do not understand life, he thought. What wisdom do I have about life? I do not yet know my own self. I must have some kind of view of life in order to know how to live my life, even if I basically do not know myself, he thought. I must have some standard with which to decide what is

---

158. Here the narrative uses the word Chosŏn for Korea.

right and what is good. Do I have such a standard, though? Am I indeed a person of self-awareness?

With these thoughts, Hyŏng-sik's foolishness and ignorance seemed to appear before his very eyes. He opened his eyes and looked at Sŏn-hyŏng. She was sitting motionless as before.

I thought Sŏn-hyŏng was an immature child without self-awareness, he thought. However, he and Sŏn-hyŏng were both children. They seemed to be a brother and sister who had lost the traditions of thought transmitted for generations from their ancestors, and were wandering about, not knowing what would be appropriate for them to choose from the confusion of Western thought. They had been thrown into a world without standards for life, or ideals of nation, and without someone to guide them in the world.

He opened his eyes again and looked at Sŏn-hyŏng. She seemed to be sleeping, her mouth half-open and her breast moving up and down as she breathed. Hyŏng-sik could not help but kiss Sŏn-hyŏng's hand where it lay on her lap. She seemed to be his sister, rather than his wife, and they were both trying to find their way, hand in hand, bereaved of parents.

We are on our way to learn, he thought. Since you and I are both children, we are going far away to a civilized nation in order to learn. Hyŏng-sik thought about Yŏng-ch'ae and Pyŏng-uk, who were sitting in the other train car. What pitiful young women! he thought.

He had feelings of affection for all three of the young women—Sŏn-hyŏng, Yŏng-ch'ae and Pyŏng-uk. His imagination took flight, and he thought of Yi Hŭi-gyŏng and his group, the students of the Kyŏngsŏng School, and innumerable students and children he had glimpsed on the streets of the capital and whose faces and names he did not recognize or know. They all seemed to be seeking and crying out for a path they should take, just like himself, and he thought of them affectionately as brothers and sisters. In his mind, he spread his arms and embraced his young brothers and sisters.

Hyŏng-sik thought that when he, Sŏn-hyŏng, Pyŏng-uk, Yŏng-ch'ae and hundreds of other people who were trying to learn, eventually returned to Korea, the latter would be transformed into a new Korea within days. He forgot about his earlier sadness, and fell asleep smiling to himself.

116

Sŏn-hyŏng did not have peace of mind, though. Her mind had become agitated while Hyŏng-sik had gone to see Yŏng-ch'ae and was away from his seat. When Sŏn-hyŏng saw how anguished Hyŏng-sik was to hear that Yŏng-ch'ae was on board the train, it seemed to her that Hyŏng-sik loved Yŏng-ch'ae more than he loved Sŏn-hyŏng. Even if it were true that, as Hyŏng-sik had said, he had gotten engaged to Sŏn-hyŏng in the belief that Yŏng-ch'ae had died, nevertheless the memory of Yŏng-ch'ae seemed to be buried deep in Hyŏng-sik's heart, and seemed to leave no room for Sŏn-hyŏng. It seemed as though Hyŏng-sik had reluctantly fallen in love with Sŏn-hyŏng only because Yŏng-ch'ae was gone, and that once he knew that Yŏng-ch'ae was still alive, his feelings for Yŏng-ch'ae were revived. Sŏn-hyŏng seemed to have been a provisional substitute for Yŏng-ch'ae. The thought made Sŏn-hyŏng even more unhappy.

Of course. He must have fallen in love with me only because Yŏng-ch'ae was gone, thought Sŏn-hyŏng, and frowned. Have I been a plaything for Yi Hyŏng-sik? she thought, and shivered. Hyŏng-sik must have gotten engaged to me in order to go and study in the United States, she thought, and jumped to her feet. I have become a concubine! she thought, and clenched her fists. She regretted having believed that Hyŏng-sik was an honest man. When he asked her, Do you love me? she should have said, No, I do not love you the least bit, and quickly turned around. The fact that she had not done so made her angry. She was irate too that she had docilely let him hold her hand. She was exasperated about everything. She fell back in her seat again. Is that the kind of man with whom I am going to the United States? she thought, and her nostrils quivered as though she were about to burst into tears.

She tried to think of how Hyŏng-sik would compare Yŏng-ch'ae and herself. Yŏng-ch'ae was very pretty. She looked bright and passionate, moreover. Sŏn-hyŏng knew that her own face was pretty too, judging from what she saw in the mirror, and from others' praise. She knew that people particularly praised her clear eyes. Whenever Sŏn-hyŏng saw another woman like Yŏng-ch'ae, she thus had the habit of looking at their face in detail, and comparing their face with her own. Earlier, when she saw Yŏng-ch'ae, she had immediately compared Yŏng-ch'ae's face with her own. Sŏn-hyŏng thought Yŏng-ch'ae very lovely. I would like to get to know her better, she thought. Then she found out that Yŏng-ch'ae was a *kisaeng* from Tabang-gol. Sŏn-hyŏng felt disgusted when she thought of Hyŏng-sik comparing her face with that of a filthy *kisaeng*. Even though Yŏng-ch'ae's face was pretty, it was the face of a *kisaeng*. Even though my face might not be as pretty as Yŏng-ch'ae's, she thought, nevertheless mine is that of a young woman from a *yangban* family. How could one dare compare them?

From the tenacity of Hyŏng-sik's attachment to Yŏng-ch'ae, it seemed that Hyŏng-sik preferred the coquettish, intriguing Yŏng-ch'ae to Sŏn-hyŏng, who was a respectable, honest-to-goodness student. What was Yŏng-ch'ae? thought Sŏn-hyŏng. Wasn't she a *kisaeng* of Tabang-gol?

Sŏn-hyŏng had begun to have doubts about Hyŏng-sik when she heard that he liked a *kisaeng* named Wŏr-hyang, and that he had followed Wŏr-hyang to P'yŏngyang. Afterwards, when he asked her shamelessly whether or not she loved him, and later took her hand in his, she had thought, He does indeed have the habits of one who frequents *kisaeng* houses!

Sŏn-hyŏng now thought him even more vile. At this moment, when Sŏn-hyŏng's worst feelings had been aroused, Hyŏng-sik seemed to her to possess all filthy and evil traits. What should I do? she thought, and shook her head as if angry. She pictured an imaginary Hyŏng-sik sitting before her in Hyŏng-sik's seat. You deceived me! she thought, and glared twice at the imaginary Hyŏng-sik. Fire rose within her once more, and she shook herself.

Sŏn-hyŏng had never hated anyone before. Fortunate Sŏn-hyŏng had no one to hate even if she wanted to hate someone. Everyone adored and praised her. She had disliked teachers at school several times, but she had never hated someone so much that the thought of them made her grimace. Hyŏng-sik was the first person she had ever hated.

She could see Hyŏng-sik's face before her. His face looked greasy and unrefined. She closed her eyes and opened them again twice, trying not to see his face, and scratched at her head, which was damp with sweat.

What was Hyŏng-sik doing now? she wondered. Was he talking about something interesting with Yŏng-ch'ae? She could see Yŏng-ch'ae smiling sweetly. Yŏng-ch'ae's white, round face looked wicked and crafty. What's so pretty about her? she thought, and lifted her foot and put it down again. In her mind she could Yŏng-ch'ae nodding her wicked face and beguiling Hyŏng-sik. Then Hyŏng-sik opened his broad mouth and laughed a disgusting laugh.

I can't stand the sight! Sŏn-hyŏng thought, and opened her two hands and put them on her forehead. Why isn't he back yet, she thought, and moved over one seat away from where she had been sitting. What could they be talking about for so long? she thought. Unable to bear the thought, she stood up, then sat down again. She wanted to fret all she wanted when Hyŏng-sik got back. Have fun you two, she wanted to say to them, and spit, and run away. What kind of fate is this? she thought, and shook her body. What should I do? She broke down and cried.

Sŏn-hyŏng too was a woman after all. Thus did she learn about jealousy and weeping.

117

It seemed as though it had been two or three hours since Hyŏng-sik had left to go see Yŏng-ch'ae. He seemed to be staying there for quite some time. The longer he was away, the more agitated Sŏn-hyŏng's mind became.

Sŏn-hyŏng had not particularly wanted to be loved by Hyŏng-sik until now. She thought she should love him as much as she could since he loved her very much. She thought she had no alternative but to love him, since a wife was supposed to love her husband, and her parents had told her to become Hyŏng-sik's wife. However, she did not feel towards Hyŏng-sik the sort of love that Hyŏng-sik asked of her, in which lovers held hands, clasped one another around the waist, and wanted to kiss one another. Thus she had not thought about how she would feel if another woman embraced Hyŏng-sik. Sŏn-hyŏng therefore did not know what it was that she was feeling. She knew the words "envy" and "jealousy." However she thought envy and jealousy were huge sins, and did not think they were emotions to be had by a nice young woman like herself who believed in Christ and was well educated. Creation teaches each person what they need to learn. People learn these lessons through experience, and not through books and words as in school. Perhaps this is because creation does not know how to speak, and can only put things into practice. Sŏn-hyŏng's lessons in life were now gradually approaching middle school level. She was beginning to learn about love, jealousy, anger, hatred and sadness. Human beings learn such lessons until their dying day, so Sŏn-hyŏng had a long way to go before graduation. Yŏng-ch'ae and Hyŏng-sik were much more advanced upperclassmen in this respect. Moreover, Pyŏng-uk had learned much about life through literature and art, which mimic the Creator, and steal from the Creator's thoughts.

People become adults the more they learn through such processes. They lose the pretty mien of the innocent child, and become what is referred to as an adult, with deliberate calculation, strength, stubbornness, and a sense of purpose. They lie very well, but can also speak truthful words, with great strength. Their thoughts grow richer and more complex. In other words, they become human beings.

Sŏn-hyŏng was still an innocent child who had just fallen from the sky the day before. Today she had tasted for the first time what it was like to be a human being. She had tasted the bittersweet taste of life for the first time, in love's burning flames, and jealousy's surging waves. There is an old saying that "even skeletons get smallpox at least once." In a similar way, this baptism of life is something that everyone receives. Though it might seem as though there could be no greater happiness than to get by without it, one would be better off not having been born a human being than not receiving this baptism. Sweet or bitter, it was a destiny that could not be avoided.

If one is vaccinated, one can more or less avoid catching smallpox. Even if one does not completely avoid catching smallpox, one will suffer only lightly if one does come down with the disease. That is why in recent years everyone gets vaccinated, and one hardly sees any people disfigured from smallpox any more.

There was a spiritual vaccine too, since there was smallpox of the spirit. Love, jealousy, disappointment, discouragement, sadness, deception, cunning, evil, lasciviousness, happiness, joy, success—all the myriad phenomena of life were a kind of spiritual smallpox. Some parents who think themselves shrewd try their best to keep their children from ever experiencing such smallpox. They cannot bear to see their children suffer. It is beyond their power to keep their children from these experiences, though. While primitive peoples might be mistaken in believing that there was a demon that caused smallpox, in the case of spiritual smallpox, there really was a demon that crept, unbeknownst to watchful parents, into the spirit of those watchful parents' children. Trying to hide all of the frightening and aspects of life from one's children was like confining one's children to a room because of germs in the open air outside. People who have not been inured to outside air, with its many germs, thus will come down with a fever and diarrhea as soon as germs enter their internal organs, and will die. However those who have been accustomed all their life to outside air, and whose organs have developed the strength to resist germs, will not be afraid even if quite a few germs enter their body. It was like the way a person who has had smallpox develops a resistance to smallpox.

Sŏn-hyŏng had been confined in a room until now. She did not even know that there were germs in the air outside. Moreover, she had not been vaccinated. The germ of jealousy had entered her now, though. And the germ of love. She did not know what to do. If she had learned about life in general from religion or literature, and had thus learned about what love was, and jealousy, she would clearly have known what to do in this situation. However this was the first time she had encountered such fearsome illnesses.

Sŏn-hyŏng lifted her head suddenly. She looked back on her thoughts just now, and shivered in shock. Her eyes grew wide. What has happened to me? she thought, and held her breath for awhile. This painful new experience was as frightening to her as dark night. What is this? she thought, shivers running through her entire body twice.

He is staying there for quite some time, she thought, looking around the train car absentmindedly.

118

Sŏn-hyŏng became afraid. Her internal organs seemed to be on fire, and sooty flames seemed to be darting from her nose. The sound of her own panting breath seemed like that of a large demon standing beside her, blowing cold gusts of air on her. Her body seemed to be falling into a dark hell, just as she had imagined when studying the Bible. She shivered once, then looked around at the people dozing here and there in the train car. They too seemed to have become frightening demons. Any moment now, it seemed as though they would open their eyes glaringly and come running at her.

Oh, how frightening! thought Sŏn-hyŏng, and covered her face with her hands. When she covered her face, she could see Yŏng-ch'ae and Hyŏng-sik. They were holding each other in a tight embrace, cheek against cheek, and looking at her contemptuously. She stood beside them and spit. Then they suddenly turned into fearsome demons and tore her apart. Oh! Sŏn-hyŏng thought, and collapsed. She shivered with inexplicable fear. She quickly thought of God, and tried to pray. The only words that came out, though, were, "God, God," and she could not say anything else. She sought God several times, then said, without quite knowing the meaning of what she said, "Please forgive me my sins." That was enough to make her fears subside, and her breathing calm. She thus imagined Christ standing beside her, and closed her eyes.

It was then that Hyŏng-sik returned with U-sŏn, and kissed her hand. Sŏn-hyŏng was by no means asleep at the time. Even though she knew that Hyŏng-sik had come into the train car, she deliberately did not open her eyes. When Hyŏng-sik's lips touched the back of her hand, she hated him so much she wanted to slap him in the face. This is what he does with *kisaeng*, she thought.

Then she fell asleep. The glaring electric lights illuminated the faces of these two suffering people all night long, as the sooty black engine car pierced through the darkness and pouring rain, its large eye wide open. There were few passengers getting off or boarding. The train went around the spur of a mountain, then through a tunnel, carrying the passengers southward as they dreamed their various dreams.

The two awoke when the train reached Samnangjin[159] Station. The short hand of the clock already pointed to five o'clock, but the sky was cloudy, and the electric lights of the station were still twinkling.

The conductor tucked his hat under his arm, and bowed his head politely.

"The train tracks have been damaged at two locations, and we will not be able to depart for four hours," he said.

Passengers who had been sleeping rubbed their eyes and made disgruntled noises, then gathered their baggage and got off the train.

"Look at the water!" someone exclaimed, looking out a train window. One could not tell whether they were exclaiming with happiness or sorrow. Train workers wearing raincoats went about their work unobtrusively near the train, ignoring the rain. The station was in a commotion, as if over a major event.

"We too should get off the train," said Hyŏng-sik. "How can we stay in the train for four hours?" He looked at Sŏn-hyŏng. Sŏn-hyŏng looked at Hyŏng-sik's lips, and thought about how he had put his lips on her hand last night.

"Of course, let's get off the train," she said, laughing inwardly, and stood up first. Hyŏng-sik disembarked, carrying his suitcase and a blanket, and Sŏn-hyŏng followed, carrying the book that she had been reading, and

---

159. Samnangjin is a township in Miryang County, South Kyŏngsang Province.

her handbag. When they went towards the ticket gate, Pyŏng-uk came running over to them.

"Are you disembarking?" she asked to neither in particular. She realized that she had forgotten to offer them morning greetings, and smiled.

"Yes, how can we wait for four hours on the train? We are going to go to an inn and rest, and perhaps look at the water."

"Then we will get off too. Please wait just a moment!" Pyŏng-uk ran in the other direction. Hyŏng-sik and Sŏn-hyŏng's eyes followed in her direction. Yŏng-ch'ae could be seen standing at a train window facing towards Hyŏng-sik and Sŏn-hyŏng, and gazing outside. She did not seem to have seen them.

What shall I do? thought Hyŏng-sik.

That wicked woman Yŏng-ch'ae, thought Sŏn-hyŏng. Pyŏng-uk ran over to Yŏng-ch'ae.

"Let's get off the train too. They are getting off," she said. Only when Yŏng-ch'ae saw Pyŏng-uk look back in the direction from where she had come did Yŏng-ch'ae see Hyŏng-sik and Sŏn-hyŏng. She shrank back immediately.

Yŏng-ch'ae walked reluctantly towards Hyŏng-sik, trying to hide herself behind Pyŏng-uk, who was walking ahead of her. Pyŏng-uk stepped aside, and Yŏng-ch'ae and Hyŏng-sik were left standing face-to-face. Yŏng-ch'ae greeted Hyŏng-sik and Sŏn-hyŏng politely, nodding at Hyŏng-sik, and smiling at Sŏn-hyŏng. Sŏn-hyŏng smiled and nodded in return. Yŏng-ch'ae and Sŏn-hyŏng both blushed all at once, though.

The four of them formed a line and went through the ticket gate. Idle passengers stared at them, and smiled or murmured. It looked as though Hyŏng-sik was traveling with three younger sisters. In the station waiting room, they gave their luggage to a servant from an inn, then followed the servant out and stood at a corner of the station and looked at the surging red waters of the Naktong River.

119

"Look at the water!" cried Pyŏng-uk, leaning over a wire.

The water! exclaimed the other three inwardly, though saying nothing.

"Look at that! Those houses are half-submerged in water!" said Pyŏng-uk, pointing to some thatched roof houses that stood along a road that branched off into the road to Masan. It was indeed a great flood. Muddy red water was everywhere, leaving only the mountains unsubmerged. One could hear water rushing in whirlpools in the middle of the river, and it seemed as though the waters would erode the flanks of the mountains on either side of the waters, until the ground at the foot of the mountains was completely swept away.

The floodwater seemed to be trapped in a narrow road, sweeping over all puddles in its path, and massing in a swell of water that looked as though it were waiting for the waters ahead of it to move on. The waters had lost their way, and invaded villages, driving away inhabitants, and occupying rooms, kitchens and shelves. People who had lost their homes in the flood climbed up the mountains seeking higher ground, carrying children on their backs and pulling the elderly by the hand. The red waters carried away the household furnishings that people had treasured and never allowed others to touch, let alone have. Moving to and fro, the waters then tossed the furnishings into the middle of the Naktong River, and sent them tumbling towards the boundless sea.

The stalks of grain that people had taken such pains to grow that summer were tossed about in the red waves and broken, or separated from their tender roots. Rice plant flowers that would have ripened with yellow grain and drooped their heavy heads in mists that filled the valleys during autumn nights—these flowers were now destroyed. The entire earth seemed to have come under the power of the red waters.

The rain had stopped, but full black clouds circled the sky, ready to burst into rain at any moment. The clouds would hurriedly flee to the east, then as if on second thought, charge towards the west. As though unable to hold back any longer, the clouds would release a few thick raindrops from time to time.

Waterfalls and streams that had suddenly appeared on the high, naked mountains seemed suspended upside down. It looked like lines of white drawn randomly against a background of black. The sound of the streams rushing down, gashing the flesh of the naked mountains and scraping at the mountains' bones, joined with the sound of the river's fearsome torrent, so that it was like listening to a resounding concert.

The soil had been thirsting for water, and drank its fill until it became soft. It seemed as though the soil would have been saturated to the very center of the earth. The sky and earth had become a world of water. What will happen? thought those who stood in this world of water, and looked up at the sky.

"Won't the floods ruin this year's harvest?" asked Pyŏng-uk, looking at Hyŏng-sik. Hyŏng-sik stood watching people scrambling to higher ground, then turned his head towards Pyŏng-uk.

"That's a good question. I wish the rain would stop now. If it goes on another day, agriculture will suffer terrible damage," he said. The three young women stared at Hyŏng-sik's mouth as he spoke. Within them moved feelings of worry and fear that transcended the self. Thought of floods and a bad harvest, the sight of billowing clouds, the sound of the water, and the sight of homeless people scrambling for safety made them forget about the self, and have common thoughts that all shared as human beings.

"If it stopped raining now, would the floodwaters recede by the end of today?" asked Sŏn-hyŏng, looking at Hyŏng-sik.

"It would probably take until tomorrow morning," he said.

"If there is no rain upstream, then the floodwaters will soon subside," said Yŏng-ch'ae. "But if it is raining upstream . . . " Yŏng-ch'ae thought of how full the waters of the Taedong River had been the year before, even though it had not been raining then.

"Are there times when floods reach the city of P'yŏngyang?" Sŏn-hyŏng asked Yŏng-ch'ae.

"Of course. Floods hardly ever reach within the city walls, but often reach the outer layer of walls that surround the city walls.[160] The year before last I took a boat through the new city streets outside the outer layer of walls that surround P'yŏngyang." Yŏng-ch'ae glanced at Sŏn-hyŏng. Sŏn-hyŏng quickly avoided Yŏng-ch'ae's glance. Pyŏng-uk listened for awhile, then smiled and thought, You two are really getting along, aren't you! When Yŏng-ch'ae saw Pyŏng-uk smiling, she took a step nearer to Pyŏng-uk and quietly took her hand in hers, trying not to let anyone notice. Pyŏng-uk squeezed Yŏng-ch'ae's hand. The four of them looked distantly at wherever it was each wanted to look at, saying nothing. They left off the common thoughts they had been sharing, though, and each became an individual self. Then they lost interest in standing there and looking. They stood there vacantly, nonetheless; then, as if having discussed the matter, all four of them eventually turned their steps towards an inn that was about a dozen paces away. "*Irasshai!*"[161] said the maidservants and the manager[162] of the inn as they led them to an eight mat *tatami*[163] room on the north end of the second floor. As they passed the rooms, they could see that each room was full of guests. All of the guests were talking. The inn was doing good business, thanks to the flood.

The four of them each took a floor cushion and sat down. Just then a sudden rain poured down on the tin roof of the inn.

What will those homeless people do? the three young women thought all at once, and frowned. The rain kept pouring down. It was quiet inside the room.

120

Crowds of homeless people were drenched in rain as they stood at the foot of the mountains, water running all over their bodies. Women holding children bent over the children and covered them with their bodies. Some

---

160. *Oesŏng* is an outer layer of walls constructed around the walls of a city.

161. "*Irasshai!*" is Japanese, for "Welcome! Please come in." The text transliterates the Japanese in Korean.

162. The text uses the Japanese word *bantō* for manager, transliterated in Korean.

163. *Tatami* is straw matting used as floor covering in a Japanese home.

children began to sob though, when for a moment, they could hardly breathe in the sudden downpour of rain. Then their mothers would sway gently with the child in their embrace, tears mixing with the raindrops that streamed in rivulets over their heads.

One old woman seemed to have resigned herself to the rain, and sat crouching listlessly in the downpour and gazing at distant mountains that were covered with rain. A middle-aged man ran in search of cover, pulling a tow-headed boy with him.

Young men and women whose faces were sunburned from weeding all summer stood and looked helplessly at where the rice paddies that they had planted with such effort had been. The red waves gradually submerged even the little that had been left of the rice paddies.

Every time thunder shook the mountains and streams, rain like a beaded curtain would descend with a roar on the mountain in front of the inn, only to be blown at an angle by the breath of the southeastern wind, and descend on the mountain in back. Then muddy water would come surging out between thickets of grass, pushing sand before it. Then there would be another clap of thunder, and another spell of fierce rain would come charging over the mountain in front of the inn. Over one hundred people stood still in the rain, not knowing what to do. They were afraid and sad at first, but after awhile they felt nothing. They just sobbed and shrank back whenever the thick raindrops struck their faces forcefully.

The bodies of several of them grew chill with cold. Their lips turned blue, and their bodies trembled. From houses sprawled before their eyes rose the smoke of fires over which breakfast was being cooked. The smoke seemed to be unable to exert any strength in the driving rain, and retreated back into the chimney almost as soon as it had emerged.

It seemed as though it would never stop raining. The rain poured down as though the entire sky were melting and turning into rain.

In the midst of the rain, at the foot of the mountain, was a straw mat propped up by an A-frame used for carrying loads on one's back. Beneath the mat was an old, wrinkled woman in an apron, holding a young woman in her arms. The young woman was biting her lip and seemed to be in pain. A young man wearing grass-stained summer trousers, his head bare with no covering for his topknot,[164] stood holding down the straw mat to keep it from flying away in the wind. He would hold down the corners of the straw sack whenever any of them started flapping in the wind.

The young woman in the old woman's arms writhed about as if in unbearable pain, and cried out from time to time. Then the old woman would tighten her embrace around the young woman, and the young man would

---

164. Korean men traditionally wore their hair in a topknot, and would cover the topknot with a hat.

look at the young woman. Water flowing down the mountain pushed muddy waters before it and flowed around the old woman as though the old woman's body were an island. The hems of the old woman and the young woman's skirts swirled in the mud.

Eventually the thunder fled to the west, the rain tapered off, and the earth and sky grew brighter. When the mountains had returned to their usual appearance, the sound of water rushing away in all directions could be heard.

The young man took off the straw mat that he was using to cover himself, and bent down and looked into the young woman's face.

"How are you feeling?" he asked. The young woman just twisted her body in pain, and said nothing. The old woman stroked the young woman's hand.

"Look at this. Her entire body is cold as ice. What should we do?" the old woman said with worry and anger, tears falling from her eyes.

"I don't know," the young man said and frowned.

The young woman writhed in pain again. "Oh, it feels as though my guts are being torn apart." She began to cry. Her entire body was covered with mud.

"Go to a nearby house and talk to someone. After all, there is such a thing as compassion, isn't there? Surely they would not turn us away."

"Where should I go? Who would take in a sick person?"

Just then, Hyŏng-sik and his group left the inn after eating breakfast, and came walking in the direction of the old woman and the young man and woman. People who were dripping with water just sat down on the ground and silently watched the group walk by. Other guests came out of the inn to look at the floodwaters, walking in twos and threes and smoking cigarettes. The sudden rains had washed dirt from the surface of the road, so that the road was smooth and flat. Here and there a few small streams of water flowed over the road. Pyŏng-uk, who was walking ahead of the others, stopped in front of the sick young woman.

"Can I help you? Are you unwell?" she asked. The young man glanced at Pyŏng-uk, then hung his head as if in shame. Hyŏng-sik, Yŏng-ch'ae and Sŏn-hyŏng too approached and stood there. The young woman who was covered with mud writhed again and cried out in pain. The old woman fell backwards, then wiped her muddied hands on her arms and waist.

"She is expecting, and the baby is due now. She has been having stomach pain since early this morning." The old woman could not continue.

"Where is your home?" asked Hyŏng-sik.

"It is under water now. That damned water . . . Please help us!"

The young woman cried out again and seemed as though she were gasping for air. Pyŏng-uk stroked the young woman's hand, then looked back at Hyŏng-sik.

"We should get a room, and take the sick woman there and have her lie down. She seems to be going into labor." Yŏng-ch'ae and Sŏn-hyŏng grimaced. Sŏn-hyŏng shivered and stepped back as though she had seen something frightening. Hyŏng-sik ran towards the inn. Everyone stood and watched Hyŏng-sik.

121

Pyŏng-uk sat down, tucking up the sleeves of her unlined Korean blouse, and her skirt, and rubbed the young woman's hand. "Yŏng-ch'ae! Let's massage her first of all." Yŏng-ch'ae too tucked up her sleeves and skirt, and went behind the old woman.

"Please stand up," she said to the old woman, and tried to put her arms around the ailing young woman.

"Please don't trouble yourself. Her body is covered with mud. You will get your pretty clothes dirty," said the old woman, and would not listen to Yŏng-ch'ae. Yŏng-ch'ae could do nothing but sit next to the old woman and stroke the young woman's disheveled hair into order. Sŏn-hyŏng sat and massaged the young woman's feet and legs. Onlookers stood around them. The three young women's white hands became stained with yellow mud.

In a little while, a perspiring Hyŏng-sik came running back. "Let's go to the inn," he said. "I told them to warm a room."

"It is said that one's parents give one life, and therefore it is filial piety not to allow the body to be harmed. I am very grateful to you. How can I ever repay you?" The old woman pulled the young woman up to a sitting position, and said to the young man, "Take her on your back, and carry her to the inn." Without saying a word, the young man took the young woman on his back and stood up, glancing at Hyŏng-sik and his group. The ailing woman put her arms around the young man's neck, and rubbed her face against his shoulder. Hyŏng-sik walked ahead of them. The mudstained old woman supported the young woman's back with one hand. Sŏn-hyŏng, Pyŏng-uk and Yŏng-ch'ae followed behind them. Onlookers followed them for awhile, murmuring, then fell away little by little.

They took the young woman to the inn, changed her clothes, and lay her down; then Hyŏng-sik went to bring a doctor, and Sŏn-hyŏng, Pyŏng-uk and Yŏng-ch'ae massaged the young woman's body. The old woman sat at the sick woman's head, weeping, then lay down herself, saying that her chest hurt. She had suffered chest pains in her youth, and today she had them again because she had been out in the cold rain all day and her body had caught a chill. Yŏng-ch'ae and Sŏn-hyŏng took care of the expectant mother, and Pyŏng-uk took care of the old woman.

The old woman would lose consciousness for awhile, then when she came to, would say, "You have been so kind. I will never be able to forget your kindness, even when I am dead and am nothing but bones. May you enjoy long life, wealth and honor, give birth to many sons and daughters, live well, and go to heaven."

The three young women lowered their heads and smiled. Yŏng-ch'ae and Sŏn-hyŏng perspired as they massaged the expectant mother's limbs, and stroked her abdomen. Yŏng-ch'ae and Sŏn-hyŏng's hands would sometimes touch. Whenever that happened, the two young women would look at each other.

"I will go to the kitchen and heat some water, and bring it," said Yŏng-ch'ae, and stood up.

"No, I will heat the water," said Sŏn-hyŏng.

"No, I will do it," said Yŏng-ch'ae, holding Sŏn-hyŏng by the hand and making her sit down.

"Keep massaging her. I will heat some water," Yŏng-ch'ae said, and stood up and left the room. Sŏn-hyŏng watched Yŏng-ch'ae leave the room. Then she closed her eyes. Sŏn-hyŏng was flustered, and hardly knew what to do. Pyŏng-uk had smiled to herself when she saw Yŏng-ch'ae and Sŏn-hyŏng talking together. Yŏng-ch'ae returned with water that she had heated, and, together with Sŏn-hyŏng, washed the expectant mother's hands and feet. As they were doing this, Hyŏng-sik arrived with the doctor. As the doctor examined the patient, the others stood around them and watched the doctor's mouth and eyes. The young man, who had been sitting silently outside the door, stuck his head into the room and watched the examination.

"There is nothing to worry about," the doctor said, and left, saying that he would send medicine. The doctor took the young man with him so that the young man could bring the medicine back. The expectant mother and the old woman were calmer now and more alert, and their faces looked more relaxed, though they still suffered some pain from time to time.

The old woman kept blessing them, saying, "How can I ever repay you for your kindness? May you enjoy long life, wealth and honor, and have many sons."

The old woman said that she had become a widow when she was young, and had endured much suffering while raising her son. Eventually her son grew up, and she acquired a daughter-in-law. They farmed, though the land they farmed belonged to someone else, and after awhile, they were able to enjoy life. The old woman built a small house with her own two hands, and even bought a dry field. Her daughter-in-law became pregnant, moreover, and the old woman thought that if she could only hold a grandson in her arms, her happiness would be complete and there would be nothing for which she envied others. Then yesterday, all their farm work had been submerged in water, and this morning at dawn, their house too had gone under the water.

"I hope my house doesn't get washed away," the old woman said, sobbing. It had taken her sixty years of hard work and suffering to get that house. If it were washed away in the flood, she might never set eyes on a house of her own again. The old woman's only wish was to hold a grandson in her arms, and die in her own home, lying on the warmest part of the heated floor, closest to the fire. They probably wouldn't be able to get so much as ten wŏn for the house if they tried to sell it, but to the family it was more precious than a palace. All the old woman could see was that small house with a stone wall around it. Every time she thought of the waves tearing down the house, the old woman felt as though her own flesh were being cut off.

"Just when you think you are going to be happy, something like this happens," the old woman said. "What sin did I commit in a former life that even my young ones have to go through disaster?"

"Don't think like that!" said Yŏng-ch'ae, trying to console the old woman. "You will live well again. Isn't there a God?" Yŏng-ch'ae thought of how she herself had needed consoling from Pyŏng-uk the night before, and was amused at the change in situations.

"Perhaps I will go to the other world now, and live well there," the old woman said, then paused, lifted her head suddenly, and looked at her daughter-in-law. "Does your stomach feel better? You would have died if not for these people," the old woman said, and blessed them again.

122

Pyŏng-uk went to the police station, and asked to see the station chief. The station chief gave Pyŏng-uk a strange look.

"Why do you want to see me?" he asked.

Pyŏng-uk told him some of the flood victims were sick, and that there was an expectant mother, and women with infants. She told him of the pitiful sight of these flood victims shivering in the rain and without a hot morning meal. She told him how she could not bear the sight of infants crying because their mothers' breasts had no milk; the mothers themselves had not eaten, and therefore could not nurse their children.

Since the train to Pusan had been stopped because of the rains and would not leave until the afternoon, Pyŏng-uk proposed holding a concert to raise money to give the flood victims some hot soup and rice, and she asked the station chief for his permission and support.

The station chief looked more and more surprised. "Is there anyone who can perform?" he asked with emotion.

"I attend music school, though I am not very good at music. And there are two women with me who can sing songs that they learned at school."

The station chief was deeply moved. "The authorities have just been considering relief plans, but since the floods happened so suddenly . . . " The station chief paused for thought. "Thank you very much. You have my permission and support, of course," the station chief said, and jumped up, put on his hat and went out.

He went to the train station and arranged with the station manager to use the waiting room for the concert, and sent a policeman to spread word of the concert through the inns and city streets. Passengers who had been waiting for four or five hours and were feeling bored, gathered in the waiting room. Here and there were a few third-class passengers dressed in white. All the chairs in the station were set out in the waiting room, and chairs were also brought from nearby inns and set up in a semicircle. The small waiting room was full. A large table was placed next to the entrance as a stage. The audience had heard that there would be a benefit concert, but they did not know who would be appearing, and their eyes were wide as they looked at the stage. After awhile, the station chief approached the side of the stage and, looking around at the audience, began to speak.

"I have asked you here for the following reasons. I would like to ask everyone to please look at the foot of that mountain. Some of our unfortunate fellow countrymen have become homeless because of the flood, and are wandering about there, drenched in the rain, with nothing to eat. Just now, a beautiful young woman came to the police station and asked if there could be a music concert to raise money for a meal for those needy fellow countrymen. I do not know how much she knows about music, but I am sure that her admirable dedication will move the hearts of all the ladies and gentlemen here, and bring everyone to tears." Tears fell from the station chief's eyes, and he could not speak. The faces of the people in the audience stung with emotion. Here and there came the sound of women blowing their noses. The station chief continued.

"We must respond to this young woman's dedication. I will introduce her to you now." The station chief summoned the three young women who were standing side by side in a corner of the room across from him. The women greeted the audience politely, beginning with Pyŏng-uk, who held a violin. Applause shook the walls of the room. Some people cried out in emotion.

Pyŏng-uk began to speak on behalf of the three of them. "We are not trying to have this concert because we know about music. We are only having the concert in the hope that you will sympathize with the flood victims. Moreover, since we do not have any musical scores in our luggage, we will perform from memory, and we will probably make many mistakes." Pyŏng-uk bent her head to the violin, placed her fingers on the strings, and began to play a tragic melody from "Aida."[165] Everyone was quiet and still. The sad music resonated in their hearts, and the violin strings seemed as though they would break at any moment.

---

165. "'*Aida' ŭi 'Pigok'*'" means literally "'The Lament' from 'Aida.'" It is not clear to which specific melody in the opera this refers.

The song was perfect for the circumstances. The listeners, whose hearts were heavy with emotion, ended up wanting to weep. Sometimes the audience's breathing would pause, then continue, following the motions of Pyŏng-uk's hand moving the bow quickly, then slowly, up, then down. Rather than my describing at length what it was like to hear that sad music, it would be better for the reader to think of "The Mandolin Ballad"[166] of Bo Ju-yi. The sad melody reverberated at length, as though it would never end; then Pyŏng-uk clasped her violin and bowed her head. There was applause louder than before, and calls for another song. Pyŏng-uk's face glowed with the color of peach blossoms.

After that, Yŏng-ch'ae sang a hymn that she had learned from Pyŏng-uk, entitled "When I think of the past, I am ashamed." Yŏng-ch'ae sang as Pyŏng-uk accompanied her on the violin. Yŏng-ch'ae's face was full of expression as she sang.

She sang with seemingly effortless skill, her voice having been well practiced and trained during ten years of singing. Even those in the audience who had not been able to appreciate the refined violin piece were intoxicated by Yŏng-ch'ae's lovely voice.

I have nowhere to shed these tears

Tears rose in the eyes of the audience when she sang these words. Next Yŏng-ch'ae, Sŏn-hyŏng and Pyŏng-uk sang a song that Yŏng-ch'ae had just now written in classical Chinese and that Hyŏng-sik had translated into Korean. The song was about the pitiful people who had become homeless and were out in the rain. The song moved the listeners even more deeply.

123

"Though the baby cries, mother's breast will give no milk. What can mother feed the baby? Cruel red waters have washed away everything they worked for spring and summer. Darkness descends in the wind and rain. Elderly parents and young couples have lost their homes. Where can they sleep? Let us give them a bowl of hot rice and soup."

The simple lyrics and moving melody brought tears to the eyes of the audience. The three young women bowed politely to warm, yet solemn applause. The station chief waited until the applause faded, then stood up.

"There are tears of emotion in everyone's eyes. On behalf of the audience, I would like to thank these three young women." He bowed his head towards Pyŏng-uk, Yŏng-ch'ae and Sŏn-hyŏng. The three returned his greeting. The audience applauded.

---

166. Stephen Owen, ed. and trans., *An Anthology of Chinese Literature: Beginnings to 1911* (New York: W. W. Norton and Company, 1996), 496.

The brief concert was over then, having lasted less than an hour. Several people in the audience put together over eighty wŏn in donations right then and there. The station chief gave the money to Pyŏng-uk. "Use this money as you see fit," he said. He was expressing respect to Pyŏng-uk. She refused the money, though. "Please take care of that yourself," she said. The station chief nodded to indicate that he accepted the money, and said that he would find the best ways possible to help the flood victims with the money. Everyone wanted to know the names of Pyŏng-uk and the other two young women, but the three young women just lowered their heads and said nothing.

Meanwhile, people who had lost their homes in the flood were sitting outside on the ground, not knowing what to do. They were becoming hungry, and starting to shiver, but they had no plans as to what to do. They could only accept whatever happened, and hope for the best.

They were powerless. Though no one could stand against the violence of nature, these people were particularly powerless. They were so powerless that everything they had built up through a lifetime of hard work could be washed away by rain overnight. It was as though they had built their lives on a foundation of sand. When the rain stopped and the water receded, they would scrape together the scattered sands, and build the foundations anew. They were like ants making a nest in the sand by digging with their weak limbs. These people who had lost everything overnight to rain and stood shivering in the rain, seemed pitiful, and yet weak and foolish too.

Looking at their faces, it did not seem likely that they would have any particular wisdom. They all looked foolish and insensitive. All they did was farm with what little knowledge they had about farming. In this manner, they might accumulate a few sacks of rotten rice over the years—that is, if God let them. If there was a flood, all of it would be washed away. They thus never got any richer, but just got poorer. Their bodies grew gradually weaker, and their minds duller.[167] If left in this condition, they would eventually become like the Ainu people of Hokkaido.

They needed to be empowered. They needed to be given knowledge. They needed to have their means of living thereby made complete.

"Science! Science!" Hyŏng-sik exclaimed to himself when he returned to the inn and sat down. The three young women looked at Hyŏng-sik.

"We must first of all give the Korean people science. We must give them knowledge." He stood up clenching his fists, and walked about the room. "What are your thoughts, after having seen what you saw today?"

---

167. In the 1917 *Maeil Sinbo* edition, this sentence simply reads, "Their minds grew gradually duller." The 1918 Sinmungwan edition changed this to "Their bodies grew gradually weaker, and their minds duller."

The young women did not know what to say in answer to Hyŏng-sik's question. After awhile, Pyŏng-uk spoke up.
"I felt sorry for them." She smiled. "Didn't you?" They had all grown much closer while working together that day.
"Yes, one pities them. What is the cause of their pitiful situation?" "It is that they do not know about modern civilization, of course. They are not empowered to make a living for themselves."
"Then what must we do to save them . . . to save ourselves?" Hyŏng-sik looked at Pyŏng-uk. Yŏng-ch'ae and Sŏn-hyŏng looked back and forth at Hyŏng-sik and Pyŏng-uk's faces.
"We must give them strength! We must give them modern civilization." Pyŏng-uk said confidently.
"And how can we do that?"
"We must teach them, guide them."
"How?"
"Through education, and through actual practice."
Yŏng-ch'ae and Sŏn-hyŏng did not quite understand the meaning of this conversation. They thought they understood, but they did not understand with as much urgency or conviction as Hyŏng-sik and Pyŏng-uk. Nevertheless, the realities they had seen with their eyes that day gave them a real-life learning experience. Such learning could not be acquired at school, or from verbose oratory.

124
Everyone was nervous. Moreover, Yŏng-ch'ae had never heard a discussion of such an important question. "How can we save them?" It was a very important question. Hyŏng-sik and Pyŏng-uk seemed very mature and impressive as they talked about this question. Yŏng-ch'ae thought about poetry in which Du Fu and Li Bo expressed concern about the world. She thought of the speech that she and Wŏr-hwa had heard five years ago, given by the principal of the P'aesŏng School. She had been young then, and had not understood the speech very clearly. Nevertheless, she remembered that the principal had said, "Your ancestors were not as foolish as you." She remembered that upon hearing these words, it had occurred to her that the people she encountered every day were indeed foolish. Yŏng-ch'ae thought that Hyŏng-sik's words and those of the principal shared some common points. She looked at Hyŏng-sik again.
"Right. We must teach and guide them through education and actual practice. However, who will do this?" Hyŏng-sik closed his mouth. The three young women felt shivers run over their skin.
"Who will do this?" Hyŏng-sik asked again more emphatically. He looked at each of them. The young women were spiritually moved, in a way

that they had never experienced before and that they could not describe in words. Shivers ran over them all at the same time.

"Who will do this?" Hyŏng-sik asked again.

"We will!" The words dropped from the young women's lips in unison without their having planned it. Flames seemed to flash before their eyes. The earth seemed to shake as though there had been a great earthquake. Hyŏng-sik sat with his head lowered for some time.

"Yes. We must do it. This is why we are going overseas to study. Who is giving us the money to take the train, and money for tuition? Korea. Why? So that we can acquire strength, knowledge and civilization, and bring them back with us. So that we can establish a solid foundation for the people's livelihood, based on modern civilization. Isn't that why?" Hyŏng-sik pulled his wallet from his vest pocket, and took out a blue train ticket.

"This train ticket contains the sweat of those people who are shivering in the rain, including the young man we saw. They are asking us to make sure that they are never put in such a needy situation again." Hyŏng-sik shook himself, as though with new resolve. The three young women trembled too.

At that moment, each one of them thought about "the work that I must do." They seemed to have become one body and one mind, without distinctions of self and other.

Ever since Yŏng-ch'ae had offered to bring heated water for the expectant mother, and had held Sŏn-hyŏng by the wrist and sat her down, Sŏn-hyŏng had begun to feel affection for Yŏng-ch'ae. When she, Yŏng-ch'ae and Pyŏng-uk together sang the song that Yŏng-ch'ae had written, Sŏn-hyŏng had liked Yŏng-ch'ae so much that she had taken Yŏng-ch'ae's hand in hers. Now when Sŏn-hyŏng, Yŏng-ch'ae and Pyŏng-uk answered that they would be the ones to help the Korean people, Sŏn-hyŏng felt even more affection for Yŏng-ch'ae. Moreover, when Hyŏng-sik conversed with Pyŏng-uk, there was a kind of solemn and dignified look on his face, and she felt sorry about the thoughts she had had about him. Sŏn-hyŏng wanted to love Hyŏng-sik and Yŏng-ch'ae always. She looked at their faces with a new perspective.

Hyŏng-sik lifted his head.

"Let us work so that when we are old, we will see a better Korea. Let us think of how we resented our lazy, powerless predecessors, and let us work so that our grandchildren thank us."

"Why don't we tell each other about our future plans?" Hyŏng-sik said smiling, and looked at the three women. Only then did the serious expressions on the three women's faces relax, and the women smiled.

"You speak first," Pyŏng-uk said to Hyŏng-sik.[168]

---

168. In the 1917 *Maeil Sinbo* edition, Pyŏng-uk says, "You speak first, Sŏn-hyŏng." The word "Sŏn-hyŏng" was changed to *sŏnsaeng* in the 1918 Sinmungwan edition, so that the sentence

"May I join you?" It was U-sŏn's voice outside the door. Hyŏng-sik jumped up, opened the door and took U-sŏn's hand. "Why are you just getting here now?" U-sŏn nodded in greeting to the women, then sat down next to Hyŏng-sik. "The newspaper company sent me a telegram telling me to take a look at the flooding in the Samnangjin area." U-sŏn rubbed his chin. Yŏng-ch'ae looked down. "How did you know we were here?" Hyŏng-sik asked. "I was at the station, and I heard about everything." U-sŏn bowed to the women. "Thank you. They are praising you effusively at the station. It is like a breath of fresh air!" U-sŏn told them what he had heard at the station in general, then said to Hyŏng-sik, "It is all right if I publish an article in the newspaper about today, isn't it?"

Hyŏng-sik did not answer, but looked at Pyŏng-uk and said, "Would it be all right?"

"Oh, my! Why would you want to publish an article in the newspaper about that?"

"How can you say that? Even a fellow like me feels greatly moved. I almost wept just hearing about it." U-sŏn had indeed been profoundly moved when he heard from a passenger at the station about the concert. U-sŏn had a cheerful and outgoing personality, and the only times he had been moved to tears were this time, and when Yŏng-ch'ae had gone to take her life. There was something U-sŏn had been wanting to say to Pyŏng-uk and Yŏng-ch'ae since he left the station.

"You were talking about something?" he asked, drinking the tea that a servant brought, and trying to find a chance to say what he wanted to say.

125

"Yes, we were going to talk about how we can save the Korean people. We were each going to talk about our goals."

"Then I would like to listen too!"

Sŏn-hyŏng and Pyŏng-uk thought U-sŏn's straw hat and the way he looked when he talked were so funny that they had to hold back their laughter. Only Yŏng-ch'ae was flustered, and blushed. U-sŏn saw Yŏng-ch'ae, but pretended not to know her.

"Whose turn is it?" U-sŏn asked.

"It seems to be my turn," said Hyŏng-sik.

means "You speak first, Mr. Lee." The word *sŏnsaeng* means "teacher;" it can also be used after a person's name or their job title, as an honorific expressing respect for that person; it can mean someone who has knowledge or experience about a certain subject; and it can be used to mean "you." Yi Ki-moon, *Sae kugŏ sajŏn* (Seoul: Tonga ch'ulp'ansa, 1996), 1137.

"Oh, then go right ahead." U-sŏn closed his eyes and lowered his head, preparing to listen. Pyŏng-uk poked Yŏng-ch'ae in the side. Sŏn-hyŏng turned her head away, trying not to laugh. "I want to be an educator. For my area of specialty, I would like to research biology." None of the listeners knew what "biology" meant, though. Hyŏng-sik himself did not really know. He had only decided on that because he thought science was important, and because biology seemed as though it would fit his interests and abilities. Pathetic was the plight of these people who had taken upon themselves the responsibility of constructing a new civilization without even knowing what biology was; and pathetic was the era that relied on them.

"You are going into music, right?" Hyŏng-sik said to Pyŏng-uk.

"Yes, I am going into music."

"And what about you, Yŏng-ch'ae?"

Yŏng-ch'ae said nothing and looked at Pyŏng-uk. Pyŏng-uk signaled with her eyes to hurry up and say something.

"I am going into music too."

Hyŏng-sik could not bring himself to say, "What about you, Sŏn-hyŏng?" Instead, he just sat quietly. Everyone smiled. Sŏn-hyŏng blushed.

"What are you going to do, Sŏn-hyŏng? You are going into education, right?" said Pyŏng-uk, smiling. They all smiled. Hyŏng-sik hung his head. Sŏn-hyŏng envied Pyŏng-uk for being outgoing and vivacious enough to have answered right away. She summoned all her strength and said, "I want to study math." She had thought of how her teacher praised her at school for being good at math. The others knew that math was a good thing, but they did not know what connection math had to life.

"It is your turn now," Hyŏng-sik said to U-sŏn.

"I would like to write, of course." No one said anything for some time. Each of them imagined their future. All of their futures reached a common intersection.

Hyŏng-sik looked at U-sŏn, who had his head down and was absentmindedly thinking of something.

"Why are you so quiet and well behaved today?" Hyŏng-sik asked, smiling. U-sŏn looked up.

"You once said to me that life is not a game, and that I look at life as a game—that I am not serious[169] about life."

"Did I say that?"

"You were right. I have considered life a game until now. The way I drink so much, and the way I fool around as much as I want to . . . these are

---

169. The 1917 *Maeil Sinbo* and 1918 Sinmungwan texts use the Japanese word *majime* (serious), transliterated in Korean.

all proof that I think of life as a game. I have inwardly looked down on you for being too serious, but I have been wrong." Hyŏng-sik realized that U-sŏn was not joking, and wiped the smile from his face and looked at U-sŏn. The young women too listened without laughing. U-sŏn had a determined look on his face, as though he had made some kind of resolution. He continued.

"I realized this today. I realized it for the first time today at the station, when I heard that you had given a concert. As I was coming here on the train, I pitied people I saw standing at the foot of the mountain, but I thought they looked funny standing there in their filthy, shabby clothes, and I even laughed. I did not think about how to help them, nor did I weep for them. As I got off the train, I thought of going to take a look at the flood, and writing a poem. I was laughing as I got off the train, not crying. When I heard about the concert for the flood victims, I was stricken with remorse. I was even more moved when I realized that three young women had given the concert." U-sŏn paused, overcome with emotion. His listeners too were silent.

"I became a person of this land today. I would like to try with all my strength and with all my heart to use my writing to contribute to society, no matter how insignificant my contribution. In less than an hour we will take our leave of one another, and it may be four or five years before I see you again. Even after you have gone far away, remember that I am not the same Sin U-sŏn that I was before. I am very happy that I was able to say this to you before you left." U-sŏn reached out his hand, and took Hyŏng-sik's hand in his own. Hyŏng-sik grasped U-sŏn's hand in return.

"I am happy to hear these words. This is not to say that you have done wrong in the past, but I am very happy about your new resolution."

U-sŏn hesitated for a long time, then said, "Yŏng-ch'ae, please forgive me for having been so rude to you in the past. I too want to become a new person from now on. I hope that you do well in your studies, and carry out important work." U-sŏn sighed deeply. Tears fell from Yŏng-ch'ae's eyes. Sŏn-hyŏng realized that everything Hyŏng-sik had said about Yŏng-ch'ae was true. Sŏn-hyŏng took Yŏng-ch'ae's hand in hers gently and thought to herself, I am sorry, Yŏng-ch'ae. Yŏng-ch'ae squeezed Sŏn-hyŏng's hand in return, and more tears fell from her eyes. Hyŏng-sik wept. Pyŏng-uk wept too. Eventually everyone wept. After the rains cleared, a clear breeze brushed against the branches of the willows that dangled outside the windows, and blew into the room, cooling the burning[170] faces of the five people there. Everyone was quiet.

---

170. The 1917 *Maeil Sinbo* text uses the words *yŏr han* (hot); the 1918 Sinmungwan edition uses the words *hwakkŭn kŏrinŭn* (hot).

126

Hyŏng-sik and Sŏn-hyŏng are now fourth-year students at the University of Chicago. They have been well, and plan to travel through post-war[171] Europe after graduating in September. Then they will return to Korea. Elder Kim and Mrs. Kim eagerly await their dear daughter's return, and are already thinking about things to do and what to feed their daughter when she returns.

Pyŏng-uk graduated from a school of music, and after that worked and made money to attend school for two years in Berlin. This winter she plans to meet up with Hyŏng-sik and Sŏn-hyŏng, and return to Korea together with them on the trans-Siberian railway. Yŏng-ch'ae graduated at the top of her class in piano and voice at the Ueno Conservatory in Tokyo, and is still in Tokyo. She plans to return to Seoul around September. Even more cause for rejoicing is that a recently arrived magazine from Berlin reports that Pyŏng-uk is a brilliant new performer in the Berlin music world, and has been very well received by critics. The magazine includes a review by an influential critic. Moreover, various Tokyo newspapers report that Yŏng-ch'ae received much applause at a large concert in Tokyo for her piano performance, singing and Korean dance. The papers also published her photograph. Hyŏng-sik and Yŏng-ch'ae are said to have received outstanding grades each year. The three young women who held a benefit concert in the waiting room of the Samnangjin Station have now become splendid ladies,[172] and the day is not far off when they will set their abilities to work in Kyŏngsŏng, and achieve recognition.

Sin U-sŏn has not set foot in the "world of flower and willows" since then, and has been concentrating on improving himself morally and intellectually, and on his writing. His literary reputation has spread throughout the nation. Moreover, his recently published book, *Korea's Future*, reached its fourth printing within two weeks after its first publication. U-sŏn's thought has acquired more depth and breadth, and his writing has become more incisive. One cause for worry is that U-sŏn still drinks too much; however, since antiquity there have scarcely been any renowned Asian writers who do not enjoy drinking. One thus cannot quite reproach U-sŏn. He has removed his famous straw hat, and now wears a panama hat white as snow, and has grown a lovely Kaiser mustache.

Kim Pyŏng-guk has grown a mulberry forest of over one hundred thousand trees in Hwangju. Last year, the forest suffered considerable damage from spring frost, but fortunately this year the leaves are full and strong. Pyŏng-guk's grandmother passed away in the summer of last year

---

171. *Chŏnhu Kurap'a*: "postwar Europe." Chapter 126 of *Mujŏng* was published June 14, 1917; World War I had not yet ended.
172. The text uses the English word "lady," transliterated in Korean as *redŭi*.

without being able to see her dear granddaughter again. Pyŏng-guk's wife has given birth to a son and a daughter, and the relationship between husband and wife is not as it was before.

Some medical students are staying at Hyŏng-sik's landlady's house. Her soy bean paste soup with maggots, and her pipe are as well known as ever. She has been getting weaker, though, and cannot visit the mineral water spring any more. She always talks about Hyŏng-sik with everyone she meets.

Yŏng-ch'ae's "mother" sold her house, went to a village near P'yŏngyang, adopted a son, and farms for a living. She has become a devout Christian, and lives a peaceful life in hopes of going to heaven. According to U-sŏn, when Yŏng-ch'ae's proprietress heard from U-sŏn that Yŏng-ch'ae had not died but was alive and had gone to Tokyo, she was so happy that she wept. Ever since then, Yŏng-ch'ae always writes to her once a month, and her "mother" writes in every letter that she now believes fervently in Christ, and tells Yŏng-ch'ae to believe in Christ too, and to come to her house when she graduates. She sends Yŏng-ch'ae money for clothes, and sometimes sends hot-pepper-and-bean paste and dried, salted sea perch.

The sad thing is that Kye-hyang, with whom Hyŏng-sik went to Ch'ilsŏngmun when he was in P'yŏngyang, became the concubine of a profligate man from a wealthy household, and caught syphilis. Her husband kicked her out of the house, and she suffers alone to this day. When Hyŏng-sik returns and hears about this, he will be very sad. That once-pretty face has become unspeakably haggard, and no one gives her a second glance.

I do not know whether or not you readers will remember him, but Yi Hŭi-gyŏng, whom Hyŏng-sik loved very much, died early, taking his valuable talents with him from the world. The dark-faced Kim Chong-nyŏl is said to have gone to Northern Jian-dao, and there has been no news of him. Dean Pae had a confrontation with the Superintendent, Baron Kim, and he is now at a mine in Hwanghae Province. They say that he has still not matured or acquired common sense, and this is indeed pitiful.

The old man outside Ch'ilsŏngmun, whom Hyŏng-sik called a "stone Buddha," is still healthy. About ten days ago, he went out on the veranda of his home, and began swaying back and forth there. The only difference is that his *kamt'u* hat[173] is older and shabbier than before.

Korea has changed considerably since Hyŏng-sik, Sŏn-hyŏng and Pyŏng-uk got on board the boat at Pusan. Korea has made substantial progress in education, the economy, literature and the media, and in the spread of modern civilization and thought. An even greater cause for celebration is the development in commerce and industry. Smoke from burning coal, and the sound of metal hammers can be seen and heard

---

173. *Kamt'u*: a traditional Korean men's hat made of horsehair, leather or cloth.

everywhere, beginning with Kyŏngsŏng. Even Korean commerce, which had deteriorated to an extreme degree, has gradually begun to prosper. Our land grows more beautiful with each day. Our arms, once so weak, grow stronger every day; and our minds, once so dark, grow steadily brighter. We will finally become as sparkling and bright as any other country. The more that this is true, the more we will have to exert ourselves. We need more great people, scholars, educators, business people, artists, inventors and religious leaders. How can one help but rejoice that Korea will be welcoming back this autumn students who are returning from countries in all the four directions, including fine people like Hyŏng-sik, Pyŏng-uk, Yŏng-ch'ae and Sŏn-hyŏng? Every year, strong workers complete technical schools en masse, and beautiful, strong boys and girls enter elementary school. This is indeed cause for rejoicing.

The world will not stay dark and cruel throughout our lifetime. Through our own strength, we will make the world brighter, more loving, more joyful, more prosperous, and stronger. And now, with happy smiles, and cries of "long live Korea!" let us bring to a close this novel, *The Heartless*, and its mourning for a world of the past.

Bibliography

Adorno, Theodor. *The Adorno Reader.* Ed. Brian O'Connor. Oxford, UK and Malden, MA: Blackwell Publishers, Inc., 2000.

An Kuk-sŏn. *Kŭmsu Hoeŭirok.* Hwangsŏng: Hwangsŏng Sŏjŏk Ŏpchohap, 1908.

Anderson, Benedict. *Imagined Communities:Reflections on the Origin and Spread of Nationalism.* Rev. ed. London: Verso, 1991.

Andrew, Dudley. "Tracing Ricoeur." *Diacritics* 30.2: 43-69.

Auerbach, Nina. *Romantic Imprisonment.* New York: Columbia University Press, 1986.

Bakhtin, Mikhail. *The Dialogic Imagination.* Translated by Caryl Emerson and Michael Holquist. Austin: University of Texas Press, 1981.

Bhabha, Homi. *The Location of Culture.* London and New York: Routledge, 1994.

Bible Committee of Korea, including Reynolds, William D.; Horace Underwood; and James Scarth Gale, trans. *Sinyak chŏnsŏ.* Yokohama: Fukuin Printing Company, for the Bible Committee of Korea, 1904.

Bible Committee of Korea, including Reynolds, William D.; Underwood, Horace; Gale, James Scarth; Pieters, A.; Scranton, William B.; Cram, W.G.; Trollope, M.N.; assisted by Yi Chang-chik; Kim Chung-sam; and Yi Sung-du. *The Holy Bible in Korean.* Seoul: American Bible Society, 1911.

Bible Committee of Korea. *Sinyak chŏnsŏ.* Seoul: American Bible Society, 1912.

Bloom, Harold. *The Anxiety of Influence.* London: Oxford University Press, 1973.

Bouchez, Daniel. "Le Roman Coréen Nam-jong Ki et L'Affaire de la Reine Min." *Journal Asiatique* 1976.

Burroway, Janet. *Writing Fiction.* New York: Longman, 2003.

Chang Kwang-chih. *Art, Myth and Ritual*. Cambridge: Harvard University Press, 1983.

Chao Yuen-ren. *Language and Symbolic Systems*. Cambridge: Cambridge University Press, 1968.

Cheah, Pheng. Paper presented at the Critical Asian Studies Conference panel "The Contagions of Liability." University of Washington, June 2, 2003.

Ching, Julia. "Yi Yul-gok on the 'Four Beginnings and the Seven Emotions.'" In *The Rise of Neo-Confucianism in Korea*, ed. William Theodore deBary and JaHyun Kim Haboush, 303–322. New York: Columbia University Press, 1985.

Cho Chin-gi. "Ch'och'anggi Munhak Iron kwa Chakp'um kwa ŭi Kŏri." *Suryŏn Ŏmun nonjip* 2 (1974). Reprint, *Yi Kwang-su Yŏn'gu*, vol. 1, ed. Tongguk Taehakkyo Pusŏl Han'guk Munhak Yŏn'guso, 448–466, Seoul: T'aehaksa, 1984.

Cho Dong-il. *Sinsosŏl ŭi Munhaksajŏk Sŏnggyŏk*. Seoul: Seoul Taehakkyo ch'ulp'anbu, 1983.

Cho Se-hyŏng. "Songgang Kasa e Nat'anan Yŏsŏng Hwaja wa Songgang ŭi Segyegwan." *Han'guk Kojŏn Yŏsŏng Munhak Yŏn'gu* 4 (2002): 157–185.

Cho Yŏn-hyŏn. *Han'guk Sin Munhak Ko*. Seoul: Munhwadang, 1966.

Ch'oe Ki-yŏng. "Yi Kwang-su ŭi Rŏsia ch'eryu wa munp'il hwaltong," *Minjok Munhaksa Yŏn'gu* 9 (1996): 376–379.

Ch'oe Nam-sŏn, translator. "ABC Kye." *Sonyŏn* 15 July 1910: 1–60.

———. "T'olsŭt'oi Sŏnsaeng ŭi Kyosi." *Sonyŏn* July 1909. Reprint, *Yuktang Ch'oe Nam-sŏn Chŏnjip*, ed. Koryŏ Taehakkyo Asea Munje Yŏn'guso Yuktang Chŏnjip P'yŏnch'an Wiwŏnhoe, vol. 10, 142–145. Seoul: Hyŏnamsa, 1973–1975.

Ch'oe Sang-hŭi. "*Mujŏng* kwa *Hyŏl ŭi Nu* ŭi Taebi Yŏn'gu–Kŭndae Sosŏl ŭi Kijŏm Kyujŏng ŭl wihan Il Koch'al." Ihwa Yŏdae Taehagwŏn, 1983.

Ch'oe T'ae-yŏng. "Yi Su-jŏng Yŏk Sinyak Maga Chŏn Pogŭmsŏ Ŏnhae." Sungjŏn Taehakkyo Kugŏ Kungmunhakhoe. *Sungsil Ŏmun* 2 (1985): 239–246.

Ch'oe Wŏn-sik. "P'alsimnyŏndae Munhak Undong ŭi Pip'anjŏk chŏm'gŏm." *Minjok Munhaksa Yŏn'gu*: 62–79.

Choi Hyaewol. "Pious Woman, New Woman: A Missionary Fiction in Korea." Paper presented for the panel "Remembering and Imagining: Tensions in the Construction of Modern Womanhood in Colonial and Postcolonial Korea," at the annual meeting of the Association for Asian Studies, New York, N.Y., March 27, 2003.

Choi Kyeong-Hee. "Impaired Body as Colonial Trope: Kang Kyŏng-ae's 'Underground Village.'" *Public Culture* 13, no. 3 (Fall 2001): 431–458.

————. "Neither Colonial nor National: The Making of the 'New Woman' in Pak Wansŏ's 'Mother's Stake 1'." In *Modernity in Korea*, ed. Gi-Wook Chin and Michael Robinson, 221–247. Cambridge and London: Harvard University Asia Center, 1999.

"Chŏk Sŏn Yŏgyŏng Nok." *Taehan Maeil Sinbo* 10–29 August 1905.

Chŏn Kwang-yong. *Han'guk Kŭndae Sosŏl ŭi Ihae*. Vol. 2. Seoul: Minŭmsa, 1983.

————. "Han'guk Kŭndae Sosŏl ŭi Yŏksajŏk Chŏn'gae." In *Chŏn Kwang-yong et al. Han'guk Hyŏndae Sosŏlsa Yŏn'gu*. Seoul: Minŭmsa, 1984: 11–20.

————. "Hyŏl ŭi Nu." *Sasanggye* March 1956: 197–216.

————. "Yi In-jik kwa Sinsosŏl ŭi Hyŏngsŏng." *Han'guk Hyŏndae Sosŏlsa Yŏn'gu*. Seoul: Minŭmsa, 1984: 36–46.

————. "Yi Kwang-su Yŏn'gu Sŏsŏl." In *Yi Kwang-su Yŏn'gu*, ed. Tongguk Taehakkyo Pusŏl Han'guk Munhak Yŏn'guso, vol. 1, 399–447. Seoul: T'aehaksa, 1984.

Chŏng Chin-sŏk. *Taehan Maeil Sinbo wa Paesŏl: Han'guk Munje e Taehan Yŏngil Oegye*. Seoul: Nanam, 1987.

Chŏng Kil-lam. *Kaehwagi Kugyŏk Sŏngsŏ ŭi P'yogipŏp kwa Munpŏp Hyŏngt'ae*. Seoul: Kaemunsa, 1987.

Chŏng Kwi-ryŏn. "Kankoku no Kindai Bungaku ni Okeru Kunikida Doppō no Juyō no Sho Yōsō: Den Ei-taku [Chŏn Yŏng-t'aek], Kin Tō-jin [Kim Tong-in], Ri Kō-shu [Yi Kwang-su] wo rei to shite." *Chōsen Gakuhō* 156 (1995): 129–209.

Chŏng Sun-jin. *Han'guk Munhak kwa Yŏsŏng Chuŭi Pip'yŏng*. Seoul: Kukhak Charyowŏn, 1993.

"Ch'ŏngnu Ŭinyŏ Chŏn." *Taehan Maeil Sinbo* 6–18 February 1906 (Kwangmu 10).

Chu Chong-yŏn. *Han'guk Kŭndae Tanp'yŏn Sosŏl Yŏn'gu*. Seoul: Yŏngsŏl Ch'ulp'ansa, 1979.

————. *Han'guk Sosŏl ŭi Hyŏngsŏng*. Seoul: Chimmundang, 1987.

————. "Yi Kwang-su ŭi Ch'ogi Tanp'yŏn Sosŏlgo." *Han'guk Kŭndae Tanp'yŏn Yŏn'gu*. Seoul: Yŏngsŏl Ch'ulp'ansa, 1980. Reprint, *Yi Kwang-su Yŏn'gu*, ed. Tongguk Taehakkyo Pusŏl Han'guk Munhak Yŏn'guso, vol. 2, 543–559. Seoul: T'aehaksa, 1984.

Chu Yŏn-uk. "Ch'unwŏn Munye Pip'yŏng Yŏn'gu." *Kyemyŏngdae Nonmunjip*. Reprint, *Yi Kwang-su Yŏn'gu*, ed. Tongguk Taehakkyo Pusŏl Han'guk Munhak Yŏn'guso, vol. 2, 189–211. Seoul: T'aehaksa, 1984.

Chung, Chong-wha, ed. *Modern Korean Literature: An Anthology, 1908–1965*. New York: Columbia University Press, 1995.

Chung, Edward Y. J. *The Korean Neo-Confucianism of Yi T'oegye and Yi Yul-gok: A Reappraisal of the 'Four-Seven Thesis' and Its Practical*

Implications for Self-Cultivation. Albany: State University of New York Press, 1995.

Clark, Allen D. *A History of the Church in Korea.* The Christian Literature Society of Korea, 1971.

Committee of Delegates. *Xin Yue Quan Shu.* Fuzhou: Mei-hwa Shu-ju, Guang xu 7 (1881).

Cornyetz, Nina. *Dangerous Women, Deadly Words: Phallic Fantasy and Modernity in Three Japanese Writers.* Stanford: Stanford University Press, 1999.

Darlow, T.H. and H. F. Moule, comps. *Historical Catalogue of the Printed Editions of Holy Scriptures in the Library of the British and Foreign Bible Society.* Vol. II. London: The Bible House, 1911.

deBary, Wm. Theodore, Wing-tsit Chan and Burton Watson. *Sources of Chinese Tradition.* New York: Columbia University Press, 1960.

Denton, Kirk, ed. *Modern Chinese Literary Thought.* Stanford: Stanford University Press, 1996.

Derrida, Jacques. *Of Grammatology.* Translated by Gayatri Chakravorty Spivak. Baltimore: Johns Hopkins University Press, 1976.

————. *Writing and Difference.* Translated by Alan Bass. Chicago: University of Chicago Press, 1978.

Deuchler, Martina. *Confucian Gentlemen and Barbaria Envoys.* Seattle: University of Washington Press, 1977.

————. *The Confucian Transformation of Korea: A Study of Society and Ideology.* Cambridge: Harvard-Yenching Institute Monograph Series, 1992

Dong Won-mo. "Assimilation and Social Mobilization in Korea." In *Korea Under Japanese Colonial Rule,* ed. Andrew Nahm, 146–182. Kalamazoo: Center for Korean Studies, Institute of International and Area Studies, Western Michigan University, 1973.

John Duncan. "The *Naehun* and the Politics of Gender in Fifteenth-Century Korea." In *Creative Women of Korea: The Fifteenth through the Twentieth Centuries,* ed. Young-Key Kim-Renaud, 26–57. Armonk, New York: M.E. Sharpe, 2003.

Duus, Peter and Irwin Scheiner. "Socialism, Liberalism and Marxism, 1901–31." In *Modern Japanese Thought,* ed. Bob Tadashi Wakabayashi, 147–206. Cambridge: Cambridge University Press, 1998.

Eagleton, Terry. *Literary Theory: An Introduction.* Minneapolis: University of Minnesota Press, 1983.

Easthope, Anthony. *Literary into Cultural Studies.* London and New York: Routledge, 1991.

Eckert, Carter J., Lee Ki-baik, Young Ick Lew, Michael Robinson and Edward W. Wagner. *Korea Old and New: A History.* Seoul: Ilchogak Publishers, 1990.

Em, Henry H. "Minjok as a Construct." In *Colonial Modernity in Korea*, ed. Gi-wook Shin and Michael Robinson, 336–361. Cambridge: Harvard University Asia Center, 1999.

Fanon, Frantz. *Black Skin, White Masks*. New York: Grove Press, 1967.

Felman, Shoshana. *What Does a Woman Want? Reading and Sexual Difference*. Baltimore and London: The Johns Hopkins University Press, 1993.

Fish, Stanley E. "Literature in the Reader: Affective Stylistics." In *Reader-Response Criticism*, ed. Jane P. Tompkins, 70–100. Baltimore: Johns Hopkins University Press, 1980.

Frye, Northrop. *Anatomy of Criticism*. Princeton: Princeton University Press, 1957.

Genette, Gerard. *Narrative Discourse*. Ithaca, New York: Cornell University Press, 1980.

Gunew, Sneja, and Anna Yeatman, eds. *Feminism and the Politics of Difference*, Boulder and San Francisco: Westview Press, 1993.

Ha Chŏng-il. "Minjok Munhangnon ŭi Chaengjŏm." In *Isip Segi Han'guk Munhak ŭi Pansŏng kwa Chaengjŏm*. Ed. Munhak kwa Sasang Yŏn'guhoe, 61–89. Seoul: Somyŏng Ch'ulp'an, 1999.

Ha Tong-ho. "Sinsosŏl Yŏn'gu ch'o." *Sedae* (1996).

Han Ki-yŏng. "1910 Yyŏn Tanp'yŏn Sosŏl kwa Nangmansŏng." *Minjok Munhaksa Yŏn'gu* 12 (1998): 126–147.

Han Sŭng-ok. *Yi Kwang-su Munhak Sajŏn*. Seoul: Koryŏ Taehakkyo Ch'ulp'anbu, 2002.

Hara Yogorō. "ABC Kumiai." Tokyo: Naigai Shuppan Kyōkai, Meiji 35.

Han Yong-hwan. "Yi Kwang-su Sosŏl ŭi Chaep'yŏngga–Yi Kwang-su ŭi Changp'yŏn Sosŏl." *Han'guk Munhak Yŏn'gu* 5 (1982).

Han Yŏng-hwan. "Yŏnam Pak Chi-wŏn kwa Ch'unwŏn Yi Kwang-su Munhak ŭi Pigyo Yŏn'gu." *Sŏngsin Yŏdae Yŏn'gu Nonmunjip*. Reprint, *Yi Kwang-su Yŏn'gu*, ed. Tongguk Taehakkyo Pusŏl Han'guk Munhak Yŏn'guso, vol. 2, 212–252. Seoul: T'aehaksa, 1984.

Hasegawa Tenkei. "Genjitsu Hakurō no Hiai." *Taiyō* Meiji 41 (1908) January. Reprint, *Meiji Bungaku Zenshū*. Vol. 43. Tokyo: Chikuma shobō, 1967: 201–205.

Hatano Setsuko. "Ri Kō-shu no Jiga." *Chōsen Gakuhō* no. 139 (1991).

———. "Yi Kwang-su ŭi Chaa." *Minjok Munhaksa Yŏn'gu* 5 (1994).

Hŏ Ung. *Kugŏ Ttae Maegimpŏp ŭi Pyŏnch'ŏnsa*. Seoul: Sae Munhwasa, 1987.

Hoffmann, Frank with Matthew J. Christensen and Kirk W. Larsen. *The Harvard Korean Studies Bibliography*. Cambridge: Harvard University Korea Institute, 1999. CD-ROM.

Hwa Chung Hwa. Kyŏngsŏng: Pangmun Sŏwŏn, Taishō 1 (1912). Facsimile reprint, *Sinsosŏl, Pŏnan (Yŏk) Sosŏl*. *Han'guk Kaehwagi Munhak*

Ch'ongsŏ I, ed. Kim Yun-sik, Paek Sun-je, Song Min-ho and Yi Sŏn-yŏng, vol. 8, 505–559. Seoul: Asea Munhwasa, 1978.

Hwang Chŏng-hyŏn. *Sinsosŏl Yŏn'gu*. Seoul: Chimmundang, 1997.

Hwang, Kyung Moon. "Bureaucracy in the Transition to Modern Democracy: Secondary Status Groups and the Transformation of Government and Society, 1880–1930." Ph.D. diss., Harvard University, 1997.

Hwangsŏng Sinmun. Kyŏngsŏng, 5 September 1898–14 September 1910. Facsimile edition. Han'guk Munhwa Kaebalsa, 1971.

"Hyangno Pangmun Ŭisaengira." *Taehan Maeil Sinbo* 21 December 1905–incomplete.

Hyun, John K. *A Condensed History of the Kungminhoe: the Korean National Association (1903–1945)*. Seoul: Koryo Taehakkyo Minjok Munhwa Yon'guso, 1986.

Hyun, Theresa. *Writing Women in Korea: Translation and Feminism in the Colonial Period*. Honolulu: University of Hawaii, 2004.

Ishida Kōzō, ed. *Shinhantō Bungaku Senshū*. Tōkyō: Yumani Shobō, 2001.

Irigaray, Luce. *The Irigaray Reader*. Ed. Margaret Whitford. Oxford, UK and Medford, MA: Blackwell Publishers, Inc., 1991.

"It'aeriguk Amach'i chŏn." *Taehan Maeil Sinbo* 14–21 December 1905.

Ivy, Marilyn. *Discourses of the Vanishing: Modernity, Phantasm, Japan*. Chicago: Chicago University Press, 1995.

Jeong, Kelly Yoojeong. "The Paradox of Korean Colonial Modernity: Images of the New Woman in Korean Colonial Literature." Paper presented for the panel "Remembering and Imagining: Tensions in the Construction of Modern Womanhood in Colonial and Postcolonial Korea," at the annual meeting of the Association for Asian Studies conference, New York, N.Y., March 29, 2003.

Kalton, Michael. *The Four-Seven Debate: An Annotated Translation of the Most Famous Controversy in Korean Neo-Confucian Thought*. Albany: State University of New York Press, 1994.

Kang Yŏng-ju. *Han'guk Yŏksa Sosŏl ŭi Chae Insik*. Seoul: Ch'angjak kwa Pip'yŏngsa, 1991.

Karatani Kōjin. *Origins of Modern Japanese Literature*. Ed. Brett de Bary. Durham and London: Duke University Press, 1993.

Keene, Donald. *Dawn to the West: Japanese Literature in the Modern Era*. New York: Holt, Rinehart and Winston, 1984.

Kendall, Laurel. *Shamans, Housewives and Other Restless Spirits: Women in Korean Ritual Life*. Honolulu: University of Hawaii Press, 1985.

Killick, Andrew. "The Invention of Traditional Korean Opera and the Problem of the Traditionesque: *Ch'anggŭk* and its Relation to *P'ansori* Narratives." Ph.D. diss., University of Washington, 1998.

Kim Byong-kuk. "February 8 Declaration of Independence." *Hankook Ilbo* English edition. 4 April 2000.

Kim Chae-yong, Yi Sang-gyŏng, O Sŏng-ho and Ha Chŏng-il. *Han'guk Kŭndae Minjok Munhaksa.* Seoul: Han'gilsa, 1994: 1–226.

Kim Ch'ŏl, Yi Kyŏng-hun, Sŏ Ŭn-ju and Im Chin-yŏng. *"Mujŏng* ŭi Kyebo: *Mujŏng* ŭi Chŏngbon Hwakjŏng ŭl Wihan P'anbon ŭi Pigyo Yŏn'gu." *Minjok Munhaksa Yŏn'gu* 20 (2002): 62–90.

Kim Chŏng-uk. *"Hyŏl ŭi Nu* Yŏn'gu." *Han'guk Munhwa* 23 (1999): 63–80.

Kim Chung-ha. "Kaehwagi Sosŏl 'Kŏbu Ohae' Sogo." *Suryŏn Ŏmun Nonjip* 5 (1975).

———. "Kaehwagi T'oronch'e Sosŏl Yŏn'gu." *Kwanak Ŏmun Yŏn'gu* no. 3 (1978).

Kim Hyung-chan. Review of Yoonmi Lee. *Modern Education, Textbooks and the Image of the Nation: Politics of Modernization and Nationalism in Korean Education, 1880–1910.* New York: Garland Publishing Inc., 2000. In *Korean Studies Review* 2002, no. 5. http://www.koreaweb.ws/ks/ksr/ksr02-05.htm

Kim, Jina. "Language, Commodity and the City: The Production of Urban Literature in Colonial Korea." *Seoul Journal of Korean Studies* 16 (December 2003): 39–74.

Kim Kichung. "'Ŭnsegye:' Art versus Ideology." *Korean Studies* vol. 5 (1981): 63–77.

———. "Hyŏl-ŭi Nu: Korea's First 'New' Novel (1)–Towards a Language of Reform." *Korean Culture* 6.1 (1985): 38–45.

———. "Hyŏl-ŭi Nu: Korea's First 'New' Novel (2)–The Power of the Press." *Korean Culture* 6.2 (1985): 17–25.

———. "Hyŏl-ŭi Nu: Korea's First 'New' Novel (3)–Verisimilitude and the West." *Korean Culture* 6.3–4 (1985): 16–26.

———. "'Mujŏng': An Introduction to Yi Kwangsu's Fiction." *Korean Studies* 6 (1982): 125–139.

———. "The Question of Betrayal." *Korea Journal* 31.4 (1991): 40–53.

———. *The Rise of the Modern Korean Novel.* Unpublished manuscript.

———. "'Ŭnsegye': Art versus Ideology." *Korean Studies* 5 (1981): 63–77.

Kim Ki-dong. "Han'guk Sosŏl Paltalsa: Kungmun Sosŏl, P'ansori." *Han'guk Munhwasa Taegye,* ed. Koryŏ Taehakkyo Minjok Munhwa Yŏn'guso, vol. 5, 1063–1113. Seoul: Koryŏ Taehakkyo Minjok Munhwa Yŏn'guso, 1985.

Kim Kyo-je. *Hyŏnmigyŏng.* Kyŏngsŏng: Tongyang Sŏwŏn, Meiji 45. Facsimile reprint, *Sinsosŏl, Pŏnan (Yŏk) Sosŏl. Han'guk Kaehwagi Munhak Ch'ongsŏ I,* ed. Kim Yun-sik, Paek Sun-je, Song Min-ho and Yi Sŏn-yŏng, vol. 8. Seoul: Asea Munhwasa, 1978.

Kim Mi-hyun [Kim Mi-hyŏn]. "'Sai' e chip chitko salgi: Paek Sin-ae ron." In *P'eminijŭm kwa sosŏl pip'yŏng,* ed. Han'guk yŏsŏng sosŏl yŏn'guhoe, 217–250. Seoul: Han'gilsa, 1995.

356   Bibliography

Kim, Nam-kil. "On Experiential Sentences." *Studies in Language* 22, no. 1: 161–204.

———. "Aspectual Verbs as Auxiliaries in Korean." *Korean Language Education* 6:99–119.

Kim P'al-bong. "Chakka rosŏ ŭi Ch'unwŏn." *Sasanggye* 6 (1958). Reprint, *Yi Kwang-su Yŏn'gu*, ed. Tongguk Taehakkyo Pusŏl Han'guk Munhak Yŏn'guso, vol. 1: 36–41. Seoul: T'aehaksa, 1984.

Kim P'ilsu. *Kyŏngse Chong.* Hwangsŏng: Kwanghak sŏp'o, 1908.

Kim Pung-gu. "Sin Munhak Ch'ogi ŭi Kyemong Sasang kwa Kŭndaejŏk Chaa." *Han'gugin kwa Munhak Sasang.* Seoul: Ilchogak, 1964. Reprint, *Yi Kwang-su Yon'gu*, ed. Tongguk Taehakkyo Pusŏl Han'guk Munhak Yŏn'guso, vol. 1: 67–153. Seoul: T'aehaksa, 1984.

Kim Pyŏng-ch'ŏl. *Han'guk Kŭndae Pŏnyŏk Munhaksa Yŏn'gu.* Seoul: Ŭryu Munhwasa, 1975 and 1988.

Kim Pyŏng-gŏl and Kyu-dong Kim, eds. *Ch'inil Munhak Chakp'um Sŏnjip.* Seoul: Silch'ŏn Munhaksa, 1986.

Kim Pyŏng-ik. *Han'guk Mundansa.* Seoul: Ilchisa, 1973.

Kim Sang-t'ae. "Challenge to Confucian Values." *Tamkang Review* 18, nos. 1, 2, 3, 4: 343–350.

Kim Sŏk-tŭk. "Uri Mal ŭi Sisang." *Aesan Hakpo* 1 (1981): 37.

Kim, Sun Joo. "Marginalized Elite, Regional Discrimination and the Tradition of Prophetic Belief in the Hong Kyŏng-nae Rebellion." Ph.D. diss., University of Washington, 2000.

Kim So-wŏl. *Wŏnbon Sowŏl Chŏnjip.* Ed. Kim Chŏng-uk. Vols. 1 and 2. Seoul: Hongsŏngsa, 1982.

Kim T'ae-jun. "Ch'unwŏn Yi Kwang-su ŭi Yesulgwan." *Myŏngji Ŏmunhak* 4 (1970). Reprint, Tongguk Taehakkyo Pusŏl Han'guk Munhak Yŏn'guso ed., vol. 1, 281–308. *Yi Kwang-su Yŏn'gu.* Seoul: T'aehaksa, 1984.

———. "Hong Tae-yong." In *Han'guk Munhak Chakkaron,* ed. Hwang P'ae-gang et al., vol. 3, 161–174. Seoul: Chimmundang, 2000.

Kim Tae-joon. "The Thought and Literary Achievement of Hong Tae-yong." *Korea Journal* 28, no. 5: 32–54.

Kim Tong-in. *Ch'unwŏn Yŏn'gu.* "Ch'unwŏn yŏn'gu." *Samch'ŏlli* 6, no. 12–7, no. 10 (December 1934–October 1935). Reprint, *Kim Tong-in Munhak Chŏnjip,* vol. 12: 357–456. Seoul: Taejung Sŏgwan, 1983.

———. "Sosŏl e taehan Chosŏn Saram ŭi Sasang ŭl." *Hak chi Kwang* 18 (August 1918). Reprint, *Han'guk Hyŏndae Munhak Pip'yŏngsa (charyo I),* ed. Kwŏn Yŏng-min, 135–138. Seoul: Tongguk Taehakkyo Ch'ulp'anbu, 1981.

Kim Tong-ni et al., eds. *Han'guk Munhak Taesajŏn.* Seoul: Munwŏn'gak, 1973.

Kim To-t'ae. *Namgang Yi Sŭng-hun Chŏn.* Seoul: Mungyosa, 1950.

Kim Yŏng-dŏk. "Ch'unwŏn ŭi Insaeng Ch'ŏrhakkwan Ko: Ki, Pulgyo Sasang ŭl Chungsim ŭro." *Han'guk Munhwa Yŏn'guso Nonch'ŏng* 26 (1975): 9–32.

Kim U-ch'ang. "Narrative Tense in the Korean Novel: a Speculative Observation." *Korean Studies Journal* 5 (1981): 79–91.

Kim U-jong. "Ch'unwŏn Munhak Yŏn'gu." *Ch'ungnam Tae Nonmunjip* 5 (1966): 205–244.

———. "Minjok Munhak kwa Hwejŏl: Yi Kwang-su Non." In *Yi Kwang-su Yŏn'gu*, ed. Tongguk Taehakkyo Pusŏl Han'guk Munhak Yŏn'guso, vol. 1: 488–513. Seoul: T'aehaksa, 1984.

Kim Yŏng-dŏk. "Ch'unwŏn ŭi Kidokkyo Immun kwa Kŭ Sasang kwa ŭi Kwan'gye." *Han'guk Munhwa Yŏn'gu Nonch'ong* vol. 5, no. 1 (1965). Reprint, *Yi Kwang-su Yŏn'gu*, ed. Tongguk Taehakkyo Pusŏl Han'guk Munhak Yŏn'guso, vol. 1: 154–190. Seoul: T'aehaksa, 1984.

Kim Yong-jik. *Han'guk Kŭndae Sisa*. Seoul: Saemunsa, 1983.

Kim Yŏng-min. "Ch'unwŏn Yi Kwang-su Kwan'gye Yŏn'gu Charyo Mongnok." *Tongbang Hakchi* no. 83 (1994): 215–236.

———. "Han'guk Munhaksa ŭi Kŭndae wa Kŭndaesŏng: Kŭndae Ch'ogi Sŏsa Munhak Yangsik ŭi Kŭndaesŏng ŭl Chungsim ŭro." In *20 Segi Han'guk Munhak ŭi Pansŏng kwa Chaengchŏm*, ed. Munhak kwa Sasang Yŏn'guhoe, 11–34. Seoul: Somyŏng Ch'ulp'an, 1999.

———. "Nam · Pukhan esŏ ŭi Yi Kwang-su Munhak Yŏn'gusa Chŏngni wa Kŏmt'o." *Tongbang Hakchi* 83 (1994): 157–192.

Kim Yun-sik. "Kaehwagi Sosŏl ŭi Munjechŏm." In *Hyŏndae Sosŏlsa Yŏn'gu*, ed. Chŏn Kwang-yong, 23–35. Seoul: Minŭmsa, 1984.

———. "Koa Ŭisik ŭi Chwajŏl." *Munhak Sasang* 232 (1992): 54–79.

———. "Kaehwagi Sosŏl ŭi Munjechŏm." In *Han'guk Hyŏndae Sosŏlsa Yŏn'gu*, ed. Chŏn Kwang-yong, 23–35. Seoul: Minŭmsa, 1984.

———, Paek Sun-je, Song Min-ho and Yi Sŏn-yŏng, eds. *Sinsosŏl, Pŏnan (yŏk) Sosŏl. Han'guk Kaehwagi Munhak Ch'ongsŏ I*. Vols. 1–10. Seoul: Asea Munhwasa, 1978.

———. *Yi Kwang-su wa Kŭ ŭi Sidae*. Vols. 1–3. Seoul: Han'gilsa, 1986.

Kim, Yung-hee. "Re-visioning Gender and Womanhood in Colonial Korea: Yi Kwang-su's *Mujŏng* (The Heartless)." *The Review of Korean Studies* 6, no. 1 (2003): 187–219.

———. "Women's Issues in 1920s Korea." *Korean Culture* vol. 15, no. 2 (1994): 26–33.

Kim Yu-sŏn. *Ch'unwŏn Yi Kwang-su ŭi Si Yŏn'gu*. Seoul: Kyŏngun Ch'ulp'ansa, 1995.

King, Ross. "Experimentation with Han'gŭl in Russia and the USSR, 1914–1937." In *The Korean Alphabet: Its History and Structure*, ed. Young-key Kim Renaud, 219–261. Honolulu: University of Hawaii Press, 1997.

————. *Koryŏ Saram: Koreans in the Former USSR.* Special issue of *Korean and Korean American Studies Bulletin.* New Haven, Connecticut: East Rock Institute, 2001.

————. "Nationalism and Language Reform in Korea: The Questione della lingua in Precolonial Korea." In *Nationalism and the Construction of Korean Identity,* ed. Timothy Tangherlini and Hyung-il Pai, 33–72. Berkeley, CA: University of California Center for Korean Studies Monograph Series, 1999.

————. "Russian Sources on Korean Dialects." Ph.D. diss., Harvard University, 1991.

Kinoshita Naoe. *Pillar of Fire.* Translated by Kenneth Strong. London: George Allen and Unwin Ltd., 1972.

Ko Mi-suk. *18 Segi esŏ Isip Segi ch'o Han'guk Sigasa ŭi Kudo.* Seoul: Somyŏng, 1998.

Ko Yŏng-gŭn. "Hyŏndae Kugŏ ŭi Munch'ebŏp e Taehan Yŏn'gu: Sŏbŏp Ch'egye." *Kugŏhak Yŏn'gu* 12.1 (1976): 17–50.

"Kŏbu ohae." *Taehan Maeil Sinbo* 20 February–7 March 1906.

Koh, Helen. "Imagining Childhood: Narratives of Formation in Korean Short Fiction of the 1970s." Ph.D. diss., University of Chicago, 2001.

Koryŏ Taehakkyo Asea Munje Yŏn'guso Yuktang Chŏnjip P'yŏnch'an Wiwŏnhoe, ed. *Yuktang Ch'oe Nam-sŏn Chŏnjip.* Seoul: Hyŏnamsa, 1973–1975.

Ku In-hwan. "Yi Kwang-su ŭi Munhak Sasang." *Hyŏndae Sahoe* 2 (1981). Reprint, *Yi Kwang-su Yŏn'gu,* ed. Tongguk Taehakkyo Pusŏl Han'guk Munhak Yŏn'guso, vol. 1: 543–567, Seoul: T'aehaksa, 1984.

Kuksa P'yŏnch'an Wiwŏnhoe. *Han'guksa.* Seoul: Taehan Min'guk Mun'gyobu Kuksa P'yŏnch'an Wiwŏnhoe, 1978.

Kureno Toshio. "Torusutoi to Shirakaba Ha." In *Nihon Kindai Bungaku no Hikaku Bungakuteki Kenkyū,* ed. Yoshida Seiichi, 306–329. Tokyo: Shimizu Kōbundō, Shōwa 46 [1971].

Kyoko Kurita. "The Romantic Triangle in Meiji Literature." In *New Directions in the Study of Meiji Japan,* ed. Helen Hardacre with Adam L. Kern. Leiden, New York, Köln: Brill, 1997.

Kuroiwa Ruikō. "A Mujō." *Yorozu Chohō* 8 Meiji 35.10.8–Meiji 36.8.22.

————. *A Mujō.* Vols. 1, 2. Tokyo: Fusōdō, Meiji 40.

Kwŏn Yŏng-min. "Ch'unwŏn Munhak ŭl Hyang Han Yŏrahop Kae ŭi Hwasal." *Munhak Sasang* 232 (1992): 111–127.

————. *Han'guk Hyŏndae Munhak Pip'yŏngsa.* Seoul: Tan'guk Taehakkyo Ch'ulp'anbu, 1981.

————. "Ilchae Cho Chung-hwan ŭi Pŏnan Sosŏl tŭl." In *Sin Munhak kwa Sidae Ŭisik,* ed. Kim Yŏl-gyu and Sin Tong-uk, Seoul: Saemunsa, 1981.

————. "Yi Hae-jo wa Sinsosŏl ŭi Han'gye." In *Han'guk Kŭndae Munhak kwa Sidae Chŏngsin.* Seoul: Munye Ch'ulp'ansa.

Kyŏngguk Taejŏn
Ledyard, Gari. "Hong Taeyong and His 'Peking Memoir.'" *Korean Studies* 6: 63–103.
———. "The International Linguistic Background of the Correct Sounds for the Instruction of the People." *The Korean Alphabet: Its History and Structure*, ed. Young-key Kim Renaud, 31–87. Honolulu: University of Hawaii Press, 1997.
———. "The Korean Language Reform of 1446: the Origin, Background and Early History of the Korean Alphabet." Ph.D. diss., University of California, Berkeley, 1966.
———. "Korean Travelers in China over Four Hundred Years, 1488–1887." *Occasional Papers on Korea* 2: 1–42.
Lee, Ann. "The Early Writings of Yi Kwang-su." *Korea Journal* 42, no. 2 (2002): 241–278.
———. "Writing for a Woman Reader: Gender, Modernity and Language in the Multilingual Letters of Yi Kwang-su to Hŏ Yŏng-suk." *Acta Koreana* 6, no. 1 (2003): 1–22.
———. "Yi Kwang-su and Early Modern Korean Literature." Ph.D. diss., Columbia University, 1991.
———. "Yi Kwang-su and Korean Literature." *The Journal of Korean Studies* 8 (1992): 81–133.
Lee, Chong-sik. *The Politics of Korean Nationalism*. Berkeley: University of California Press, 1965.
Lee, Chung Wha. *Abŏnim Ch'unwŏn*. Seoul: Sŏnmunsa, Tan'gi 4288 [1955]. Reprint, *Kŭriun Abŏnim Ch'unwŏn*, Seoul: Usinsa, 1993.
———. *Kŭriun Abŏnim Ch'unwŏn*. Seoul: Usinsa, 1993.
Lee, Grant. *Life and Thought of Yi Kwang-su*. Seoul: U-Shin Sa, 1984.
Lee, Iksop and S. Robert Ramsey, *The Korean Language*. State University of New York Press, 2001.
Lee, Jin-kyung. "Autonomous Aesthetics and Autonomous Subjectivity: Construction of Modern Literature as a Site of Social Reforms and Modern National-Building in Colonial Korea, 1915-1925." Ph.D. diss., University of California, Los Angeles, 2000.
Lee Ki-baik. *A New History of Korea*. Translated by Edward W. Wagner with Edward Shultz. Cambridge: Harvard University Press, 1984.
Lee Ki-moon. "Kaehwagi ŭi Kungmun Sayong e Kwanhan Yŏn'gu." *Han'guk Munhwa* 5 (December 1984): 65–84.
———. *Kugŏ Ŭmunsa Yŏn'gu*. Seoul: T'ap Ch'ulp'ansa, 1985.
———. *Kugŏsa Kaesŏl*. Seoul: T'ap Ch'ulp'ansa, 1978.
Lee, Peter H. *Anthology of Korean Literature: From Early Times to the Nineteenth Century*. Honolulu: University of Hawaii Press, 1981.
———. *Korean Literature: Topics and Themes*. Tucson: University of Arizona Press, 1965.

————. *Pine River and Lone Peak: An Anthology of Three Chosŏn Dynasty Poets*. Honolulu: University of Hawaii Press, 1990.

————. *Studies in the Saenaennore: Old Korean Poetry*. Rome: Istituto Italiano per Il Medio del Estremo Oriente, 1959.

Levinson, Stephen C. *Pragmatics*. Cambridge: Cambridge University Press, 1983.

Lew, Walter. "Jean Cocteau in the Looking Glass: A Homotextual Reading of Yi Sang's Mirror Poems." *Muae* 1 (1995): 118–147.

Liang Qichao. "On the Relationship Between Fiction and the Government of the People." Trans. Gek Nai Cheng. In *Modern Chinese Literary Thought*, ed. Kirk Denton, 74–81. Stanford: Stanford University Press, 1996.

Liu, Lydia. *Translingual Practice: Literature, National Culture, and Translated Modernity—China, 1900–1937*. Stanford: Stanford University Press, 1995.

Mako Den Fukuin Sho. Trans. James Curtis Hepburn. Romaji edition. In *Shinyaku zensho*. Yokohama: R. Meiklejohn and Co. for the American Bible Society, 1880.

Mansebo. Seoul: Mansebosa, 17 June 1906 (Kwangmu 10)–29 June 1907 (Kwangmu 11). Fascimile edition. Seoul: Asea Munhwasa, 1985.

Manyōshū. Edited by Takaki Ichinosuke, Gomi Tomoyoshi, Ōno Susumu. Nihon Koten Bungaku Taikei. Vol. 4. Tokyo: Iwanami Shoten, Shōwa 32 (1957).

Marran, Christine L. "The Allure of the Poison-Woman in Modern Japanese Literature." Ph.D. diss., University of Washington, 1998.

McCann, David. "The Structure of Korean Sijo." *Harvard Journal of Asian Studies*. Vol. 36 (1976): 114–134.

————. *Form and Freedom in Korean Poetry*. Leiden: Brill, 1989.

McCarthy, Kathleen Louise. "*Kisaeng* in the Koryŏ Period." Ph.D. diss., Harvard University, 1991.

————. "*Kisaeng* in the Koryŏ Period." *Korean Culture* 15, no. 2 (Summer 1994): 4–13.

Min Pyŏng-su, Cho Dong-il, Yi Chae-sŏn. *Kaehwagi ŭi Uguk Munhak*. Seoul: Sin'gu Munhwasa, 1974.

Minatoya, Lydia. *The Strangeness of Beauty*. New York: W. W. Norton and Company, 1999.

Minjok Munhwa Ch'ujinhoe, ed. *Sinjŭng Tongguk Yŏji Sŭngnam*. Seoul: Minjok Munhwa Ch'ujinhoe, 1969-1971.

Mong Mong. "Ssŭrŏjŏ kanŭn chip." *Taehan Yuhaksaeng Hakpo* no. 3 (25 May 1907): 60–65. Facsimile reprint. Han'guk Munhŏn Yŏn'guso ed. *Han'guk Kaehwagi Haksulchi*. Seoul: Asea Munhwasa, 1975.

Morohashi Tetsuji. *Dai Kanwa Jiten*. Vol. 12. Tokyo: Taishū Shokan, 1976.

Munhak kwa Sasang Yŏn'guhoe. *Isip Segi Han'guk Munhak ŭi Pansŏng kwa Chaengjŏm*. Seoul: Sohyŏng Ch'ulp'an, 1999.

Mushanokoji Saneatsu. "Jiko no Tame oyobi so no Hoka ni Tsuite." *Shirakaba* Meiji 45: 95–102.

Nam Ki-sim. "Hyŏndae Kugŏ Sije e gwanhan Munje." *Kugŏ Kungmunhakhoe* 55–57 (1972): 213–238.

Nam Ki-sim and Ko Yŏng-gŭn. *P'yojun Kugŏ Munbŏp Non*. Seoul: T'ap Ch'ulp'ansa, 1985.

Natsume Sōseki. *Botchan*. Trans. Alan Turney. London: P. Owen, 1973.

Nihon Kokuritsu Kokkai Toshokan. *Meiji Taishō Shōwa Honyaku Bungaku Mokuroku*. Tokyo, 1972.

Noh Yang-hwan. "Yŏnbo." In *Yi Kwang-su Chŏnjip*. Pyŏl kwŏn. Seoul: Ushinsa, 1978: 150–194.

"Nonsŏl." *Tongnip Sinmun* 7 April 1896.

Oh, Bonnie B.C. "Kim Iryŏp's (1896–1971) Conflicting Worlds." In *Creative Women of Korea: The Fifteenth through the Twentieth Centuries*, ed. Young-Key Kim-Renaud. Armonk, New York: M.E. Sharpe, 2003.

Orbaugh, Sharalyn. "Structure and Stylistics in the Short Works of Shiga Naoya." Ph.D. diss., University of Michigan, 1989.

Ōtani Morishige. *Chosŏn Hugi Sosŏl Tokcha Yŏn'gu*. Seoul: Koryŏ Taehakkyo Minjok Munhwa Yŏn'guso, 1985.

Owen, Stephen. *An Anthology of Chinese Literature: Beginnings to 1911*. New York: W. W. Norton and Co., 1996.

Paegak Ch'unsa. "Tajŏng Tahan: Sasil Sosŏl." *T'aegŭk Hakpo* 6–7 (1907).

Pai, Hyung-il. *Constructing "Korean" Origins: A Critical Review of Archaeology, Historiography, and Racial Myth in Korean State Formation Theories*. Cambridge: Harvard University Press, 2000.

Paik Nak-chung. "Sŏyang Myŏngjak Sosŏl ŭi Chuch'ejŏk Ihae lŭl Wihae: Tolsŭttoi ŭi *Puhwal* ŭl Chungsim ŭro." *Wŏrha Yi Tonmyŏng Sŏnsaeng Hwan'gap Kinyŏm Munjip*, 1982. Reprinted in Paik Nak-chung. *Minjok Munhak kwa Segye Munhak*, II. Seoul: Ch'angbisa, 1985: 176–203.

Pak Hwan, "Kwŏnŏp Hoe ŭi Chojik kwa Hwaltong," *Rŏsia Hanin Minjok Undongsa* (T'amgudang, 1995)

———. *Rŏsia Hanin Minjok Undongsa*. Seoul: T'amgudang, 1995.

Pak Pyŏng-ch'ŏn. *Han'gŭl Kungch'e Yŏn'gu*. Seoul: Ilchisa, 1983.

Palais, James. *Confucian Statecraft and Korean Institutions: Yu Hyŏng-wŏn and the Late Chosŏn Dynasty*. Seattle: University of Washington, 1996.

———. "Political Participation in Korea." *Journal of Korean Studies* 1.1 (1979): 73–121.

Panha. "Mongjo." *Hwangsŏng Sinmun* 12 August 1907–17 September 1907.

Pihl, Marshall. *The Korean Singer of Tales*. Cambridge: Harvard-Yenching Institute Monograph Series, 1994.

———. "The Tale of Sim Ch'ŏng: a Korean Oral Narrative." Ph.D. diss., Harvard University, 1974.

Pinghŏ cha. "So Kŭmgang." *Taehan Minbo*, 14 January 1910–6 March.

Preminger, Alexander, Frank J Warnke, and O.B. Hardison, Jr., eds. *Princeton Encyclopedia of Poetry and Poetics*. Princeton: Princeton University Press, 1974.

"Pyŏngin Kanch'in Hoerok." *Taehan Minbo* 19 August–12 October 1909.

Renaud, Young-key Kim, ed. *The Korean Alphabet: Its History and Structure*. Honolulu: University of Hawaii Press, 1997

Ricoeur, Paul. *Oneself as Another*. Translated by Kathleen Blamey. Seoul: The University of Chicago Press, 1992.

Riffaterre, Michael. *Semiotics of Poetry*. Bloomington: Indiana University Press, 1984.

Ricatte, Robert. "Les Misérables: Hugo et ses personnages." In Victor Hugo. *Oeuvres completes*. Vol. XI. Paris: Le Club Francais du Livre, 1969: I–xxi.

Robinson, Michael. *Cultural Nationalism in Colonial Korea*. Seattle: University of Washington Press, 1988.

———. "Colonial Publication Policy and the Korean Nationalist Movement." In *The Japanese Colonial Empire: 1896–1945*, eds. Ramon Myers and Mark Peattie, 312–343. Princeton: Princeton University Press, 1984.

———. "National Identity and the Thought of Sin Ch'ae-ho: *Sadaejuŭi* and *chuch'e* in History and Politics." *Journal of Korean Studies* 5 (1984): 121–42.

Ross, John. *Yesu Sŏnggyo Chŏnsyŏ*. Mukden: Moon-kwang Printing House, Guang xu 13 [1887]. Facsimile edition. Mukden: Korean Bible Society, 1956.

Rutt, Richard. *The Bamboo Grove*. Berkeley: University of California Press, 1971.

Rutt, Richard and Chong-un Kim. *Virtuous Women: Three Classic Korean Novels*. Seoul: Royal Asiatic Society, 1974.

Ryan, Marleigh Grayer. *Japan's First Modern Novel: Ukigumo*. New York: Columbia University Press, 1967.

Sang Ho. "Ka T'aegŭk Hakpo chi Ch'angsi." *T'aegŭk Hakpo* 1 (1906).

Schalow, Paul. Introduction to *The Great Mirror of Male Love*, by Ihara Saikaku. Trans. Paul Schalow. Stanford: Stanford University Press, 1990.

Schmid, Andre. *Korea Between Empires, 1895 to 1919*. New York: Columbia University Press, 2002.

Setton, Mark. *Chŏng Yagyong: Korea's Challenge to Orthodox Neo-Confucianism*. Albany: State University of New York Press, 1997.

Shimazaki Tōson. *The Broken Commandment*. Translated by Kenneth Strong. Tokyo: University of Tokyo Press, 1974.

Shin, Gi-wook. "The Paradox of Korean Globalization." Working Paper, Stanford University, Asia/Pacific Research Center, January 2003.

Shin, Michael D. "Interior Landscapes: Yi Kwang-su's 'The Heartless,' and the Origins of Modern Literature." In *Colonial Modernity in Korea*, ed. Gi-Wook Shin and Michael Robinson, 248–287. Cambridge: Harvard University Asia Center, 1999.

Sibley, William F. "Naturalism in Japanese Literature." *Harvard Journal of Asiatic Studies.* 28 (1968): 157–169.

Sin Tong-uk. "Ch'unwŏn ŭi Munhak Pip'yŏng." *Han'guk Hyŏndae Munhangnon.* Seoul: Pagyŏngsa, 1981. Reprint, *Yi Kwang-su Yŏn'gu,* ed. Tongguk Taehakkyo Pusŏl Han'guk Munhak Yŏn'guso, vol. 2, 621–627. Seoul: T'aehaksa, 1984.

Sinhan Minbo. San Francisco: Sinhan Minbosa, 10 February 1909–28 December 1961. Facsimile reprint, Seoul: Asea Munhwasa, 1981.

Skillend, William. *Kodae Sosŏl: A Survey of Korean Traditional Style Popular Novels.* London: School of Oriental and African Studies, University of London, 1968.

———. "Tears of Blood: a Novel by Yi In-jik with Notes and a Translation by W. E. Skillend." Department of Chinese and Japanese Language Teaching Materials, Columbia University, 1964.

Sŏ, Carolyn P. "Modern Korean Fiction Under Colonialism: Structure and Dynamic in the Works of Four Women Writers." Ph.D. diss, University of California, Los Angeles, 1995.

———. "Seeing the Silent Pen: Kim Myŏngsun (1896–c.1951), A Pioneering Woman Writer." *Korean Culture* vol. 15, no. 2 (Summer 1994): 34–40.

Sŏ Chŏng-ju, ed. *Han'guk Yŏsŏng Sosŏlsŏn.* Vol. I: 1910–1950. Seoul: Kabin ch'ulp'ansa, 1991.

Sŏ Chŏng-su. *Chondaebŏp ŭi Yŏn'gu.* Seoul: Hansin Munhwasa, 1984.

Sŏ Yŏng-ch'ae. "*Mujŏng* kwa Sosŏljŏk Kŭndaesŏng." *Munhak Sasang* 232 (1992): 92–110.

So Chae-yŏng. *Im Pyŏng Yangnan kwa Munhak Ŭisik.* Han'guk Yŏn'gu Ch'ongsŏ 40. Seoul: Han'guk Yŏn'guwŏn, 1980.

Sohn, Ho-min. *The Korean Language.* Honolulu: University of Hawaii Press, 1999.

———. "Retrospection in Korean." *Ŏhak yŏn'gu* 11.1 (1975): 87–103.

Song Ha-ch'un. "*Mujŏng* ŭi Hyŏndae Sosŏlsajŏk Ŭiŭi." *Inmun Nonjip* 28 (1983): 1–20

Sŏng Hyŏn-gyŏng. "*Mujŏng* kwa kŭ Ijŏn Sosŏl." *Ŏmunhak* 32 (1975). Reprint, *Yi Kwang-su Yŏn'gu,* ed. Tongguk Taehakkyo Pusŏl Han'guk Munhak Yŏn'guso, vol. 2, 471–493. Seoul: T'aehaksa, 1984.

Sŏng Hyŏn-ja. *Sinsosŏl e Mich'in Manch'ŏng Sosŏl ŭi Yŏnghyang.* Paksa Hagwi Nonmun 5. Seoul: Chŏngŭmsa, 1985.

Song Min-ho. "Ch'unwŏn Ch'ogi Chakp'um ŭi Munhaksajŏk Yŏn'gu: *Mujŏng, Kaech'ŏkcha* kkajinŭn Sinsosŏl ida." In *Yi Kwang-su Yŏn'gu*, ed. Tongguk Taehakkyo Pusŏl Han'guk Munhak Yŏn'guso, vol. 2, 69–100. Seoul: T'aehaksa, 1984.

Song Myŏng-hŭi. *Yi Kwang-su ŭi Minjokchuŭi wa P'eminijŭm.* Seoul: Kukhak charyowŏn, 1997.

Sŏng Nag-yun, Yi Ton-hwa, U Pŏm-jin. "Ka i Pijang." *Taehan Maeil Sinbo* 30 September 1905–5 October 1905.

Song Paek-hŏn. "Ch'unwŏn 'Sonyŏn ŭi Piae' Yŏn'gu." In *Yi Kwang-su Yŏn'gu*, ed. Tongguk Taehakkyo Pusŏl Han'guk Munhak Yŏn'guso, vol. 2, 174–188. Seoul: T'aehaksa, 1981.

Song Young-Bae. " 'Relativism' and Iconoclasm in the Late Chosŏn Dynasty: Hong Tae-yong's Argument for Reform." *Seoul Journal of Korean Studies* 7 (1994): 71–97.

Sŏwŏn Anwŏn Taegunp'a Chŏnju Yi ssi Sebo. Seoul: P'yŏngan Pukto Chŏngju kun Yiŏn Silli Chokpo P'yŏnch'anhoe, 1976.

Steiner, George. *Tolstoy and Dostoyevsky.* Chicago: University of Chicago Press, 1985.

Suh Dae-sook. Center for Korean Studies, University of Hawaii, Honolulu, Hawaii. Interview, May 1988.

T'aegŭk Hakpo. Tokyo: T'aegŭk hakhoe. August 1906–December 1908. Facsimile reprint, *Han'guk Kaehwagi Haksul Chi*, Seoul: Asea Munhwasa, 1975.

Taehan Maeil Sinbo. Seoul: Taehan Maeil Sinbosa, July 1904–August 1910.

Taehan Minbo. Seoul: Taehan Hyŏphoe, 2 June 1909–31 August 1910. Facsimile reprint, Seoul: Asea Munhwasa, 1975.

Takeuchi, Chizuko. "Ch'oe Nam-sŏn: History and Nationalism in Modern Korea." Ph.D. diss., University of Hawaii at Manoa, 1988.

Thion'go, Ngũgĩ wa, "The Language of African Literature." In *Colonial Discourse and Post-Colonial Theory: A Reader*, ed. Patrick Williams and Laura Chrisman, 435–455. New York: Columbia University Press, 1994.

Tolstoy, Leo. *Resurrection.* Translated by Aline Delano. New York: Thomas Y. Crowell Co., 1911.

———. "The Kingdom of God is Within You. What is Art? What is Religion?" Translated by Aline Delano. N.Y.: Crowell, 1899.

———. *What is Art and Essays on Art.* Translated by Ayler Maude. Oxford: Oxford University Press, 1930.

Tompkins, Jane P., ed. *Reader-Response Criticism.* Baltimore: Johns Hopkins University Press, 1980.

Tongguk Taehakkyo Pusŏl Han'guk Munhak Yŏn'guso, ed. *Yi Kwang-su Yŏn'gu.* Vols. 1, 2. Seoul: T'aehaksa, 1984.

Tongnip Sinmun 4 April 1896–4 December 1899. Facsimile edition, Seoul: Chungang Munhwa Ch'ulp'ansa, 1969.

U Si Saeng. "Hyanggaek tamhwa." *Taehan Maeil Sinbo* 29 October 1905.

Wagner, Edward. "The Civil Service Examination Process as Social Leaven: the Case of the Northern Provinces in the Yi Dynasty." Paper presented at the International Symposium Commemorating the 30th Anniversary of Korean Liberation, Seoul, Korea, 11–20 August 1975.

Waley, Arthur, trans. *The Book of Songs*. Edited with additional translations by Joseph R. Allen. New York: Grove Press, 1996.

Walker, Janet. *The Japanese Novel of the Meiji Period and the Ideal of Individualism*. Princeton: Princeton University Press, 1979.

Wells, Kenneth. *New God, New Nation: Protestants and Self-Reconstruction Nationalism in Korea 1896–1937*. Honolulu: University of Hawaii Press, 1990.

West, Stephen and Wilt L. Idema, ed. and transl. *The Moon and the Zither: The Story of the Western Wing*. Berkeley: University of California Press, 1991.

"Wiguk Kidomun." *Korea Daily News* 19 November 1905.

Williams, Raymond. *Marxism and Literature*. New York: Oxford University Press, 1977.

Wordsworth, William. "The Prelude." In *English Romantic Writers*, ed. David Perkins, 213–263. New York: Harcourt, Brace, Jovanovich, 1967.

Yanagida Izumi. *Meiji Shoki Honyaku Bungaku no Kenkyū*. Tokyo: Shunjusha, Shōwa 6.

Yang Mun-gyu. "Han'guk Kŭndae Munhaksaron ŭi Insik kwa Chaengjŏm." In Ed. Munhak kwa Sasang Yŏn'guhoe. *Isip Segi Han'guk Munhak ŭi Pansŏng kwa Chaengjŏm*. Seoul: Samyŏng Ch'ulp'an, 1999: 35–59.

Yi Chae-sŏn. "Ch'unwŏn ŭi Ch'ogi Tanp'yŏn kwa Sŏgan Hyŏngt'ae." *Ch'oe Nam-sŏn kwa Yi Kwang-su ŭi Munhak*. Seoul: Saemunhaksa, 1981. Reprint, *Yi Kwang-su Yŏn'gu*, ed. Tongguk Taehakkyo Pusŏl Han'guk Munhak Yŏn'guso, vol. 2, 575–587. Seoul: T'aehaksa, 1984.

———. *Han'guk Hyŏndae Sosŏlsa*. Seoul: Hongsŏngsa, 1982.

———. *Han'guk Kaehwagi Sosŏl Yŏn'gu*. Seoul: Ilchogak, 1972.

———. "Hyŏngsŏngjŏk Kyoyuk Sosŏl esŏ ŭi 'Mujŏng.'" *Munhak Sasang* 232 (1992): 80–91.

———. "Kaehwagi ŭi Uguk Sosŏl." In Min Pyŏng-su, Cho Tong-il, Yi Chae-sŏn. *Kaehwagi ŭi Uguk Munhak*. Seoul: Sin'gu Munhwasa, 1974: 133–189.

Yi Ho-suk. "Wiakchŏk Chagi Pangŏ Kije rosŏ ŭi Erot'ijŭm: Na Hye-sŏk Non." In *P'eminijŏm kwa Sosŏl Pip'yŏng*, ed. Han'guk Yŏsŏng Sosŏl Yŏn'guhoe, 79–121. Seoul: Han'gilsa, 1995.

Yi In-jik. "Kwi ŭi Sŏng." *Mansebo* 10 October 1906–31 May 1907.

————. "Sahoehak." *Sonyŏn Hanbando* 3 (1 January 1907).

————. *Kwi ŭi Sŏng*. Vol. 1. Hwangsŏng: Kwanghak Sŏp'o, Yunghŭi 1. Facsimile Reprint, *Sinsosŏl, Pŏnan (yŏk) Sosŏl*. *Han'guk Kaehwagi Munhak Ch'ongsŏ I*, eds. Paek Sun-je, Song Min-ho and Yi Sŏn-yŏng, vol. 1, Seoul: Asea Munhwasa, 1978.

————. *Kwi ŭi Sŏng*. Vol. 2. Hwangsŏng: Chungang Sŏgwan, Yunghŭi 2. Facsimile Reprint, *Sinsosŏl, Pŏnan (yŏk) Sosŏl*. *Han'guk Kaehwagi Munhak Ch'ongsŏ I*, eds. Paek Sun-je, Song Min-ho and Yi Sŏn-yŏng, vol. 1, Seoul: Asea Munhwasa, 1978.

————. "Tears of blood." Translated by William Skillend. In *Korean Classical Literature: An Anthology*, ed. Chung Chong-wha, 159–221. London: Kegan Paul International Ltd., 1989.

Yi Kwang-nin. *Han'guk Kaehwa Sasang Yŏn'gu*. Seoul: Ilchogak, 1981.

Yi Kwang-su. "Ai ka." *Shiragane Gakuhō* (1909). Reprint, *'Gaichi' no Nihon Bungaku Sen*, ed. Kurokawa Sō, vol. 3, 21–26. *Chōsen*. Tōkyō: Shinjuku Shobō, 1996.

————. "Chakcha rosŏ Pon Munhak ŭi Simnyŏn." *Pyŏl Kŏn'gon* January 1930. Reprint, *Yi Kwang-su Chŏnjip*, ed. Noh Yang-hwan, vol. 10, 583–584. Seoul: Usinsa, 1978.

————. "Ch'ŏnan'gi." *Tonga Ilbo* 5–6 January 1926. Reprint, *Yi Kwang-su Chŏnjip*, ed. Noh Yang-hwan, vol. 7, 289–349. Seoul: Usinsa, 1978.

————. "Chohon ŭi Aksŭp." *Maeil Sinbo*, 23 November 1916–26 November 1916. Reprint, *Yi Kwang-su Chŏnjip*, ed. Noh Yang-hwan, vol. 1, 542–545. Seoul: Samjungdang, 1971.

————. "Chŏnjaenggi ŭi Chakkajŏk T'aedo." *Chosŏn Ilbo* 6 January 1936. Reprint, *Yi Kwang-su Chŏnjip*, vol. 10, 490–492. Seoul: Usinsa, 1978.

————. "Chosŏn Mundan ŭi Hyŏnhwang kwa Changnae." *Tonga Ilbo* 1 January 1925. Reprint, Yi Kwang-su. *Yi Kwang-su Chŏnjip*, vol. 10, 399–402. Seoul: Samjungdang, 1971.

————. "Chosŏn Ŏmun Yech'an." *Chosŏn Ilbo* 29 October 1935–3 November 1935. Reprint, *Yi Kwang-su Chŏnjip*, vol. 9, 458–461. Seoul: Samjungdang, 1971.

————. "Chosŏn ŭi Munhak." *Samch'ŏlli* March 1933. Reprint, *Yi Kwang-su Chŏnjip*, vol. 10, 464–468. Seoul: Samjungdang, 1971.

————. "Chosŏnŏ ŭi Pin'gon." *Chosŏn Ilbo* 3 October 1933. Reprint, *Yi Kwang-su Chŏnjip*, vol. 9, 353. Seoul: Samjungdang, 1971.

————. "Chosŏn Saramin Ch'ŏngnyŏn ege." *Sonyŏn* 6 (June 1910). Reprint, *Yi Kwang-su Chŏnjip*, vol. 1, 532–536. Seoul: Samjungdang, 1978.

————. *Ch'unwŏn Sŏgan Munbŏm*. Seoul: Samjungdang, 1939. Reprint, *Yi Kwang-su Chŏnjip*, vol. 9, 196–327. Seoul: Usinsa, 1978.

————. "Haesamwi rosŏ." *Ch'ŏngch'un* 6 (1 March 1915): 79–83. Reprint, *Yi Kwang-su Chŏnjip*, vol. 9, 137–139. Seoul: Usinsa, 1978.

———. "Hŏnsinja." *Sonyŏn* 3. 8 (August 1910). Reprint, *Yi Kwang-su Chŏnjip*, vol. 1, 565–568. Seoul: Usinsa, 1978.

———. "Hyŏngsang Sosŏl Kosŏn Yŏŏn." *Ch'ŏngch'un* 12 (1918). Reprint, *Han'guk Hyŏndae Munhak Pip'yŏngsa Charyo* I, ed. Kwŏn Yŏng-min, 97–98. Seoul: Tandae Ch'ulp'ansa, 1981.

———. "Ilban Insa ŭi P'iltok hal Sŏjŏk Sujong." *Maeil Sinbo* 9 November 1916. Reprint, *Yi Kwang-su Chŏnjip*, vol. 10, 323–325. Seoul: Usinsa, 1978.

———. "Ilgi: Na ŭi Sonyŏn Sidae." *Chosŏn Mundan* no. 7 (April 1925). Reprint, *Yi Kwang-su Chŏnjip*, vol. 9, 328–334. Seoul: Usinsa, 1978.

———. "Ingwa." *Chogwang* January 1936. Reprint, *Yi Kwang-su Chŏnjip*, vol. 9, 615. Seoul: Usinsa, 1978,

———. "Injoin." *Tongmyŏng* 1 April 1923. Reprint, *Yi Kwang-su Chŏnjip*. Vol. 7, 644–647. Seoul: Usinsa, 1978.

———. *Insaeng ŭi Hyanggi.* Seoul: Hongji Ch'ulp'ansa, 1936. Reprint, *Yi Kwang-su Chŏnjip*, vol. 8, 227–273. Seoul: Usinsa, 1978.

———. "Kagawa Kōchō." *Kokumin Bungaku* October 1943. In *Shin Hanto Bungaku Senshū.*

———. "Kamsa wa Sajoe." *Paekcho* 2 (May 1922). Reprint, *Yi Kwang-su Chŏnjip*, vol. 8, 227–234. Seoul: Usinsa, 1978.

———. "Kim Kyŏng." *Ch'ŏngch'un* 6 (1 March 1915): 113–126. Reprint, *Yi Kwang-su Chŏnjip*, vol. 1, 568–573. Seoul: Usinsa, 1978.

———. "Kŏmdungi ŭi sŏrum." Seoul: Sinmungwan, 1913. Reprint, *Yi Kwang-su Chŏnjip*, vol. 7, 601–644. Seoul: Samjungdang, 1971.

———. "Kŏmdungi ŭi sŏrum mŏri mal." Seoul: Sinmungwan, 1913. Reprint, *Yi Kwang-su Chŏnjip*, vol. 10, 543–4. Seoul: Samjungdang, 1971.

———. "Kŭmil a Han Ch'ŏngnyŏn kwa Chŏngyuk." *Taehan Hŭnghakpo* 10 (1910). Reprint, *Yi Kwang-su Chŏnjip*, vol. 1, 525–526. Seoul: Usinsa, 1978.

———. "Kŭmil a Han Yongmun e Taehaya." *Hwangsŏng Sinmun* 24, 26, 27 July 1910.

———. "Kŭmil Chosŏn Yaso Kyohoe ŭi Kyŏlchŏm." *Ch'ŏngch'un* 11 (October 1917). Reprint, *Yi Kwang-su Chŏnjip*, vol. 10, 20–24. Seoul: Samjungdang, 1971.

———. "Kŭ tŭl ŭi Sarang." *Sin Sidae* January–March 1940. Reprint, *Ch'inil Munhak Chakp'um Sŏnjip*, eds. Kim Pyŏng-gŏl and Kim Kyu-dong, 20–60. Seoul: Silch'ŏn Munhaksa, 1986.

———. "Kŭ ŭi Chasŏjŏn." *Chosŏn Ilbo* 22 November 1936–1 May 1937. Reprint, *Yi Kwang-su Chŏnjip*, vol. 6: 299–437. Seoul: Usinsa, 1978.

———. "Kŭ ŭi Chasŏjŏn." *Chosŏn Ilbo* 22 November 1936–1 May 1937. Reprint, *Yi Kwang-su Chŏnjip*, vol. 6, 299–437. Seoul: Samjungdang, 1971.

368   *Bibliography*

————. "Kyuhan." *Hak chi Gwang* (January 1917). Reprint, *Yi Kwang-su Chŏnjip*, vol. 8, 532–537. Seoul: Usinsa, 1978.

————. "Mal tŭtkŏra." *Yi Kwang-su Chŏnjip*, vol. 9, 468. Seoul: Samjungdang, 1971.

————. "Mo, Mae, Ch'ŏ ege." *Samch'ŏlli* (July 1940). Reprint, *Ch'inil Munhak Chakp'um Sŏnjip*, eds. Kim Pyŏng-gŏl and Kim Kyu-dong, 88–93. Seoul: Silch'ŏn Munhaksa, 1986.

————. "Mujŏng tŭng Chŏn Chakp'um ŭl Ŏ hada." *Samch'ŏlli* July 1937. Reprint, *Yi Kwang-su Chŏnjip*, vol. 10, 520–524. Seoul: Samjungdang, 1971.

————. "Mujŏng." *Taehan Hŭnghakpo* (March 1910–April 1910). Reprint, *Yi Kwang-su Chŏnjip*, vol. 1, 561–565. Seoul: Usinsa, 1978.

————. "Mujŏng." *Maeil Sinbo* 1 January–14 June 1917. Facsimile reprint, Seoul: Kyŏngin Munhwasa, 1984.

————. *Mujŏng*. In *Han'guk Hyŏndae Sosŏl Ch'ongsŏ*, vol. 1. Seoul: T'aeyŏngsa, 1985.

————. *Mujŏng*. In *Yi Kwang-su Chŏnjip*, vol. 1, 15–209. Seoul: Samjungdang, 1971.

————. "Mumyŏng." *Munjang* (1939). Reprint, *Yi Kwang-su Chŏnjip*, vol. 8, 15–57. Seoul: Usinsa, 1978.

————. "Munhak e taehan Sogyŏn." *Tonga Ilbo* 23 July 1929–1 August 1929. Reprint, *Yi Kwang-su Chŏnjip*, vol. 10, 452–9. Seoul: Samjungdang, 1971.

————. "Munhak iran Hao?" *Maeil Sinbo* 10 November–23 November 1916. Reprint, *Yi Kwang-su Chŏnjip*, vol. 1, 547–555. Seoul: Usinsa, 1978.

————. "Munhak kanghwa." *Chosŏn Mundan* nos. 1–5 (October 1924–February 1925). Reprint, *Yi Kwang-su Chŏnjip*, vol. 10, 378–394. Seoul: Usinsa, 1978.

————. "Munhak kwa Munsa wa Munjang." *Han'gŭl* June–October 1935. Reprint, *Yi Kwang-su Chŏnjip*, vol. 10, 471–479. Seoul: Samjungdang, 1971.

————. "Munhak ŭi kach'i." *Taehan Hŭnghakpo* March 1910. Reprint, *Yi Kwang-su Chŏnjip*, vol. 1, 545–547. Seoul: Samjungdang, 1971.

————. "Nae ka Sokhal Yuhyŏng." *Munye Kongnon* no. 1 (May 1929). Reprint, *Yi Kwang-su Chŏnjip*, vol. 8, 400. Seoul: Usinsa, 1978.

————. "Nae So wa Nae Kae." In *Simun Tokpon*, ed. Ch'oe Nam-sŏn, Seoul: Sinmungwan, 1916. Reprint, *Yi Kwang-su Chŏnjip*, vol. 8, 472–474. Seoul: Usinsa, 1978.

————. "Na: Sonyŏn P'yŏn." Seoul: Saenghwalsa, 1947. Reprint, *Yi Kwang-su Chŏnjip*, vol. 6, 438–507. Seoul: Usinsa, 1978.

————. *Na ŭi Kobaek*. Seoul: Ch'unch'usa, 1948. Reprint, *Yi Kwang-su Chŏnjip*, vol. 7, 219–288. Seoul: Usinsa, 1978.

———. "Na ŭi Mundan Saenghwal Samsimnyŏn." *Sinin Munhak* (July 1934). Reprint, *Yi Kwang-su Chŏnjip*, vol. 10, 589–591. Seoul: Usinsa, 1978.

———. "Nae ka Sosŏl ŭl Chuch'ŏn Handamyŏn." *Tonga Ilbo* 5 January 1931. Reprint, *Yi Kwang-su Chŏnjip*, vol. 10, 586–587. Seoul: Samjungdang, 1971.

———. "Nimne ka Kŭriwŏ." *Chosŏn Mundan* 5 (March 1925). Reprint, *Yi Kwang-su Chŏnjip*, vol. 9, 488. Seoul: Usinsa, 1978.

———. "Nongch'on Kyebal." *Maeil Sinbo* 26 November 1916–18 February 1917. Reprint, *Yi Kwang-su Chŏnjip*, vol. 10, 62–97. Seoul: Usinsa, 1978.

———. "Obscurity," translated by Lyndal Weiler. In *Modern Korean Literature*, ed. Chung Chong-hwa, 427–467. New York: Columbia University Press, 1995.

———. "Okchung Hogŏl." *Taehan Hŭnghakpo* January 1910. Reprint, *Yi Kwang-su Chŏnjip*, vol. 1, 573–575. Seoul: Usinsa, 1978.

———. "Ŏrin Hŭisaeng." *Sonyŏn* February 1910–May 1910. Reprint, *Yi Kwang-su Chŏnjip*, vol. 1, 556–561. Seoul: Usinsa, 1978.

———. "Puhwal ŭi Sŏgwang." *Ch'ŏngch'un* 12 (March 1918). Reprint, *Yi Kwang-su Chŏnjip*, vol. 10, 26–7. Seoul: Samjungdang, 1971.

———. "Sanghae sŏ." *Ch'ŏngch'un* no.3–4. (1914–1915). Reprint, *Yi Kwang-su Chŏnjip*, vol. 9, 130–134. Seoul: Usinsa, 1978.

———. *Sarang. Hyŏndae Kŏlchak Changp'yŏn Sosŏl Chŏnjip*. Seoul, 1939. Reprint, *Yi Kwang-su Chŏnjip*, vol. 6, 15–298. Seoul: Usinsa, 1978.

———. *Sejo Taewang*. In *Sinsŏn Yŏksa Sosŏl Chŏnjip*. Vol. 5. Seoul: Pangmun Sŏgwan, 1940. Reprint, *Yi Kwang-su Chŏnjip*, vol. 4, 484–603. Seoul: Samjungdang, 1971.

———. "Sin Ch'eje ha ŭi Yesul ŭi Panghyang." *Samch'ŏlli* January 1941. Reprint, *Yi Kwang-su Chŏnjip*, vol. 10, 257–259. Seoul: Usinsa, 1978.

———. "Son'garak." *Yŏngdae* no. 2 (September 1924). Reprint, *Yi Kwang-su Chŏnjip*, vol. 8, 236–237. Seoul: Samjungdang, 1971.

———. "Sonyŏn ŭi Piae." *Ch'ŏngch'un* no. 8 (June 1917). Reprint, *Yi Kwang-su Chŏnjip*. Vol. 8. 1978: 58–65.

———. "Sosŏlga ŭi Chunbi." *Chogwang* September 1936. Reprint, *Yi Kwang-su Chŏnjip*, vol. 10, 493–495. Seoul: Usinsa, 1978.

———. "Sosŏl Sŏnhuŏn." *Chosŏn Mundan* 3 (December 1924). Reprint, *Yi Kwang-su Chŏnjip*, vol. 10, 572–4. Seoul: Samjungdang, 1971.

———. "Sŏul ŭi Kyŏul Tal." In Ch'oe Nam-sŏn, ed. *Simun Tokpon*. Seoul: Sinmungwan 1916. Reprint, *Yuktang Ch'oe Nam-sŏn Chŏnjip*, Koryŏ Taehakkyo Asea Munje Yŏn'guso Yuktang Chŏnjip P'yŏnch'an Wiwŏnhoe, ed., vol. 8, 581–582. Seoul: Hyŏnamsa, 1973–1975.

———. "Taegu esŏ." *Maeil Sinbo* 22–23 September 1916. Reprint, *Yi Kwang-su Chŏnjip*, vol. 9, 134–137. Seoul: Usinsa, 1978.

———. "T'agorŭ ŭi Wŏnjŏng e taehayŏ." *Tonga Ilbo* 20 January 1925. Reprint, *Yi Kwang-su Chŏnjip*, vol. 10, 560–561. Seoul: Usinsa, 1978.

———. "Talch'ul Tojung ŭi Tanjae Insang." *Chogwang* April 1936. Reprint, *Yi Kwang-su Chŏnjip*, vol. 8, 515–517. Seoul: Usinsa, 1978.

———. "Tananhan Pansaeng ŭi Tojŏng." *Chogwang* April–June 1937. Reprint, *Yi Kwang-su Chŏnjip*, vol. 8, 445–457. Seoul: Usinsa, 1978.

———. "The Heartless," translated by Kim Kichung. In *Modern Korean Literature: An Anthology*, ed. and comp., Peter H. Lee, 2–15. Honolulu: University of Hawaii Press, 1990.

———. "Toksŏ wa Kojŏn." *Chosŏn Ilbo* 29 September 1935. Reprint, *Yi Kwang-su Chŏnjip*, vol. 9, 454–455. Seoul: Samjungdang, 1971.

———. "Tol pegae." Seoul: Saenghwalsa, 1948. Reprint, *Yi Kwang-su Chŏnjip*, vol. 8, 276–311. Seoul: Samjungdang, 1971.

———. "Tonggyŏng Chapsin: Pokt'aek Yugil ŭi Myo lŭl Paeham." *Maeil Sinbo* 27 September–9 November 1916. Reprint, *Yi Kwang-su Chŏnjip*, vol. 10, 316–319. Seoul: Samjungdang, 1971.

———. "Tongjŏng." *Ch'ŏngch'un* 3 (1914). Reprint, *Yi Kwang-su Chŏnjip*, vol. 1, 580–582. Seoul: Usinsa, 1978.

———. "Tuong kwa Na." *Chosŏn Ilbo* 20 November 1935. Reprint, *Yi Kwang-su Chŏnjip*, vol. 1, 595–596. Seoul: Usinsa, 1978.

———. "Uri Munye ŭi Panghyang." *Chosŏn Mundan* 13 (November 1925). Reprinted in *Yi Kwang-su Chŏnjip*, vol. 10, 428–430. Seoul: Samjungdang, 1971.

———. "Wigo ŭi Sahu Osimnyŏn Che e." *Chosŏn ilbo* 23 May 1935. Reprint, *Yi Kwang-su chŏnjip*, vol. 10, 591–2. Seoul: Usinsa, 1978.

———. "Wŏnhyo Taesa." *Maeil Sinbo* 1 March–31 October 1942. Reprint, *Yi Kwang-su Chŏnjip*, vol. 5, 337–541. Seoul: Usinsa, 1978.

———. "Wusŏn Su ka Toego, Yŏnhu e In i Yoera." *Hak chi Kwang* June 1917. Reprint, *Yi Kwang-su Chŏnjip*, vol. 10, 242–244. Seoul: Usinsa, 1978.

———. "Yasogyo ŭi Chosŏn e Chun Ŭnhye." *Ch'ŏngch'un* 9 (1917). Reprint, *Yi Kwangsu Chŏnjip*, vol. 1, 17–19. Seoul: Samjungdang, 1971.

———. "Yesul P'yŏngga ŭi P'yojun." *Tonggwang* May 1926. Reprint, *Yi Kwang-su Chŏnjip*, vol. 10, 442–443. Seoul: Samjungdang, 1971.

———. "Yi Kwang-su ŭi 'Kwŏnŏp Sinmun' 'Taehanin Chŏnggyobo' Kigomun." *Minjok Munhaksa Yŏn'gu* no. 9 (1996): 355–375.

———. "Yujŏng." *Chosŏn Ilbo* 1 October 1933–31 December. Reprint, *Yi Kwang-su Chŏnjip*, vol. 4, 15–91. Seoul: Usinsa, 1978.

———. "Yun Kwang-ho." *Ch'ŏngch'un* no. 13 (April 1918). Reprint, *Yi Kwang-su Chŏnjip*, vol. 8, 96–104. Seoul: Usinsa, 1978.

Yi Kwang-nin. *Han'guk Kaehwasa Yŏn'gu*. Seoul: Ilchogak, 1969.

Yi Sang-hyŏp. *Chae Pong Ch'un*. Kyŏngsŏng: Tongyang Sŏwŏn, Taishō 1. Reprint, *Sinsosŏl, Pŏnan (Yŏk) Sosŏl. Han'guk Kaehwagi Munhak*

Ch'ongsŏ I, eds. Kim Yun-sik, Paek Sun-je, Song Min-ho and Yi Sŏn-yŏng, vol.10. Seoul: Asea Munhwasa, 1978.

Yi Sŏn-yŏng. "Ch'unwŏn ŭi Pigyo Munhakchŏk Koch'al." *Sae Kyoyuk* 134 (1965). Reprint, *Yi Kwang-su Yŏn'gu*, Tongguk Taehakkyo Pusŏl Han'guk Munhak Yŏn'guso, vol. 1, 191–204. Seoul: T'aehaksa, 1984.

———. *Yŏksa Chŏn'gi Sosŏl*. Seoul: Asea Munhwasa, 1979.

Yi Su-jŏng. "Maga ŭi Chŏn han Pogŭm Sŏ Ŏnhae." Facsimile reprint. Sungjŏn Taehakkyo Kugŏ Kungmunhakhoe, ed. *Sungsil Ŏmun* no. 2 (25 February 1985).

Yi Ŭng-ho. *Kaehwagi ŭi Han'gŭl Undongsa*. Seoul: Sŏngch'ŏngsa, 1975.

Yu Beong-cheon. *Han Yong-un and Yi Kwang-su*. Detroit: Wayne State University Press, 1992.

Yu Yang-sŏn. "Kuhanmal Sahoe Sasang ŭi Sosŏrhwa Yangsang." *Chindan Hakpo* no. 59 (1985): 115–133.

Yun Chŏng-wŏn. "Ch'up'ung Ilchin." *T'aegŭk Hakpo* no. 3 (1906): 45–47.

Yun Hong-no. "Yi Kwang-su Munhak ŭi Yŏn'gusajŏk Pansŏng." In *Yi Kwang-su Yŏn'gu*, ed. Tongguk Taehakkyo Pusŏl Han'guk Munhak Yŏn'guso, vol. 1, 514–525. Seoul: T'aehaksa, 1984.

Yun Pyŏng-no. *Han'guk Kŭn-Hyŏndae Munhaksa*. Seoul: Myŏngmundang, 1991.

Yun Pyŏng-sŏk. "1910 Nyŏndae Yŏnhaeju Chibang esŏ ŭi Han'guk Tongnip Undong." *Kugoe Hanin Sahoe wa Minjok Undong*. Ilchogak, 1990.

Index

CORNELL EAST ASIA SERIES

Order online: www.einaudi.cornell.edu/eastasia/CEASbooks, or contact Cornell East Asia Series Distribution Center, 95 Brown Road, Box 1004, Ithaca, NY 14850, USA; toll-free: 1-877-865-2432, fax 607-255-7534, ceas@cornell.edu

SB/8-05/1.6M pb/.45M hc

CPSIA information can be obtained
at www.ICGtesting.com
Printed in the USA
LVHW042004210322
713996LV00002B/42